COLOUR FILMS IN BRITAIN
THE NEGOTIATION OF INNOVATION 1900–55

SARAH STREET

A BFI book published by Palgrave Macmillan

First published in 2012 by
PALGRAVE MACMILLAN

on behalf of the

BRITISH FILM INSTITUTE
21 Stephen Street, London W1T 1LN
www.bfi.org.uk

There's more to discover about film and television through the BFI. Our world-renowned archive, cinemas, festivals, films, publications and learning resources are here to inspire you.

Palgrave Macmillan in the UK is an imprint of Macmillan Publishers Limited, registered in England, company number 785998, of Houndmills, Basingstoke, Hampshire RG21 6XS. Palgrave Macmillan in the US is a division of St Martin's Press LLC, 175 Fifth Avenue, New York, NY 10010. Palgrave Macmillan is the global academic imprint of the above companies and has companies and representatives throughout the world. Palgrave® and Macmillan® are registered trademarks in the United States, the United Kingdom, Europe and other countries.

Cover image: *The Ladykillers* (Alexander Mackendrick, 1955), Ealing Studios/© Canal+
Designed by couch
Set by Cambrian Typesetters, Camberley, Surrey and couch
Printed in China

This book is printed on paper suitable for recycling and made from fully managed and sustained forest sources. Logging, pulping and manufacturing processes are expected to conform to the environmental regulations of the country of origin.

British Library Cataloguing-in-Publication Data
A catalogue record for this book is available from the British Library
A catalog record for this book is available from the Library of Congress
10 9 8 7 6 5 4 3 2 1
21 20 19 18 17 16 15 14 13 12

ISBN 978–1–84457–312–7 (pb)
ISBN 978–1–84457–313–4 (hb)

CONTENTS

ACKNOWLEDGMENTS

I first became interested in colour when researching a project on set design. Many people and institutions have helped along the way and it has been a pleasure to work on something so fascinating and challenging. This book was part of an Arts and Humanities Research Council (AHRC) project, and so I first must thank the Research Council for making the scope of this, and the other outputs associated with the project, achievable. Simon Brown, Vicky Jackson and Liz Watkins worked with me on 'the colour project' for three years, and in particular we benefited from collaborating and connecting with other scholars and archivists from all over the world. Colour and the Moving Image, the conference we hosted in Bristol in July 2009, was a pivotal event in the development of our work, providing great intellectual stimulation at our project's halfway point, and prompting ideas for future directions in colour studies. I have been assisted in the production of this book my many supportive individuals. Simon Brown researched and wrote the Technical Appendix that is so important for understanding the specifications of the many colour processes mentioned in the text. I thank him for his efficiency, moral support and diligence throughout. Sonia Genaitay assisted with the production of the frame enlargements; she was generous with her time at the BFI National Archive and always willing to share her expertise on early colour films. Liz Watkins researched information for interviews with Ossie Morris and Chris Challis that we conducted during the project, as well as transcribing key interviews with technicians from the BECTU History Project that proved to be an important source of information about the many professionals involved with colour film production and processing. Vicky Jackson prepared the index and we had many stimulating conversations about the exhibition of Kinemacolor; she was awarded her PhD in 2011. Several other people also provided invaluable advice, information, materials and enthusiasm that have been important throughout the preparation of this book: John Belton, Edward Branigan, Ian Christie, Barbara Hall, Scott Higgins, James Layton, Luke McKernan, Richard Misek, Nathalie Morris, Steve Neale, Duncan Petrie, Andrew Spicer and Joshua Yumibe. Sue Simkin accompanied me on research trips to the USA, and I thank her for assisting with research on the Natalie Kalmus papers that proved to be both interesting and entertaining. Rebecca Barden at BFI/Palgrave Macmillan has been a great editor to work with, and her enthusiasm for the project at an early stage was extremely helpful. Joy Tucker was an excellent copy-editor. Apart from the AHRC, additional financial support has been received from the University of Bristol in bringing the project to completion. All images reproduced for this book are for the purposes of criticism or review. The International Olympic Committee gave permission to use the frame enlargements from *XIV Olympiad: The Glory of Sport* and Coats plc for *Queen Cotton*. Finally, I must honour my dear parents Carol and Lindsay. My mother was an avid reader of *Picturegoer* in her youth. My parents loved the cinema and were proud of my career as a film academic. I dedicate this book to their memory.

INTRODUCTION

The introduction of colour into films was as natural and logical an improvement as the introduction of sound, and I think we can expect as rapid an advance in technique as attended the introduction of sound. (Alexander Korda, 1937)[1]

Like many British film producers, Alexander Korda put his faith in colour with the arrival of three-strip Technicolor and other colour systems that were being showcased in the mid-1930s. This was not the first time that colour films generated excitement among film industry professionals. In the previous three decades colour was a focus of experimentation for many pioneers for whom it became something of a 'holy grail' in the development of motion picture technology. British inventors were at the forefront of experimenting with colour and numerous processes were introduced, discussed, discarded or taken up by the film industry. In the early 1900s the majority of films were coloured by hand-painting black-and-white prints or by tinting them with coloured dyes.[2] Photographic systems aimed to record the visible colour spectrum but the majority made little commercial headway; by the end of the 1920s the number of coloured films had decreased. It was not until the late 50s that colour regained its primary place as the dominant aesthetic choice for film-makers and audiences, a trend that more or less continued to the present. Korda was excited about the prospects of colour in 1937 because there was a revival of interest as several processes contended for prominence, some of which were British. It was not clear that Technicolor would become the most commercially

successful system or that British directors and technicians would be responsible for producing so many visually striking and technically innovative Technicolor films. The time was right for another phase of colour activity which occurred in Britain in World War II and into the subsequent decade.

Korda was, however, incorrect in his prediction that the advance in technique would be as rapid as in the first years after the introduction of sound. Instead colour's story is of intermittent trial and error, intense debate and speculation before gradual acceptance. While the technological details of the processes have been documented and described by historians, far less scholarly work has been undertaken on the economic and cultural impact of colour films, and there has been no thoroughgoing study based on primary sources and film analysis of the British experience. Although there are studies of Technicolor in the USA in the 1930s and of the French attitude towards colour aesthetics in the 40s, examining British colour cinema within intertwined national, cultural and economic contexts has not previously been attempted.[3] In addition to investigating the technical specificities of a variety of colour techniques and processes, this book aims to elucidate how innovative technologies that represent a challenge to prevalent aesthetic regimes are negotiated, and with what consequences. As emergent technologies, colour processes constantly had to make a case for their superiority in a market dominated by cheaper, black-and-white films that tended to be admired by critics as more aesthetically pleasing. As is the case with contemporary innovative technologies, colour systems had to negotiate a space for themselves, often facing fierce opposition from competitors who had vested interests in preserving the status quo. While seeing the world in colour was a part of everyday life, on screen it was a complex engagement with notions of realism and the attractions of film spectacle.

As well as presenting histories of colour processes, this book analyses the textual aesthetics of colour films and considers their place in British film culture. Taking colour as a primary referent, the analyses of many different films demonstrate how colour influenced approaches to film narrative, aesthetics and particular genres. The focus is on British films, although significant examples of colour films produced in other countries are referenced. The British example provides a context for addressing broader concerns about technology transfer, and the ways in which film industries negotiated the potential advantages of technologies such as Technicolor. This raises questions such as the extent to which the adoption of a colour process led to economic advancement, or whether a technology invented and developed in one country and subsequently applied by another national film industry resulted in its improvement, diversity of application or any particular distinguishing features. The methodological approach combines economic and technological histories, supported by detailed textual analyses to consider how far British directors, artists and technicians were responsible for extending the technological and aesthetic range of several processes, particularly Technicolor. The latter is particularly significant because Britain was the first country to seriously collaborate with the company outside the USA. Related issues are whether the technology in question was the most advanced at any given time in terms of technical capability, or whether ideologies around colour influenced which processes were actually taken up. Contesting the application of colour by those who sought to control its impact is a recurring pattern throughout the decades. Indeed, many commentators invested colour with nationalist ideologies, arguing that British colour films contained specific aesthetic effects that differentiated them from those produced in Hollywood. These provided a context for the many distinctive contributions made by British directors and technicians to the development of colour as they negotiated its innovatory potential within an intricate matrix of national debate, traditions of aesthetic taste and economic competition.

British cinema was indeed both complex and particular in its response to the potential for innovation presented by colour. In the silent period and into the 1930s directors, artists and technicians explored many processes, most notably Dufaycolor, that were considered to be particularly conducive to British film-making, and short film trials took place with various systems. The arrival of Technicolor enabled British cinema to exploit a latent tendency to experiment with realism, genre and *mise en scène* in a more sustained basis. John Huntley's *British Technicolor Films* was published in 1949 as a celebration of the strides made by British film-makers with Technicolor.[4] He confidently declared: '25 colour features have been made in Britain. In one year alone Hollywood makes about 40 Technicolor pictures. Yet somehow when we speak of colour in the cinema, it is very often these 25 English movies that we recall most clearly.'[5] Critic Dilys Powell shared his estimation of the quality of British Technicolor films, distinguishing Britain for demonstrating 'initiative, originality and intelligence in the use of the colour film' typified by the 'poetic' experimentation of films such as *Henry V* (1944).[6] French critics such as Roland Dailly similarly perceived in British cinema a particular 'quality' usage of Technicolor as they debated how their own cinema might respond to colour after World War II.[7] Despite admiring the British usage of Technicolor, the French were wary of being dominated by Hollywood. Having to cope with a backlog of orders after the war, Technicolor did not pursue an aggressive campaign in France. Until 1955 the colour process used in French films was Gevacolor, a Belgian former affiliate of the German Agfacolor, but only 2 per cent of production was colour. The cinema of 'quality' persisted as an aesthetic style associated with black and white.[8] The availability of colour did not result in its automatic adoption by a national cinema, and the French case is a perfect example of how ideological, as well as technological and economic, factors are of key importance in influencing attitudes towards colour.

The British case was different; from the 1930s interest in colour gathered momentum and the British colour films so admired by French critics were at the forefront of innovatory techniques and aesthetics in the

40s. British experimentation with Technicolor was appreciated by its American inventors and by critics writing in technical journals such as *American Cinematographer*. Writers in the *British Journal of Photography*, who reviewed the majority of colour films screened in British cinemas, charted developments from a comparative, transnational perspective, commenting in detail not only on British films but also on Hollywood features and short films. Expertise with, and imaginative use of, Technicolor assisted Britain's postwar drive to export its films. Although hardly numerous in comparison with Hollywood's output, prestigious titles given a 'roadshow' release, such as *Henry V* and *The Red Shoes* (1948), were appreciated as contributing meaningfully to Technicolor's record as the most dominant colour process.[9] During the years when Anglo-American film relations veered from being collaborative and amiable to suspicious or even hostile, a few key British films occupied a particular niche as far as colour was concerned. This reflected well on how a colour process primarily identified with the USA could be developed by another national cinema. Unlike France, Britain was not so hostile towards Hollywood and showed an interest in Technicolor from an early stage, sending technicians to America to learn the latest innovations on several occasions.

The introduction of new technology can result in different national variants in terms of application, as Charles O'Brien's study of early sound cinema in France and America demonstrates.[10] He notes how the French emphasis on reproducing a performance staged for recording resulted in a preference for direct sound. Hollywood cinema, on the other hand, emphasised tight synchronisation to make sure sound served storytelling intelligibility as far as possible. Compared with colour, sound was introduced very fast, totally transforming the major film industries in a few years. O'Brien explains how this rupture exaggerated a particular conception of silent cinema as an art form in comparison with sound films:

> When sound and image were recorded at the same time – as in the highly popular talkies and *films parlants* ('talking films') – certain cinematographic and editing effects familiar to silent-era cinema became difficult or impossible to duplicate. Multiple superimpositions, lens-filtered images, color tinting and toning, and other cinematographic techniques with tendencies toward two-dimensionality, which had been a hallmark of silent-era cinema, proved incompatible with the phenomenology of the synch-sound film. Inevitably three-dimensional and relentlessly linear in temporality, synch-sound images entailed a straightforward, naturalistic narration and visual style.[11]

These developments militated against an imaginative application of colour in the first years following the introduction of sound, and the stress on naturalism rendered problematic attempts to resuscitate experimental practices with applied colour that were identified with silent cinema.

Colour's much slower introduction permitted many false starts and phases of optimism about its aesthetic possibilities as the merits of different processes were debated over many years. The lack of a clear direction provided a space for experimentation but also for chromophobic forces to gather momentum. Much as with the elevation of silent cinema to the status of art cinema once sound was introduced, for many observers black-and-white films appeared aesthetically superior when colour was on the agenda but was far from totally accepted. Cultural preferences for black and white are underpinned by philosophical positions such as Immanuel Kant's privileging of line and form over the addition of colours that might cause distraction. Roland Barthes wrote about colour as 'a coating applied *later on* to the original truth of the black-and-white photograph. For me, colour is an artifice, a cosmetic.'[12] As we shall see, the somewhat paradoxical identification of black and white with realism rather than colour was at the heart of many attempts to describe colour as 'natural' and capable of enhancing the realism critics so prized as fundamental to a successful aesthetic contract between art work and viewer. For some, this could have negative consequences for attempts to create a new language of cinema through colour. Writing in 1924, theorist Béla Balázs feared colour made film-makers prioritise fidelity to nature above artistic purpose. Seven years later he was more positive, seeing colour as introducing 'perspectival depth' and 'opening up space' in a creative way.[13] Rudolf Arnheim was another theorist who initially privileged black-and-white cinematography but started to reconsider his views on colour once three-strip Technicolor was invented. In its capacity for introducing visual complexity through organising an image by variations in hue and saturation he subsequently began to appreciate colour's artistic potential.[14] Here is the rub: to draw attention to itself colour had to be different, yet for complete acceptance it needed to take care to support, rather than challenge, dominant aesthetic preferences.

The space given in this book to reflection on colour, its merits and shortcomings, constitutes a key frame of contextual reference. As Dudley Andrew's study of responses to colour in France has shown, the history of technology must go beyond being a history of invention. He asks: 'What happens when the brute issues of technology, economics and film praxis interact with a contemporaneous discourse about the ideological implications of change? Can this effect the change? Discourse is surely a social *fact*, but should we also treat it as an historical *factor*?'[15] His study of reactions to colour technologies in France is instructive in that prevalent ideological regimes delayed the introduction of colour technologies for some time, instead identifying the French 'cinema of quality' with black and white. This book traces exactly these facets in which colour's technical development was profoundly influenced by contemporary debates and ideologies around colour. British cinema is particularly fascinating in this regard because of its identification by many contemporary film critics with realism. One of this book's key arguments is that film-makers operating within colour 'restraint', and therefore not a world away from the sentiments of those who prized black-and-white art and films, explored a great deal of latitude within that construct. The films they produced proved to many critics that British experimentation with colour was exceptional. The boundaries between realism and spectacle were indeed stretched as film-makers negotiated established aesthetic regimes while at the same time exploiting colour's artistic potential.

Colour Films in Britain: The Negotiation of Innovation 1900–55 is based on archival documents, interviews with cinematographers and other professionals who worked with colour, and film analysis, supplemented by a Technical Appendix by Simon Brown. Due to the complexity of many of the technical specifications of the various processes discussed it is advisable for those unfamiliar with colour technology to consult the Appendix in the first instance. The reader will find key details explained, such as the differences between additive and subtractive processes, as well as some of the fundamental principles of colour cinematography. Every process mentioned in the book has a detailed entry in Appendix 2 (Technical Appendix by Simon Brown) to which readers are directed in the chapters should they wish to read further about its history and specifications. The concentration is on films intended for theatrical release, although processes developed for the amateur market are taken into account from technical and economic perspectives.

The period 1900–55 has been selected as the key years when significant colour experimentation occurred in Britain, from early pioneers including William Friese-Greene, G. A. Smith, Charles Urban and J. Stuart Blackton in the silent period to Adrian Cornwell-Clyne, Len Lye and cinematographers Jack Cardiff, Ossie Morris and Chris Challis in the 1930s–50s. While it might appear arbitrary to begin with 1900 and end with 1955, the dates are intended as approximate markers of the early development of 'natural', photographic colour processes and ending with the serious take-up in the 1950s of Kodak's 35mm Eastmancolor monopack colour negative film stock, heralding the demise of Technicolor's three-strip system, which had been the foundation of so many distinguished British colour films. Of course, that was not the end of interesting colour films. Technicolor processing continued after its famous beam-splitter cameras – tellingly described by cinematographer Jack Cardiff as analogous to a 'Rolls Royce', a prestigious, high-quality British car manufacturer – were no longer used.[16] Analysis of the subsequent decades of Hammer's Eastmancolor aesthetic; post-new wave colour films of the 1960s including *Tom Jones* (1963) and *Blow-Up* (1966); Nicholas Roeg's colour experimentation in films including *Performance* (1970) and *The Man Who Fell to Earth* (1976); the colour look of the 'heritage' cycle of costume films in the 1980s, through to experimentation with digital colour in British films as varied as Michael Winterbottom's *Code 46* (2003) or Sally Potter's *Rage* (2009) would indeed produce fascinating results.[17] This book is intended to establish the historical foundations upon which analyses of post-three-strip colour technologies inevitably depend.

The following chapter summaries serve as a guide to the book's chronological phases, as well as to the themes which relate to the overall conceptual framework outlined above. Chapter 1 concentrates on Kinemacolor, an additive photographic process which enjoyed commercial success in Britain in 1908–14. Its development and exploitation by G. A. Smith and Charles Urban is examined within the broader context of the late nineteenth-century and early twentieth-century cultures of invention. Kinemacolor set a precedent for later experiments, and was part of a growing fascination with colour in cultural and commercial spheres. During this period many of the discourses that reverberated in subsequent decades were established around the nature of screen colour. Processes were judged according to a variety of factors including fidelity to reality, their technical competence, or spectacular novelty value. Kinemacolor was known for its popular topical films of royal subjects and foreign places, but was susceptible to a technical problem known as 'fringing'. The main problem was 'time parallax' whereby if an object changed position during the time it took to expose the records these appeared misaligned when projected, resulting in 'fringing' around the moving object as a coloured, ghostly trail following figures when they moved. This fault also dogged other processes and concentration on it as a major deficiency persisted into the 1920s after Kinemacolor ceased to be commercially viable. The chapter concludes by arguing that the legacy of Kinemacolor is nevertheless very important in establishing a precedent for the benefits and problems of early colour film experimentation. Subsequent film-makers looked back to it in order to learn from Charles Urban's talents at commercial exploitation. On the other hand, they also took note of the technical difficulties evident with Kinemacolor and tried to avoid repeating them in their own experiments.

Moving on to the 1920s, the second chapter concentrates on two different photographic processes: Prizmacolor and Natural Colour. The focus on Prizma is illustrated by an extended examination of *The Glorious Adventure* (1922), a celebrated feature film that attracted a great deal of publicity, not least because it was directed by British-born film-maker J. Stuart Blackton who had made his name working in the American film industry. The film is significant not only for its use of Prizma, but also because it represents a high level of Anglo-American collaboration and the deployment of a female star, society beauty Lady Diana

Manners. The analysis suggests that Blackton was astute in making a virtue of 'fringing' by exploiting it as a special effect in scenes of the Great Fire of London. The film is an excellent example of the mixing of colour styles, demonstrating how applied and photographic methods were not necessarily distinct during this period of colour hybridity. The chapter's second case study is of Claude Friese-Greene's experiments which were also steeped in the legacy of Kinemacolor and lessons learned from Prizma. 'Fringing' was, however, also a problem with Friese-Greene's mainly topical films, which were generally unsuccessful in spite of receiving much rapturous publicity. Scholarly attention has recently focused on *The Open Road* (1925) following restoration work undertaken by the British Film Institute which presents the films with most of the technical faults 'tidied up'. Although they were not widely exhibited in the 1920s, the marketing of Friese-Greene's films became caught up in the fervour of patriotic lobbying about the future of the British film industry on the eve of the Cinematograph Films Act 1927, which required distributors and exhibitors to handle and show a certain percentage of British films in the hope that American competition might be reduced. Friese-Greene's films aimed to use colour to convey the charms of the British countryside, establishing a precedent for later appreciations of processes such as Dufaycolor, which became identified with being especially appropriate for filming in Britain.

Chapter 3 concentrates on the early 1930s when, due to the development of a number of three-colour processes – most famously three-strip Technicolor – colour was again very much on the agenda. It was not clear that Technicolor would dominate and several additive and subtractive processes were being patented and presented to the film industry. Dufaycolor and Gasparcolor in particular jockeyed for attention, establishing a small but significant foothold in the short and advertising film market. Dufaycolor became identified with a limited, restrained colour palette that many deemed to be appropriate for an 'English' colour aesthetic. The chapter surveys the major contours of debate, with discussions about the extent to which colour should appear to be obtrusive in a film attracting the most controversy. A consensus was, however, emerging that the principle of colour design was a good one, whether used to rein in the spectacular potential of colour images or to produce a strikingly conceived artistic design. The 1930s was a decade when the future of the British film industry continued to be a topic of concern for politicians as well as the industry. Many prominent feature producers considered colour to be an important marker of quality, as well as enhancing the aesthetic and commercial potential of British films.

The arrival of three-strip Technicolor in Britain is documented in Chapter 4, particularly the intervention of Natalie Kalmus and the Color Advisory Service. Credited as 'color consultant' on most Technicolor films from 1933 to 1949, Natalie Kalmus was the ex-wife of Technicolor co-founder Herbert Kalmus. She headed the Color Advisory Service, which producers were obliged to consult as part of their contract to use Technicolor. A new phase of Anglo-American collaboration was, of necessity, inaugurated by Technicolor's success with three-strip technology and imbibition printing. Technicolor's introduction coincided with incentives for bigger-budget film-making as a result of protective state legislation. Competition between colour systems caused a new intensity around debates about the desirability of film colour. Natalie Kalmus's ideas about 'color consciousness' were well received because they reinforced some of the discourses already in circulation, most notably expounded by figures such as the British film historian and colour theorist Adrian Cornwell-Clyne. The chapter analyses *Wings of the Morning* (1937), the first British three-strip Technicolor film, and *The Thief of Bagdad* (1940), a visually spectacular, experimental fantasy film that plays with colour symbolism and special effects. Acknowledging its legacy as a seminal three-strip Technicolor film, co-director Michael Powell later recalled: 'The Archers thought in colour from *The Thief of Bagdad* onwards.'[18] Both films showcase colour in different ways and represent major steps forward for colour design and Anglo-American cooperation with Technicolor.

In spite of scarcities and the problems of producing colour films during wartime, Chapter 5 demonstrates how, contrary to what might be expected, the war was pivotal in terms of promoting technical advancements and establishing the cultural case for an expansion of colour films in the postwar world. Experiments in the short, sponsored film market which produced many notable colour films such as *This is*

Colour (1942), shot by Jack Cardiff, are the main focus. The chapter also surveys the views of a number of key commentators who documented responses to British and American colour films during wartime, most notably E. S. Tompkins, who wrote a regular 'Colour Enthusiast at the Cinema' column in the *British Journal of Photography*. It is suggested that 'colour control' could not operate in quite the same way or with a similar degree of constraint as in the immediate prewar years. This opened up a space for a national variant to develop during a time when the demand for colour accelerated as part of broader social, cultural and utopian aspirations for the postwar years.

A number of key British colour feature films in which the wartime context assumes thematic significance are analysed in Chapter 6. It presents detailed, comparative analyses of how colour functions in *Sons of the Sea* (1939), made in Dufaycolor, and *The Great Mr Handel* (1942), *The Life and Death of Colonel Blimp* (1943), *This Happy Breed* (1944), *Henry V*, *Western Approaches* (1944) and *Blithe Spirit* (1945), made in Technicolor. In their different ways the films demonstrate the advances that were taking place in the deployment of colour in feature film narratives. As a rare example of a feature film made in Dufaycolor, *Sons of the Sea* provides an opportunity to assess its properties in comparison with the norms that were being developed for Technicolor. The notion of 'restraint' is examined, demonstrating how an approach to colour design that might be thought of as subdued nevertheless deployed colour as emphasis in certain scenes or sequences and involved occasional displays of spectacle. *Western Approaches* is an example of how technical difficulties promoted ingenuity when colour was mobilised to 'sell propaganda', as it was in *Henry V*. The analysis of *Blithe Spirit* demonstrates how an obtrusive colour design functioned in relation to narrative, as well as to prevailing cultural and social preoccupations with the themes of death and spiritualism. The film's colour was of fundamental importance in expressing its thematic concerns, in particular its use of green and in visually coding conflict between characters. In this regard it is an example of colour design constituting an integral element of film form, theme and address.

A survey of the immediate postwar context follows in Chapter 7, which notes a revival of technical experimentation in the colour field. Technicolor's consolidation of its dominant market position was, however, never seriously threatened. These years saw the rise of a talented cinematographer who had gained experience with Technicolor cameras since the late 1930s. Jack Cardiff was given the chance to work on *A Matter of Life and Death* (1946), a highly unusual film with scenes in monochrome and Technicolor to demark the film's two worlds of, respectively, heaven and earth. The film's striking, creative play with colour is examined, noting its seminal status as indicative of the confidence in colour that was gathering momentum at the end of the war. Admired by many commentators in America, it also marks the growing perception that although few in number British colour feature films had matured during the war and were making a distinctive contribution to colour film aesthetics.

Chapter 8 is the first of three chapters which examine colour's role in different genres, arguing that it became an important register of generic repetition and difference. This involved establishing internal consistencies rather than simply reproducing colours deemed to have specific symbolic resonances. After presenting initial examples from the silent period to demonstrate some enduring themes and approaches, colour film spectacles of events including the 1948 Olympic Games, the 1951 Festival of Britain and the 1953 Coronation are discussed. An extended analysis of *XIV Olympiad: The Glory of Sport* (1948) provides an opportunity to examine how three different technologies (three-strip Technicolor, Technichrome and monopack) function in one film with variable results. *Scott of the Antarctic* (1948) and *The Magic Box* (1951) are then analysed, since as biopics they share some similar conventions to the films about contemporary events. *The Magic Box* is particularly appropriate, since the film is a dramatisation of the life of colour film pioneer William Friese-Greene. The *World Windows* (1937–40) series of travelogues shot by Jack Cardiff introduces the final section on fiction films about Empire, including *The Drum* (1938), *The Four Feathers* (1939) and *Men of Two Worlds* (1946). The chapter concludes by arguing that while colour often enhances genre in expected ways, it can still surprise the viewer, breaking away from the constraints generic film-making might otherwise impose.

Often seen as a 'natural' genre for colour, particularly in relation to Douglas Sirk's Hollywood melodramas, the films analysed in the following chapter demonstrate interesting examples of British colour melodramas. The case studies bring to prominence films not normally accorded sustained attention such as *The Man Within* (1946), *Saraband for Dead Lovers* (1948) and *Footsteps in the Fog* (1955). A differently inflected canon of British melodramas is thus proposed. The chapter also presents analyses of *Jassy* (1947), *Blanche Fury* (1948) and *Gone to Earth* (1950), films that establish a broad comparative frame of reference while drawing on a range of theoretical perspectives on melodrama and colour. The final chapter concentrating on generic colour analysis is on musicals and comedies. Comedy is seldom examined with colour as the primary referent. Yet the examples included from *The Importance of Being Earnest* (1952), *Genevieve* (1953), *The Titfield Thunderbolt* (1952) and *The Ladykillers* (1955) show that on occasion it could be very important as part of a film's comedic address. Colours such as red are used differently than in, say, melodramas, providing more support for Eisenstein's ideas about colour relating primarily to context rather than to a universal symbolism per se, as noted with reference to many case studies in this book. The example of the musical *London Town* (1946) is instructive on the consequences of box-office failure for colour films, and how particular countries became identified with specific colour genres in this period. In this case a considerable number of American musicals were released but British producers tended to avoid the genre after the failure of *London Town*.

Having established a pattern of comparative textual analyses, Chapter 11 continues with this method by examining films less tied to conventional notions of genre. An introductory section on colour films notable for their consistent displays of nature, particularly floral imagery, informs a broader discussion of realism and spectacle. This was a recurring theme in debates about the affective impact of colour imagery which can also be related to ideas about the affinities between colour and music. Experimentation is the key element in Powell and Pressburger's *Black Narcissus* (1947), *The Red Shoes* and *The Tales of Hoffmann* (1951). These films permit analysis of the connections between colour, dance and music, as well as interrogating the idea of the 'composed film' in which a film is shot to match previously composed music in a holistic way. Contemporary commentaries on the relationship between colour and music, and the potential of the 'dance film' to transform film art inform a discussion of their impact on feature films. Particularly striking sequences are analysed, including the 'stalking' sequence towards the end of *Black Narcissus* as an early example of the composed film. The analysis of *The Red Shoes* compares the celebrated Red Shoes ballet sequence with a short film of Hein Heckroth's designs that formed a template for the feature film. This provides a rare opportunity to track the evolution of the colour design from pre-production to shooting. *The Tales of Hoffmann* is the final example of attempts to unite colour, dance and music in an aesthetic collaboration that represented a high-point of colour experimentation in postwar British feature films.

The final chapter returns to questions raised in the book about the nature of creative and technical collaboration with colour. It follows several celebrated cases when cinematographers developed innovative methods of colour design: Jack Cardiff's cinematography on *Pandora and the Flying Dutchman* (1950), a film not normally discussed in relation to colour or particularly highly regarded by contemporary critics, and Ossie Morris's extraordinary experimental work on *Moulin Rouge* (1953) and *Moby Dick* (1956). These films demonstrate the highly collaborative creative contexts within which innovators with colour operated and how technical challenges inspired creative exploration at the highest level. The book's conclusion ties the arguments together in relation to British colour cinema. Looking back on the history of colour films in Britain one is struck by parallels with our contemporary experience of digital technologies. As in the silent period of applied colour, the image is subject to ever more extreme degrees of manipulation, with infinite choices available to 'colourists' in extending the range of emphasis in applying the concept of colour design. Yet the principles of harmony, control and balance are enduring ones, again proving that historical precedent is instructive in our understanding of how innovation is negotiated in many different economic, aesthetic and cultural contexts. Indeed, the key to understanding British colour aesthetics is to appreciate the complex matrix of negotiated relations that interact with each other as colour technologies are developed and marketed. Significant economic contexts include the cost of colour technologies and the British film industry's relations with Hollywood, at times fraught and competitive, while on other occasions cooperative and mutually beneficial. In developing a British approach to colour, film-makers and technicians were also influenced by taste cultures that derived from older aesthetic traditions including British romantic and landscape painting or pictorial approaches in early colour photography. These traditions encouraged a positive reception for technologies developed in Britain, such as Kinemacolor and Dufaycolor, that celebrated the colours of the British countryside in travelogues. At the same time, when three-strip Technicolor was invented British directors and technicians were at the forefront of experimentation, seeking to graft their own stylistic preferences and identities on an American technology. Along with Alexander Korda, many predicted that colour would pervade all films in a relatively short period of time. The journey down the yellow-brick road was, however, far from straightforward, involving a number of blind alleys and lost causes along the way. It is hoped that this book goes some way towards understanding the often tortuous path of colour in the first half of the twentieth century, as well as celebrating its aesthetic variety and enduring fascination for film-makers, technicians, critics, audiences and scholars.

1 COLOUR IN SILENT BRITAIN
THE KINEMACOLOR STORY

In May 1924 *Collier's: The National Weekly*, a popular American magazine known for its investigative journalism and vivid colour illustrations, published an article by D. W. Griffith entitled 'The Movies 100 Years from Now'. The preamble criticised contemporary colour film processes as deficient, arguing that in the first decades of cinema history:

> We have been merely exploring and speculating. Only through one method will color be naturally and properly given to objects and persons in the motion pictures. This is a method which will develop a film so sensitive that it will record the natural tints and colors as the picture is being photographed … One hundred years from now the color of a woman's eyes and hair, the tint of the sea, the hues of the rainbow itself will be a natural part of every motion-picture play.[1]

Griffith's article had been read and annotated by Charles Urban, by then a veteran in colour film exploitation who was particularly renowned for the short-lived but undoubtedly significant **Kinemacolor (see Technical Appendix)** process first developed in Britain. In the margin Urban wrote defiantly: 'Why wait 100 years? Kinecrom does it now.'[2] Since the beginning of the silent era, these claims had been made. Urban's response reflected the intensely competitive commercial culture of colour experimentation during this period in which hundreds of patents were registered but few processes exhibited.[3] Indeed, perfecting colour film became a holy grail for many inventors, entrepreneurs, film pioneers, social reformers and educationalists who were convinced from varying, yet often overlapping, perspectives that only through colour could cinema fully realise its potential as a medium capable of achieving a convincing mimetic relationship to the world.

Conflicting ideological assumptions were behind this drive in which colour became enmeshed in wider debates in the late nineteenth century to the early twentieth century about realism, aesthetics, physiology, psychology, class, modernity and commerce that were not confined to motion pictures. Commentary on colour films – tinted and toned and 'natural' photographic processes such as Kinemacolor – reflected and developed discursive contexts applied to the invasion of colour in everyday life, as seen in magazines, posters, magic lantern slides, wallpapers, dyes and in consumer goods. As Tom Gunning noted, aspirations for colour cinema depended on two apparently contradictory attributes, on the one hand delivering a 'true', Bazinian representation of the world 'as it is', while on the other transcending that reality principle with its brilliance, its spectacular impact to shock, thrill, surprise and draw attention to itself.[4] In the silent era and particularly concerning applied colour techniques, Gunning argues, the latter tendency was more dominant but, as we shall see, even understandings of colour which depended on valuing its indexical qualities were not free of judgments which drew attention to the novelty and nature of colour on screen, indeed, as a 'spectacle of reality'.[5]

Silent cinema historians note how applied techniques such as hand and stencil colouring, tinting and toning were extensive, as a general estimate evident in up to 80–85 per cent of motion picture productions,

1895–1930.[6] This makes the silent period especially fascinating since it contrasts markedly with the period 1930–55 when colour was nowhere near as all-pervasive. As noted below, some processes were more widespread than others, and by the closing years of the silent era tinting and toning was the most prevalent method. Studying colour film in the early years of cinema is, however, fraught with difficulties since many nitrate prints vulnerable to deterioration did not survive. The colours of those that did are long-since faded and in order to get a sense of how they might have looked researchers must take into account contemporary variations in standards and styles, dyes and exhibition conventions which differed from country to country. In addition, much early coloured film was not preserved in colour but as black-and-white duplicate negatives and prints with a written record of the colours. As Paul Read notes: 'The image has good archival permanence but there is no visual record of the colours, either as faded by time, or as originally seen.'[7] In addition, as Gunning has commented, it is perhaps 'an impossible quest for historians to get back, not so much to the original object, as to the original experience' of viewing colour films, a sentiment echoed by Cherchi Usai: 'Colour in the moving image is the most unstable component of an inherently ephemeral medium; anything we can say about it comes from a contradictory mediation between memory and present visual experience.'[8] Yet important studies have been produced, particularly concerning American cinema, as well as of Kinemacolor in Britain.[9] Documentary evidence exists in film trade papers and in advertising materials, and surviving nitrate prints have been restored by professionals informed by the conventions of film colouring during the period.[10]

R. W. Paul may have been the first person to exhibit colour films. He demonstrated a hand-coloured film of an 'Eastern Dance' at the Alhambra Theatre, London, in April 1896, two weeks before Edison's celebrated presentation of the *Serpentine Dance* in the first programme of the Vitagraph in New York. Paul also coloured a version of his film of the 1895 Derby, and a few months later it was reported that: 'The colouring of the pictures is almost a matter of course now, and the mingled effect of the many separately coloured positives makes every tint harmonious and pleasant.'[11] While the effects were beautiful, hand-colouring was a time-consuming, highly skilled technique developed from expertise in painting magic lantern slides, often undertaken by groups of women who would painstakingly colour images frame by frame. Other British inventors were at the forefront of colour development. Cecil Hepworth, for example, used gel tinters over projector lenses as early as 1903, a technique which originated in stage and magic lantern practices and was influential in the development of colour tinting, along with hand-colouring emulsions of film prints with translucent, aniline dyes. Hepworth also advertised brown, red and blue toning in a 1903 catalogue.[12] While it is difficult to trace the chronological development of various applied techniques and photographic processes with complete accuracy, it seems that in Britain and elsewhere costly and labour-intensive hand-colouring was replaced by mechanised methods developed in France such as Pathécolor, a stencil colour process introduced in 1905–06 and Gaumont coloured films in 1908.[13] Tinting and toning were first evident around the turn of the twentieth century, and dyeing techniques soon became the most common means of incorporating colour into the moving image. Of the various methods, hand-coloured films were generally the most expensive, and toned films tended to cost more than tinted.[14] The market was competitive, as trade paper advertisements reveal. *Egypt: Cairo to Khartoum*, offered by the Charles Urban Trading Company in June 1907, for instance, was 'beautifully tinted in sections at no extra charge', whereas *The Fountain of Eternal Youth*, a Gaumont film available from late November was described as: 'Full of brilliant and fascinating incidents and coloured in glowing shades … No Christmas bill complete without it', cost extra for colouring.[15]

A survey of British trade papers for the years 1907–09 demonstrates something of the extent of colouring by hand, tinting or toning (or combinations of applied methods) for films released in Britain.[16] While detailed commentary on the use of colour is relatively rare beyond general remarks such as 'beautifully toned and coloured', some impression can be gained of what was considered unusual or particularly effective, as well as the circumstances in which colour was applied. One film, for example, called *Jim's Apprenticeships* (Pathé Frères; tinting) involved a boy's disastrous attempts at different jobs. The description noted: 'The conclusion, represents Jim in the publican's cellar up to his knees in wine – good colouring giving the proper amber hue.'[17]

Achieving the 'proper hue' was praised in other films and some consistency is evident for the application of particular colours for scenes such as blue for night or for the sea in travelogues, and red for fire in Hepworth's *Baby's Playmate* which featured a red-tinted fire scene.[18] Trick films used colour effects as part of their spectacular generic expectation, as in *The Magic Eggs* (Gaumont) which featured eggs performing tricks 'meanwhile changing colours' at the wave of a fairy's wand.[19] Two-colour tinting and toning effects were noted as 'really remarkable' in *The Highwayman* (Pathé Frères) in a review that makes an interesting comment on the extent to which the colour achieved:

> the closest approximation to natural tints, which we imagined would be impossible to get without colour photography. By the use of two colours for tinting, which act together, seem to produce a third, Pathes [*sic*] have in this subject obtained really fine effects of a blue sky, and of grass etc., though the colouring in parts is inclined to be a little high.[20]

This anticipates later discourses about photographic colour needing to convince on the grounds of 'natural verisimilitude' and that it should not be garish, even in a film that was not a travelogue. This is somewhat at odds with hand-coloured films which aimed to engage spectators with 'dazzling "spectacular realities" that seem to leap from the screen'.[21] Indeed, a 'shift towards restraint' in the discussion of colour is perceptible around 1907–08 in the USA as part of a reaction against Pathé's incursion into the market with its highly coloured films and in relation to wider discursive educational, ideological contexts which promoted a more subdued colour style.[22] Commentary on *The Highwayman* in the British trade press would appear to support the idea that a general trend in this direction was occurring. As Urban was astute in realising, photographic processes such as Kinemacolor gained notoriety at an appropriate moment when opinion was conducive to what they could offer in terms of providing different experiences of colour attraction, occasionally spectacular for trick films but more typically 'natural' and less obtrusive for travelogues and dramas.

Benjamin Pask's concise table of 314 patents registered for colour processes in Britain 1893–1930 includes 180, or 57 per cent, listed as British.[23] The various colour 'patent wars' instigated commercial rivalries that lasted for many years, such as between William Friese-Greene of **Biocolour (see Technical Appendix)** and Charles Urban that culminated in the notorious court appeal ruling in 1914 that hastened Kinemacolor's demise. Based on the south coast near Brighton, figures such as William Norman Lascelles-Davidson, Benjamin Jumeaux and Otto Pfenninger were also important in the early years of developing natural colour systems, as well as Colin Bennett, who exploited a Friese-Greene patent and was later credited for developing Cinechrome. Friese-Greene's experiments involved two different methods: a light-splitting prism behind the camera lens passing through filters, and a process in which successive frames were dyed red and green.[24] These enterprising figures to some extent revived the cultures of popular fervour around invention more commonly associated with the celebration of nineteenth-century technologies including railway construction and the excitement generated by the 1851 Great Exhibition. The second half of the nineteenth century has often been depicted by historians as a period of anxiety as Britain's industrial and technological competitiveness was seen to be threatened by other countries such as Germany and the USA.[25] From this perspective G. A. Smith and William Friese-Greene's efforts constitute evidence of a more thriving culture of invention in the first years of the twentieth century. The primacy of many British inventors in motion picture technology and the specialist interest many had in colour promised to revive Britain's creative and commercial reputation.

As discussed in more detail subsequently in this chapter, Kinemacolor enjoyed a brief, but spectacular intrusion into the commercial market as a photographic, **additive process (see Technical Appendix)** that specialised in topical films of royal occasions and travelogues, 1908–14. Kinemacolor had to compete with Gaumont's three-colour Chronochrome additive process first demonstrated in Paris in November 1912, as well as with a host of other patented ideas. The greatest number of patents relating to colour motion pictures were filed in 1912, spurred on by Urban's success with the Delhi Durbar films.[26] The amount of energy and enterprise directed towards colour during this period is impressive and on occasion pre-dates subsequent well-known experiments. Edward Thornton, for example, filed a great number of patents and is credited for inventing a camera in 1911 using three lenses and a dye imbibition process very similar to that later successfully developed by Technicolor.[27] The British interest in colour was established at an early stage, from R. W. Paul to William Friese-Greene and Charles Urban, making distinctive contributions in the field. The race to perfect photographic colour processes was at the heart of conflicts between inventors, who worked tirelessly to achieve 'natural' colour, inspired by a range of approaches which included tinting alternate film frames red and green; putting rotating coloured filters on projectors; using light-splitting prisms with cameras and sensitising film stock. As McKernan's research on Kinemacolor has demonstrated, commercial success in the context of photographic colour processes is a relative concept, since revenue must be offset against the considerable expenses involved in development and exploitation.[28] Yet even though other British photographic processes such as Cinechrome and **Polychromide (see Technical Appendix)** were exhibited, Kinemacolor was by far the best known, facilitated by Urban's aggressive showmanship and publicity. Combined with the number of films made, their profitability for a few years and the effectiveness of their intrusion into the public consciousness, it is not therefore surprising that out of the fervour of colour experimentation Kinemacolor emerged as the most notorious process.

The quest for colour involved mixed motives which combine varying degrees and emphases in Branagan's models of historical explanation for technological innovation. Inventions do not just appear out of nowhere. They are the result of the interaction of a range of complex factors. These include the brilliance and tenacity of particular individuals, but, in addition, other reasons mean that some inventions are taken up while others, like the many colour patents that were never exploited, remain unknown. But crucially Branagan's models, therefore, include the 'adventure' narrative of individual agency; technological issues; theories of industrial exploitation; and the role of ideology.[29] 'Adventurers' such as Friese-Greene and Charles Urban indulged in the rhetoric of scientific discovery, presenting themselves as pioneers on the brink of enlightenment. While it is tempting to present the history of colour film as a succession of shorter- and

longer-lived triumphs of individuals such as Urban or Herbert Kalmus, it is clearly necessary also to understand significant technological problems and breakthroughs, as well as the impact of prevailing economic and ideological contexts. As Branagan points out, Kinemacolor's emergence as the most celebrated, sustained example of a commercial, non-applied process in the silent period was in part influenced by prevailing views about the efficacy of science, in particular the 'optical desirability of color in motion pictures' related to notions of realism.[30] Faith in mimetic reproduction was also related to contemporary ideologies around education and moral 'uplift', since believing the camera to be capable of exceeding human vision was linked to the desire to influence 'character forming processes' through scientific endeavour.[31] Such claims were based on acknowledging the moving image's power to influence as no other media had done before, for good or for evil. In the wake of the technological revolution Urban presented Kinemacolor as another triumph of man's ingenuity. As we shall see, the rhetoric deployed by Urban to promote Kinemacolor was imbued with claims about the process's educational role as 'The Marvel of the Age', revealing new worlds to audiences in films recording nature, foreign countries, royal processions and military ceremonies normally outside their direct experience.[32]

The history of Kinemacolor has been recounted by several historians, most notably in McKernan's study of Charles Urban and Hanssen's research on contemporary notions of 'natural' colour based on the *Catalogue of Kinemacolor Film Subjects, 1912–13*.[33] Before considering the relationship between Kinemacolor and the multifarious, complex discursive formations with which it was inextricably involved, a brief recounting of how it managed to achieve such notoriety in a relatively short time is necessary.[34] G. A. Smith worked with Urban to produce a practically viable process based on **Lee and Turner**'s three-colour additive principles patented in 1899 **(see Technical Appendix)**. Stymied by challenging technical problems, Smith developed a related two-colour process that was patented in 1906 and formed the basis of the claim to 'approximately' reproduce natural colours with Kinemacolor. He also was responsible for adapting orthochromatic stock so that it was more responsive to light from the red area of the spectrum, a technological breakthrough which assisted subsequent two-colour processes. Towards the end of 1907 some trial demonstrations took place, and in May 1908 selected dignitaries were invited to the newly opened Urbanora House to view colour films in a prestigious gathering that was to become a familiar means of advertising Kinemacolor. On 23 February 1909 the public was introduced to the process which was publicly named Kinemacolor for the first time at the Palace Theatre, London, before being exhibited all over the country and abroad.

Smith publicised his work to the scientific community at a meeting of the Royal Society of Arts in December 1908, detailing his decision to abandon three-colour experimentation in favour of a two-colour process that featured revolving shutters containing red and green filters on both camera and projector. In his opinion this was capable of approximating the range of the spectrum when projected at a high speed (30–2 fps) and working in conjunction with the principle of persistence of vision.[35] Smith's paper was then discussed and in view of the problems later experienced by Kinemacolor, some of the issues raised appear to be prescient. After seeing some demonstration films, Sir Henry Trueman Wood, Secretary of the Society, remarked that 'while the reds were admirably rendered, the darker blues, and some of the greens, were not quite as true to nature as theoretically they might be'; greys and browns, on the other hand, were 'admirably and perfectly truly rendered'.[36] Thus began a trend of criticism to which every colour process was subsequently subjected: how 'true' was it to 'reality'? Why were red and brown 'admirably rendered', whereas other colours were not considered to be as well reproduced as, say, in the Lumière brothers' Autochrome photographic plates, which were receiving very favourable publicity in 1907–08 and, Smith admitted, gave 'wonderful' colour records using a triple system?[37] The main problem he had found in trying to develop a three-colour process for moving images was 'time parallax'. If an object changed position during the time it took to expose three records these appeared misaligned when projected, resulting in colour fringing around the moving object.[38] Working with only two records helped reduce fringing but was less successful in adequately reproducing a full range of colour, particularly blue. The problems of exaggerating the scope of a two-colour process came back to haunt

Urban in a series of legal wrangles in 1913–14 with Bioschemes, a company formed to front William Friese-Greene's campaign against Smith's 1906 patent. In December 1913 Bioschemes petitioned for the patent to be revoked. The petition was dismissed but when Bioschemes appealed the company succeeded in getting the patent revoked in March 1914, largely on the grounds that claims to render the colour blue were inaccurate. In the following month Urban liquidated the Natural Color Kinematography Company and soon departed for America. Although Kinemacolor films continued to be shown, the monopoly was lost, and the case contributed to Kinemacolor's decline.[39]

In the preceding years Kinemacolor, however, enjoyed notoriety by being demonstrated to prestigious audiences including the royal family, numerous titled personages and representatives of society's elite. Urban began his campaign to develop the process as a quality product designed to appeal to discerning exhibitors and audiences attracted by the novelty of colour as a scientific, spectacular attraction he hoped would transform cinema into an educational, 'uplifting' institution. Colour was thus equated with quality and prestige, rather than being considered vulgar or associated with lower-class taste. Urban's marketing of Kinemacolor was influential in advancing ideas about British colour cinema as tasteful, for the discerning, patriotic viewer. The connection with royalty was of fundamental importance to Kinemacolor's success. Members of the royal family were frequently invited to special screenings and they featured as subjects in films of national events such as the funeral of Edward VII in May 1910, the Coronation of George V in June 1911 and Investiture of the Prince of Wales in July 1910. The royal tour of India and Coronation Durbar at Delhi filmed in December 1911–January 1912 was probably Kinemacolor's most celebrated triumph of capturing the pageantry, spectacle and magnitude of ceremonial occasions and glorifying the British Empire which, as McKernan has noted, coincided with a policy of 'increased visibility' for the British royal family and popular demand to see them on screen.[40] The Delhi Durbar was a magnificent ceremonial event to anoint King George V as Emperor of India. As such it represented the apotheosis of British imperialism preserved 'for all time', as *The Bioscope* put it, by Kinemacolor, 'the modern Elixir of Life'.[41] Urban's 'scooping' of such occasions was a unique selling point that served two convenient objectives: first, to brand Kinemacolor as a high-class, quality product that presented moving images of people and places audiences would seldom, if ever, have seen before; and, second, the very novelty of seeing those people and places on screen paradoxically, and for some time, detracted from Kinemacolor's technical shortcomings and perceived lack of full-spectrum reproducibility. The aura of royalty, exotic places and cultures made up, to some extent, for technical imperfections; audiences were arguably drawn in by the spectacle of royalty rather than colour per se, although these attractions tended to reinforce one another. Chapter 8 refers back to Kinemacolor's foundational legacy in linking films of royalty and national occasions with colour at a time when filming the Olympic Games in 1948 and the Coronation in 1953 were very much experiments in colour cinematography.

For long, prestigious Kinemacolor films, on occasion, lecturers would accompany touring companies to introduce and provide informative commentary for specific titles such as the Durbar film. Advertising leaflets were also issued to exhibitors. These described Kinemacolor's superior technical attributes and why the process was so important. Urban's control over commentary on the films by means of published programmes and lecture notes written for the purpose of supporting film screenings also acted as a brake on criticism which might otherwise have focused attention on Kinemacolor's problems, listed in a series of detailed, retrospective articles on colour cinematography published in the *British Journal of Photography* in 1922.[42] These included only being able to obtain a full exposure at maximum light conditions which limited what could be shot; the irregularity of the panchromatic stock; an unwieldy camera until Charles Raleigh (author of the articles who was involved in developing Prizma) constructed a smaller Debrie model embodying the colour shutter; variable printing results; the special projector that needed to be very robust because of the high speed requirements; complaints about 'off colour' resulting from a lack of synchronicity between the colour values of the film and the colour shutter; pictures showing an over-pronounced tone of either red or green; and, the most notorious failings, flicker and fringing. With regard to fringing, Raleigh explained that:

If Kinemacolor had kept to scenic … this eyesore would never have been noticed, but familiarity breeds contempt, and when bold barons fought and fair maidens danced they were all wreathed in gaudy ribbons of red and green, which, however, in the maypole dance was very effective and always brought applause.

As we shall see in Chapter 2, fringing was a problem that dogged subsequent processes such as Prizma and Claude Friese-Greene's experiments in the 1920s; fringing rather than colour rendition became the most problematic issue for additive systems. As Kinemacolor cameraman William T. Crespinel explained: 'If one waved a hand, it would appear as red and blue-green for the reason that there was a lapse of time between the red and blue-green exposure in the camera. Had both images been photographed simultaneously, there would have been no lapse of time between exposures.'[43] The Delhi Durbar films were generally praised, but one report singled out an incidence of unintended spectacle when soldiers walked 'with the red stripes on their trousers and their red coats following along behind them'.[44] A reviewer in *The Bioscope* warned Smith and Urban about exaggerating Kinemacolor's capabilities after seeing some films demonstrated in which 'the least expert in the audience could tell that a leaden blue was not the veritable hue and tint of a young lady's arm, or that a cornfield was all one dull, sandy yellow'.[45]

While these problems were considerable the demise of Kinemacolor cannot be attributed simply to its technical shortcomings in comparison with later processes. As McKernan points out, in spite of the difficulties it was nevertheless for a few years a very commercially successful natural colour process whose legacy must be considered in relation to the contemporary context of viewing colour films.[46] One has to take into account the cases when people were extremely impressed by what they saw, such as when Theodore Brown visited the Palace Theatre in 1910 and marvelled at the 'pleasurable intoxication' resulting from seeing actuality films of phenomena in which 'delusive nature has at last been captured'.[47] As Raleigh noted in relation to the maypole dance, defects such as fringing did not necessarily matter; in fact, they could be said to enhance the spectacle in a pragmatic approach later exploited by J. Stuart Blackton in the scenes of the Fire of London in *The Glorious Adventure* (1922) shot in

Prizma. As detailed in the following chapter, the spectacle of flickering flames was enhanced by the effect of fringing. It is worth pointing out that fringing was not only experienced by photographic methods. If successive frames were unevenly hand-coloured, fringing could result, an unintended effect which enhanced the impact of the popular dance films much as with the example of fire scenes in which the sensation of colour movement was compelling for its dynamism.

What is curious is that even though the Bioschemes court case drew attention to Kinemacolor's inability to render blue, Kinemacolor was occasionally admired for achieving blue tones, as one report of the Delhi Durbar film attests: 'Even the sky, which throughout serves as a frame for the human spectacle, is a thing to wonder at; it is one pure sheet of palpitating light, blue with a blueness of which one can only dream here in grey England, deep, intense, unruffled, like one gigantic sapphire.'[48] Even though the colour palette achieved with Kinemacolor was clearly deficient as far as blue and purple were concerned, projecting the film onto a light blue screen helped overcome these problems and may explain the enthusiastic comments about blue.[49] In addition, giving evidence to the court in the Bioschemes vs Natural Color Kinematograph Co. Ltd case, G. A. Smith made the point that even though an image of a Union Jack flag might not have very blue sections, more grey or even black, the viewer's cultural expectation to see blue could indeed convince her/him that it was actually present.[50] This example draws attention to the complex factors that come into play when trying to assess the impact of colour; the power of suggestion and symbolism are important influences on colour perception. Commentary in the *Catalogue of Kinemacolor Subjects, 1912–13* mentions dark blue in *Children Forming the US Flag* as 'unmistakeable' and the sea in *Telemachus: A Mythological Play* as 'a superb blue'. *Floral Friends* was said to convey a cornflower in 'remarkable vivid blue' in spite of the difficulties of obtaining the colour.[51]

One must indeed chart a careful evaluative course amid a wealth of contradictory detail about Kinemacolor, not least found in Urban's archive which contains many scrapbooks of advertising materials, press reviews and reports on Kinemacolor screenings all over Britain and abroad. The phrases used are often similar, inviting the suspicion that many descriptions were taken from the catalogues produced by the Natural Color Kinematograph Company. Colour vision is, indeed, variable, and the excitement around Kinemacolor might well have induced those who saw the films to imagine a fuller range of colours than they actually saw. One report recounted how after a demonstration colour specialist Professor Lippmann insisted on seeing the Kinemacolor projector 'to see with his own eyes that only two colours were actually employed. He did not believe it possible that such a combination of tones and shades could be obtainable in this manner.'[52] The wonder of natural colour film was sufficiently novel as to invite positive appreciation from many audiences, particularly when the films were carefully presented and contextualised by the company's publicity.

In a world in which many lower-class people did not have access to bright-colour clothing, for example, and most colour was seen in advertising materials, its appearance in film was all the more notable.[53] While colour was clearly making an incursion into everyday life for those able to purchase coloured wallpapers, clothes and jewellery, one cannot assume that these commodities were available to all. Admissions to Kinemacolor programmes varied and not all exhibitors charged higher prices for tickets. Some halls explicitly stated in newspaper advertisements that they were keeping their normal prices for Kinemacolor screenings – for example, the King's Theatre Greenock (May 1912); His Majesty's Theatre, Dundee (September 1912); The Cinema de Luxe, Walsall (March 1913); and The Palace, Durham (August 1913). But higher prices were charged in some halls, such as the Electric Theatre in Bath which increased its prices in April 1912 on the afternoon Kinemacolor arrived. It appears, however, that a significant number of venues chose not to increase prices and this trend occurred throughout the years when the process was being screened in Britain, presumably in an attempt to broaden its appeal.[54] Urban's pitch to higher-class audiences was, however, likely to connect with those able to afford the growing commercial availability of colour in other spheres. For this reason new fashion ranges were promoted by Kinemacolor as the only way to fully appreciate the styles in films such as *Advance Styles in Ostrich Plumage*:

All those who have seen monochrome representations of the latest fashions in dress or in hats, will have realised how powerless black and white motion photography is to reproduce with fidelity and conviction these wonderful creations of the modiste's art, or to import a true idea of their actual appearance. Thus it is, in this field of colour photography holds undisputed sway, by this process alone is it possible to present on the screen convincing reproductions which are so true to actuality as to awaken the envy and admiration of every woman in the audience.[55]

In this case audiences are invited to admire the fashions and be envious of the women wearing them, implying that purchase of the items would not necessarily be possible for everyone. Indeed, the description ends by remarking on the 'perfect detail' of the hats on display and flesh tints of the models as being 'so life-like … as to complete the illusion that one is gazing, not on a picture screen, but, as through a window upon an actual scene'.[56] The choice of words is interesting, implying a spectator who gazes from afar, as if from the perspective of someone looking in from a street onto a scene, perhaps seeing an opulent house or shop beyond their own experience or financial circumstances.[57] A similar sensibility is evident in *Kitty, the Dressmaker*, a Kinemacolor film about a 'humble' dressmaker's assistant who has a dream in which she is 'richly dressed, wearing furs'.[58]

McKernan notes that: 'Those who criticise Kinemacolor now for its inadequate colour reproduction are ignoring both the prevalent cultural conditions and the physiological processes that enriched the colour effect.'[59] These included the vicarious acquisition of culturally coded sensibilities with which colour became inextricably associated. In these circumstances an approximation of colour was most probably acceptable to many viewers when combined with the magnificence of a ceremonial occasion, or showing an exotic, foreign location which had been photographed in bright sunshine. These images were less tied to commercial exploitation of commodities or fashions but rather depended on the revelation of new experiences of colour at home and abroad. The description of *A Visit to the Seaside*, the first 'scenic picture' shot in Kinemacolor in Brighton, remarked of a shot of the Cameron Highlanders' Band that: 'In colorless Britain one must go to the Army to find rich, glowing hues.'[60] Films taken in India featured elephants adorned with 'crimson

velvet … at times the whole screen seems to be filled with a riot of gorgeous color as has never been seen before'.[61] But apparently limitless interpretations of such scenes were not acknowledged by the judge in the 1914 Lords Appeal case when Kinemacolor's claims to 'approximately' render all colours from a two-colour method were considered to be empirically unproven, therefore invalidating the patent on which the process was based.[62]

Kinemacolor was shown extensively in London, particularly at the Palace Theatre leased by Urban in 1911, and there is evidence of considerable dissemination in the provinces. In 1910–14 Kinemacolor films were exhibited in approximately 250 venues in a total of 161 regions across the country, and there is further evidence of screenings in the regions until at least May 1916. Runs were typically short, supplied by touring companies.[63] An exclusive licensing system meant that exhibition in London and elsewhere was largely subject to Urban's control. In August 1912 exhibitors were offered, for example, a programme entitling a licensee to choose ten reels, representing one and three-quarter hours of projection, for £30 a week. With the programme came instruction on musical accompaniment, the installation of modern 'sound effects' and 'the worth, and method of judicious and skilful advertising'.[64] The aim was to market Kinemacolor as a means by which exhibitors might draw in the 'upper strata of local society' to their cinemas, as well as retaining their typical patrons. Urban's mission involved bringing colour to cities 'where the prevailing hues are grey, black and brown', a modern invention being marketed as providing relief from the drudgery of industrialisation.[65] Provincial Picture Palaces, an independent company, was initially granted exclusive rights outside London to show Kinemacolor in its circuit until the Natural Color Kinematograph Company Ltd (NCKCL) sold licences individually to exhibitors. Kinemacolor (London District) controlled exhibitions in the metropolis, particularly those located in the immediate vicinity of the Palace Theatre. For a time this exclusive system ensured Kinemacolor exhibitions in Britain and overseas could be monitored, although it is likely that in the long term the costs of hiring films and equipment held back mass expansion after the initial, novelty phase. Exhibition and patent rights were also sold all over the world and Kinemacolor did comparatively good overseas business in Japan and, for a time, in America. But after a promising start it proved impossible to repeat the popular success of the Delhi Durbar films, although something of a brief revival was experienced with wartime screenings of *With the Fighting Forces of Europe* (1914) that was arguably popular more for its subject matter than for its colour. The financial costs of specialised exhibition facilities and prestige venues proved in the long run to hasten Kinemacolor's demise. In an attempt to offset exhibitors' reluctance to purchase special projection equipment when the majority of them did not show Kinemacolor films for long periods, the NCKCL developed a projector that could also show black-and-white films. Even so, a long-term commitment to Kinemacolor was rare, a notable exception being T. J. West's run for approximately two years at the Shaftesbury Hall, Bournemouth.[66] The rest of Europe proved to be an even more difficult market. After selling the patent rights to a French company in 1912 Urban bought them back at a profit and built the Théâtre Edouard VII in Paris, a costly enterprise that ended in financial disaster.[67] After the patent was invalidated in 1914 the exclusive licence system broke down; thereafter Kinemacolor was available to all producers and exhibitors. Yet the process did not thrive in a free market since it required considerable technical expertise and financial investment. Urban was forced to retrench, particularly on his worldwide operations, and during World War I shifted his priorities to war propaganda, including successful Kinemacolor screenings of *With the Fighting Forces of Europe* and *Britain Prepared* (1915). He collaborated with Henry Joy on perfecting yet another colour patent for Kinecrom, a process that was designed to address Kinemacolor's technical shortcomings with a non-fringing projector known as Urban-Duplex.[68]

The majority of Kinemacolor films were actualities or topical films that could be regarded as a limitation when the film industry was poised for saturating the market with fiction films. An analysis of the Kinemacolor catalogue 1912–13 indeed demonstrates that the majority of films were non-fiction of the British countryside; numerous animal and bird studies; royal events; and many films of military parades and natural scenery in countries including the USA, Canada, European countries, Sweden, India and Egypt.

The emphasis on British locales places Kinemacolor within traditions of landscape painting which can be seen to have had a longer-term influence on perceptions of a British approach to colour cinema. While only a very small percentage of Kinemacolor films survive, often in tantalising fragments such as scenes from the Delhi Durbar film, the catalogue's descriptions of individual films nevertheless gives an impression of what was perceived to be of colour interest to exhibitors and audiences. Eirik Hanssen's study draws attention to the catalogue's great value as a source that reveals a sense of what was achieved with Kinemacolor in terms of film form, genre and address, as well as the ways in which it connected with contemporary discourses around colour.[69] The films demonstrated trends of silent cinema from Gunning's notion of 'the cinema of attractions' to ideas about natural colour processes exemplifying a close relationship between an object and photographic indexicality.[70] As such the films demonstrated different approaches to engaging spectators by establishing regimes of verisimilitude appropriate for a particular genre. Some films were geared towards showing 'attractions' such as magic tricks or travelogues of faraway, exotic places which induced the pleasure of surprise, while on other occasions they presented close approximations of familiar sights such as the seaside, trees, flowers and everyday objects which induced the pleasure of recognition. *Italian Flower and Bead Vendors* announced Italy to be 'the land of colour'. It showed stalls and wares with vendors selling coloured beads. Another travelogue that made a spectacle of place and colour was *Kingston, Jamaica*, which again featured a marketplace and an exotic fruit, the ackeé, 'somewhat resembling the banana in colour, but having black berries which are not edible … the close views of this fruit are wonderful examples of the powers of Kinemacolor'.[71] In such films unusual objects and locales were so presented that the spectacular values of place and colour were mutually reinforcing.

Trick films in particular made colour an obtrusive feature and were obviously intended to punctuate colour presentation with surprise as cinematic attractions.[72] Films featuring speed magnification such as *From Bud to Blossom* are discussed in Chapter 11, which takes a long view of film colour aesthetics, but it is important to convey a sense here of the variety of Kinemacolor's output. *A Kinemacolor Puzzle*, for example, had two rotating coloured discs revolving in kaleidoscopic fashion yet 'in spite of the rapid movement the colors of the discs are perfectly distinct'. The film was described as being 'in considerable request'. There was clearly great confidence in Kinemacolor's ability to reproduce colours 'true to nature' that would immediately invite audiences to compare what they saw on screen with their own experience of colours for particular foods or objects. The catalogue's description of *Refreshments* noted that: 'If any needed to be convinced that Kinemacolor is *not* a system of artificial coloring of the film itself, this section would surely suffice.' The film showed a man pouring water into a tumbler of claret and 'as the claret diffuses itself in the water, the liquid gradually assumes a deeper hue. The actual process of diffusion and the change in color of the contents of the tumbler are depicted exactly as if the real thing was happening before our eyes.' The same film featured an orange being cut and squeezed: 'It is *exactly* the color of orange juice and is so like the actual thing that one's mouth positively waters as one watches the picture.' Such claims were risky, although in this case orange was a colour that tended to reproduce well in Kinemacolor. *Studies in Natural Colour* went even further by showing the contrast between an ordinary orange and a blood-orange.[73]

The emphasis on differentiating Kinemacolor from applied techniques was an important element of Urban's rhetorical presentation of 'natural' colour, in particular emphasising the aim of photographic processes to convey changes in hue or saturation in mimetic rather than symbolic fashion associated with, say, tinting an image in its entirety to convey a generic mood for a frame or scene rather than to 'capture' the colours of particular objects. Publicity boasted that, unlike applied colour methods, Kinemacolor 'instantaneously catches the most unexpected tints with wondrous sweetness and represents the dominant colors not only in their own richness and brilliance, but also in their finest and most delicate shades, presenting an endless combination which in scale of splendour is rivalled only by the band of the spectrum'.[74] These aims transcended genre, the emphasis being on exposing applied methods as somehow fooling audiences with inaccurate, 'false', unscientific representations of reality. This was demonstrated in *Gerald's Butterfly*, a comedy film that depicted a boy who paints a butterfly that fools a naturalist when it is dangled over a hedge. The naturalist

pays for being taken in by the painted butterfly since his attempts to catch it result in a greenhouse being damaged and him getting thrown into a pond. The catalogue's description offsets this narrative of disaster wrought by deception with praise for the film's reproduction of flowers and the countryside as 'so realistic that it was almost possible to fancy that one could smell the new mown hay'. By means of a dramatic scenario the film can be seen as presenting a somewhat reflexive position on Kinemacolor's relationship to applied methods of colouring film by hand.[75] While the naturalist suffers for being taken in by the fake painted butterfly, audiences were encouraged to delight in Kinemacolor's approximation of flowers and the countryside as a more accurate mode of representation. The emphasis on natural colour eliciting a sensual response from audiences ('tasting' the orange or smelling the hay) was a typical claim that linked with Goethe-based theories that conceived of colour perception as subjective, interactive and experiential.[76] It also engaged with theories which linked sensory experience to colour. The idea that colour intensified the spectator's pleasure and could even elicit a physical response resonated in subsequent discussions about the impact of screen colour. While some saw this as an opportunity to explore colour's educational potential, others claimed colour's enhanced sensorial potential as a point of aesthetic difference from monochrome. Colour was seen to produce psychological and physiological effects, constituting a 'synaesthesic' approach which emphasised its impact on emotions, senses and health. These connections were investigated by Loyd Jones, a technician who developed a number of colour technologies at the Kodak Research Laboratories in Rochester, New York, from the 1910s–50s.[77]

One must, however, be careful not to construct an impression of this period as one in which colour processes were necessarily distinct in people's minds. While Urban encouraged notions of specificity around Kinemacolor comments on films coloured by other means reveal similar tendencies and aims. *The Glories of Sunset*, a Gaumont film, seems to have presented variable colour effects:

As the sun sets the toning gradually becomes deeper, giving a most beautiful effect. The various scenes shown represent the sun just before it disappears, entitled 'Last

Rays', the sun having set, entitled 'First Shadows' and concludes with a striking view of the bay by moonlight with a ship in full sail passing across, the silver reflection on the water.[78]

Sunsets of Egypt was a Kinemacolor film that also took pride in showing 'the red glow of the sun and the changing colours in the sky ... the after-glow of the setting sun fills the sky with the richest and most glorious colors imaginable'.[79] Such examples draw attention to the mutual effect processes were having on each other during a time when the achievement of 'spectacular realism' was a shared goal of colourists using a variety of different approaches. Kinemacolor's success increased exhibitors' interest in other forms of colour film. *The Bioscope* reported in October 1911:

> Within the year – almost within the last six months – Mr Charles Urban's Kinemacolor process has come right to the front, and has become a formative influence upon the future of the business, the importance of which cannot be over-estimated. 'Colour' has now become a *sine qua non* of the picture theatre programme, and one cannot pass along the streets without seeing from the announcements of exhibitors that they are fully alive to this, and, if they have not a Kinemacolor licence, they are making a special feature of tinted or coloured films in order to cope with the public demand.[80]

The flurry of experimentation clearly had an impact on applied methods. Kinemacolor drew attention to colour and increased demand for interest in other systems, particularly stencil methods, 1909–16.[81] As films became longer, often dealing with complex narratives and different temporalities, **tinting and toning (see Technical Appendix)** could be motivated by an extended range of imperatives. Examples of tinting used for melodramatic effect as well as for creating a frame differentiated by a combination of tinting and toning can be seen from frame enlargements from *At the Villa Rose* (1920). While this is a restored version of the film it nevertheless communicates something of the variety possible with dye methods which outlasted Kinemacolor by being used until the early 1930s. Rachael Low argues that for some time blue tints made up for technical deficiencies in lighting and stock which made night-shooting difficult. Once the latter improved, tinting was

At the Villa Rose (1920): tinting and toning for melodramatic effect; tinting and toning; blue tinting

not so necessary for night effects, but was nevertheless used creatively and to convey a sense of realism. One example cited is Hitchcock's *Downhill* (1927), in which a sequence conveying the central character's delirium was dyed sepia, while his imaginings were in green.[82] When the BFI National Archive restored another Hitchcock film, *The Lodger* (1927), in 1984, it was done using tinting and toning to replicate the original technique that had iron blue and amber tint for exterior scenes to produce an eerie, smog-like effect for the London night scenes.[83] H. G. Wells appreciated the artistic potential of tinting and toning, declaring:

Colour in the films is no longer as it is in real life, a confusing and often un-meaning complication of vision. It can be introduced into the spectacle for effect, slowly flushing the normal black and white with glows of significant hue, chilling, intensifying, gladdening. It can be used to pick out and intensify small forms. It can play gaily or grotesquely over the scene with or without reference to the black-and-white forms.[84]

This recognition of the principle of colour design rather than aiming for realism confirmed colour's key contribution to establishing silent film as an art form.

It is generally acknowledged that Urban's personal interest was in non-fiction and that Kinemacolor's difficulties in filming in studios in less than very bright light conditions meant that dramas were not particularly suited to the process. Yet a number of fiction films were made from 1910, generally, but not exclusively, reflecting Urban's preference for high-brow, historical or literary subjects including *By Order of Napoleon*, *The Flower Girl of Florence* and *The Fall of Babylon*. As subsequent film history attests, the historical/costume genre was conducive to colour subjects, and Kinemacolor films similarly made the most of emphasising the spectacle of *mise en scène* in titles such as *Telemachus: A Mythological Play* in which: 'The staging of the palace scenes, and the costumes are exceedingly fine, while the outdoor episodes are set in the most beautiful surroundings.' *A Love Story of Charles II* ended with a portrait of Charles II in which 'the detail of the costume is well reproduced, especially a leather gauntlet'. Urban's decision for Kinemacolor to 'march with the times' by making more fiction films was confirmed in 1912 when a number of new fiction titles

were announced, with an emphasis on historical films 'staged wherever possible at the places where the actual events occurred and no pains will be spared in the preparation of any dramatic subject in the effort to secure realism and attractiveness'.[85] Authentic staging provided an opportunity to combine the pleasures of the travelogue with drama, with Nice in France or Brighton on the south coast of England as favoured locations because of the favourable natural light conditions.

There were also comedies, one of which betrayed contemporary ideological fascinations with racial difference. These used colour to reinforce orientalist perceptions common in literature and painting which depicted different races and skin tones as 'exotic other'.[86] The catalogue description of *The King of Indigo* remarked that the comedy turned on 'the complexions between men of different races'. The King of 'Indigo' and his Vizier travel by car to receive the freedom of the City. They enlist the services of two tramps to bring them refreshments but the tramps drug them, put on make-up and take their place at the ceremony. The pretence is later discovered when the King turns up after the tramps 'laden with honour and the gold cup' have fled to a nearby inn to celebrate. The comedy was intended to revolve around awareness of different complexions; the tramps' ruse revealed when, as the catalogue notes, the 'dusky' King and Vizier appear at the end. Similar sentiments are evident in *Scenes in the Indian Camp at Hampton Court, 18 June 1911* that was noted in the catalogue for reproducing 'swarthy skins' of 'native warriors' in comparison with differences in shades of the European visitors' complexions. Such judgments are consistent with what was to become the litmus-test of subsequent colour processes to render variations in flesh tones. As with these examples from Kinemacolor films, it is the 'dusky' or 'swarthy' complexions that are seen as exceptional, as well as 'differences in shades of complexions' being remarked upon for curiosity value. One of Kinemacolor's functions, then, was to bolster contemporary ideological predispositions towards accentuating racial difference, since it was promoted as being capable of rendering flesh tones more accurately than with monochrome. In the case of *The King of Indigo* the masquerading tramps' identities were revealed when the real 'dusky' King appeared. The film's comedy derived from the audience's superior knowledge of the 'true' skin colour of the foreign visitors, knowledge that had been revealed to them by Kinemacolor. The characters in the film that mistook the tramps were not so enlightened; they were only made aware of the truth when confronted with the King and Vizier, a narrative resolution that is consistent with Kinemacolor's claims to show the world 'as it is', in this case by accentuating a world of racial and ideological differences.

Although it is generally acknowledged that the Bioschemes case accelerated Urban's financial difficulties and hastened Kinemacolor's decline, its brief years of experimentation, demonstration and exploitation had, in retrospect, a profound impact on the history of colour film. Its legacy was evident in subsequent years when Kinemacolor served as a paradigm of successful and less successful commercial development. Its public profile mobilised some consistent cultural, ideologically motivated discourses about colour aesthetics which resonated down the decades. Reviewing contemporary colour experiments in 1922, Charles Raleigh declared it to be 'the forerunner of what so many of us have been striving for'.[87] J. Stuart Blackton drew on its example when developing Prizma, as did Claude Friese-Greene with a revival of his father's patents for his Natural Colour process in the 1920s. He was careful not to make grandiloquent claims in the style of Urban, who had convinced many through the power of words that Kinemacolor was unbeatable. For a while this drive undoubtedly assisted dissemination, but once other problems conspired against Kinemacolor the showman's rhetoric proved unable to sustain public interest for more than a few years. Technicolor No. 1, first presented in 1917, was an additive, two-colour process in combination with a prism-based beam-splitter which solved fringing during shooting. Yet misalignment still occurred on projection, pushing Technicolor towards **subtractive methods (see Technical Appendix)** and **imbibition (see Technical Appendix)** printing.[88] **Morganacolor (see Technical Appendix)**, first developed as a home movie process in 1931, was a two-colour additive process similar in principle to Kinemacolor but never progressed beyond the demonstration stage. Kinemacolor is thus part of the *longue durée* of colour's history constituting an apposite precedent in technical experiment and commercial exploitation. It is tantalising to think what it must have been like for those who saw Kinemacolor for the first time. Journalist and spiritualist W. T. Stead, who drowned on the *Titanic* in April 1912, saw Kinemacolor films at the Scala Theatre in June 1911. He congratulated Urban on 'the magnificent exhibition of artistic pictures … The only fault they have is that they spoil you for all other living pictures for evermore.'[89] For Stead and Urban, Kinemacolor had no 'ghostly rivals', a judgment that typified the ebullient confidence that was as much a part of its success as it was of its downfall.[90] The different approaches taken by subsequent entrepreneurs in colour motion pictures will be explored in the next chapter.

2 COLOUR ADVENTURES WITH PRIZMA AND CLAUDE FRIESE-GREENE IN THE 1920s

PRIZMA AND *THE GLORIOUS ADVENTURE*

When *The Glorious Adventure*, a British film made using the **Prizmacolor (see Technical Appendix)** process, was released in 1922, it was greeted negatively by David Robertson, an artist writing in *Motion Picture Studio*, and who subsequently engaged in a debate on the film with its producer, James Stuart Blackton. Robertson levelled a by then familiar criticism of attempts to produce colour films:

> No picture is likely to retain the interest of its viewer unless it allows ample scope for the imagination. The eyes must discover the blanks for the mind to fill in, and when you present a film which is leaden in its colouring, you banish that recreation of the imagination which the mind needs … Colour does not make a film more instructive, educational, or realistic, but rather detracts from the first two and distorts the last.[1]

Blackton replied that Robertson's opinions were not representative of audiences, artists and critics, who appreciated the film which represented a 'pioneer experiment' in colour cinematography. In particular, he rejected the opinion that colour was not 'realistic' since, 'Colour is not to be considered merely as a pictorial asset. Its contribution to dramatic realism and to the psychology of drama in countless ways is a big subject.'[2] These comments are illustrative of the confusion which raged around colour, and continued to do so well into the reign of Technicolor. Blackton was proud of how colour was obtrusive in *The Glorious Adventure*, an

integral aspect of the drama as well as a key to psychological realism. That this had been achieved with a newly developed process invested the film with further novelty, a 'glorious adventure' indeed for those who shifted allegiance from additive approaches to subtractive. In retrospect, both the film and Prizmacolor were important markers of two-colour, subtractive process experimentation, contributing to the development of Vitacolor, Magnacolor, Multicolor and Cinecolor, the latter being the only two-colour process which retained currency into the 1940s.

The Glorious Adventure and Prizma are more than just footnotes in the history of colour cinematography on the road to Technicolor's domination. In this chapter *The Glorious Adventure* will be examined in the context of how colour on screen was debated and interpreted in the early 1920s. Janus-faced, Prizma connects with earlier developments as well as to subsequent processes. As an example of the silent British costume/heritage drama, *The Glorious Adventure* raises important issues of the British colour experience. These relate to transnational experimentation with early colour systems, as well as to specific aesthetic and technical concerns which had a broad significance. The film has tended to be written off by critics, who failed to appreciate its multifarious approach to colour. The aesthetic choices demonstrated a practical awareness of how to work creatively within the constraints of prevailing systems and critical assumptions about what constituted 'good' colour.

The Glorious Adventure represents Anglo-American collaboration on many levels. It was directed by J. Stuart Blackton, born in Sheffield, but whose film career was forged with Vitagraph, a company he co-formed in New York. He was particularly associated with innovative stop-frame animation, and with devising streamlined, cost-effective ways to run a studio. He was convinced that colour and Prizma were the way forward for cinematographic art. Prizma's roots go back into the legacy of Kinemacolor, with the key figures William Van Doren Kelley and William T. Crespinel being fundamental to its development. William Van Doren Kelley was responsible for several important patents, including **double-coated stock (see Technical Appendix)** and **dye toning (see Technical Appendix)**. Working in partnership in New York with Carroll H. Dunning and Wilson Salisbury, he developed a subtractive system known as 'Kesdacolor' in 1918, which was an important precursor to Prizma, resulting in a one-minute film, *Our American Flag*, shown in September 1918.[3] Crespinel was an expert cinematographer who had worked with Kinemacolor in Britain and America. He was employed by Blackton at Vitagraph in 1915, and then worked with Kelley on Prizma from 1917. *The Glorious Adventure* was filmed by Crespinel at Stoll's Cricklewood Studios, near London. He recalled his experiences in an interview conducted by his son in 1977 on shooting the first full-length film using a subtractive process.[4] On a technical level, Prizma is significant for its anticipation of **bipack (see Technical Appendix)** colour systems, and for offering an ingenious printing method with its double-coated film, one side 'toned blue-green by an iron solution, and the opposite side toned red-orange with uranium'. It also had the advantage of not needing a special projector.[5] Even so, it was more expensive than black-and-white film (estimated at eight times as much per linear foot for prints)[6] and, as with Kinemacolor dramas and later many prestige colour films, was marketed as high class and geared to attract a clientele to match.[7] As Blackton boasted, 'Instead of drab monotone, we have the life, richness and variety of nature's own colours. We have the sense of reality that springs from not merely the colour, but the depth and stereoscopic values.'[8]

A one-reel travelogue, *Everywhere with Prizma*, had been shown in New York in 1919 at the Rivoli Theatre, and *Bali the Unknown*, a four-reel film made in Prizma, was premiered in New York in February 1921.

The first screening of Prizmacolor in Britain was reported in 1921 as a private event for exhibitors, held at the Alhambra in London, where the programme included films of Niagara Falls, the Kilauea Volcano of Hawaii, a film about fashion and studies of fruit and flowers, first seen in monochrome and then in colour to demonstrate Prizma's qualities. This latter display was a common means of showcasing colour, since nature and natural beauty persisted as the 'litmus test' of successful colour film exhibition well into the Technicolor period as part of 'the cinema of attractions' in non-fiction film well after 1907. While enthusiastic about Prizma's potential, the report on the screening noted that it was probably not yet ready to record fictional subjects, since 'fringing' presented a problem with figure movement.[9] *The Times*'s reviewer, however, recorded that 'in all of them [the pictures] the colour reproduction was wonderfully good'.[10]

A report on the latest Prizma patent in 1920 demonstrated that work had progressed on developing a camera in which, according to Crespinel, 'the lens image is divided into three identical images in such a manner that the camera can be used with the same strength of artificial lighting as is employed for ordinary monochrome films'.[11] Despite this claim an American report included an intriguing comment by Walter Murton, the art supervisor who worked on *The Glorious Adventure*. Murton argued that the film had too many colour effects spoiled by too-high lighting, 'which frequently resulted in a stained-glass color effect rather than the more subdued colors of nature. For in nature objects refract the rays of light that shine upon them and must never be given the effect of shining thru them, as they would thru a colored lantern slide.'[12] In view of the colour displayed in the film as noted below, these comments indicate a confused response to the resulting effects rather than constituting evidence of Prizma's failure to produce anything interesting with colour. Colin N. Bennett also noted that the film strained lighting 'to its uppermost limit', resulting in medium and close-shots supported by artificial light that cast harsh, 'unnaturally placed' shadows, while much of the rest of the film was open to the criticism of under-exposure.[13] As well as perfecting the camera, costly experimentation continued with building accurate double-printing machines, as well as machines for the continuous automatic tone-dyeing of both sides of the film. Charles Raleigh of the *British Journal of Photography* commented that 'They certainly had pluck, having sunk not far from three-quarters of a million dollars in the chase.'[14]

In addition to claiming technical advances and the ability to reproduce 'the life, richness and variety of nature's own colours', Blackton's enthusiasm for Prizma invested it with a particularly nationalist discourse, claiming that 'Our (British) natural colours are far richer than those in America, and better results should be obtained.'[15] His decision to return to Britain in 1921, and to utilise Prizma on a historical melodrama, reinforced his belief that British films had a strong future in the international market since:

> Americans – to take one big market – are tremendously interested in English life, literature, history, and romance. Then there are the Dominions, with the Imperial values of British pictures that go with them, and in all the countries of the world British pictures will carry their own messages of International value.[16]

The Glorious Adventure was produced and distributed by Stoll Picture Productions, an important British film company founded in 1918 by theatrical impresario Sir Oswald Stoll, who had a reputation for exploiting theatrical talent for the screen as well as for transforming music halls to serve 'more upscale custom'.[17] Blackton's British films have generally received a mixed press. His ambition and talent for gregarious showmanship are offset against the films' alleged shortcomings. Rachael Low's verdict is typical when referring to Blackton's most well-known British films, *The Glorious Adventure* and *A Gypsy Cavalier*, both released in 1922, the latter being a tinted print rather than shot in Prizmacolor:

> The films were ambitious costume spectacles with huge sets, crowd scenes, involved plots and enormous casts supporting the fashionable and celebrated leading players. The films were monumentally slow and dull and the use of colour disappointing, and despite society *premières* they were not especially successful.[18]

In her biography of her father, Blackton's daughter did not consider *The Glorious Adventure* to be an example of her father's best work. While recognising the film as 'a milestone of importance on the road to cinema advancement' and as 'a good yarn' with some 'rousing moments', she rather dismissed it as 'strictly melodrama, not my father's forte'.[19] The film was publicised as an event of momentous importance for the motion picture industry: 'The Dawn of a New Day in the Kinema World'.[20] Reviews in Britain were quite favourable, while teething problems with the process were noted, as in the *Film Renter and Moving Picture News*, which commented that Prizma worked best for achieving 'exquisitely beautiful reproductions of natural scenes, and gorgeously coloured Court dresses'.[21] The scenes of the Great Fire of London, commented on by the majority of reviewers as genuinely spectacular, were much appreciated, but, in spite of claims to the contrary, the doubts expressed after the screening to exhibitors at the Alhambra in 1921 about a tendency towards 'fringing' were confirmed by the observation that whenever characters moved quickly, 'detail becomes lost, and colour merges and becomes blurred and indistinct'. On the other hand, for shots picking out detail such as fruit on the court banqueting table, 'Prizma achieves its most brilliant and true-to-Nature touches in still-life studies.'[22] *Kinematograph Weekly* pronounced that the novelty of colour was most definitely an appealing aspect of the film: 'There are a number of beautiful shots and some excellently coloured and well photographed close-ups.' With an eye to box-office appeal the story was, however, considered to be 'difficult to follow and moves far too slowly'.[23] Although the film was geared for international distribution and Blackton thought it would do well overseas, one report noted that the focus on British history was not fully appreciated by American audiences.[24]

Viewing the British Film Institute's restored version of *The Glorious Adventure* allows some of these comments to be considered from the perspective of how Prizma was demonstrated in the context of historical melodrama.[25] The film begins in the Cromwellian period, introducing Hugh Argyle and Lady Beatrice, a young couple who are separated when Hugh goes away to sea. The Restoration of the Stuarts occurs and Lady Beatrice, played by society beauty Lady Diana Manners, waits for Hugh's return. The castle where she lives is temporarily occupied by Charles II and his court, which provides the occasion for outdoor scenes of pageantry and revelry. A parallel narrative strand shows Hugh at sea being tricked by rogues who steal his inheritance

The Glorious Adventure (Prizmacolor, 1922): the 'Golden Swan' on the horizon in Prizmacolor

papers and throw him overboard. One of the rogues, Roderick, double-crosses another called Bullfinch so that he alone is blamed for murdering Hugh. On arrival in London Bullfinch is put in prison and Roderick pretends to be Hugh in order to claim the inheritance and marry Beatrice. Meanwhile, Beatrice's financial difficulties force her to marry a condemned criminal (Bullfinch) so that he can assume her debts. Having been rescued by fishermen, Hugh also appears in London and attempts to recover his inheritance claim from the scheming Roderick. The film climaxes with the Great Fire of London and after the resolution of several interlinking plot twists, Hugh and Beatrice are finally united.

The film raises several key issues which are important in considering colour during this period. The first is that with many processes a single, indentifiable aesthetic signature was not always evident. What we get is a mediated, multiple application of colour which imported conventions already in current use. As such, colour style in the 1920s demonstrates a great degree of hybridity in which films often use multiple colouring techniques, as in *The Phantom of the Opera* (Rupert Julian, USA, 1925).[26] Although Prizma was marketed as a subtractive process, on occasion the film demonstrates approaches to colour associated with tinting and toning. So, while Prizma is the 'star' of the film aesthetic

The Glorious Adventure:
the young 'Lady Beatrice Fair'
(Violet Virginia Blackton)

approaches from applied colour persist with the bathing of frames with a single colour. Similarly, but adding colour contrast, the scene just before Hugh departs to go to sea presents an opportunity for colour spectacle with a shot of him in the dark, bathed in blue light, as Beatrice runs to wave him goodbye wearing a cloak in shades of red. The set of the *Golden Swan* ship provides another occasion for an establishing shot with the ship on the horizon framed with deep blue sea and red clouds. The almost translucent qualities of this shot are an example of the lantern-like, 'stained-glass color effect' criticised by art supervisor Walter Murton for being 'unnatural', but which stand out as visually striking and similar to **Pathécolor (see Technical Appendix)** stencilling.[27] Also, the inter-titles are colour-coded like tinted films, so that

this scene is announced with a blue title card, and the next with a yellow one, as we learn that the Restoration of the Stuarts has occurred while Beatrice grows up. In this way colour guides the film's episodic structure as the more up-beat 'tone' of the next scene is declared.

As with most colour processes, Prizma was subject to close analysis, and one of the 'litmus tests' for colour was how it reproduced flesh, particularly with stars who were normally seen in monochrome. The representation of a star to audiences used to seeing their image in monochrome required careful treatment. Some commentators were unconvinced that this was desirable, as artist Paul Nash later remarked: 'You may think it thrilling to see your pet star *as* in real life, but you may soon wish you had kept your illusion.'[28] Lady Diana

The Glorious Adventure:
Lady Beatrice (Diana
Manners) with red flower

Manners was the youngest daughter of the Duke of Rutland. She married Duff Cooper, a future Member of Parliament in 1919, and gained a reputation for being a fast-living society beauty who acted on the stage and in films. Quite apart from the colour, her presentation in *The Glorious Adventure* was a spectacle in itself. The revelation of 'Lady Beatrice Fair', as the title describes her, is accentuated by a medium close-up of her face against a dark background which demonstrates Prizma's ability to render skin tones in the context of an English drama. This produces an image marked by complementary contrast which makes the face stand out almost stereoscopically. Reports on the production keenly anticipated how Prizma would render Lady Diana's appearance:

When one gazes on the perfect blue of her eyes and the tinted alabaster which her perfect complexion suggests, one realises that Stuart Blackton has done well to arrange to film *The Glorious Adventure* in Prizma colour. For the natural tints of Lady Di, he assures me, will live on the screen. It is anticipated that this colour process will even reveal such detail as the flush of anger on the cheeks.[29]

Colour was referred to in Felix Orman's adaptation of his scenario published in *Picturegoer* with the star described as being 'enveloped in a draped gown of soft satin of exquisite colouring; her head was crowned with a mass of golden hair … her wide blue eyes now smiled'.[30]

The Glorious Adventure:
Stephanie's red cloak as
distraction for Bullfinch

Blackton's concern to go beyond presenting colour as a pictorial asset led him to use it for dramatic interest. The narrative features colour at several key points but as we shall see in a complex, rather than a straightforwardly symbolic manner. At first Beatrice does not recognise Hugh when he returns to London. The villain Roderick pursues her and tries to break into her bedroom. Hugh comes to her rescue and after gaining her trust as a gallant stranger, he tells Beatrice that if any more trouble occurs she should send a white rose to the landlord at the inn where he is staying. A colour motif is therefore introduced to assist the plot and in contrast to the deep red clothes worn by the villain Roderick when we first see him in London. Beatrice falls in love with her protector (she unaware that he is Hugh), who offers to marry her when he learns of her financial difficulties and in view of his imminent inheritance. She waits for him in the garden, clutching a red flower and smelling it, creating a sensual link between colour and fragrance and apparently changing the association of red with danger. But this is not entirely the case since danger is still present because Roderick's gang of thieves overhear this

plan and capture Hugh. In addition, a white rose has earlier been suggested as the way to alert Hugh when Beatrice is in danger. Making conclusions about consistency in colour symbolism is therefore problematic in this film. Indeed, flowers were frequently filmed to display 'natural' colour in silent cinema. As noted by Gunning, colour is associated with the figurative and ephemeral in that flowers represent 'a brilliant moment rather than something that is constant'; they are brilliantly saturated but they fade.[31] This instability around meaning is further demonstrated when, in a further twist, the thieves send Beatrice a box with a white rose and a threatening message. Such play with colour, symbolism and narrative can be related to Eisenstein's observations that interpretations of colour must always be related to context which means that meaning will inevitably shift: 'The problem is not, nor ever will be, solved by a fixed catalogue of colour-symbols, but *the emotional intelligibility and function of colour will rise from the natural order of establishing the colour imagery of the work, coincidental with the process of shaping the living movement of the whole work.*'[32]

Blackton anticipated this view, clearly exploiting the opportunities offered by colour for experimenting with symbolism.

Play with colour – particularly red – also occurs in the lead-up to the climactic scenes of the Great Fire of London. Beatrice marries the prisoner Bullfinch, who awaits his fate in jail. The marriage scene uses close-ups very effectively, as the menacing Bullfinch contemplates his bride. Although she is separated from him by a door, she can see his face through the bars and vice-versa. Suspense is created as physical contact occurs when he puts the wedding ring on her finger but instead of letting go of her hand he pulls it through the bars towards him. To distract him, the character Stephanie taunts Bullfinch by waving her red cloak, using colour to assist plot and to create a visually arresting display as he tries to grab hold of it and releases Beatrice's hand. The colour red and fire are used at other key points in the film, as an earlier title, 'Playing with Fire', announces, followed by shots of Soloman Eagle (Tom Heselwood), a fanatic who we later see start the Great Fire of London. Indeed, the various threads of the narrative are brought together when the Great Fire breaks out, producing scenes which for many distinguished the film and its colour. The

flames and light are particularly effective when they appear as dynamic, flickering shades of orange and red, often shown through doorways and windows. In this respect, any indication of 'fringing' does not matter, since the vitality of the flames and their changing hues are enhanced by the sensation and sight of movement.

The debate on 'fringing' was not a new one, going way back into the Kinemacolor and Biocolour period when 'fixing' colour during movement became the most difficult challenge for achieving what was perceived as successful, 'natural' colour rendition. Indeed, Charles Urban criticised the first, additive Prizmacolor process when it was demonstrated to him at the Prizma factory, Jersey City, in 1916. He reported that the films were shot in such as way as to conceal 'fringing', often avoiding movement or restricting it to action either to or from the lens:

> The most severe test which can be applied to any color process known is to march a body of red-coloured soldiers across the lens of an ordinary march step and reproduce the same without excessive color fringing … Referring directly to the Prizma exhibit which I saw yesterday afternoon, the photographer has been exceedingly careful

The Glorious Adventure: fruit bowl shot in Prizmacolor

in his selection of subjects, both as to color, harmony, lack of action, and insistence on distance … The portraits of beautiful ladies were most pleasing, only the slightest movements of the hands, body, eyes, and facial muscles were discernible. If one of these ladies started to raise her hand, the moment the hand began to raise [sic] the picture ended abruptly, and any movement close-up in these pictures, as recorded by Prizma methods, would have occasioned very extreme fringing. All of the pictures taken showed action either to or from the lens, at a calculated distance, to the sacrifice of distinctness and detail.[33]

Another reviewer identified the prevalence of 'composed' shots as displaying colour most effectively, also noting, however, a 'bleeding effect' in which 'red becomes predominant, and the retina transfers the colour to objects which are white or neutral'.[34]

In a few years Prizma tried to address these shortcomings by developing the subtractive process used in *The Glorious Adventure* and the verdict of the *British Journal of Photography* was that great progress had been made in this regard.[35] Yet as we have seen, judgments of colour were still focused very much on whether 'fringing' was evident and, even though the fire was praised for its dramatic force, the shots of static, brightly coloured objects were considered to be one of the film's best features, such as a close-shot of a bowl of fruit. Even though colour was essential to the story at certain points (the use of colour for the various roses, for example, and the association of red with the rogue Roderick), reviews tended not to comment on colour as an integral element of narrative. Once colour became the focus of discussion the standard ways of assessing its merits persisted, as reviewers drew on established terms of discourse. Criticism of 'unstable' colour was not confined to additive and subtractive processes. A report in 1921 on 'Tinting Troubles', for example, identified problems with varying quality of dyes and a lack of uniformity between batches of a film. If films were tinted on racks there could be unevenness and streaking, or even spots and irregular markings as a result of drops of water on the surface of the film becoming more or less saturated with the dye before drying.[36] Yet these imperfections were clearly not considered to be as serious as 'fringing', which threatened to disrupt the illusion of cinema being capable of capturing, in Blackton's words, 'a sense of reality'.[37]

In the film's publicity much was made of period authenticity, the beauty and colours of the costumes and the extent to which designs from the period were well researched. Blackton's wife designed the costumes, claiming that she 'studied for months' in libraries and museums, superintending 'every step in the progress of the making of the costumes'.[38] Blackton liked to quote from *Conquest*, a popular science magazine, which praised *The Glorious Adventure* for 'every dress, every piece of tapestry and every colour in the gorgeous sets', and how 'the reproduction of nature's own colours on the screen has given to the film a resemblance to stereoscopic depth entirely lacking in the old black and white pictures'.[39] Such reportage tended to shift the focus away from questions of narrative to observations about costumes and sets which required the eye to appreciate them as static objects rather than as narrative/plot elements. In view of the problems most processes experienced at the time with 'fringing', such commentary made sense, to draw the viewer's attention to an appreciation of colour as an enhancement to the presentation of static objects. This required that for some parts of a film principles of continuity were sacrificed to ponderous shots which enticed the eye with the spectacle of colour. There are several such exterior shots of the castle gardens in which colour features, providing an opportunity to observe Prizma's ability to render shots of 'the life, richness and variety of nature's own colours' as Blackton put it.[40]

Blackton's daughter recalled that while in London audiences were impressed by Lady Diana Manners' aristocratic connections, her social magnetism held less sway elsewhere. The 'restrained' approach to exteriors, sets and performance style went with a narrative which veered from being ponderous to full of suspense. When she observed a young couple watching the film at a Leeds cinema she noted how they responded to the film's various shifts in pace:

They were silently attentive through the early part of the picture, but grew restless as Lady Di and her lover moved ever so politely through a series of mishaps that were to lead them finally to near-cremation in the crypt of St Paul's Cathedral, while all London blazed around them, and the molten metal from the fabulous dome oozed down to form a sizzling, engulfing, lethal lake at their very feet.[41]

This was a preferable way, however, to show off a process rather than to draw attention to how colour appeared to shift with movement. Indeed, the acting style adopted by Diana Manners was suited to the repression of movement and gesture. While this can be linked to her theatrical affiliations and aristocratic demeanour, it is also indicative of prevailing film performance styles of 'restraint' with 'passion', which Christine Gledhill has argued typified British cinema of the 1920s.[42] When she was interviewed by *Picturegoer* during training for her role in *The Glorious Adventure*, she confirmed that this was her favoured method, arguing that: 'Repression in one's movements without exaggerated gestures I feel represents the highest plane of screen art.' The report went on to note that,

> Blackton worked on the vivid personality of Lady Di, and taught her the art of registering the emotions of horror, surprise, and sorrow. Always she was the confident, self-possessed aristocrat. There was no temperament here. She clenched her slender bejewelled hands and mirrored fear in depths of her expressive blue eyes with an assurance which told of her descent from a line of fighting ancestors who for centuries faced the world with courage and self-reliance.[43]

That this performance style suited colour made both the actress and the scenario appropriate for Prizma since it detracted from exaggerated movement and gesture which would have drawn further attention to 'fringing'. Yet it nevertheless explains some criticisms of the film as 'slow'.

Blackton's claim to have achieved 'stereoscopic values' through colour with Prizmacolor in *The Glorious Adventure* revives an area of debate which by then had a long association with colour film.[44] Kinemacolor films such as *Pleasure Seekers at Manly, New South Wales, Australia* (1912), for example, featured a diving exhibition which was noted for its 'stereoscopic quality'.[45] The impression is that colour would emphasise planes of depth in much the way that deep-focus photography allows the detail of a shot to be appreciated from the foreground into the background. Joshua Yumibe notes how stencilling colour processes created the impression of three-dimensionality, and how the marketing of colour often commented on a resulting stereoscopic effect. In some cases this produced 'a projective dimensionality that proceeds from the

background into the foreground of the image, out toward the viewer'.[46] Colour thus 'leaps from the screen' as a sensational effect which is similarly evident in *The Glorious Adventure*, with shots designed for colour spectacle, such as the ship on the horizon with blue sea and red clouds, and even more obtrusively when the flames of the fire are seen through doorways and windows, appearing to come towards the viewer as the fire gets out of control. In this way the apparent shortcomings of the Prizma process unwittingly assisted in making sure that a display of colour was necessary, and that apparent 'imperfections' such as fringing did not matter in shots which depended on flickering, unstable colour in projective, 'stereoscopic' scenes.

Blackton directed Lady Diana Manners again in *The Virgin Queen* (1923), but this was only partly shot in Prizmacolor. Compared to *The Glorious Adventure*, the film was not considered to demonstrate a move forward for Prizma, as noted in the *British Journal of Photography*: 'The colour process is used only for occasional passages in the story, chief among which are a super-royal banquet and the burning part of Woodstock Palace … they appeared to us as inferior to much that was shown in the previous all-colour film *The Glorious Adventure*.'[47] It is interesting to note that the scenes using Prizma were exactly those considered to be most successful in *The Glorious Adventure* – static shots of food and the drama of flickering flames. The first showed off colour reproduction as pictorial display while

The Glorious Adventure: making the most of 'fringing' with shots of flames through windows and doorways

the second avoided criticism of 'fringing' because, as argued above, filming fire actually benefited from the imperfection. Blackton returned to the USA and some short films were made using Prizmacolor. Complaints about 'fringing' persisted, and the company got into financial difficulty. According to Crespinel, keeping the laboratories in Jersey was a mistake when most film production had gravitated to Hollywood.[48] Kelley started work on a new imbibition process called Kelleycolor and in 1928 the Prizma patents were acquired by Consolidated Film Industries, part of Republic Pictures, and the name of the process was changed to Magnacolor.

CLAUDE FRIESE-GREENE AND NATURAL COLOUR IN THE 1920S

Blackton's fortunes with Prizma were keenly followed by Claude Friese-Greene, son of William, pioneer in cinematography and colour, who died in 1921. William's passion for colour was passed on to Claude who continued experimenting in the early 1920s, inspired by a letter from his father which exhorted him to:

> Remember, in colour, although so simple, all the great discoveries of the new world will be found. I don't mean only the brilliant colours, but the dusky ones as well; and as we can photograph the passing of the fleeting colours now, nothing will be lost, for we have a chance of a permanent record, as well as the colours impressions of the mind's eye, so one can compare the mind's eye impressions with the permanent records, and by those contrasted in your learning, which all comes down to a truthful record of Nature, and what you leave out and judge to convey, is your picture, whether it's from nature or your mind's eye.[49]

The failure of earlier processes loomed large in Claude's thinking, as he refined his father's two-colour additive Biocolour process, drawing on four patents registered by William in 1918–21. Fringing was an obvious fault to try to avoid, as well as making exaggerated claims about being able to present the full range of the spectrum, an issue which had contributed to the downfall of Kinemacolor. Colour Photography was formed with a capital of £25,000 to develop the process and Spectrum

Films to produce the films. The production manager was Felix Orman, scenario writer on *The Glorious Adventure*, and equipment manufacturer William Vinten was Engineering Adviser. Claude presented his results in papers to the Royal Photographic Society in 1924 and 1925 and a number of reports in the film trade press also featured the details of **Natural Colour (see Technical Appendix)**.[50] The camera had an attachment, a rotating disc with two apertures, one filled with a colour filter passing light from the red side of the spectrum and the other partly filled in with some opaque material, leaving a small white opening in combination with a small portion of filter, also passing light from the red side of the spectrum. The disc was rotated at half the speed of the shutter. The panchromatic negative was developed the same way as black-and-white films except that the colour-sensitive negative had to be developed in total darkness or with a safe light, and a machine stained each alternate picture orange-red and blue-green. The 'unique selling points' in marketing were that the process was relatively cheap because an ordinary camera could be used with the attachment, exposures could be made from lower-light situations than the bright sunlight normally required for natural colour cinematography. Less light than other colour processes was required in projection as well and conventional equipment could be used, the only difference being that the projection speed needed to be faster than normal for black-and-white film.[51]

The films were first demonstrated on 25 March 1924 at the Holborn Empire, London, at Urbanora House on 29 April and then in New York in June. The programme consisted of a dance prologue, 'The Awakening of the Wood Nymphs', featuring Russian dancer Lydia Kyasht. The first film was *Moonbeam Magic*, based on a 'biblical legend' by Felix Orman about an eastern prince's desire for colour, which provided the opportunity for a shift from monochrome to colour. The second film, *Dance of the Moods*, challenged viewers to judge the quality of the colours achieved with the process in comparison with the same performance seen live beforehand by the Margaret Morris Dancers. It seems that the dancers were, however, accompanied by coloured lighting, perhaps casting doubt as to the effectiveness of the experiment whereby the film would be compared to 'natural' colours. Finally, *A Quest for Colour* was a colour film record of scenery in Spain and Britain. Claude had learned from Charles Urban, presenting the films to a specially invited audience which included representatives from the government as well as painters including Augustus John. He avoided making grand claims, locating the process as the achievement of a soft, pleasing effect rather than an accurate representation of the full range of the spectrum. Reviewers, however, noticed the absence of yellow, which was particularly notable in a shot of a sunflower and for the brass instruments being played by the guardsmen.[52] J. Dudley, President of the Royal Photographic Society, also noticed the problem of conveying yellow. Claude responded in the discussion after the screenings at Urbanora House that yellow was a 'very evasive' colour in a two-colour process since although it was theoretically possible to obtain it from red and green, the need to convey blue meant that green tended to look blue-green, which militated against yellow.[53]

An interesting difference of opinion on the films became evident when John Campbell, Chairman of Photographic International, who had experimented with a similar approach to colour cinematography as early as 1911, was printed in *The Bioscope* arguing that Claude's films tended to avoid effects that would show fringing: 'The movements were strictly controlled, and, in the topical scenes, the point of focus was always at or near the horizontal axis. Where cross-movements did occur they were in the far distance, which, of course, reduced the fringing, but at the expense of the picture.'[54] Colin N. Bennett disagreed, saying that: 'All those members of the audience to whom I talked were agreed that rapid and close-up movement had successfully been demonstrated on the screen without noticeable fringing at all. Actually, flicker and fringing of colour sensations were both so slight that it took the special methods of the initiate to spot them.'[55] As with Prizma and Kinemacolor there was great sensitivity around the issue of fringing, so much so that other reviews confirmed that care at least had been taken to avoid rapid movement.[56] The *Manchester Guardian* summed up the pros and cons of Claude's experiments:

> While [the process] still suffers from the limitations of a two-colour process, the reds and greens which consequently predominate are not so crude as in earlier experiments. It has also minimised the danger of 'fringing' but with the exception of certain still-life photographs the colour effect is neither natural nor pleasing to the eye, while the high speed of projection necessary induces much of the unpleasant eye-strain and headache which caused the wane of Kinemacolour [*sic*] in public favour.[57]

A major breakthrough in screen colour had clearly not been achieved.

Claude Friese-Greene took the films to the USA for similar demonstrations and there were reports of his ambitions to establish a branch in New York and produce feature films with D. W. Griffith and Graham Cutts.[58] On his return to Britain, however, Sir Beresford White, Chairman of Spectrum Films, announced that even though the process could have been sold 'at a high price' in America, it was important that it stayed in Britain where a number of topical films were to be produced.[59] The result was *The Open Road*, twenty-six short films of a motor tour of Britain exhibited to the film trade in October 1925. Reviews of the nine-reel demonstration were enthusiastic:

> Views of the seashore, the beautiful scenery of the Doone Valley, the mists drifting across Exmoor, cattle winding up a narrow lane near St Ives, were shown in soft and beautiful colouring, without fringing, without distortion, or loss of perspective. Some still-life studies of Wedgwood ware and delicate pottery, as well as some interior shots of work in a pottery, revealed fineness of detail, sharpness of contrast, and subtle degrees in shade. Among the outdoor examples is a wonderful fountain photograph, where the camera has actually caught the atmospheric colours of the rainbow in the fine cloud of water.[60]

While it was possible to regulate the quality of projection carefully for such demonstrations, as had been the case with the earlier test films, once shown in cinemas it was not easy to ensure that *The Open Road* was shown to its best advantage. A letter to Claude in May 1926 from Will Day of Kinutilities, a cinematographic equipment supplier, documents the problems:

> I really think it is my duty to write and let you know that they are running your picture, *The Open Road*, at our local cinema in Highgate, and the public are complaining very seriously of the terrible eye strain. My own children, and also my wife, said they have never seen anything so awful in all their lives. The film is evidently being run too

The Open Road (1925): little movement in shots in Friese-Greene's Natural Colour

The Open Road: pictorial views and spectacular scenery

slow, and as they said, all they could see was red and green flashes and no sign of picture at all. This being the case I thought I would let you know, as there is nothing more harmful to your process than this sort of exhibition. Unless the picture is run at its proper speed it will kill the whole of your future, and give a bad name to your system where it should not be, and I feel sure after hearing this you will look into this matter, as it is more serious perhaps than you would think.[61]

At that time Claude was away working on a production and his brother Kenneth looked into the matter. Claude reported to Day in July that he hoped the problem had been rectified and that Day would report again to him if the same issue reoccurred.[62]

Film historian Rachael Low's verdict on *The Open Road* films as 'little more than elementary scenics' is perhaps over-harsh.[63] She would not have had the opportunity to see the restored versions of the films released on DVD in 2006. Although these are far from what audiences would have seen in 1925, since they reduce the faults which clearly contributed to the process's rapid demise, they convey something of Claude's intentions and also indicate his strengths as a cinematographer. A new preservation negative was made using a digital intermediate so that colours could be combined, flicker could be controlled and motion depicted at twenty-four frames per second.[64] The two

colours used are reproductions of the original films found in the only nitrate show reel known to exist. On one level the DVD is an inaccurate record of what contemporary audiences would have seen. It does, however, permit us to judge whether rapid movement was avoided in order to detract from any fringing which might occur, as well as appreciate something of the 'showcase shots' commented on in reviews such as the spectacular sunset.

The topical film genre in many ways lent itself to displaying colour processes with fringing problems on movement since shots were often static, designed to display spectacular scenery. *The Open Road*'s inter-titles, such as 'We had to stop to admire the view', encouraged the spectator to adopt a contemplative attitude towards the images which involved little or no movement. Curious anticipation was encouraged as the viewer momentarily waited for the following shots which would then be studied closely. These were often presented as pictorial compositions, the emphasis being on high-angle shots presenting a view – slow movement or no movement at all, or a slow pan of the camera to show a complete vista of scenery. Claude's cinematographic style was thus based on the principle of revelation, such as in the second shot of a sunset in which the camera follows the car as it slowly drives along and after a few seconds the sunset appears in the background. The comments in the press about a lack of quick movement are borne out

The Open Road: some
impression of fringing is
retained in DVD restoration

by the DVD, which shows many fairly static
compositions, including a man painting a landscape or
the Wedgwood pottery display. While the DVD retains
some examples of fringing on movement – as when
swimmers glide off a slide into a pool, hounds wag their
tails in a hunting scene, children dance merrily in a ring
or a monkey in a zoo rapidly moves – on many occasions
this is avoided by the shot construction. Examples of this
demonstrate the 'stereoscopic' effect commented on in
the press whereby a person would walk slowly towards
the camera, emphasising depth of field. The car likewise
repeats similar movements on its journey as it is driven
down country lanes. The film was shot in sunshine and
hot weather, indicated by the parasols seen carried by
people filmed in various locations. This suited the mood
of the film, as with the languid sunbathers at Torquay
beach. Many images appear posed and the subjects seem
to be aware of the camera's presence.

The two-colour limitations are clearly evident in
the DVD, with emphasis on orange and turquoise-
green. Deep blue, yellow and bright reds are not
evident, except perhaps for the soldiers' coats in the
Changing of the Guards sequence which appear redder
than shots of other iconic red objects such as the
London trams, which show up as orange. Colour
deficiencies are thus most noticeable when familiar sights
invite unfavourable comparison with the viewer's
everyday knowledge, such as when the grass at the Oval

cricket ground or at Cardiff Castle looks brownish and
dull. A close-up of two roses from Blore Hill, where a
battle in the Wars of the Roses took place, is clearly
lacking since the rose which is supposed to be
Lancastrian red looks closer to orange. One inter-title is
bold enough to invite the viewer to appreciate 'nature's
colours' before a shot of a pier at the seaside. On the
DVD at least this rather falls flat since the colours appear
muted and the sea in the background is greyish. While
this may have been true to nature, spectators'
expectations may well have been for more vibrant hues,
although this is difficult to ascertain. Another shot of a
rainbow is perhaps more successful, since the sight of the
vague glow of different hues is rather as rainbows often
appear in the distance, with their colours blurred rather
than clearly defined shades of the spectrum.

Claude Friese-Greene's experiments were
thwarted by a number of interlinked factors. As we have
seen, in spite of his efforts to combat the problems
experienced by previous two-colour additive processes,
perceptible faults persisted. Following on from
Kinemacolor and Prizma, his process was subject to the
same intense scrutiny by the trade press, even though he
tried to off-set criticism by never claiming to show all
colours of the spectrum. At the end of 1925 Claude's
faith in colour was resolute, writing articles in
publications including the *Times of India* arguing that
women in particular were 'demanding more refined
shades and greater variety of colour in their own dress
and in home furnishings' and so were ready to see
colour on screen for a more restful, natural effect. For
those working in cities, colour film would 'cheer and
brighten a dull existence'.[65] Reflecting on the past in an
article in the trade press published in 1934, Claude,
however, concluded that 'the time was not ripe' for the
widespread introduction of colour film since 'the silent
black and white picture was then still a sufficient
attraction without the added appeal of colour … The
speed of silent film – 16 fps – was too slow for the two-
colour processes and cinema proprietors were not willing
to have their machines speeded up.' He concluded that
the only viable way forward was colour values being
'embedded in the emulsion', as in the subtractive
approach being developed by Technicolor.[66] Shortly
before his death he shot the first few reels of *The Great
Mr Handel* (1942), a Technicolor biopic discussed in
Chapter 6.

Yet technical issues were not the only reasons Natural Colour failed to gain ground after 1926. The severe crisis in the British film industry is a key context which explains Claude's approach both to the marketing of Natural Colour and to his attitude towards potential American investors. Like his father, Claude was passionate about the British film industry's need to counter American competition. The rhetoric deployed to advertise the films was steeped with patriotic fervour, reproducing such sentiments from the trade press as advertising copy for *The Open Road*:

> There should be a tremendous future for these pictures, for, coming at the moment when the whole country is clamouring for British pictures, these beautiful films of the glorious countryside, showing in actual colour places that one reads about day after day, will be certain to appeal to picture palace audiences all over the kingdom. Indeed, they should circulate all over the world. It is the plain duty of exhibitors to support films such as these, for they are one hundred per cent entertainment.[67]

After the first demonstration films in 1924 it seems that Claude did not follow through with his campaign to sell the process in America. The decision for it to remain based in Britain to produce topical films may well have been motivated by the prevailing context whereby British films were being encouraged to counter Hollywood's domination and when producers were seeking protection from the state. The timing of Claude's experiments coincided with the lobbying activities by the film trade from 1924 onwards in the run-up to the first Cinematograph Films Act, 1927.[68] These encouraged an attitude which hardly welcomed collaboration with American directors, and the crisis also made exhibitors wary of deviating from sure-fire bets at the box office.

The hyper-concentration on the technical performance of colour processes also perhaps led to a conservative attitude towards content. Claude concentrated on topicals for patriotic and financial reasons, but one senses that this was part of his overall philosophy which emphasised the therapeutic value of colour films in bringing nature closer to city-dwellers. Pastoral romanticism is certainly evident in *The Open Road*, even if the film's premise is motivated by the journey of a motor car and some cities are featured. When reading reviews of *The Open Road* it is striking how similar the responses are to opinion on Kinemacolor's topicals and other travelogues produced in the 1910s. For all its faults, *The Glorious Adventure* was operating in a different diegetic space, needing to graft colour to the imperatives of plot, character, action and stars. The furthest Claude came to attempting a dramatic scenario with colour was in *Moonbeam Magic*. One review conveyed something of its ingenuity when the appearance of colour effects is described: 'The young Prince appealed to Elizur to use his magic and make the world beautiful with colours. Elizur retired to his chamber and invoked the deity to give him power to charm colours from the moonbeams. In this he succeeded and turned the coloured moonbeams into liquids in his magical cauldron and then coaxed the liquids back into the moonbeams. The flashing coloured moonbeams then painted beautiful colours over the face of the earth.'[69] This narrative provided less invitation for judgment according to standards of colour 'fidelity' as had occurred with the comments on the lack of visible yellow for the sunflower or deep blues for skies and seas in *A Quest for Colour*. Although topicals were interesting, as the entertainment industry developed in the 1920s the box-office success of American feature films was a seductive commercial example many British producers sought to emulate. Based on similar approaches of revisiting older patents and responding to past criticisms, Prizma and Friese-Greene's Natural Colour demonstrated the limits of contemporary experiment. It was another ten years before Technicolor's research into three-colour subtractive methods and imbibition dye transfer gained commercial and aesthetic prominence. As we shall see in the following chapter, this left room for other significant interventions in the continuing quest for colour.

3 DEBATING COLOUR IN THE 1930s

One should remember that the inventor and scientist may offer the user a perfect process, but unless the user exercises discrimination, accepting a new group of artistic formulae conditioned by the technical facts, it is just as possible to fail by misuse of a new medium as it is to inaugurate a splendid advance in film history. (Adrian Klein, 1935)[1]

With the appearance of subtractive two-colour Technicolor in 1922, the introduction of dye-transfer printing in 1928 and the three-colour camera in 1932 some predicted 'black-and-white films will soon be a thing of the past', while others were more cautious, worrying that 'with the screen a blazing riot of colour it is impossible to concentrate fully on any particular individual'.[2] Indeed, there were chromophiles, cautious chromophiles and chromophobes in the British colour adventure. Adrian Cornwell-Clyne published three editions of *Colour Cinematography* (1936, 1939 editions under the name of Adrian Klein, and 1951 as Cornwell-Clyne), a classic technical book which also discussed the principles and theory of colour.[3] Writing in the 1951 edition, Cornwell-Clyne revisited what he had written about the future of colour in 1939. In the latter edition of his book he asked himself the following question: 'Will the colour film altogether supplant the black-and-white film?' He replied that a rapid change-over was unlikely and that it would be very surprising if in five years' time half of films were in colour. In 1949 only about one tenth of all films were made in colour, and Cornwell-Clyne wrote that 'it will still be surprising … if one-half of all films are made in colour in the year

2000'.[4] Costs were the main reason given, but he also identified a particular form of criticism which is consistent with the remarks cited earlier about Prizma and which had appeared in the 1939 edition of his book: 'any slight distortion from the condition of neutral balance is very quickly spotted as *unnatural*'. Because of this hyper-sensitivity to 'wrong' colour, Cornwell-Clyne recommended that 'The quality of the colouring should be such as hardly ever to call attention to itself. The first colour film to be received with universal acclamation will be that one in which we shall never have been conscious of the colour as an achievement.'[5] By 1951 the nationalist cast of this view was extended further when Cornwell-Clyne declared that audiences did not want 'vivid' colour 'which may be due to a national liking for the restrained and rather sad tones typical of the British sentiment for colour … The average cinemagoer is attracted primarily by the individualities of their favourite stars and by the story and treatment, and the question of colour is only a subsidiary factor of final polish.'[6] While Cornwell-Clyne's comment would appear to be in complete variance with J. Stuart Blackton's earlier claim when promoting Prizma that British natural colours were particularly rich, he is referring to an ideological proclivity as well as an aesthetic sensibility towards restraint, rather than to colour imagery per se.

Colour continued to be a 'glorious adventure' for many in Britain from the 1920s into the 30s, continuing the instances of unstable hybridity around colour noted in the last chapter. This chapter will discuss the many processes that competed for technical and aesthetic prominence during this period when the sheer variety of approaches prompted extended debate on the future of colour cinema. As such the period constitutes a fascinating interregnum between the co-existence of both additive and subtractive colour experimentation and the commercial rise to prominence of three-strip Technicolor. Although many of the films no longer exist, surveying the commentary they inspired which focused on their colour rendition permits an archaeology of colour film to be assembled. As well as constituting a record of technical innovation, this is also a register of the different ideological standpoints being expressed about colour. As we shall see, these often oscillated wildly before a consensus emerged that the principle of 'colour design' was a good one, whether used to rein in the spectacular potential of colour images or to produce a strikingly conceived artistic design. Colour design was an important concept because it acknowledged that film colour, as in painting, could be planned to create particular effects. It also acknowledged colour's potential to transform an image, whether to reduce potentially disruptive effects or to highlight colour as a symbolic register.

In the early 1930s it was far from clear that Technicolor would come to dominate the market. The subtractive, two-colour Technicolor features *Toll of the Sea* (1922) and *The Black Pirate* (1926) had been shown in Britain, and the company's progress was followed as the development of a three-colour method was announced.[7] *Toll of the Sea* had a glowing review in *Kinematograph Weekly* that described the film's colour as its 'chief charm'. The way this was expressed is interesting in terms of demonstrating how discourses around tastes were gravitating towards praise for 'entirely natural' colour in 'a continuous series of brilliant pastel studies that are a sheer delight to the eye'. There was also an appreciation of how colour supported narrative and vice-versa: 'The production has obviously been carried out with a view to displaying the colour qualities of the process to the best advantage, but the slender dramatic thread is artistically woven and the dramatic values very well balanced against the technique.'[8] When *The Black Pirate* was released in Britain in March 1926 reviewers also judged its colour with admiration. The two-colour system was appreciated for rendering 'cool and restful tones', and was likened to the work of Dutch painters.[9] Technical specialist and

former Kinemacolor cameraman Colin N. Bennett also observed that its colour effects appeared as 'refined down to more of an artistic suggestion than a robust reality', more 'faint infusion' than the vibrant colours he had observed with Gaumont's three-colour Chronochrome.[10] Although other two-colour Technicolor films such as *Whoopee* (1930) were admired in Britain, the process was considered expensive and needing excessive light levels.[11] As Higgins explains, 'subtractive systems were limited to reproducing a narrow slice of the spectrum. Based on two colors, usually cyan and magenta, these processes translated the *mise en scène* into compositions of bluish green and pinkish orange. Flesh tones and saturated primary hues were problematic.'[12] When Simon Rowson reported to the Cinematograph Exhibitors' Association conference in 1930 he considered Technicolor's lack of precise definition to be problematic, as it was before the introduction of the imbibition printing process in 1928. He nevertheless gave a reassuring forecast for colour in the long term, predicting that as soon as technical issues had been resolved black-and-white films would 'disappear from our screens as rapidly and as completely as the "talkie" superseded the "silent" film'.[13] By contrast, 'high-brow' critics writing for journals such as *Close-Up* preferred to promote cinema as differentiating itself as an art form primarily by *lacking* colour and sound.[14] Such thinking was consistent with the modernist views of writers including Rudolf Arnheim whose early film theory text, *Film as Art*, dismissed colour and sound as 'wax museum ideals' that debased film's destiny to make a distinctive contribution to art through black-and-white silent film.[15]

Claude Friese-Greene's 'Natural Colour Process' used for *The Open Road* travelogues (1925) has already been analysed, but a few other processes which similarly depended on two or more images being recorded to obtain different colour records of the same picture on one film are worthy of mention. In 1914, the company Cinechrome was formed by Colin N. Bennett (who was a technician and a technical film reporter, see comments above on early Technicolor), and various patents were worked on including those of William Friese-Greene. An additive process, it used a double-width film perforated down the middle and with identical exposures side-by-side, one green and the other red. Kodak produced the special wide film stock and the beam-splitter camera with two lenses placed behind the prism divider. A film of the Prince of Wales's visit to India was shot using **Cinechrome (see Technical Appendix)**, and it was exhibited successfully in 1922 to the Royal Society of Arts. But the need for a special projector to cope with the unusually wide film limited its potential for further commercial development. Cinechrome was renamed **Cinecolor (see Technical Appendix)** in the mid–1920s (a British process not to be confused with the American subtractive Cinecolor), once it became possible to have two half-size exposures within the normal frame area, again using a beam-splitting lens and prism device.[16] **Zoechrome (see Technical Appendix)** was a three-colour process using a four-lens camera with a complex method of printing and dye-toning that was never taken up by the industry.[17]

British producer Maurice Elvey developed an additive process called **Raycol (see Technical Appendix)** in the late 1920s which involved two quarter-sized colour records in opposite corners of the same frame. For projection, a special lens had to be used and the results were greeted with some enthusiasm by the film trade. *The School for Scandal* (1930), a short film produced in Raycol by Albion Productions and directed by Elvey was, according to Coe, 'the first sound colour film to be made in England', and 800 cinemas purchased the Raycol projection lenses. After some modifications *The Skipper of the Osprey* (1933) was shown but Raycol was criticised for 'poor definition, pastel shades and colour fringing'.[18] Another report noted that 'some attractive pictures resulted, especially those rich in reds, such as barge and smack sails, hunting scenes etc. But here the need for special lenses in the projection room and their very fine adjustments formed an obstacle to a wide use of the process.'[19] Nevertheless, Raycol had attracted attention, not least from novelist Elinor Glyn who wanted to use it in 1929 for a colour adaptation of her novel *Knowing Men*. But after a dispute with Elvey over her intention to make both colour and black-and-white versions of the film, she turned to another short-lived additive two-colour process called **Talkicolor (see Technical Appendix)** that had been developed by Dr Anton Bernardi, one of the inventors of Raycol. Talkicolor was also, however, flawed by insurmountable technical problems and Glyn was subsequently involved in an ultimately unsuccessful attempt to exploit a process called **Morganacolor (see Technical Appendix)**.

Pagliacci (1936) was a black-and-white British film but featuring a process known as British Chemicolor for the prologue and final sequence, both of which depict a comic opera troupe's stage performances while touring in Italy. Based on the German Ufacolor process, British Chemicolor did not require a special camera and used bipack negative film. Printing involved chemical toning of double-coated film.[20] The film's theme of backstage drama encouraged the interspersion of stage scenes shot from the viewpoint of the audience within the diegesis, as well as from backstage and outside the theatre. In the final sequence, for example, several shots of the performance are intercut with those of the audience, creating a contrast between the often vivid colours of the actors' costumes and the more 'natural' reverse shots of the audience. The cinema audience is thus encouraged to compare the two styles of colour – the theatrical, spectacular mode for the performance with one costume a deep red/orange and another with a green and red diamond pattern – and the more generally subdued colours for the shots of the audience. This contrasting display is rather like a combination of applied and photographic colour since the prologue features a shot in shades of red to depict a sunset (as with tinting), and the later shots of the audience from the viewpoint of the troupe appear as a photographic process. A similar two-colour process using Agfa bipack stock was the French **Harmonicolor (see Technical Appendix)** process.[21] In March 1936 a demonstration film was trade shown in London called *Talking Hands* (directed by Ivor Campbell and produced at studios in Walton-on-Thames). A report on the screening noted that the colour range was good and worked well to depict the unusual device of a story told through the hands of card players. This meant, however, that there were not exterior shots which, for the reviewer, would have presented a better guide for judging the merits of Harmonicolor. The film does not appear to have survived, but it serves as an interesting example of a two-colour system which according to contemporary reportage was making good progress with 'excellent blacks' and without a tendency towards the dominant orange and blue-greens of many other two-colour processes.[22]

Dufaycolor (see Technical Appendix) was an additive system used for several British newsreels, advertising films and one feature, *Sons of the Sea* (1939), directed by Maurice Elvey, who had been involved with Raycol. *Sons of the Sea* will be analysed in Chapter 6 on wartime feature films in colour, whereas Dufaycolor's short films will be the focus of attention here. Indeed, it was by no means clear that subtractive approaches were superior. When D. A. Spencer gave the Presidential Address before the Royal Photographic Society of Great Britain in 1937 he explained that:

> In additive processes the color rendering can be more accurate than in subtractive systems. This is because no known magenta or blue-green coloring matter fulfils the theoretical requirements of subtractive processes as closely as do the available projection filter colors those of additive systems. Generally speaking, additive materials are cheaper and easier to process both at the negative and at the positive stage. Their big disadvantage is that they require considerably more light for successful projection than do subtractive films.[23]

Dufaycolor had many supporters, including artist Paul Nash, who appreciated its 'understated' and 'natural' qualities.[24] These terms continued to be important in the evaluation of colour technologies. The coupling of 'natural' with 'understated' can be related to the writings referred to at the beginning of this chapter which sought to rescue cinema's artistic potential from the danger of being debased by high colour. Colour expert Adrian Klein (who later changed his name to Cornwell-Clyne) who had been involved in the development of **Gasparcolor (see Technical Appendix)** was recruited by the Dufay-Chromex company in 1937, where he produced a number of short films, working with renowned directors. For many it seemed that Dufaycolor was Britain's chance to produce colour which could be distinguished from Technicolor, and which was identified with a British 'look' suitable for subjects such as scenery and royal pageantry. These themes were, however, by no means the extent of Dufaycolor's catalogue, and enthusiasts for the process were attracted by its potential for experimental film-making and animation. Animation was a particularly attractive form for colour experimentation and popular shorts such as those produced using a subtractive process called **Dunningcolor (see Technical Appendix)** by animator Anson Dyer in the mid-1930s. Colour is usually easier to control when using animation than with

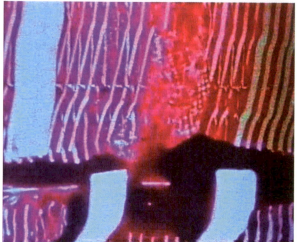

A Colour Box (Dufaycolor, 1935): animated colour vibrancy with Dufaycolor; animated abstraction to music and with Dufaycolor; colour contrasts

*The HPO – Heavenly Post
Office* (Dufaycolor, 1938):
animation by Lotte Reiniger

live action. The impressive results encouraged Disney
to support Technicolor in the early 1930s, as well as
animators who wanted to work with Dufaycolor and
other colour processes. Animated films made using
Dufaycolor stock included the General Post Office-
sponsored films such as Len Lye's *A Colour Box* (1935)
that presented Dufaycolor in an entirely different way
from its use in live-action films. Instead of being
characterised by pastel colouring, this hand-painted film
relished in the visual pleasures of pulsating, vibrant
colours that positively danced in syncopation with the
Cuban soundtrack. Other notable applications were
Norman McLaren's *Love on the Wing* (1938) and Lotte
Reiniger's *The HPO – Heavenly Post Office* (1938). The
heavily accented blue of Lotte Reiniger's *The HPO –
Heavenly Post Office* features an angel in the sky
observing people receiving 'heavenly' telegrams and
silhouetted animals and shapes that defined her signature
style. The qualities of the Dufaycolor animated films are
distinctive, especially when compared with the part-
Dufaycolor live-action short film *The King's Stamp*
(William Coldstream, 1935), which details the designing
of the King's Jubilee stamps. After an opening sequence
in black and white, the first colour sequence features the
stamps being printed. The printing rolls and gumming
machines are shown, as the stamps are rolled off
cylinders with oranges and blues dominant. A black-and-
white sequence detailing the history of stamps from the
Victorian period follows, with colour used to display the

'Penny Black' and the 'Tuppenny Blue' stamps. A
further historical sequence follows in black and white,
with colour returning at the end to show off the 1935
stamps in close-up. Although interesting, this rather
ponderous display of colour intermittently placed in an
otherwise monochrome film cannot really compete with
the arresting, inventive playfulness of the Dufaycolor
animated films.

Simon Brown has described how Dufaycolor was
presented in Britain in 1931 as a revised process from
the original French invention by Louis Dufay, which had
subsequently been developed in collaboration with T.
Thorne-Baker, a British scientist who worked for the
Spicer-Dufay company which had been established in the
UK a few years earlier to exploit the process.[25] Although
Dufaycolor had great potential as a cheaper process than
Technicolor (although not as cheap as black and white),
there were problems – for example, the *réseau*, or mosaic
pattern fundamental to the process' technical
specification, was visible in projection as tiny diamond
shapes. While for most commentators this was a flaw,
some actually appreciated the resulting effect which gave
the image an almost impressionistic look 'similar to
that seen on a half-tone block' and 'by no means
aggressive'.[26] In its early stages of development, it was
difficult to produce copies from a master, but this
potentially disastrous obstacle was overcome by the mid-
1930s.[27] Dufaycolor film, however, needed greater than
normal illumination when projected in the cinema, as
well as louder sound amplification. This was confirmed
by R. Howard Cricks, a specialist in screen projection,
explaining that whereas a Technicolor print could be
made sufficiently thin to be projected at relatively low
screen intensities, Dufaycolor required a certain
minimum intensity because much of the light was
obstructed by the silver image behind the other two
réseau elements. On the other hand, he also pointed out
that provided a Dufaycolor print was sufficiently dense
through over-printing, higher screen intensities could be
withstood without the colours appearing 'glaring'. This
was not the case with Technicolor, since very high
screen intensities tended to make the colours appear
'unnaturally brilliant'.[28] This did not, however, solve
Dufaycolor's overall difficulties, since both projectors
and cameras required adjustments, particularly for
shooting interiors. As we have seen, projection issues
hindered the progress of earlier processes such as

Kinemacolor. In addition, commentaries on Dufaycolor which concentrated on the visibility of the *réseau* tended to detract from its distinctive look. The timing of its development, in tandem with the arrival of three-strip Technicolor, was perhaps unfortunate since Dufaycolor had many enthusiastic supporters who appreciated the charm of the *réseau*, with its affinities to the Autochrome, an earlier colour technique which involved dyed starch grains on a photographic plate.[29]

Problems with shooting interiors meant that Dufaycolor was primarily used for the short film market, and in this regard some notable films were indeed produced, particularly those that concentrated on exterior, pastoral, 'heritage' scenes which the process was better equipped to portray. The range of films is impressive, including *Calling Mr Smith* (Franciszka Themerson, 1944), a propaganda short produced by the Polish Film Unit. As Brown notes, this film was experimental in its use of live action and animation and used 'bold swathes of colour in a purely sensational way' – for example, with recurring instances of red in different shots to communicate the all-pervasive threat of Nazi oppression in a range of contexts.[30] Experimentation with Dufaycolor progressed with advances such as reducing 35mm prints to 16mm, which encouraged short film production and increased the exhibition of advertising films. High-profile names were attracted to work with the process. As well as Len Lye, other notable directors included Humphrey Jennings, who directed *Farewell Topsails* (1937) and *English Harvest* (1937, re-edited as *The Farm*). Brown has observed how *Farewell Topsails* uses colour as metaphor:

> Throughout the film there is subtle colour contrast between the browns and greys of the shore, and the blues of the sea. Topsail schooners transported chalky china clay, so Jennings' palette is deliberately bleak, the browns of industry and the suits of the men in the village, the chalky grey-white of the clay, and then the blue of the sea and the black of the ship. The blue of the ocean contains within it the rhetoric of the spectacular. Partially, this is due to the inherent romanticism of the ocean itself, but Jennings exploits this by juxtaposing its vividness in contrast with the dour earth colours of the shore … The lack of colour on shore to contrast the bright blue of the ocean gives a sensual dimension to the plight of those without jobs and future.[31]

This lyrical, evocative style is also evident in *English Harvest*, a film that describes the introduction of mechanisation to harvesting methods. The colours are pale, even bleached-out, for the fields and trees, even though some of the shots of the sky are blue. Since the farmers wear brown, black and white, the opportunity for a wider colour range is not presented in the film which is more an evocation of the rural pastoral than a display of colour.

Jennings's final film in Dufaycolor was *Design for Spring* (1937, rereleased as *Making Fashion* in 1938, produced by Adrian Klein). It was a showcase for fashion designer Norman Hartnell's spring collection, as well as for the colour film. Although Jennings did not seek to deploy colour overtly for its own sake, its appearance nevertheless constituted a visual sensation experienced by contemporary audiences as spectacular, particularly since screen colour was still relatively rare. The colour direction was by Joan Bridge, and 'colour harmony make-up' is credited as Max Factor, the company more usually associated with Technicolor. It is quite a daring film, since it invites the viewer to compare colours named in the voice-over with what is seen on screen. This exposes Dufaycolor to scrutiny, and on several occasions it does not emerge favourably as capable of achieving an 'accurate' colour record. As with many films documenting industry, the viewer is taken through the various stages of development from design to display. At the start of the film, the designer is inspired by statues in the British Museum, and by the blues and whites of Wedgwood china. In one scene a blue fabric is compared with the blue of the designer's drawing, as details of the craft and skill involved in fashion design are described and the principle of colour accuracy is established as important for the craft and for the film. It is, however, the show of Hartnell's spring collection which invites the greatest scrutiny of colour as the voice-over describes the gowns with their names often specifically referring to their colours. The Ascot dress, for example, is described as having 'pale pink lace' but this appears more whitish, and the 'navy blue fox' trimming on the sleeves of the next outfit looks black. 'Dark wine' gloves show as black and 'lavender' looks pale blue. A 'soft pink' coat looks too orangey and the models' lips show as more orange than red.[32] Even though the colour descriptions are clearly variable, the spring collection is nevertheless a spectacle of fabrics and textures, including a sparkly,

Making Fashion (Dufaycolor, 1938): a jacket inspired by a matador's costume

sequinned evening dress in emerald green. Other costumes are black and white, which deflects attention from Dufaycolor's reproduction of the named colours of the gowns. A later shot of a horse guard shows his jacket more orange than red, which is another instance of Dufaycolor simply not delivering a well-recognised colour. This also occurs with a jacket inspired by a matador's costume. The final shot declaring spring has arrived shows a close-up of a very pale daffodil which typifies the film's apparent refusal to shrink away from showing familiar objects known by everyone for their colours. This is perhaps symptomatic of the confidence around Dufaycolor during the late 1930s when many looked to it as a suitably 'British' system when compared with Technicolor, which generally looked more saturated. Equating Dufaycolor with a national colour aesthetic assists our understanding of how colour technologies were negotiated in Britain during this period. 'Natural', quality film-making was associated with colour tastes that gravitated towards restraint, delicacy of hue and shooting the British countryside.

Dufaycolor was particularly suited to outdoor shooting, and the catalogue of films made with the process features a majority of titles which can be described as travelogues such as *Lakeland Heritage* (1938), *Garden of the Sea* (1942) and *Our Inheritance* (1945). Newsreels featuring the royal family were also vehicles for the display of Dufaycolor, which further identified the process with themes of English heritage, patriotism and nation. In this sense many of the films, their locations and subject-matter, can be compared to earlier colour processes, particularly Kinemacolor, which relished in the presentation of shots which picked out details such as brightly coloured flowers, as well as filming military parades and royal subjects. These subjects were good vehicles for colour, since they mostly did not necessitate rapid camera movement and concentrated attention on a subject that was, in itself, a visual spectacle made all the more so because of the impact of colour. As we have seen, this, however, placed emphasis on the quality of colour rendition, so that commentary often fixated on perceived notions of fidelity to 'reality' even though, somewhat ironically, the films often presented themes and events not witnessed by the majority of the population. Humphrey Jennings appreciated Dufaycolor's suitability for documentary work, especially for shooting in poorer light conditions,

and the mobility of the 'ordinary' camera. With this in mind, he predicted: 'In the future I believe that colour film stories will have to be constructed far more in terms of the locations than has been the practice with black and white films,' even producing a 'new realism' particularly suited to British cinema.[33] Such an observation contributes to the notion that Dufaycolor had the potential to enhance a British school of colour film-making. Some even went so far as to argue that Dufaycolor was more 'natural' than subtractive processes such as Technicolor because the micro-colour primary filters (the *réseau* or mosaic) on the film resembled the construction of the human eye with its separate sensitive nerve terminals contributing towards the primary colour sensations of red, green or blue. Three-strip Technicolor required a greater degree of human intervention whereas Dufaycolor was 'subject to the laws of nature in so far as they operate within the limits of photographic science'.[34] This style of discourse about colour can be compared with earlier comments about Kinemacolor, when it was promoted as a 'natural' system as opposed to applied colour. The imperatives for making this argument were to firmly establish Kinemacolor as an accurate, indexical 'window on the world', and operating in a pioneer spirit of the pursuit of scientific truth.[35] With the stress on Dufaycolor's ability to 'capture' nature, it is perhaps not surprising to see that some of the tropes of earlier discourses around colour were repeated twenty years later. As Kinemacolor's positive reception as a 'natural' process had shown, the casting of Dufaycolor as demonstrating a 'natural', British colour aesthetic gave it a potential advantage over Technicolor.

Experimentation took place on several fronts, and the advertising sector became an important outlet for short colour films. As with photography, colour advertising became a site of experimentation during this period in the face of criticism from those who were wedded to black-and-white 'artistic' aesthetics. Dufaycolor was used for advertising films and sponsors included Morris Motors, the Co-Operative Wholesale Society and the Guide Dog Association. Len Lye's *Rainbow Dance* (Gasparcolor, 1936) and *Trade Tattoo* (Technicolor, 1937) were made for the General Post Office. The latter used an innovative approach in not being filmed with a Technicolor beam-splitting camera. Instead Lye substituted the matrix elements with black-and-white out-takes from various GPO films to form one colour record and he painted onto celluloid for the other record. As Enticknap explains, the result was intricate and startling: 'The combination gives the impression of toned black-and-white photography in one shade with superimposed animations of a different colour when the constituent elements were combined.'[36] The films are witty, working to surprise the audience by gradually revealing their purpose, indeed often keeping this knowledge to the end. The three-colour **Brewstercolor (see Technical Appendix)** process was demonstrated in 1935 by Revelation Films for *Let's Look at London*, the first of a travelogue series of twelve films advertising London and intended for worldwide release. A contemporary report by Elliott Hammett noted the following comments about the film which had been shot using three Brewstercolor cameras brought back from New York by Revelation's Chairman, Charles A. Cochran:

> It reflects great credit on the system employed that the colour was natural and definition quite good despite the movement and unrehearsed conditions. While the scenes were only a little better than the customary two-colour range, within the studio, where it was possible to control the lighting, a much wider range was immediately apparent. This included a very good yellow – a colour very seldom seen on the screen. The characteristic sheens of the various fabrics were beautifully rendered, there was no mistaking a tweed for a velour, or satin for velvet. The complexions of the mannequins [the film featured a mannequin parade and cabaret show as well as exterior 'sights'] were noticeably good, too.[37]

The only criticism was that blacks 'were a little dead, and surges of colour and a preponderance of purple were occasionally observed. Now and then the registration was not perfect and the definition of exteriors might have been better.' Another review reported that: 'Vibration was noticed in one or two scenes (due to camera motor). To me, the finest colour was a yellow velvet seen in a mannequin parade, whilst the green in the exteriors was very true, and the general fidelity of the colours very pleasing.'[38] So the verdict was broadly enthusiastic, and indicative of the huge potential identified at the time for colour film in advertising. Not everyone was, however, convinced that advertising needed colour. One correspondent writing in *The Commercial Film*, for example, warned against using

colour: 'The temptation to photograph in garish colours objects and designs which are better left in monochrome should be sternly resisted by our national advertisers.'[39] Such caution was, of course, disproved in World War II, when colour cinematography in short films benefited from technical developments as well as from a culture that was heightened to appreciate colour positively in a variety of contexts.

When he was technical director of Gasparcolor Adrian Klein prepared the way by arguing that any three-colour process was perfect for advertising: 'The inclusion of colour in the advertising film is so obviously advantageous as to be self-evident, and it is unnecessary to advance various arguments in favour of the colour film.'[40] He hoped that the addition of colour would help advertising films reach larger and 'better class' cinemas, especially since colour would enhance the entertainment appeal of advertising films. He warned, however, that such colour films should not appear as mere animated posters, but instead be seen to deploy 'imagination and charm' in their execution. He also advocated that knowledge about colour was essential in order to achieve this aim:

> It is essential that the colour direction be in the hands of competent artists assisted by technicians intimately acquainted with the peculiar conditions as to illumination for colour photography, and who possess specialised knowledge of pigments and dyes and their reproductivity. Above all, the actual advertising should be as far as possible indirect, actual reference to the product being reserved to the last few feet of the film, and then only presented in good taste.[41]

The appearance of colour in advertising films redirected critical attention towards how colour presented a 'spectacle of reality' whereby, as Brown notes: 'The commercial producers, subordinating ideas of film as art to film as advertising, had no hesitation in using the sensual pictorial tropes, spectacle and realism of colour in order to better sell their products to a resistant public.'[42] This shift in the presentation and reception of colour had a lasting impact on subsequent developments, including Technicolor, which depended less on an imperative to represent reality as on being a particular brand of film colour that developed its own aesthetic styles and conventions.

Rainbow Dance (Gasparcolor, 1936): animated, silhouetted figure dancing to sound and colour

Rainbow Dance

Gasparcolor specialised in advertising films as well as animation films, including Hungarian artist George Pál's *Puppetoons* series (1932–47).[43] Adrian Klein was head of the London office of Gasparcolor Ltd from 1934. Gasparcolor was a subtractive process first developed in Germany by Hungarian chemist Belá Gaspar. It was distinguished by its multilayer printing whereby the film was coated with three layers of emulsions with dyes (two on one side, one on the other). As such it was 'the first 35mm integral layer tripack film (known as monopack and multilayer) to be used commercially', therefore representing a tremendous advance.[44] Animators found it particularly suitable as a film stock capable of rendering deep, saturated colours, as can be seen in films such as Len Lye's *Rainbow Dance* which featured a silhouetted figure (Rupert Doone) dancing his way through various scenarios to a piece played by Rico's Creole Band. The film's opening very much sets the tone whereby the credits are accompanied by a rainbow shape which cascades with colours. A storm (with rain represented by pulsating, coloured vertical streaks) is followed by a rainbow which sets the figure on his travels, as he dances his way around the world. The film is an advertisement for the Post Office Savings Bank, but along the way it shows a number of vibrant scenes in which the music synchronises with colour and movement. It is endlessly inventive and dazzling. The dancer's silhouette progresses across frames and through

colours, mostly moving but with the occasional moment of stasis. It is a wonderful example of how colour was used by such artists for abstraction in a playful spirit of extending the colour box beyond notions of restraint and narrative cinema.

Another notable Gasparcolor title is *On Parade* (1936), a puppet film advertising Horlicks, a hot, malted milk bedtime drink. It was made, like *Puppetoons*, by George Pál who made several films advertising the same product. *On Parade* features a colonel in charge of lethargic soldiers in need of revival so that they can go on parade. Horlicks comes to the rescue, energising all concerned, including the colonel's horse. The light-hearted touch whereby the film uses the product it is advertising judiciously, visible but not detracting from the film's entertaining qualities and colour interest, marks it as a text-book example of Klein's theories. As with other Gasparcolor films, the colour is vibrant, particularly the blue skies and tunics worn by the soldiers, contrasted with their orange trousers. When we first see the colonel he is presented as a display of colour, emerging from a canon barrel where he has been asleep. His black feet, orange legs, blue tunic, orange and black hat and yellow skin establish the film's dominant colours. Blue and orange are deeply saturated, whereas the green in a few shots of trees is darkish. Varying camera positions, such as a low-angle focusing on the patterns formed by the marching soldiers' orange legs,

result in a sense of creative dynamism which is also evident in shots which depend on internal framing to accentuate colour contrasts and dimensionality – for example, a shot of the soldiers framed by an arch. On another occasion we see the soldiers through glass and from a high angle as they drink their Horlicks. The film is a simple, witty and humorous advertisement that is as much about celebrating Gasparcolor as the product it is promoting.

Klein directed *Colour on the Thames* (1935) in Gasparcolor, which features a journey down the Thames. The film begins with a small child in a red bathing suit playing in the sunshine on the riverbank, and the camera proceeds down-river, into the Pool of London, past ships and then towards London Bridge. Several of the shots are clearly intended to display colour – for example, one shot in particular dwells on the yellow-coloured writing of a ship's name against its black hull, while another pans from a red, white and blue funnel to the red and black hull of another ship. A gently paced film, the journey into London provides an excellent vehicle to display Gasparcolor, with its rendering of the red funnels and blue skies in particular.

In the trade press colour was debated as ever, and with each process similar judgments were made about the extent to which 'natural' reproduction of colours was evident and, harking back to earlier debates, whether movement caused 'fringing'. D. A. Spencer's Presidential Address to the Royal Photographic Society of Great Britain in 1937 outlined the 'producer's dilemma' around colour in that while many critics advocated a restrained, 'unnoticed' approach, in order to justify the additional expenditure and novelty value which could be exploited to draw in audiences, colour must feature as a visible attraction. While cartoons were recognised as being extremely suitable vehicles for colour on account of the high degree of control possible during production and because the form does not equate with visible standards of 'realism', Spencer suggested that colour newsreels might constitute a focus for research into the 'physio-logico-psychological' reactions to colour film.[45] He recommended that the impact of colour on audiences should be tested in colour newsreels rather than more expensive feature films: 'The news in colour would have just that much more specific interest for the audience.' In other words, realism would be enhanced by colour.[46] This rather avoided confronting the broader aesthetic questions raised by the 'producer's dilemma', but it is indicative of how colour encouraged greater discussion of short films, in part because of their greater attractiveness and practicality in terms of inviting colour inventiveness. The 'producer's dilemma' was a problem shared by Technicolor, as Herbert Kalmus demonstrated new three-colour developments in animated shorts such as Disney's *Silly Symphonies* series and then in a live-action short, *La Cucaracha* (1934). The financial outlay was less than with most feature films, and the failure of a short film was arguably less damaging in terms of reputation. Spencer's colour newsreel idea played safe; it can be related to Urban's advocacy of Kinemacolor as enhancing realism in short subjects. During this time British colour shorts nevertheless provided producers and artists with a vital arena for testing colour's potential that was noted by many contemporaries. Veteran British director George Pearson, for example, thought that colour provided British directors with a chance to lead the world in developing innovative short film subjects: 'I think that the short film will return again, *via colour*, to the screen and will become as inherent and entertaining a part of the programme as in the early days of the industry.'[47] Britain's studio structure was not as vertically integrated as the Hollywood studio system in which the major companies dealt with production, distribution and exhibition. It is possible that the British film industry's weaker financial base and less vertically integrated structure shifted attention to short film-making as a practical, more economical site for experimentation with colour. British studios facing fierce competition from Hollywood were less able to risk finance and reputation on producing expensive colour feature films so it made sense rather to exploit a rich national tradition of innovation in short film-making, from travelogues to the GPO Film Unit.

The merits and problems of each process were extensively discussed, particularly when they could be directly compared. National events such as the Coronation in 1937 were filmed with various processes, Dufaycolor, **British Realita (see Technical Appendix)** (a short-lived additive process which had originated in France), Technicolor and Kinechrome. A report in the trade press concluded that:

> The full-bodied colours of Technicolor made their version a thing of beauty … Dufaycolor was totally different from that of Technicolor – the bright colours more subdued but the dark tones, particularly the glossiness of the

horses, somehow richer. The brilliance of Technicolor may, perhaps, have been preferable for this particular subject, but I have the feeling that for a feature-length film one would prefer the softer, less tiring colours of Dufay.

Realita was deemed to be less impressive and Kinechrome had 'remarkably good gilt colours' in the opening shot of the state coach but 'the rest of the film did not maintain quite the same standard', with a good range of blue tones.[48] *The Times* report noted Technicolor's advantage in filming close-ups and 'slow' (presumably meaning slow pans) shots of Windsor Castle and the royal portraits, but less success in filming crowd scenes. Gold, so important in such events, was not considered to film well in any process which tended to accentuate pink tinges, or with an impression of brassiness. The Dufay film was judged not to have the same degree of 'theatrical richness' as Technicolor. Crowd scenes contained some ruddy faces, and the range of colour for uniforms was praised, even though khaki tended to have a pinkish tinge in Dufaycolor.[49] These evaluations confirmed the accumulation of praise for Dufaycolor and its association with a British colour aesthetic based on a preference for soft, 'natural' colour that was differentiated from Technicolor's brighter 'theatrical richness'. While the latter description was not meant to be highly critical of Technicolor, such a judgment can be linked to Arnheim's view of colour as constituting 'waxwork museum ideals'. Dufaycolor, on the other hand, with its capacity for conveying quality and realism down to the glossiness of a horse's coat, firmly placed it in keeping with aesthetic values that favoured colour restraint.

Apart from debating the technical advantages and disadvantages of each particular system, views still differed on whether colour was desirable at all. F. Watts, production chief at Pathé, worried that colour newsreels would distract from news stories, and that the technical difficulties of filming in colour might prevent a cameraman obtaining the best pictures as events unfolded before the camera.[50] From this perspective additive processes such as Francita-Realita and Dufaycolor had an advantage over Technicolor because they took less time to process. When the Coronation was filmed on Wednesday, 12 May, for example, only British Realita was able to issue a 'flash' copy that evening, and by midnight the following day three West End newsreel cinemas were able to show the film. The Technicolor film was shown in a short version on the Friday, and the Dufaycolor film was available on Sunday, 16 May.[51]

When the British film industry was going through a period of expansion, followed by a financial crash in 1937–38, the risks and opportunities presented by colour acquired a compelling force. Producers such as Alexander Korda were enthusiastic, making several films in Technicolor, including *The Divorce of Lady X* (1938), *The Drum* (1938), *The Four Feathers* (1939), *Over the Moon* (1939) and *The Thief of Bagdad* (1940). He argued that, despite the extra costs, colour was particularly attractive to female cinemagoers. Yet even with his appreciation for colour Korda emphasised that 'its greatest triumph is that it is no longer remarkable'.[52] By the end of the 1930s Technicolor aesthetics had shifted somewhat from the early 'demonstration' mode described by Scott Higgins towards the 'unobtrusiveness' that followed after *The Trail of the Lonesome Pine* (1936).[53] The latter was praised in Britain for 'admirable restraint', capturing the outdoor scenery in a 'true' way.[54] C. P. Metcalfe, President of the Cinematograph Exhibitors' Association, was also inclined to the view that when used in an obtrusive, dominant fashion, colour could be a problem: 'Applied as it often has been it mars a good film, because instead of being used to give a sense of greater reality to the subject of the film it has been applied in such a way as to call attention to itself … Audiences should be almost unaware of its presence.'[55] Arthur Dent, managing director of Wardour Films, was unconvinced that all films should be made in colour. He argued that, even though producers were claiming that when applied judiciously colour did not create a distraction from a film's story, colour could not be ignored: 'With the movement of the action there is the changing of the dispositions of the colours, and don't tell me you aren't supposed to be watching the colours! If the producer didn't want you to see the colour he'd make it in black and white – it would cost him less anyway.'[56] He preferred black and white's rendition of facial detail: 'I have yet to see a colour picture which can bring out that sense of the dramatic in the face as well as it can be done in monochrome.'[57] Artist Paul Nash considered that commercial films were wasting an opportunity with colour since they were obsessed with naturalism rather than imagination.

He argued that an obsession with naturalism drew attention to technical deficiencies since precision in this regard was unobtainable.[58]

Yet some commentators were prepared to go further and consider how colour invited a different approach to techniques, such as lighting. Bernard Knowles, who assisted Technicolor cinematographer Bill Skall on *The Mikado* (1939), advocated that instead of assuming lighting should be flat for colour, thought should go into colour distribution within a frame. He also saw that the introduction of colour presented challenges and opportunities for greater cooperation between art directors, directors and cinematographers. Unusually, he argued that the scriptwriter's approach was most radically affected by colour since 'He must not only visualise the story but must be able to appreciate how the telling of that story in colour is going to affect his writing of it … Colour must be written before it can be used intelligently.'[59] Indeed, these principles can be seen at work in *The Mikado*, the first screen adaptation of the Gilbert and Sullivan operetta produced and adapted by Geoffrey Toye and directed by Victor Schertzinger. The subject's theatrical origins were highly appropriate for colour cinematography, and care was taken with sets and costumes to display shades that were praised for being 'exquisitely lovely'.[60] The lavish advertising campaign highlighted the film as a 'screen event', which was all the more notable for its Technicolor.[61] Examples of colour being 'written' for the film include the contrasting costumes worn by Nanki-Poo (Kenny Baker) when posing as a minstrel dressed predominantly in brown and his rival Koko (Martyn Green) who wears red, black and purple, colours more typically associated with authority which in this context refer to him being the official fiancé of Yum-Yum (Jean Colin), the young woman who Nanki-Poo loves. She wears light blue and cream and generally soft, pastel shades in contrast to the woman Nanki-Poo is supposed to marry whose colours are predominantly grey and black. Even when Nanki-Poo is revealed to be the Mikado's son and thus abandons his minstrel costume, he wears a beige outer garment with red and blue silk underneath. Colour is thus inscribed in the characters' robes in a consistent manner. The film features many sets which were similar to how they would have been planned for stage performances. However, when shot in Technicolor opportunities were clearly

taken to display colour effects such as shots of lanterns throwing warm shades of yellow and orange to provide strategically located illumination within the frame. Although the film featured a variety of such colour effects it was praised for its 'pastel' approach, and this was taken to be evidence of British cinema developing a particular palette in the deployment of colour.[62]

With hindsight these comments resonate with responses to the multifarious approach to colour in *The Glorious Adventure*, with its mixture of styles, the advantages and disadvantages of 'fringing' and an attempt to play with colour symbolism. Such debates persisted into the 1940s, reflecting a range of opinion around colour that demonstrated continuities with the silent period in their discussion of realism, form and the technical challenges posed by colour. As elsewhere, Britain's colour adventure demonstrated a *longue durée* in which experimentation was accompanied by protracted discussion, often masking nationalist discourses and repeating earlier rhetorical positions. Like Blackton and the characters in *The Glorious Adventure*, many got burnt, while others persisted in grappling with the aesthetic and technical challenges posed by capturing elusive, yet 'glorious' colour on screen.

The Mikado (Technicolor, 1939): Nanki-Poo (Kenny Baker) and Yum-Yum (Jean Colin); *The Mikado*'s stage-like set; soft, pastel palette showing fine gradations of colour

4 GLORIOUS TECHNICOLOR COMES TO BRITAIN

When Disney cartoons in three-colour **Technicolor (see Technical Appendix)** were seen in British cinemas, the 'era of colour' was seen to have arrived.[1] Other commentators were concerned about colour in fiction films, complaining that 'with the screen a blazing riot of colour it is impossible to concentrate fully on any particular individual'.[2] It was feared that audiences might be distracted by colour although the potential to transform cinema appeared tantalising. Colour presented directors, cinematographers and art directors with opportunities to exploit it as an expressive technique and to use it as a device to support narrative, underscore character etc. This chapter discusses the arrival of three-strip Technicolor in Britain and the impact it had on prevailing practices as well as on aesthetic regimes. An analysis of *Wings of the Morning* (1937) and *The Thief of Bagdad* (1940), films which demonstrate notable, varied and, on occasion, remarkable uses of Technicolor, will serve as case studies to demonstrate how concentrating on colour invites a combination of analytical and theoretical perspectives that reveal the complex challenges posed by colour to film scholarship. While Technicolor has received attention in contemporary commentary, histories of film technology, film theory and criticism, this has by no means formed an extensive corpus and research has mostly been focused on Hollywood cinema. The following chapters explore its history in Britain as a technology that gained far more prominence than earlier experiments with colour film. The short and feature films discussed constitute analytical models that examine colour as the dominant register within specific historical, generic and aesthetic contexts.[3]

Positive responses in Britain to earlier developments with two-colour Technicolor have been noted in Chapter 3, but these had not incorporated a key technical breakthrough introduced in 1928. Through the use of a printing technique known as **imbibition and dye transfer (see Technical Appendix)**, a single print was then produced that did not need a special projector for exhibition.[4] After further experimentation three-strip Technicolor was introduced in 1932 as a three-colour (red, green, blue) subtractive process whereby a beam splitter behind the camera's lens reflected light via filters onto three negatives. The three-strip technology overcame many of the technical problems that had bedevilled previous colour systems and became the dominant one applied in the USA and Britain for the next twenty years or so. Although the majority of British films were made in black and white, once Technicolor was introduced in the mid-1930s it became by far the most widely used colour process around the world until the mid-1950s. Filming in Technicolor was expensive, but it was used in Britain for key films including *Wings of the Morning*, *The Drum* (1938), *Sixty Glorious Years* (1938), *The Four Feathers* (1939), *The Thief of Bagdad*, *Henry V* (1944), *Western Approaches* (1944), *Caesar and Cleopatra* (1945), *A Matter of Life and Death* (1946), *Black Narcissus* (1947), *Scott of the Antarctic* (1948), *The Red Shoes* (1948), *Moulin Rouge* (1952) and *The Ladykillers* (1955). As detailed in Chapter 5, it was also used for short and informational films, but the concentration in this chapter will be on two early, seminal British feature films.

When Technicolor was exported to Britain, application of the process was overseen by Natalie Kalmus, ex-wife of co-developer of Technicolor, Herbert Kalmus. In her position as head of the Color Advisory Service, Natalie Kalmus was credited as 'color consultant' on most Technicolor films from 1933 to 1949. While she often worked with others and delegated responsibilities, there is no doubt that she exercised a profound influence over the ways in which Technicolor was used for many years.[5] Crucially, she developed guidelines for use of the process, advocating a theory of 'color consciousness' through the use of charts for each film that operated like a musical score and associated colour intensity with dominant moods or emotions. A chart was produced after reading a script; consultations would take place with producers and members of a studio's art and costume departments, and further adjustments would be made on the set and into post-production. As the company explained, the function of the colour consultancy service was to 'offer suggestions where color enhances dramatic mood and story value. Under Mrs Kalmus's direction, Technicolor has tested literally thousands of fabrics and color combinations and this information is made available to producers.'[6]

Many British cinematographers recall that Kalmus could be obstructive when they wanted to experiment with colour, and some commentators, including Martin Scorsese, credit cinematographers such as Jack Cardiff with developing a British use of Technicolor that was distinct from its application in the USA. As this and subsequent chapters demonstrate, there were indeed very distinctive uses of colour, but these must be understood in relation to overall developments in colour cinematography. As well as cinematographers, art directors were key production personnel who negotiated the details of working with colour in collaboration with Kalmus and Joan Bridge, who was also credited as colour director on many British films. While many contemporary commentators claimed aesthetic uniqueness in the ways in which Technicolor was used in British films, it is clear that these form an aspect of nationalist discourse which claimed differentiation from Hollywood. I argue that the issue is not a simple question of isolating differences between British and Hollywood Technicolor, but involves understanding the negotiation of convention and innovation that faced both cinemas. When British film-makers used Technicolor they did so in the knowledge that the process involved conforming to a particular set of technical conventions while at the same time providing scope for experimentation. It was to be expected that any perception of strictures around colour, such as those provided by the Color Advisory Service, would be resented as interference from Hollywood. Ivor Montagu, for example, thought that expert advice on every shade for costumes, interior and exterior settings, tended to flatten-out the impression of colour, resulting in a 'muddle'. Instead he advocated a style that harked back to silent cinema when colour would be used for emphasis, to accentuate the drama of a particular scene or shot. Only when this occurred, he argued, would colour take its place as 'the thing of the future'.[7] In view of the later experiments with colour conducted by Powell and Pressburger discussed in subsequent chapters, this would appear to be an apposite description of how British colour films were to develop.

Assessing the contributions of the many people involved in this complex mix of nationalist discourse, aesthetic judgment and technical enterprise demands a methodology which adequately takes into account competing claims on the origin of screen colour. Opinion often reflected Britain's love–hate relationship with Hollywood at a time, particularly in the 1930s and 40s, when British films aspired to international distribution, sought to establish cooperative links with the USA and enhance the reputation of British films as prestige products suitable for 'roadshow' distribution. Since the introduction of protective legislation for the British film industry in 1927, Anglo-American film relations could be strained. The Cinematograph Films Act required exhibitors and distributors to show and handle a certain percentage of British films. This threatened Hollywood's domination of the British market, although ways were found to circumvent the legislation by establishing companies in Britain as well as owning cinemas that booked mainly American films. In 1938 the Cinematograph Films Act was renewed to include measures to encourage American companies to finance high-budget films registered as British. At the same time British companies hoped their films would be distributed by Hollywood studios and thus provide them with a greater share of the domestic and international markets.[8] This economic background is crucial in understanding the ebb and flow of Anglo-American film relations which had an impact on how technologies developed both in the USA and in Britain were received. Technicians clearly admired American ingenuity in inventing Technicolor, but wanted to make clear their own contribution towards its technical and aesthetic development. Somewhat paradoxically this involved both admiring and cooperating with Technicolor while at the same time seeking to establish an independent creative space. Criticism of Natalie Kalmus was a symptom of what at times appeared to be a frustrating position whereby the existence of norms around the use of colour appeared to be impossible constraints. Claims made, for example, by cinematographers that they flouted the approach laid down by Technicolor, need to be considered as a response to the Corporation's much-publicised attempts to 'control' colour via the consultancy service and ideas developed around 'color consciousness' which underpinned its operation.

As we have seen, from the first instances of the application of colour in silent cinema via various manual, mechanical and photographic processes, commentators were fascinated by its impact on audiences, particularly the disruptive aesthetic potential of its sensual, synaesthesic effects.[9] The development of Technicolor was no less affected by concerns to control the impact of colour in order to make it acceptable to an industry that had developed the majority of its mainstream aesthetic norms on principles of supporting classical narrative. In keeping with this general approach but, as we shall see, allowing for a degree of experimentation with colour, Natalie Kalmus developed her theory of 'color consciousness' to guide the work of the Technicolor consultancy service. This involved being aware of the impact of colour at every stage in a production, just as an artist considered the principles of colour, tone and composition in a painting. This was first published in 1935 and reflected an art historical/painterly approach whereby: 'The design and colors of sets, costumes, drapes, and furnishings must be planned and selected just as an artist would choose the colors from his palette and apply them to the proper portions of his painting.'[10] For Kalmus, colour appreciation and study were key to the judicious use of colour in motion pictures. There was a somewhat utopian element to her ideas since she argued for film as an opportunity to unite music, graphic art and acting in 'one expression of more ultimate art'. On the other hand, her desire to insert a degree of

control over colour did not encourage this broader aim to a great extent. As we shall see, the role of colour as a unifying, 'organic' property featured more centrally in the writings of theorists such as Eisenstein. Kalmus, however, steered a course which celebrated colour but warned against its excessive demonstration: 'A super-abundance of color is unnatural, and has a most unpleasant effect not only upon the eye itself, but upon the mind as well. On the other hand, the complete absence of color is unnatural.'[11]

These general ideas were elaborated by particular systemic codes. She argued that colours and neutrals augment each other and that the psychology of colour was very important. Drawing on traditional colour theories she proposed that a mood could be 'keyed' by colour, making the audience more receptive to an emotion. She demarked 'warm' colours (red, orange, yellow – indicating excitement, activity and heat) from 'cool' colours (green, blue, violet – associated with retiring, rest, ease, coolness). The addition of white could have interesting consequences, indicating youth, gaiety and informality. The addition of grey, on the other hand, introduced subtlety, refinement and charm. The addition of black added strength but could also be considered to introduce a 'baser' look. Here she is referring to how colour, according to the influential Munsell system, first published in 1921, is characterised by hue, value and chroma (saturation). Hue is the everyday colour name and its lightness or darkness is its value (high for lighter; low for darker), and saturation refers to the intensity of a colour which is usually weakened by the addition of grey.[12] Colours such as green were associated in Kalmus's scheme with nature and the outdoors; violet, indigo and blue were considered to be 'quiet' colours associated with tranquillity and passivity. In accordance with these tenets, Kalmus prepared colour charts that were the foundation of a film's colour design. She explained: 'The preparation of this chart calls for careful and judicious methods, but through application of the rules of art and the physical laws of light and color in relation to literary laws and story values.'[13]

Any analysis of Technicolor must acknowledge Kalmus's broad principles of 'color consciousness', since they can be seen to operate at a textual level and indeed can go some way to reveal how colour scoring guides the viewer to understand the dynamics of a particular dramatic situation. Kalmus had expertise in the area of costume design, since she believed that costume colours should be associated with character, frequently that of the lead female performer, whose costume colour was often repeated in flowers in a scene. The 'color consciousness' scheme emphasised how colour separation was an important fact of design whereby different hues were placed beside each other. In addition, the 'Law of Emphasis' stated that 'nothing of relative unimportance in a picture shall be emphasised', which implied that colour was not meant to draw attention to itself. But it had a role in achieving the effect of making actors stand out among interesting and varied sets that were not 'flat'. To achieve this aim colour was used in a similar way to how the function performed by lighting created the impression of depth in black-and-white cinematography. Colour complements and juxtapositions – orange/blue, for example – were another strategy favoured by Kalmus who demonstrated how the placing of two such colours together resulted in the first emphasising in the second the characteristics which are lacking in the first: 'The orange will appear more red than it really is,' so that hue changes when different colours are placed one over the other or side by side.[14] Kalmus's guidelines were supported by rigorous technical rules which included high-key light levels made possible by the use of arc lamps, and a very low contrast ratio, particularly in shadow areas which required extra care to avoid distortions to colour caused by under-exposure.[15] Processing in the lab was another aspect of the operation that was strictly controlled so as to achieve the 'correct look' for Technicolor. The number of available Technicolor cameras in Britain in 1937 was limited to four, and the large, cumbersome and heavy 'blimp' that was necessary to reduce noise made planning complex tracking movements with soundtrack very difficult.

While Kalmus's interventions at the level of production are fundamental in assessing the use of colour in the specific context of Technicolor, it is important to recognise that analyses must draw on a more extensive conceptual register in order to fully appreciate colour as being capable of exceeding the requirements of story or of achieving a balanced graphic composition. Colour is a complex register and subject to many variables in application as well as in reception. The latter is a fascinating area which demonstrates that

understandings of the meanings associated with colour relate not only to narrative norms, but also to cultural context. As David Batchelor has observed: 'The rainbow is a universally observable and consistent natural phenomenon, and yet its representations, both verbal and visual, are strikingly inconsistent. Rainbows are always seen through the prism of a culture; they are marked by the habits of language or the conventions of painting.'[16]

Other theorists have similarly taken an approach which is less tied to the immediate concerns of narrative, or to the proposition that the relation between colour and object is fixed. As Eirik Hanssen has argued:

> Colour in cinema is characterised by a tension and alternation between autonomy and integration, independence and connection. Colours can be imagined independently, and without borders, but can only be perceived and exist within a context; colour always represents a 'matter of relationships'.[17]

Eisenstein, for example, theorised colour as part of a holistic but mutable system, although his theoretical writings were more explicit about the specific correspondences between colour and sound as an aspect of his conception of film montage. Eisenstein was concerned with how colour evades fixity of meaning, emphasising instead how context can alter the association of colour quite markedly.[18] While acknowledging that certain cultural associations are resonant with particular colours, when placed within a particular narrative context or as a contrapuntal discourse, colour can become disassociated from object. The sign-meaning connection is thus disrupted, often creating a new association between a particular colour and the object in question. As we shall see, this is a feature of notable usages of Technicolor when application was guided by particular, and often shifting, usage within the context of a narrative. Related to these questions of the inherent instability of meaning represented by colour, its appearance in film was greeted with a mixed response, not least from the industry.

Colour was not universally welcomed in terms of economics or style. The historical context for the appearance of Technicolor during a period when colour on screen was unusual, invested it with an element of novelty which at times was emphasised by the industry, while on other occasions it was not privileged. As the British film industry was seeking to establish a firm economic base from which to develop its own export strategies, relations with Hollywood encompassed co-production, star trading and the transfer of technological processes.[19] During the period in the early to mid-1930s, when Technicolor was seeking to establish itself as the leading commercial three-colour subtractive process in the USA, Herbert Kalmus was keen to export it to Britain. The nature of this exportation was tied into the ways in which the company sought to retain control over its application; colour control was an economic as well as an aesthetic strategy. Equipment was therefore never sold outright. Instead, the cameras were rented out to companies that wanted to use them, and it was compulsory for Technicolor's consulting service to be used as part of the contract. In November 1929 it was announced that Technicolor had plans for two studios abroad, one in Berlin and the other in London.[20] Sir Herbert Ingram and a syndicate prepared to subscribe £250,000 for debentures in the British company to be known as Technicolor Ltd, a company limited by shares. Draft agreements were drawn up empowering the company to execute and accept the licence under Technicolor patents, and to build and operate a laboratory and Technicolor cameras.[21] Yet the negotiations were frustrated and eventually abandoned because of the economic slump, as Kalmus reported at the end of 1930 in a cable to one of the negotiators in London: 'Just now entire industry in slump and every would be competitor of Technicolor much worse off than Technicolor so what chances have they in London now.'[22]

By the mid-1930s the financial situation had improved and in April 1936 Natalie Kalmus accompanied the process to Britain when *Wings of the Morning*, the first British feature film to use Technicolor, was shot at Denham Studios and on location in Ireland and at the Epsom Downs. The link between Technicolor and Denham was forged because London Film Productions (LFP), the company directed by Alexander Korda, had been interested in colour from the early 1930s. Indeed, LFP's major financial backer, the Prudential Assurance Company, had been persuaded to invest in films on the promise of developing the **Hillman colour (see Technical Appendix)** process owned by Colourgravure, a subsidiary of Gerrard

Industries, a box-making company that subsequently became involved with British Technicolor.[23] As shown in Chapter 3, there were many attempts to develop this and other processes in the 1920s and 30s, such as Dufaycolor, Raycol, **Spectracolor (see Technical Appendix)** and Gasparcolor, and the film trade papers of this period are full of discussions of each process's technical strengths and weaknesses. After the coming of sound, which had totally revolutionised the film industry, discussions of colour fixated on the extent to which its widespread adoption might have similar effects. In May 1935 there was a debate in *Today's Cinema* on the likelihood of colour's widespread usage even though the cost issues were considerable: 'If ordinary films in colour should prove as great an improvement on black and white as cartoons in colour have done, then black-and-white films will soon be a thing of the past.'[24]

Indeed, Technicolor's success with Disney cartoons, and perfections of the three-colour process in feature films, as demonstrated with *Becky Sharp* (1935), made an impression in the UK. The reviewer in *Today's Cinema*, for example, wrote: 'Words fail adequately to describe the stereoscopic effect that colour has given to many of the scenes while yet escaping in some miraculous fashion all sense of the tawdrily theatrical.'[25] After the press screening it was declared a triumph by the trade paper under the headline 'Another Revolution?' in a leader article that declared: 'Blotchiness, fringing, tonal inconsistency, were quite absent … Three-colour Technicolor may be capable of improvement, but even at its present stage it is definitely ready.'[26] What is notable about these contemporary comments is that Technicolor was considered acceptable only when the process was perceived as having overcome flaws such as 'blotchiness' or 'tonal inconsistency' that drew attention to colour, judgments that are in keeping with the notion that colour must not be aberrant. Links were formed with Technicolor only when the American company appeared to have overcome some of the technical problems which had been the focus of reviews that associated colour with imperfection, of failing to achieve 'correct' or 'natural' tones and thus distract audiences from being totally drawn into the fictional world on screen.

Even so, the industry was still not totally won over, and debates continued as to whether colour was worth the extra costs incurred for producers and, with some additive processes, exhibitors who needed special projection equipment. When Sidney Bernstein added a question on colour to his questionnaire to cinema audiences in 1937 ('Do you like coloured feature talkies?'), 62 per cent of people surveyed were in favour of colour film. Ten years later this picture had changed, demonstrating the increased popularity of colour film in the interim period resulting in 80 per cent of people surveyed saying that colour was a reason for going to a film (3 per cent said colour was a reason for staying away, and 17 per cent did not know either way).[27] In the 1930s, however, the aesthetic effects were also a cause of ambivalence, since many reviewers of colour films insisted that successful colour was used as an aid to storytelling and not as a spectacular property in itself.

In this vein, one *Picturegoer* reader complained that the colour effects in the two-strip Technicolor film *Ring Up the Curtain* (US title *Broadway to Hollywood*, 1933), were 'introduced in rather haphazard fashion and, consequently, break the continuity of the film. This fault must be avoided.'[28] Comments such as this were in keeping with Natalie Kalmus's strictures, since her designs for three-strip colour films used colour in such a way as to make it distinctive but not distracting. As Scott Higgins has shown, however, in the early years of three-colour Technicolor development in the USA, the 'demonstration mode' prevailed in which colour was used to create a spectacular impact and in some cases departed from being tied strictly to narrative development in films such as the two-reel *La Cucaracha* (1934) and full-length feature film *Becky Sharp*. As Higgins observes, both films 'employ color in particularly forceful ways, displaying the processes's chromatic range and drawing attention to its potential for underscoring drama. They are films inspired by a fleeting belief that color would usher in a bold new form of cinema.'[29] As the process became less of a novelty it was to a certain extent 'reined in' to a more restrained aesthetic approach that favoured tone and value rather than the contrast of hue, as the film industry was encouraged to appreciate that its use did not represent a break with classical style.[30]

In Britain producer John Maxwell was similarly cautious, arguing that colour was 'an embellishment' that would be used when 'perfected' and only then 'on appropriate occasions'.[31] This is hardly surprising in terms of Maxwell's reputation for an economical approach to production at British International Pictures

in comparison with Korda's association with bigger-budget films. The reviewer for *Picturegoer* who saw *La Cucaracha* had a mixed response, commenting that 'I have never seen better blues nor more artistic pearl greys,' but 'one still feels a sense that it is not natural. Facial colours are prone to be too ruddily yellow and the feast of colour is far too wholesale.' The desire for a 'natural' rendition of colour was frequently expressed in reviews, the same writer noting that when Technicolor was introduced into a feature-length film it should be throughout, not just in sequences, since 'I know of nothing more annoying than being switched from black and white to colour and back again; the effect is to engender a wholly artificial atmosphere.'[32] There were also concerns that watching colour films might be bad for people, some commentators claiming that in dark auditoria bright colours would give audiences headaches as well as causing an unnecessary distraction from the action of a film.[33] In the case of replicating blood in war films, another objection was raised that 'only a few could stand it [the scenes in colour], not the majority'.[34] Such comments are indicative of the confusion caused by the possibility of more widespread use of colour and betray fears about its disruptive potential. On the other hand, it could not be easily dismissed since the novelty value of colour, with its claims to deliver both heightened realism and spectacular fantasy, promised to place producers ahead of the technological game. Its fascination for contemporary audiences was also manifest when one of J. P. Mayer's respondents to his request through *Picturegoer* for 'motion picture autobiographies' commented: 'When I've been to a film [especially one in Technicolor] I always walk home feeling disgusted with the drab town I live in, the paint-work of doors etc. seem awfully dull and dresses look plain after seeing the glorious scenery and stylish clothes in the film.'[35]

This attitude was prevalent in the reception of the three-strip process in Britain by one of its leading producers, Alexander Korda.[36] In the 1930s Kalmus made several visits to the UK and British financier Sir Adrian Baillie went to Hollywood to see the Technicolor laboratories and the completion of *Becky Sharp*.[37] Technicolor Ltd was established in 1935 under the direction of Kay Harrison. In the next twenty years it showed an increase in production each year, with the exception of 1940 which was affected by the impact of the outbreak of war. In the first full year of operations

Technicolor Ltd produced and sold 13.5 million feet of film; in the year ended 1955 this figure was 209.5 million.[38] The first primary shareholders of the company were Herbert Kalmus, St George Syms, a solicitor, and Kay Harrison of Gerrard Industries, a company which had become interested in film investment via connections with Korda's London Film Productions.[39] Both the Prudential Assurance Company and Technicolor financed the erection of a modern plant that was designed to develop the process in the UK and which was opened in January 1937.[40] Soon after the formation of Technicolor Ltd a party of key personnel was sent to Hollywood to study the technical specifications and operation of the laboratories.[41] In March 1936 reports were published of the first Technicolor film to be made in the UK which coincided with plans to build the Technicolor laboratory on the Great West Road, Harmondsworth, Middlesex. A month later Natalie Kalmus arrived in London to supervise the use of the process in the production. She confidently predicted that in two years every major feature film would be made in colour.[42] Her 'color consciousness' article received widespread coverage in Britain, which demonstrates the extent to which the guidelines laid down by her were in currency at the same time as the process had been exported and the British company established.[43] She was generally regarded as the Technicolor expert who also knew about art, a combination which attracted a degree of curiosity that was partly to do with her gender, as one trade press commentator reported after interviewing her:

> Mrs Kalmus I found a most delightful and enlightened character … Indeed I'd like to see her in Technicolor herself for she's by no means a flat personality. It is clear that she has the technical side of the game at her fingertips and can be depended on not only to look after that angle but the creative colour angle as well.[44]

This kind of reportage continued throughout her career and Technicolor clearly took advantage of her 'star' value as an ambassador for the process who was in a fairly unusual position as a woman heading a complex and key operation in the company's development.[45] It suited them to publicise her technical knowledge for this purpose, on one occasion putting her name on an article written by a male colleague in the company.[46] Her work attracted widespread reports in fan magazines and she encouraged tie-ins between Technicolor and department stores such as Harris and Company, Dallas, by advising on colour combinations for new fashion ranges, as well as giving radio interviews.[47] Her relationship with Herbert Kalmus, their secret divorce in 1921 and bitter law suit in 1948, adds to her reputation as a fascinating, yet mysterious figure in film history.[48]

Conflicts and misunderstandings could easily result when she advised on British productions. Freddie Young recalled Natalie Kalmus visiting the studio when *Sixty Glorious Years* (1938) was being shot and declaring the shade of the exterior blue sky to be 'wrong' on the basis of 'instinct'. His view was that she failed to take into account the impact of studio lights which made any such judgment problematic. He concluded that she was ignorant and persuaded Herbert Wilcox to thereafter ban her from the studio.[49] On the other hand, there is certainly evidence of her being involved at quite a detailed level when the film was being planned. As Natalie Kalmus's papers reveal, she was sent the script and corresponded with Maude Churchill, wardrobe mistress, regarding a number of possible laces dyed particular shades, submitted as swatches to Kalmus for her selection and then the chosen ones returned.[50] The papers also reveal that Kalmus prepared charts for *The Divorce of Lady X* (1938) which were photographed and sent to England in 1935. In an unusual record of how this actually worked she advised in a long memo how the company should work with the photographs in anticipation of her arrival to supervise the production.[51] The authoritative tone of such correspondence, as well as its particular details, confirms that Kalmus worked well with art directors including Vincent Korda. Although the documents on her dealings with Technicolor Ltd are not voluminous they nevertheless reveal a productive and mutually respectful relationship with managing director Kay Harrison. While she might have enjoyed being in Britain for social pleasures such as going to the races, the idea that Kalmus was not much involved with British productions can to some extent be challenged by reading letters from the beginning of World War II.[52] Soon after she had returned to Hollywood after overseeing the production of the first British three-strip films, Harrison wrote that they missed her expertise and that her presence 'alone made it possible for this company to have efficient colour direction during the initial stages of its development'.[53] In practice, therefore, it appears that Kalmus was not as obstructive as was often assumed and that experts such as Joan Bridge, who worked in Britain as colour consultant at first with Kalmus and then on her own, developed a nuanced approach that planned colour for specific projects and as appropriate to technology and genre. Indeed, generic norms for colour influenced the range of possibilities for a particular production. Technical constraints were also important since working with a process over many years inevitably generated notions of good and bad practice as the insightful and technically informed reports in the *British Journal of Photography* attest.

'AS FINE A PIGMENTATION AS HAS YET APPEARED': *WINGS OF THE MORNING*

Wings of the Morning was chosen, like other early showcase Technicolor Films, for the colour potential of its locale and settings. It features the story of Marie (Annabella), daughter of an Irish gypsy king, who in the late nineteenth century marries Lord Clontarf, a nobleman who is killed in a riding accent. Marie believes that a curse has been put on her descendants and she leaves for Spain to join her people. She returns to Ireland fifty years later with 'Wings', a prize horse she hopes will win the Derby. She is joined by her great-granddaughter, Maria (also played by Annabella) who has escaped from a revolution in Spain in disguise as a boy. Still in this attire she meets Kerry (Henry Fonda), a Canadian horse trainer, who agrees to train 'Wings' after Maria's disguise has been discovered and they have fallen in love. In an extended final sequence, 'Wings' wins the Derby, and the curse on Marie's family is finally lifted.

Cinematographer Jack Cardiff recalled that the film 'portrayed Ireland and gypsies and the Derby horse race, so it was very colourful'.[54] This judgment reflects early discourses on colour which linked it with the 'exotic' and 'otherness', as in some of the Kinemacolor films discussed in Chapter 1. Indeed, the films I discuss in this chapter are linked by their use of colour to highlight questions of racial difference and exoticism within generic contexts which favoured the foregrounding of colour: the outdoor melodrama and empire film. Undoubtedly the genre of a film or its status as mainstream narrative cinema had key implications for the scope permitted for the obtrusive intervention of colour.[55] On the basis of his

Wings of the Morning (Technicolor, 1937): soft greens and browns

knowledge of classical painting and lighting structures, Cardiff had been selected as the cinematographer at Denham who would serve as camera operator when Technicolor was used. In addition to learning the craft of working with the large cameras, Cardiff worked with Ray Rennahan, Technicolor's cameraman who was brought over from America to shoot the film. Although *Wings of the Morning* was registered as a British film it nevertheless had a huge amount of American participation quite apart from the Technicolor connection. The producer was Robert T. Kane, an American who had been involved in European productions by Paramount and Fox, with his company New World Pictures that had a financial connection with Fox. Harold Schuster, the director, was also American. Although he was better known as an editor, Schuster took over the direction of the project from Glenn Tyron after some initial shooting had taken place. All of the major technical roles were performed by Americans with the exception of Jack Cardiff as operating cameraman and art director Ralph Brinton. The film was shot in England and Ireland, but it was processed in the USA.[56] Once the laboratory was completed at Harmondsworth, Middlesex, in January 1937, British Technicolor productions could be serviced there as well as prints of American colour films for British distribution.

Natalie Kalmus explained the logic behind the use of colour in the film:

> We have tried to preserve one level of colour throughout. Over half the picture was filmed out of doors, so that in these scenes the predominant color is the soft and restful green of the English [Irish] countryside. This approach demonstrates the principle of colour scoring whereby a scene's dominant mood or emotion is underscored by color. Even in the gypsy prologue to the picture, where some of the costumes are very vivid, they are offset by the masses of green. When we cut from these exterior scenes to interiors we try to preserve the same 'high level'. Our sets are brown, grey and green – warm, rich shades of color for walls, furniture, tapestries and curtains, but all soft and tending to absorb light rather than reflect it. In this way the colors of the interiors and exteriors are kept at the same level.[57]

Indeed, Jack Houshold, a technician who worked for Technicolor and was involved with the BFI National Archive's 1990 restoration of *Wings of the Morning*, commented that it was 'very much a grey picture', which gave it a particular look that detracted from the colours being perceived as garish or hyper-spectacular.[58] What is achieved instead is 'softness' through colour with an emphasis on 'warm' hues of brown, green and mauve/blue. These are keyed in to the pastel-shaded costumes worn by Annabella, the lead actress, as was common in Technicolor films. Ray Rennahan, expert Technicolor cinematographer who had been brought from Hollywood to supervise the production with Jack Cardiff as operator, explained that light make-up was needed in front of Technicolor cameras, and that Annabella was a very suitable actress since 'her light-gold hair, brown eyes, and fine, clear skin and complexion are exceptionally valuable attributes for a star of color films'.[59] Indeed, the poster advertising *Wings of the Morning* announced it as being filmed 'all in the new, natural Technicolor'. The theme of naturalness is maintained in interior scenes – for example, there is an obtrusive shot of a fire which was typical of how many Technicolor films sought to highlight details that emphasised colour through the visual pleasure of seeing natural phenomena. The use of colour in some instances can be interpreted as expressive since high-key lighting was not used throughout, although, as we have seen, naturalness and balance was the goal of Kalmus's design. While this approach was highly influential for the film, the combination of consistent tones with variable, expressive values again highlights the inherent mutability of colour and meaning. The design of the film, to preserve one level throughout, cascades colour over a range of objects and within a variety of contexts, as in a yellow accent for an exterior shot of Kerry and Maria as their relationship develops into romance. The perhaps unintended effect of this demonstrates how colour shifts from sequence to sequence in such a way that stretches the boundaries that one would assume might be the goal of a strategy of consistency. As Steve Neale has noted, there is an inherent contradiction 'between colour as an index of realism and colour as a mark of fantasy, as an element capable, therefore, of disrupting or detracting from the very realism it is otherwise held to inscribe'.[60] In this sense discussion of the efficacy of colour in *Wings of the Morning*, and in other early British Technicolor

films, is illustrative of the tension between measuring the success or failure of colour against its perceived naturalism while recognising at the same time its suitability for spectacle and artistry.

Contemporary critics of Technicolor included artist Paul Nash who described *Wings of the Morning* as an example of 'the inane pursuit of naturalism, colour for its own sake, and the naive attempts at colour harmony, do obviously slow up the picture'.[61] This comment is interesting in terms of the film allowing colour a space to operate outside of conventional imperatives of continuity, on occasion taking longer over a scene because of the need to display colour effects, such a close-up of a gypsy dancer's swirling burgundy and orange skirt. Others, however, praised the film's colour and for many it pointed the way forward for British films. While some found fault with the film's pace and occasional lapses in logic, the majority agreed that the use of colour was remarkable. The review in *Variety*, for example, recommended a shorter, brisker style and considered the ending to be weak. Nevertheless, the summary comment is typical of critics' reactions to the film: 'It will be hailed as fine a pigmentation as has yet appeared.'[62] The *Kinematograph Weekly* reviewers praised the film's photography, describing it 'as good as anything yet seen on the screen, if not better', and because the colour was 'not overdone'.[63] Kane was interviewed, declaring that colour was not the star of the picture but it 'adds a considerable quota to the entertainment, enhances the value of the film and generally lends it a quality of its own'.[64] In his handbook on Technicolor published in 1949 John Huntley commented with similar sentiments that

> There is nothing garish or glaring and even the brilliant scene of the Downs is wonderfully soft in tone. A certain degree of blurring, due to technical defects in the colour process which have since been rectified, if anything adds to the charm of the location scenes; the sharp outlines of modern colour film often results in a too violent effect which destroys the gentle colour tones found in early films.[65]

While such descriptions can be related to Technicolor in its restrained mode, they can also, as noted above, illustrate the expanding repertoire of colour imagery to a variety of contexts and shifting associations. The sequence on the Epsom Downs quoted

Wings of the Morning:
dancer in burgundy and
orange skirt

by Huntley, for example, is remarkable for its use of red as punctuating the spectacle of the Derby.[66] It opens with a poster announcing 'Derby Day!' in bright red letters, and proceeds to establish London as a city signified in terms of an iconography of 'landmark London', as Charlotte Brunsdon has noted operating in other films.[67] This singles out red London buses; red and black uniforms worn by the guards at Buckingham Palace, and the Pearly King and Queen travelling to the Derby in a carriage, with the Queen wearing a large hat with predominantly red feathers. In keeping with Eisenstein's theory of montage, the juxtaposition of these shots adds complexity to the meaning of red. While the Pearly King and Queen represent a local, cockney tradition, the marching guards connote a national tradition of royalist pageantry. They also demonstrate how texture (the rigidity of the cloth worn by the guards and Pearly Queen's exuberant feathers) impacts on colour, as well as movement and light. This accent on colour serves as a prelude to the Derby itself, which is also punctuated with red, the colour in particular being isolated as spectacle within a frame –

for example, in a minstrel show performer's red jacket, and the predominantly red costume worn by a female spectator who features in the montage displaying the Derby's feast of visual attractions. These images, which are cumulatively presented to highlight the building of excitement before the start of the race, are inter-cut with shots of a radio commentator in a booth reporting highlights of the Derby's visual spectacle which form an aural commentary for the film as he tells listeners (and viewers) what he is seeing. It is as if the wonders of Technicolor are not enough, that audiences need to be *told* about its ability to capture the full spectacle of the Derby. This is perhaps again reflective of anxieties associated with Technicolor's early application and the tension between a desire for colour to be noticed but at the same time for it to be perceived as 'natural' and appropriate to narrative context. An ideological association of colour with race is also referenced as the radio commentator declares: 'No Derby is complete without the people of Romany, dark-skinned faces, flashing teeth and gay, picturesque clothes with all the colours of the rainbow,' as we see the gypsies who have

gathered to support 'Wings', the horse owned by gypsy Marie, and the caravans are singled out for their colour contrasts. One reviewer complained that this sequence was 'too gaudy' whereas the rest of the film was so impressive you could 'almost forget that it was shot in colour'.[68] This comment does not, however, acknowledge the extent to which colour is emphasised in less overt, but nonetheless striking ways in the pre-Derby sequences.

There are many establishing shots of the Irish landscape which emphasise Technicolor's ability to record natural beauty as scenic spectacle. There are also arresting images which draw attention to colour such as close-ups of an owl with large, yellow eyes; of a cockerel with its red comb; or of a bowl of fruit containing oranges and purple grapes, following Kalmus's use of colour juxtapositions, featuring centre-frame on a table while two characters are in conversation. In the latter instance, the characters are incidental dinner guests who are intrigued by Lord Clontarf's attraction to the gypsy Marie as they whisper 'Bewitched!' Conversations between major characters would not usually feature such a distracting addition of colour in a Technicolor film, but in this case *because* of the characters' relative unimportance the contrasting colours of the fruit are all the more dominant. These examples contradict Paul Nash's dismissive judgment of

the film as failing to exploit contrasts. They also demonstrate how, in a film whose primary attraction is its colour, scenes negotiate conventional imperatives of continuity by occasionally slowing up the action to display features such as the close-up of the owl to which Nash objected.[69] Also distinctive are the film's various interiors, allowing use of colour which departs from the high-key lighting often associated with Technicolor. The dark stable scene when Maria, dressed as a boy, stays overnight with Kerry, allows for subtle changes of tone which are a prelude to daybreak when the light streams in and another luscious landscape is depicted in Technicolor. In this way the sequences that emphasise colour are experienced relationally in order to have maximum impact. Colour is used here to reinforce other formal elements such as lighting to declare temporal development into the new morning. This can be seen as an example of Technicolor being tied to 'time tested' cinematic functions: 'In instances where lighting, composition, or music might have highlighted a dramatic development, colour could now be counted on as well.'[70] This function of colour in *Wings of the Morning* can, however, be seen to be doing more since it showcases an unusually high number of pictorial landscape shots which offer colour as visual spectacle and which are not strictly necessary to advance the story.

Wings of the Morning: colour and sensation as Marie (Annabella) warms her hands by the fire

Wings of the Morning: cueing a flashback: Jenepher (Helen Haye) remembering Ireland

Wings of the Morning also connects colour with physical sensation. In one shot a direct link is made between a fire and the corresponding feeling of warmth as Marie warms her hands in a room in which the colour of the fire is the dominant chromatic accent. In this case colour movement and variation of value is key since the flames of the fire are dynamic, inviting synaesthesic suggestion by encouraging the audience to *feel* the impact of the warm fire through *seeing* its 'warm' colour. This impression of warmth is further emphasised by the scene's narrative context, since Maria feels out of place in the castle as the other female guests shun her; the fire reminds her of a natural environment in which she feels more comfortable. An emphasis on colour as sensation also features in relation to the blind character Jenepher (Helen Haye) who touches the fabrics of Maria's clothes when they are propped-up on her upturned trunk as she unpacks her things when she has come to stay in the castle. Maria says that she wishes Jenepher could see the dresses, to which she replies: 'I see a great deal of the beauty of life. Sometimes I think because I'm blind there's more perfume in gardens or in the heather when the wind blows over it.' Since there have been so many pictorial, establishing shots of the Irish countryside, this sensation is evoked several times in the film, as the impact of the colours of the natural environment, particularly with the mention of heather, are being emphasised when they are not actually being shown. A striking follow-up to this occurs later in the film when Kerry has arranged a party

for Maria at the castle. Singer John McCormack entertains the guests with three songs. One of them, 'Killarney', provides the occasion for a montage of scenic images which is located with the point of view of Jenepher, since there is a transition from her to an out-of-focus image of Killarney, which gradually becomes clearer as she acquires a 'memory' image of the scene while McCormack sings of the region's natural beauty. A montage of shots proceeds as a travelogue and is concluded by a gradual return to the main party sequence with a transition again from an out-of-focus image to Jenepher. While it was common for montages and transitional passages to motivate colour spectacle, this example is nevertheless unusual. For Paul Nash the presentation of Killarney resulted in a 'vulgar' version of the picture postcard, perhaps missing the point that these images have the added inflection of memory in this particular context, which provides a clear motivation for their vivid presentation.[71] They also are directed at the audience, to a collective experience of Ireland, with the words of the song matched by particular images, such as the castle.

Costumes are also used to display colour, since when young Marie first visits Clontarf castle her dress is distinguished by a daisy pattern which is differentiated from the less decorative costumes worn by the non-gypsy women. One of the gypsy dancers has an orange underskirt which is shown as her outer dress swirls up as she dances for the guests, emphasising the spectacle of the dance as well as the revelation of colour. For part of

Wings of the Morning:
Jenepher's memory of
pastoral Ireland

Wings of the Morning: Maria
(Annabella) in burgundy dress

the film Maria is disguised as a boy, a plot device explained by her need to escape undetected from revolutionary Spain to Ireland. Once in Ireland and used primarily for comic effect, she continues to dress as a boy, but once her disguise has been discovered by Kerry she abandons wearing the drab suit. This enables a transformation whereby her femininity is announced by a blue chiffon dress and then by a red evening dress as she walks down a staircase to be revealed as a woman to Kerry, whose point of view is emphasised as he 'sees' her differently for the first time. Since (as the young Marie) she has previously worn red in the film's early, outdoor sequences, the dress appears as natural for the character but is now invested with a more sexualised connotation, especially when it has been immediately preceded by the blue dress, which was not cued into the male point of view. In keeping with Kalmus's rule, the cool blue of the first costume has given way to the activity and passion associated with red. Cinemagoers found this scene memorable for its colour accent, as shown by one of the respondents to a question about film preferences placed in *Picturegoer* magazine by J. P. Mayer for his study of audiences in the 1940s. A female, shorthand typist, aged thirty-four, recorded: 'I shall never forget the dramatic appearance in *Wings of the Morning* of Annabelle [*sic*] coming downstairs into a room of subdued tones (after one had got used to seeing her disguised in drab boy's clothes) clad in a burgundy evening gown.'[72]

STAGGERING 'THE AMERICANS AND THE TECHNICOLOR COMPANY': *THE THIEF OF BAGDAD*

After *Wings of the Morning* the use of Technicolor varied between the restrained mode represented by films such as *The Divorce of Lady X* and *Over the Moon* (1939) and a bold, demonstrative use of colour in *The Thief of Bagdad*. Colour was influenced by genre, as we shall see with these examples and in subsequent chapters. Some genres, such as melodramas, musicals and especially fantasy, allowed scope for obtrusive colour designs. Michael Powell claimed that cinematographer Georges Périnal's lighting for *The Thief of Bagdad* 'had staggered the Americans and the Technicolor Company'.[73] Powell also attributed his interest in the potential of colour to *The Thief of Bagdad*: 'The Archers thought in colour from *The Thief of Bagdad* onwards'.[74] The design of this film provides a contrast with *Wings of the Morning* and is a key film in the history of British Technicolor and for the use of special effects such as back-projection, travelling matte, 'blue screen' compositing, hanging miniatures and Academy Award-winning colour cinematography by Georges Périnal and Osmond Borrodaile.[75] Rather than eschewing the idea that colour might be the star of a film, *The Thief of Bagdad* positively relishes this approach. Colour is used for spectacle many times in the film – for example, a shot of a sunset which is immediately followed by a similar natural image of a fire; the combination of these two shots facilitates the editing but also presents images that are arresting for their beauty in a spectacular display of natural occurrences in varying hues. From the outset colour is declared as a dominant register for both narrative and symbolic ends, in this case the dynamic between primaries red and blue. At the opening of the film, we see a ship's red sail and, as we get closer, the large blue eye motif painted on the side of its hull, as was common for ships in the Middle East. This is first seen from a distance but then becomes larger and larger until a close-up of the eye fills the screen. This image then dissolves into a shot of Jaffar (Conrad Veidt), a man waiting on the quay, who is wearing a red turban with only the upper-half of his face visible. The final close-up of his face and blue eyes creates a colour link between the eye motif and the character, thus establishing the theme of looking which recurs throughout the film.

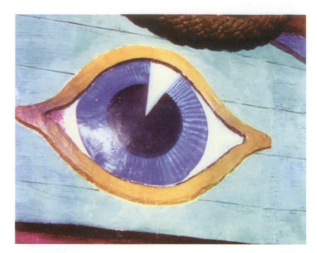

As Kahf has observed, the film plays out the struggle between Jaffar and Ahmed (John Justin), the King of Bagdad, for the 'scopic possession' of the Princess (June Duprez) with whom they are both in love.[76] We learn from a flashback that Ahmed was persuaded by his Grand Vizier, Jaffar, to disguise himself as a poor man in order to become acquainted with his subjects. Jaffar has Ahmed arrested and while incarcerated in jail he meets Abu (Sabu). They escape and flee to Basra, where Ahmed sees the Princess and falls in love with her. Jaffar is determined to marry the Princess and when he discovers that Ahmed also desires the Princess, Jaffar uses a spell to make him blind and turn Abu into a dog; Ahmed can only regain his sight when Jaffar can 'take' the Princess in his arms. The motif of the eye is therefore an important thread throughout the narrative and colour is integral to expressing the conflict between the two characters for the possession of the woman. As Kahf has suggested, this has distinct ideological connotations in terms of both patriarchy and Orientalism:

The Thief of Bagdad's hero Ahmed has been symbolically castrated (blinded) by the rival Jaffar, an evil Eastern father figure as well. Ahmed's ability to engage in the voyeuristic look of the camera has been suspended. In order to maintain visual pleasure, Jaffar must rape her ('take her in my arms') for Ahmed to see again. Psychoanalytically, Ahmed has projected his sadistic scopophilic impulse onto Jaffar so that he can remain a

The Thief of Bagdad (Technicolor, 1940): close-up of eye motif on ship; Jaffar (Conrad Veidt) dissolve shot to establish theme of looking; further link shot to establish theme of looking

The Thief of Bagdad: the
Princess (June Duprez) and
a blue rose

The boldness of the colour used for *The Thief of Bagdad* is perhaps explained by developments in Technicolor processing which featured in reviews of the film. The use of colour was clearly designed to be obtrusive, as one reviewer noted: 'Color has been used here with enormous success, to enhance the flavor of the magic and to entrance the eye.'[79] One dress designer who reviewed the film even went so far as to predict that the film would 'have a great influence on improving the general color taste of women all over the world'.[80] The reviews were mixed as to the desirability of such a spectacular display of colour. Some were extremely positive, as in Bosley Crowther's review in the *New York Times*, which commented that 'the color alone makes this picture a truly exciting entertainment'.[81] On the other hand, some critics found that, apart from the colour, the story was far from gripping.[82] There was considerable anxiety, therefore, around the reception of *The Thief of Bagdad*, since, along with special effects, colour was the film's major attraction.

pure and uncomplicated hero and pair with her at the end at a safe distance from the disturbing ambivalence of Jaffar's no less genuine attraction for her.[77]

Later in the film the image of the eye again becomes important with the 'All-Seeing Eye', a magical red jewel that when gazed into reveals other locations, which Abu, restored to being human, steals from a temple and allows him to locate Ahmed from whom he has become separated. When they both look into the red eye they observe the Princess who is about to smell a blue rose which will make her forget her hatred of Jaffar. Here the colour blue is 'cool' (as in Kalmus's strictures), since it makes her forget her anger and hatred of Jaffar, but as this film shows, the meanings that are often attributed to colours are indeed variable and fluid. Here, red is the route to insight for Ahmed and Abu while at the same time for the Princess blue signals magic that should not be trusted and danger, more usually associated with red. Red and blue are also used in the deadly mechanical creature that kills the Princess's father, again bringing more ambiguity to the mix. As Eisenstein observed, in such instances the relationship between colour and object is not a fixed one and it can 'even assume absolutely *contradictory* meanings, dependent only upon the general system of imagery that has been decided upon for the particular film'.[78] It is fitting that at the end of the film we see Sabu on a flying carpet with a rainbow behind him – colour being spectacular to the last in this film.

Yet the fact that it was produced is testament to a renewed sense of confidence about film colour at the end of the 1930s. Unlike the many previous attempts to promote colour as the dominant aesthetic preference, Technicolor had infiltrated the feature film market. While domination was out of the question, the number of established producers who were willing to raise the extra finance required had a spin-off effect on film stars, directors and technicians. As Hollywood sought to protect its overseas markets against the impact of protective legislation for Europe's film industries, Technicolor was caught up with the strategy of taking advantage of quota laws that favoured big-budget film-making in collaboration with British companies. The establishment of Technicolor Ltd and the consequent number of visiting experts from Hollywood, including Natalie Kalmus, represented a new phase of Anglo-American film relations. The next chapter shows how, although this was disrupted by World War II, the desire for colour films did not recede. Far from being a disaster for Technicolor the war can be seen as a pivotal period in terms of overcoming technical obstacles and taking advantage of experimental opportunities available in the sponsored short film market. In this context British film-makers were able to keep colour very much on the agenda for postwar expansion while producing some of the most significant colour films to date.

5 COLOUR ENTHUSIASTS
COLOUR TRANSFORMATIONS IN WORLD WAR II

A Matter of Life and Death, released just after the end of World War II in 1946, features the character Conductor 71 (Marius Goring), who passes from heaven to earth. In this film, discussed in greater detail in Chapter 7, heaven was shot in monochrome (Technicolor with the colour printed out rather than using conventional black and white), and colour was used for earth. As a rose acquires its colour the character remarks: 'One is starved for Technicolor up there.' Many viewers would sympathise, having seen Technicolor films make advances towards the end of the 1930s, then to be curtailed by the disruptions caused by the outbreak of war. Indeed, on the eve of World War II the expansion of colour film was debated by many technical experts and film reviewers. This trend was not new, since the merits and problems of successive processes had been the subject of discussion for many years in both the silent and sound periods. This chapter concentrates primarily on short film-making during the wartime years in Britain (Chapter 6 deals with wartime features), when the advancement of colour was threatened by scarcity, disruptions and, on the part of some, scepticism as to its necessity. When war-weary audiences needed to be entertained and propagandised, a steady stream of films that were not expensive or overtly preoccupied with aesthetic experimentation was surely required. On the other hand, as I shall argue, colour became a highly desirable format for features and shorts, and despite wartime conditions considerable advances in the deployment of Technicolor were observed by contemporary commentators. Focusing on contemporary discourses that circulated around colour, I argue that, in spite of the problems of shooting and

processing colour films, World War II was a pivotal period which prepared the way for the considerable advances made in colour cinematography in the postwar years.

By the time of the outbreak of war in September 1939, seven British feature films had been released in Technicolor (*Wings of the Morning* (1938), *The Divorce of Lady X* (1938), *The Drum* (1938), *Sixty Glorious Years* (1938), *The Mikado* (1939), *The Four Feathers* (1939) and *Over the Moon* (1939)). In addition, a number of shorts had been produced, most notably the film of the 1937 Coronation, *Cavalcade of the Navy* (1939) and the *World Windows* travelogue series shot by Jack Cardiff (1937–39, not generally released before the war).[1] A greater number of American films shot in Technicolor had been seen, but compared to the overall total of titles trade shown they nevertheless represented a very small percentage.[2] Technical developments occurred on the eve of war, most notably the availability of faster Eastman stock for Technicolor which reduced the light levels necessary for shooting, as well as increasing the scope of back-projection effects and providing improved colour rendition, particularly for greens.[3] While in the mid-1930s some predicted that colour would revolutionise the industry much as sound had done towards the end of the previous decade, by 1938–39 a more cautious tone was adopted since shooting and processing Technicolor was expensive compared to black and white. In addition to the limited number of available cameras (only four) and the high light levels required, attention focused on the variable quality evident in screening colour films in different cinemas, resulting in a recommendation that for the most effective exhibition of colour films higher than usual screen intensity was required, and that this should be standardised across the country's cinemas.[4] This issue was also raised by Adrian Klein who argued that to maximise the quality of colour film suitable projection was a high priority, even to the extent of proposing that a grey surround to the screen was preferable to black because by adding white, grey tends to have the effect of rendering the colours on screen of greater value. His other recommendations included that a smaller, bright screen was preferable to a larger, under-lit one, and that standardisation across the country's cinemas was an important goal. During this period he was also one of the few writers who highlighted set design as a key factor in determining colour choices for the screen.[5]

The quest for standardisation was complicated by the fact that it was not yet clear which system would dominate the commercial market. Additive systems such as Dufaycolor were disadvantaged in this respect because they required more light than subtractive processes such as Technicolor during projection. Although Dufaycolor required less light than other additive processes it was still difficult to demonstrate the process in smaller cinemas where the light was still not bright enough. In any case critics of Dufaycolor were alert to spotting the *réseau* traces which, ironically, were more visible with the correct amount of light when projected so that, rather than show off its qualities, correct illumination tended to draw attention to its perceived deficiencies. The technical explanation is that, as in black-and-white film, in subtractive processes whites were areas of clear gelatine. For an additive processes to show a colour rendering of similar saturation and brilliance as much as three times more light was required on the gate, or a bigger aperture projection lens.[6] One report went so far as to claim that in 1939 50 per cent of Britain's cinemas, mostly the smaller venues, ran low-intensity screen illumination, thus lowering the quality of colour projection.[7] Such discussion demonstrates the extent to which colour was seen as desirable but difficult, and subject to variation. Although it was still a relatively novel feature which depended to a certain extent on surprising audiences with its capacity for infinite variety, at the same time these observations in trade and technical journals reveal a desire to enhance and control how colour could be used on screen. The concept of

'colour control', therefore, exceeded Natalie Kalmus's well-publicised strictures for Technicolor.

General reportage on colour films tended to praise those which did not appear to draw unnecessary attention to colour. A review of *The Divorce of Lady X*, for example, praised the Technicolor photography since 'it is as near as lifelike as makes no difference', while criticising the opening charity ball and hunting sequences as 'merely an obvious instrument for the exploitation of colour'.[8] Nevertheless, reports of the film's exploitation showed that colour was indeed seen to be a notable feature by exhibitors. The colour angle was exploited by the manager of a cinema in Nuneaton, as reported in the *Kinematograph Weekly*: 'In the window of local dyers and cleaners, an array of colourful materials was accompanied with the poster: "The gorgeous colours worn by Merle Oberon in *The Divorce of Lady X*". A similar kind of caption linked up a full window display of paints and wallpaper appearing in local decorators.'[9] Although *The Divorce of Lady X* was noted for 'tasteful' colour, it was most certainly used in precise ways to display costumes, including the white fancy-dress ball gown worn by Oberon embellished with large blue flowers, a blue feathered fan and silk shawl. This was fully appreciated by Alexander Korda, who acknowledged that the film was in good part a vehicle for costume and colour display.[10] What is most impressive is how Technicolor renders the textures of Oberon's outfits and accessories, highlighting, for example, how these create contrasts within and between colours, from silken pyjamas whose sheen is caught by the light, to a bejewelled ornament glistening on a black hat. On one occasion she wears a white fur coat over a black cocktail dress which again creates contrasting textures when the sensation of the coat's almost ebullient mobility, visible as she emerges from a taxi, serves as counterpoint to the more the formal contours of the black gown worn underneath. While such opulent attire would hardly have been available to all, the shades, fabrics and textures nevertheless communicated an appreciation of the variety and potential of colour. Although not referring to this film in particular, interviews conducted for Annette Kuhn's project on cinema audiences in the 1930s demonstrated how the textures and details of different garments, including their colours, were fondly remembered, and that such recollections were 'often coloured by a sense of lack'.[11]

Indeed, interest in colour was not confined to motion pictures, since in 1930 the British Colour Council (BCC) had been incorporated. It was an organisation that produced a reference code and indexes naming colours for use in a variety of industries. Its major publication in 1934 was the *Dictionary of Colour Standards*, aimed for application in the textile industry and subsequently adopted as the source of standard reference nomenclature for colour in a range of institutions such as the Royal Horticultural Society, the British Army and the Royal Mail.[12] It selected 220 colours – available in silk ribbon examples and as a separate volume naming the colours, such as Union Jack Red, Bottle Green and Sky Blue, which were based on Lovibond Colorimeter readings.[13] In 1941 the BCC published a special horticultural colour chart in collaboration with the Royal Horticultural Society which aimed at even further refinements to convey whether particular colours were full hues, shades or tints. The impact on the film industry was more indirect than direct, in the sense that the industries adopting the nomenclature produced costumes and wallpapers used in productions – although, of course, adjustments for shooting in colour had to take place. The existence of the BCC offers an important indication of the growing culture of colour that influenced the developing context for its use in cinema. A report, however, claimed that the circus scenes of *Incendiary Blonde*, an American film released in 1945, occasioned the BCC's exploitation of three 'Texas' colours for autumn collections of cosmetics, clothing and shoes.[14] The trend towards standardising nomenclature linked with related discussion on how particular effects could be achieved in photography, such as moving emphasis away from colour contrast towards variation of saturation and brightness in order to yield harmonious results.[15]

While the disruptions to film production caused by the war were a setback for the rapid development of Technicolor in Britain, short and feature films were nevertheless made using the process, and some colour titles were rereleased to make up for the shortage. Approximately 10 per cent of cinemas closed during the war and, even though domestic feature film production was curtailed, the short film market expanded and average weekly cinema attendance increased from 19 million in 1939 to 30 million in 1945.[16] A report by Bernard Happé, who worked at the Technicolor

laboratories in the UK, recorded the difficulties caused by the reduction of normal production hours, the loss of laboratory workers called up to fight in the war, the decrease in footage and delays in the supply of chemicals, especially dyes that were crucial to the processing of Technicolor films.[17] Kay Harrison, manager of Technicolor Ltd, reported to Natalie Kalmus in Hollywood, that wartime conditions had some beneficial repercussions:

> Technicolor has been riding a bit of a storm since the outbreak of war which created many uncertainties regarding our future. All of the American producers were obliged to hold up all their plans for distribution of their pictures here, as they were unable to determine what amount of money they would be able to remit back to America, but today the news has been published and for the time being they will be permitted to withdraw 50c on the dollar. The other 50c will have to remain in England, and it is hoped that a substantial part of this will be devoted to motion picture production in England, and I believe that something along these lines will follow. With the money which they have frozen here, it is hoped by the Government – and certainly by ourselves – that some of it at least will be devoted to making really good pictures for release in America, and Technicolor stands in a good position as there are more than ordinary reasons why productions should be in colour if they are seeking an American outlet.[18]

The Technicolor plant in Britain stayed open and made up for the loss of manpower called up to fight in the war by employing women who by 1943 made up more than half of the employees.[19] During World War II the Technicolor plant experienced shortages in chemicals, especially dyes, which encouraged experimentation to affect economies. An account by Happé documents the many ingenious and innovative experiments with chemicals undertaken at this time.[20] In addition, the plant was restricted to operating with four cameras, one transfer machine and four matrix printers. Technicolor's plant was kept working to capacity during the war and with the exception of 1940 there was an increase in production over the previous year from 1937 to 1955.[21] Some commentators claimed that British studios were more efficient in wartime because of 'a new spirit of planned production' which had become necessary when the working week was reduced to forty-seven hours (from sixty to eighty hours) because of the blackout.[22]

Discussion of colour continued; if anything, the debates became even more intense, since the promise of colour became invested with a utopian discourse about cinema's potential to make significant technical, aesthetic and ideological progress in the postwar world. Perhaps because of wartime austerity, the cultural fascination with colour (and the perceived lack of it) created an intensified interest in colour on the screen and in everyday life. A report on wartime conditions in London sent to Hollywood confirmed this view:

> It is the opinion of the distributors that Technicolor will be called upon more and more in times of war owing to the type of pictures which these conditions will encourage. In this country Technicolor, because of all its qualities to portray drama and the gaiety of things, will be, in the opinion of many, in increased demand by the people who will seek relief from their problems.[23]

In a context of material scarcity Technicolor could also remind people of restricted pleasures in an unusual way, as one report on a screening of *Moon Over Miami* (1941) in London recorded 'scenes' in the audience when 'a glorious close-up of an egg frying in Technicolor' was seen. The report continued: 'Egg-a-fortnight England returns night after night to scream at the sight of that almost forgotten delicacy.'[24] Discussions included reference to colour and emotion, synaesthesia and psychology – for example, critic V. Chamberlain discussed experiments with senses and colour in the *British Journal of Photography*:

> The associations between emotion and colour are interesting … In recent years we have seen attempts to turn music into colour on the cinema screen … It will not be long, we hope, before in many ways the world will become more colourful. With the coming of changing fashions, cheap dyes and colour photography we may well have in store for us all a new colour age.[25]

While the tone established earlier in the 1930s for praising films which did not use colour to distract from narrative persisted, some commentators bemoaned that by and large, experimentation with colour cinema had

not occurred. As *The Times* correspondent observed on the eve of war: 'The achievements of what might almost have been a new art are quite ridiculously meagre … With all its vast economic resources the cinema industry has scarcely ventured to make the humblest experiments in the exploitation of colour.'[26] The war did, however, result in many notable colour films, and as American studios released their schedules for 1945–46 British exhibitors predicted that 'within two years colour will be almost universally used for any important subject'.[27]

The most extensive and lively debates on colour films in Britain took place in the *British Journal of Photography*, a well-established technical journal which started in 1854. While its primary focus was on still photography, it also recorded developments in motion pictures and colour. The main correspondent was E. S. Tompkins who began a regular column entitled 'The Colour Enthusiast at the Cinema', which ran more or less monthly from March 1942 to October 1947. Another contributor, although not nearly on such a regular basis, was Darrel Catling who directed short films sponsored by the British Council including *Colour in Clay* (1942). The commentaries constitute a fascinating record of responses to colour films – British, American and others – released during the war. They are also highly interesting because they are written from an informed perspective of, in the case of Tompkins, someone who saw practically every colour film available, offering opinions based on a breadth of knowledge about cinematography and of the comparative development of Technicolor in Britain and the USA. Tompkins's main motive for writing the articles was to advise amateur cinematographers of best practice in commercial cinema. Tompkins explained how such amateurs could be instructed and inspired by fiction films in his first 'Colour Enthusiast' article:

> Much may be learned by the amateur about the potentialities of colour, either in still or moving pictures, by studying the successes and failures of the film producers. The colour photographer is often the most responsive member of a cinema audience, able to ignore weaknesses of plot or playing, and content to glory in the lavish exploitation of the Technicolor process, with its capacity of filling dark winter days with a feast of brightest colour, and of bringing to a drab war-time world vivid glimpses of the brightly glowing scenes beyond.[28]

At the time key developments had encouraged the expansion of home movie-making in colour with the introduction in 1935 of 16mm Kodachrome film, which was then extended to 8mm and to 35mm for miniature cameras. One such amateur was Rosie Newman, a wealthy Londoner who shot striking footage of wartime Britain. As many noted at the time, Kodak's marketing of 16mm Kodachrome was right to identify it as an extremely significant development. The advantages were that colour rendering was 'extremely faithful' and, perhaps most important of all, the film could be handled in exactly the same way as black-and-white film, not requiring special filters for shooting or projection, the speed of the film being about half that of normal panchromatic reversal stock. A most important aspect of Kodachrome was its dye-coupling developer, which produced the coloured images. As one report noted: 'The outstanding fact is that a tri-pack silver image had without separation been converted into colour. Other methods to achieve this end may be devised or material alterations be made in the present methods. The miracle has, however, at last been worked.'[29] In 1938 it was estimated that more than half amateur substandard cinematography was in colour, and that in the new climate of enthusiasm for colour 'the old school of natural colour inventors' were encouraged to revive obsolete processes in the hope of attracting speculative investors.[30]

Tompkins was very much a chromophile, taking issue with Adrian Cornwell-Clyne, author of *Colour Cinematography* discussed in Chapter 4, and at that time a director of Dufay-Chromex. *Cinema* had published an article written by Cornwell-Clyne entitled 'Colour Films are too "Glorious"', in which he argued that the most desirable commercial application of colour was to render it as more or less monochrome, in keeping with prevailing discourses about the need for an overall restrained approach. Tompkins's response was 'In Defence of "Glorious" Colour', an article in which he took issue with Cornwell-Clyne's argument that contemporary directors had no sense of how to use colour expressively, and citing *The Life and Death of Colonel Blimp* (1943) as an example of a film that in its wartime sequence reduced colour to a minimum while introducing subtle touches for lips, eyes and details on uniforms.[31] He developed an argument here and in subsequent articles for a *relative* appreciation of colour,

that is to say an understanding which depended on the contextual presentation of colour which bears striking similarity to Eisenstein's theories on colour.[32]

Another sparring partner in the wartime debate on colour was documentary film-maker Darrel Catling, whose article 'Let's Clean Up Colour' criticised how he thought most films failed to use colour 'imaginatively', that their directors failed to understand the need for 'control' to be exercised as well as creativity.[33] Catling's approach in directing *Colour in Clay* (Gaumont British Instructional, shot by Jack Cardiff), a film about English porcelain, had indeed been to exercise restraint, using the 'cooler' end of the spectrum and aiming for consistency in colour choices between shots to avoid a jarring, uneven look.[34] Tompkins replied, informing Catling that his knowledge of current films failed to appreciate the work of Natalie Kalmus's 'color control' department, or the extent to which Technicolor films demonstrated an artful deployment of colour in popular genre films. He reiterated arguments he had made the previous year, in which he defended the deployment of 'hot' colour in 'theatrical' films such as musicals which demanded 'exaggerated colour' as a marketable and appropriate choice. Far from indicating ignorance about colour, he argued that these choices demonstrated ingenuity, planning and expertise.[35] Such advocacy of colour was linked to the development of greater 'colour consciousness', not only as far as directors, cinematographers and art directors were concerned, but also regarding the audiences of popular cinema:

> Colour must continue to be recognised as a useful tool for lowbrow story-telling. We cannot afford to see it become just one more misguided highbrow experiment ... Colour will only improve by constructive preaching to the unconverted, in the form of steady step-by-step improvements in its use in the popular cinema.[36]

The experience of seeing colour films in wartime was all the more impressive because of prevailing conditions of the blackout and reduced interior lighting, as well as the stressful psychological pressures of life on the Home Front. Early in 1943 Tompkins recorded the following impression in his 'Colour Enthusiast' column:

> The fourth blackout winter of the war has been brightened for millions of cinemagoers by the colour films

of the last few months, and the colour worker who has not seized the opportunity of keeping colour-conscious, and watching the reactions of his fellow-men to colour in the commercial cinema, has been missing valuable chances. One of the writer's most lasting impressions of this winter's blackout is going to be that of a laughing, happy crowd streaming out of an only-just-disenchanted cinema, into a very inky night, and striding off into the blackness, chanting happily, 'Sing me a Song of the Islands'. One wished, above all, that Betty Grable and the rest of those responsible could have shared the experience, and could have seen this evidence of the strength of the coloured spell they wove.[37]

Indeed, his patience was tried by those who criticised American genre films for using 'unrealistic' colour at a time when the chances of seeing fully saturated colours in everyday life were reduced. He wrote: 'Our reactions to Technicolor ought to be of gratitude for a beautiful record of something that we lack, rather than a narrow-minded accusation that its record is false.'[38] This sentiment was echoed by one of J. P. Mayer's respondents who stated that: 'When I've been to a film [especially one in Technicolor] I always walk home feeling disgusted with the drab town I live in, the paint-work of doors etc. seem awfully dull and dresses look plain after seeing the glorious scenery and stylish clothes in the film.'[39] Like this cinemagoer, Tompkins placed great emphasis on the relative power of colour to enhance everyday experience and as a stimulant to 'happiness'. He quoted examples, including a personal experience when travelling which he then related to the cinema:

A few years ago a travel agency used an advertisement which simply said, 'Colour makes you happy!' and which used as a background a coloured Egyptian scene from one of their cruises. I never really appreciated this advertisement, in spite of an absorbing interest in colour photography, until one February morning a few years ago when I awoke in the train just outside Athens and found myself almost hysterically happy at the warm, sunny, coloured world into which I had come, straight from the rigours of a north-European winter. Since then I have never doubted the reality of the inborn craving which we all have for colour or the power of its brightness and warmth to bring happiness to our lives.[40]

Tompkins went on to reference how cinema similarly exploits colour in films, such as the opening sequence of *Week-End in Havana* (1941) in which a wintry New York street is transformed with a shot of a coloured cut-out window display in a shipping agency of Carmen Miranda's Banda da Lua orchestra. As Tompkins observes:

The camera then tracks through the window and approaches one member of the band. The film cuts to a similar animated shot and the characteristic music swells as the camera takes in the whole orchestra in action, with a final pan to pick up Carmen Miranda herself, the most colourful personality of them all. Such scenes represent the fullest exploitation of colour as a stimulus of simple childlike happiness.[41]

Here colour is linked with music and an intense, emotional experience at the cinema is understood to be both possible and desirable.

As well as in British and American Technicolor feature films, the short film market provided another notable arena for experimentation with colour during wartime. Tompkins noted how small news or magazine cinemas were often excellent venues to view colour shorts, such as the American Fitzpatrick travelogue series, with an 'up to date apparatus, small, well-lit screen, and a narrow auditorium giving a good view from all seats and without the necessity for very bright wall lighting'.[42] Other key titles imported from the USA included Warners' dance shorts *The Gay Parisian* (1941) and *Spanish Fiesta* (1942), as well as propaganda films about the forces including *At the Front in North Africa* (1943, first shown in Britain in 1945) and *The Fighting Lady* (1944), a US Navy film shot on 16mm Kodachrome and then printed in Technicolor. Notable British shorts included those sponsored by organisations such as the British Council and Imperial Chemical Industries (ICI).

The British Council films provided an outlet for experimentation in colour film during wartime, and were shown in many British cinemas. They were made by a number of production units for commercial, propaganda and instructional films, the latter becoming the most common in the war. They were shown in Britain, the empire and in the USA, with different linguistic commentaries facilitating their export. For the production personnel, the films provided the occasion for experimentation with colour. The British Council was able to call on experts in related fields to cinema, such as Ralph Vaughan Williams who composed music on some of the films, and for commentaries spoken by those familiar to radio listeners including Alvar Lidell, Frederick Grisewood and Joseph McLeod. Titles which featured colour included *Green Girdle* (1941), produced by Basil Wright and directed by Ralph Keene. Jack Cardiff was the cinematographer on this film, which featured parks and recreation spaces around London. The propaganda message was that recreation must not suffer during wartime, with the colour photography focusing on the tints of autumn. *The People's Land* (Strand Films, directed by Ralph Keene, cinematographer Geoffrey Unsworth, 1943) was a cooperation between the British Council and the National Trust. Exterior locations featured predominantly in other British Council films, and were an obvious way to display colour by linking it with natural beauty, landscape and a nostalgic evocation of English pastoral settings. These arguably increased in sentimental and propaganda value during wartime, as well as illustrating continuities with earlier colour film experiments with nature. *World Garden* (1941) and *Gardens of England* (Strand Films, cinematographer Geoffrey Unsworth, 1942), for example, challenged viewers to judge the accuracy of the colours in comparison with their own experience by focusing on flowers and natural imagery with which they would be familiar.

Of particular note from the British Council's group of films sponsored in wartime is *Queen Cotton* (Merton Park Studios, directed by Cecil Musk; cinematographer Jimmy Rogers, with Jack Cardiff as Technicolor Adviser, 1941), geared towards overseas distribution but also shown in Britain. It features the operations of cotton spinning in Lancashire, and how fabrics are produced, culminating with a fashion show of a collection which was exported to South America. The film opens with pastoral shots of Lancashire, followed by Manchester, the 'great city of textiles', as the male voice-over commentary informs us. It is also explained that the collection was created by designers, and one early scene, designed to convey the opulence of the dress, shows a model being fitted in a gown with a pale orange and black pattern. In addition, a medium close-up shot introduces a direct colour correspondence when we see

Queen Cotton (Technicolor, 1941): colour correspondences with fashion. Courtesy North West Film Archive

the fitter's arm as she adjusts a detail on the dress which at the same time reveals that she is wearing a large, bevelled glass bracelet in the same shade of pale orange, as the camera catches its multifaceted, glistening shape against the background of the dress. In this instance the film's ostensible instructional remit is overtaken by a sheer aesthetic pleasure in the sight of colour correspondences, as well as showing how objects which are similarly coloured look different when reflected off different surfaces and textures.

As with many instructional films, a good deal of time is, however, spent explaining how the cotton industry worked, and the scientific basis of innovation in the creation of synthetic dyes. Technical details follow, such as how synthetic substances are experimented with in order to create fast dyes for cotton, while at the same time showing different fibres, colours and testing chemicals in the laboratories to see how cotton can be mixed productively with other substances. The film becomes especially vibrant with colour in a long sequence showing the looms, operated it seems by women wearing patterned dresses (as opposed to the white-coated women seen in the earlier 'scientific' scenes), which the commentary tells us are weaving 'a symphony in cotton for the people of the world'. The shots of the spinning machines show colours being added and weaves produced; eventually the sequence develops so that the shots of the machines working are alternated with full-frame shots of different coloured textiles. The film then progresses to a new stage, focusing on large pails of coloured dyes which are used for printing machines. It is emphasised that artists design the prints that are used for mass production, with the printing process described as 'capturing the colours of the rainbow' as the colours are fixed onto rolls of cotton. These are then seen in all their variety of multitudinous colours and patterns, before the film ends with a fashion show. The voice-over commentary (now by a woman) emphasises that although the collection is intended for export, fashion is not 'exclusively the property of a few wealthy women', and refers to the British Cotton Board's Colour, Style and Design Centre as an organisation which encourages fashion for all women, for lines designed by top names but which cost 'shillings' rather than 'guineas'.

This would have resonated with wartime audiences since from 1942 utility clothing was designed by top names in the fashion world, including Norman Hartnell, Digby Morton, Peter Russell, Victor Stiebel, Bianca Mosca and Edward Molyneux. The 'utility scheme' concentrated on textiles that would wear and clean well to produce clothes that were sold at a regulated price without purchase tax. Such incentives meant that gradually utility clothing began to dominate the market and 'one of the most remarkable features of wartime dress is the extent to which utility and non-utility clothing resembled each other. It was not that one was fashionable and the other was not: fashionable dress was provided within the utility scheme itself.'[43] As Jonathan Walford explains, the term 'utility' conjured up a rather unfortunate image of dowdiness and utilitarianism when, in fact, 'the Utility scheme actually improved the overall quality of ready-to-wear clothing in Britain'.[44] Colour was very much a feature of wartime clothing with trends emerging such as recorded in *Vogue*'s commentary on pastel shades for spring and summer of 1942, with the development in spring 1943 of 'mixing and matching' of colours and, finally, the introduction of bold, vivid contrasts in 1944.[45] The 'Make do and mend' campaign encouraged people to be creative and, as Kirkham explains, experimenting with colour was an integral aspect of adding individual touches to an otherwise restricted choice in garments:

> Colourful, intricate and often witty small prints enlivened the fabrics used for frocks and blouses and fashionable details were used to ring the changes ... The colours were

far from drab and the dresses [observed in Leicester's costume museum] came in a variety of colours including grey and purple, tartan, dark red, maroon, purple, multi-coloured (floral), black and white (stripes), red and white (stripes), yellow (with white spots and black circles), red (with white trims), and purple, green, red, yellow and white mixed together in an exotic print, while the materials include cotton, wool, moyagashel, and synthetic materials including artificial and watered silks. Professional dressmakers had to conform to changing governmental regulations but if a woman was sufficiently skilled and could obtain the fabric, she could make what she wanted at home; many women worked miracles from old curtaining, bedspreads, disused clothes or fabrics sent home by men serving abroad.[46]

Apart from the fashions on display, as Tompkins noted when he saw this film, the wartime context was present in the film as indicated by 'little touches in the commentary and photography which identify the film as the product of a land at war; the barrage balloon floating over the docks, and the crowd from the fashion display coming out into the gathering gloom of the black-out to the sound of singing troops marching by'.[47] The final shots are of women in Lancashire leaving the mill, some of them wearing a variety of colours demonstrating that colour was not absent from everyday clothing. The related theme of weaving featured in another British Council film, *Border Weave* (Turner Films, directed by J. L. Curthoys, cinematography Jack Cardiff, 1942). This again concentrated attention on colour and how tweed clothing is made in various stages from spinning to specimen inspection, and ending with a shot of a young woman stepping off a curb in Edinburgh wearing one of the tweed coats the film has shown being made, against a background of the Pipe Band of a tartan-kilted Scots Regiment. Once again, national discourses are linked with industry, productivity and colour.

The British Council shorts also featured industrial themes, such as *Teeth of Steel* (Technique Films, directed by Ronald H. Riley, cinematographer Geoffrey Unsworth, music by Vaughan Williams and commentary by John Laurie, 1942). Colour is given a prominent address in shots such as the opening credits with a mechanical shovel made all the more strikingly visible against the bright blue sky background. The film is then characterised by a repetitious deployment of

variated 'hot' colours which show the specifics of the industrial process, as noted by Tompkins who observed that: 'There are some interesting scenes in low-key of the drying of the ore by firing it in its stacks, and of the pouring of the smelted metal, the latter pictures being taken solely by the coloured light of the molten metal. These shots open up a wide field for the use of colour in the recording of industrial processes.'[48] A follow-up film, *Steel* (Technique Film Productions, cinematographers Jack Cardiff and Cyril Knowles, 1945), was also directed by Riley. This documentary further exploited colour's potential to render different effects with molten iron, furnaces in action, the casting of steel ingots and transformation of materials in a series of sequences that made the whole process suspenseful and exciting to watch.[49] Indeed, on viewing the film it certainly does feature many shots of red-hot coke, molten metal and the spectacular sight of flickering fire and flames. As an instructional film there is much detail about the various stages in the making of steel. The repetitive, stark contrasts between the blackness of the dark factory, its machines and the vibrant mutations of yellows and oranges create interesting colour effects. Even though these occur in many shots on each occasion they are linked with another part of the process, involving different shapes of the metal as it is treated. The 'electric arc' process is especially dramatic since it introduces the only sight of blue which is immediately followed by the red-hot furnace. The technical process is almost presented as a sort of alchemy in which the viewer is caught up in the transformation of the iron ore into processed steel in a series of laborious and dangerous-looking procedures which banish impurities from the metal. The series of films showed how incurring the extra expense of making films in Technicolor was more than justified because of how colour enhanced the visual spectacle of industrial processes in such a way as to make them both entertaining and instructional.

The fascination with colour was perhaps demonstrated most strikingly when Jack Cardiff shot *This is Colour* (ICI, produced by Basil Wright, 1942), a short film focusing on experiments with coloured dyes which towards the end exceeds a purely instructional imperative when the commentary declaring 'Now let all the colours dance' heralds a sequence that more resembles an abstract, experimental film. As with *Queen Cotton*, this film contains much that is of instructional

This is Colour (Technicolor, 1942): vats of coloured dyes; celebrating design with rolls of patterned fabrics

This is Colour: colour and consumption

This is Colour: colour and the environment

This is Colour: proving colour is better; swimmers in black and white

Swimmers in colour

This is Colour: all the colours dancing towards the end of the film

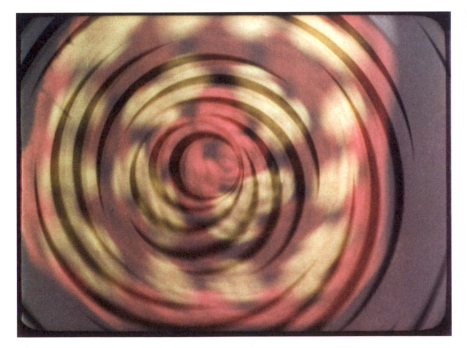

Colour abstraction in an instructional film

address. It opens with a description of how colour works, is created from light, and then progresses to information about the history of when synthetic dyes were invented. The theme of the film's early sections is in the spirit of documenting an exciting scientific quest – for example, showing how to create green as a colour-fast dye and mixing various dyes to produce different colours. The film then progresses to a section on colour vats, with the camera panning past machinery – red, blue and yellow liquid dyes in vats that are seen being absorbed onto rolls which are converted into patterned fabrics. The saturated colours are striking in this sequence, one after the next producing a different style and combination of colours. A woman's voice-over commentary takes over from the previous male one and the film focuses on colour in everyday life. A poetic rhyme describes different uses of colour which we are shown, including curtains, lampshades, china, pencils, tapestries, rugs, carpets, notepaper, cups and plates, telephones, candles, hot water bottles, wallpapers and railway posters. We are reminded of how colour surrounds us and pervades everyday life: 'Almost everything you use you can pick and choose from a hundred hues.' The message becomes even more explicit when the voice-over tells us that 'Colour means people can never be standardised,' and we see shots of flats with different-coloured curtains, and are reminded how colour is important for operating railway signals and in offices. The same ideological imperative that was evident in other films is present here, whereby colour is seen to be something which can be used by artists and individuals in different ways, while at the same time it is shown to assist industry and commerce. Shots of people diving into a swimming pool are interspersed with the same in black and white, to show how 'Colour is a holiday by itself – if you take it away beauty is lost,' as we experience the shock of colour present and then absent. There is an almost messianic tone as we are told we are living in a 'new age, a golden age of colour'. The last section of the film is given over completely to a celebratory display of shots which relish colour, its patterns, as we see 'all the colours dance'. The film has become almost experimental in its aesthetic pleasure in just showing colour, shapes and patterns, which is a long way from the tone of the film's instructional opening. In many ways this is an extraordinary film, produced in wartime and celebrating colour as a leveller, an essential element of modern life and to be appreciated on many different levels. Michael Powell saw it and remembered it as 'using all sorts of devices like pouring pots of yellow paint and wonderfully photographed and lit'.[50]

ICI sponsored another film, *Discovery of a New Pigment* (c. 1940, ICI Dyestuffs Group) that featured colour itself, in this case detailing the discovery of Monastral blue made by ICI in 1935 from copper phthalocyanine. The decision to make the film was interesting, especially in view of its projection on substandard equipment lit with metal filament lamps which were deficient in the blue end of the spectrum. Nevertheless, the film was another example of how, in its desire to educate and advertise, industry was prepared to tackle scientific themes such as this which only made sense being filmed in colour. Cornwell-Clyne explained how Monastral blue was 'ideal for purposes of colour photography' since unlike other blues such as ultramarine, cobalt and Prussian blue, it absorbs most red and yellow light and reflects blue and green.[51] As Philip Ball also notes this makes Monastral blue 'the ideal cyan colour for three-colour printing'.[52]

Catling's *English Village* (cinematographer Frank North, 1943) experimented with the new monopack film because the few available Technicolor cameras were in great demand. Despite practical difficulties of having to send the film to the USA for processing, and numerous delays during production, the film is an interesting example of how necessity sparked ingenuity in short film-making.[53] Although many critics placed emphasis on the representational codes associated with the realist aesthetic of black-and-white photography, wartime subject-matter was quite suited to colour. Situations such as the need to show aircraft or ships clearly in training films lent themselves to colour cinematography as blue skies provided striking backgrounds for aeroplanes, and the blueness of the sea provided visual relief in naval scenes, as in Pat Jackson's popular, suspenseful documentary-style drama about the 'Battle for the Atlantic', *Western Approaches* (1944). When producer Ian Dalrymple, head of the Crown Film Unit, was making the case to film *Western Approaches* in colour to Jack Beddington, Head of Film at the Ministry of Information, he argued that colour 'sells propaganda'. He claimed that 'colour automatically adds 100 per cent value – due to uniforms, flags and other patriotic emblems, insignia', and that 'Films of the sea shot around these shores are usually drab to look at', so colour was imperative for the first British naval subject they were able to film. The arguments succeeded, and even though there were considerable difficulties producing the film, its box-office success and critical reception at home and abroad more than justified it being financed by the Treasury.[54] A number of Army, Navy and RAF training films were also shot during wartime using Technicolor. Colour also came into its own for medical training films, one shot by Jack Cardiff was entitled *Plastic Surgery in Wartime* (1941). Such accomplishments in achieving definition through colour are resonant with earlier debates in the silent period on colour's 'stereoscopic' properties. Fiction films, particularly Westerns, which opted for the often difficult challenge of location shooting in Technicolor rather than resorting to more easily controllable back-projection or

process shots, were also enhanced in this way, a connection that was picked up by contemporaries.[55] Ingenuity in achieving effects in exterior locations included using filters on the camera lens, as for the silhouette effects in *For Whom the Bell Tolls* (1943).[56]

Although colour films constituted a small percentage of the total shown in the UK, output did not fall off during wartime, as the adjacent table of the number of films (mainly features) trade shown in the UK demonstrates.

The shortage of British colour films placed even greater emphasis than usual on American Technicolor films screened in British cinemas.[57] As we have seen, the reportage in the *British Journal of Photography* was broad in its coverage of colour and largely appreciative of Hollywood's films. Interestingly, this coincides with a far less strained period of Anglo-American diplomatic and film relations than was the case in the 1930s. Throughout his extensive commentaries, Tompkins praised box-office winners which deployed colour effectively – for example, C. B. DeMille's *Reap the Wild Wind* (1942), *Heaven Can Wait* (1943) and *For Whom the Bell Tolls*, as well as colour classics such as *Gone with the Wind* (1939), *The Wizard of Oz* (1939) and *Fantasia* (1940). British feature films were also appreciated since, despite the difficulties affecting film production, some very significant Technicolor films were produced in the UK during wartime, as detailed in the following chapter.

YEAR	FILMS	REISSUES	TOTALS
1939	585	18	603
1940	502	38	540
1941	545	28	573
1942	555	50	605
1943	437	100	537
1944	442	110	552
1945	444	100	544

YEAR	US COLOUR FILMS (INCLUDING REISSUES)	BRITISH COLOUR FILMS (INCLUDING REISSUES)	TOTAL COLOUR FILMS (INCLUDING REISSUES)
1939	5	4	9
1940	16	2	18
1941	16	1	17
1942	13	3	16
1943	26	3	29
1944	27	6	33
1945	23	4	27

Source: Kinematograph Year Books.

6 BRITISH COLOUR FEATURE FILMS IN WARTIME

One noticeable feature of war-time film entertainment has been the sweeping popularity of the colour film, which has gone far in convincing exhibitors that colour suitably employed is in itself a box-office attraction. Probably the reaction of the public is due largely to the care shown by producers in the selection of vehicles, and to a certain extent, that most of the pictures have been 'escapist' in theme. It is evident, however, that colour will enter more effectively into the post-war picture, first because of the greater skill of the technician; and secondly, because of its appeal to a public tired of the drab monotony of war-time experience.[1]

As the above quotation attests, exhibitors tracked developments in colour during wartime, concluding that technical advances in the various processes, particularly Technicolor, and evidence of the positive impact of colour on box-office returns, resulted in an economic and cultural climate that was conducive to its further exploitation. As we have seen, experimentation with colour was significant during World War II, particularly in the short film market. But key British features were also produced in Technicolor – these and one in Dufaycolor and will be discussed here in relation to each other, to the wartime context and to developments in colour more generally. *Sons of the Sea* (Dufaycolor, 1939), *The Thief of Bagdad* (1940), *The Great Mr Handel* (1942), *The Life and Death of Colonel Blimp* (1943), *This Happy Breed* (1944), *Henry V* (1944), *Western Approaches* (1944) and *Blithe Spirit* (1945) were the key British feature films released in wartime. *Queen Victoria* (1942) was a composite reissue of Herbert Wilcox's previous films

about the monarch and production started on *Men of Two Worlds* in 1943 but the film was not released until 1946. To make up for the relative shortage of British colour films, several were reissued during the war: *Wings of the Morning* (1937, rereleased 1940), *The Divorce of Lady X* (1938), *The Drum* (1938) and *The Thief of Bagdad* (all rereleased 1944).[2] *The Thief of Bagdad* has already been discussed for its bold colour design and special effects in relation to the early development of Technicolor features in Britain, but its release at the beginning of the war links its reception to the contemporary context whereby the film's narrative about overthrowing an oppressive tyrant resonated with current events. Publicity for *The Mikado*, released in October 1939, was adapted so that the film appeared to have a wartime message by playing with the 'I've Got a Little List' line in one of the songs. Cinema posters for the film were produced whereby Hitler was caricatured with the heading 'We've Got HIM on our List'. In this way films were marketed to accentuate contemporary relevance at any opportunity.[3] The films discussed in this chapter can similarly be related to the war in terms of content, but the focus here is on how their colour designs were notable, contributing to the enhanced perception of colour's potential that the wartime context provoked.

EXPERIMENTS IN 'RESTRAINT': *SONS OF THE SEA* AND *THE GREAT MR HANDEL*

Dufaycolor's aspirations as a legitimate, rival process to Technicolor were in many respects demonstrated in *Sons of the Sea*, particularly the claim that the process was suited to shooting British locales. Directed by Maurice Elvey on the eve of the war and starring Leslie Banks, Mackenzie Ward, Simon Lack and Kay Walsh, the film was greeted enthusiastically by reviewers, who referred to its display of 'flawless' Dufaycolor cinematography in 'delicate pastel shades'.[4] The film clearly had much to offer, with its setting in the Royal Naval College, Dartmouth, and patriotic themes of duty and respect. The narrative mobilised noble sentiments when Captain Hyde (Leslie Banks) takes command of the College after the mysterious murder of his predecessor. In possession of secret information about enemy minefields, it becomes clear that Hyde was the intended victim. He is pursued by a German posing as a naval intelligence agent called Newton Hulls (Mackenzie Ward). Hulls charms his way into the confidence of several characters at the College, including Hyde's son Phillip (Simon Lack) who is experiencing a personal crisis concerning his commitment to the Navy. The resulting conflict between father and son is exploited by Hulls who seeks information about Hyde's whereabouts when he leaves for a secret meeting concerning the minefields. Hyde is nearly killed and when Hulls's true identity is discovered, suspicion falls on Phillip as the possible informant. But, and perhaps improbably, Phillip has so impressed Hulls with his loyalty to his father (he did not betray him) that he clears his name, in admiration for the young man who is then welcomed back by the College, reunited with his father and feels renewed commitment to his naval vocation.

Dufay's signature style of restraint, delicacy and pastel shades is indeed evident throughout the film. The subject-matter – life at the College and associated pastoral settings – lends itself well to the aesthetic developed by Dufaycolor of understated tastefulness which was often compared to what some considered the more vulgar, garish tendencies of Technicolor. As we have seen, the latter was not always the case, and judgments that repeated this criticism were often motivated by nationalist resentment at Hollywood's domination of British cinema culture. Yet there are perceptible differences between the two processes, as is made clear by a close analysis of *Sons of the Sea*. Grass appears as more yellowish than green and, although exteriors have clearly been shot in bright sunshine, with harsh shadows and even a tendency for a bleached-out

Sons of the Sea (Dufaycolor, 1939): ensign against the sky; Britannia against the sky

look, skies are seldom blue, and certainly not as one would expect in Technicolor. A low-angle shot of the red, white and blue ensign against a cloudy sky attempts colour contrast, but this still appears rather muted. A shot of a statue of Britannia against the sky is perhaps more striking. The exterior shots have the effect of communicating hot, summer days, but the grey/light skies evoke humidity in an overcast manner which can seem strange, even oppressive. The absence of a 'colour control' schema is evident on several occasions as with the white/cream suit and tie worn by Hulls at the beginning of the film. This is shown next to one of Alison's (Kay Walsh) pale yellow dresses, which flouts Kalmus's views on colour complements and contrasts. The suit does, however, have a symbolic function in that when Hulls is walking with Phillip they come across a ferret in the grass whose colouring resembles Hulls's light-coloured suit. Phillip remarks that ferrets are 'all right to look at but they're cruel little devils', prefiguring the revelation that Hulls is a spy and confidence trickster.

Interior settings, more difficult to shoot in Dufaycolor than exteriors, have an extremely limited colour range. The predominant impression is of browns and greys, almost sepia tones. Strong colours hardly appear; even the sports car featured in the film is a dark shade of maroon rather than bright red, and flags have muted, rather than bright reds and blues. Since the film has a naval theme, uniforms are worn by several characters. Yet coloured ribbons indicating decorations against the background of the uniforms hardly show up, in fact not nearly as well as, for example, they do in *The Life and Death of Colonel Blimp*, a Technicolor film discussed in a subsequent chapter which, although associated with restraint, has some striking colour shots. The lipstick worn by Alison, one of the few female characters in *Sons of the Sea*, is not at all bright red, contrasting starkly with, for example, Merle Oberon's more obtrusively rouged lips in *The Divorce of Lady X*, a film nevertheless noted for Technicolor 'restraint'. Although Alison is seen wearing red trousers on several occasions their saturation is inconstant between scenes. This is problematic for Dufaycolor, since such inconsistencies could have been less noticeable if the actress had worn a greater variety of costumes. In this way the film's realist address (she probably would not have changed her clothes that much) has taken precedence over the need to be alert to Dufay's potential shortcomings (why do the trousers look a little different across several scenes?). The muted appearance of lipstick and make-up, and less frequent display of female costuming have implications for the role of colour in contributing to specific representations of gender. Even though she is practically the only woman in the film Alison is not objectified, in fact the reverse since she is seen several times looking at the sailors through a telescope in the observatory with a masked shot of the men replicating her line of vision.

To take another example of how Dufaycolor differs from other processes, a shot of a bowl of fruit appears as quite 'restrained', particularly when one compares this with similar shots which were common in Technicolor films such as *Wings of the Morning*. In this particular shot from *Sons of the Sea* an orange has a darkish coloured skin, and a banana tends more towards

Sons of the Sea: Alison (Kay Walsh) showing Dufaycolor's rendering of red lipstick; Alison looking through a telescope; fruit bowl in Dufaycolor

green/dark yellow than one might expect. This is dangerous territory when viewing colour films, since objects known very well to the audience automatically provide a vivid basis for comparison when shown on the screen. Everyday knowledge notwithstanding, it is interesting to consider the extent to which audiences would have compared colour processes in 1939–40, since the number of Technicolor films shown in British cinemas had certainly not been great. But viewing *Sons of the Sea* today (restored by the British Film Institute in the 1980s), the number of observable differences from the better-known Technicolor norms are striking. The film bears out the perceptible strand of British screen colour considered desirable by many in the 1930s. Its release at the beginning of World War II was before the Japanese attack on Pearl Harbor in December 1941 that brought the USA into the war. This pivotal moment in Anglo-American relations provides a useful background political context for subsequent changes in intensity within debates about British vs American colour.

The Great Mr Handel is probably the least well-known British Technicolor feature of the wartime period. It is somewhat at odds with the others: it was not particularly successful at the box office, had a reputation for slowness and for not being particularly experimental with colour.[5] Claude Friese-Greene, the film's main cinematographer, had a history of experimentation with colour. In the 1930s he shot the colour sequences in *Radio Parade of 1935* in Dufaycolor, but he had little experience with Technicolor. Jack Cardiff was establishing a reputation as the British Technicolor expert and so shot the first reels of *The Great Mr Handel* and advised on the photography, with Claude Friese-Greene taking over as he became more fully acquainted with the process and experimented with low lighting for candlelit effects in interiors and to obtain a soft tone for exteriors. In Hollywood the film was appreciated for its 'subdued' shades, and Natalie Kalmus selected it for screening to guests who visited her home in Bel Air, which presumably indicated admiration for the film.[6]

The film's story of the composer's tortuous path towards the divine inspiration which resulted in the composition of 'The Messiah' established its predominantly serious and reverential tone. Although the colour evokes an overall impression of 'restraint' it is nevertheless used for key scenes such as when Handel is composing at night with bright colours and silhouetted figures visible in the background through the window, in a series of religious scenes which create a stained-glass effect. Intended to evoke the composer's creativity, they stand apart from the rest of the film's colour design. Using visually arresting shots to evoke musical creativity was a common stylistic strategy in biopics about composers, in this case intensifying colour to convey the fullest expression of Handel's artistic achievement. Costumes and sets are, however, subject to repetitious schemes, such as the red coats frequently worn by Handel and features such as red curtains which stand out against the overall pastel shades of the *mise en scène*. In all the film could be said to be typified by a limited palette – red, blue and gold – which nevertheless makes it an interesting experiment. As E. S. Tompkins noted: 'There is some variation in lighting and colour values from shot to shot and some rare cases of over-emphasised crude colouring; but these small imperfections merely draw attention to the general excellence of the rest of the production. Outstanding film.'[7] Another reviewer noted the co-existence of different schemes within the film: 'While full value was given where necessary to the essential bright colouration of scenes and dresses, this superficial brilliance did not outweigh the general tonal effect of the sober hues and low-lit scenes which afforded such aesthetic satisfaction to so many critics.'[8]

Claude Friese-Greene's involvement may have contributed to the overall tone of the colour, since in places it almost replicates the two-colour systems of previous periods of colour experimentation, and with which he was personally associated. The film's serious themes must also have been influential, linking the historical narrative with the present in its highlighting of the virtues of duty, perseverance and self-sacrifice. It is interesting that the next two British Technicolor films, *The Life and Death of Colonel Blimp* and *This Happy Breed*, were also identified primarily by their 'restrained' colour. Yet, as the following analyses demonstrate, this was never a straightforward indication of dullness, or denoting a particular *lack* of colour design and sensibility. What was emerging was a sustained experimentation with hue, saturation and accent in particular sequences and scenes, and these constituted the qualities that came to be identified with Technicolor films made in Britain.

THE LIFE AND DEATH OF COLONEL BLIMP: A 'BLACK AND WHITE FILM COLOURED'?

Colonel Blimp was surrounded by controversy on first release, not least because Winston Churchill attempted to halt production since he saw its caricature of bungling 'Blimpishness' (loosely based on the David Low newspaper cartoon figure first introduced in 1934) as threatening to morale.[9] In addition, an inappropriate poster campaign for its US release which implied that it was a bawdy romp struck entirely the wrong note for its effective marketing overseas, and claims that Theo, its sympathetic German character, rendered it pro-German meant that the film's aesthetic merits were overshadowed by its reputation as puzzling and unnerving.[10] Discussion of the film's Technicolor was hardly at the forefront of contemporary debate and the film has never been analysed entirely from this perspective. It is interesting, however, that *Colonel Blimp* is the second candidate for a major restoration of a Powell and Pressburger film championed by Martin Scorsese after *The Red Shoes* (1948) in 2009.[11] The wartime context of release is, however, crucial from many perspectives which as we shall see are important for an understanding of its deployment of colour.

Rather than being seen as a national cinematic aberration, *Colonel Blimp* has been appraised by Andrew Moor for in many ways conforming to the dominant myths of the Home Front and, in spite of its reputation for anti-realism, romantic sentiment and quirkiness, nevertheless including sequences that contain:

> key motifs of wartime British cinema, such as the London blackout and the mobilised woman. The film also undertakes an 'incorporative' mission, drawing together a new army to fight Nazism. It is therefore sympathetic to the over-riding ideology of its time … the film gestures towards representing a united nation, chronicling a shift from a once dominant form of leadership to a more broadly hegemonic sense of collaboration.[12]

In relation to film style, Moor's analysis identifies the film's hybridity and its foregrounding of different musical motifs to convey the fluctuating contours of debate between reactionary and progressive forces. These are also reflected in *Colonel Blimp*'s negotiation of the imperial adventure genre.

As far as colour is concerned, Moor references the work of cinematographer Georges Périnal who had worked on previous Technicolor films in the empire/adventure genre: *The Drum*, *The Four Feathers* (1939) and *The Thief of Bagdad*. Moor notes that: 'The bright colour code of Powell and Pressburger's film clearly reproduces Périnal's earlier style' rather than anticipating the more overtly symbolist colour experimentation associated with *A Matter of Life and Death* (1946) and *Black Narcissus* (1947).[13] Indeed, in his autobiography Michael Powell described *Colonel Blimp* as 'a conventional film, a black and white film coloured' which was approved of by Technicolor.[14] In the commentary (recorded before Powell's death in 1990) that was included in the Criterion Collection's DVD release of a restored *Colonel Blimp* in 2002, Powell, however, described it as a 'very colourful film'. Even so, discussion of the film's colour has been overshadowed by the cinematography of Jack Cardiff for Powell and Pressburger's more celebrated later experiments with Technicolor. Cardiff was employed on the film's second unit, and has commented on his successful lighting strategies and 'inserts' for particular scenes. He recalled, for example, his work on the time-compression scene in which Clive Candy's hunting trophies are displayed on a wall in his aunt's house:

> This particular insert was more interesting than usual. It was a drawing-room wall, on which there was a collection of stuffed animal heads, all with large branches of horns. It was difficult to light without casting multiple shadows, and I spent more time than usual arranging the lights.[15]

Perhaps because Cardiff's input was restricted to such examples and as far as his own career was concerned his work on *Colonel Blimp* resulted in an invitation from Michael Powell to shoot *A Matter of Life and Death*.

The film's colour has been neglected in comparison with the attention it receives in commentary on The Archers's other Technicolor films. But that is not to say that the colour was not remarkable or subject to a 'system' in *Colonel Blimp*, an idea which emerges as significant from sources such as art director Alfred Junge's writings on colour and by the occasional reviewer commenting on an 'uneven' use of Technicolor that was elaborate and spectacular.[16] While audience responses are difficult to recover, one of Mass

Observation's questionnaires from November 1943, asking people about their favourite films seen in the previous year, resulted in several naming *Colonel Blimp*, with female respondents in particular mentioning colour as distinctive. The comments describing this included: 'Almost perfect technicolour [*sic*] putting American colour to shame'; deploying a 'restrained' use of colour; 'the colour was the most pleasing of any I have yet seen'.[17] Rather than take these comments to indicate that the colour was unobtrusive and therefore relatively insignificant, I want to analyse exactly what was meant by an awareness that something different was going on in the colour design for *Colonel Blimp*. Martin Scorsese's commentary on the Criterion Collection DVD of *Colonel Blimp* similarly notes that the British deployment of Technicolor was different, in his view because of chemicals and water used in printing, as well as the lower exterior light levels creating a soft effect which was particularly suited to Périnal's cinematographic approach.[18] Indeed, when asked about the existence of a 'British School of Technicolor' many claimed that national differences were influenced by factors such as the light, the weather, the water and processing. Technicolor's Frank Littlejohn said that 'we found that the composition of the water had a damned important effect on the characteristics of transfer'.[19] It is plausible that these factors contributed towards an appreciation of British colour films that favoured a soft, restrained aesthetic. This was informed by aesthetic preferences and taste cultures found in other arts, particularly British traditions of landscape painting.

In 1942 the *British Journal of Photography* reported on proceedings recently published in the *Journal of the Society of Motion Picture Engineers* which described some of the overriding contemporary norms for Technicolor cinematography. The idea of a 'colour score' was described in the following terms: –

> The colour design of the sets and the selection of the sets and the selection of colour for costumes may be compared with a musical composition. Harmony and discord, brilliance and softness must all have attention for scenes which are to please the eye. Consequently the set colours must be chosen with care for hue, chroma, and value (which we shall interpret as meaning hue, saturation, and brilliance) having in mind the costumes to be used, the colour context in which the scene is placed, and the

requirements of the script. The plan finally adopted could be called the colour score and the Technicolor organisation have a Colour Control Department to advise upon this important aspect of their production.[20]

Colonel Blimp provides an opportunity to experiment with this approach, particularly in the presentation of a variety of values (lightness or darkness) and saturation (intensity of a colour).[21] As I shall argue, the film's complex narrative pushed it further, however, which supports contemporary observation that a different style of Technicolor was present.

Some precise observations about colour in *Colonel Blimp* came from the *British Journal of Photography*'s 'Colour Enthusiast' E. S. Tompkins, who observed that there was a carefully planned system for the film.[22] In his review of the film he noted in particular how the film's structure invited a different approach to colour in each section:

> The colourful Edwardian shots at the beginning of the retrospective part of the story are truly 'rich but not gaudy', a note which is carried into the German sequences which follow. There is a dramatic chilling change in colour values in the gymnasium preliminaries of the duel, where a blueness of décor and general lighting conveys the cold of the early winter morning, a cold which seeps off the screen out into the tense spaces of the auditorium. In the 1914–18 sequence the khaki of the uniforms is echoed by a general brownness and drabness of settings, which is very effective even though it may be slightly overdone.[23]

Indeed, *Colonel Blimp* presented Alfred Junge with the challenge of designing for Technicolor cinematography. When Junge was commissioned by the art periodical *The Artist* in 1944 to write about his craft, he described how *Blimp* gave him the opportunity to grapple with designing three different time-frames within the same film (1902, 1918 and 1942) as well as for colour. One set in particular demonstrated how Junge's designs were often inspired by a close study of character. The room kept for Clive Candy (Roger Livesey) in his aunt's house (which later becomes his own on the death of his aunt) was of crucial importance in all three periods covered by the film. A thread that runs through Candy's life is competition and hunting: as a child he wins trophies at school and collects butterflies; as he grows up his

The Life and Death of Colonel Blimp: colour and spatial design for the hallway

The Life and Death of Colonel Blimp (Technicolor, 1943): colour accent for 1902, 1918 and 1942

'treasures' become stuffed animals he has shot, hung as trophies of adventure on the wall. Junge's designs for the room include all these carefully planned details, showing other subtle changes in the room as time advances, such as the introduction of electric light instead of paraffin lamps, different furniture and redecoration. Junge decided not to go overboard on this last aspect because he considered that Candy's character would not favour modern design. He opted for tones of beige for the wallpaper, in order for the mounted stuffed animals' heads to stand out as important symbols of character which as we have seen were carefully shot and lit by Jack Cardiff.

Junge also noted that Technicolor needed very much to be taken into account during the design phase; for example, red colours would appear to be stronger, or furniture near a fire ought not to be too reddish 'as it would attract the eye too much'. The film has several shots of lit fires in fireplaces, and candles being lit on a table which draw attention to achieving the effect in colour. There is one recurring shot, for example, when Theo has dinner with Clive and his army friends just after the end of World War I, when we see candelabra with three lit candles obtrusively placed in the foreground of the shot. The focus of the scene is their conversation, but the eye is drawn to the candelabra as it dominates the table. However, in other instances Junge was concerned to privilege the demands of narrative and character over what might be easiest for Technicolor cinematography. When designing the hall in Candy's house, for example, he decided that 'it had to be just right in character with his small staircase leading up to the next floors … A more square shaped hall would be easier for action and lighting, especially as Technicolor needs stronger and more lamps, but to me we had to overcome all the difficulties to get the proper surrounding for the characters.' Junge avoided strong, florid colours and designed every set on a lower key than he expected the film to reproduce. Yet the colours nevertheless had to be interesting: 'I had to tempt the camera to make more of my colour scheme than the actual scheme itself did.'[24] As well as Junge's key input into designing the film's colour, there is evidence that Natalie Kalmus, credited for 'colour control' as with all Technicolor films of that period, worked on the script and completed a 'colour synopsis' in spite of the fact that she was at that time back in the USA.[25]

As Tompkins and Junge observed, the different time-frames created an opportunity to display different approaches to colour within the same film. From the very start, colour is distinctive with the tapestry behind the credit sequence, first seen in a close shot with the camera tracking out to reveal more of the characters, scenes and allusions, accompanied by a witty description of the Colonel changing its lettering from 'mortal' to 'immortal'. Khaki appears many times in the film, but rather than indicating drabness, as observed by Tompkins this is often contrasted with different colour details, as in the early scene of uniformed men racing their motorcycles shot from below against a vivid blue sky. The addition of red for lapels, decorations or insignia stands out against khaki, details that pervade even the World War I section of the film where the colour design is at its dullest and in which the red crosses on the nurses' uniforms serve the same punctuating, embellishing purpose. The first flashback to 1902 with its British and German locations and introduction of two major characters, Theo (Anton Walbrook) and Edith (Deborah Kerr), features more opportunities for colour detail and contrast. The first sight of Edith is particularly interesting. She is wearing a dark green coat with an ermine collar and lapels, which contrasts with her red hair. Her hat is in the same green, embellished on top with the shape of a bird, appears to lean onto her forehead, also in green, as a humorous, almost grotesque detail since it prefigures Clive Candy's proclivity for hunting.[26] Red continues the punctuating function of colour in the Hohenzollern Café sequence

with its red menus, musicians' uniforms and the woman serving drinks wearing a red blouse. Edith has a red silk bow in her hair, just showing underneath another of her elaborate hats. A correspondence with this accent occurs at the beginning of the duelling sequence when we see a close-up of the red code-book for duellists with its red cover.[27] In the first flashback also the German uniforms have bright red frontispieces, another detail which marks this section of the film as, in Tompkins's words, 'rich but not gaudy'. The costumes (designed by Joseph Bato) carry most of the colour interest as, for example, when Edith is visiting the nursing home and her green blouse is differentiated from the red and blue costumes which are worn by the other visitors and soldiers. Another instance is Edith's outfit when she is packing, just before Theo tells Clive that he loves her. She is wearing a blue skirt, a pink and white-striped blouse with a blue bow at the neck, and her belt is red and shiny. The colour of the belt in particular dominates the look of the scene because of its width and its shiny, reflective surface. It is as if the colour palette is becoming more and more vibrant towards the end of the section, to create a shock for the contrasting second flashback to World War I.

The opening of this section is immediately dark and with an almost bleached-out appearance. Khaki uniforms dominate, but Candy's is embellished with red lapels and the colours of his decorations. Andrew Moor has noted the resemblance between Junge's set of a deserted battlefield on Armistice Day and Official War Artist Paul Nash's paintings, which share a similarly monochrome palette.[28] Paul Nash would have approved of this approach, since his criticism of Technicolor features in the 1930s was that they failed to exploit 'the infinite variations of contrast', preferring the understated effects achieved by Cinecolor and Dufaycolor.[29] This accent definitely predominates until we move forward in time to the immediate postwar sequence which begins with a close-up of a newspaper headline from June 1919 announcing 'No More Khaki for Looms: First Peacetime Cloth for Bridal Gown'. This refers to the imminent wedding of Clive and Barbara (also played by Deborah Kerr) who, as the daughter of a West Riding mill owner, will have her bridal gown manufactured by the family firm. The following montage of shots showing the looms of a mill in action were designed to emphasise the coloured fabric worn by the woman operator, and to suggest that the production of khaki uniforms had given

The Life and Death of Colonel Blimp: our first sight of Edith (Deborah Kerr)

The Life and Death of Colonel Blimp: red accent in the Hohenzollern Café

Clive Candy (Roger Livesey) and colour accents within the restrained palette for 1914; shot from *Queen Cotton* (1941) interspersed into 1919 sequence in *The Life and Death of Colonel Blimp*. *Queen Cotton* image courtesy of Coats plc

way to the manufacture of more vibrant patterns.[30] This shot is actually taken from *Queen Cotton*, the instructional film produced in 1941 discussed in Chapter 5, on which Jack Cardiff had been Technicolor adviser. In *Colonel Blimp* a few shots from *Queen Cotton* are used to indicate a shift from wartime austerity in 1919 rather than when they were actually filmed in 1941. Our first sight of Barbara once again introduces a costume which is noticeable for its colour: a floral-patterned top in green and pink, which links her with the sequence's opening pastoral scenes. One particular scene featuring

this garment, when Barbara agrees to marry Clive, was filmed against an early example of coloured back-projection, which Powell noted was unusual for the time.[31] When Theo reappears as a prisoner, the German uniforms are grey-coloured and the prisoners' military hats have bright red bands. These contrast with the British khaki uniforms but rather than conveying an overall image of 'monochrome colour' they operate according to a variety of emphases in value, hue and saturation within, say, shades of grey and brown.

In the final sequence, which starts with the approach of World War II, Theo returns to Britain after the death of his wife and rejection by his two Nazi sons. When he makes his case to be allowed to stay in the country he is wearing a khaki-coloured coat, as if he has rejected Germany in every possible way (including sartorial) and showing his affinity with the English. Angela 'Johnny' Cannon (Deborah Kerr) wears a uniform, but her red lipstick again provides the colour addition which has by now become standard in the film. Even in scenes in which the colour palette is not that varied, as for example when Theo visits Clive in his house, the varieties of brown and grey create contrasts within a narrow range but which are nevertheless distinct as between the varied browns of leather belts, the wood-panelled walls, the patterned wallpaper, Angela's khaki uniform, her reddish hair and Theo's dark suit contrasted with Clive's striped woollen suit in different shades of grey.

An interesting colour detail in this final section was noticed by Tompkins:

> One small scene deserves mention for its intriguing use of colour for dramatic ends. The ATS driver [Angela] is seen driving her car up to traffic lights in the black-out. She tries to get over before the lights change to red. Her passenger [Theo] asks her about Colonel Candy and she starts to describe him enthusiastically, so much so that we see the light on the faces go through a whole cycle of colours before she becomes conscious of the signals again. This is a small but subtle scene which, like so many of Disney's cartoon touches, is completely dependent on colour for its effect.[32]

This is a small but important detail which testifies to Tompkins's alertness to colour in films of this period and when multiple viewings were not possible. The 'whole cycle of colours' is a bit misleading, since while green and red are certainly shown as reflected on Angela's face when she fails to jump the lights, the other incident involving lights in the scene is when a car approaches 'with a badly fitted mask' on its lights, creating a glare rather than a colour effect.[33] Michael Powell recalled the difficulties of creating the effect of the blackout for this scene, with the low light levels necessary to convey the realism of the incident.[34] Vibrant colour is also introduced when we see Angela later playing darts in the

The Life and Death of Colonel Blimp: colour effect with traffic lights; after the colour effect has passed

Roadhouse Café, Western Avenue. The scene is introduced by a close-up of a red and green juke-box, perhaps signalling the modernity with which she is associated and has begun to invade Clive's life. In this set most of the tables and chairs are red-painted, and the waitress is wearing a floral-patterned overall in red, green, white and pink shades. The film ends as it began, with the coloured tapestry which as Andrew Moor has observed serves as an emblematic register of the film's 'creative dialogue between the historical, the mythical and the topical, a stitched-together collocation of heterogeneous signs, jostling with and against each other'.[35] The same could be said for colour, as it too has contributed to the film's richness in terms of theme, address and structure. Grey jostles against brown, and red creates a through-line with its embellishing, arresting appearance in so many different scenes. It defies the

The Life and Death of Colonel Blimp: vibrant colours of the juke-box are highlighted

film's temporal divisions, however, since it appears in all three sections, mostly associated with military uniforms, but also with female costuming such as the scarf Barbara wears when visiting her new home in London, or even as seen on the capes of the actors in *Ulysees*, the play Clive goes to see in London on his return from Germany after he parts from Edith and Theo. Red lettering on wartime posters is also visible, as well as on the montage of copies of *Picture Post* which are shown to chart Clive's contribution to the war effort in the film's 1940s section. Such examples attest to the film's colour interest. Far from being 'a black and white film coloured', there is play with Technicolor which revises the notion that films which err on a 'restrained' approach lack chromatic density, contrast or design. This is also demonstrated in *This Happy Breed*, the next major British feature film to be released during the war.

THIS HAPPY BREED: THE COLOURS OF ENGLAND

As we have seen, critics would often praise British films for using colour in a non-garish, unobtrusive fashion and with an affinity to the dominant realist aesthetic of black and white, such as this comment on *This Happy Breed* which claimed Ronald Neame's cinematography 'experimented with the use of entirely muted tones to express the essential drabness of the lives of the people involved in the story'.[36] The association of British colour with realist codes gave it a *gravitas* that took advantage of high-brow,

modernist thinking on the aesthetic superiority of monochrome. On the other hand, as was the case with *Colonel Blimp*, realist colour was a specific style that used colour in a particular way, rather than rendering it unnoticeable. As Neame explained, the 'look' for *This Happy Breed* was a deliberate aesthetic choice to give the film a 'modern touch' and, 'in order to make Technicolor less glorious we exaggerated the age and shabbiness of everything; tidemarks round the bath, stains on the walls. With shades of grey and brown to "dirty down" the sets and costumes, I was able to light the picture so that everything looked drabber than normal.'[37] Even though realism was the declared goal, these comments demonstrate colour being used as an *active system*, rather than as an unobtrusive aesthetic style. And on closer analysis there are many instances of striking colour in the film which are all the more noticeable for their placement within a *mise en scène* otherwise dominated by less saturated and toned-down, pastel shades. For his first experience of working with Technicolor, Neame was supported by Guy Green as camera operator and Harold Haysom of Technicolor. Colour control was exercised by Joan Bridge on behalf of Natalie Kalmus.

Colour is far from absent, especially for decorations, flags, posters and costumes. Particularly in the first section of the film in the immediate years after the end of World War I, scenes of jubilant crowds cheering soldiers as they parade through London include colour vibrancy for flags (the Union Jack and Stars and

This Happy Breed (Technicolor, 1944): realist tones for the house interior

Stripes), as well for the coloured streamers being waved. Colour is emphasised when the final shot of the crowd scene cuts to a black-and-white image in a shop window. As the camera tracks out the image is surrounded by coloured flags in the display, and we see that the photograph is an advertisement for 'Tickler's Tours' of the battlefields. Such a stark contrast between colour and black and white emphasises the presence of the former even though in terms of narrative the switch is explained by the context of a wry comment on an early example of the war being commercialised. E. S. Tompkins was critical of some of the crowd scenes for failing 'to record the inevitable strangeness of crowd costume', but praised the film's cinematography and W. Percy Day's special effects.[38] There is a similar display of flags when the family visit the fair at Wembley and colour as decoration features as time moves onwards to Christmas 1925. Contemporary commentary was not at all specific, and even Neame's remarks about a bath with tidemarks are not borne out by the film in which no such shot appears. Also, there is never the impression that Ethel does not keep a tidy or clean house. But the specifics of the house are important in terms of colour, even though they are generally unobtrusive. Throughout the film the house has different wallpapers, to indicate the passing of time in a subtle way, as the patterns change with new trends in home decoration. While the patterns on the wallpapers are never very strong, they nevertheless are subtly coloured using contemporary designs which are evident in restored versions of the film.[39] Stronger colours show up well against them, making the *mise en scène* one in which colour is obtrusive through contrast and scoring. The inclusion of brightly coloured Christmas decorations, for example, makes such a contrast with the décor but with colour correspondences, however, present between the decorations and the costume of two major characters such as the colour blue resonant with Frank's tie and Ethel's cardigan.

The women's clothing has colour interest since there are consistent approaches for particular characters. Frank's mother Nora, and his daughter Queenie, for example, are generally associated with non-conformity. Nora always has a contrary opinion and at times meddles with intra-family squabbles. The first time we see her, when the family move into no. 17 Sycamore Road, she is wearing a dark blue coat and a hat with mauve and red flower decorations which contrast with Ethel's green suit

This Happy Breed: colour emphasis in a Christmas scene

with a plain, simple band on her hat in the same shade. In the first half of the film, when she is associated with rebellion, Queenie in particular wears stronger, more saturated colours than the other female characters, as when she wears a royal blue dress with a polka dot pattern on the collar and sleeves which contrasts with Sylvia's green suit. Queenie works in a dress shop and knows about fashion, even making her own dress for a Charleston competition. She is the film's 'modern woman' who defies convention by running off with a married man, to be reclaimed by Billy, the dependable sailor who waits for her to realise her mistake and with whom she is reunited, as well as with her family, by the end of the film. Queenie's dresses are never plain and in one scene we see her wearing a silk dressing-gown with flower patterns. This association with modernity, exoticism and difference are in marked contrast with her mother's outfits which are generally more practical and, particularly as the film advances in time, increasingly typified by greys and browns.

The film features several celebrations which invite the inclusion of colour. The post-World War I scenes have already been mentioned, but the various family weddings are occasions when 'best' clothes are worn and which create colour interest. The principle of colour design is evident. On occasion the colours of one character's costume will be 'reversed' with another – for example, as when Queenie's pink dress and blue hat are seen alongside Phyllis's blue dress and pink hat. During the General Strike marchers parade the streets with red placards, and a brief scene introducing Reg's impending marriage is conveyed by a close-up of a red advertisement for Bravington jewellers which he sees on the Tube. Another association between colour and modernity occurs with a close-up of a poster advertising *Broadway Melody* which is made all the more obtrusive since it appears just before we see an extract from the film in black and white. While the novelty of the sound film does not impress Sam, who finds it difficult to understand the American accents, Vi is enraptured. Yet presented in this way with a full-colour poster followed by the black-and-white talkie, it is surely colour that is being showcased here, rather than the sound film which by the time of *This Happy Breed*'s release was far less of a novelty.

As World War II approaches and Queenie has left and been rejected by her mother, the colours of the film become more muted; the range on display becomes more limited than in the film's earlier sections. Indeed, when Queenie returns with Billy she is wearing a black coat and we never see her again in quite the range of shades we have come to expect of her character. When she sails to Singapore to join Billy, now her husband, the colours of her clothes resemble those associated with Ethel (beige, grey, brown). But in spite of the film's considerable colour interest contemporaries concentrated on the drab tones used for the décor, particularly the shots of the empty house at the beginning which also close the film when the family has moved out; while similarly structured they nevertheless reveal subtle changes of décor to demonstrate the passing of time (the wallpaper in 1919 has a flower pattern whereas in 1939 it is patterned with light streaks of colour). American reviews commented on the 'different' look for Technicolor in *This Happy Breed*. It was described using such terms as 'misty Technicolor, which subdues rather than glamorises'; 'subtle and striking use of Technicolor, so different from the fashion in which it is employed by Hollywood cameramen', as well as comments about the colour being 'unobtrusive' and 'muted'.[40] One reviewer credited the film with having a superior colour style to that deployed in Hollywood, but no specific details were given as to what this might mean.[41] As we have seen, Neame's comments concentrated on décor rather than costume or other elements of *mise en scène*. He continued his experiments with colour for *Blithe Spirit*, a film which required a very

different approach to colour design, in view of its unusual subject matter, setting and characters.

BLITHE SPIRIT AND THE LURE OF TECHNICOLOR IN WARTIME BRITAIN

Blithe Spirit was the fourth of director David Lean's collaborations with Noël Coward, following *In Which We Serve* (1942), *This Happy Breed* and *Brief Encounter* (1945). *Blithe Spirit*, Coward's successful play, had been written in five days when he was in Wales after his London home had been damaged in the Blitz.[42] The film version of *Blithe Spirit* has not received much critical attention in comparison with David Lean's other films. By all accounts it was not a 'happy' picture for Lean who rather dismissed it as a 'high', polite upper middle-class comedy, one of Noël Coward's frothy drawing-room entertainments which in retrospect seems to be somewhat out of kilter with Lean's developing concerns.[43] Coward's verdict was that the film 'wasn't

Blithe Spirit (Technicolor, 1945): poster, 'In Blushing Technicolor'

entirely bad, but it was a great deal less good than it should have been'.[44] Rex Harrison plays Charles, a writer researching material for a book, who invites a local medium Madame Arcati (Margaret Rutherford) to his house to conduct a séance. The spirit of Charles's dead wife Elvira is unwittingly summoned and she materialises after the séance, but is only visible to Charles and not to his second wife Ruth. Much of the comedy is constructed around the disruption caused by Elvira's presence and Ruth's initial misunderstanding of Charles's strange behaviour before she accepts that Elvira has materialised. Outside New York the film did not do well in the USA – Sheridan Morley blamed posters announcing the film to be 'In Blushing Technicolor' ('Blushing' written in red, the implication being that not only was the film in colour but that it was also risqué, as indicated by the image of a scantily clad ghost) had erroneously pitched the film as 'misleadingly sexy … an orgy of tasteless publicity'. Other theories about the film's relative failure include the idea that the theme of death may have been insensitive at the end of World War II (it was released in May 1945, as the war was ending).

Yet *Blithe Spirit* merits reconsideration on many levels. There is much more to say about the film, particularly its striking colour design which contributes towards a distinctive Technicolor *mise en scène*.[45] Far from the film being of little interest in cinematographic terms, it is not a poor relation to its theatrical origins (in particular its play with viewpoint). Also, the charge that warrants closer scrutiny is that audiences were put off by the film's so-called insensitive treatment of death within a society comedy. This is not very convincing considering that Coward's play, written in 1941, was a very popular success as one of the longest-running plays in London theatre history.[46] Lahr notes how ghosts feature in other plays by Coward, particularly *Cavalcade*, *Post-Mortem* and *Shadow Play*, with *Blithe Spirit* further expressing his fascination with ghosts as a dramatic device which acquired even greater symbolic significance in the context of World War II when the reality of death was intensified. Lahr observes that:

> In making a spectacle of coming to terms with ghosts, the stage acts out an ancient shamanistic function of winning power over the dead. The ghosts who are materialised in *Blithe Spirit* are ghosts of ruthless passion and tyrannical

order, forces that vied as much for control of Coward's life as Charles Condomine's. In the battle between the ghostly suffocation of the wives and Charles's manipulative charm, the play becomes a paradigm of survivor guilt. In the end Condomine engineers a victory over the ghosts, and puts fear, guilt and mourning behind him.[47]

An important difference between the play and film, however, is that whereas in the play Charles survives the ghosts, in the film he joins them in the afterlife. In both play and film the materialisation of the ghosts highlighted the importance of addressing the reality of death, of the dramatic function of ghosts to disturb the status quo by awakening past memories and reviving buried passions.

As well as chiming with contemporary concerns, there is evidence that audiences liked the film which was relatively successful at the UK box office, although reviews were rather mixed.[48] In Josh Billings's annual survey of the British box office published in *Kinematograph Weekly* in December 1945, *Blithe Spirit* was high up the list and described as being 'in the money'.[49] According to Lean, the film was a big success in India.[50] There is anecdotal evidence that British audiences liked it, one of the reasons being its comedy and Technicolor cinematography. One respondent to J. P. Mayer's survey of cinema audiences in the 1940s wrote that '*Blithe Spirit*, not advertised as hysterically funny, made me nearly sick with laughter, the diologue [*sic*] was impeachable [*sic* – impeccable?], of course, the cast was chosen admirably, and it was filmed magnificently [*sic*].'[51] Colour is mentioned by another of Mayer's respondents as providing 'the added attraction of technicolour [*sic*]'; other positive comments include *Blithe Spirit* as: 'one of the best [films] I have ever seen'.[52] Even critics who otherwise were not that impressed with the film were intrigued by its use of colour. The *New York Times* reviewer, for example, picked-out the striking presentation of the ghost: 'In Technicolor, and a chartreuse make-up, with heavily rouged lips and matching finger nails, Kay Hammond is effectively eerie as the ghostly protagonist.'[53]

We are left, therefore, with some key questions that justify a closer look at *Blithe Spirit*. First, it is important to recognise the film's thematic connections with other films released at this time which draw on similar themes, preoccupations and ideas of 'the uncanny'. As I shall also demonstrate, the use of colour was a key register in the film's exploration of these themes, requiring a different approach to that which had been used for Lean's previous Technicolor film, *This Happy Breed*. *Blithe Spirit* can be related to British and American films released at around the same time dealing with themes of spirituality, split personalities and alter egos, which include the *Topper* cycle (USA, 1937, 1938, 1941) of popular comedies in which a character can hear and see ghosts. The theme was also evident in *Here Comes Mr Jordan* (USA, 1941), a comedy in which a man whose death is 'mistaken' is cremated prematurely but then permitted to live out his allotted span on earth by inhabiting the body of a corpse. *A Guy Named Joe* (USA, 1943) involves a dead pilot returning to earth to serve as guardian to his former girlfriend's new suitor. *The Ghost and Mrs Muir* (USA, 1947) featured the materialisation of a ghost when a woman buys a house which is haunted by its former occupant. Several British films were also preoccupied with the afterlife, death and the spirit world – for example, *The Halfway House* (1944) and *A Place of One's Own* (1945), a melodrama in which a woman is taken over by the spirit of a dead person who occupied the house in which she is living. Perhaps the boldest film of all which features *both* death and the afterlife was Powell and Pressburger's *A Matter of Life and Death*, in which a pilot whose plane has crashed hovers between life and death as a celestial court decides whether he ought to be permitted to live on earth with the woman he loves. Placing *Blithe Spirit* in relation to these films makes it less of an oddity, less of a stage-bound adaptation and more in tune with wider prevailing cultural preoccupations.

With these films in mind, it is useful to note that the war and immediate postwar years were characterised by a revival of spiritualism and concern about the individual's battle to maintain a coherent, stable identity after the societal strains and psychological fractures caused by World War II. There had been a similar upsurge of interest in spiritualism after World War I. The 1930s saw the 'high water mark' of the Spiritualist movement, with a growth in the number of churches affiliated to the Spiritualists' National Union, as well as the formation of many local book clubs and 'unofficial' groups. During World War II the movement experienced a number of setbacks through men leaving to serve in the forces; wartime disruptions to regular meetings and availability of venues, and a loss of confidence among members when predictions about another war being prevented proved to be false. In addition there were prosecutions of spiritualists believed to be bogus, one of the most publicised cases occurring in 1944 when medium Helen Duncan was imprisoned for nine months for 'pretending to communicate with deceased persons to deceive and impose on certain of HM subjects'.[54] In this context the figure of Madame Acarti becomes all the more fascinating for her resolute belief in the afterlife as her enthusiasm for her 'talent', personal conviction and eventual success in banishing the spirits is demonstrated with affection in *Blithe Spirit*. This is contrasted with sceptic Charles Condomine's calculating move to use her in his experiment only to discover that ghosts do exist and that he cannot banish the past or feelings of guilt. As Lahr observes, Charles is 'a modern man' who 'displays the estrangement of the community of the living from the community of the dead', an attitude he is forced to revise.[55]

Blithe Spirit was the fourteenth British feature film to use Technicolor. It can be related to early Technicolor in the UK in its affinities as a society comedy with Korda's *The Divorce of Lady X*, and for its tendency towards experimentation with hue and saturation. This is all the more striking in Britain where social realism was widely accepted as the defining characteristic of 'quality' cinema. Similar comments were made about *Blithe Spirit*, filmed by Neame and along the lines of his camera never escaping 'into a wallow of "glorious" Technicolor. The pastel suggestiveness, the subduedness of the color so completely attuned to the undertones of the piece, are an object lesson in Technicolor's employment.'[56] In his Technicolor cinematography Neame was concerned to achieve as much contrast as possible without over-accentuating colours when not appropriate. The latter was a tendency of the process as Neame explained:

> In black and white, if negative contrast is increased the blacks look more black and the whites look more white, shadows go heavier and highlights stronger. In colour, something else happens as well – the reds look more red, blues look more blue, pink faces look more pink … and before you know where you are you are faced with very glorious Technicolor.[57]

Blithe Spirit: colour and nostalgia for the Condomines' house

Blithe Spirit: Madame Arcati (Margaret Rutherford) at the séance

He claimed that this was tolerated in Hollywood since 'they are prepared to sacrifice more subtle tones of colour for clarity of vision'.[58] The lighting required for Technicolor was very high key (using a key light of 800 foot candles as opposed to the usual 100 foot for black and white). One of the respondents in J. P. Mayer's contemporary studies of audiences wrote that colour in *This Happy Breed* and *Blithe Spirit* was,

> streets ahead of the American … the colours blended so perfectly in every way that it made you want to see them through twice just for the colour alone. There were no blinding and dazzling conglomerations of colours here, no ultra tanned specimens of man and woman-hood, no red, yellow, or mauve and green stripes to insult your colour sensitivity, here was the beautiful house, the sunlit lawns, not too green, but just right to bring back a terrific nostalgia for the country.[59]

This comment is striking for its recognition of a colour system operating in both films and of the need to study them closely to gain a full appreciation of how – and here the respondent must be referring to *Blithe Spirit* – colour can evoke nostalgia as well as exhibit a style considered to depart from the Hollywood model. Yet, despite enthusiasm for the films having 'no blinding and dazzling conglomerations', colour in *Blithe Spirit* was generally more saturated than in *This Happy Breed*, as is clearly evident with the experimentation with hues of

green for Elvira and Ruth, as well as for flowers which are an important element of the film's *mise en scène*. There was also experimentation with shooting the séance scenes in flickering firelight when Neame used a lower-key light than usual for Technicolor (500 foot candles instead of 800), 'but the effective light was reduced to about 400 foot candles by the use of paraffin torches held in front of the lamp to create flicker'.[60] Thus, this scene abandons the Technicolor cinematographer's more typical aim to banish shadows, in this case *accentuating* them in order to convey the dramatic atmosphere necessary for the staging of the séance. Madame Acarti, wearing a red dress, turns off the lights so that the firelight creates flickering shadows on the back wall. As she moves out of view to the other side of the room her own shadow forms a large silhouette on the wall; her corporeality has been transformed into a dark, spectral vision in seconds. In this way, as the red dress changes into a black shape, the intrusion of Technicolor and its mutable qualities appropriately convey the film's thematic preoccupation with the fantastic, the uncanny and otherworldliness.

While Lean was bound to the contractual arrangement with Technicolor to utilise the colour consultancy service provided by Natalie Kalmus and Joan Bridge, as with many other directors and technicians, he was dismissive of their expertise.[61] Yet some very typical Technicolor norms are used in the film. As we have seen in Chapter 4, Natalie Kalmus's

Blithe Spirit: Elvira (Kay Hammond) proves her materialisation by moving a vase of flowers

article on 'color consciousness' guided the application of Technicolor for many decades.[62] In this schema green is a 'cool', 'retiring' colour. She acknowledged, however, that hues can change a colour and its suggestion, so there is leeway in these 'types' which is clearly the case with green and, as noted above, its juxtaposition with another colour such as red, which is very evident in *Blithe Spirit*. Hitchcock, for example, used a jade-green (pale jade) to suggest ghostliness in a number of films, most strikingly in *Vertigo* (1958). His choice was influenced by his recollection of the use of green light on the London stage as being associated with the appearance of ghosts and villains. Allen argues that this particular use of jade is remarkable because 'although green, jade is a green that has been crossed with a blue to render it cool and decidedly unlike the earth tones that green customarily evokes'.[63] In this sense, green displays a strange dualism which can be likened to the uncanny in that it can combine two apparently contradictory elements, acquiring a double semantic capacity to mean its opposite, signifying at once life, nature, earthiness *and* ghostliness, other worlds and death. Elvira is the embodiment of this dualism when Charles calls her 'ethereal, not quite of this world', while, as we have seen, Ruth describes her as 'earthy'.

As Eisenstein observed in his writings on colour which insist on how colour meanings fluctuate according to their deployment within different filmic contexts, green 'is directly associated with the symbols of life – young leaf-shoots, foliage and "greenery" itself – just as firmly as it is with the symbols of death and decay – leaf-mould, slime, and the shadows on a dead face'.[64] We see both associations in *Blithe Spirit* with the garden's verdant, 'natural' green lawn displayed prominently the morning after the séance, which contrasts markedly with Elvira's apparitional, green-tinged costume. In its embodiment in the character of Elvira, green forms a structuring design for the film. In relation to questions of viewpoint and point of view, it becomes an excessive register, almost present by association with the uncanny when Elvira is not visible to Ruth, and also when she is not literally present but continues to haunt Charles. The availability of multiple meanings attributed to a colour in the film, and its association with a female character, is also consistent with cultural constructions of femininity as quixotic, 'unknowable' and haunting.

As noted above, colour juxtaposition is used in *Blithe Spirit* with colour complements red and green. As Kalmus observed, when this happens 'each color tends "to throw" the other toward its complement – the juxtaposition of the colours makes each one more vivid: when any two colors are placed together, the first emphasises in the second the characteristics which are lacking in the first'.[65] Colour is used to stand in for Elvira, as in the striking scene when Charles asks Elvira to pick up a vase of flowers to prove that she really has materialised as a ghost. The choice of object to stand in

Blithe Spirit: Ruth (Constance Cummings) wearing a green dress with red embellishment

Blithe Spirit: Elvira (Kay Hammond) plays games with her materialisation in a bedroom scene to confuse Ruth

for her is significant in that cut flowers are briefly resplendent before dying. Elvira's materialisation is also a reminder of the uncanny co-existence of life and death which Charles and Ruth are forced to confront and eventually accept. In these shots we see the flowers from Ruth's viewpoint and then from Charles's, in the latter case Elvira is present and Ruth's blue costume stands out as contrasting with Elvira. Elvira's green and red appearance (green hues used for ghostly effect; red for nails and lips) is not commented on by Charles, but the colour associations are passion (red) and death (green). This has an enhanced uncanny resonance when for the séance Ruth wears a green dress with red embellishment, almost in sartorial anticipation of Elvira's materialisation and the film's questioning of boundaries between life and death. This colour link between the two women suggests that in spite of their differences they are often doubled. There is even a suggestion earlier in the film when Charles and Ruth are talking about Elvira that to obtain Charles's fullest expression of love his wife would need to be dead, as Ruth comments when talking about Elvira, 'If I died?', just before she puts on her green dress for the séance. In addition, the women are often shot together by over-the-shoulder shots which link them in intriguing ways. When Ruth wears a dress that is completely red, however, this is commented on by Elvira as being very much in bad taste. In one scene when Charles cannot tell Ruth that Elvira is laying on the bed he puts Ruth in the ridiculous position (to him and to

the audience) of talking to a vacant chair beside the bed, while Elvira looks on in amusement. In this case Elvira claims the upper hand in both sartorial and spiritual matters. It is as if Ruth's choice of the red dress is a vain attempt to 'trump' Elvira by showing her anger; in essence they conduct their conflict through colour. It is worth noting, however, that even in her choice of red Ruth is not entirely divorced from associations with Elvira since she has red nails and lips, and Madame Arcati's reddish costume worn early in the film can also be equated with the spirit world. The red and green colour 'doubling' is in anticipation of when Ruth herself becomes a ghost and of how she and Elvira both are summoned back to the afterlife when Madame Arcati finally succeeds in effecting their dematerialisation. In a final, witty twist, the conflict through colour at least is apparently over when all three are united at the end of the film (which does not occur in the play in which Charles does not die but on his return to the house is reminded by crashing vases and pictures that the women continue to haunt him). The afterlife has triumphed in the film's final shot of Elvira, Charles and Ruth sitting on a wall, equally bathed in bleached-out grey/white/ greenish hues.

In conclusion, *Blithe Spirit* is extremely significant as a wartime colour feature in terms of its relation with other films of the period about spirituality, death, the uncanny, character doubling and questions of point of view. Its colour is distinctive and an essential part of the film's address, with many examples of changing hues, deep saturation and obtrusive design through colour. While *This Happy Breed* has tended to dominate discussion of David Lean's early colour films, *Blithe Spirit* was the film which, in keeping with its fantastical premise, deployed colour to spectacular effect. It, thus, deserves to be located not as a poor relation to British social realist drama, but as an example of the 'lost continent' of British films which eschewed realism in favour of horror, gothic fantasy and the uncanny. Its colour design is also striking at a time when experimentation with Technicolor was notable in other non-realist films, including Gainsborough's *Jassy* (1947) and *Blanche Fury* (1947), Powell and Pressburger's *Black Narcissus* (1947) and Ealing's *Saraband for Dead Lovers* (1948), all of which support the idea that there was a particularly distinctive usage of Technicolor in British films.[66] When 'colour enthusiast' E. S. Tompkins saw *Blithe Spirit* it is no surprise that he appreciated its technical experimentation both for its 'Englishness' and as a 'dazzling series of scenes in colour'.[67] While *Blithe Spirit* clearly accorded with some of Natalie Kalmus's observations on 'color consciousness' it extended them by exploring a life/death dualism that is paradoxically embodied in the materialised ghost of Elvira. As we have seen, the character's appearance at a key moment in the film causes a central narrative disruption which is in large part associated with the colour of her costume and continues to constitute an anarchic, troubling presence throughout the rest of the film. It is worth pointing out in this context that a lead female character would normally never wear the same costume for an entire film, as Elvira does in *Blithe Spirit*, thus according the particular choice of grey/green as significant in its repetitious appearance. In addition, Elvira's excessively pale facial make-up is also at odds with Technicolor's claim to render complexions of 'natural' beauty for lead female stars.[68] Far from demonstrating the 'blushing' Technicolor claimed in advertising to typify the film, Elvira's skin tones are ashen and in keeping with her general demeanour of ghostliness. In combination with the film's central narrative meditation on the afterlife and the uncanny, in *Blithe Spirit* grey and green are therefore fully expressive of the problematic enterprise of separating life from death and, in the spirit of Eisenstein, of equating a colour with a single, unchanging cultural meaning.

WESTERN APPROACHES: SELLING PROPAGANDA IN COLOUR

The protracted production context of *Western Approaches*, the Technicolor documentary-drama directed by Pat Jackson and shot by Jack Cardiff about 'The Battle of the Atlantic', has been documented fairly extensively.[69] Of particular note is Anthony Aldgate's detailed discussion of how the Treasury funded the film after Ian Dalrymple, head of production at the Crown Film Unit, persuaded Jack Beddington, director of the Ministry of Information's Films Division, to shoot the film in Technicolor, even though this choice made the film more expensive and difficult to shoot.[70] One of the key arguments deployed by Dalrymple was that colour 'sells propaganda', making the following points in a memorandum to Beddington written in January 1942:

1. Colour is still sufficiently a novelty to attract patronage. In other words, it sells propaganda.
2. The first British *naval* subject in Technicolor will attract enormous notice.
3. For the Adminalty's purpose … colour is used considerably for recognition.
4. Colour will have a most salutary effect on revenue.
5. Films of the sea shot round these shores are usually drab to look at.
6. In propaganda films, colour automatically adds 100 per cent value – due to uniforms, flags and other patriotic emblems, insignia etc.
7. It will be particularly useful to distribute the film in the United States.[71]

Although the film was not released until 1944, the various stages of its pre-production history revealed key developments towards the official acceptance of colour as an aid to propaganda in wartime. In the early stages of discussion private financing was a strong possibility from the Rank Organisation, but the decision was taken that the film would be funded entirely by the Treasury. Officials were not only persuaded by the appropriateness of colour for the subject but also by its potential to increase profits both at home and overseas. But the film did not come cheaply, with costs escalating hugely during production from the first direct-costs estimate of £16,000 to £86,292. The reasons for this were because the film ended up being longer than originally planned;

there were many delays during production; labour costs for the merchant seaman increased during location shooting; studio work was also involved; and the film was in colour. Although precise figures do not exist, it was a clear success at the box office and with critics which contributed to its reputation as one of the most popular wartime propaganda films.

Jack Cardiff's account of filming *Western Approaches*, in which he described the experience as 'the most despairing struggle a film unit ever had', details the many delays, seasickness and difficulties of recording sound with the auxiliary lightweight blimp for the Technicolor camera:

> This emergency blimp is the *bête noire* of any cameraman who has ever used it, as, being light and abbreviated for soaring on a crane or being carried up rocky mountains, it is fitted in one piece, like a hat, over the camera, and laboriously strapped together. For the most trifling operation like changing a view finder matt, it all has to come off again. This is fidgety enough on land, but at *sea* in a rolling lifeboat ...[72]

Due to Pat Jackson's work on the script, the film's story was in essence a tribute to merchant seaman, with its story of the rescue of twenty-two men adrift in the mid-Atlantic after their ship has been torpedoed.[73] The reason the film was popular was in large part because of its suspense element: the survivors from the *Jason* wait in their lifeboat to be rescued by the *Leander*, a ship which has picked up their distress signal. But the German submarine has also picked up the signal and waits for the ship in order to achieve another sinking. The men in the lifeboat become aware of the submarine and attempt to warn their rescuers of the trap which awaits them. They send warning signals to the *Leander* which dodges the first torpedo. But it then is hit by a second, and the men abandon ship except for the captain and some of the sailors. The U-boat surfaces when it believes the ship to be totally abandoned and the remaining men on board the *Leander* sink the submarine. The survivors from both ships are then taken on board the damaged *Leander* which is joined by the convoy. At the film's conclusion the fate of the Germans on the U-boat, who we see jumping into the sea, is unknown.

The actors were real seamen, which gave the film an authentic sensibility. The lifeboat scenes were shot off the coast of Wales near Holyhead; there was also location shooting in the Atlantic, at the docks of New York, as well as in Fishguard and Liverpool. At every turn the crew was faced with obstacles. Cardiff found it difficult to film in such a range of weather conditions – sometimes skies would be blue and on other occasions dull:

> Now a person seen up against a summer's blue sky, bathed in radiant sunlight, is, to use a technical term, a pushover; but take away the radiant sun and blue sky, and an unrecognisable silhouette is smudged against the grey horizon. On groups of seamen this was just right for atmosphere; but on a close-up I could not get enough exposure to see who it was, unless I shot with the lens wide open – but then that over-exposed the sky behind.[74]

Varying weather conditions added to these problems, leading Cardiff to experiment with the incandescent (orange) lamps. In normal usage these had a blue filter added so that the yellow light became white, but when the weather was dull he removed the blue filter. To offset the orange he over-exposed the negative 'to clean the dirty grey sky to a white one, and allowing for the laboratory to print on the blue side to correct the complementary yellow, so making the white sky blue, I was able to save waiting so long for sunshine'.[75] The length of time it took to shoot the film (six months for the lifeboat scenes) also created difficulties, since tanned complexions in summer became less so in winter months, even though in screen time far less time had passed. Filming at sea meant that the camera equipment needed to be protected, salt water being particularly dangerous and liable to cause corrosion. Cardiff's recollections of using the camera are particularly vivid:

> The Technicolor camera is the swanky apotheosis of movie machines, bred in million dollar Hollywood, delicately coloured, with superb high-precision machinery and a prism which is set to a fraction of an inch and diligently watched for the most microscopic speck of dust, which would show as a large coloured blob on the screen. This prism is always placed, with tense caution and bated breath, into the camera, keeping a perfect balance while doing so. This meticulous operation was a sight to be remembered in a lifeboat on stormy seas. Reloading the camera with fresh film was always a nightmare, with the

ubiquitous gremlins having glorious fun, making the boat
heave right over and throwing gallons of water over us as
we staggered drunkenly about, lifting the blimp off and
threading up the film somehow under a flapping
tarpaulin.[76]

Other tales of the difficulties of the film's production
include a broken mast, induction problems with
electrical cables, the drifter accompanying them ahead
appearing in the shots and working in the dangerous
Atlantic waters in wartime.

When filming on the cargo ship to New York the
shortage of available Technicolor cameras and the
dangerous circumstances of the voyage meant that
Cardiff had to shoot the monopack film using a black-
and-white camera. Jackson referred to the stock as
'untried' and 'unsatisfactory', as well as there being
problems matching the scenes shot with monopack and
those using the Technicolor three-strip camera.[77] There
were delays in printing and Technicolor 'had become
thoroughly disillusioned with their experiences over the
film', so much so that Kay Harrison informed
Beddington that monopack stock would not be offered
to any more productions until after the war.[78] The
problems mainly resulted from the stock's need for very
precise temperatures when travelling to be processed.
Jackson recalled:

We could only send what we'd exposed from New York.
Well, so that meant that the aircraft taking it to Los
Angeles was going to at least stop at two aerodromes, in
the temperature which would probably rise to hundreds in
the sun, and they weren't going to look after this very
carefully, however refrigerated it was. In point of fact, we
lost about 30% of the Monopack.[79]

The damage to the stock resulted in magenta streaking.
With monopack the single strip was a form of
Kodachrome which at that time could only be processed
in Hollywood. Darrel Catling described the entire process
as had applied to his film *English Village*, but which would
have been the same for *Western Approaches*. Catling's
account is worth quoting in its entirety since it provides a
detailed description of the procedures involved:

After processing the strip becomes a reversal positive in
colour. From this a 'print' is made on negative stock

(being colour sensitive) and reversed, to make it a positive.
This black and white cutting print is sent to us in
England, together with the pilots. Pilots are short lengths
specially shot at the end of each scene, and subsequently
separated so that colour prints can be made from them.
They are used as a guide both to the cutter, and to the lab
technicians when ultimately grading (or timing, as they
call it) before making the matrices, and the eventual
answer print.

In monopack the pilots could be chopped off the
colour master and used just as they are, but this would
afford no guide as to the eventual colour resulting from
matrix printing. So separation negatives are made from
these sections of the colour master, matrices made from
the negatives, and the colour pilots proper from the
matrices – just as in the three-strip shooting principle.

When the black and white print has been cut in
England it is returned to America where the colour master
is matched to it, and the separation negatives made from
this matched master. The matrices are then made in the
normal way. Next, a black-track answer print is made; this
is a print in colour, but with no sound. The colour print,
and the matrices, are then sent to England. After this we
record the commentary, and the music, synchronise the
two tracks, dub them to make a mixed track, together
with the colour print, to Technicolor's English laboratory,
and they (already having the matrices) proceed to make a
combined print in colour.[80]

This meant that although monopack was an advantage
in replacing the heavy, 'special' three-strip camera there
were considerable delays at that time and these were
made all the more difficult in wartime. Jack Cardiff
considered monopack to be inferior to three-strip since
it had a 'decidedly blue bias necessitating correction in
the lab'.[81] Adrian Cornwell-Clyne also considered that
monopack had not lived up to expectations.[82] A flaw in
the final reel of *Western Approaches* revealed flare in a
close-up shot. This was objected to by Technicolor,
but Dalrymple decided not to take their advice to shoot
the scene again but to proceed with release, in view of
the long delays already incurred during production
and so that the film could play its fullest role as war
propaganda.[83] The film was eventually printed and
released, nearly three years after the initial idea to
film a record of 'The Battle of the Atlantic' had
been mooted.

The colour is significant in *Western Approaches*, not least for the different shades of blue for the sea, which was recognised at the time as adding depth and visual relief to what might otherwise have been dull black-and-white images.[84] Indeed, the ability of Technicolor to work effectively in exterior settings is announced from the film's beginning, when the pink titles are printed against a cloudy sky and the letters change to red as the sky in the background gets darker into the night. As the clouds pass from the left-hand side of the frame to the right, a sense of momentum is created, in effect, establishing the dominant colour tones for the rest of the film which are blue, grey and black with touches of red for particular objects which provide contrast. Indeed, the scenes at sea dominate the film, using colour contrasts sparingly; but, when evident, they appear as striking – for example, a shot of a wounded sailor with a bloodied bandage on his head, the blue sea contrasted with a sailor's buff coat, the red on the ship's flag and a red fire hydrant. A spectacular sunset is also a feature marked by its red colour, which is followed by a succession of blue-bathed night shots which created a visually stunning contrast. The latter is notable as a display of colour but it is placed strategically in the narrative since it comes just before the men in the lifeboat hear the nearby submarine charging its batteries and a little later the U-boat spots the lifeboat through the periscope. The spectacular sunset and blue night shots therefore act as the closure of the film's opening section, before the suspense narrative is established. Other scenes stand out – for example, New York in the fog, as viewed from the convoy setting out on its transatlantic voyage. Interiors are also interesting for their blend of colours, as in the scene in New York when the officers discuss the convoy at a long table, with their uniforms providing colour interest for decorations, much in the same way that was observed in *Colonel Blimp* and also appreciated by E. S. Tompkins in his review of *Western Approaches*.[85] The circumstances of its production on location for most of the time at sea meant that even though credited for 'colour control' it is unlikely that Natalie Kalmus would have had much, if any, input into the colour design.

Colour was mentioned by many reviewers. Bosley Crowther of the *New York Times* wrote that *The Raider* (the film's US title) was 'a gripping re-enactment' whose colour 'renders the sight of sea and shipping, of the

Western Approaches (Technicolor three-strip and monopack, 1944): shades of Technicolor blue for the sea; sunset shot; contrasting night-time shot

derelict lifeboat and the vessel's crew, all the more real and impressive, for the colour is exceptionally good'.[86] William Whitebait's review in the *New Statesman* criticised the unevenness of the colour in some sequences, 'so that a picture postcard blue may suddenly intrude among more subtle graduated shots'.[87] This is indeed noticeable in sections of the film – for example, there are distinct differences between shots in their sky tones when the men in the lifeboat first see the U-boat's periscope above the sea's surface and the *Leander* in the distance. Since the men are stranded in the lifeboat, it is, however, possible to view these contrasts in a positive way in the sense that they convey something of the seemingly unending endurance that they are suffering as they wait to be spotted by a rescue ship, day after day and night after night. In this reading customary temporal regimes are upset which makes the sky contrasts create an effect which is not just about 'mistakes' in matching the shots. When reviewed by E. S. Tompkins the uniformity question was examined with the following conclusion:

> The results are far better than one would imagine possible … There are occasional lapses, but most of them are of such an incidental nature that they pass unheeded. No ordinary cinemagoer, for example, will be disturbed by the sudden realisation that the out-of-focus sea in the background in one or two of the dramatic shots of the gun duel between the *Leander* and the U-boat is far bluer than the sea looks in any of the general shots. There is no serious mixture of shots with and against the light, and there is enough evidence of real care in matching weather and light so as to get a reasonable and acceptable uniformity in colouring.[88]

Writing in the *News Chronicle*, critic Richard Winnington considered the colour to be an achievement, particularly in its relation to sound:

> I have seen this film three times and its quality becomes more marked with each viewing. It is perhaps the feel of the sea itself evoked at moments with an exquisite blend of colour, sound and shape – the flapping of a sail, the cry of a bird, the clanking of chains, the elusive changing face of the Atlantic. In this delicate use of sound, embracing at times the best Technicolor effects of the sea ever photographed, lies perhaps the film's great freshness.[89]

This assessment indeed captures the film's lyrical combination of sound, music (composed by Clifton Parker) and colour image.

Dalrymple had been proved right that colour sells propaganda, not least to the funders. But apart from its colour interest *Western Approaches* was a successful film because of a variety of factors. The parallel scenes of the three locations (the lifeboat, the *Leander* and the U-boat) create high suspense. The shots are not over-long, providing short scenes of the men interacting with each other. Often shot in close-up, as with the various vignettes of the sailors at leisure on the *Leander* or on the lifeboat, the men are presented as 'types' in the manner of Eisenstein's use of *typage*. Since they were not professional actors this suited the film's documentary feel without stretching their capabilities to deliver long lines of dialogue. In addition, the recurring shots through the U-boat's periscope assisted the suspense narrative as they provided a striking visual linkage with both the lifeboat and the *Leander*. As a learning experience, it was quite unlike the films Jack Cardiff had previously shot, even though he was well used to location shooting from the *World Windows* series. As he put it:

> As films go, although I have taken my camera all over the world: on live volcanoes, in fever-ridden jungles, scorched deserts, and on the perishing heights of the Himalayas, I have never had a job that was so onerous and nerve-breaking. I think I agree with one of our seamen who has been torpedoed already in this war. He said, quite seriously, that he would rather be torpedoed again and really cast adrift in a lifeboat, than have that film experience again.[90]

This may be a rather extreme view, but in later accounts Cardiff also dwells on the uncomfortable physical and practical difficulties he experienced while shooting the film.[91] Despite the problems experienced by the crew during production, and the delays caused by processing the monopack stock, it is without doubt one of the most significant Technicolor films to have been produced by a British team during World War II.

HENRY V: PROPAGANDA, COLOUR AND ENTERTAINMENT

The link between propaganda and colour was probably most evident in *Henry V*. While the film's production history has been researched by scholars, including its origins, high budget, role as wartime propaganda and box-office success in Britain and abroad, the contribution of colour has not been considered as a subject in itself.[92] Laurence Olivier was released from national service to star (a request denied to Powell and Pressburger when they wanted him for *Colonel Blimp*) and subsequently direct the film, indicating its perceived high propaganda value in governmental circles. Olivier had not made a film in colour previously, and the cinematographer, Robert Krasker, was also new to colour. The credits do not reference the colour control service of Natalie Kalmus in the usual fashion, but the film nevertheless owes its distinction in large part to its colour cinematography. Krasker was assisted by Jack Hildyard who had also worked as camera operator on *The Divorce of Lady X* and *The Mikado*, so there was certainly expertise in filming with colour, and Hildyard's experience working on these earlier films would appear to have been influential. Indeed, the film was generally considered to be a triumph for Technicolor. E. S. Tompkins reviewed it from the perspective of colour and made his usual astute observations, such as identifying different schemes for the English and French settings:

> When the King goes to Southampton a transparency device is used to link the makebelieve of the Globe with the more modern makebelieve of the large-scale motion-picture set. The settings from this stage onwards, in spite of their mingling with outdoor scenes, have an air of very consistent and most telling artificiality about them. The embarkation and the siege of Harfleur are both in this key. With the first scene at the French Court we are introduced to a different colour scheme, all high-key and in pastel shades. The contrast with the English colouring is pointed and is conveyed in Technicolor of both types, each perfectly uniform in quality. There is further contrast in the night scenes in the two camps, all of which retain their individuality as French or English in their colour treatment, even though in low-key.[93]

The film of course provides many other occasions to display colour, particularly the battle scenes; regalia of the horses; coloured flags shot from below against deep blue skies; painted tents, etc. When first released in the USA in 1946 reviewers commented on the Technicolor, with some claiming that the film was superior to a Hollywood production, as the *New Yorker* wryly observed: 'Even the horses are more tastefully dressed than most of the girls in a Hollywood spectacle.'[94] The association of British Technicolor films with a quality, 'heritage' aesthetic is clear from this comment, and recalls the appreciative comments on Dufaycolor's reproduction of the horses' coats in the Coronation film discussed in Chapter 3. Indeed, this anticipates the heritage films identified by Charles Barr and Andrew Higson as being of fundamental importance in British film-making.[95] These were identified with precisely the qualities that critics heralded as marking British cinema's coming of age during World War II: 'At last there was a national cinema able to exploit effectively those two distinctive objects of pride, British understatement and the rich British heritage.'[96]

While Tompkins's remarks are a good guide to aspects of *Henry V*'s colour design there is more to be said on the variants used and how in this particular context colour certainly sells propaganda. The subject-matter – with military regalia requiring colour to differentiate the French and British soldiers – calls for a vibrant, visually pleasing palette. Yet this is never over-gaudy and for all its historical detail the film nevertheless subscribes to generally restrained Technicolor norms with accents on ceremonial attire and painted scenic backdrops. The differences in emphasis noted by Tompkins are observable, and to these should be added the considerable colour interest in costumes, not only in the battle scenes. In the beginning, for example, the Prologue announcing the play is spoken by a man dressed in a yellow cape which stands out from the predominantly brown and red tones of the audience at the Globe. When King Henry is seen for the first time he is dressed in a red cloak with gold and white detail; thereafter in the film he is generally associated with red. The framing of the figures as they discuss the English claim on France accords with Kalmus's ruling on complementary colours: Henry's plush, red attire is contrasted with another man's blue and green costume, and with Westmoreland's yellow coat which is in turn highlighted by the wide black ribbon holding the medal

Henry V (Technicolor, 1944):
colour contrast and costume
as the claim on France is
debated; Westmoreland's
contrasting yellow costume

On other occasions colour simply embellishes the frame as flags are waved (red and white English; blue with gold *fleur de lys* for France) against the blue sky, with armour and decorative gold braid and tassels on costumes glinting in the sunshine. In this way colour not only emphasises form with its contrasting schemes, but also suggests and highlights texture, in this film particularly velvet and golden, decorative fabrics. The film opens with the sight of a play-bill floating in the sky until it settles and announces the performance at the Globe in 1600. The swirling paper is striking against the blue sky; this spectacle is repeated at the end of the film when the cast list is detailed in a similar fashion after falling from the sky. Details such as this emphasise the film's symmetrical design, and colour is no exception in this respect. The night scenes when Henry goes

Henry V: flickering flames at
night when Harry is
incognito; St Crispin's speech

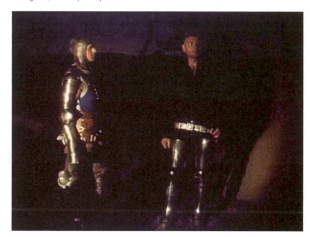

he wears around his neck. The French Ambassador, however, wears a blue and yellow coat and trousers; his tunic is green and he also has white gloves and ruff. Throughout the film King Charles of France wears a darkish green/grey tunic, embellished with the *fleur de lys* symbol in white (a detail which is repeated as wall decoration in the French court). The colour differentiation for English and French soldiers is generally consistent in the film, with French identified by shades of blue such as Bourbon in dark blue. The comic character Pistol wears red, in keeping with this emphasis on national *typage* through colour. In the final love scene (shot in high key) between Henry and Catherine, she is wearing blue which contrasts with his red velvet tunic.

incognito to survey the troops maintain colour interest as muted tones are seen in the dark, flickering flames are glimpsed in tents and armour glints in the moonlight effect. When day dawns for Henry's 'St Crispin's Day' speech, the contrast is emphasised by higher-key lighting which delivers what has been absent in the previous scene. Coloured tents are shown off as well as the horses dressed in their regalia and close-ups of red drums being beaten as the troops rally before the battle. The spectacle of this pageantry is very clearly delineated in colour; the film would have been far less impressive in black and white. The link to contemporary events was further established when, for its New York premiere, *Henry V* was accompanied by a seventeen-minute Technicolor newsreel of the Victory parade in London, reported as being only the second newsreel to have been made in Technicolor.[97]

As the war years had produced a desire for colour in a culture of scarcity and austerity, Britain was clearly not 'starved' of Technicolor. As technical developments in three-strip colour continued, and monopack was becoming available, other systems, notably Agfacolor and a revival of Dufaycolor, also accentuated the belief that colour had a crucial role to play in the postwar world. As the blackout ended advocates for a society that was more informed about colour were optimistic that better light levels in people's homes and in workplaces would lead to a greater appreciation of colour's multifarious potential which could be explored by both amateur and professional cinematographers.[98] World War II was a transformative event on many levels, not least in providing a recurring, popular interest in colour which fuelled a national investment in developing an alternate mode of Technicolor. The positive reception of British colour films at home and abroad created interest in what directors and technicians were doing with colour. A British colour aesthetic was being developed and appreciated. In broader terms, these examples demonstrate how cultural and material contexts impact on aesthetics and influence *how* technology works.

7 INTO A POSTWAR WORLD OF COLOUR
A MATTER OF LIFE AND DEATH

After the war the future seemed highly promising for colour films. Writing in the *Observer*, critic C. A. Lejeune predicted that colour was the key to cinema's bid to remain ahead in the competition with television, and all that needed to happen for it to fully transform the industry was for some of the 'great' directors – Welles, Ford and Hitchcock – to fully utilise colour.[1] Several topics dominated debates about colour during the period 1945–50 which will be outlined as context for an examination of British colour films during this period in the following chapters. As some of the difficulties of producing colour films experienced in wartime eased, it appeared that there was scope for reviving older processes as well as the development of newer ones which might offer competition to Technicolor. The cost of colour films continued to be a concern, and many looked to Kodachrome 35mm 'monopack' stock as a potential breakthrough in this regard. Monopack was revolutionary because it recorded three emulsions sensitive to the primary colours on a single base. This was much cheaper than three-strip Technicolor since it did not require a special camera. Agfacolor, Ansco Color (an American variant of Agfacolor), Gevacolor and Ferrania Color (Belgian and Italian variants of Agfacolor) already demonstrated great progress since they depended on integral tripacks or monopacks which automatically separated the colours of an image when exposed in an ordinary camera. Preferring to express the 'cinema of quality' in black and white, the French film industry made very few colour films, and these used Gevacolor rather than Technicolor in the postwar years.[2] Although 35mm monopack stock was used by Technicolor its use was not yet widespread, largely due to problems during processing and the high cost of creating release prints.[3] As we have seen, Darrel Catling's experience in 1944 of filming *English Village* with monopack left him unimpressed with delays experienced in processing his film in America.

There was revived optimism about the fortunes of Dufaycolor because somewhat ironically, and in view of impending developments with Eastmancolor stock, the process did not require a special camera. British Tricolour was announced as a new British process in 1947, based on patents of British colour expert Jack Coote. The Tricolour camera was similar to Technicolor's three-strip technology, and with refinements in processing and development Tricolour was acquired a few years later by Dufay-Chromex and renamed **Dufaychrome (see Technical Appendix)**.[4] Financial difficulties, however, prevented the company from being able to make significant advances in developing the process. With hindsight, it seems strange that Dufay should have gone in this direction when most in the industry were looking to monopack solutions to bring down the costs of colour cinematography; to produce an imitative rival to Technicolor at this stage in the game was surely misguided. On the other hand, this should be interpreted in the context of postwar optimism about colour, since perfecting the successful principles already proven by Technicolor provoked aspirations to strive for still greater perfection that might be attained by other companies and processes other than Technicolor.

American two-colour processes that were demonstrated and discussed at this time included Trucolor (Magnacolor) and Cinecolor, the latter being a particularly important development which enjoyed some success until the late 1940s.[5] Radiantcolor was a short-lived two-colour process tested in the UK in 1947 which used Gevaert bipack stock.[6] An agreement was subsequently struck with Cinecolor so that films made using that process were only handled for the European market by the Radiantcolor laboratories.[7] Indeed, some argued that two-colour processes had a window of opportunity, particularly during the 'Dalton Duty' crisis 1947–48 when there was disruption in the supply of Technicolor films and to production, resulting from the ban on Technicolor monopack stock which was only available from the USA. The Treasury is reported to have refused to grant a permit to Rank for the purchase of £3,000 worth of Technicolor stock for *Blue Lagoon* (1949) in respect of location shooting in the Fiji islands. The 'Dalton Duty' crisis of August 1947 was when a 75 per cent *ad valorem* duty was placed on American films by the British government, and Hollywood retaliated by boycotting the British market. The dispute was resolved in March 1948.[8] Further, in a context of public demand for colour films, it was argued that two-colour processes were better than black and white, although as R. Howard Cricks predicted: 'As soon as the public gets accustomed to seeing the majority of films in colour it will learn to distinguish between the wide range of pleasing colours obtainable with three colours, as opposed to the lack of primary colours in the two-colour process.'[9]

With this wealth of potential in the colour field Technicolor co-existed with many other possibilities, although the majority of colour films nevertheless continued to be made in Technicolor.[10] In an attempt to compete, some of the two-colour processes were developed into three-colour systems; for example, *Honeychile* was trade shown in the UK in 1951 as an example of Republic's three-colour Trucolor which also made use of the new Eastmancolor negative. Howard Cricks's verdict in the *Kinematograph Weekly* was fairly positive:

> Every colour in the spectrum was produced pleasingly, and, on the whole, I would say, accurately, except that in the case of highly saturated colours some loss of saturation

occurred. Flesh tones were especially good, and grass and trees were green (and not, as is so often the case, brown), even though the green was at times bluish.[11]

Technicolor films released at about the same time did not appear to be so closely scrutinised for their colour, usually eliciting comments such as that *The Magic Box* (1951) had 'excellent' colour, or *Where No Vultures Fly* (1951) was 'brilliantly photographed in Technicolor'.[12] This would perhaps indicate the degree of acceptance received by Technicolor at this point, having graduated to being a standard, rather than an experimental colour process and notwithstanding the activities of the many aspirant rivals referred to above.

Problems associated with the non-standardised exhibition of colour film nevertheless persisted into the postwar years, so that claims to 'accuracy' for colour reproduction were often flawed when films were shown in a variety of cinemas all over the world. Even after careful shooting and processing, a colour film could be ruined by being projected in a cinema with imbalanced arc lights, with a yellowish screen or with projectors with older and newer arcs which resulted in jarring changes between reels. Concern was even expressed for cinemas which displayed luminous colour signs, clock faces or allowed in a ray of sunlight, lest they should invite immediate comparison with colours on screen, working from the theory that colour appreciation might be lessened with the visibility of striking examples of comparative, 'real' colour.[13]

Debates in trade and technical journals which typified commentary on colour in the 1930s and during the war continued immediately afterwards. In March 1946 Darrel Catling turned his attention again to colour in an extended article in the *British Journal of Photography* entitled 'Talking Colour'. It provides a guide to how colour changes were being received, and the extent to which optimism about colour was animating contemporary experts, critics and amateur film-makers. As in earlier articles, Catling argued for what he called 'colour continuity' in which the colours featuring at the end of a scene are followed by complementary colours at the start of the next. Care over such details required planning and thought, a tendency he lamented was absent in many films which used colour as mere decoration. On these grounds he criticised *Caesar and Cleopatra* (1945) for lacking 'the authoritative stamp, style, and character of a master director … It is stagey and lacks the essence of cinema.'[14] He had seen examples of Agfacolor, and initially was not impressed because of its 'browniness', 'mistiness' and inability to render 'firm' black. Seeing *Munchausen* (1943), however, changed his view somewhat, since as a fantasy film it benefited from changes in locale and trick shots, and he noted that 'some thought was … given to the colour planning to avoid, as much as possible, revealing the system's weaknesses'.[15] Even so, at that time Agfacolor was hampered by being unable to produce cheap prints for commercial release purposes. It did put the 'monopack' principle at the centre of debate, however, since, as noted earlier, for many this constituted a revolution in the way colour films were shot.

E. S. Tompkins also reviewed the current state of developments in 1946, lamenting the fact that lower-grade colour, or the 'cautious neutralising' of colour continued to be greeted with greater enthusiasm – even to the extent of the revival of two-colour systems and praise for the reduced saturation of Dufaycolor – than three-colour Technicolor. With this preference in mind he predicted that monopack would have a positive reception but that Technicolor should continue to offer the best product since: 'Even though the ordinary member of the audience many not be colour conscious enough to detect small stepping down in quality, it seems desirable to keep colour reasonably correct and to aim at education of the public rather than to play down to their deficiencies of colour appreciation.'[16] This view was indicative of the arguments made in the previous decade about audiences needing to acquire 'colour consciousness'. It also attests to Technicolor's perceived maturity which helped it weather competition from the other systems which aspired to dominance in the immediate postwar years. There were even recommendations that if industrial managers adopted particular colour strategies when decorating factories or painted heavy boxes green rather than black, workers would respond positively by increasing productivity and perceive the newly painted boxes to be lighter than they had been before, even though they were the same weight as when they had been painted black. Such was the optimism around inculcating awareness of the possibilities of colour in everyday life and in the service of capitalist enterprise.[17] The broad interest in colour

across many spheres of life was reported in journals such as the *British Journal of Photography*, which gave so much attention to colour films. This attests to the prevalent belief that colour was a major influence in industry, culture and society.

The debates were not confined to the UK but formed a broader, international discussion on colour. British photography specialists such as Catling and Tompkins frequently referred to their counterparts in the USA, engaging with similar discussions published in the *American Cinematographer*. When, for example, Herb A. Lightman, a writer who reviewed many British and American colour films, quoted Russell Metty's claims that the heavily contrasted lighting design in *Arch of Triumph* (1948) was only possible because the film was shot in black and white, Catling strongly disagreed. Instead, he argued that Technicolor had reached such an advanced point that 'colour commands the entire range from white, through the greys, to jet black. Moreover, colour prints usually achieve a *richer* black than that reached by monochrome.'[18] In quoting films that used colour effectively, such as *Black Narcissus* (1947), Catling made the case for colour as an exciting and flexible choice for 'artists' working in cinema, so much so that when more widely available 'there will have to be a very good reason for making a film in black and white'.[19]

Although many distinguished films were subsequently made in Technicolor, for many it seemed that the dominant aesthetic preference, as in other countries, nevertheless remained with black and white, or with 'cautious neutralised' colour that posed little threat to clear narrative comprehension. This is striking in Britain, where documentary realism was widely accepted as a defining characteristic of 'quality' cinema in wartime black-and-white films such as *In Which We Serve* (1942), *Millions Like Us* (1943) and *The Way Ahead* (1944), admired by critics. So the colour films that were successful (or at least were remarked upon by critics for their use of colour) were spectacular interventions in a conventional, economy-driven, aesthetic system. Pre-monopack colour was still expensive, and it suited film producers to use it on occasion rather than totally adopt it. In this sense, arguments made for black and white's aesthetic superiority chimed with economic imperatives. As we have seen, critics would often praise British films for using colour in a non-garish, unobtrusive fashion and with an affinity to the dominant realist aesthetic of black and white. From another perspective, in debates about the problems facing the British film industry in the 1930s and 40s in respect of Hollywood's domination, Technicolor was understood as part of the broader hegemonic process of 'technology transfer', as had occurred with the transition to sound. It is not surprising that in all of this Technicolor is often remembered as brasher than it actually was, since it was associated with Hollywood and broader discourses about national difference. The claims that the British use of colour was somehow more tasteful than its application in the USA are partly explained by a desire to differentiate colour in a similar way to how discourses about stardom sought to place British stars on a more refined, class and theatrically based pedestal. Like other commentators Kay Harrison, manager of Technicolor Ltd, attributed a specific 'look' of British films to the softer and more subdued light of the region. He commented: 'We haven't a hard, bright light and so our taste is not for strong and vigorous color. The color we shoot outside is soft, and we carry the same idea with us when we shoot inside.'[20] This particular look was particularly noticeable when compared with films shot in California but set in the UK, such as *Lassie Come Home* (1943) which involved settings posing as English and Scottish. Bright blue skies and deep blue waters created a 'dreamland', an over-romanticised effect indoors and outdoors which in the context of this particular film did not really matter for achieving the desired impact.[21] There clearly was a perceived colour 'look' to British films that was influenced by prevailing discourses around colour taste. Restraint was favoured, although as we have seen this could often make colour noticeable in particular scenes and for achieving effects. As the following chapters demonstrate, this could operate somewhat differently depending on generic context. But the additional impact of objective factors (light, water) mentioned by many involved in producing Britain's colour films during this period must also be taken into consideration to fully understand Britain's colour aesthetic.

While discussion of the creation of screen colour tends to concentrate on production, processing often had a decisive impact on colour control and quality. In the pre-Technicolor period it was noted how laboratories were often required to make up for deficiencies in a negative, including under-exposure, flat or hard lighting or mechanical defects, as well as to execute tinting and toning.[22] Technicolor's imbibition dye-transfer process required accuracy and consistency but also flexibility. As cinematographer Chris Challis explained:

> Its great advantage was that the negative was black and white and you could even force one record in processing if you were in trouble … Then when it came to the matrices you had enormous control over how you printed it. You could also superimpose, which they did, a faint black and white image which could vary in intensity. They did it originally to help definition; they took it off the blue record which was the sharpest of the three negatives and they put a light black and white key which helped refine the definition over all the print. Of course it also helped the contrast, because with the Technicolor print, they could desaturate the colour until it was black and white. You had infinite control.[23]

This view is confirmed by those who worked in the laboratories, names which have seldom featured in previous accounts, including Dave Davis, Bernard Happé, Ron Hill, Jack Household, Frank Littlejohn, Les Ostinelli, Len Runkel and Syd Wilson.[24] Interviewed as part of the Broadcasting, Entertainment, Cinematograph and Theatre Union (BECTU) History Project, their recollections shed light on the complexities and challenges of colour processing and laboratory practices as crucial elements of colour film production. Bernard Happé joined the Technicolor laboratories in 1936 and was a technical manager from the 1960s to 1974. Technicolor's philosophy of 'branding' its product with a clearly recognisable 'look' associated with high-quality production values was reflected in the intricate procedures around its 'unique selling point', imbibition dye transfer. Happé described how matrices were exchanged between Technicolor plants in Britain and Hollywood to ensure the same results from the same matrix.[25] Operations in the laboratories were meticulous, as Happé explained:

> Materials from each printer in positive control were checked for alignment under microscopes and then for registration on screen for size, shape and definition … You transferred the yellow, cyan and magenta images separately and unless you got them down correctly with the matrix

and blank in the right condition you'd have nasty coloured fringes and so register control was an important part of the operation.[26]

Another key function was grading whereby density and colour values were altered from shot to shot during processing to achieve consistency, balance or a particular desired effect.

Like many cinematographers, Happé was dismissive of interference from Natalie Kalmus, claiming that her contact with the laboratories was 'negligible'. But he acknowledged that to some extent the principle of colour control, or at least expertise, was important since working with Technicolor was far from straightforward in terms of needing to know how particular colours such as white required adjustment (in this case 'Technicolor whites' were dyed in coffee) before filming to render the correct hue. Dyes were crucial to the imbibition dye-transfer system since the emulsion of the blank film absorbed the dye from the matrix. Dyes were, however, subject to variation and until the 1960s there was no standardisation of pre-mixed substances. Although dyes were transferred as yellow, cyan and magenta, they were 'complex mixtures of dyes which were normally available as textiles and they had to be compounded with various proportions of different dyes'.[27] During World War II the Technicolor plant experienced shortages in chemicals, especially dyes, which encouraged experimentation to affect economies. An account by Happé documents the many ingenious and innovative experiments with chemicals undertaken at this time.[28] In addition, the plant was restricted to operating with four cameras, one transfer machine and four matrix printers. For the postwar expansion more printers were purchased and the first Technicolor cameras were manufactured in Britain. At the same time other laboratories such as Denham, Humphries, Kay, Olympic, Radiant and Reed's took advantage of new colour stocks including Eastmancolor, Gevacolor, Ferrania Color and widescreen processes to gain reputations for expertise, having equipped themselves with new or adapted developing and printing machines.[29] CinemaScope, other widescreen formats and 3-D challenged the Technicolor imbibition process because their increased magnification showed up discrepancies in colouration or density between individual prints. These technical challenges and awareness of competition provoked intense experimentation at

Technicolor Ltd and the laboratories adapted dye-transfer printing for Eastmancolor's single negative, demonstrating the longevity of Technicolor's processing of colour films long after the demise of three-strip cameras.[30]

In the response of technicians, the issue of authorship features prominently in discourses about Technicolor. In the USA, cinematographers boasted about how they flouted Kalmus's strictures as to the application of Technicolor, and this seems also to have been the case in Britain with Jack Cardiff, Oswald Morris and Chris Challis claiming that they challenged or even ignored the stipulations laid down by Technicolor. Indeed, Cardiff has often given detailed accounts of his interest in Technicolor and the specific occasions when he pushed the boundaries established for the process by the company. As he put it, he was 'the *enfant terrible* of Technicolor, the real bad boy that broke all of their rules, but eventually they came to appreciate what I was trying to do'.[31] On several occasions he claims that innovative lighting and filter techniques he tried out were frustrated or blocked by Technicolor, especially when effects could be 'corrected' at the printing stage. These instances point to strains in Kalmus's system that emphasised colour control although it must be acknowledged that the strictures laid down did impose a degree of regulation which as time went on became standardised within the industry. At the same time the ambitions expressed about challenging Technicolor's authority revolve around seeking to exert another kind of control over colour at the level of production and as a means of enhancing the status of the cinematographer as a key figure in Britain's response to Hollywood. Cinematographers in Hollywood also sought recognition for their application of Technicolor, so to some extent this phenomenon is about the recognition of technical expertise among a broader international community of cinematographers.

'BRITAIN'S FINEST CINEMATIC ACHIEVEMENT': *A MATTER OF LIFE AND DEATH*

Cardiff's first sustained experiment with Technicolor was *A Matter of Life and Death* (1946), a feature film which used colour in a bold, structural manner when the scenes of heaven were shot in monochrome (three-strip Technicolor with the colour printed out) and conventional black and white, and the earthly world was shot in colour. Jack Cardiff was not that experienced in black-and-white cinematography and he recalled that it was the laboratory's idea to use 'Technicolor black and white' for the transition scenes, discussed in more detail below. It suited the desired aesthetic style because it produced 'an iridescent sheen on it like a beetle's wing'.[32] While this stylistic choice might appear to be innovative, it was nevertheless inflected with the dominant discourse of restraint since the transition scenes from the world in colour to black-and-white heaven were deliberately shot in monochrome Technicolor, to avoid 'the visual shock such changes have evoked in certain films in the past'.[33] In diegetic terms colour was however associated with a loss of control and sexuality (the pilot's reluctance to take his place in heaven because he has fallen in love on earth, after being killed in a plane crash), themes which also convey the idea that colour can be troubling and chaotic. This points to a central paradox in discussions about Technicolor: those who advocated 'color consciousness' aimed to apply colour with care and control while at the same time demonstrating colour's inherent instability of affect and meaning, knowledge which had the potential to frustrate such a goal.

As a landmark British Technicolor film, *A Matter of Life and Death* deserves extended analysis from a colour perspective. Although the film was not appreciated by many British critics, who favoured a realist style, its significance as a colour film was noted by technical specialists, most notably Herb A. Lightman, writing in *American Cinematographer*, and E. S. Tompkins in the *British Journal of Photography*.[34] For Lightman it was 'Britain's finest cinematic achievement' and for Tompkins its photography (rather than narrative) was remarkable as 'one of the most significant pieces of entertainment in Technicolor for years'. Michael Powell recalled that: 'We were going to play with Technicolor on the screen in a way that nobody had ever played before.'[35] Indeed, even at the film's opening credits it is visually arresting in terms of colour. The Archers' infamous target logo, with nine thrusting arrows, blends from black and white into colour as a witty touch preceding the credits proper with blue background, the letter 'A' in red; 'Matter of Life and' in white, and 'Death' in black. Supporting Cardiff's

cinematography were camera operator Geoffrey Unsworth; special effects team Douglas Woolsey, Henry Harris, Technicolor Ltd and with additional effects by W. Percy Day; and art director Alfred Junge assisted by Arthur Lawson. The effects are striking in many scenes, including the opening sequence of the universe, with the voice-over commentary observing stars, the milky-way from outer space, before focusing in on the Earth to establish the World War II context. The infamous 'stairway to heaven' (the film's US title) designed by Alfred Junge and built as a set at Denham Studios, and with effects work by Percy Day, also features as a high-point of experimentation with miniatures and travelling matte shots.[36] Lightman was bowled over with admiration: 'Never has this reviewer seen such perfection of mechanics in the execution of travelling matte shots and double printing.'[37]

The parallel action sequence of Peter (David Niven) in his burning aircraft having what he thinks is his last conversation with June (Kim Hunter) in the aerodrome's control-room is remarkable for the colour correspondences between the two locations. As Peter talks to June the flames of his burning plane are visible outside the window and are reflected on part of his face. Similarly, as June replies the red, pulsating signal lights of the aerodrome's beacon are also visible through the window of the control-room. This linkage through colour, combined with the sequence's low light levels, obscuring much surrounding detail except for intermittently highlighting each character's face, adds to the mood of intensity and heightens suspense. The facial colour contrast between the two characters is also established through colour in this early sequence, with June's dark hair and eyes, white complexion and red lipstick contrasted with Peter's more tanned face and blue eyes. There are many such comparative close-ups in the film, particularly towards the end as June's tears provide evidence of her genuine love for Peter which convinces the heavenly court to grant him long life on earth. These levels of experimentation with lighting were remarkable, linking with Cardiff's later aesthetic signature of innovative lighting in *Black Narcissus*.

A Matter of Life and Death has seven colour sequences and six in black and white/dye-monochrome. As noted above, the strategy to use the latter was a deliberate one for the transition scenes. Michael Powell was impressed by the appropriateness of Jack Cardiff's

A Matter of Life and Death:
'One is starved for Technicolor
up there'

A Matter of Life and Death
(Technicolor, 1946):
Conductor 71 (Marius
Goring) starved for
Technicolor; the rose about to
be transformed; the rose
acquires colour

remark that the resulting 'look' of the dye-monochrome
was 'sort of pearly'.[38] Lightman explained how the
process worked:

> Any reproduction of a black and white photograph in a
> Technicolor picture is a dye-monochrome reproduction of
> the neutral original, the neutral effect being obtained by
> identical printings of the three reproduction colors used in
> the Technicolor process. For the scenes to be
> photographed in dye-monochrome, a black and white
> negative was photographed, and from this three identical
> negatives were made which were used as if they were
> separation negatives. The transition effects from black and
> white to color were actually long dissolves 'synced' to the
> exact frame, so that there was absolutely no jump in
> action. The most unusual aspect of the effect is that,
> although the sets were lighted for color, the black and
> white reproductions of these scenes maintain a smooth
> velvety quality devoid of the flatness one might expect.[39]

This process facilitated non-jarring transitions, when care
is taken for the transition shots to be gentle, as when the
tally of people 'delivered' to heaven merges from having
some colour to monochrome, or the white hospital wall
at the end of a colour sequence followed by the heavenly
staircase in monochrome. Here the process is assisting in
making the switch easy on the eye, but in addition the
choice of settings is crucial. As noted previously,
commentators on films which featured both black and

white and colour objected to harsh contrasts between the two; even in the trailer for *Becky Sharp* (1935), which demonstrated the difference between a close-up of Miriam Hopkins in black and white and then in colour, the transition was effected by a dissolve rather than a cut. The transition in *The Wizard of Oz* (1939) showed Dorothy's house swirling through the air in sepia rather than the harsher tones of black and white, before she enters the world of colour. *Shine on Harvest Moon* (US, 1944) was a black-and-white musical about Broadway stars with a colour epilogue. To lessen the shock of the introduction of colour a diegetic device was deployed whereby two stage hands work on a spot-light in preparation for the number 'Harvest Moon'. They request coloured lights and operate a disc of coloured 'gels' in front of the lamp. One report noted that even with this transitional device the change was quite a shock: 'It is quite intriguing to see black and white characters come to life as tinted flesh and blood, but need they have given Miss Sheridan quite so much yellow in her dress, hat and fan, to contrast so vividly with the blue backing and to provide quite such a violent eyeful.'[40] While these stylistic reasons for creating a smooth and gentle shift between heaven and earth were becoming conventional, it is also the case that in terms of *A Matter of Life and Death*'s questioning of boundaries between worlds, time and materiality, the technique served a thematic purpose central to the film's subject-matter. From this perspective, a 'pearly', ethereal touch was appropriate. As Lightman remarked: '*Dissolves* from color to monotone, as well as from full sets to miniatures are so smooth that it is difficult to tell where one scene ends and the other begins.'[41]

It would, however, be a mistake to downplay the role of colour in the earthly scenes, even if they are not introduced with a jolt. When, for example, the rose in Conductor 71's buttonhole blends from monochrome to colour, he makes the remark in a French accent: 'One is starved for Technicolor up there.' After this we indeed get a celebration of colour that suits his decadent demeanour much more than black and white. The impression is of a *longing* for colour, that the world is incomplete without it, just as in wartime people had to put up with material deprivation, emotional loss and hardship. Close-ups of the transition, with the pink rose contrasted with the deeper red of the jewel on his ring, are followed by a medium-shot which shows him

surrounded by deeply-saturated red rhododendrons. What is remarkable is the cumulative impact of colour as the scene unfolds. The arrival of colour, itself a spectacle, reaches a crescendo as Conductor 71 (Marius Goring) is framed by an abundant display of nature. Although gradual, the colour at the end-point of the transition is most certainly striking. It is interesting in this context to relate this key moment of colour's arrival with the fascination with floral imagery demonstrated in many films. Tom Gunning observed that flowers often featured in colour films of the silent period because they show 'a brilliant moment rather than something that is constant'; they are brilliantly saturated, but they fade.[42] In this and other examples, cinema and photography drew attention to their ephemeral nature as media well placed to document things that pass.

Colour sequences which established a particular mood were facilitated by wide-angle photography, such as the shots of Saunton Sands in North Devon. It was important to establish a credible setting which could at first be mistaken for heaven when Peter Carter is washed up by the tide, having bailed out of his plane without a parachute. As Powell explained, the setting and colour were crucial in creating an atmosphere evocative of other-worldliness:

> It had that pearly look of an English August morning, like nothing on earth, which was just as well because David Niven thought he was in Another World. As we stood upon the low cliffs above the sands and looked directly down onto where the waves were lazily breaking, we could see the blue sky and the cirrus clouds above us reflected in this enormous mirror made up of sand and water.[43]

In another scene which depended very much on engaging with the film's premise that time could – literally – be stopped, Jack Cardiff used a lemon rather than an amber filter on the arc lights when June and Dr Reeves (Roger Livesey) are playing table tennis and the frame freezes.[44] What might otherwise be interpreted as an example of Technicolor 'restraint' is, therefore, used to banish any sense of warmth, creating an 'unreality' effect which enhances the film's 'otherworldly' theme. As pointed out in a discussion of 'warm' and 'cold' colours in an editorial in the *British Journal of Photography*, the popular understanding of these was opposite to the science, whereby 'hotter' light sources, or those

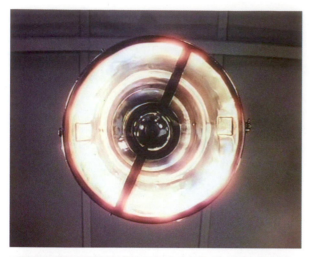

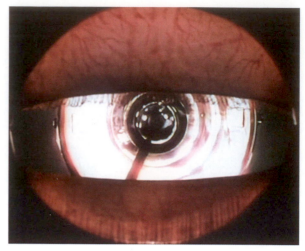

A Matter of Life and Death: experimental effect as graphic design similar to shot above left

A Matter of Life and Death: Peter's (David Niven) viewpoint as he is being wheeled into the operating theatre; Peter about to lose consciousness

operating at a higher colour temperature give a bluish tint, with 'yellow-green' being the coolest, which is what Cardiff was aiming for here with his filter experiment.[45]

As Peter hovers between life and death he experiences hallucinations connected with a brain injury that take place in space but not time. As in the table tennis example, time is 'stopped' in conventional terms (June and Dr Reeves are immobile), but it continues for Peter when he is visited again by Conductor 71. As Damian Sutton has observed, this approach can be related to Deleuze and Bergson's concept of *durée* which questions the conventional markers of time passing in neat, chronological blocks. Instead, they argue time is heterogeneous, an experience that can vary and be subject to differing experiential planes (an hour can pass very fast or it can seem 'like a lifetime'). Following this line of thought, in *A Matter of Life and Death*: 'Time itself appears to be interrupted and the present exists only as an internal experience … Time, no longer governed by movement or sound, is simply duration: as long or as short an impression of being as it needs to be.'[46] This observation can be linked with dreams and dreaming, similar to the themes explored in *Blithe Spirit*. Both films share a preoccupation with questioning boundaries between life and death, as well as with Freud's conception of the uncanny; in life we know death and vice-versa. Laura Mulvey explains how: 'The threshold between life and death becomes a space of

A Matter of Life and Death:
abstract colour transition shot

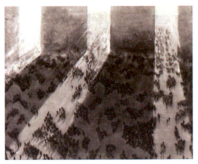

A Matter of Life and Death:
designer Alfred Junge's
drawing introduces the
transition to heaven

A Matter of Life and Death:
live action blurs with the
drawing as the transition is
completed

uncertainty in which boundaries blur between the rational and the supernatural, the animate and the inanimate.'[47] The technical care taken over achieving a particular look for the transition scenes makes sense in terms of these ideas, since in the spirit of *durée* the progression between heaven and earth is not jarring.

This preoccupation is particularly striking in the sequence when Peter is wheeled into the operating theatre for brain surgery. The use of close-ups and colour do much of the work in suggesting these themes. Several close-ups dominate the sequence as Peter's bandaged head is shown as he lies on the stretcher. His viewpoint of the ceiling and the light above the operating table makes the environment strange, in keeping with the tendency of close-ups to de-familiarise. This is further emphasised by the lack of sound, as Peter cannot hear the nurses' voices. His distance from everyday life is also given a spatial dimension as June looks anxiously into the theatre, separated from the event by a window. This sequence stands out as conveying the intensity of Peter's life and death experience; through his viewpoint we 'see' objects made strange. Kracauer observed that:

> Any huge close-up reveals new and unsuspected formations of matter, skin textures are reminiscent of aerial photographs, eyes turn into lakes or volcanic craters. Such images blow up our environment in a double sense: they enlarge it literally; and in doing so, they blast the prison of conventional reality, opening up expanses which we have explored at best in dreams before.[48]

To invoke Deleuze, the facial close-up combines 'a reflecting, immobile unity' and 'intensive expressive movements', which can be observed here since, although Peter is under anaesthetic, the close-ups gather momentum as he lapses – *moves without moving physically* – into another world.[49] As the anaesthesia mask approaches in close-up, with its red, almost lip-like appearance, there is again a contradictory insinuation (kiss of life or death?) in that the mask comes at Peter's face as if to smother him, while giving him what he needs in order to survive the operation.

The close-up of the mask being applied to Peter's mouth occasions a loss of conventional time/consciousness. We have seen this occur before, but without the assistance of the anaesthetic which creates a rational explanation for what is to follow. Because we have seen Peter's lapses out of time before, however, this scene takes on a similar quality of hallucination which takes us to black-and-white heaven where the celestial court is preparing to debate his case as to whether he should be claimed for heaven or allowed to remain on earth. What is striking here is that to make the distinction/separation of hallucinatory incidents, we have the intrusion of colour, as Peter passes out of consciousness. The famous shot of his eyelid closing is followed by a shot of pure colour affect in reds and purples combined with the sensation of movement within the frame. The camera is static but what passes before it is a screen of colour rolling upwards, eventually becoming monochrome as Alfred Junge's drawing completes the shot. This is then animated into the figures in heaven as the fully black-

and-white world assumes dominance. Although colour has been used before in the transition between worlds this example is more spectacular, encouraging us to pause, to look and think again. The colour is not related to a particular object, as is most common in cinema, and so is therefore devoid of obvious symbolic meaning. Instead, the moving, coloured frame is connected to Carter's lapsing consciousness – not into oblivion but into heaven. Since the colours in the frame move upwards the sensation is unlike the effect of a wipe to suggest transition from one locale to another.[50] For the viewer, the combination of travelling with Peter on his journey into the operating theatre; the close-ups aligning us with his viewpoint and finally the sensation of intense colour movement, combine to produce a haptic, embodied experience for spectators as they follow Peter's journey into a celestial world, which by this time has actually become quite familiar.[51]

In many respects *A Matter of Life and Death* was a remarkable film to be produced at the end of the war, and in a context of scarcity. The confidence it demonstrated about the efficacy of colour is indicative of the years when cinemagoing was more popular than ever, with attendances in Britain reaching an all-time peak of 1,635 million in 1946. Even though there were aspirant rivals to threaten Technicolor's dominance, in Britain Technicolor Ltd was doing reasonably well. The company had been incorporated as a private company in July 1935 and converted into a public one in July 1952. It operated under licences from the Technicolor Motion Picture Corporation which contained provision for cross-royalties for prints made from American and British productions. The company provided cameras, equipment and personnel to producers in the British Commonwealth (excluding Canada) for photographing films in Technicolor; in addition it processed negatives and made coloured prints. According to Frank Littlejohn, who worked for Technicolor Ltd, the company made prints of films for the European market: 'So our licence although never officially extended became a licence which enabled us to print virtually for anywhere.'[52] Technicolor Ltd's profits during the war period to 1951 are detailed in the following table.

YEAR ENDED 30 NOVEMBER	£ PROFITS*
1942	51,859
1943	46,152
1944	104,496
1945	173,753
1946	122,239
1947	123,927
1948	178,823
1949	377,725
1950	436,689
1951	454,008

* After charging depreciation of fixed assets other than freehold land, directors' enrolments and all other working expenses, adjustments but before charging tax.[53]

In the USA, British films and the activities of Technicolor Ltd were reported in generous terms, with commentary often noting that the British deployment of the process was somewhat different from prevailing Hollywood conventions. The aesthetic boldness of *A Matter of Life and Death* was in good part responsible for this attitude. The following chapters will examine other key films in relation to different generic contexts and during a period when some of the most notable British Technicolor films were produced and C. A. Lejeune's hopes about 'great' directors turning to colour were in good part realised.

8 COLOUR GENRES IN POSTWAR CINEMA 1
TOPICAL SPECTACLES – BIOPICS AND THE EMPIRE GENRE

From its early usage, colour was associated with particular styles and genres. The tendency to link colour with fantasy and spectacle resulted in its overt demonstration in films about empire, for coverage of national events and in musicals, historical biopics and melodramas. These genres used forms of colour spectacle to vivify momentous events and historical figures; show-stopping numbers and the characters in shocking, emotionally moving melodramas. This chapter contends that colour established and developed specific generic affinities over the decades and that this was necessary in order for colour to establish itself as a viable screen technology. At the same time, discourses around colour insisted that it enhanced realism, even though the dominant aesthetic preference for conveying this idea was black-and-white photography. The complex negotiation between these two discursive aspects of colour – realism and fantasy – will be explored and the opportunity taken to consider how colour relates more broadly to theories of genre. Once particular genres developed associations with colour and conventions for its deployment, for example, it is possible to chart the contribution of colour in the 'repetition and difference' dynamic posited by genre theorist Steve Neale as central to the nature of generic development. This idea is that audiences are most satisfied when new films satisfy their generic expectations by repeating elements that they have previously enjoyed, and at the same time offer something new. In this way genre is a dynamic concept, driven by the delivery of popular, tried and tested elements as well as innovations that surprise the audience. While it is clear that technology has always

been a dominant element in the promotion of genres such as the Western (widescreen), musicals (colour) and science fiction (special effects), it is useful to consider in detail the role it plays in establishing the 'regimes of verisimilitude' or systems of expectation and hypothesis, that underpin the generation and regeneration of popular cinema forms.[1] Also, in terms of establishing the aesthetic techniques required to produce recurring iconographic tropes, a technology such as Technicolor became inextricably bound up with the establishment, development and commercial exploitation of particular genres. The genres most usually associated with colour did not, however, gain equal prominence in different national contexts. Colour musicals, for example, were far rarer in Britain than in the USA. As 'colour genres' became identified with particular countries, discussions of colour were intertwined with discourses on national cinemas and associated assumptions about 'non-realist' colour as inferior. E. S. Tompkins recognised this with his plea for critics to abandon their critique of screen colour as a poor relation to perceived norms of realism. He recommended that: 'Once it is realised that the use of colour in [such] musical comedy or extravaganza films is artificial, it need never annoy again, and the enthusiast can settle down to enjoy the skill with which this particular use of colour is made.'[2]

While this chapter's focus is on examples from postwar cinema, earlier periods are relevant to how colour's generic conventions became established for the screen. Regarding an association with pageantry and national spectacle, for example, colour was used for filming events including the Delhi Durbar in 1911, the

Coronation ceremonies in 1937 and 1953, the Olympic Games in 1948 and films made to commemorate the Festival of Britain, 1951. Biopics concerning monarchs such as *Victoria the Great* (1937, the last reel) and *Sixty Glorious Years* (1938) were shot in Technicolor. This tradition of filming in colour for events and themes deemed to be of historic and national importance was influential in the decision to shoot *Scott of the Antarctic* (1948) in Technicolor, as well as *The Magic Box* (1951), produced for the Festival of Britain to commemorate William Friese-Greene's pioneering experiments with cinematography, including colour.

As well as being associated with national spectacle, historic events and personages, colour also featured in films about empire and for overseas adventures such as the many Kinemacolor travelogue films shot all over the world; the *World Windows* series of travelogues (1937–40); Alexander Korda's features *The Drum* (1938), *The Four Feathers* (1939) and *The Thief of Bagdad* (1940); and in *Men of Two Worlds* which was filmed in Africa during the war and released in 1946. Comparative analysis of colour in these films will ascertain the extent to which it was applied differently in varying generic contexts. While an iconographic formula was rare, the nature of film production meant that colour was engaged with the 'repetition and difference' tendency of film genres. When Technicolor was first introduced in both the USA and the UK its value as spectacle was exploited in marketing, as it was with earlier processes. As we have seen, the creation of a desire for screen colour in a culture of wartime scarcity resulted in the privileging of colour in the immediate postwar years for certain productions, particularly but not exclusively to those with the 'prestige' tag. Tracing such links across time helps to locate the generic deployment of colour as a key factor in technological change. Colour needed genre and vice-versa. The higher cost of colour film meant that becoming a key component of generic convention, as with the musical, was essential to justify its deployment. The commercial viability of colour over a long period of time, therefore, depended to some extent on it being located within a particular set of generic expectations so that a degree of stability (repetition) co-existed alongside incentives for experiment (difference).

COLOUR SPECTACLES OF ROYALTY, THE OLYMPIC GAMES AND THE FESTIVAL OF BRITAIN

What exhibitor of black-and-white moving pictures would dream of appealing to the public by offering to show them (in monotone) any of these ceremonies? Even when the pictures of the events were still in this strictly limited sense of the word 'topical' the monotone exhibitor found them unsatisfactory and only moderately successful from a monetary point of view. The reason is not far to seek. These pictures lacked the one essential to a truthful reproduction of brilliant ceremonial – they could not convey the slightest idea of the beauty of color of the original.[3]

The Natural Colour Kinematograph Company's most publicised and successful films were their colour records of royal ceremonials, which included the funeral of Edward VII in 1910, the unveiling of the Queen Victoria memorial and the Coronation of King George V in 1911. As detailed in Chapter 1, perhaps the most famous Kinemacolor film of all, the filming of the royal tour of India in 1911–12 which included the Coronation Durbar at Delhi, represented Kinemacolor's most ambitious claim to be 'the only process in existence reproducing the actual scenes in living, vivid colours'.[4] Reportage on the films revealed the elaborate pageantry audiences experienced in witnessing royalty in colour. Kinemacolor was presented as a superior form of entertainment for discerning, up-market audiences, which included the royal personages themselves when they attended screenings at the Scala, the theatre leased by Charles Urban specifically to showcase Kinemacolor. When the press reported on the Kinemacolor record of Edward VII's funeral the colour effects were noted as being particularly striking in view of the contrast highlighted in the films between the mourners dressed in black and the soldiers' tunics in red; foreign uniforms featuring greens and blues; the colours of the Union Jack; ceremonial golds and the green trees. These colours were deemed to 'produce an extraordinary faithful copy of the actual scenes'.[5] In its 1912–13 catalogue of Kinemacolor films, such subjects were singled out as being uniquely identified with the process with its claims to present 'the revivication in all the glowing hues of majesty' of important state events.[6]

The films described in the catalogue provide a sense of how colour featured in the ceremonial films and in addition how the company sought to catch the attention of exhibitors in the hope that they would then take out a Kinemacolor licence. Any sort of identifying insignia such as the colours of a flag or of a ship's hull or funnel was noted, such as in *Launch of SS Olympic*, which apparently had its hull specially painted in red and white 'in order that a good Kinemacolor result might be obtained'.[7] Staging a scene for colour was also apparent in films where specific contrasts were favoured, such as between khaki and 'the more brilliant hues of British uniforms' in *Lord Kitchener reviewing Egyptian troops at Khartoum*, and between khaki and highland dress in *Children's Empire Day review by Lord Roberts*.[8] The deployment of Kinemacolor to enhance and improve on the experience of people who gathered to watch the ceremonial spectacles was emphasised in publicity and reports. The colour record was presented as offering a unique window on the world by filming from angles above eye-level, thereby providing views of marching soldiers from a very different perspective and in so doing creating patterns which emphasised colour differentiation and depth of field. A sense of using the camera to glimpse royal personages and dignitaries as they had never been seen before is conveyed by the comment on *Nobility leaving Chelsea for Westminster* regarding peers needing tickets to attend the Coronation ceremony in 1911: 'The camera cruelly records the peer's agitated fumblings and searchings in the unaccustomed recesses of his ermine robe for the missing ticket.'[9] The *Royal Visit to Bombay* was the first film in Kinemacolor's Indian series, when George V and Queen Mary visited India in December 1911. In the majority of the descriptions of these films specific colour details were noted as with other Kinemacolor films listed in the catalogue. What is remarkable is the recurrence of specific details and techniques which were becoming part of Kinemacolor's recognisable repertoire. *The Pageant Procession*, for example, commented on an elephant procession in India, shot in 1911: 'One is adorned with a fine dark-red cloth with embroideries; others are covered with crimson velvet … at times the whole screen seems to be filled with a riot of gorgeous colour as has never been seen before.'[10]

McKernan has observed that: 'For producer and audience fidelity to nature through colour came to be equated with fidelity to the crown and the imperial idea.'[11] In this context, communicating the full, *true* majesty of British royal pageantry was only made possible with the addition of colour. Urban was astute in pushing these connections between colour and British patriotism which were also strong in subsequent decades. Brian Winston argues that there are profound connections between technological processes and 'deeply social factors' which have far-reaching consequences.[12] There is no doubt that filming the Delhi Durbar cemented the special relationship between Kinemacolor and royalty. They were partners in promoting patriotism, with Kinemacolor providing a new way to promote royalty and vice-versa. Not only did the films inspire admiration for the spectacle of monarchy, but they also provided an opportunity to see the King and Queen closer than would normally be possible, although the shots could hardly be regarded as approaching intimacy. The special relationship between Kinemacolor and royalty was emphasised in films which delivered *close* views, or shots of the King and Queen advancing *towards* the camera.[13] As with the example cited earlier of the film which showed the peer fumbling for a ticket to the Coronation ceremony, Kinemacolor films were conscious of the need to promote images of figures in positions of power and authority as subject to human frailty much in the same way as anybody else. Far from implying weakness, this further inculcated patriotic loyalty. W. T. Crespinel recalled that at one point in the Coronation procession film, the King was seen to acknowledge the camera, presumably because he heard it clicking, by nodding slightly and smiling, looking into the lens. One projectionist apparently used this moment for comic effect by calling 'Hy, George!' just before the King looked at the camera and to give the impression that he was responding to the call.[14] Such incidents encouraged the 'aristocratic–proletarian' alliance whereby people were mobilised to recognise similarities between themselves and royal personages as human beings. In this instance the projectionist's joke implied that the King *would* respond in such a light-hearted and friendly way to a call from the crowd.[15]

The Kinemacolor films provided evidence of the wonders of Empire, as noted in the *Evening News*:

The Kinemacolor pictures of the Coronation were amazing, but those of the Royal Indian tour are stupendous. Nothing so soul-stirring, so varied or so beautiful has ever been seen anywhere outside the actual places they depict. A picture that touched the audience with pride and patriotic fervour was that of the Indian Mutiny Veterans, but when the great Durbar itself was over there came the picture of the evening – one which shows the might of the Empire more than the majesty of all the ceremonies – the Review of 50,000 troops of all arms.[16]

While colour features prominently in descriptions of travelogue films which were not part of a military display or royal ceremonial tour, they are inflected with overtones which similarly express the imperial idea in no uncertain terms. This is evident in films such as *The Piegan Indians*, described as showing the tribe's attire as 'picturesque and barbaric ... their multi-coloured robes and brilliant feathers, are perfectly reproduced by the Kinemacolor process'.[17] Differences in skin complexion were also noted as being of interest in the Kinemacolor film catalogue, as with reference to *The King's Camp and the Ruling Chiefs' Receptions*, which revealed 'slight differences in complexion between one Indian and another. A harder test of color photography, or one more triumphantly met, could scarcely be conceived,' once again demonstrating what was considered to be of note when the films were being promoted.[18]

As Hanssen has also observed, the link between colour and exoticism relates to a broader western cultural position which equates colour with 'otherness'. Hence the many contrasts cited in the Kinemacolor Catalogue between films about 'grey, colourless cities' such as London or Berlin, and the strikingly bright colours of Italy, Spain or India.[19] The difference between 'home' and 'abroad' was emphasised in films which offered 'the brightness and beauty of color' of Indian scenes, in contrast to a 'notoriously gloomy city' such as Manchester.[20] In this way colours were identified with particular nations and Kinemacolor was seen to offer an important function in helping people make particular distinctions. The ideology around Kinemacolor as a 'natural' process in turn worked to naturalise ideological discourses around race. These created a degree of fixity in respect of certain applications of colour which inculcated expectations such as red as a ceremonial register. This could be extended to a number of contexts, however, including details such as the painting red of an elephant's forehead and trunk in *Preparations for the Calcutta Pageant*.[21] This was just as well, since red was a colour rendered

reasonably well in Kinemacolor, which in turn encouraged other suitable subjects such as sunsets and the spectacle of seeing claret being added to a tumbler of water.[22] As noted in Chapter 1, when defending Kinemacolor's claim to render 'natural' colour in the infamous court case that hastened its demise, G. A. Smith argued that the Union Jack did not necessarily always contain a clear blue, whereas red was the primary means of its identification which Kinemacolor reproduced well.[23] What is so interesting about reading reports on Kinemacolor screenings is that the quality of colour rendition was often praised, and colours such as blue were referenced as being visible even though we know that Kinemacolor's palette was limited.[24] The pomp and circumstance of military parades and royal ceremonial events, combined with Urban's 'hype' around Kinemacolor, no doubt encouraged reviewers to 'see' colours that perhaps were not as marked as their accounts would have us believe.

Subsequent colour processes were showcased by filming royal events. The 1937 Coronation was filmed in three-strip Technicolor, along with other processes, which at the time were trying to gain a footing in the market (see Chapter 3). This was rather different from Kinemacolor's sustained engagement with royal events and spectacles of imperial power, yet there are continuities with the rhetoric around colour when it was mobilised for such a purpose. Kinemacolor cinematographer W. T. Crespinel, who worked with the process in Britain and America and shot *The Glorious Adventure* (1922) in Prizma, made the historical continuity clear by writing an article in *American Cinematographer* in 1937 which detailed Kinemacolor's approach to filming the 1911 Coronation ceremonies. The importance of securing 'unique' placements for the cameras was emphasised, as well as making sure prints were ready to be shown in the shortest time possible between the filming of the event and public exhibition. There were specific technical difficulties of working with Kinemacolor which in retrospect made Crespinel all the more proud of its achievements. There was no available panchromatic negative stock, for example, necessitating a special process to sensitise the stock to more colours.[25] The choice of several colour processes (Dufaycolor, Technicolor, Realita and Kinechrome) to shoot the Coronation was in recognition of how such occasions could serve as advertisements. The newsreel, feature and short film markets were each potential converts (newsreels were already being made in Dufaycolor), and reports of the various processes' success at 'capturing' the full range of ceremonial colours heightened the impression that it was just a matter of time before colour was a requirement of all films.[26] The conjunction of a new monarch being crowned and colour entering into a new phase established a generic, contextual relationship between technology and monarchy.

The Royal Wedding of 1947 provided Technicolor and the Rank Organisation with an opportunity to produce a special three-reeler film of the wedding presents. The Canadian Film Board produced *Royal Journey*, a five-reeler of the Royal Tour of Canada using Eastmancolor negative safety film (monopack).[27] It was, however, the Coronation in June 1953 that attracted the greatest interest in demonstrating new colour processes.[28] At the time rivals to Technicolor were being showcased, including Warnercolor, Gevacolor, Ansco Color and Agfacolor. Warnercolor used Eastmancolor multilayered stock that was processed by Warners as part of the company's decision in the early 1950s to go 'all out for colour'.[29] The first Warnercolor feature film was *Carson City* (1952), but British colour expert R. Howard Cricks was disappointed, pronouncing the result to be 'little better than that obtainable by a two-colour process'.[30] George Ashton of the *British Journal of Photography* was more impressed, considering the film to be superior in quality to *Royal Journey* largely because the lighting conditions were more favourable and the interiors shot by John Boyle were 'excellent'.[31] It was announced that a Coronation film would be made in Warnercolor and the resulting film, *Elizabeth is Queen* (1953), was released by Associated-British Pathé as a short feature. The twenty or so cameras used to film the event experimented with a new zoom lens which was used for shots taken from opposite Buckingham Palace. The technical advantages of the Eastmancolor stock meant that hand-held cameras could be used for shots taken among the crowds. The film was processed at Denham Laboratories. Previously Eastmancolor could only be processed in the USA, but Debrie Multiplex developing machines were adapted to handle it, so the film was ready as soon as possible for public exhibition.[32] In an interesting example of media symbiosis, the television coverage of the Coronation was used as a means of speeding up the editing of the

Warnercolor film footage, since, while the latter was being processed, the cutting teams watched the event on television so that they could get an advance sense of content and continuity.[33]

Elizabeth is Queen was praised in reviews, particularly for scenes shot in the Abbey 'where there is a riot of noble colour', as well as for exterior shots which obtained very good results in dull weather conditions that were not conducive to colour cinematography.[34] A review in the *Monthly Film Bulletin*, however, deemed the television coverage to be superior, criticising both *A Queen is Crowned* (1953) and *Elizabeth is Queen* for having 'portentious and uninformative commentaries and superfluous introductory sequences', and for missing an opportunity to take interesting shots of the crowds and their reactions to the event. The films were also criticised for appearing to have been hastily edited which was unnecessary in view of the television record's immediacy, the implication being that the colour films should not have attempted to compete in this regard since the television record was so impressive. The colour was generally thought to be disappointing, with the exception of the shots in the Abbey which 'most effectively caught in both films the shining white gowns of the Maids of Honour and the simple white gown which the Queen wears for her Anointing', providing a contrast with 'the shimmering velvets and glittering cloth of gold'.[35] Other reviewers were more admiring of the colour in both films, especially when compared to *Coronation Day* (1953), the less successful British Movietone colour newsreel which used Gevacolor film and was critiqued for having underexposed shadow areas visible as 'a rich magenta'.[36]

Elizabeth is Queen devotes a lot of attention to the 'dressing' of London for the Coronation, more so than the ceremony in the Abbey, which is less extensively recorded than in *A Queen is Crowned*. This allows viewers to remark on the preparations with banners and flags adorning shops, buildings and streets in a show of all the colours of celebration. One report described this somewhat lengthy lead-up to the ceremony as 'contrived', with the colour balance and definition disappointingly variable. On the other hand, the Eastman stock coped well with the low light conditions in the Abbey, benefiting from a faster stock which was tested during the run-up to the event.[37] Both films focus on the golden carriage and soldiers, and as the reviewers commented, there are no close-ups of faces in the crowds. Associated-British Pathé also made *Royal Review* (1953), a 3-D colour newsreel film of the Coronation procession and subsequent celebrations outside London, using 'Stereo-Technique' cameras and Eastmancolor. The film was never shown because the majority of cinemas were not equipped to project films in 3-D, but extracts were broadcast on British television in 2009, with the producer and cinematographer recalling their film and its context of production.[38] The film featured close shots of the Queen and of the golden coronation carriage, as well as those which emphasised, as the Kinemacolor films had done, the 'layering' of marching troops in a stereoscopic fashion from above, with particular colour details, particularly red and the Union Jack, becoming all the more obtrusive for the combination of colour and depth.

The event was also filmed in Technicolor as a short feature and released as *A Queen is Crowned* through Rank's General Film Distributors. Every Technicolor camera available in Europe (eighteen in total) was deployed for the filming, including some placed in Westminster Abbey to record the ceremony. Pathé also obtained permission to shoot in the Abbey, where the challenge was to film in the lower light levels. In acknowledgment of the importance of facilitating a colour record of the Coronation, official cooperation was granted for both films, even to the extent of David Eccles, Minister of Works, examining previous films of royal pageantry so he could advise Castleton Knight, producer of *A Queen is Crowned*, on the most advantageous positions for the cameras. Filming in the Abbey had not been possible previously, and the film made the most of the novelty of being able to shoot the ceremony's exceptional grandeur, visible from high camera angles as the royal procession advanced towards the altar.

Aside from recording the monumental nature of the event, the film was very much about showcasing the ceremonial display of colour. Eyewitnesses remembered that the event was very much about the display of colourful processions inside and outside the Abbey.[39] The opening credit sequence features as background shields with red and gold dominating, before a contrasting prologue about the nation which resembles a travelogue of pastoral scenes of the countryside, the White Cliffs of Dover, Edinburgh Castle, Balmoral etc.

For critics such as Cyril Ray of the *Sunday Times*, who described this as 'a sugary survey of a sceptred isle where it is always Sunday afternoon', this was too much, even unnecessary.[40] It is not only the images which create the tone since the idyllic, picture-postcard Technicolor views are accompanied by Olivier's voice-over commentary, quoting the 'This Happy Breed' speech from *Richard II*. Olivier's commentary serves as a guide to the images which is integral to establishing the film's reverent, patriotic tone. The degree of emphasis subsequently placed on colour in Laurence Oliver's commentary is, however, unusual. On several occasions he mentions the colours we see; Technicolor's ability to render gold, red, purple and blue is drawn attention to in aural as well as visual terms. This attendance to the detail of colour resonates with Charles Urban's accompanying written commentaries for Kinemacolor's coverage of royal events, as well as his instructions to exhibitors on how to introduce such titles by emphasising their novel colour content. While this emphasis might not always have been wise with Kinemacolor since drawing attention to colour invited a degree of scrutiny that could be counter-productive in view of the process's technical shortcomings, Technicolor was on surer ground by the early 1950s with its reputation for quality. The splendour of the 1953 Coronation is indeed enhanced by highlighting key details such as the contrasting colours of different uniforms and ceremonial dress; the golden Coronation carriage; the crown and light reflected off jewels. Before the ceremony begins, for example, we see the crown on a plush red velvet cushion and against a red background. While the red is obtrusive, Olivier draws our attention to the crown's purple velvet cap, a colour contrast which might have been missed in view of the overwhelming impact of the red. The first shots in the Abbey show from a low angle the heraldic banners of chivalry hanging in the Henry VII chapel whose colours of gold, blue, crimson, gold and cream are mentioned in Olivier's commentary. The coloured stained-glass of Westminster Abbey features prominently in shots which accentuate the magnificence of the setting. Details are selected for the film viewer which would have been difficult for those present to appreciate at close scrutiny, such as the five swords of state displayed against a purple background. The blue carpet in the Abbey, also shot from above, emphasises colour contrasts and patterning created by the slow

A Queen is Crowned
(Technicolor, 1953):
procession from high-angle
shot

movement of the procession and during the various
stages of the ceremony. As the procession proceeds
towards the altar, for example, the excessive length of
Princess Elizabeth's long red, gold and white train can
be seen all the more clearly because of the high camera
angle. These colour contrasts are also shown well in
Elizabeth is Queen. For the anointing ceremony her gold
cape is also highlighted as a ceremonial, sartorial detail
that is remarkable for the quality of its colour rendition.

These details constitute 'colour showcase shots',
repeated many times and in different contexts in *A
Queen is Crowned*. The wealth of magnificence of the
soldiers' uniforms and visual splendour provided by the
procession of visitors from the rest of the world and
Commonwealth meant that these shots were plentiful.
Particular views were also on occasion composed
specifically to highlight colour contrast, as with a low-
angle shot of several vertical red ceremonial banners
which appear to frame Nelson's Column which can be
seen in the background. The criticism that the film-
makers missed an opportunity to pick out enthusiastic
supporters in the crowd, or indeed any close details of
the royal supporters, is perhaps explained by the
assumption that a Technicolor film should foreground
striking colour detail wherever possible. With so much
on offer regarding the procession and ceremony the
appearance of royal supporters was not considered to be
sufficiently spectacular in colour terms. The crowds are
instead depicted from afar, and towards the end of the
film they appear as multitudinous tiny dots, rushing

forward as the royal family appears on the balcony of
Buckingham Palace. This emphasis was to be expected,
especially when *A Queen is Crowned* had to compete
with the Warnercolor film since both were judged in
great part on their ability to render the colours of the
ceremony. Competition with black-and-white television
was another reason for both films to be structured
around displaying colour. By contrast, in *XIV Olympiad:
The Glory of Sport* the depiction of enthusiastic
supporters of the various sporting events was an
important part of the coverage, even though the
Technichrome record was clearly deficient in so doing.
Perhaps because of the length of that film, and the need
to create heightened suspense around the different
events, the closer view of people cheering on the
competitors was essential. The decision to exclude close
shots of the crowds watching the coronation procession
is interesting in comparison. It was clearly considered
more important to produce repeated colour showcase
shots of the seldom-seen golden carriage or the Queen
of Tonga in her splendid pink ceremonial costume than
the reaction of the general public.[41] Generic convention
also played a part since if Castleton Knight was advised
on how previous films had filmed royal occasions this
approach is exactly what would have been suggested
as appropriate. Physical distance from royalty was
maintained, with the film providing a unique means of
getting closer without transgressing decorum.

Dubbed versions of *A Queen is Crowned* were
produced as fast as possible so that the film had extensive
overseas distribution. Exhibitors in Britain and
internationally were encouraged by the Rank
Organisation to be ingenious with showmanship stunts
in advertising the film, with cash awards and holidays
given for the most imaginative campaigns.[42] The various
campaigns were reported, including one displaying a
monochrome picture of the Coronation with the
announcement: 'See this in Technicolor!'[43] With the
existence of television coverage of the event which was
seen by 20 million people in Britain, it was all the more
important to differentiate the films by focusing on the
novelty of them being shot in colour. One reviewer
heralded it as a generic breakthrough:

> History served piping hot, it brilliantly combines the
> dignity and clarity of the finest documentary with
> pageantry and splendour far more dazzling and thrilling

XIV Olympiad: The Glory of Sport (three-strip Tecchnicolor, Technichrome and monopack, 1948): three-strip Technicolor. All images from this film are copyright IOC

than any so far witnessed in the most sumptuous British and Hollywood romances. Her Majesty, queenly and compellingly feminine, rightly dominates the proceedings in the mighty real life role and strengthens her hold on the widest public in the world. No professional player could possibly put over such a terrific *tour de force*.[44]

A *Queen is Crowned* was a box-office success (although not particularly so in America), was widely shown and generally recognised by contemporaries as being of great historical importance. As Chapman has argued, its popularity and the reverence with which it was held by the majority of cinemagoers and reviewers reveals levels of popular support for the monarchy which are no longer as prevalent.[45] Far from being a film which is solely about celebrating the past, it can be related to Britain in the early 1950s with its emphasis on the Commonwealth and the waning of postwar austerity. Howard Thomas, Chairman of the Newsreel Association, noted that exhibitors played a key role in promoting patriotism: 'We all know that the exhibitor has his eye on the box office, yet every one I have met is proud that the film he is supporting will help to strengthen the links of our monarchy in the remotest parts of the Commonwealth.'[46] Marcia Landy argues

that the film's focus on objects including jewels, the crown and sceptre, clothing etc. are important in locating it as a document that speaks very much to its immediate socio-economic context:

> The spectator is made aware of the opulence of the occasion, the monetary value of places, objects, and garments, and the exalted position of the personalities involved. Tradition is harnessed to commerce. The voyeuristic camera seeks out the major actors and brings the spectator into a privileged position in relation to them. The spectacle reveals more about contemporary history and the 1950s emphasis on affluence than about Britain's glorious past.[47]

Colour film was also used to commemorate another key postwar event, the 1948 Olympic Games. *XIV Olympiad: The Glory of Sport* was a feature-length film with a £250,000 budget produced by the Olympic Games Film Company, which had been formed by the Rank Organisation specifically for the event.[48] The extensive nature of the Games with many events and locations, and a shortage of regular three-strip Technicolor cameras (only three were available), necessitated the use of three different colour processes:

monopack for the winter games in St Moritz, Switzerland (this footage had to be processed in the USA); three-strip Technicolor for the opening and closing ceremonies at Wembley; and Technichrome for the Torch Ceremony in Greece and Games at Wembley, Henley, Herne Hill, Torquay and Windsor. Technichrome was a new bipack stock using red and a blue-green and was used in adapted Newall cameras. Castleton Knight, an experienced producer of Gaumont-British newsreels who was charged with directing *XIV Olympiad*, considered it an achievement that the differences between the different technologies did not appear to affect the film: 'I think it is remarkable that not one of the many thousands of press notices even hinted that there had been more than one colour process. This was more than we dared hope for.'[49] He went on to explain that care was taken so that changes between processes could not be easily identified by, for example, cutting from the green grass in Wembley to a close-up of a discus athlete to direct attention away from the paler grass as the process switched from three-strip to Technichrome, which as a two-colour process did not

render green very well. One reviewer, however, judged Technichrome in far from congratulatory terms: 'Monopack stands up well and compares very favourably with the standard method but the Technichrome or bi-pack system obviously needs considerable experimentation before it can be adopted widely for commercial film-making.' The faults identified were that green was poorly rendered, giving a specific example towards the end of the film when 'in one shot you see the grass of the Stadium in a muddy sage-green and the film then changes to three-strip for the closing ceremony and you see the same grass in a bright emerald'.[50] On viewing the film this is indeed evident, and the shot change to the discus athlete referred to above most certainly presents a stark change in the rendering of green as the film shifts from three-strip to Technichrome. Even though in this case, as Castleton Knight noted, attention is on the athlete, the colour difference is so stark that it cannot be offset by the spectacle of the sports event. In fact the entire footage of the Games at Wembley has a bleached-out look, unable to present strong colours, so that grass appears as brownish grey/green and the track

XIV Olympiad: The Glory of Sport: opening shots in Greece in Technichrome; Winter Olympics shot in monopack

XIV Olympiad: Winter Olympics shot in monopack

a dull orange. Clothes worn by spectators that were probably red and which showed up as vibrant in the three-strip film of the opening ceremony appear in Technichrome as dull, with any reds appearing orange.

Technichrome was also used for the opening shots on location in Greece. This proceeds to the Olympic torch ceremony, with the torch being carried by a succession of runners to Wembley. The Greek setting suited the two-colour process since the blue sky and bright sunlight provided effective filming conditions for shots of the three lead Greek female dancers in their contrasting costumes in blue, orange and white. Once the torch is lit the smoke from the flame appears as blueish, a detail devised by Stan Sayer who adapted the fuel so that the smoke was more clearly visible.[51] The film then switches to monopack for the winter games, a change which is assisted by the stark contrast between locations, from the bright sunlight and warm colours of Greece to the stark, white snow and mountains of St Moritz. Monopack was generally very effective for this sequence, with red being a particularly dominant colour for the competitors' regalia as the Games opens and for details such as the red Swiss flag with a white cross. The skies are variable, with little blue visible except in a few shots, and the green of the trees is very dark. But the overall effect is of white crispness and, where colour details are visible (as with red or blue), it is much more saturated than with Technichrome. The setting clearly helped since the white of the snow creates an effective background for the formations of skiers shot from

above, as well as for particular events such as bob sleigh races, the high jump and skating. While red and blue are the commonest colours, a greater variety is introduced by the skating events. The first green in this section of the film is a skater's dress, followed by a Canadian female skater's yellow dress contrasted with her partner's black outfit. A feature is created out of colour when she skates towards the camera, gradually filling the screen with the yellow of her dress. A repeat of this shot is attempted later on when we see the champion skater Barbara Ann Scott in the distance in what appears to be a white dress until she approaches the camera when it is revealed to be yellow. This instance of apparent colour instability indicates how variations in light and shot affected monopack's ability to render a colour in varying conditions. A more successful example is when we see clearly an American skater's gold dress with a red underskirt, a detail that shows up obtrusively against the white background of snow and ice.

The opening and closing ceremonies in Wembley shot in three-strip Technicolor certainly stand out as capable of rendering more brilliantly saturated colours for details such as the grass, flags and the respective national colours of the competitors' sportswear as they march around the stadium before the Games open. With the change to Technichrome everything appears toned-down, and in the shots of the marathon and the rowing events which take place outside the stadium, one is reminded of two-colour films of an earlier period when the prevalent tones were also dull oranges and browns.

XIV Olympiad: skater Barbara
Ann Scott in yellow dress

XIV Olympiad: three-strip
Technicolor ceremony shot

This is particularly noticeable when the increasingly exhausted marathon runners are seen pounding down country roads where grass and trees appear in muted, brownish-grey hues. While the decision to use Technichrome for the main events was dictated by circumstances, it is also likely that the gripping nature of the sports depicted was considered sufficient to offset the process's technical deficiencies. Variations on camera angles, slow-motion and other effects were designed to create suspense and to convey the emotional intensity experienced by competitors and spectators alike.

The film is notable for many other technical details including the design of special mobile tubular steel camera towers located in strategic locations in the Wembley Arena. Care had to be taken to avoid the filming interfering with the events or the view of the spectators, and noiseless electric camera trolleys were built as another example of how filming the Games necessitated ingenuity on the part of the technical team, which numbered a vast 25 camera crews, supervised by noted Technicolor technicians including George Gunn, Douglas Hague and Stan Sayer. The swimming events presented a problem of having to comply with regulations laid down by the swimming and diving associations regarding lighting levels that were not supposed to cause unnecessary reflections or distract the competitors. These were not conducive to filming in colour, but once the paint was scraped off the ceiling of the Empire Pool a greater amount of natural light eased the situation. Technichrome and black-and-white

cameras were used for the swimming events and, unusually, a woman, Norma Candy, directed the camera crew. This sequence is impressive, especially since it features some underwater shots; the blue water of the pool provides the main colour interest, particularly in overhead shots which display it as background to the events as the swimmers race in symmetrical formation down the clearly demarked lanes. The first shot of the sequence, for example, presents an entire screen of blue, with pulsating light reflecting off the water followed by the fleeting sight of a competitor diving into the pool which reminds us today of a Hockney painting. The competitors generally wore black costumes so there was not so much of a sense of 'wrong' colour as with the exterior shots in the stadium, with the exception of shots of the spectators which had similarly low levels of colour saturation in relation to their clothing. *XIV Olympiad* is also notable as a 'composed film'. The music was composed and recorded before shooting so that 'in some cases we had to adapt the music track to the picture, and in others we had to cut the picture to the music'.[52] Instances of the former were the hammer-throwing sequence, and of the latter the marathon coverage. Shot in three-strip Technicolor, the Olympic flag, with its rings in blue, yellow, black, green and red, showed up very well in the opening ceremony and again featured as the final shot of the entire film as an apposite way to declare it as a celebration of sport and of colour.

A few years later a number of short films were made to commemorate the Festival of Britain at London's

South Bank (3 May–30 September 1951), described in *Festival in London* (Crown Film Unit) as 'a milestone between past and future … a diverse place of serious fun and light-hearted solemnity'. The Festival included attractions such as the Dome of Discovery, a 'Fun Park' at Battersea Pleasure Gardens and displays of industry, technology and modern design. Although it has not received the profile of *Family Portrait*, Humphrey Jennings's black-and-white film made to commemorate the Festival, *Festival in London* was shot in Technicolor to celebrate the Festival's promotion of civic pride, new technology, modernist design and consumerism. It used colour to enhance its address, providing a particularly interesting comparison with *Brief City*, a black-and-white film which featured similar shots of the Festival's buildings and exhibits and whose commentary mentions that colour was a very important aspect of the Festival's design.

Festival in London aims to capture the experience of the Festival, with its impressive temporary structures containing exhibits celebrating historic figures, contemporary technologies and inventions, as well as art, sculpture and modern design. The 'open house'

activities on the South Bank and the funfair alongside the Thames also feature as highlights. Colour details are selected for concentration such as coloured baubels decorating a high steel barrier and blue and red balloons being released into the sky. The Festival's most dramatic piece of decorative sculpture, the tall 'Skylon' made of aluminium, steel and wire, which tapers to a point at its top as if cutting into the sky, is shown in several shots. The colour photography displays its golden colour glistening in the sun, an effect which is entirely missing from similar shots of the Skylon in the black-and-white *Brief City*, which make the object seem flatter, perhaps more sinister as it appears as a spacecraft on standby for blast-off. The latter also contains shots of the baubles which look dull in comparison with their coloured appearance in *Festival in London*. The Festival's attempts to interlink past traditions or 'values' as the commentary refers to them, with the present and future recalled by shots such an extreme close-up of a judge's red robes, shown in a slow panning shot which begins with red filling the screen, the camera panning slowly upwards to reveal the regalia in its complete dimensions. Towards

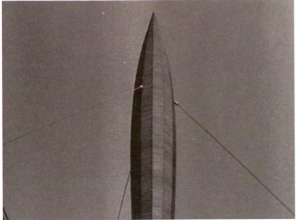

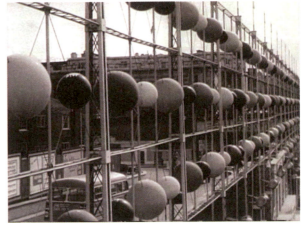

Festival in London
(Technicolor, 1951): the
Skylon in Technicolor; *Brief
City* (black and white, 1951),
the Skylon in black and
white. Courtesy Crown
Copyright/BFI

Festival in London: coloured
baubels on the boundary
fence. Courtesy Crown
Copyright/BFI; *Brief City*:
coloured baubels shot in
black and white

the end of the film a firework display provides another
platform for colour as a suitable homage to the Festival's
aims of providing education, enlightenment and fun.
This privileging of colour for dramatic effect was lost on
the *Monthly Film Bulletin* reviewer, who described the
Technicolor cinematography as 'refreshing, but it is
hoped that this is only the programme opener for a
more serious and permanent record of, in particular, the
South Bank Exhibition. As the years go by the film will
increase in nostalgic appeal, like snapshots of enjoyed
events, but what is provided here is little more than a
series of snapshots.'[53] The 'snapshot' effect is indeed a
feature of the film, but instead of constituting a limited
record, it was integral to the film's style of juxtaposing

shapes, camera angles and colours to convey in particular
a sense of the Festival's engagement with modernist
design and attempt to align visuals with the music
track.[54]

COLOUR AND THE BIOPIC

Linking colour with ceremonial occasions, themes and
personages deemed to be of national importance
extended to the biopic. Herbert Wilcox showcased
Technicolor for the final reel of *Victoria the Great* in a
way that was particularly in keeping with matching
colour to royal pageantry for the Diamond Jubilee

celebrations. The timing of the release of Wilcox's film was crucial, since it became caught up in enthusiasm for royal events after the Coronation of King George VI and Queen Elizabeth on 12 May 1937. As we have seen, the latter provided a showcase for four different colour processes (Technicolor, Dufaycolor, British-Realita and Kinechrome) which recorded the occasion for newsreels. The Technicolor film was received with most enthusiasm, described as a 'thing of beauty', although Dufaycolor was praised for its ability to convey 'the dark tones, particularly the glossiness of the horses'.[55] Soon after the Coronation, announcements for the release of *Victoria the Great* appeared which advertised that the final reel of the Diamond Jubilee was in Technicolor, the rest of the film being in black and white. The Coronation was attended by representatives from the British Empire, and the newsreels showcased colour as appropriate for the pageantry of imperial display. Wilcox also emphasised this association with colour by choosing to highlight Victoria's imperial role which was very much in keeping with the conventions established by Kinemacolor.

The trade press, with an eye on the box office, was generally enthusiastic about *Victoria the Great*. The *Kinematography Weekly* reviewer described the Technicolor reel as 'brilliant if not perfect'.[56] Some commentators, however, found this a distracting gimmick from the film's overall image of decorum, good taste and Englishness. Writing in *The Spectator*, Basil Wright commented: 'The rather vicious brightness of the Technicolor Diamond Jubilee forms an unfortunate ending to a good-looking film.'[57] Critic James Agate was similarly unimpressed, pronouncing: 'At the end it breaks into colour, with an effect like that of a picture book on which a six-year-old has been messing about with a box of paints. The result is to make the last half-hour of the picture look like something enamelled on pottery and marked "A present from Blackpool".'[58] Comments such as this equate colour with vulgarity and Agate also links it with class, a discourse which as we have seen can be traced back to early discussions of colour in the silent period. There is also the implication in these criticisms that to insert colour in an otherwise black-and-white film was an unwelcome intrusion even though the effect was clearly intended to place spectacular emphasis through colour on the Diamond Jubilee. Equating colour with the apotheosis of empire

in this way places ideological imperatives above fears that audiences might not, as many contemporaries feared, appreciate the appearance of colour in the final reel. The film's box-office success attests to the degree to which the novelty of colour did not have a negative impact on the film's commercial prospects; it might indeed have had the opposite effect.

Enthused by his experiment with colour and convinced of its suitability for regal subject-matter, Wilcox immediately filmed *Sixty Glorious Years* entirely in Technicolor. The issue of colour again received a somewhat mixed response, although the film was generally regarded as being very fine and the comments on colour are not quite so critical. Since the whole film is in colour it lacks the spectacle of surprise which the sudden appearance of a colour reel represented in *Victoria the Great*. Also, by the time of release, Technicolor was gaining ground in technical and critical terms. Huntley singled out Technicolor's appropriateness for conveying 'a magnificent cavalcade on British history'.[59] These examples exhibit the generic proclivity for colour as royal spectacle, as being able to convey the exoticism of empire, travel and the variety of history. As an adjunct to Anna Neagle's star persona, these generic forms consolidated her position as a regal ambassador for British cinema. What is interesting about Wilcox's approach was that he used colour to capitalise on the appeal of Neagle's established image.[60] Colour provided the perfect means of enhancing the 'private life' approach to monarchy that had proved to be so popular with films such as *Nell Gwyn* (1934), which had followed after the international box-office success of Korda's *The Private Life of Henry VIII* (1933). While black and white reinforced dominant generic codes of realism, colour offered the spectacle of domesticating royalty, inspiring comments such as Huntley's appreciation in *Sixty Glorious Years* of 'the reposeful chromatic pattern of the interior set in Apsley House, as against the bright outdoor colours of the Highland scene'.[61] This approach extended the range of spectacle as interior, 'domestic' scenes acquired a greater sense of intimacy through colour. In this sense, colour was applied to *enhance* an impression of realism by familiarising audiences with Victoria and Albert's home life.

Other notable biopics were filmed in Technicolor, including *Scott of the Antarctic* (directed by Charles Frend for Ealing, 1948) and *The Magic Box* (directed by

John Boulting and produced by Ronald Neame, 1951). Both were associated with national events – *Scott of the Antarctic* was shown at the Royal Command Film Performance towards the end of 1949 and *The Magic Box* was the British feature film industry's contribution to the Festival of Britain, 1951. In *Scott of the Antarctic* Jack Cardiff shot studio scenes in three-strip Technicolor and Osmond Borradaile shot footage in the Antarctic using monopack. Other locations were used to 'stand in' for the Antarctic, so Borradaile also went to Switzerland and Geoffrey Unsworth to Norway. Perhaps to suit the subject-matter and chosen approach of conveying a 'semi-documentary style', the film is hardly a Technicolor extravaganza. Colour is used primarily to showcase natural phenomena, such as spectacular natural light effects in the sky; a shot of the sun low on the horizon as it appears after the title 'The Return of the Sun'; and for stunning pink and blue skies. Flags have symbolic national significance at key points in the narrative, such as when Admunsen's red and blue Norwegian flag is discovered at the South Pole, a poignant reminder of earlier shots of the flag before his expedition set out.

Using colour to convey the intense cold and varieties of whiteness in the Antarctic was also achieved, as one reviewer noted: 'The photography is superb, whether the camera is roving the gleaming white glaciers and blue ice-sheets or concentrating on the cold, greenish tent interiors.'[62] The monopack film's 'pronounced blue bias' perhaps accentuated 'the essence of the awesome remoteness of the coldest place on earth'.[63] Cardiff experienced technical problems in matching the varied presentations of the polar landscape with studio shots.[64] He was keen to acknowledge the expertise of Technicolor in processing the different hues which were an effect of varying light conditions in the Antarctic and Norway, the latter being bathed with a more amber tinge because of the sun.[65] When reviewing the film in 1949 Roger Manvell was particularly impressed by the achievement of variable colour for the ice, naming Technicolor as:

> wonderful … for the Antarctic is a region of colour with the black shining sea breaking through the ice-packs, the blue sky seen through the clean air against the blue-white snowscapes, a place where dawns and sunsets can turn glaciers into incredible scenes of red and gold, the crevassed ice glistening like great frozen ribs or burnished

tree-roots. Mountains seem made of steel, and the mists and snow, blown like human breath in the wind, turn this harsh inhuman land into a painter's fantasy. The colour is a revelation.[66]

Other reviewers were similarly appreciative of the colour, such as Frank Majdalany writing in the *Daily Mail* of the Technicolor as 'poetically exciting'.[67] Cardiff recalled how he used a green filter for shots inside the tent, and was keen that this was an overall colour, including the men's faces. This effect was not approved of by Technicolor but it heightens an impression of the all-pervasiveness of the bitter locale, the men becoming, as

Scott of the Antarctic (Technicolor, 1948): Jack Cardiff uses green filter shots in a tent scene

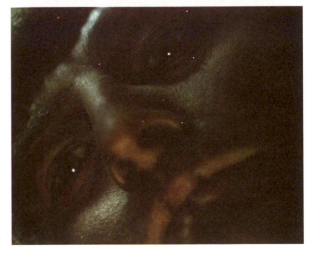

it were, part of the environment they seek to conquer.[68] This is particularly striking since the green tinge combines with the rugged colouring of their weather-beaten skin and further emphasises how their visages have been changed by the climate. In terms of colour symbolism, green as used here can also be taken as a portent for the team's tragic fate.

The Magic Box was an appropriate biopic to be made in colour because its subject, William Friese-Greene (Robert Donat), was one of the first to experiment with colour cinematography. Yet there is also an element of irony, indeed tragedy, since the process chosen for the biopic – Technicolor – succeeded where his own Biocolour and his son Claude's related process Natural Colour failed to become commercially viable. The film refers to colour on several occasions, but the main narrative focus is on Friese-Greene's quest for motion pictures. A flashback structure enables the major periods of his life to feature, intertwined with his battles to keep solvent and the toll of constant indebtedness on both marriages. The film opens in 1921 with Friese-Greene visiting his estranged second wife Edith (Margaret Johnston), on his way to the film industry meeting when he famously collapsed and died while making a speech. In this first scene he tells Edith that he's finally 'got colour … practically perfect … the real thing', which introduces his ceaseless passion for cinematographic invention, even when elderly and with failing health. This occasions the first flashback to 1897, which opens with a dazzling display of colour, since the setting is a firework display for Queen Victoria's Diamond Jubilee. At the fair Edith sees moving pictures for the first time and is then taken by a friend to a laboratory where she meets William Friese-Greene. Reference to colour continues since before we see him we see colours reflected on a ceiling from a prism he is manipulating, followed by a bath of red chemicals and the mixing of blue and red in a vial. Although no explanation for these processes is offered, the impression is of serious scientific pursuits taking place, as Edith's voice-over narration recalls his 'obsession' with colour.

Spectacular colour introduces the second flashback after briefly reverting to 1921 and William at the film industry meeting. When he hears someone say 'Forget the past' the screen fills with a pink distortion of his face in a dissolve to begin the flashback to his early career as a photographer in Bristol and meeting his first

wife Helena (Maria Schell). Of all the flashbacks, and probably to reflect William's youthful ambitions and commitment to his profession, these sequences feature the broadest array of colours and higher-key lighting, particularly the scene when Helena and William sing Gilbert and Sullivan in a local choral society. Helena is chosen with one of the other singers to select costumes for a forthcoming performance to be conducted by Sir Arthur Sullivan. They consult William as to the best colour for their sashes (wine), since he is the acknowledged expert on colour. This sets up the classic melodramatic device of William failing to show up for the special concert because he has forgotten the time when engrossed in his first meeting with William Fox-Talbot; the choir is without a male solo and Helena is humiliated.

The sequence when William finally manages to shoot moving pictures has colour interest since the Technicolor shots of the park show a sunny day and green grass, as well as William filming his relatives. These contrast starkly with the stuttering black-and-white images later shown in the laboratory when a jubilant William hauls in a passing policeman to share with him the wonder of his discovery. The irony of this sequence is that it celebrates Technicolor, the invention for which Friese-Greene was not responsible. As a film to mark the occasion of the 1951 Festival of Britain *The Magic Box* thus serves several purposes. It celebrates a British inventor, motion pictures and colour. While the personal drama of Friese-Greene is tragic, since he died in debt and with a contested legacy as the inventor of motion pictures, the narrative of technological achievement is demonstrated by the film itself. Even though the history of Technicolor plays no part in the film, its association with the success-story of cinematographic technologies is marked by its performance in the film. One review praised the Technicolor as 'the best I have seen in any British picture except *Black Narcissus*'.[69] The film was not, however, a box-office or financial success despite a generous funding arrangement from the National Film Finance Corporation.[70] Reviews blamed the picture being 'over sold'; the number of stars was said to be distracting; the film's release was badly timed after the Festival of Britain had ended, and the narrative considered 'too drab'.[71] The stories of heroic failure represented by *Scott of the Antarctic* and *The Magic Box* clearly proved to be less popular than Herbert Wilcox's regal biopics.

COLOUR AND EMPIRE

While the pronounced associations between Kinemacolor and empire have already been acknowledged, it is important to note that by the time three-strip Technicolor features were being made in the mid- to late 1930s, it seemed obvious to producers such as Alexander Korda to use colour for conquest/adventure films set in far and distant lands. Kinemacolor's filming of royal pageants, especially the Durbar in India, provoked comments which isolated how colour featured in ceremonial contexts. Bringing the full-colour splendour of royal events, processions and the sights of foreign lands to the spectator was Kinemacolor's forte, featuring prominently in the marketing of the process. In terms of ideology, this emphasis reinforced assumptions about the equation of colour with exoticism, otherness and empire. The film of *Preparing for the Durbar in the Chiefs' Camps* (1911), for example, noted: 'Natives working differently-colored stones into various designs' and how 'the different classes of workman may be distinguished by the colors of their turbans'.[72] The observation that other cultures deployed colour according to design was also noted in *Scenes in Delhi, the new Capital of India* (1911), in which Chandni Chowk, the major avenue lined by shops, was described as:

> a living mosaic ... after a while the kaleidoscopic crowd can be resolved into separate units, each unit being an independent blend of orange and magenta, green and violet, or silver and scarlet ... What will impress the artistic visitor is the natural love of picturesque effect, and the correct taste in color possessed by the Hindus. In spite of the extraordinary variety of colors to be seen in the streets, one seldom sees any 'color discords'.[73]

This remark is interesting for its appreciation of 'colour consciousness' observable as operating in other cultures, although of course the impression can also be taken as another pat on the back for Kinemacolor in 'capturing' the magnificence of India. A shared, pan-cultural interest in colour thus emerges in reviews, although these often remarked on how such vivid displays were not evident in western locations.[74]

The *World Windows* (1937–40) series of travelogues shot by Jack Cardiff also exploited colour to enhance the exoticism and visual splendour of foreign locations, including India.[75] Chris Challis was one of his camera assistants (the other was Ian Craig) and he remembers the films being appreciated as 'much better than any other travel films'.[76] These continued in the tradition of Kinemacolor's strategy of harnessing a colour process to broader ideological discourses about empire. The films were funded by Count von Keller (F. W. Keller), a wealthy, well-travelled German and 16mm amateur cinematographer who had moved to the USA. He approached Kay Harrison in the UK about making a series of professional travelogue films in Technicolor which were then co-produced with his wife Countess von Keller and distributed by United Artists. Jack Cardiff was appointed cinematographer and the titles included *Wanderers of the Desert* (dir. Hans Nieter), *The Eternal Fire* (dir. Nieter and Pietro Francisci), *Arabian Bazaar* (dir. Nieter and John Hanau), *Petra* (dir. Nieter), *Jerusalem* (dir. Nieter) and *Ruins of Paimera and Balbeck* (dir. Hanau). Shooting in different locations all over the world presented technical challenges such as making sure there was enough light when filming in St Peter's in Rome by exposing the same film in reverse through manipulating the Technicolor camera.[77] The equipment taken on the expedition included cranes and camera dollies, which was unusual for travelogue films. Difficult terrains were navigated, such as taking the camera 4,000 feet up volcanic Mount Vesuvius for *Eternal Fire*. Accounts of the expedition recounted the feats of technical ingenuity achieved and personal hardships endured by the team. In addition, these emphasised a sense of adventure of filming in exotic locales normally inaccessible to tourists, a point often repeated in the films' voice-over commentaries.

Jack Cardiff explained how the films were intended to offer more than the

> ordinary stereotyped travel record, namely to suggest the intrinsic characteristics of each country or place visited, to have a pictorial composition *symbolising* rather than recording the nature of the country. In the sound department the voice was included as little as possible, but music was used, and an endeavour was made to harmonise it with the character of the scene depicted.[78]

This analysis is interesting in that it reveals how the films were a conscious projection of the western traveller's experience of foreign lands rather than constituting an unmediated 'window on the world' which was a more common claim for such films. Liberated from a strictly realist imperative, the films seek to offer something *beyond* the tourist gaze. By emphasising the difficulties of obtaining permission to film in several sites and the importance of collaborating with religious leaders, linguists and local officials, the *World Windows* expedition was invested with a spirit of imperial adventure which is also evident in the genre of empire feature films.[79] A photograph of the team on location has the caption: 'Empire Builders'.[80] As outsiders having to combat fatigue, strange experiences and cultures, the crew became immortalised as heroes of the travelogue, willing to do anything for their films. Nieter, for example, recorded how this involved persuading Muslim leaders that filming them did not transgress religious rulings against the portrayal of the human form:

> It took me a fortnight of endless discussion with the Bedouins before I found my solution in the argument that Mahomed [sic] only forbade static portrayal, but in a film they would live and move for ever. This argument was accepted to the extent that from that moment we and the camera ceased to exist for them so that everything we filmed was part of their actual lives.[81]

This statement is indicative of the attitude adopted by the team. The solution to a cultural problem is presented as being quickly solved by exploiting an apparent loophole and, by implication, a degree of gullibility on the part of the religious leaders. The idea that filming henceforward became 'invisible' and 'part of their actual lives' seems implausible, as incredible as the assumption that colonial presence was part of the natural order of things.

The films adopted some consistent strategies. Jack Cardiff's claim that voice-over commentary was kept to a minimum is not quite the case. According to Chris Challis, outline scripting took place before shooting began.[82] Several of the films open with rolling text, often in stylised writing which is clearly intended to communicate a sense of strangeness that goes with the locale. The commentaries emphasise the places and peoples as foreign to western eyes and experience, as in the opening of *Wanderers of the Desert*: 'This is the mysterious Arabian desert', and later refers to desert patrollers who are descendants of the Bedouin tribe as 'strange and superstitious'. The audience is led into a

land about which, it is claimed, 'little or nothing is known' which prefaces a commentary that praises the tribe for absorbing western influences by using guns to patrol the desert, having benefited from the influence of Lawrence of Arabia. The mystery of the East is conveyed in classic orientalist terms, with the men described as 'dusky demigods' while the women erect tents and make bread which we are told 'may seem crude to western eyes'. Shots taken at dusk show tribe members dancing but the sound was post-recorded (composed by Ludwig Brav) so it is hard to tell whether it truly relates to what was heard. There are no close-ups of faces and the whole impression in this and the other films is of the camera as distanced from its subjects, thus maintaining a voyeuristic gaze whereby we are familiarised with foreign places and people in such a way that cultural and racial difference are accentuated. In acknowledgment of the crew's 'outsider' status and mentality, Jack Cardiff recalled how making this particular film made him feel 'like Dr Livingstone in darkest Africa when I saw their reaction to the portable gramophone we played to them. They couldn't have been more awestruck if Allah had descended from the sky.'[83] Another distancing technique via technology can be observed at the opening of *Ruins of Palmyra and Baalbek* when men leading camels in the desert are followed by the camera which has been placed on a vehicle that moves at a much faster pace. The spectacle of the crew and the accompanying 'fleet of six high-powered American cars, including two specially-built trucks to carry our camera equipment' could hardly have gone unnoticed.[84]

Several of the films feature ruins whose history is recounted in detail via the voice-over commentary. *Petra* opens with a series of shots which pan across the mountains on the approach to Petra, the deserted city carved into the rock face by the Nabataeans which was once an important junction for the silk, spice and other trade routes that linked China, India and southern Arabia with Egypt, Syria, Greece and Rome. The film creates a drama out of this history in visual terms as well as via the commentary. There are successive shots which emphasise the theme of hidden mysteries as details are picked out, such as the entrance to cave dwellings, carvings made by the Romans and shots of the ruins from the perspective of dark recesses in the rock, creating frames within shots to make the central image more startling. Cardiff's cinematography was influenced by his own experience of Petra, as when exploring the site for the film he was overwhelmed by details such as 'a large temple carved like an exquisite pink cameo out of the mountain itself ... I know of nothing more astonishing than this sudden unexpected sight'.[85] Colour also intrudes obtrusively towards the end when flowers including 'masses of dazzling pink oleanders' and 'kniphofia – "red hot pokers"', are shown growing in the fields.[86] A wealth of architectural detail selected by the camera is also a feature of *Jerusalem* and *The Eternal Fire*. In both these films the camera functions as a wandering explorer, creating suspense as hidden areas are revealed, such as a temple and the Garden of Gethsemane in *Jerusalem* and the ruins of Pompeii in *The Eternal Fire*. Specific trick techniques were employed in the latter film to accentuate a dramatic tone, such as mock doors opening to reveal the first sight of the ruins, and some fountains shown as still working. Both camera, music and voice-over commentary draw the spectator into the past, as if the inhabitants are still there by taking us through specific spaces such as the Temple of Jupiter and the amphitheatre.

The nearby modern city of Naples is not shown, except for fishermen and a final sequence of southern Italians dancing. This provides varied colour interest with their costumes featuring many colours. The celebration of life and colour in such close proximity to the dangerous volcano creates dramatic tension through juxtaposition. The spectacle of the molten lava flowing down the mountainside is perhaps the most dramatic sight in *The Eternal Fire*. Cardiff explained that he exaggerated the impact of the lava's trail by halving the speed of the camera (twelve frames a second instead of twenty-four), which quickened the action, and over-exposing the shots to heighten the lava's red-hot appearance.[87] Contrasting locales accentuated the film's overall suspenseful tone: 'The film included views of the city of Pompeii against the background of the blazing mountain. The sense of a buried city wonderfully restored was cleverly conveyed in the film, and the colours of the gardens and of the shore of the bay of Naples were well brought out.'[88] The idea behind this, and other films in the series, was to show through Technicolor a vivid sense of past civilisations, using colour, camera movement and commentary to animate the spaces in a visual and aural *tour de force*. An example

of this approach was recalled by Cardiff: 'On my suggestion we did a "double take" with the camera, panning over a background that was untouched by human hands, continuing the pan past some steps, then jerking the camera back to the steps as if a discovery of something made by man.'[89]

The film in the series which makes a particular spectacle of colour is *Arabian Bazaar*. The opening credits have a silken-textured, purple background before presenting scenes of the bazaar visited, we read in the accompanying text, by the Bedouin Arabs from the desert once a year. When a conjurer takes out successive handkerchiefs in a magic trick, each is differently coloured, making a spectacle which causes the commentary to observe how the scene is colourful in every sense. Other shots pick out colour details such as on carpets which are for sale, the red costumes worn by dancers and a string of amber beads shown against black. It is striking how, although the camera is unusually close to the subjects, very few, if any of them look at the camera. Perhaps this is what Nieter was referring to when he claimed that the filming became 'part of their actual lives', although this lack of engagement with the technology could be interpreted as challenging its authority.

Colour film was seen to enhance loyalty to the empire by bringing audiences closer to and familiarising them with its 'real' colours while at the same time communicating an idea of difference. This was argued in 1937 by patriotic producer Dallas Bower:

Arabian Bazaar (Technicolor, *World Windows* series, 1937–40): marketplace shot

The two-dimensional monochromatic cinema is unsuitable in subjects of an Eastern character. The 'gorgeousness' of the East, the popular idea of lavish splendour with which the average Western mind associates, say, India, is an association indissolubly bound up with colour ... With the evolution of a successful and practical colour system, however, a very different case presents itself. Something of the 'unreality' of the East is then available for the Westerner.[90]

Alexander Korda's Technicolor films similarly engaged with this mode of presenting by means of generic stereotype particular associations between colours and empire. His fictions of imperial spectacle operate in the spirit of orientalist imagination. The 'unreality' of the East is not, however, a monolithic strategy since, as the following analyses demonstrate, at times there are slippages in presentation, nuance and impact. While colour can be seen to reinforce dominant myths about empire, it cannot consistently be contained within the realms of imperialist or racist discourse.

Korda's first empire film in colour was *The Drum*. It was a box-office success in Britain and the USA. Technicolor was singled out as the most distinctive feature by many reviewers, and as fitting for its genre and theme. Set in the north-west frontier of India, the film details the British strategy of 'divide and rule' in territories which were historically difficult to control. This involved exploiting conflicts between native tribes, taking advantage of pro-British factions and offering military protection to them in exchange for economic advantages. Captain Carruthers (Roger Livesey) finds himself in such a role, charged with negotiating a treaty in Tokot, a fictitious town situated on the border of the contentious frontier province of Afganistan, with the Khan, a local ruler. The Khan and his son Azim (Sabu) are pro-British, whereas the Khan's brother Ghul (Raymond Massey) is pro-Muslim and promotes the use of guns against the British. Ghul murders the Khan, plans to kill Azim and to massacre the British troops at a feast he has invited them to attend. Azim's admiration for the British is symbolised by a pact he makes with a young British soldier, Bill Holder (Desmond Tester), to warn each other of danger by beating a special drum signal which Bill has taught Azim. Azim learns of Ghul's plans and uses the signal to warn the British. In the ensuing conflict Ghul is shot, order is re-established and Azim is appointed as the pro-

British ruler. The crisis averted, the film nevertheless exposes the empire's vulnerability. As an example of the imperial romantic adventure film, *The Drum* is thus a paradoxical text in which empire is celebrated but ultimately exposed as unstable and on the wane.[91]

Most of the locations were filmed in Wales, with only a small percentage of footage shot in India. According to E. S. Tompkins, due to the shortage of three-strip Technicolor crew and cameras, the Indian scenes were shot using the two-colour Multicolor process.[92] The predominantly dusty, yellowish tones of the landscape feature often. The convention of presenting an establishing shot whereby the vast expanse of the landscape is surveyed, followed by a dissolve to a closer shot of the locale before a scene commences is repeated on several occasions. The length of the shots is designed so that maximum impact of the colonial vista is rendered impressive through Technicolor cinematography; in this respect a common shot is the desert shot from below to show a stark contrast with the blue sky. Although the British are mainly seen wearing khaki uniforms, when performing as the military band and for the regimental dinner the Scottish regiment wear bright red jackets, contrasted with dark blue and green tartan. Apart from the colour details associated with some of the characters described below, other colour incidental highlights include turbans worn by the local men.

The Drum suggests some complex relations between colour, gender and race. Steve Neale has noted some classic links between colour and femininity, observing how: 'The female body both bridges the ideological gap between nature and cultural artifice while simultaneously marking and focusing the scopophilic pleasures involved in and engaged by the use of colour in film.'[93] It is notable that colour features in this way more in respect of native female and male characters rather than for Carruthers' wife Margery (Valerie Hobson), who consistently wears 'cool' colours of pale blue or beige, or a dark maroon dress, with very little or no exposed flesh. This emphasises her role as a sensitive, non-sexualised and passive character who bonds with Azim and represents the white women of conscience frequently depicted in imperial fiction, as discussed by Dyer.[94] On the other hand, a longish sequence shows Ghul watching – and appreciating – a woman dancing whose movements are slow and sensual, and she is dressed in a red, blue and gold costume which sparkles in the light. The inclusion of gold in Technicolor shots was a frequent means of drawing attention to colour, to an area in the frame designed for specific visual attention. The reinforcement of colour through texture is a similar idea, emphasising depth, contour and shape.

Although the feminisation of native men in films of empire is a familiar trope, as Jaikumar points out, in *The Drum* it works as one of 'several maneuvers that collapse the distance between coloniser and colonised to grasp the film's tentative redefinition of imperial relationships'.[95] This involves the depiction of Azim by Indian actor Sabu, who is frequently seen without a shirt, with the camera focusing on his bare torso which contrasts with the blue of his turban and billowing whiteness of his 'harem pants'. These shots caused controversy in India, where riots were reported when it was screened on account of the bare torso being 'inauthentic' for the Pathan character played by Sabu.[96] Brian Winston has analysed the ideological proclivity of Technicolor to render Caucasian skin tones as unnaturally white.[97] The eroticisation of Sabu's body in *The Drum* shifts the focus to darker skin being equated with beauty and desire. In terms of viewpoint, the latter is located within the homo-social, bordering on the erotic, attachment between Azim and Bill. Jaikumar interprets this as an example of a fissure in colonialism whereby conventional power relations between white and non-white characters are threatened by the close bonds that develop between them:

> In visual terms, Sabu's feminisation maintains him in a position of subjugation while admitting an erotic susceptibility of the camera and audience to his image. Thus historically, a commercialised pull of fascination with the native's image is concomitant with admissions of imperial vulnerability to subject lands and peoples.[98]

Although ultimately discredited, the eloquent and clever character Ghul occupies a similarly ambivalent space in terms of gender, race and ideology. Although his flesh is not exposed he is a compelling figure in terms of his pivotal role in dominating much of the narrative. This is arguably assisted by the fact that Ghul is played by Raymond Massey, known for acting roles associated with eloquence, sagacity and insight. In sartorial terms he is visually arresting; his clothes are frequently elaborate, coloured and bejewelled, evoking connotations of

opulence, grandeur and authority. It is characters such as these that disturb the stability of empire, an enterprise with which colour is complicit. Just as colour was effective in evoking patriotism in Kinemacolor's films of British royalty, it is also compelling in its association with Ghul. The context of colour's application is again seen to be all-important, demonstrating how it can disturb conventional, ideologically driven associations.

The Four Feathers was the second Korda film in the empire genre. The very premise of the film, that to be given four white feathers is a sign of cowardice, presents a variation on white as being symbolically equated with superiority, conquest or purity. The film takes place largely in the Sudan, in the period leading up to the British victory at the Battle of Omdurman in 1898. After resigning his army commission when his regiment is ordered to fight in the Sudan, Harry Faversham (John Clements) is given a white feather by each of his three friends and a fourth at his own instigation, to represent the incredulous response of his fiancée Ethne (June Duprez) to his decision. To disprove their charges of cowardice, he travels to Egypt and disguises himself as a member of a local tribe. He evades detection in part because he does not have to speak (tribe members were rendered mute after being punished by the ruling tribe), following his comrades and rescuing each of them from death by committing extreme acts of bravery. The film shows that bravery need not be demonstrated in conventional ways, and by the end Faversham has more than proved himself to be a hero by saving not only his friends but assisting the British Army in their struggle to defeat the insurgents. As such the film shares the same ideological imperatives as *The Drum* by suggesting that although the empire is profoundly unstable and dangerous, British military intervention and the endorsement of particular codes of masculine chivalry are necessary to keep order.

While the film has been cited in discussions of British genre cinema, apart from general observations about it being shot in Technicolor, the specifics of colour have not been isolated as part of its address.[99] This is perhaps explained by the fact that although interesting, colour is not a particularly obtrusive feature. The cinematographer was Georges Périnal, with scenes in the Sudan shot by Osmond Borradaile. As noted by E. S. Tompkins: 'There is some lovely colour work in the production and great restraint is shown in the use of colour, which is always an added interest rather than a definite distraction.'[100] As in *The Drum*, the Sudanese landscape is depicted in many recurring panning shots which contrast the sandy tones of the desert and soldiers' khaki uniforms with a vivid blue sky. This landscape is contrasted with the ordered gentility of England, since the film reverts there on several occasions to focus on Harry's fiancée. Several scenes take place at night, a bold move in terms of early three-strip Technicolor which was criticised by Tompkins as being 'less expert' in terms of shadow lighting than contemporary Hollywood productions.[101] With little emphasis on ceremonial occasions *The Four Feathers* does not indulge in a display of military colours and regalia, with the exception of shots of flags in the Sudan as the troops are gathering. When Harry resigns his commission his uniform is black and as the central character he spends the majority of the film in disguise, living rough, battling with the sun and wearing dishevelled clothes. Contrary to how Sabu is filmed in *The Drum*, there are low-angle shots of the native insurgents which show them as very dark-skinned and menacing. Posing as a member of the Sanghali tribe, Harry's skin is not very dark and it is never a problem for the audience to identify him. As with other instances of cinematic masquerade, western audiences are granted a privileged viewpoint which inevitably communicates a sense of cultural superiority since the local people in the narrative implausibly do not question the disguise. This film is an interesting example of how colour has no particular role in instilling patriotism through overt displays of military regalia and pageantry. Instead, the more subtle differentiations of skin tones and the symbolism of the white feathers are more significant. Usually taken to signify cowardice, the film works to overturn that association as the feathers inspire Harry on his honourable quest and in so doing the virtues of his chivalry and 'whiteness' ultimately prevail.

The Thief of Bagdad has already been referenced as an important showcase film for early three-strip Technicolor. Unlike *The Drum* and *The Four Feathers*, as a Technicolor fantasy the film is not specifically located in British imperial history. In relation to the discussion of empire films it, however, raises similar questions about colour and ideology. The 'Eastern other' is equated with colour, the spectacular landscape and special effects communicating an exaggerated

perspective that confirmed stereotypical images of the empire as full of exoticism, adventure and danger. Technicolor's 'natural' alignment with these ideas, and the by then quite embedded assumption that if colour was to be used obtrusively then it was appropriate in this context, resulted in the repetition of particular tropes which became equated with the empire genre. Once again we see British/European actors masquerading as native characters (Conrad Veidt as Jaffar, June Duprez as the Princess and John Justin as Ahmed), which arguably impacts on their performances and the responses of western audiences. Sabu is cast as a mischievous thief, a child-like, yet eroticised figure who spends some of the film transformed into a black dog because of a spell cast by the evil Jaffar. The transition shot when this happens creates an uncomfortable moment when Sabu's face dissolves into that of the dog, thus equating him visually with an animal in a shot which is based on showing similarity between Sabu's features and those of the dog. Incidents such as these are naturalised as comic elements, which make for disconcerting viewing today.

Men of Two Worlds, produced by Two Cities films during wartime and directed by Thorold Dickinson, constitutes a different example of the colour film set in colonial territories, in this case Tanganyika, a former part of German East Africa which was assigned to Britain as a mandated territory under the League of Nations in 1919. Dickinson researched and wrote the script in collaboration with novelist Joyce Carey who had been District Officer in West Africa, associate producer Richard Vernon, cameraman Desmond Dickinson and art director Tom Morahan. They went to Africa in order to write an 'authentic' script, aiming to break new ground with the film which explores a clash of two worlds when Kisenga (Robert Adams), a young black pianist who has been living in Britain for fifteen years, is invited back to Africa to teach. He is committed to assisting District Commissioner Randall (Eric Portman) and Dr Caroline Monroe (Phyllis Calvert) in educating the local people and gets involved in trying to persuade a tribe, from which he originates, to relocate to escape a rapidly spreading sleeping sickness. He is opposed by witch doctor Magole (Orlando Martins), who curses him for his interference and accuses him of betraying his people. Kisenga's father dies and Magole says it is his son's fault. When Kisenga becomes ill the people believe that Magole is right, but his recovery proves to them that the witch doctor's spell of death has failed and he is discredited. They realise that they must follow Kisenga's advice and move from the sickness, representing a victory for Kisenga and his white colleagues against what are depicted as dangerous forces of ignorance and superstition in colonial territories.

'Two worlds' is definitely the theme of the film, which opens in London. Red London buses are prominent in a panoramic 'landmark London' shot and we hear the striking chimes of Big Ben. The first scene is at the National Gallery where Kisenga is performing as a concert pianist. His return to Africa is in stark contrast to this, as we see the landscape from an aerial shot. Realism is the aim of much of the colour cinematography, with shots of the local settlements in abundance, and with no English actors masquerading as natives. Many sequences were shot on location, particularly in East Africa for the village setting on the plains. Dickinson recalled the difficulties of shooting in a variety of locations before returning to Denham to complete the film.[102] Throughout the film much of the lighting is low key, with details such as firelight, shots of a full moon and a dark blue sky constituting arresting colour contrasts. An account of the production detailed how such shots as these were achieved at Denham, where a complete village was built as the set for the tribal dances:

> To get the effect of the sudden transition from firelight to moonlight took a few rehearsals as the extinguishing of the orange arc lights on the gantries had to synchronise with the dousing of the fire by water … The sudden complete contrast of glowing firelight and soft, brilliant moonlight, added to the colourful costumes make these sequences some of the finest of English Technicolor achievements.[103]

There are many shots which feature light emanating from within the diegesis, such as soft illumination from cars' headlights and coloured light from lanterns. These techniques enhance the film's deployment of 'natural' colour sources with very little studio work.

The most striking colour effect appears twice concerning red. When Kisenga is challenged by Magole he cuts his arm and the flowing blood is shown as very bright red, almost artificial. Later, when Kisenga is ill, we see his hallucinations in a strange sequence featuring an orchestra and an African tribe. This relates to the film's theme of western culture pitted against ancient tribal rituals, expressed as an opposition between the classical music played by Kisenga and the thudding drumbeats of African music. In a very unusual effect, blood splatters the screen to such an extent that red practically covers the entire frame. This explosion of colour is indicative of similar moments of crisis in films when colour is used to convey a particularly traumatic experience, such as rape or loss of consciousness. In a film which is otherwise concerned to operate within realist conventions such effects have a great impact. In this case Kisenga's very blood is thrust into the camera as his life slips away. As he regains consciousness he hears the local children sing a song he has taught them, which aids his recovery. Back from the brink of death, the film ends with the apparent triumph of the forces of enlightenment. On the other hand, the violence of the blood splattering on the camera lens creates a rupture that arguably cannot be contained by the film's formal closure. Its explosive nature, particularly in relation to the style of the rest of the film, alerts us to how colour can exceed symbolic resonance, confirming Godard's succinct observation that 'it's not blood, it's red'.[104]

While this example is not commented on by Huntley, it is unusual that *Men of Two Worlds* is singled out in his book *British Technicolor Films*, published in 1949, for more detailed colour commentary than many of the other films discussed in the volume. Huntley singles out the contrasts between the interiors of mud huts which were coloured to replicate 'rich red earth' and 'the luxurious tropical colouring of the outdoor sequences'. Huntley also mentions 'the use of colour for dramatic emphasis', congratulating Joan Bridge for her work in creating colour gradations between characters for dramatic effect:

> Two figures are seen in the foreground; one in green, the other in tan. This colour motif is emphasised when the camera picks up the two principals. As Kisenga and Saburi, his sister, both in white, push their way through, they part the two foreground figures, thus accenting in colour the verbal clash to come a moment later when Kisenga confronts Magole. The latter is clothed in slate blue, which is again in complete contrast to the white tropical suit worn by Kisenga.[105]

Men of Two Worlds was, therefore, seen by contemporaries as attempting to experiment with colour within a generic framework that was considered appropriate.

The examples discussed in this chapter demonstrate how genre influences colour and vice-versa. Films about royalty, historical figures and the empire were extremely popular in Britain, so it is not surprising that colour was used to 'complete' and 'make real' emotions and ideologies circulating around British history, spectacle and empire. Genre can be seen to operate as a constraining force in the sense that colour impact is reduced when presented as a convention associated with genre, such as scarlet military uniforms in the empire genre, or the 'already familiar' exotic locations whose colouring equates with expectations generated from print culture, travelogues and even personal experience. The veracity of these images is thus compared with other registers and the pleasure of recognition is in being presented with something that appears to be visually convincing in terms of colour. It does not follow that such images necessarily go *unnoticed*, since recognition can operate almost as a Barthesian *punctum*.[106] Also, some of the films discussed can be seen to boldly divert from the imperative of establishing verisimilitude, on occasion presenting colour to shock or 'surprise' the viewer, which cannot be explained by generic codes. Instances of this would be the blood splattering the camera lens in *Men of Two Worlds*; the sudden appearance of a Technicolor reel towards the end of *Victoria the Great* that some viewers found to be in bad taste or disconcerting, even though the scene was for a royal celebration and in keeping with the norms of filming royal occasions established earlier in the century with non-fiction Kinemacolor. Other examples include the colours reflected on the ceiling from Friese-Greene's prism, and the Olympic athlete skating towards the camera wearing a yellow dress that gradually dominates the screen to such an extent that the figure and her context are completely engulfed by the colour; in Godard's terms, it is not a dress but yellow.

We have also seen how to facilitate instances of dominant or obtrusive screen colour particular shots and camera techniques consistently feature, including panning shots for the presentation of exotic locations in the empire genre. High camera angles are particularly important in the films of the 1953 Coronation and the 1948 Olympics. Such shots are in part motivated by a fascination with showing colours and the patterns they make from perspectives not available to spectators attending the events. In the spirit of the 'cinema of attractions' and taking advantage of this idea that the film record offers something *more*, the film coverage of the Coronation was presented as a superior experience to the more conventionally privileged viewpoint of those actually at the ceremony. Since the films were competing with television's black-and-white coverage, colour featured as one of the major attractions, as evident from Olivier's commentary which made sure people did not miss important colour details such as the purple velvet cap on the crown. While this is clearly evidence of a confidence about the quality of Technicolor in the early 1950s, some of the films reveal insecurities around the process, which related to its expense and intermittent scarcity. While those who viewed *Scott of the Antarctic* were pleased with the results achieved by a mix of locations and light conditions, the more extreme case of having to use even more formats for *XIV Olympiad: The Glory of Sport* was less successful.

The fiction and non-fiction films confirm that genre in a broad sense works to fix some of the ideological meanings associated with colours. In so doing they also, however, reveal the contradictions which are inherent in this proposition. While critics such as James Agate equated the vibrant colour reel of *Victoria the Great* with gaudiness, and lower-class aesthetic sensibilities ('a present from Blackpool'), short films and newsreels which celebrated royalty and the military in bright colours were deemed to be appropriate for celebrating tradition and pageantry. This example of more saturated colours being more acceptable in one form (non-fiction film) than another (a mainstream royal biopic with a major British star as Queen Victoria) also relates to the tenacity of ideas about the desirability of colour restraint in fiction film that persisted for so long. Operating outside of the conventional realms of colour control, shorts and non-fiction films perhaps had more leeway to include colour showcase shots than genre fiction films. Yet, as the following chapter will demonstrate, genres such as melodrama permitted some interesting experiments with colour design and British films in the postwar period were particularly open to pushing the boundaries of restraint.

9 COLOUR GENRES IN POSTWAR CINEMA 2
THE COLOUR OF MELODRAMA

The study of colour in relation to melodrama has concentrated on examples from Hollywood cinema. The genre's tendency to foreground emotional dilemmas and the impact of social and ideological pressures upon individuals promotes a particularly affective response from the viewer who gets caught up in the characters' inner turmoil and repressed desires. The modes of expression in melodramas characteristically highlight, even exaggerate, *mise en scène*, colour and music in ways which distinguish the genre. In 'Tales of Sound and Fury', a seminal article on melodrama, Thomas Elsaesser cited Douglas Sirk's recollection that deep-focus lenses were effective in *Written on the Wind* (1956) because they gave 'a harshness to the objects and a kind of enamelled, hard surface to the colours. I wanted them to bring out the inner violence, the energy of the characters, which is all inside them and can't break through.' This constitutes a compelling example of the interrelationship between film, style and technique which attracted many theorists to studying the genre from a variety of theoretical perspectives from the 1970s.[1] Mary Beth Haralovich, for example, has analysed Douglas Sirk's *All That Heaven Allows* (1954) as a case study of how colour can contribute to the genre's challenge to the conventions of Hollywood cinematic realism. In particular, she notes the tendency for colour to assist the excesses of *mise en scène* in exposing contradictions in 'the ideological bases of social life' depicted in the films:

> Costumes, settings, lighting, and the arrangement of characters in the frame – all help to define the characters and their relationship to each other and to the conflict the film is working through. But the realist narrative space of melodrama also makes evident the social pressures and ideologies that participate in the definition of the characters and the conflict.[2]

Haralovich demonstrates how, for example, in *All That Heaven Allows* a red dress can function to separate an object or character from the setting 'in order to emphasize the narrative or to comment on ideologies'. At the same time, the subsequent addition of red objects can 'complicate the realist narrative space, interfere with the emotional trajectory of melodrama, and trouble the attention to the narrative that is important to the conventions of color film practice'.[3] This analysis depends on seeing colour as part of establishing a film's verisimilar conventions but also as mutable, obtrusive and troubling. This is different from simply noting that colour can on occasion be 'spectacular' because melodrama's investment in presenting realist narrative space is more marked than in musicals or in fantasy genres. Subtle shifts in colour emphasis, hue and saturation are therefore part of the emphatic and mutable colour systems of melodrama, since it is in these differences that colour extends a film's visual style and complexity.[4]

Classic theories of melodrama concentrated on examples from Hollywood, with Elsaesser arguing that 'visual orchestration' was 'fundamental to the American cinema as a whole' in which spectacle was privileged as an aesthetic discourse, supported by the 'additional melodic dimensions' of the spoken word.[5] Melodramas provided generic contexts that were, however, conducive to colour experimentation in a number of postwar British films including *Jassy* (1947), *Blanche Fury* (1948), *Footsteps in the Fog* (1955), *Saraband for Dead Lovers* (1948) and *Gone to Earth* (1950). These permit an analysis of colour in relation to both melodramatic modes and to contemporary aesthetic and technical discourses circulating around Technicolor films released in Britain. Working with melodrama encouraged directors and technicians to experiment further with British colour aesthetics. British costume melodrama has been primarily identified with Gainsborough Studios and the popular run of box-office successes following *The Man in Grey* (1943) and *The Wicked Lady* (1945). These films were frequently dismissed by high-brow critics as sensational and trite, but they were very popular with audiences and have been appreciated by critics since the 1980s as significant registers of contemporary issues and as a commercially astute studio strategy for repeating a successful formula in spite of low budgets.[6] The films nevertheless looked sumptuous, with period costumes designed by Elizabeth Haffenden and lavish-looking sets by key figures such as Maurice Carter, John Bryan and Andrew Mazzei. Their thrilling scripts were adapted from popular novels and, even though their narratives were located in the past, the dilemmas facing the characters often chimed with war and postwar concerns, particularly in relation to class and gender. Released in a context of postwar austerity, these tales of female transgression appealed to audiences who relished their visual styles which privileged pleasurable looking, excess and exoticism.[7] Although only one of the films considered here was produced by Gainsborough, the chosen examples demonstrate how the British historical costume melodrama was exploited by different studios and creative teams. Following the box-office failure of *London Town* (1946), a British Technicolor musical, and in response to critics who often failed to appreciate Hollywood's colour musicals, it made sense to use Technicolor in more commercially proven British generic contexts.

Gainsborough's first colour melodrama in this tradition was *Jassy*, starring Margaret Lockwood and directed by Bernard Knowles who had previous experience with Technicolor directing *The Mikado* (1939) for which he learned about the advantages of colour distribution in the frame, and that colour

separation could make the job of lighting an easier one for the cameraman.[8] The cinematographer was Geoffrey Unsworth, who had worked with Technicolor as an assistant and as a camera operator on a number of films, including *The Drum* (1938), *The Thief of Bagdad* (1940), *The Life and Death of Colonel Blimp* (1943), *A Matter of Life and Death* (1946) and on Gainsborough's first colour film *The Man Within* (1946), a smuggling story set in the early nineteenth century, based on Graham Greene's novel. According to John Huntley, *The Man Within* was a wasted opportunity since there was,

> little imaginative use of colour … so much could have been done … Technicolor films are often viewed in black-and-white in the studio cinema during the 'rough cut' period. Those who saw the picture in this state say that *The Man Within* looked just as good in monochrome; that colour added little or nothing to the emotion and drama of the film.[9]

On the other hand, as Murphy notes, colour invested the film with a 'different atmosphere' from earlier Gainsborough films.[10] Huntley failed to appreciate that *The Man Within* was actually a significant experiment with colour and lighting. It can be seen to have laid the groundwork for Geoffrey Unsworth's initial approach to colour which deployed it to exaggerate mood with low-key lighting and colour-bathed frames, and which can be compared with Chris Challis's cinematography in *Footsteps in the Fog*. While *The Man Within* is not a female-centred historical film, it is an important precursor to colour experimentation in subsequent melodramas, so it deserves brief consideration here.

The Man Within uses colour to enhance setting in many of its outdoor scenes, especially for expressionist-like effects in the mist when low-key lighting combines with colour lighting effects to exaggerate the central character's experience of fear and disorientation. The story is told in a series of flashbacks by Francis Andrews (Richard Attenborough) as he is being forced under torture to provide information about the leader of a group of smugglers. He describes his relationship with his guardian Carlyon (Michael Redgrave), who rescues Andrews from school when he is orphaned, and takes him on board *The Good Chance*, a smuggling vessel under his charge. He admires Carlyon greatly but this relationship is strained when one of the sailors plants money on Andrews to make Carlyon suspect him as a thief. Francis is beaten by Carlyon and Francis betrays the smugglers by writing a letter to the customs authorities, informing them of their landing spot on the Sussex coast. When they land they are ambushed and a local man is shot. Convinced that Carlyon is chasing him Francis runs in search of refuge, struggling in the mist which has enveloped the landscape. A blue-bathed screen accentuates his experience of disorientation and desperation as he tries to find shelter but is also running from Carlyon who, the film implies, may or may not actually be there. The effects include one shot in which Francis runs into the centre of the frame and disappears into the mist; the screen becomes enveloped by colour as his figure vanishes. This establishes an impressionist viewpoint since we are not sure whether Francis's guilt has caused him to hallucinate. On several occasions Francis again appears to be haunted by Carlyon, seeing him behind doors, or reflected in a mirror, and he becomes terrified that he will seek revenge for the betrayal. Combined with the blue effect, low-key lighting is very effective for several scenes in the mist which accentuate the film's brooding atmosphere of dark shadows and sinister shapes. Technicolor's aim was to develop stocks to enable shooting in lower light levels, and progress had been made at the end of the 1930s and again towards the end of the 1940s.[11] This facilitated the aim of many colour cinematographers to demonstrate lighting skills developed when working with monochrome, while taking advantages of colour's ability to convey separation and enhance dimensionality. In a case such as this, however, the alignment of the blue mist with the character's terror and confusion renders the effect plausible as a psychologically motivated colouring which contradicts any idea that in terms of symbolism blue might be associated with calmness.

Other colour effects are fairly conventional, such as different costumes for the two women in the film. Francis hides in a cottage, where he encounters Elizabeth (Joan Greenwood), the daughter of the man who was shot. Dressed in plain, black mourning clothes, she is contrasted with Lucy (Jean Kent), mistress of the Public Prosecutor, a woman he encounters in a pub where he is persuaded to give evidence of the shooting so that the smugglers can be convicted. She wears a green bejewelled dress intended to be indicative of the charge made against her in court as a 'loose' woman with whom Francis has associated. At the end of the film Francis refuses to betray Carlyon; he is released and Carlyon admires him for his bravery. Critics were puzzled by the film's mixture of costume drama with complex Freudian psychology. Basil Wright wrote that it 'foxed my critical faculties', commenting on its 'artificial settings, stylised to the *nth* degree'.[12] Others were less impressed and the film has not received much subsequent critical attention, let alone been viewed for its interesting attempts to deviate from Technicolor norms as a precursor to *Jassy* and subsequent attempts to exploit colour in historical melodrama.

Jassy did not experiment to quite the same degree as *The Man Within*. Yet it certainly continued with the idea of colour exuding atmosphere and realistic detail, and was promoted as a significant development of the studio's established style for period melodramas. Set designer Maurice Carter was given 'the biggest budget I'd ever had for sets'.[13] The press book linked the sets directly to a particular approach to colour design which was identified as being specifically British:

> Gainsborough have used the method which they believe is partly the reason for British Technicolor films proving so much more harmonious than the often more blatant colouring of the Hollywood product. They have made their sets subjective to colouring, in other words they have designed the colouring to blend with the Technicolor itself to bring warmth to pale colours – as opposed to the usual Hollywood method of designing vividly coloured sets only to have them brightened again by the normal process of the colour cameras.[14]

British Technicolor is thus linked again with 'harmony' and restraint, although critic C. A. Lejeune's response was typical of those who did not appreciate the style or genre: 'It would have been better, I should have thought, if some cool and gentle hand had held back the Technicolor *Jassy* until such time as the quality of British films had ceased to be a burning international topic.'[15] While this comment is not necessarily a criticism of colour, it is indicative of the ways in which particular critics considered Gainsborough melodramas not to be good advertisements for British cinema, particularly at a time when the Rank Organisation was poised for an assertive campaign in the American market. While more recent critics have noted that *Jassy* was filmed in Technicolor, comments are seldom detailed and it has not received the attention given to earlier black-and-white melodramas or to subsequent films which had more obtrusive colour designs. Petrie notes, for example, how in terms of using low-key lighting in conjunction with colour which could be identified as 'expressionist', *Jassy* is not as overtly experimental as *Blanche Fury*, another melodrama with which it is often compared even though it was not a Gainsborough production and was photographed by Guy Green.[16] While the analysis of the impact of low-key lighting on colour is a key area, it is also important to note changes in colour made possible by higher registers which make subtle changes visible as well as the colour relationships between costumes and sets. As Darrel Catling argued in the *British Journal of Photography*, colour was able to achieve high degrees of tonal contrast and that 'the few venturesome, imaginative lighting men … despite opposition from the colour laboratories … have proved that colour possesses a flexibility sufficient for it to respond to their most delicate touch'.[17] Gainsborough was perhaps cautious about appearing to deviate from a successful generic formula or to present Margaret Lockwood for the first time in colour without great care. Yet it was the nature of that formula which determined that Technicolor's purpose was to heighten the verisimilar sense of period 'authenticity' which was so important to costume melodrama, and at the same time deploy colour as both emphatic and mutable emphasis to underscore the narrative's various conflicts and resolutions.

Set in the 1830s, *Jassy* opens with an event which triggers the fate of the major characters when Christopher Hatton (Dennis Price), a feckless aristocratic gambler, loses Mordelaine, his ancestral home, in a dice game to the unscrupulous Nick Helmar (Basil Sydney). Christopher moves with his family to a farm where his son Barney (Dermot Walsh) meets and becomes attracted to Jassy (Margaret Lockwood), a gypsy with second sight. Her father is shot by Nick Helmar and she is sent away to work in a school where she befriends Dilys (Patricia Roc), Helmar's daughter. They both go to live at Moderlaine when Dilys is expelled from school after attempting to elope with a soldier and Jassy is dismissed for trying to protect her. Christopher commits suicide after further disgracing the family by continuing to gamble and being discovered to be a cheat. Jassy loves

Barney but he is attracted to Dilys who marries the son of a neighbouring landowner. Even though she does not love him Jassy marries Nick on condition that Mordelaine becomes hers as part of the marriage settlement. Nick is angry when it is clear that Jassy will not live as his wife. While recovering from a horse riding accident he is poisoned by Lindy (Esme Cannon), Jassy's faithful dumb servant who knows that Jassy hates Nick. Jassy is arrested, but during the trial Lindy's voice is miraculously restored and she confesses to the murder. Jassy gives Mordelaine to Barney and the implication at the end of the film is that he has come to love her.

The film's opening titles have a red background, a colour which appears to be connected with the importance of Mordelaine. As in many Gainsborough melodramas, the country mansion setting is extremely important. This is indicated in the press book, which details the work of scenic artist Albert Juillon who painted the large wall tapestries, and the exterior shots of Mordelaine, shot at Blickling Hall at Aylsham in Norfolk.[18] Christopher's wife wears an orange/red dress as mistress of Mordelaine in the opening scene before he loses the game and they are forced to move out. There is indeed a case to be made that red features in *Jassy*, as it does in many melodramas, as a particularly important colour. When we first encounter Jassy as the gypsy being taunted near the farm, she is in dull browns and beiges. This is somewhat unusual since in other Technicolor films, such as *Wings of the Morning*, gypsies are normally adorned with hyperbolic colour; Jassy's colour association with red is, however, held back until later in the film. She subsequently wears more elaborate costuming to match her transition from being a despised gypsy to owning a magnificent country house. Before she gets there, however, it is typical to see her in blue, such as when Jassy meets Barney's mother in the farmhouse. Blue is a colour more associated with Dilys and perhaps is used to underscore their friendship at this point as, for example, when Jassy is a 'between maid' at the school she wears a long blue apron. Towards the end of the school sequence, when Dilys attempts to elope and Jassy rescues her after she is rejected by the soldier, the entire scene is bathed in night-time blue and Jassy wears a blue cloak. It is not until she arrives at Mordelaine with Dilys that she wears red, as if the colour goes with being mistress of the house and so prefigures the material security acquired by her eventual ownership of the property. The tendency to chart a character's changing fortunes through colour was common in Technicolor films.[19]

Jassy's costume thus becomes more emphatically associated with Mordelaine, and as her character rises to prominence. This is supported by the viewer's prior knowledge of her history, as well as of her presentation as being clever, sensible, sensitive and having special gifts which overrides the fact that at that point in the narrative she has lost her job, has no status and is a guest in the house subject to the whim of her quixotic friend Dilys. Later on, in the scene when she goes to fetch Dilys which provides Lindy with an opportunity to poison Nick, Jassy again wears red, as if to mark another decisive moment in the plot. The idea of colour accent is appropriate here, since the deeper saturated, emphatic red worn by Jassy appears at such key moments – on arrival at Mordelaine with Dilys, and for her journey when she leaves Lindy alone with Nick. In these particular contexts as a colour register within the film red can exceed its immediate temporal moment, that is to say it can acquire anticipatory, portentous qualities which in retrospect become evident, as with a motif. I use the term 'emphatic' to indicate such incidents, since by linking red in these examples with what Jassy *is to become*, colour's function within the visual excesses of melodrama can be demonstrated. It also supports theoretical observations of Eisenstein which stress the shifting, contextual relation of a colour to the imperatives of a specific fiction rather than to symbolism in general.[20]

The maroon dress Jassy wears on several occasions when playing chess with Nick can be seen to have another function. As a brownish-crimson colour, maroon is an intermediate colouring for Jassy, since once installed in Mordelaine she has no control over her destiny or power over Nick. As such it is a mixture of the colours she was first seen wearing – browns and beiges – and the red referred to above; it is transitional rather than emphatic. The chess game is, however, a fitting metaphor for her relationship with Nick which involves manoeuvring him into a passive position. In this period it would have been very unusual for a house to be made over to a woman on marriage. Jassy's actions are therefore not only out of revenge for her father's death, but against the patriarchal system Nick represents. She confounds expectation on several levels, not least that of

gender. He agrees to make the property over to Jassy but as soon as the deeds are signed she makes it clear that their marriage will not include sex, an outcome he clearly did not anticipate and does not challenge with violence. Even though Jassy's ostensible reason for securing Mordelaine is out of love for Barney, her actions nevertheless involve manipulating Nick into an unusually weak position. This is all the more impressive in view of Mordelaine's significance as the centre of desire for several characters: Nick delights in taking it from Christopher; it is presented as the thing Barney loves most; it is the location for Jassy's extraordinary bargain achieved on her own terms, and securing the house facilitates her eventual reunion with Barney.

As noted above, the lighting set-ups for the film were not particularly low key, with the exception of the scenes towards the end of the film when Nick is poisoned and in the courtroom scene when shadows are visible on the dock. In this scene the brightest colour touches are for the judge's red robes and for Jassy's lipstick. Although she is dressed in black her lipstick shows up as more red than in previous scenes when she is presented as not very made-up, the colour contrast being accentuated by the black. As the first time audiences would have seen Margaret Lockwood in colour, care would have been taken not to shock them by presenting an image which did not accord with her star persona. While by this time Lockwood had become identified with 'wicked lady' roles, she was keen to be appreciated as an actress who was associated with a particularly British type of stardom which was differentiated from the Hollywood model. This stressed acting ability and versatility rather than being a glamorous 'dame' in danger of becoming typecast in 'bodice ripping' melodramas.[21] Although the colour images of Lockwood in *Jassy* are not jarring, close-ups such as when she is reciting a poem to one of the schoolmistresses who is surprised at her literacy, are shot brightly to 'reveal' her beauty in Technicolor. In keeping with the part of Jassy, the emphasis is on 'natural' beauty since she is very different character from the more overtly sexualised Barbara Skelton in *The Wicked Lady*. At the same time, and perhaps paradoxically, audiences are reassured that Lockwood maintains the power to surprise, even shock. In this particular example she is therefore 'presented' to the audience through a close-up which appears to elongate time through arresting

Blanche Fury (Technicolor, 1948): Blanche (Valerie Hobson) lapsing out of consciousness in shots reminiscent of *A Matter of Life and Death*

attention. Lighting and colour therefore provide visual emphasis as a dual register in relation to the plot as well as to extra-textual discourses.

Geoffrey Unsworth also worked on *Blanche Fury*, shooting the exterior shots. It was an ambitious production directed by Marc Allégret, who had previously worked in France, and produced by Cineguild in 'a serious attempt to combine the quality of production lavished on big-budget literary adaptations with the passion and intensity of the wartime Gainsborough melodramas'.[22] The film's interior scenes were photographed by Guy Green whose previous work was noted for his 'meticulous low-key, high-contrast style' in black-and-white films.[23] This approach was also demonstrated in *Blanche Fury*, whose press book contains Green's account of what he was trying to do, also reproduced by Huntley.[24] He argued that while musicals could fully exploit colour as an element of generic expectation, care must be taken with dramatic subjects in which colour should 'reflect the emotional content of the scene. It must help the audience to forget that they are in a cinema at all. It must not be a glorious spectacle all on its own.'[25] He then makes some very interesting points about the differences between black and white and colour, with black and white described as:

far enough removed from reality for the audience to accept without question certain conventions, and the cameraman with an infinite number of shades from black to white at his disposal can blend an appearance of reality into whatever dramatic effect he is seeking. In fact this result should be better than reality.[26]

He is referring to the conventions of cinematic realism which in terms of a comparison with colour can create problems for audiences versed in 'reading' films in a particular way. As Stanley Cavell observes, the cultural power of black and white to 'dramatise reality' as a continuum from the traditions of nineteenth-century drama are challenged by colour in spite of the knowledge that colour is capable of representing the world as we literally see it. His point is that paradoxically the colour film-world is a less knowable one than that presented with more familiar conventions of the 'black and white axis of brilliance ... along which our comprehensibility of personality and event were secured'.[27] Green recognised this problem, arguing that colour could not be fully exploited because audiences' perceptions were limited to comparing what they saw on screen with their everyday surroundings. This confined colour work to conventions of naturalism and

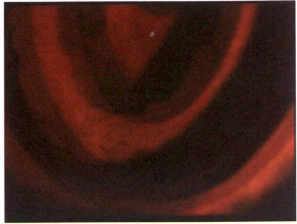

discouraged film-makers from the colour compositions possible in painting. The moving image presented problems in that 'separation and colour combinations change within a scene. The dramatic effect tends to disintegrate with movement if it is based on colour composition.' He felt the most he could do was continue to suggest dramatic effects with lighting.[28]

In spite of this *Blanche Fury* has received attention for the impact of Green's lighting on colour, as well as the film's play with colour contrast, harmony and saturation. As discussed in the introduction to this chapter, the melodramatic genre was enmeshed with establishing realism, particularly in terms of promoting a sense of periodicity and the locales in which the narratives take place. At the same time the quality of excess and visual hyperbole required to convey intense emotional conflicts, meant that even with these caveats colour would not necessarily be confined to a minor role as 'only an appearance'.[29] Watkins examines the interplay between red and blue as shifting registers which chart the tumultuous relationship between the two central characters Blanche (Valerie Hobson) and Philip Thorn (Stewart Granger). She draws on contemporary discourses around the idea of colour-music and Elsaesser's observations on melodramatic elements 'as constituents of a system of punctuation, giving expressive colour and chromatic contrast to the story-line, by orchestrating the emotional ups and downs of the intrigue'. In addition, Watkins argues that 'the emphasis of colour, through an increase in saturation or a move from accent colour to dominant hue can underscore the dramatic emphasis of a sequence by

marking difference within the colour design'.[30] With reference to the previous discussion of *Jassy* it is important to note that red similarly features in *Blanche Fury* as a colour which subtly shifts in inference, becoming primarily associated with Blanche's transgression.[31] Red was a colour rendered particularly strongly with Technicolor which tended to accentuate 'warmer' colours. It was often placed as a primary in contrast with others, as well as with black which gave three-strip prints a sense of sharpness and three-dimensionality.[32]

As with *Jassy*, a large country house and a struggle for its possession are at the centre of the narrative. Historical costume melodramas frequently intertwined stories of intra-familial conflict, patrimony, patriarchy, female transgression and sexual desire. Clare Hall is the property at stake for Philip Thorn, the illegitimate heir of the Fury estate who has been rejected by his family and works as a steward on the estate. After difficult years in servitude, Blanche is invited by her wealthy uncle to Clare Hall to be governess to her niece, Lavinia (Susanne Gibbs), and once installed she becomes attracted to Philip although she is forced to marry the legitimate heir Lawrence (Michael Gough). Blanche and Philip become lovers. He is determined to be recognised as the heir to the estate but a lawyer advises him he does not stand a chance. Disguised as a gypsy, out of desperation and revenge Philip kills Lawrence and his father. Blanche conceals her knowledge that Philip is the murderer and intends to stay silent until she suspects that he plans to murder Lavinia, who is now the heir, by encouraging her to ride her horse over jumps that are

dangerously high. Realising that Philip loves Clare Hall more than anything else, even her, Blanche goes to the police and Philip is convicted for murder and sentenced to death. At the same time as Philip is being hanged Lavinia is killed in a riding accident as she attempts the high jump. Blanche dies giving birth to Philip's son, who then becomes the rightful heir to Clare Hall.

Blanche Fury announces itself as a momentous drama from the start, with the titles in red letters and the house silhouetted in semi-darkness in the background, to the stirring sounds of Clifton Parker's foreboding score. The opening shot features a tree silhouetted in front of a cloudy blue sky and with a whistling wind audible, merging into the sound of galloping horses which then appear to rush into the frame from the bottom right. This sets up a series of shots similarly conceived with dark shadows and more silhouettes as the horses gallop through gates; the riders dismount and dash into the house. We see a doctor run upstairs to assist a sick woman lying on a bed. An out-of-focus shot aligns us with her viewpoint as she lapses in and out of consciousness. This is maintained as we see

the doctor daubing a mask with chloroform in close-up and then the camera pans upwards to the right and the screen becomes filled with pulsating, orange/red circular formations, with a voice in the background repeating dialogue we have already heard: 'She's weak, isn't she?'. The screen then becomes black and we enter a flashback which presents Blanche's story. This surreal effect is reminiscent of David Niven's lapsing out of consciousness in *A Matter of Life and Death*, discussed in Chapter 7. As with that example, it presents an unusual instance of the screen-as-colour, while creating an intriguing opening as we are curious about the nature of the woman's illness, it not having been made explicit that she is in childbirth. The film ends with Blanche's death as we return to this scene which is now imbued with plot significance.

When Blanche arrives at Clare Hall her red lipstick is noticeable. This was marketed as 'Fury' lipstick by Dorothy Gray, and endorsed by Valerie Hobson in advertisements.[33] Red is a colour with which she is subsequently associated, particularly her 'Fury Red' satin-striped taffeta evening dress which was described in

the press book as 'the most wonderful colour ever to splash across the Technicolor canvas'. It is associated with her affair with Philip after she is married to Lawrence, establishing her as a rebellious woman who then becomes embroiled in his revenge plot. Such details were exploited by exhibitors, one manager in York tying-in with a fashion house so that mannequins modelling the 'Fury Red' dress paraded in shops and factories, as well as in the cinema before the film was shown. It was estimated that about 10,000 people saw the dresses during the campaign.[34] Such incidents attest to the extent to which colour was considered to add commercial value to a film since the actual replication of the dress could be more completely achieved than with black-and-white films. Philip, on the other hand, is primarily identified with blue, particularly the walls of his quarters where he illicitly meets Blanche when they conduct their affair and which contrast with Blanche's red dress and ruby necklace. Although red and blue can be said to be the dominant colours with which the couple are associated, their affinity and tempestuous relationship is marked by instances where each of the colours becomes implicated with both characters. An instance of this is the red-patterned gypsy scarf Philip gave to one of his lovers and which was then returned to

him by her in anger. He uses this as a disguise when he shoots Lawrence and his father. Such instances constitute what Watkins refers to as sites of tension around the colour red.[35]

In addition to the dynamic relationship between the couple being expressed through variations in hue, saturation and intensity of both blue and red, colour is notable in the film for exterior shots. The *Kinematograph Weekly* reviewer wrote of its 'breathtaking beauty … there are many exquisite panoramas and equine shots and a hair raising fire sequence'.[36] When Blanche and Lawrence's wedding party is taking place, barns on the estate are burnt down by gypsies who have been evicted. The shots of swirling flames seen against the black sky and reflected on the faces of the wedding guests who look on in horror are reminiscent of the burning of the Atlanta Depot scenes in *Gone with the Wind* (1939). The press book for *Blanche Fury* highlighted the fire sequences as being 'transformed into visions of exquisite beauty by Guy Green's skilful handling of the Technicolor camera. The fierce colouring and drama … is in sharp contrast to the pastel tones achieved by the cameraman when photographing the other, more tranquil scenes.'[37] *Gone with the Wind*'s producer David O. Selznick favoured a

Blanche Fury: barns on the
estate are burned; swirling
flames against the black sky
for contrast, reminiscent of
the burning of Atlanta scenes
in *Gone with the Wind*
(Technicolor, 1939)

similar 'multifunctional' style which applied saturated colours to reflect a happy or particularly dramatic mood, and desaturated for sombre moments. The contrast between colour styles within a film, usefully referred to as 'selective emphasis' by Patrick Keating, ensured maximum impact for colour when stressing moods such as joy or, as above, natural disaster.[38] On a more literal narrative level, *Blanche Fury* might also be compared with *Gone with the Wind* because the child Lavinia dies in a horse riding accident which is similar to the fate of Rhett and Scarlett's child Bonnie.[39] Some American reviewers were not so impressed, however, such as the comment in the *Motion Picture Herald* which praised the photography in *Blanche Fury* as 'outstanding', but 'on the whole there is little in this Rank production to greatly excite American audiences'.[40]

The next film to be considered is *Footsteps in the Fog*, a melodrama based on a novel by W. W. Jacobs, set in the Edwardian period. Produced some time after *Jassy* and *Blanche Fury* it shares some interesting generic similarities to make the three films benefit from comparative analysis. It was made at a later stage in Technicolor's history and when widescreen technologies were being showcased (the aspect ratio was 1.66:1 whereas *Jassy* and *Blanche Fury* were 1.37:1). The trend was on the increase with 60 per cent more films being offered in widescreen formats in a survey comparing 1954 with 1955 (including films scheduled for release to the end of 1955).[41] With an American producer (Mike Frankovich) and director (Arthur Lubin), *Footsteps in the Fog* was made by Columbia's British operation and therefore registered as a British film with a cast to match. The narrative is about Lily (Jean Simmons), a housemaid who discovers that her employer Stephen Lowry (Stewart Granger) has poisoned his wife. She blackmails him and he is forced to elevate her position to housekeeper. He attempts to kill her when she is walking in the fog, but he murders the wrong woman by mistake, a policeman's wife. A cane found at the scene of the crime is identified as belonging to Stephen, so he is tried for murder but then acquitted because witness testimony is considered to be unreliable and Lily provides him with an alibi. Stephen is defended by David (Bill Travers), a lawyer friend who becomes suspicious of his relationship with Lily. David wishes to protect Beth Travers (Belinda Lee), a woman he loves but who has fallen for Stephen, with whom she has plans to marry.

When Lily hears of this she tells Stephen that for self-protection she has sent a letter to her sister denouncing Stephen as the murderer of his wife. She agrees to tell her sister to burn the letter when Stephen pretends that marrying Beth is simply a plan so he can obtain enough money for him to go to America with Lily and eventually marry her. Anxious to put an end to her blackmailing, Stephen, however, plans to condemn Lily by ingesting small doses of poison to give the impression that she is trying to murder him and that she killed his wife. The letter Lily wrote to her sister is discovered but, believing Stephen has told the truth about wanting to marry her, she persuades the police that it is a forgery. It is later discovered to be genuine and the police come to arrest Stephen who dies by mistake, after taking too much poison. Lily is taken for questioning by the police as a possible suspect for Stephen's murder.

Footsteps in the Fog has a specific approach to colour which uses it to heighten a suspenseful atmosphere while at the same time demonstrating some of the effects noted in the other melodramas, on occasion with a different intention. The predominant tones are greys and browns, but with high contrast between black and white rather than primary colours as in *Blanche Fury*. In this sense there is a degree of resemblance to the restrained mode identified by Higgins from early three-strip Technicolor in which 'a finely tuned design can draw attention to, and get use from, relatively minute and precise changes in color'.[42] When she reviewed the film, critic Dilys Powell remarked at the colour as being unusually interesting for this emphasis on 'the plush-and-mahogany of the establishment in which the master, having disposed of his wife, lolls about in a maroon-figured dressing-gown, while it leaves the courtroom scene effectively unemphatic'.[43] On the other hand, the choice to draw attention to black and white in a colour film makes them unusually obtrusive. As Catling pointed out, 'colour commands the entire range from white, through the greys, to jet black. Moreover, colour prints usually achieve a *richer* black than that reached by monochrome.'[44] The film opens with the funeral of Stephen's wife, and he is seen in black formal attire with a white dress shirt which is almost luminescent in contrast to the deep Technicolor black of his jacket. This stark highlight recurs on several occasions as his white collar can be seen glinting and sharp as he ascends the stairs, a detail that is suggestive of the gothic/horror genre. Thus presented, he becomes a menacing figure, shot from below almost Dracula-like as he thinks he has triumphed over his wife. In one shot a close-up of his feet draws attention to glistening, streaks of white highly visible in the semi-darkness as light reflecting mirror-like off his highly polished black shoes as he creeps, having heard noise, to his dead wife's room to discover Lily trying on her clothes. To include another layer of chromatic complexity, Lily's servant uniform is also black and white, providing an early colour link between them and in anticipation of their mutual interest in concealing the truth about Mrs Lowry's murder, in his case because he is guilty and in hers because knowledge of this gives her power over Stephen.

The horror connection is further marked by details such as the dead rat used as proof by Lily that the medicine bottle Stephen has hidden contains poison, providing her with evidence of Stephen's guilt. In keeping with gothic melodramas, a portrait of Mrs Lowry hangs above the fireplace and is shown on several occasions as if she possesses superior knowledge, at one point Lily saying it gives her a 'queer feeling … almost as if she is trying to tell me something'. Her sombre, grey dress contrasts with her reddish hair and the brooch she wears makes David suspicious of Lily when he sees that she has appropriated it, since when she begins to blackmail Stephen she helps herself to Mrs Lowry's clothes and jewels. A black cat stalks the house, much to Stephen's annoyance, since we know from its inclusion in the painting that the cat was Mrs Lowry's pet. Lily is fond of the animal whose presence accentuates the ambient horror since Stephen's reaction to it is of fear, as if the cat embodies his dead wife's spirit as she watches him from her portrait.

The dominating sombre colour design is maintained consistently throughout the film with the exception of scenes outside the house in connection with David and Beth. When, for example, they are out motoring, a scene, which is a rather comic interlude, is filmed with higher-key lighting, and colour complements which rarely appear elsewhere in the film are visible, in this case Beth's green jacket and David's green scarf contrasted with a bright red carnation in David's buttonhole. Compared to Stephen and Lily, David and Beth are cast as 'normal' people who are not consumed by ambition and guile. The colour design

therefore reflects their normality even if as characters they are far from compelling. Shingleton's set designs emphasise this contrast between the Lowry home, with its dark, brooding atmosphere, and the Travers mansion with its 'high, neutral coloured ceilings, flowerladen tables, and sparkling chandeliers, presenting a vivid effect of happiness and opulence'.[45] Despite their different class backgrounds, the shared 'outsider' status of Stephen and Lily is underscored by shared colour referents. The clean, brilliant whites of Stephen's dress shirt have already been noted; in early scenes Lily's servant uniform has a starched, white apron that similarly picks up the light. Stephen wears a black and red silk dressing gown for many subsequent scenes when he is in the house. The idea of red linking the two characters relates to their physical relationship which is implied, as noted by Josh Billings: 'Both the characters are unscrupulous, but a compelling physical affinity exists between them and the stars neatly manipulate the salient thread.'[46]

As soon as Lily becomes confident that she has a hold over Stephen she wears his dead wife's clothes – at first a gold dress, but when she attains her most powerful position, just after Stephen is acquitted of murdering the policeman's wife largely due to her testimony, she appears at the top of the stairs in a red dress. She is then seen wearing the dress lounging on a sofa as she hears Stephen did not love his wife and married for money. They are linked by red at this point since they share the same ambition to rise above their circumstances. The red of her dress is particularly striking after the general sombreness of the rest of the film's colour design. Her lips appear pale in comparison which is unusual in a Technicolor film which tended to show up lips brightly. The effect of this is that in spite of her efforts at a material transformation into the lady of the house she seems not yet fully confident in that position in spite of her power over Stephen. It also relates to how colour in melodrama can relate to critique, as with the example cited at the beginning of this chapter by Mary Beth Haralovich of a red dress commenting on ideology. In the case of *Footsteps in the Fog*, Lily has dared to elevate her position to housekeeper and aspires to possess Mrs Lowry's house, clothes and husband. Even though she achieves some of these things, her class background means that the transition of power is incomplete. Stephen urges her to

Footsteps in the Fog
(Technicolor, 1955): Lily (Jean
Simmons) at the top of the
stairs wearing a red dress

Stephen (Stewart Granger)
chasing Lily in the blue-tinged
fog

go abroad where she can 'pass' for a lady in a way that is impossible in England. David is suspicious of her elevation and tells Stephen that to avoid accusations of impropriety she cannot stay in the house alone with him. Wearing Mrs Lowry's dress therefore looks unconvincing since its incongruity draws attention to a social world which excludes her even though she has managed to gain a semblance of its material properties through blackmailing Stephen. The relative paleness of Lily's lips could also be related to the type of femininity she represents: she is not a vamp, and a degree of sympathy for her is obtained in her struggle for survival in a strictly hierarchical class society.

In the pivotal scene when Stephen chases after the woman he thinks is Lily in the fog blue becomes important as the dominant colour register. This is set up just after Lily has made it clear that she wants to stay with Stephen rather than go abroad as he has suggested. Dressed in a grey cloak, she goes out into the foggy night. As the door opens a deep, saturated blue night sky can be seen, and the following scenes in the fog as Stephen chases after the cloaked figure have an overall blue haze. This suggests confusion and disorientation, since once outside the house figures cannot be easily recognised and the expressionist-like, blue-bathed images resemble tinted and toned images from the silent period. Stephen chases after the figure with malevolent intent as the sound of footsteps guide him when he cannot trust sight alone to identify his target. The camera angles are low which further emphasise the difficulty of vision encountered; it is as if Stephen is chasing a phantom. The widescreen also accentuates the

impression of disorientation, since the fog-ridden space appears to have limitless depth. In a shot reminiscent of *The Man Within*, the cloaked figure disappears in the fog like a vanishing ghost into the centre of the frame. A recurrent cinematographic strategy in this sequence is for the camera to be slightly in front of Stephen, tracking with him for some time followed by a shot from his viewpoint behind the woman he is following as she walks briskly along. This creates a sense of continuous action which in widescreen appears to flow with movement and which is accentuated by the suspenseful music. The usual signifiers of identity are absent as distinctive colour cannot guide Stephen; one cloak appears as another and one woman as another. The density of the fog conceals the fact that Stephen is near a pub where witnesses later claim to have seen him standing above the murdered woman as the fog clears and they can see his face; he would not have committed murder if he had known he was so near to them. The fog is therefore both an ally and a threat since he assumes it can conceal his crime but at the same time he cannot be sure he has not been identified.

In all three films a woman rises in social prominence, and this rise is charted by colour changes in costume and using red for emphasis. As we have seen in relation to *Jassy*, the colour red is associated with crucial moments which signal her ascendancy and when her action provokes an important narrative resolution. *Blanche Fury* and *Footsteps in the Fog* use the same device of linking red with female sexuality by having them wear a red dress when their illicit liaisons are at their most intense. In both films the women are linked with dangerous men whose sexual desire for them is not as strong as their quest for money, status and property. *Jassy* sticks closely to the traditions of Gainsborough melodrama, while *Blanche Fury* has some interesting colour effects, most notably the out-of-consciousness introduction to the flashback and a degree of homage to *Gone with the Wind*. As we have seen, the elements of generic hybridity (gothic melodrama and horror) in *Footsteps in the Fog* influence colour and make it unusual, particularly in the contrast of black and white at the beginning of the film operating as strong colour statements made all the more obtrusive when viewed against 'restrained' background colour cinematography. The stalking sequence in particular deploys variations on blue and the diffusion effect of the fog setting, in combination with the 1.66:1 widescreen dimensions exploited impressively by cinematographer Chris Challis.[47] As such the film is pushing in its colour design against some of the expectations established for melodrama and in so doing anticipating some of the Eastmancolor conventions in Hammer horror films. It is another example of British films working within broad generic traditions to produce distinctive colour aesthetics.

Ealing Studios' first colour film was *Saraband for Dead Lovers* (dir. Basil Dearden), a costume melodrama based on a novel by Helen Simpson which drew on historical events towards the end of the seventeenth century surrounding the political machinations of Hanoverian Prince George Louis's claim to the English throne (he later became King George I). In order to further advance the claim Sophie-Dorothea (Joan Greenwood) is forced to leave her home in Celle for Hanover to marry George Louis (Peter Bull), a man she does not love and who has a ruthless, ambitious mother, the Electress Sophia (Françoise Rosay). Sophie-Dorothea has an affair with Count Philip Konigsmark (Stewart Granger), a Swedish soldier of fortune who is charged with leading the army on a campaign with the Prince's brother. When the affair is discovered Philip is killed in a swordfight after being betrayed by a jealous former lover, Countess Platen (Flora Robson). Sophie-Dorothea is imprisoned for the rest of her life in the Castle of Ahlden.

Saraband for Dead Lovers was an ambitious project for Ealing, with much care and attention lavished on production design by Michael Relph, and colour cinematography by Douglas Slocombe. To some extent it was experimental in aspiring to unite narrative with music and colour, as well as to challenge Ealing's reputation as being primarily associated with realist drama.[48] While Balcon's vision for the film was to extend Ealing's repertoire, it was nevertheless, as Harper argues, somewhat caught between conflicting desires to be 'soberly realistic, or sumptuously symbolic'.[49] In terms of establishing an approach to colour design Douglas Slocombe's interest was in experimenting with low-key, high-contrast lighting and exploiting Technicolor's tendency to render deep blacks.[50] He did this in spite of being advised by Technicolor Ltd that the stock did not respond well to this approach. He recounted how Dearden and Relph agreed that they should nevertheless try for the low-key effects and sets were lit for high contrast, much as they would have been if Slocombe had been shooting in black and white. He reported that:

> The results were extremely encouraging and taught me amongst others, a surprising thing: the wonderful richness of the Technicolor black and white! The blacks, particularly were so warm that I decided to treat a lot of the picture after the fashion of the Dutch old masters and let the thin shafts of 'window light' pick out the salient parts of the sets and action while the rest of the picture dwindles off into complete blackness.[51]

Relph drew inspiration from painters in equating strong, dramatic lighting effects with low-contrast, 'almost monochromatic' colour, and flatter lighting designs with a wider range of colours to create contrast and intensity.[52]

Johnston's reading of the film notes how blue is associated with the Hanoverian court, indicating a cold and ruthless regime under which Sophie-Dorothea suffers. Blue is also influential later in the swordfight sequence when Philip is killed as he fights his stalkers against a disorientating, atmospheric background created by contrasts of blue-grey and deep black. Johnston also offers a detailed account of the Hanover Fair sequence when Sophie-Dorothea struggles through the crowds which are presented as menacing, with dizzying conglomerations of colours looming towards her in disturbing close-ups and evocative of a nightmare in which colour 'visually represents the chaos within

Saraband for Dead Lovers (Technicolor, 1948): accent on red as Sophie-Dorothea (Joan Greenwood) travels to her wedding

Sophie-Dorothea struggling through the crowd, surrounded by colour

Sophie-Dorothea's mind in this wild, unruly fair, and she is pulled into the centre of this colourful world'.[53] This sequence is indeed impressive for its creation of both spectacle and horror around colour. As Relph noted: 'We wanted to create the nightmarish effect which the wild atmosphere of the fair would have in the girl's mind … Lit by the strongly contrasted lighting from flares and torches, the effect was one of violent clash and conflict, the exact atmosphere we wanted.'[54] Combined with close-ups and fast cutting, colour exaggerates the impression of grotesquery as Sophie-Dorothea passes knife-throwers, fire-eaters, tightrope walkers and jostling hoards of revellers wearing devilish masks. The music also accentuates the sense of claustrophobia and confusion, much as in one of Michael Powell's experiments with the 'composed film'.[55] The film's script confirms that the composer, Alan Rawsthorne, attempted to match the dialogue to the score, an approach which is obviously extended to this particular non-dialogue sequence.[56] It approaches closure with a succession of blue, red and yellow gloved hands frantically hammering at the door, concluding an event in which colour appears to conspire against Sophia-Dorothea. There is so much of it in multiple configurations, and since most other people appear to be enjoying the revels, there is perhaps also an element of class association with colour since her confusion is of someone out of their normal environment, unable to enjoy what most people do and unversed in the communal experience of carnival.

Her terrifying encounter with the general populace marks her as other, a royal personage hidden behind a mask as she is jostled by the revelling hoards. This sequence is an excellent one through which to discuss colour as complicit in delineating a dangerous, volatile setting in which conventional colour associations are overturned.

There are many other points of colour interest in the film, however, which work to augment, nuance and even challenge perceived consistencies within the overall colour design. Sue Harper has noted how 'the sets are unrestrained in their use of crimson … the colour red operates as an alternative sensual pleasure to the dry intrigues of the Protestant Hanoverian court'.[57] Red is indeed deployed interestingly in *Saraband for Dead Lovers* but in multiple contexts which create tension and multivalence around its meaning. It is invested, for example, with horror and disgust when it is consistently worn by George Louis when he seeks to exercise his conjugal rights over Sophie-Dorothea. His appearance in bright red bedclothes is rendered even more grotesque by the removal of his wig on such occasions; his appearance is visibly transformed for this purpose. Rather than denoting 'alternative sensual pleasure', in this case red is menacing, an association which has been previously indicated by the deep, red background for a close-up of Sophie-Dorothea's downcast face as her carriage takes her to her wedding ceremony. This foreboding sensation is accentuated when during the ceremony a thunderstorm breaks out and Sophie-Dorothea looks up at the coloured stained-glass windows above being pelted with rain. These are then featured in close-up to reveal the appearance of tears streaming down the face of the stained-glass virgin, as if in sympathy with Sophie-Dorothea's misery. Relph described this as a deliberate effect to make 'ironic comment on the sanctifying of this enforced union'.[58] Although she wears red on occasion, any effect of total saturation is offset by the addition of a pink skirt or gold detail, or when it is of a much darker shade, such as the cloak worn when she illicitly visits Philip and he tells her of his plans for them to leave Hanover. Such multiple instances and contexts create a tension around red, since it is Sophie-Dorothea's colouring (she has red hair) and can be related to our sense of her as a repressed personality. Rather than connote the sense of terror and sexual exploitation of her husband's 'rights', to which she succumbs in passive resignation, when associated with her there is a greater sense of ambivalence. Set against the Hanoverian blue she often wears, it connects with her own desire for Philip, in opposition to the court and what it represents. In the brief sequence when we see her pass the time at court while Philip is away with the army, we glimpse her in a succession of red dresses adorned with jewels and gold braid. Any sense of pleasure in courtly activities that a 'warm' colour such as red might otherwise connote is, however, qualified by the futility her expression indicates. A further nuance is introduced by another red-haired character, Countess Platen, whose desperation for Philip's affection leads her to unscrupulous measures which lead to his death. From these instances we can therefore conclude that red is a complex and changing colour which defies prescriptive meaning.

Slocombe's preference for Technicolor black does indeed accentuate a sense of foreboding mystery and intrigue, such as in night-time scenes or for the swordfight. But it is also used consistently for the Electress Sophia, a stern figure who has repressed her own desires for her son's advancement. She is always seen in a jet black dress, relieved only by details such as ermine trimmings. Combined with her pale complexion and severely brushed-back hair, she embodies female sacrifice for male ambition, confirmed by her warning to Sophie-Dorothea that 'royalty may not look for happiness'. The implication is that Sophie-Dorothea

must follow her example and that any deviation from duty, such as the affair with Philip, is punishable. For much of the time Philip wears a black frockcoat with white cuffs and ruff, but not with quite the same impression of formality or deep blackness as with the costume worn by the Electress. His attire is inconsistent: he also is seen in grey or with a gold breastplate, blue trousers and a fur jacket on his return from fighting abroad. There is little in the way of a discernible design around his costuming that facilitates the effectiveness of scenes such as the swordfight which depend on shades of grey and black contrasting with fleeting details such as a glimmer of light on a face, or the flames from an overturned lantern seen burning on the ground that also illuminates partial details in the frame.

Gone to Earth is the final melodrama considered in this chapter. Designed by Hein Heckroth and shot by Chris Challis, the film lives up to expectations of colour display established in previous Powell and Pressburger films. It is based on a novel by Mary Webb set in late nineteenth-century Shropshire. Hazel Woodus (Jennifer Jones), whose mother was a gypsy, lives with her blind father Abel (Edmond Knight) who plays the harp and makes coffins. She meets the local squire, Jack Reddin (David Farrar) when his horse and cart accidentally runs into her and she goes to his house afterwards. Hazel is aligned with nature, loving animals and keeping a pet fox. She marries the caring local minister Edward Marston (Cyril Cusack) who wants to protect her, but their relationship is not sexual. Reddin pursues her relentlessly, tempting her into meeting him illicitly. She disapproves of his hunting wild animals and struggles against being physically attracted to him. She looks for guidance from her late mother's spell book which tells her that hearing fairy music at the top of a mountain signals an affirmative sign. She mistakes the sound of her father playing the harp for the fairy music, and goes to meet Reddin. They begin a passionate affair and Hazel writes to Edward that she is safe but has transgressed, and asks him to look after her fox. He discovers that she is living with Reddin and goes to fetch her home. On their return the couple are ostracised by Edward's mother and chapel elders who disapprove of Hazel's behaviour. The pet fox escapes and is chased by the local hunt, including Reddin. Attempting to rescue it, Hazel catches up with the fox, picks it up and runs from the hounds, but she stumbles and falls into a deep well to

Gone to Earth (Technicolor, 1950): pastoral imagery, skylines and silhouettes

her death. The cry, 'Gone to Earth!', first heard at the beginning of the film is repeated as the film ends, but this time with tragic implications.

Repetitive shots of the landscape in particular relish their presentation in Technicolor. The most common set-up is a low-angle shot of dark trees which appear silhouetted against the blue sky and billowing clouds, or shots at dusk with the grey, yellow and orange sky in the background as the sun sets. On occasion, we also see semi-dark figures against terrain or skies marked by brilliant colour formations. David O. Selznick's influence in the early stages of the film's production is perhaps evident here, since these shots are reminiscent of the under-exposed shots of characters silhouetted against the sky in *Gone with the Wind*.[59] In this respect the film's skylines can also be compared with their similarly dramatic, silhouetted presentation in another Hollywood melodrama, *Duel in the Sun* (1946). In this way *Gone to Earth*'s celebration of the Shropshire countryside depends on colour variation for the sheer number of pictorial, pastoral shots to be acceptable. Their accompaniment by natural sounds such as the wind blowing through trees is reminiscent of the visual presentation of landscape and sounds in *Black Narcissus* (1947), a film which as we have seen is particularly evocative of place and space. When Hazel climbs rocky terrain to 'God's little mountain', so that she can listen for the fairy music that will inform her decision whether to meet Reddin, she puts a multicoloured silk shawl on top of one of the highest rocks as part of the spell she

has read in her mother's book. A high camera angle shows the shawl billowing in the breeze, and then from a lower angle to emphasise its importance in summoning the spirits. Its bright colours are highlighted, a detail which is all the more noticeable since the scene takes place at midnight and with the background landscape looking stark, even sinister in the semi-darkness.

Hazel's costuming links her with 'earthiness' and nature, such as the green dress she wears when she travels to town to visit her aunt and cousin, or with 'warm' colours such as the orange circles which pattern her shawl or the yellow dress she wears for the chapel social and Shropshire County Fair. Her rustic demeanour is challenged by the clothes she finds at Reddin's house, most notably the low-cut red dress which has a very full skirt with a large yellow flower pattern. This contrasts with the colours, more practical shapes and materials of her previous costumes and serves as a somewhat crude indication of their passionate relationship. He uses the dress to tempt her the first time she is in his house after the accident with the cart. The dress is one of many in a trunk, presumably belonging to the woman in the painting seen on the wall above the trunk. In this scene the orange-amber glow from the fire accentuates the impression of smouldering passion, as it bathes their faces as he presses the red dress against her body in anticipation of her wearing it as his lover. A combination of low-key and coloured lighting maximises the flickering firelight effects which, combined with the red dress, produce a non-naturalistic composition in which red-orange hues totally dominate the frame. When he leaves the room for her to try on the dress he watches her through the window as she holds it against her body.[60] It is not unusual that Hazel wears white on her wedding day to Edward but the next time we see her in a white dress, ironically, is when she goes to meet Reddin. As she waits for him we see his shadow enter the frame and gradually cover her body, thus progressively rendering the white fabric grey, as if in anticipation of his subsequent sexual conquest. The choice of a white dress visibly changing colour before our eyes is unusual. The red flowers she is holding fall from her hands when they embrace and a close-up shows Reddin tread them into the ground; the crushed petals indicate the imminent loss of her virginity.[61]

By contrast, Hazel's marriage to Edward is portrayed in terms of him being almost paternal in his

Gone to Earth: Hazel
(Jennifer Jones) in firelight
scene with red dress; flowers
crushed as symbolic of the
loss of Hazel's virginity

physically. The skirt also serves a practical purpose a little later when Hazel runs clutching the fox, the red showing clearly against the green fields since it is important that she can be picked out at a distance to intensify the suspense created by the sight of the hounds catching up on her. The choice of colour for her costuming in addition identifies her with the fox and her associations with wild animals. It also relates to the film's stereotyping of her gypsy heritage which depicts her as an outsider, prone to superstition, sexually alluring and passionate. This is less nuanced or progressive than the depiction of gypsy characters in the Gainsborough melodramas such as *Jassy*, in which Margaret Lockwood plays a highly intelligent woman who is able to climb the social ladder.[63]

The melodramas discussed in this chapter had varying success at the box office, *Jassy*, *Blanche Fury* and *Footsteps in the Fog* attracting good takings in comparison with *Saraband for Dead Lovers* and *Gone to Earth*. Whether the latter two films' variation from the melodramatic formula first established at Gainsborough was responsible for their relative failure is difficult to assess. All five films deployed colour as part of their melodramatic address and colour featured as an important feature in their marketing. *Saraband for Dead Lovers*, for example, was advertised in different issues of *Kinematograph Weekly*, each time introducing a different character and with different colour backgrounds.[64] Harper and Johnston suggest that the film's combination of realism and colour as symbolism was largely responsible for its poor box-office returns.[65] Yet this was hardly problematic in other films which combined 'restraint' with 'demonstration', and *Jassy* was popular even though it is the least experimental in terms of colour. The film's failure probably has more to do with the at times obscure historical details about the Hanoverian claim on the English throne, and Stewart Granger's casting as a likeable character which might have disappointed audiences more familiar with him as a rogue. *Gone to Earth* was also a film whose commercial prospects were affected by factors other than colour, which was highly praised by critics.[66]

Box-office considerations apart, this analysis of several key British postwar melodramas demonstrates the variety of colour effects achieved during a period when colour sought to make big strides in technical and aesthetic fields. Gainsborough, Ealing and Alexander

caring protection of her, making no sexual demands on her when she does not return his physical affection. They sleep in separate rooms, on one occasion Edward makes a tentative move to encourage her to be sexually responsive, but she appears to be uninterested so he returns to his room. As his door shuts the screen becomes totally black, as if to indicate that there is no possibility of passion in their relationship, signalling finality.[62] When Edward storms to Reddin's to fetch Hazel he is told by Reddin that she belongs to him since their union has been physical. Back in Edward's house and after his mother has left, the next morning Hazel wears a pinkish-red skirt with a brown/maroon blouse. This costuming and their embrace could be an implication that they have come to love each other

Korda were all keen to take advantage of the optimism created around colour, even to the extent, in the case of Ealing, of declaring a new direction for the studio. While the most detailed scholarship on Technicolor has concentrated on Hollywood films from the 1930s – including the seminal period melodrama in colour, *Gone with the Wind* – the British examples show that experimentation with Technicolor was by no means confined to the USA.[67] As in Hollywood, cinematographers wedded to technical conventions of lighting for monochrome were intrigued by colour's possibilities to extend their repertoire of effects. The plots of melodramas with their characters' personal dilemmas and emotional conflicts encouraged stylistic innovation as an aid to establishing affective registers. Combined with music and lighting, colour intensified the expressive potential of *mise en scène*.[68] As well as providing a 'scoring' function of registering the changing fortunes of a character, or of consistent usages of a particular colour such as red to connote symbolic themes such as female sexuality as we have seen in the instances of red dresses, colour occasionally pushes beyond these imperatives.

Guy Green's observations noted earlier that motion picture movement challenged rigid conceptions of colour design tended to over-exaggerate the need for caution with colour. His work on *Blanche Fury* indicates that he was not averse to using colour for expressive effect. Although it is the case that movement creates variation of hue which can be further disturbed by low-key lighting, the notion of a dominant accent once established pertains in many instances. It is encountering a colour in different contexts which leads to subtle shifts in meaning, or introducing a degree of irony, as with Hazel's white dress in *Gone to Earth*. As Haralovich noted, in melodrama the world of the fiction as initially established can easily become de-stabilised. The narrative importance given to properties, objects and clothes in melodramas invests them with more than satisfying a realist stylistic imperative. The notion of movement is useful when considered in a different sense from literal physical movement of characters within a frame. As destinies change characters can move on, or take steps backwards in a sense of movement through time and circumstance rather than literal physical movement. Seemingly inconsequential details of *mise en scène* become invested with irony, even poignancy when we see them, and their colours, in a different light as the

narrative develops. The repeated return to the portrait of Mrs Lowry in *Footsteps in the Fog*, for example, accumulates meaning each time we see it. Portraits were often used in melodramas to trigger tumultuous events, or to indicate mysteries that have yet to unfold. At first the portrait in *Footsteps in the Fog* indicates a wife Stephen may have loved. The camera is placed behind him so we cannot see his face as he looks up at it. When we finally do see his expression his smile indicates that he is far from a grieving widower. Mrs Lowry's red hair, which stands out as colour detail in view of her otherwise grey appearance, acquires ironic significance once red has been established elsewhere in the film as important in relation to Lily's gradual assumption of power in the household. Attempting to assume her identity, Lily wears Mrs Lowry's clothes and jewels, an item of the latter actually seen in the portrait. The film's final shot of the picture indicates that she has finally attained the upper hand since Stephen is dead and Lily will go to prison.

The notion of movement referred to by Green appears to be confined to figures or objects, rather than to a camera's slow pan to reveal a stunning landscape, as in *Gone to Earth*. In such shots and also in still, pictorial compositions, landscape is showcased through colour. This can be terrifying and disorientating, as in *The Man Within* or *Footsteps in the Fog*, or evocative of sensation, as in the fire sequence in *Blanche Fury* or the Hanoverian buildings silhouetted against deep blue skies in *Saraband for Dead Lovers*. These images fully convey the 'sound and fury' of melodrama since they constitute an excessive pictorial address which invites sensual, affective engagement. The environment becomes implicated in the narrative and vice-versa. Selznick's decision to reduce the number of landscape shots in the remake of *Gone to Earth* as *The Wild Heart* perhaps indicates a different level of tolerance for such shots in Hollywood, where showcasing stars was more important. On the other hand, it was certainly not the case that Hollywood films, particularly those in the 1930s from the 'demonstration mode', were averse to such techniques, not least Selznick's own *Gone with the Wind*. American critics were, however, often puzzled by the incidence of landscape shots in British films which they considered slowed up the action. As demonstrated with films such as *Wings of the Morning*, using colour to accentuate pictorial imagery was an approach rooted in silent British cinema and which has been identified as a precursor to 'heritage' cinema of the 1980s onwards.[69] A broader tradition of British landscape painting would appear to provide a significant cultural context for the longevity of these aesthetic choices in British colour cinema.

Genre was a key influence on the ways in which colour was deployed in postwar cinema. It is perhaps ironic that the popularity of low-budget black-and-white Gainsborough melodramas emboldened the studio to film in Technicolor, since the commercial viability of colour was crucial for any studio or director wishing to work with the process. As we have seen, Technicolor historical melodramas encouraged expertise to be stretched in interior lighting set-ups, location shooting, art direction and costume design. As three-strip Technicolor reached the end of its monopoly, some seminal films had been produced as British tales not only of sound and fury but also of colour.

10 COLOUR GENRES IN POSTWAR CINEMA 3
MUSICALS AND COMEDIES

The genres examined in the previous two chapters are not particularly surprising for their affinities with colour. Historical pageants, films of national and international events, fantasy spectacles, empire films, biopics and costume melodramas exploited colour as part of their appeal and affective regimes. Although their makers were aware of dominant critical opinion which equated British cinema with colour restraint, these films' generic imperatives nevertheless encouraged showcasing colour in interesting and innovative ways which on occasion created dynamic interplay between restraint and demonstration that made colour stand out all the more obtrusively. This chapter will consider two genres from a colour perspective which had very different histories in Britain, the musical and comedies. In the 1930s musicals starring Jessie Matthews were very popular, as were those featuring Gracie Fields and George Formby. In the 1940s and subsequently the genre did not, however, feature prominently in British cinema. Different varieties of comedy on the other hand performed consistently well at the domestic box office, constituting a staple output of a national cinema dominated by Hollywood.[1] Locating the comparative performance of colour in these two genres foregrounds the impact of Technicolor in relation to discourses about national specificity and the international film market. It also permits analysis of a genre seldom considered in terms of colour, since the nature of comedy is frequently identified with purely verbal address or slapstick/physical performance. The extent to which colour contributes to comic effect, or occupies an assertive space in the *mise en scène* of comedic fiction are central issues this chapter will address.

The musical was a genre in which colour became a central component of expectation as the 1940s progressed. E. S. Tompkins noted the high percentage of Hollywood musicals in relation to the total number of colour films seen in Britain, frequently commenting on the technical brilliance of colour designs which were freed from conforming to conventions of realism established in other genres.[2] As an admirer of Technicolor even Tompkins was, however, not averse to lamenting how the musical genre frequently failed to combine 'polished technique' with good scripts.[3] The narratives of musicals were easily critiqued for their frivolity even if many of the colour effects were innovative. In the 1930s there were two British colour musicals, the largely black-and-white *Pagliacci* (1936), which showcased British Chemicolor, and *The Mikado* (1939) in Technicolor. These were opera-based and although distinguished in their ways for demonstrating their respective processes, the films did not initiate a trend for British colour musicals. During the war British audiences saw Hollywood musicals which developed the form in such a way that by 1945 it was practically unthinkable to plan a musical that was not in colour. At a social level, Hollywood musicals were a key element of the cinema's growing popularity during the war and postwar period and participated in the cinematic construction of the American Dream 'as a key signifier of possibility, affluence, escape and transformation'.[4] By 1955 musicals were the most popular genre of American films in Britain.[5]

Analyses of musicals have concentrated on the extent to which the numbers relate to the plot, at times being irrelevant while on other occasions able to progress the narrative. Musical numbers are also capable of offering critical commentary on events or expressing the emotional intensity of a character's dilemma.[6] Although in formal terms attention has focused on the display of technical virtuosity such as extreme low and high camera angles for Busby Berkeley's backstage musicals which 'tend to disrupt the established relationship between the viewer and the film', in contemporary commentaries colour was seldom mentioned beyond the commonplace observation that colour musicals were 'bright', even 'garish'.[7] Yet we can see from the many examples quoted by Tompkins in his viewing of Technicolor films in wartime that musicals facilitated colour display in very particular ways. He was astute regarding the impact of genre on colour, pointing out that genres in which quick, 'staccato' cutting was common, such as thrillers, needed care as far as colour was concerned since 'a colour scene needs slightly more time to sink into the mind of the audience than does black-and-white'.[8] The comment prefigures Cavell's observations about the strangeness of colour for audiences, with the paradoxical consequence that colour strained established conventions of cinematic realism which had their foundation in black-and-white cinematography.[9] The incidence of long shots within musical numbers thus allowed colour to have sufficient time to become obtrusive, or to assist the showcasing of a star. He cites an example from a Rita Hayworth vehicle, *My Gal Sal* (1942), in which she,

> begins to sing in full long-shot, right at the back of the stage. As she sings she walks down the stage and finishes in big close-up still singing, the lights do not alter visibly in the course of the movement nor does the camera move. There is, however, a definite warming of the colour and a hardening of the definition towards the end of the travel.[10]

In this case a close-up is achieved seamlessly and without editing; colour is the emphatic feature which makes final sense of the figure walking towards the camera.

Other examples of colour experimentation within the musical genre include *Lady in the Dark* (1944), shot by Ray Rennahan to showcase Ginger Rogers' first appearance in colour. She plays a magazine editor undergoing psychoanalysis to understand her dreams which are shown with different colour accents.[11] *Something for the Boys* (1945), a Carmen Miranda vehicle, similarly contained interesting effects such as a highly saturated red dress giving 'an almost stereoscopic separation of the figure from the blue background', combined with contrasting, subdued colour for night effects rather than 'the former all-pervading blue'.[12] Colour with 'real imagination' was evident in *Ziegfeld Follies* (1946), in which one character literally goes red with anger, and red-coloured lighting is integral to the success of a corridor scene for Judy Garland's entrance.[13] Films such as these further identified the American musical with colour experimentation. The fascination with American life, cities and culture was also enhanced by colour, as described by one of J. P. Mayer's respondents who went to the cinema four times a week with the following result: 'I do get very dissatisfied with my way of life and neighbourhood. After seeing marvellous places like New York, Hollywood, California, Cuba, Washington … on the screen, especially in Technicolour [*sic*], it makes me very miserable and unhappy sitting in my stuffy little office all day.'[14] One woman took inspiration from the Technicolor musical for 'ideas of poise, self-confidence and also dress sense … it enables you to pair off colours, which you would not dream of wearing unless you had seen how lovely they look'.[15] Comments such as these illustrate the extent to which Technicolor was becoming an integral aspect of American cinema's appeal, especially in a context of postwar austerity and into the comparatively more affluent 1950s.

Inspired by the optimism around colour at the end of World War II the Rank Organisation hired Wesley Ruggles, an American director best known for black-and-white comedies, for *London Town* (1946), the first major British musical in Technicolor. With a big budget and shot at the recently de-requisitioned Shepperton Studios, it was intended to capitalise on the popularity of veteran variety comedian Sid Field who stars as Jerry, a provincial comic just arrived in London with his young daughter Peggy (Petula Clark) to appear in a revue called 'London Town', only to discover that he is the understudy. Upset at seeing her father's disappointment night after night when he is not called to star in the revue, Peggy plays a trick on the principal comedian Charlie (Sonnie Hale) so that Jerry has to take his place. Jerry is such a success that he is promoted

London Town (Technicolor, 1946): opening titles and colour

to permanent lead and Charlie is offered a new role in a touring show. Jerry's romance with his leading lady Patsy (Kay Kendall) flourishes and the film ends with sketches and numbers from 'London Town', the show-within-the-film which has been interspersed with the narrative.

The cinematographer on *London Town* was Erwin Hillier, who described his first experience with Technicolor on the film as 'one of the worst mistakes I made in my life'. Ruggles was apparently colour-blind, uninterested in exploring cinematic technique and way past his prime.[16] Hillier's regrets about the film were due to its poor commercial performance and critical reputation rather than with having to work with Technicolor per se. The film was a box-office flop and severely criticised by the press as over-long, badly scripted and a poor relation to the Hollywood musical. Huntley's verdict was typical: 'It seems that the category of Technicolor productions at which Hollywood is so adept remains as the one type in which this country consistently fails to please – musicals.'[17] E. S. Tompkins found merit in the sets and some of the colour to be effective, except for the make-up, lighting and photography of the female stars.[18] The *Monthly Film Bulletin* summed up the major problems:

Ruthlessly impartial editing – to eliminate much of the ballet and to trim Field's individual sketches – is its chief lack. A few touches of neat camera-handling plus some lavish production work and extravagant costuming do not conceal the lack. Field is a comedian high in the tradition of the English music-hall, but more intelligent scripting would eliminate much which is repetitive in his set-piece sketches.[19]

Viewing a print restored in the 1980s by Paul de Burgh, the film has some interesting colour work which cannot be seen to contribute to the film's other admitted failings. The opening titles sequence makes a stunning impact, with different-coloured neon lettering for the cast and crew, as well as 'Technicolor'. The camera pans 360 degrees to survey the names which are on a number of billboards shot against a dark night sky to replicate a rooftop viewing experience. This sequence establishes colour as the central attraction and this is carried into several of the numbers from the show 'London Town' which have colour-codes, such as the yellow accent on costumes and the set for 'Spring'. Outside of the show the sets are restrained in their colour design as in a nightclub scene which is carefully composed with men in black-and-white formal dress and

London Town: 'Spring' set
and yellow accent

women in de-saturated shades of reds, blues and purple. Colour features very obtrusively for one important plot point – Peggy's trick which prevents Charlie from appearing on stage. She places a bar of novelty soap in his dressing-room which temporarily dyes his face green; as an integral part of the sight gag, colour has conspired in a crude way to move the plot along. It also assists in demonstrating some of the film's retrogressive ideological predispositions as with a golf sketch in the revue with Sid Field remarking on lilac as a beautiful colour and speaking with a camp accent in an exaggerated performance of a homosexual stereotype designed to generate laughter.[20] The cockney 'Any Old Iron' number is accompanied by brash, bright colours, including a donkey and cart decked with multicoloured ribbons. The scene is followed by far more restrained tones for a society marionette show which is subdued and de-saturated, implying an equation of brash colour with lower-class behaviour. In these instances colour contributes to the comic intention of the scenes, as well as reinforcing stereotypes which today appear anachronistic.

The failure of *London Town* appears to have sealed the fate of British musicals in the postwar period as competition with Hollywood was thereafter mostly avoided in this genre. Towards the end of the 1940s films in the 'London series' of star vehicles for Anna Neagle and Michael Wilding featured the occasional song and dance, including the Technicolor *Maytime in Mayfair* (1949), but they could hardly be described as full-blown musicals. As Harper and Porter point out, the few British musicals that were made in the early 1950s such as *The Story of Gilbert and Sullivan* (1953) or Powell and Pressburger's *Oh ... Rosalinda!!* (1955) were 'out of touch with the times' and 'harked back to a bygone age'.[21] The rest of this chapter turns to a genre seldom considered in terms of colour: comedy. As genre theory rightly cautions, it would be unwise to declare strict boundaries between genres, as shown by the examples above from *London Town* which include 'comic moments' within a musical.[22] A focus on mainly comedic narratives, however, allows colour to be considered from a slightly different perspective than usual.

The well-established, music-hall traditions of British comedy flourished in black-and-white films released during the 1930s and over the course of World War II. The comedians were well known, guaranteed to attract audiences by their very notoriety rather than needing new technology to boost their appeal. These comedies were primarily aimed at the domestic market, 'indigenous' product, often made on low budgets, as opposed to 'exportable' films which were more likely to be made in colour to appeal to the American market.[23] This was particularly the case with Korda's films and, as we have seen, British Technicolor was held in high esteem by American critics. It is not surprising then that the first British Technicolor ventures into comedy were Korda's star vehicles for Merle Oberon, *The Divorce of Lady X* (1938) and *Over the Moon* (1939). These were not very successful at the box office, particularly in comparison with *The Drum* (1938), *The Four Feathers*

London Town: cockney
number with bright,
saturated colours

London Town: society
marionette number with
colour restraint

(1939) and *The Thief of Bagdad* (1940), films that were more highly dependent on colour spectacle for their impact and yielded good returns overseas. As we have seen in Chapter 6, *Blithe Spirit* (1945) was a society comedy which made use of colour in very specific ways, most notably to dramatise the conflict between the two lead female characters. Colour was an integral element of the film's witty, light-hearted comic style which nevertheless managed to raise serious issues that resonated with the experiences of wartime audiences. The Technicolor comedies to be analysed here are *The Importance of Being Earnest* (1952), *Genevieve* (1953) and two Ealing comedies, *The Titfield Thunderbolt* (1952) and *The Ladykillers* (1955). They present an opportunity to evaluate the role of colour in enhancing their particular strands of comedy as well as to reflect more broadly on how different generic imperatives influenced film colour design.

The *Importance of Being Earnest* was director Anthony Asquith's first Technicolor film, and it was shot by Desmond Dickinson in a generally restrained style which privileged the colours of costumes and flowers. Even though the interior and exterior sets are important, the generally close shooting style, which concentrates on the figures, means that dialogue and costume are the main features to command attention. This cinematographic approach makes sense of the film's opening shots which feature a woman in a theatre box looking at the stage through opera glasses which focus on Jack Worthing (Michael Redgrave). A blurred

image becoming sharp replicates the woman's viewpoint as her glasses reveal Redgrave's comic figure as he scrubs himself clean in the bath while humming a tune. This overturns expectations established by the opening shot which shows the credits against a red theatre curtain. The device of the woman with opera glasses signals that what we are about to see is anything but a filmed play since the close shooting style exploits the specificity of cinematic presentation. In so doing it allows costume and colour to be appreciated, which is important in view of the verbally dexterous, effervescent comic style which permits several key costume changes and a high degree of visual interest in the outfits worn by the main characters, both male and female. For one reviewer this was not entirely successful since 'magnifying the proceedings and characters' for cinematic presentation had the effect of associating Wilde's 'glittering epigrams' too readily with the speakers 'who are plainly quite incapable of giving birth to them'.[24] This criticism interestingly points to the fact that troubling differences were perceived in the filmic presentation in that the centre of attention was not totally on the language. Yet this approach emphasised colour and costume as operating in collusion with Wilde's witticisms, as well as the quality of individual screen performances.

The first scene between Algernon (Michael Dennison) and Jack shows them in contrasting attire. To underscore the frivolity of his character, a dapper Algernon wears a yellow waistcoat and checked jacket with a white cravat. Jack is in a dark green dressing gown, shirt and red bow-tie and his general appearance is much darker than that of Algernon, a contrast which suits the mood of the scene in which they reveal each other's deception. The costumes were designed by Beatrice Dawson, who had a reputation for being creative with colour from her work on the historical drama *Trottie True* (1948). The contrasting approach is again evident in the scene when Jack meets Lady Bracknell (Edith Evans). In view of Evans's popular association with Lady Bracknell on stage and the character's central importance to Wilde's play, the impact of her grand entrance is enhanced by her flamboyant attire. Earnest's grey suit with a blue/grey silk cravat and a white gardenia in his buttonhole does not detract attention from the significant visual impact of Lady Bracknell's floral-patterned bolero with puffed sleeves, purple silk sleeveless dress gathered at the waist, with bows on the shoulders, topped with a highly decorative purple hat adorned with blue feathers. Harper comments that this costume is 'deeply inappropriate for a dowager, and it indicates the character's self-deception'.[25] On the other hand, some reviewers thought it inappropriately 'grotesque' and even 'outrageous'.[26] Its appearance at this moment contrasts markedly with her subsequent plainer, more serious costumes which are perhaps more in keeping with a dowager. Although Lady Bracknell's costume is different in colour from the green of Gwendolen's (Joan

Greenwood) silk dress, the shape and styles are similar in their highly puffed sleeves, boleros, the almost luminescent sheen reflecting from the material, and elaborate feathered hats. The hint of similarity creates an ironic costume link with the line later delivered by Algernon that: 'All women become like their mothers. That is their tragedy. No man does. That's his.' The different colours assist the comedy here since the green is appropriate in this context for Gwendolin's youth while the purple of Lady Bracknell's connotes a mature, authoritarian and matriarchal demeanour of which Jack is clearly afraid.

Costume and colour are very finely attuned to underscore character, as with Cecily (Dorothy Tutin), whose white puff-sleeved dress with a pale blue waistband and pink flower embellishment is later described by Lady Bracknell as 'sadly simple'. Her life in the country, freedom to day-dream and the absence of an overbearing mother influences the lack of fussiness of her costume. This contrasts markedly with the pink silk dress adorned with embroidered detail, lace, ruffles and hat worn by Gwendolen when she visits. In this way colour and costume are actively deployed to collude with the comedy of incongruity as the two women dressed respectively in white and pink prove to be far from innocent or without guile in their sparring verbal conflict until the misunderstanding over the identity of 'Earnest' is resolved. There is also an unusual degree of play with male costuming, as with the jaunty appearance of Algernon's check-patterned suit and yellow bow-tie with red spots worn when visiting Cecily. The black attire worn by Jack when he pretends that his fictitious brother Earnest is dead contrasts markedly with his subsequent outfit which could not be more different: a white suit with striped pale blue, pink and black banding and straw hat. All of these costumes are seen clearly because of the cinematographic strategy of close shots which direct attention more centrally to their details and colouring, or literally highlight facial details in Technicolor, such as Jack's blue eyes remarked on by Gwendolen. Colour thus enhances the presentation of the stars, particularly Joan Greenwood, who was especially popular in the black-and-white Ealing comedies *Kind Hearts and Coronets* (1949) and *The Man in the White Suit* (1951), although she had first starred in colour for non-comic roles in *The Man Within* (1946) and *Saraband for Dead Lovers* (1948). By contrast, the part of Cecily was

The Importance of Being Earnest (Technicolor, 1952): our first view of Lady Bracknell (Edith Evans) wearing a purple hat

Dorothy Tutin's first screen appearance so there was no established black-and-white image which required careful re-presentation in colour.

Some generic differences between comedy and melodrama can thus be identified as having significant implications for colour design. In this example the shots are closer, preventing the background *mise en scène* from being quite so significant in its potential to critique or draw attention to the social constraints under which the characters suffer in melodrama. On the other hand, the generally higher-key lighting of comedies permits, even encourages, the colours and details of costumes to be obtrusive. Although the witticisms of the dialogue provide a central pleasure in Wilde's play, on screen these are supported by comedic play with visual detail, as with Lady Bracknell's first costume or the excessive fussiness of Gwendolen's green and pink dresses. The costumes' different materials additionally invest colour with a tactile sensibility such as the delicate play of light reflecting off silk. In this and other ways the precise, artfully crafted comedy of language is matched by an equally sophisticated colour design which similarly involves inflections of meaning, play with contrast and repetition, and the suggestion of subtext.

Melodramas and comedies both involve affect. Melodramas present characters in states of emotional turmoil which are so powerful that the audience experiences degrees of vicarious acquisition, hence the equation of 'melodrama' with 'tears'. Comedy, on the other hand, deals with affectivity from another perspective, to generate laughter but often tinged with pathos so that the experience depends on comedy co-mingling with other emotions. Another British comedy, *Genevieve*, illustrates such further observations about the relationship between colour and comedy. The film was one of the most popular British comedies of the 1950s, filmed largely on location by Chris Challis.[27] This was fairly unusual for a Technicolor film since the varying light conditions on location created technical difficulties. The film nevertheless has a bright, 'modern' feel as it follows the fortunes of two couples on a vintage car race from London to Brighton. Alan (John Grigson) and Ambrose (Kenneth More) are motor enthusiasts whose long-suffering partners Wendy (Dinah Sheridan) and Rosalind (Kay Kendall) accompany them on the race. Despite being friends, both men are fiercely competitive and much of the film's comedy is constructed around

their respective schemes to prevent each other from getting to Brighton and back. It is also based on the women's presence as observers of their partners' obsession with their cars, 'more often united in condemning the childishness of the whole thing'.[28] The generally high-key appearance of the majority of the shots allows colour detail to be clearly visible, offering high-contrast images which are not complicated by shadow or variation in hue. Alan and Wendy's contemporary, compact London mews house is a good example in which modernity is equated with bright colours, such as the red wall lights and practical, unfussy white bedroom furniture. These details of *mise en scène* underscore the presentation of 'modern' marriage based on equality; new designs for progressive attitudes. But this equilibrium is soon strained by the men's enthusiasm for their cars, and a colour detail is significant in signalling a key change in Wendy's attitude. At first she refuses to go on the race because she has been invited to a cocktail party she would rather attend. Alan is disappointed and sulks upstairs but she changes her mind when she comes across an antique hat in a box in a cupboard, presumably worn in previous years for the race. The soft, 'feminine' pink of the hat and its association with earlier times and attitudes, is shown to full effect in a close-up of Wendy admiring herself in a mirror when trying it on. The music and her expression combine to evoke a nostalgic memory of the race which changes her mood entirely. Her decision to let Alan to go alone to Brighton is thus overturned and the film thereafter explores the limits of her loyalty as she is driven to Brighton in the car which frequently breaks down, she spills coffee on her dress and puts up with a number of schoolboy pranks which typify Alan's rivalry with Ambrose.

Simple colour-coding links the men with their cars: Alan's red jumper goes with his car's red seats and chassis, while Ambrose wears a yellow waistcoat when we first see him, in keeping with his yellow car with green seats, and a green tie when the race has begun. When Rosalind arrives to join him for the race she has a yellow hat and when Wendy's pale blue Victorian dress is ruined by the spilt coffee she puts on a much more practical outfit of check trousers and a reddish-pink jumper and hat. Such details provide a sense of colour correspondence which is important in delineating the world of the hobbyist for whom getting the details right

Genevieve (Technicolor, 1953): the shiny, red car is ruined

is crucial as well as fully entering into the spirit of the race with its physical challenges to both people and technology. Rosalind in particular struggles to keep decorum after falling into the water. In spite of her dishevelled appearance she redoes her red lipstick as the car starts to move forward. This detail repeats an emphasis previously established for her character on make-up, contemporary fashion and independence. The race takes its toll particularly on the women at whose expense much of the comedy is constructed (especially their clothes getting dirty), as in the humiliating incident when a news cameraman films Wendy, initially without her knowing, as she is changing her clothes after spilling the coffee. The women's attempt to rise above the petty rivalry that drives the men's obsession is ultimately defeated since as Geraghty argues the film works 'to endorse male enthusiasm and to suggest that it is linked to their greater feeling for tradition, which is, in the end, justified'.[29] From this perspective the comedy of Rosalind's defiant gesture of putting on red lipstick in a rickety, moving car and the visible ruination of Wendy's much-loved period costume acquires pathos as they are forced to succumb to the men's competitive desire and values associated with another era.

Technology is assisted in its presentation through colour, not only for the cars but also for the equipment needed to enhance their performance. When Alan repairs his car at a garage in Brighton the high-key lighting shows up background details of oil cans and iconic signs such as 'Goodyear Tyres', with its bright yellow letters and blue background. Care of the cars involves commitment which extends beyond time and money, the implication being that they almost rival the women for the men's affection. The portrait of the obsessive male hobbyist which the film delivers does not confine itself to owners of vintage cars. When Alan's car breaks down the driver of a modern, red sports car happily offers to tow him. He is as proud of his new car as Alan is of 'Genevieve'; when the latter runs into the back of the sports car the owner is devastated. The shiny, red paint is scratched, and the boot is dented. While this might appear to be an insignificant detail the spectacle of state-of-the art, aerodynamic technology being damaged relates to more than the impossibility of keeping cars in perfect condition. It constitutes an example of comic suspense by building something up to be knocked down; colour is an essential element of the moment we know is somewhat inevitable when the two cars will collide.[30] The car's red appearance, made all the more spectacular because of its highly polished surface, is ruined in an instant as a close-up of the damage completes the 'joke'.

Ealing's *The Titfield Thunderbolt* was the studio's first comedy in colour, directed by Charles Crichton and shot by Douglas Slocombe. There are similarities with *Genevieve* with the theme of past technologies and the encroachment of modernity, as a much-loved old railway engine is taken out of the museum by a group of local enthusiasts who are determined to keep the railway going after being informed that the branch line must close. Also like *Genevieve*, the narrative oscillates between triumphs and setbacks as the enthusiasts are opposed by commercial interests who want to make money from launching a rival bus service. When the original engine is sabotaged by them, the ancient but workable engine known as the 'Titfield Thunderbolt' has to save the day. Continuation of the service depends on the train run by amateurs passing a test imposed by the Ministry of Transport and the final sequences of the film are devoted to the various obstacles they encounter in a race against time. The film is generally considered to be one of the least successful Ealing comedies, signalling the beginning of the studio's demise. Charles Barr notes how the pace and style of the film, including the colour, 'operate in simple reinforcement of the script's image of the train and of the community; slow, uncomplicated, and picturesque'.[31] There is little of the experimentation evident in *Saraband for Dead Lovers*, also photographed by Slocombe, but the film was a very different project with other motivations for colour.

The first title announces 'Ealing Studios' against a mauve background and with a drawing of a circular railway track with a red-painted train engine. This serves as a quaint emblematic impression of what is to follow, since the train which comes to the rescue after the current one is sabotaged is first seen in a coloured drawing, fondly treasured by one of the men as a nostalgic reminder of the 'Titfield Thunderbolt' in its heyday. The colours of the ancient engine are red, green and gold, in contrast to the darker appearance of the first engine, the predominantly cream coach being promoted as 'alternative transport'. In this way the engine's special qualities in bringing the community together in defiance of the line closure are particularly signalled by red, a colour which is associated with the local squire (John Gregson), whose grandfather built the railway and who wears a red tie for many of the early scenes. Red also punctuates a key moment when the locals have been given the go-ahead to operate the railway for a trial period. One of the scheme's backers, Valentine (Stanley Holloway), a rich eccentric, picks a red rose for his buttonhole at the start of the first day of operation. A close-up of the rose is an unusual shot; the only other close-ups are reserved for the train's red wheels. Red also underscores a mood of optimism when the community are preparing the station for operation, since they plant red flowers, paint benches and make the station fit for purpose. In contrast to the many other usages of red discussed in this and other chapters, the colour is used here rather one-dimensionally to connote the optimism of the plucky community members who wish to resuscitate the railway. It is thus a colour associated with pride and defiance, standing for tradition and its defence and thus underscoring Ealing's dominant ideological preoccupations.

The film's theme of evoking nostalgia for past traditions is also emphasised by many long shots of the countryside as the train passes through lush, green fields with blue skies and billowing clouds. These contrast starkly with the low-key, night-time sequence when the first engine is de-railed. Colour is not used to generate specific comic effects, with perhaps the exception of a sight gag when, in a great hurry, George Blakeworth (Naunton Wayne), the town clerk, puts on dark trousers over grey, white and yellow-striped pyjamas which have been prominently displayed hitherto in the scene. He suspects that the community-run engine will be sabotaged the night before its efficiency is tested by the Ministry, and rushes out in the dark to see if he is right when he hears suspicious noises outside. The comedy is created around the incongruity of this image: previously the clerk has been shown in a three-piece dark suit, carrying a briefcase and wearing a bowler hat (as a stereotypical bureaucrat), and his line delivered on departure to his wife, 'It doesn't do for a man in my position to make a mistake', acquires added humour because of the trouser/pyjama sight gag. The officious demeanour epitomised by the smart, formal suit and the pyjamas' contrasting softness and warmth, largely created by their material and the yellow stripes, could not be more different. The film certainly does not have the variety of colour evident in the films previously discussed, but it is of interest because it was Ealing's first attempt to film a comedy in colour. At a late stage of Ealing comedy it can be said to correspond with, as Barr puts it, 'the common identikit view of the genre, formed in retrospect, as something nice and wholesome and harmless, quaint and static and timeless'.[32] The conservatism of its theme is perhaps accompanied by a similar approach to style. After all, the most successful Ealing comedies were in black and white and *Saraband for Dead Lovers* had not been a box-office success. As the star of the film, however, the train was appropriately coloured and since there was no particular character development or inclusion of relationships as in *Genevieve*, the scope for a more complex colour design was limited.

The Ladykillers (dir. Alexander Mackendrick) had a very different cinematographic style, shot by Otto Heller in 'expressionistic' Technicolor.[33] The film's comedy is based around the incongruity of a criminal gang led by 'Professor' Marcus (Alex Guinness) occupying rooms in a rickety and crumbling Victorian house owned by Mrs Wilberforce (Katie Johnson) in King's Cross, London, under the pretence of being musicians in need of rehearsal space. The gang steals money from a payroll van, concealing it in a trunk which they ask the kindly Mrs Wilberforce to collect from the station. Unaware of their criminal activities, she believes it to be luggage and after a tortuous journey home involving several delays, she returns with the trunk and

The Ladykillers (Technicolor, 1955): the 'operations room'

the gang stash the money in their instrument cases. Mrs Wilberforce is ignorant of the crime until a cello case bursts open when it gets wedged in the front door as the gang leave the house. Their attempts to persuade her to keep silent fail and she resolves to tell the police. The gang decide that one of them must kill her and draw straws to decide who will commit the deed. By this time several of them are fond of her so try to avoid taking action, even when they have drawn the short straw. In a series of accidents caused by their prevarication and in-fighting, each of the criminals dies. Mrs Wilberforce goes to the police and tells them about the crime but assuming she is an old lady with an active imagination they are unconvinced and she keeps the money.

The comic basis of this situation is strong in comparison with *The Titfield Thunderbolt*. The darker tone in theme and style is highly appropriate for a comedy which locates criminality within the walls of a respectable elderly woman's home. As with other Ealing colour films, most notably *Saraband for Dead Lovers* and *The Titfield Thunderbolt*, title cards provide an emblematic guide to the film and its colour design. Blue-patterned wallpaper forms the background, to which is added a pink rose. When it appears the film's title is adorned with blue, green and red detail, and a gun is added beside the rose as the titles follow on from each other. The creeping embellishment of detail anticipates the juxtaposition of gentility and criminality, and the suspenseful score accentuates the mood of black

Red signals on the railway line

comedy. The colour design follows a similar dynamic with contrasts between pastel colours worn by Mrs Wilberforce and her friends, the genteel, pale-patterned wallpaper in some of the rooms and the darker forms, colours and objects associated with the gang and the 'operations room' they inhabit. The *mise en scène* of the house is a highly appropriate setting for the allegorical nature of the film's 'entrancing portrait of a Victorian civilisation lingering on, tottering, into the postwar world'.[34] Repeated high-angle chiaroscuro shots of the house show the oddity of its placement in King's Cross among shops and other markers of modern city life. Subsidence causes pictures not to hang straight, the plumbing requires a hefty bang on the pipes to work and the sitting-room is cluttered with ornaments. As a

London house, it could not be more different from Alan and Wendy's compact, modern mews residence in *Genevieve*, and the contrasting colour design underscores the uneasy co-presence of a bygone age and modernity.

For a film which is marked for much of the time by low-key lighting, primary colours are nevertheless outstanding and work to accentuate contrast. Red is a key colour throughout the film, both within the house and outside. Mrs Wilberforce's front door has a thick, red velvet curtain to one side, and the carpet and runner up the stairs are red. In the sitting-room her chair is burgundy, matched by a heavy drape over the mantelpiece above the fireplace. In exteriors, red features prominently for the telephone box near the house, which is seen in several shots. It becomes particularly integral to the comedy when Professor Marcus is told about Mrs Wilberforce's progress once the trunk has been collected and other members of the gang crowd into the box to hear the news. At King's Cross station the mail trains are red, contrasting with the blue van intercepted by the gang which carries the money in shiny silver boxes. Red London buses are visible in the background for some of the street scenes and in the extremely low-key lit sequence by the railway line towards the end of the film, red signals stand out in the darkness. Again, these accentuate the collision of worlds delineated in the film which oscillates between the claustrophobic interior spaces of the house and the bird's eye shots which highlight its seemingly stubborn, continued existence in the locale.

Additional details accumulate to form a palette which is visually arresting for colour contrast, repetition and surprise. Bright colours are a feature of *mise en scène* rather than for costume which generally supports characterisation – for example, Major Countney's (Cecil Parker) red bow-tie, check jacket and ochre waistcoat indicate a man struggling to maintain respectability even though he has fallen in with criminals. Together with his foreign accent Louis Harvey's (Herbert Lom) dark suit, hat and white tie mark him as different, even sinister, and Mrs Wilberforce's beige suit and neat boater hat with floral detail typify a genteel elderly woman. The visibility of bright colours enhances the comedy created by the parrot, General Gordon, who has to be retrieved by one of the gang when it escapes, and also for the fruit which spills all over the road when Mrs Wilberforce gets into an altercation with a barrow-boy which is one of the delays that causes the gang anxiety as they await her return to the house with the trunk. In this way colour is woven into a sequence marked for its comic suspense since the audience has knowledge not possessed by the character who is blissfully unaware that she is carrying stolen goods.

These examples show how colour was, to a greater or lesser extent, integral to generic address and development. After the failure of *London Town*, Hollywood's domination of the market for Technicolor musicals was assured, even though the film is not without colour interest. As far as comedies were concerned colour became important for films outside the revue, comedian-centred and sketch-based model that had been so popular in the 1930s and during World War II. For comedies dealing with broad themes such as conflict between different generations, genders or ways of living, there was more scope for colour to accelerate the comedic impulse of particular scenes or sequences. The visual pleasure of *The Importance of Being Earnest* was heightened by colour as a register that extended, underscored and rendered more complex visual 'puns', ironies and subtext. In the case of *Genevieve* colours are applied consistently to emphasise the men's identification with their vintage vehicles and the anachronistic car race serves as an astute comic metaphor for probing gender in 1950s Britain as well as conflicting attitudes towards modernity. The two Ealing comedies similarly deploy colour to underscore their broader societal themes using different stylistic approaches. *The Ladykillers* in particular highlights colour within a low-key, black-comedy aesthetic in which the force of the primary colour red dominates in a range of different contexts which is more complex than its deployment in *The Titfield Thunderbolt*. Although such an assertive combination of comedy and colour was far from the norm, these examples show that the 'repetition and difference' dynamic of genre equated well with colour's similar capacity for supporting, but also subverting established cultural meanings when located within comic situations, techniques and performances.

11 COLOUR AESTHETICS IN POSTWAR CINEMA
IMAGE, SOUND, COLOUR

Following on from the generic experiments with colour detailed in Chapters 8 to 10, this chapter will focus more centrally on questions of film colour aesthetics, asking how colour explores and extends the range of aesthetic possibilities in film. What aesthetic choices does colour make possible, encourage and, conversely, what does colour make problematic? Analysing such questions involves considering technical difficulties of working with colour such as depth of field, movement and lighting, as well as colour's relation to narrative forms and conventions. The long time it took for colour to become the norm and its association with both realism and cinematic spectacle kept open radical aesthetic possibilities which in notable films pushed against a closed approach to convention. This allowed for very specific contexts that were particular to each film's use of colour to broaden the range of options available to directors, cinematographers, set and costume designers. As we have seen, the reception of colour, particularly Technicolor, in critical commentary demonstrates how colour was often greeted with a confused response which sought to contain its potential for aesthetic experiment. Although working with Technicolor involved negotiating with the Color Advisory Service and within the boundaries of classical narrative, this chapter demonstrates how British film-makers exploited colour's great potential for aesthetic innovation in many celebrated films.

In the first part of the chapter, analysis will focus on flowers/natural phenomena and colour film, referencing debates about 'natural' colour and nature from the silent period to create a context for understanding the longevity of particular aesthetic tropes that fascinated film-makers for decades. The choice of this example arises from the concentration of much early commentary on the potential of colour film to replicate nature, be spectacular and appeal to the senses. Many commentators saw colour as the most effective method of illustrating natural phenomena, even though it was also acknowledged that its capacity for non-naturalistic representation was a major part of its appeal for audiences (as explored in previous chapters). Case studies will include the use of flowers in Kinemacolor and other silent films. Natalie Kalmus's utopian ideas about colour and their perhaps surprising affinity with those of Eisenstein are noted, drawing on examples from *The Thief of Bagdad* (1940), the association between flowers, colour and ghostliness in *Blithe Spirit* (1945), and spectacular natural imagery in *Black Narcissus* (1947). This leads into the second part of the chapter in which the relationship between colour, sound and music will be explored with case studies of *Black Narcissus, The Red Shoes* (1948) and *The Tales of Hoffmann* (1951), drawing on the ideas of Adrian Klein and Sergei Eisenstein as primary analytical referents. *Black Narcissus*, for example, presents an example of 'the composed film' in a key sequence towards the end of the film in which editing, montage, music, movement and colour demonstrate Eisenstein's conception of organic unity in cinema. The ballet within the film *The Red Shoes* is another oft-cited example of the 'composed film' which will here be subject to detailed scrutiny, with an emphasis on the relationship between colour and music. Colour's contribution was of fundamental importance in promoting cinema as a total art form in the spirit of the *gesamtkunstwerk* idea that inspired Powell and Pressburger.

'ALL THE HUES OF NATURE'

As noted in the more general analysis of *A Matter of Life and Death* (1946) when Conductor 71 (Marius Goring) passes from heaven to earth a rose acquires its colour, and he famously remarks: 'One is starved for Technicolor up there.' Close-ups of the transition, with the pink rose contrasted with the deeper red hue of the jewel on his ring, are followed by a medium-shot, which shows him surrounded by rhododendrons. What is remarkable is the cumulative impact of colour as the scene unfolds. The arrival of colour, itself a spectacle, reaches a crescendo as Conductor 71 is framed by an abundant display of even deeper hues. Tom Gunning observed that flowers often featured in colour films of the silent period because they 'show a brilliant moment rather than something that is constant'; they are brilliantly saturated, but they fade.[1] Cinema and photography drew attention to their ephemeral nature as media well placed to document things that pass in a context of tumultuous industrial and technical change. Some films, such as Pathé's *Les Fleurs Animées* (a 1906 trick film inspired by an 1847 féerie book) featured novelty devices such as petals plucked from a flower coming back to life with women's heads in place of their buds. The rose in Conductor 71's buttonhole becoming coloured represents a continuum of a long tradition of mechanical virtuosity with which the wonder of colour cinema was implicated.

The first part of this chapter explores how floral imagery forms a consistent aesthetic trope in colour films from the silent era well into the arrival of sound, the introduction of Technicolor and beyond. Other elements similarly dominated discussion about colour films including skin tones, skies and clouds, but the temptation to prove the success of a particular process by demonstrating its capacity to film (and manipulate) floral imagery ('all the hues of nature') was great for many film-makers experimenting with colour. I argue that the 'cinema of colour attractions'[2] persisted within the dominant context of classical narrative, and in spite of commentators such as Adrian Cornwell-Clyne

declaring that the best colour work was relatively unnoticeable: 'The first colour film to be received with universal acclamation will be that one in which we shall never have been conscious of the colour as an achievement.'[3] Opportunities existed for moments of intense creativity in the application of colour that spanned across decades rather than being confined to the silent period.

In the first instance, colour's affective potential was discovered through the idea that cinema was uniquely placed to capture reality. Early discourses on colour film were obsessed with the extent to which fidelity to nature could be achieved. Technical difficulties with early natural (that is non-painted, tinted, toned or stencil) colour processes meant that concentrating on static objects reduced the danger of fringing (colour 'bleed' with movement). As we have seen, Kinemacolor claimed to be a natural process involving film stock sensitised to colour. The colour was only visible to the eye when projected at high speed, using red and green filters. Charles Urban marketed it from 1906 as a superior process that offered an educational 'window on the world'. The marketing also emphasised that the achievement of 'true' colour was entirely down to motion picture technology:

> For a proper realization of the astounding advance made by Kinemacolor in the art of the camera, it must be clearly emphasized that the colors obtained are due to the agency of LIGHT only. No painting, handwork, stencil-work or similar devices are used. The colors are, as it were, lying latent in the photographic picture, and are brought into visibility at the moment of exhibition.[4]

As Eirik Hanssen points out, these claims were of fundamental importance in Kinemacolor's bid to be the most accurate process for representing unmediated 'trace' or 'index' – a window on the world of nature that was seen to be scientifically (and therefore educationally) superior to applied colour processes.[5]

To avoid fringing, obtrusive camera movement was avoided in Kinemacolor films so that particular objects were filmed almost as photographs with the aim of demonstrating 'good', that is to say acceptable in a context of technical difficulty, colour rendition. But movement of another kind accentuated the appeal of *From Bud to Blossom* (1910), a celebrated film in which speed magnification was used. In order to accentuate Kinemacolor's claim to technical superiority, it had to *exceed* the requirements to simply film things as they appeared to the eye. Single photographs were taken of stages of a flower's growth and then projected to make nature's achievement visible in a few seconds. The Kinemacolor catalogue explained:

> This picture enables us to realize in a degree that it would be impossible by any other means that growth in both the plant and animal worlds follows the same general principles, although this cannot always be detected by the unaided human vision. One of the queerest things one notices in the film is the effort that the plant appears to be making as it opens its buds. Leaves and stem move in sympathy and it seems as thought the plant was making a mighty effort to realize the principle aim of its existence.[6]

What is remarkable about this claim is how film technology is promoted as a means of making us see nature better – visual perception is exceeded to reveal the secrets of natural phenomena.[7] 'True' nature but presented by an unnatural means. One viewer of the film expressed this paradox, while also noting how this experiment appeared to invest the flower with spiritual properties: 'Delusive nature has at last been captured. By a clever mechanical trick in the preparation of the films, the floral subjects appeared to come and go as spirits out of thin air; but their dissolution came only after they had shown themselves as solid coloured realities.'[8]

While replicating floral imagery was often considered to be a test for 'good' colour, we find in this example that this was in fact extremely mediated by technology in a hyper-realistic way. Such human manipulation of nature allowed for claims about filmic superiority and specificity in the sense that technology permitted an accentuation of human perception which resulted in a spectacular aesthetic experiment. At the same time nature was allied with human agency and also associations with magic, spirituality and otherness since what was produced was outside normal human experience. Antonia Lant documents how such films had a particular appeal for women, based on accounts by Mary Field and Germaine Dulac from the 1930s of seeing and producing 'germination' films depicting plant growth.[9] She observes that such subject matter 'pointed to the ways in which film projection itself was a process

of metamorphosis', a comment which acquires particular significance in the context of Kinemacolor with its emphasis on projection as the technical harbinger of colour vision.[10] It also points to a connection between spectacular nature and the feminine, a trope that was demonstrated in later colour films, such as the association of the ghost Elvira in *Blithe Spirit* with flowers, as she demonstrates her 'presence' to a character who cannot see her by carrying a vase of flowers across a room.

This approach of making floral imagery perform a sort of litmus test for the success of a particular colour process was not confined to the silent period and, when fringing had been overcome, discourses about colour continued to be preoccupied with the technical advantages and disadvantages of each particular system and views differed on whether colour was desirable at all. As we have seen, under the direction of Natalie Kalmus, Technicolor's consultancy service emphasised careful planning, harmony and control. To be 'colour conscious' meant avoiding 'a super-abundance of color' while applying methods such as underscoring character and narrative, and introducing colour complementaries. Less often noted were her ideas on using colour film as an opportunity to unite music, graphic art and acting in 'one expression of more ultimate art', which were more fully articulated by theorists such as Eisenstein – whose ideas have already been referenced in this book regarding the importance of interpreting film colour as contextual rather than overtly symbolic.[11] As also noted by Tom Gunning, there are no fixed codes around colour, particularly in the silent period since:

> The colour establishes a kind of dialogue with the film as we watch it. We suddenly see the colour through the narrative, or the narrative through the colour, and not just the narrative, but the action, the objects, the people or the places with non-narrative films. There's a kind of reciprocal process by which these two layers of the film interact, and the dominant element in this interaction is … the *changes* of colour.[12]

This position advocates a self-referential approach whereby a particular film can establish its own internal consistency in a manner that departs from colour's broader cultural associations. Kalmus's remarks thus represent continuity with the silent era when the need to present colour film as superior involved negotiating a paradoxical position in which claims about heightened realism, and colour completing cinema's ability to present 'a window on the world', were illustrated by spectacular experiments that demonstrated the opposite. Like flowers, colour's mutability provided opportunities for film-makers, both in relation to narrative and to the presentation of visual spectacle, to experiment with colour as an element of technical and aesthetic manipulation towards 'more ultimate art' appealing to the senses through music and images in a total, enveloping experience. While Kalmus's 'color conscious' strictures tended towards non-spectacular conventions, her more utopian aspirations for colour were realised by several Technicolor films discussed in this chapter.

To explore these connections, I will now turn to some examples from British Technicolor films: *The Thief of Bagdad*, *Blithe Spirit*, *Black Narcissus*, *The Red Shoes* and *The Tales of Hoffmann*. Even as late as 1953 Technicolor was advertised for its ability to produce

Technicolor Ltd advertisement in *Kinematograph Weekly*, 29 October 1953

colour attracts…

Colour by TECHNICOLOR
TECHNICOLOR LIMITED
HERBERT T. KALMUS, CHAIRMAN

striking natural images, such in an advertisement featuring a cactus with a pink flower which has attracted a butterfly. 'Colour attracts …' is the caption, with the green base of the cactus contrasted with the pink flower which has a blue sky background above yellow for the ground. The fantasy film genre invited a non-naturalistic approach to colour, as noted by E. S. Tompkins in the *British Journal of Photography*: 'To succeed, the fantasy film must start where life and the stage finish; must go further than a mere picturisation of stage tricks; and should show effects and happenings which are impossible in normal human experience.'[13] Noted for its groundbreaking special effects (blue-screen compositing, hanging miniatures), *The Thief of Bagdad* celebrates colour as integral to its design as well as to its narrative in unexpected ways for the spectacular representation of natural imagery. A blue eye motif establishes the theme of vision from the opening of the film. Both are associated with a major, powerful character, Jaffar (Conrad Veidt), made clear by a dissolve from the eye to his face and our introduction to him by seeing only his eyes. Jaffar is associated with magic and an important instance of this comes later in the film when he creates a blue rose designed to make the Princess forget her love of the character Ahmed and to fall in love with Jaffar instead. Intrigued by the unnatural appearance of the magical blue rose, the Princess cannot resist smelling it and forgets the past in an instant. Here sensual experiences and curiosity are encouraged by colour; the strangeness of the colour provokes her to smell the rose to see if it is different from the norm. Referred to by Natalie Kalmus as a 'quiet color', here blue functions differently in its association with danger and with the evil character Jaffar. The film has thus established its own regime of colour association, subverting more typical symbolic conventions for blue and exemplifying Eisenstein's concern to make colour an integral aspect of a film's organic unity in an experimental manner. While Natalie Kalmus's thoughts on colour as being an integral element working towards 'more ultimate art' might not appear to be central to her operation of the consultancy service, this example shows perhaps more tolerance for experimental ideas than she is usually credited for.

As noted earlier, the comment about Kinemacolor's *From Bud to Blossom* in which 'the floral subjects appeared to come and go as spirits out of thin air', is resonant with *Blithe Spirit*. Here flowers (and their colours) actually stand in for Elvira, a dead woman who is haunting her husband, Charles. The 'trick' of the film (awarded an Oscar for special effects) is that she is only visible to him and not to his second wife Ruth. In a key scene Charles wants to prove to Ruth that Elvira really has come back to haunt him. He asks Elvira to walk towards Ruth carrying a vase; two shots are filmed from Ruth's viewpoint followed by one from Charles's. While performing a perfectly good plot point in this context, the flowers are an apposite stand-in for a dead character. Their association with an ephemeral existence of being resplendent before dying is reinforced by the spectacle of green together with different hues of red, pink and purple. Elvira is dressed in grey/green, reminding us of the apparent contradictory symbolism around green as both nature and life but also decay and death. The trick shots resonate with examples referred to earlier of silent films that used nature and colour to advertise cinema as a mechanical form of magic.

As will be demonstrated in the more extensive analysis below, *Black Narcissus* draws on floral imagery to convey abundance, spirituality and the 'other worldliness' of the Himalayas. Once again trickery is involved since the exteriors were filmed in Horsham, Surrey, rather than in the exotic locale where the film is set. Again working within the context of the film the shots which concentrate on natural beauty, presented and framed as colour spectacle, are associated with a world unknown but revealed to us by cinema. This is in the tradition of the travelogue, demonstrating again how the cinema of colour attractions persisted beyond the silent period. A notable instance of this was in the *World Windows* series of films made in 1937–40 – for example, *Arabian Bazaar*, shot by Jack Cardiff and again featuring abundant floral imagery to convey a sense of eastern 'otherness'.

To summarise this initial consideration of colour aesthetics, colour films were frequently judged against perceived standards of realism or accuracy, especially in silent cinema when colour was pronounced as 'wrong' if a film showed fringing, blotchiness or inconsistent colour rendition. In travelogues and films documenting the wonders of nature, early film-makers nevertheless devised ingenious ways of demonstrating colour so that in addition to capturing nature's beauty cinema itself was displayed as something wondrous and specific. In terms of presenting an entertaining display, films exaggerated

the qualities of nature, drew attention to them to show off a new world of colour on screen. That space for a cinema of colour attractions persisted well into the Technicolor period, when film-makers drew on earlier modes of presenting natural and floral imagery in films that pushed against convention. Critics of this approach argued that audiences were bored by gratuitous displays of colour. Artist Paul Nash, for example, objected to incidental shots of natural beauty in *Wings of the Morning* (1937), since he thought they slowed down the film.[14] Genre was, of course, important in presenting opportunities for experimentation and films such as *The Thief of Bagdad* invited an expectation of technical and narrative ingenuity. In comparison to the conversion to sound the acceptance of colour was slow. Since colour had to establish its credibility over and over again for many decades, the persistence of residual tropes in establishing aesthetic practices was hardly surprising. Those 'starved' of Technicolor continued to judge its sporadic appearance within dominant critical paradigms of naturalism. Yet, as this chapter will continue to demonstrate, there were impressive exceptions as early approaches to colour that permitted considerable latitude and innovation continued to be evident in subsequent decades. This allowed for nature's abundance to provoke daring colour compositions, and for colour to combine with music in locating cinema as an art of the senses. The Technicolor 'system' was not closed to instances of colour spectacle, and many British cinematographers and directors perhaps unwittingly enabled the ideas of Natalie Kalmus and Sergei Eisenstein on colour to come together in surprising ways.

BLACK NARCISSUS: COLOUR DESIGN AND MUSIC

Perhaps Jack Cardiff and set designer Alfred Junge's greatest challenge in creating an environment that was perfectly suited to character, colour and dramatic action was *Black Narcissus*, which won Academy Awards for colour cinematography and art/set direction. Adapted from Rumer Godden's novel, *Black Narcissus* was set in the Himalayas but Powell decided against location shooting on the grounds that a studio environment provided greater opportunity to produce a precisely controlled effect: 'The atmosphere in this film is everything, and we must create and control it from the start … If we went to India and shot a lot of exteriors, according to the usual plan, and then came back to Pinewood and then tried to match them here, you would have two kinds of colour and two kinds of style.'[15] So the Himalayas were re-created at Pinewood and at Leonardslee, a sub-tropical garden in Horsham, Surrey. Under Jack Cardiff's direction colour vividly captures the exoticism of Leonardslee's azaleas and rhododendrons. The gardens of Leonardslee are highlighted for their colour as part of the film's creation of Mopu as the eastern 'other'. As the previous section of the chapter has argued, spectacular realism exaggerated natural beauty with a range of formal devices including close-ups. In *Black Narcissus* the vibrancy of the flora is of fundamental importance in suggesting eastern exoticism. In this way, colour's capacity to make the viewer both recognise something yet somehow find it surprising found perfect expression. As *Black Narcissus* and the other films discussed in this chapter demonstrate, music was similarly crucial in producing the unified cinematic experience of colour *and* musical attractions advocated by Eisenstein.

The atmosphere that proves to be so seductive to the English nuns who establish 'The convent of St Faith' high in the mountains was suggested by set designer Alfred Junge's early drawings of the old palace at Mopu that was formerly used as a harem. Junge also created significant interior details in his designs. Of particular note are the erotic wall paintings of the voluptuous women of the harem that cause the nuns embarrassment, which are created with a bold red, green and blue palette that influenced the scoring of colour for the costume designs, particularly for Kanchi (Jean Simmons) who represents sexuality and 'the East'. Junge's designs, in combination with Technicolor, produce a key effect in the film of combining the past with the present while at the same time symbolising the sexual longings experienced by the nuns who are profoundly unsettled throughout their stay at Mopu. W. Percy Day's special effects were also of crucial importance in creating the film's atmosphere, incorporating a new, economical method for the matte process which dispensed with shooting tests before the actual shooting of scenes. The film could thus be developed and printed straight away.[16]

Black Narcissus (Technicolor, 1947): Sister Ruth (Kathleen Byron) putting on red lipstick and in red dress

The film's themes of losing control, of temptation and sexuality are communicated well through the use of Technicolor. Cardiff recalls, for example, how the reddening effects of the process had to be counteracted by making the actors put on pale lipstick. On the other hand, Sister Ruth's (Kathleen Byron) rebellion is symbolised by a flagrant use of the colour red with the extreme close-up of her putting on lipstick and the red dress she procures illicitly when she decides to leave the Order. Red, of course, signifies sexuality, change and activity. Colour is used quite literally to show Ruth's fall from grace, which is a common association of colour, as pointed out by David Batchelor.[17] In the scene when Ruth declares her love for Mr Dean (David Farrar), we see colour used for an extreme effect when the screen becomes flooded with red as she faints when he rejects her. Here colour can be

Black Narcissus: Sister
Clodagh (Deborah Kerr)
being spied on as the stalking
scene unfolds; Sister Ruth
transformed

seen to operate as an excessive register, colouring
everything in the frame and with the association of anger
and jealousy as she cries, 'Clodagh, Clodagh, Clodagh'.
In this case the colour red, which has previously
connoted uncontrollable passion and rebellion, becomes
the most dominant, affective register in a way that is
reminiscent of Robert Jones's use of such devices in the
early Technicolor 'demonstration mode' film *La
Cucaracha* (1934).[18] The equation of red with female
hysteria was repeated in Hitchcock's *Marnie* (1964).
The reds in *Black Narcissus*, and in other Powell and
Pressburger films, were particularly striking and
appeared more saturated when contrasted with black, as
with the black screen seen directly after Sister Ruth's
red-drenched fainting episode. A similar device is used to
heighten the saturation of Sister Clodagh's (Deborah
Kerr) emerald green necklace, shown in one of her

flashbacks to her past life in Ireland, as the scene
concludes by fading to black as she runs out into the
night.

Cardiff's use of low-key lighting was remarkable,
using little or no fill lights to produce expressionist
effects not normally used for Technicolor. He explained
how for this technique he drew inspiration from
Vermeer and Caravaggio: 'They both lit with very simple
light. Many painters did, but with Vermeer and
Caravaggio you were very conscious of it; they really
used the shadows. Caravaggio would just have one
sweeping light over everything so that you were aware of
the single light.'[19] Cardiff recalls how in *Black Narcissus*
he insisted on using fog filters and diffusing techniques
not readily approved of by Technicolor. He had already
done this in *A Matter of Life and Death* and although
Technicolor was at first disapproving the company
appreciated the results he had achieved in that film.
A striking example of this technique in *Black Narcissus*
occurs in the 'stalking' scene towards the end of the film
when a tired and distraught Sister Clodagh goes to ring
the bell at dawn, just before she is attacked by Sister
Ruth from whose point of view most of the sequence is
shot. In this sequence Cardiff went ahead with his tonal
experiments, using a slight fog filter on the camera
(unusual for Technicolor) and guided by a 'painterly'
imperative, drawing on the expressive tones of Van
Gogh and the greens and reds of Rembrandt's paintings.
In addition to the fog filter, he used green filters in the
filler light and also pinkish colours for the sun effects.
This sequence begins early in the morning as dawn
breaks, with Sister Clodagh watching for Sister Ruth
outside the convent. Pink, mauve and greyish colours
form the dominant palette when tension builds as Ruth's
point of view is accentuated as she watches Clodagh's
every move. At first we see Clodagh from afar, as a
silhouette with dawn breaking in the background. The
pinkish tones are visible and are used throughout the
sequence not only to show the beginning of a new day
but also more symbolically to underscore the build-up of
tension and sinister presence of Ruth. The next shot
indicates a malevolent point of view as the camera tracks
from behind a wall to indicate Clodagh being spied on
from afar as her silhouette gradually attains centre
placement in the frame. The music builds to an agitated
choral swell to accompany the revelation of the stalker in
an extreme close-up of Sister Ruth, whose instability is

indicated by her glowering look, dishevelled hair and stark, white face. The music resumes with low-toned violins striking an ominous, repetitive rhythm which builds gradually as we follow an exhausted Clodagh into the chapel which is lit to accentuate the mauve/pinkish light intruding into the top half of the frame, with the lower portions darker in tone. We briefly glimpse Ruth running up the stairs, looking all the more terrifying as she forms a streaking dark shadow against the pink light of dawn and the music again builds to an agitated choral swell. On hearing a noise, Clodagh realises that she is being watched and looks around for the intruder. With Ruth now apparently gone, the tension gives way to some calmer moments as Clodagh leaves the chapel and washes her face, getting ready to perform her duty of ringing the bell. But the high-angle camera and touches of pink light indicate that Ruth is still watching from above, as six o'clock approaches and a weary Clodagh staggers over to the bell tower. Her exhaustion is conveyed as she steadies herself by reaching out to the wall and Cardiff's diffused camera is noticeable as an impressionist technique which emphasises her weariness and disorientation. The sequence reaches its dramatic climax with the struggle at the tower when Ruth tries to push Clodagh over the precipice and Ruth falls to her death.

Black Narcissus: the Young General (Sabu); Kanchi (Jean Simmons)

In addition to Cardiff's key work with colour, the music for the 'stalking sequence' was composed by Brian Easdale before the film was shot, representing an early example of Powell and Pressburger's experiments with 'the composed film'.[20] In this sense *Black Narcissus* can be related to Eisenstein's conception of organic unity, in which colour performed a key role in relation to sound:

> For it is color, color and again color to the very end, which can solve the problems of proportion and abduction to produce a general unity of sound and visual factors. The higher forms of organic relationship between the melodic outline of music and the tonal structure of systematically blended color shots are possible only with the appearance of color in the cinema.[21]

It is perhaps here that the undeveloped, utopian aspects of Kalmus's thinking on colour were realised, since, as previously noted, in spite of her position as overseeing 'color control' for Technicolor films, she sympathised with aims for colour as 'one expression of more ultimate art'. In the 'stalking' sequence this technique is clearly demonstrated as the 'composed film' operates as a sequence which is united by a precise combination of editing, musical punctuation, movement within the frame, juxtaposition through lighting and, of course, colour. After initial objections Technicolor appreciated what Cardiff was trying to achieve and consented to leave the scene as shot.[22]

Used in conjunction with low-key lighting, Jack Cardiff's 'painterly' use of Technicolor is capable of conveying subtleties of mood that would have been impossible had a different cinematographic approach been deployed. He was anxious to present the colour compositions judiciously, to achieve the impression of the eastern 'other' without exaggerating:

Black Narcissus: the cueing of
Sister Clodagh's flashback;
Sister Clodagh's memory
unfolds

It will be obvious that all these sugar-icing effects could be horribly calamitous if used without great care. We know how those over-blue night effects and hideous blood-orange sunsets nauseated cinemagoers, and here was a problem; the effects had to be exaggerated to a point almost of incredulity in order to plant the fact that the Nuns are in constant psychological conflict with the wild, unearthly beauty of their surroundings, yet the photography must never become vulgar and gaudy. Nearly every scene must show such exotic, hot-house sensuality that one should appreciate that mysterious influence of impending disaster without the colour becoming 'chocolate box'.[23]

Colours are associated with the character of the Young General (Sabu) in his excessively splendid silks and jewels and, as we have seen, of Kanchi. On other

occasions, as the analysis of the sequence when Sister Ruth 'stalks' Clodagh demonstrates, colour is used in an expressive way via the privileging of a pink, mauve and grey-black colour palette to create suspense. When a similar colour palette is used for Calcutta at the beginning of the film it connotes order and regimentation; by the end of the film these same colours are highlighted, particularly accentuating the pink, to illustrate the extent to which order has completely broken down at St Faith. This usage of colour applies Eisenstein's theory whereby colour is perceived relationally to context:

For convergence between sound and colour can only take place through the visual image, i.e. through something psychologically specific but essentially changeable, subject as it is to the mutations imposed by its content and by the overall conceptual system. What is unique in an image and what can blend essentially with it are absolute only in the conditions of a *given* context, of a *given* iconography, of a *given* construct.[24]

Colours therefore alter their meaning according to context. The precise, controlled vision of the East created by Alfred Junge similarly shifts meaning in curious ways. On some occasions it functions as the mysterious 'other' of the western imagination, while on others it is strangely familiar to the West, as in the vivid flashback when Clodagh's memory is visually linked by shots of the blue sky and blossoms at Mopu and the stunning landscape of Ireland that forms the backdrop to her own 'exotic' appearance in her former life, occasioned by a dissolve to introduce the flashback. For the audience, this shot has the added spectacle of seeing Deborah Kerr as film star, revealed, after her costume as a nun has deprived them of the sight of her red hair, a colour which Ray Rennahan, cinematographer on *Wings of the Morning* and many other films shot in Technicolor including *Gone with the Wind* (1939), declared was particularly suited to reproduction in Technicolor.[25]

These examples show that there was indeed an adventurous and at times innovative approach to the application of Technicolor in Britain. While this chapter has so far concentrated on particular examples, there are other films which are notable for their negotiation of colour film aesthetics within British cinema including *Blanche Fury* (1947), *Saraband for Dead Lovers* (1948)

Black Narcissus: Sister
Clodagh in Ireland

and *Moulin Rouge* (1953), the latter (discussed in Chapter 12) being particularly striking for cinematographer Ossie Morris's innovations with Technicolor through the use of colour coding for characters by using filtered lights, fog filters on the camera and smoke effects on the set to replicate the style of Toulouse-Lautrec's post-impressionist paintings.[26] Nevertheless it is important to bear in mind that at the same time experimentation was occurring elsewhere, not least in the USA when, as Scott Higgins points out, 'the 1940s brought a confidence in colour which rendered [such] obvious emulation of black-and-white technique less important'.[27] The export of Technicolor to the UK provoked a variety of responses, not all of them welcoming. While for some colour had the potential to ensure the cinema's advancement as an art form, others were cautious about its threat to dominant cinematic codes which placed film form as subservient to story. Torn between celebrating the novelty value of colour and reining in its expressive potential, producers, directors, cinematographers, art directors and stars could not, however, ignore its impact as a new technology which heralded new economic and aesthetic challenges. Perceptions of Natalie Kalmus's position as imposing rigid 'color control' over British films reflect wider debates about the status of the British film industry in the 1930s and 40s. While for many commentators Technicolor represented another instance of Hollywood's domination, it also provided an opportunity to explore product differentiation since, as we have seen, external control was never entirely

possible or indeed desirable. Higgins concludes that 'The general principles endorsed by the professional press and proffered by Natalie Kalmus never mandated a single, undifferentiated approach to color.'[28] Indeed, Kalmus delivered a service with which cinematographers and art directors negotiated, and in their different ways everyone involved sought to impose some level of control over colour. Since the impact of colour is subject to many variables from the quality of the print to the cultural context of reception, this aspiration remained (and remains) as elusive as colour itself. Yet drawing on Natalie Kalmus's ideas of 'color consciousness', films such as *Wings of the Morning*, *The Thief of Bagdad* and *Black Narcissus* demonstrate how the scoring of dramatic action and the enhancement of cinema's expressive potential could be explored with colour playing a fundamental, integral role. In the context of a British cinema that was primarily associated with black-and-white, 'quality' social realism, this was indeed remarkable. This was demonstrated most clearly in Powell and Pressburger's next colour films, *The Red Shoes* and *The Tales of Hoffmann*.

THE RED SHOES: COLOUR, DANCE AND MUSIC

Films of ballet and dance offered potential as leading the way in screen colour experimentation and perfection. Some of the earliest applied colour films demonstrated the spectacle of colour and dancing figures such as Robert Paul's exhibition at the Alhambra, London, in April 1898 showing an 'Eastern Dance', and exhibitions of serpentine dance films with their displays of successive colours visible on the dancer's costume with its billowing sleeves and as, like a winged creature, she moves her arms high and low.[29] As we have seen, photographic processes such as Kinemacolor, Prizma and Friese-Greene's Natural Colour, used for *The Open Road* (1925), were criticised for 'fringing' evident with quick movement of figures and objects. In view of this, dance films were not such frequent subjects, and early sound films had their own preoccupation with privileging dialogue over movement. *Pagliacci* (1936) was a British film made with a prologue and final sequence in British Chemicolor, both of which depict an opera troupe's stage performance.

It was perhaps predictable that Technicolor should highlight its technical achievements by using dance in one of its earliest three-strip films. The first live-action Technicolor three-strip short was *La Cucaracha*, a film which, as Higgins has noted, demonstrated Technicolor's technical and dramatic potential in ways which highlighted its superiority over the two-colour process. Brazenly showing off red, green and blue, it used strong and varied hues and bold colour accents, making colour an integral part of the narrative. The film deploys colour foregrounding which ascribes a graphic design function to colour which is of fundamental importance in the dance numbers. Higgins describes Robert Jones's approach as colour designer for the film: 'Jones mixes strong hues by juxtaposing them within the frame or by alternating colors across shots. This flamboyance makes color into something of an attraction.'[30] *La Cucaracha* thus demonstrated analogies between colour and music, what Jones termed 'mobile color, flowing color' which he likened to 'a kind of visual music'.[31] In this philosophy, colour's similarity to music, with its range of variation, emotional intensity, motifs etc., is emphasised, using it to convey mood, even if Jones's particular approach can be criticised for being somewhat crude. Such discourses on colour aesthetics were debated in *American Cinematographer* by contributors including William Stull, who argued that in the wake of *La Cucaracha* and *Becky Sharp* 'cinematographers, art-directors and directors must learn to compose their pictures in color, as well as in line, mass and chiaroscuro … Color must be used, not only as color, but as a dramatic, emotional tool, to build and maintain mood.'[32] This practice was demonstrated in *The Unfinished Dance* (1947), a Hollywood film set in the ballet school of the Metropolitan Opera Company which deployed colour for dramatic effect in its narrative, which included a young ballerina's desire for a red coat worn by another dancer, as well as using colours such as yellow to make significant characters stand out against the background. Robert Surtees, who was working for the first time as colour cinematographer on the film, explained how the production team learned lessons from *Henry V* (1944) in creating a pastel, low-contrast effect 'by the careful choice of complimentary colors in the wardrobe and set walls … If a blue was used on the wardrobe of the main actor the clothes of the people around him were of a tone somewhat lower

in scale, such as gray, then the walls were of a neutral coloring.'[33] While these effects are fully in keeping with prevailing Technicolor norms rather than the more overtly spectacular effects achieved in *La Cucaracha*, they nevertheless indicate that for films involving ballet colour was considered important for accentuating dramatic impact and supporting an aesthetic design based on complementary colours. What is interesting here is that the concept of 'pastel' colouring, the acknowledgment that it was most fully demonstrated in a British film and that it did not depend on toning-down colour. Rather, the careful deployment of colours in relation to each other militated against any one colour, unless the narrative determined that this was necessary, appearing to be 'wrong' or outstanding.

Darrel Catling also wrote about ballet and dance films as having great potential for the application of very precise colour control.[34] After the experimentation exhibited in the demonstration films *La Cucaracha* and *Becky Sharp* the turn towards restraint in colour design over the next few years meant that 'colour-music' experiments were not much in evidence. When reviewing *Spanish Fiesta* (1942), an American Technicolor short film featuring the Ballet Russe de Monte Carlo and dancer Leonide Massine, who later was in *The Red Shoes*, Catling lamented the fact that relative colour values did not appear to have been considered:

> The colour strengths in nearly every shot were equal over the whole screen in every dimension; the foreground figures, mid-stage figures, and those in the background, were dressed not merely in a series of colours of similar strengths, but actually in the same series of colours … It is a cardinal point of colour work that the central foreground figures must be separated from the background and background action.[35]

In effect he was advocating colour variation to be achieved by devices such as careful selection of lighting; the spacing of action in relation to depth of focus and by camera angle or movement. Indeed, directors filming ballet sequences often thought the choreographer had done most of the work and that all that was required was to simply film the event. This underestimated the multiple possibilities presented by the ballet film to engage the audience not only with the dancing but also with colour as a contributory aesthetic experience in support of both music and movement. For Catling, the key devices to achieve such effects were lighting to emphasise action and mood, as well as judicious use of camera angles and editing to 'make the implicit character of the dance become explicit'.[36] The emphasis on design and control was striking in his analysis, which concluded with a call to arms intended to inspire film-makers to be creative with colour in the ballet film:

They [film-makers] have too long been misled by the expression 'natural colour' – as if Nature did all the work, and man's job was merely to record it. We must start from scratch and build with all the materials and tools at our command – for it is somewhat tantalising to foresee what grand results are possible and yet have to sit by and see them missed.[37]

E. S. Tompkins added to the debate by observing that too many ballet films used close-ups so that the full agility of the dancers' steps was missed by the audience.[38] This problem is evident in a scene featuring a dancer in *Pagliacci*, where the film's focus on opera presumably contributed to the decision not to highlight the dancer's steps. This example highlights the dramatic and cinematic challenges of filming dance, since to 'capture' a performance in its entirety generally demanded formal strategies which contradicted conventions of narrative cinema which emphasised stars and facial expression. Part of *La Cucaracha*'s success is that as a short film its function as a demonstration film takes precedence over the expectation of a compelling narrative. American musicals in general were perceived to be improving their overt engagement with colour control just after the war, successful examples being *Yolanda and the Thief* (1945), *Ziegfeld Follies* (1946) and *Night and Day* (1946). Minnelli's *Yolanda and the Thief* contained a dream ballet sequence with surrealistic sets and colours which mutually supported each other.[39] In his review of *Ziegfeld Follies* Tompkins noted that:

There are touches of colour used with real imagination and with most telling effect, which would be quite impossible in monochrome. Thus we remember Keenan Wynn going red with anger in his telephone sketch. Lucille Bremer's yellow costume in the 'Limehouse Blues' scene is similarly vital to the effect, while Judy Garland makes her entrance in her song and dance from a red-lit

corridor, and coloured foam is used in vast and somewhat unpredictable quantities in Kathryn Grayson's final number.[40]

In *Night and Day* the 'I've Got You Under My Skin' number featured dancers against a blue backing and floor 'in a lovely flowing routine in which the colour has an integral and most telling part'.[41] As we shall see, *The Red Shoes* demonstrated both Catling and Tompkins's recommendations for a successful ballet film in its attention to lighting, camera movement, close-up and, most significantly, focus on the dancer's feet wearing the red shoes that haunt both the aesthetics and themes of the entire film.

Writing from a less specific perspective regarding the ballet film or musicals, Adrian Cornwell-Clyne had long been an advocate of what he termed 'colour-music'.[42] Although, as we have seen, he preferred restraint in colour design for popular narrative cinema, in his early writings he was interested in experimentation with non-representational light projections that were coordinated with music. Although apparently disconnected from his ideas about narrative cinema, the writings on 'colour-music' point to an approach which is useful when considering the ballet film. The theory behind this idea was that music and colour were similar in that they evoked mood and caused sensation. Like Eisenstein, Cornwell-Clyne rejected the idea that specific colours could be related, as in Newtonian tradition, in a precise way to musical notation. While he acknowledged that psychologists often attributed particular affective values to colours, Cornwell-Clyne was concerned to stress that,

context must play such a very important part in deciding the approximate mood awakened by a coloured mass of light. It is insufficient to assert that red and red-orange will be exciting. The luminosity of a hypothetical red might be less than that of a blue-green preceding it, and less than, say, a light-violet succeeding it. In which case, the effect of the red might be momentarily restful; an effect due to its luminosity context.[43]

As for practical application, it was intended that 'colour-music' displays would take place in cinemas such as at the New Gallery Cinema, London, where concealed coloured lamps changed rhythmically in time with the music playing between film performances. But the principles established by Cornwell-Clyne were to have important implications for his later reflections, which suggested a variation on the idea of 'colour control'.[44]

In *Colour Cinematography* Cornwell-Clyne proposed the idea of 'colour scores' to be used by art directors when planning a colour composition for a film.[45] These were to be completed *after* the music had been recorded, which was a similar idea to that of the 'composed film' referenced earlier in relation to *Black Narcissus* and demonstrated even further in *The Red Shoes* and *The Tales of Hoffmann*. 'Colour scores' were not, however, intended only to relate to scenes with musical accompaniment, but to the film as a whole. Using Munsell's charts of colour samples, typified by the scales of hue, value and chroma, Cornwell-Clyne advocated an art director completing a colour score that communicated scene by scene 'the sequential dynamic of the film, and the colour harmonies should have direct psychological relationship to the film fluxion and to the musical treatment'.[46] While it is unclear as to what Natalie Kalmus's colour charts looked like, Cornwell-Clyne was in effect advocating a similar idea with coloured transparencies indicating costume colours superimposed on drawings which also showed the colours of a set. Kalmus also compared her chart to 'a musical score'.[47] In view of Cornwell-Clyne's comments on colour and context this holistic approach, which implied tonal variation and mutability, can be usefully compared to that of Eisenstein, whose views on the desirability of 'organic unity' for film, colour and music, have already been noted in the discussion of *Black Narcissus*.

The idea of 'colour scores' also bears striking resemblance to set designer Hein Heckroth's practice for *The Red Shoes* of using sketches and paintings to 'compose' the ballet sequence within the film. These were made into a short film which served as a guide for shooting the actual sequence. Working with Heckroth artist Ivor Beddoes produced sketches which resembled colour strips outlining each scene. Composer Brian Easdale monitored the relationship between images and music and if one compares Heckroth's template with 'The Red Shoes' ballet sequence in the final film they are very similar in terms of the synchronisation of music and image.[48] When Heckroth's sketches were complete and Easdale's score composed, Sir Thomas Beecham and the Royal Philharmonic Orchestra recorded the music before any filming took place.[49] Often presented as innovative, as British designer Edward Carrick explained in an address to the Royal Society of Arts in 1950, using a film of sketches as a template for the final shooting of a film had been advocated in Germany in the 1920s.[50] In the second edition of Carrick's practical manual on set design, published in 1949, he urged film-makers to appreciate that: 'Colour has an emotional value and [that] when cutting from one scene to another in a sequence it has to be done with the same consummate care as would be taken with instrumental parts in the orchestration of a piece of music.'[51] Echoing Catling, Carrick elaborated this by pointing to the necessity of distinguishing between foreground and background in planning colour sequences, with the background analogous to the bass, and the foreground action likened to a treble theme. The best pre-planning also considered the impact of light in turning two-dimensional sketches into complete sets since in creating the 'third dimension' light reflects on surfaces, actors and costumes and thus changes the appearance of colours. From many aspects *The Red Shoes* served as an excellent model for these ideas and may indeed have provoked Carrick into writing his chapter on colour in the second edition of his manual since it is illustrated with examples of Heckroth's designs and references the 'story strip' of the ballet sequence. These observations recognised that dimensionality in colour design was different from the planes of a black-and-white composition. The addition of colour required very careful planning so as to avoid the background, as it were, upstaging the foreground, while at the same time constituting colour interest. Thus, in the early scene of the students waiting to see 'Heart of Fire' the majority dressed in darkish colours with the exception of a young woman sitting next to Julian in a yellow jumper and another directly behind him in pale blue. Thus, the centre of interest is surrounded by colour while the background is not distinctive. This approach was especially important in a context of narrative cinema which depended on reducing the extent of spectacle in the frame which was not related to narrative interest. The ballet film, however, offered a greater number of possibilities in this regard because of its more openly theatrical address and function as a spectacular event – in Carrick's terms, bass and treble in a symbiotic relationship rather than either one or the other dominating a scene. In *The Red Shoes* the ballet sequences invite this approach more than elsewhere, but that is not to say that colour interest in the rest of the film is limited.

Although *The Red Shoes* has a colour in its title, and is generally regarded as a significant Technicolor film, no analysis has concentrated on colour. While Jack Cardiff often recalled specific details about working with colour for previous films such as *A Matter of Life and Death* and *Black Narcissus*, there are few detailed recollections about *The Red Shoes*. What we know of Cardiff's technical experiments concerns the acceleration of camera speed to film dancers as they leapt in the air. He was convinced that the camera's job was to enhance, but not dishonestly represent, ballet movement, arguing that: 'Film adaptation of Ballet must be regarded as a separate art … [film] must be allowed full expression in what is a perfect subject for the abstract stylisation and dream fantasy that a film can so well express.'[52] Cardiff also used two powerful, prototype 225 amp Mole Richardson arc lamps, which were more suited to shooting in Technicolor than the 150 amp arcs he normally worked with.[53] In addition, a powerful 300 amp water-cooled spotlight capable of creating 1,200 foot candles one hundred feet away from the subject, which made 'a searchlight look like a fountain-pen torch', was used in the ballet sequence.[54] It is as if the theatricality of much of *The Red Shoes* discouraged specific commentary which might have singled out colour as contributing to the film in unexpected ways; perhaps the unfamiliar world of ballet and exotic Riviera settings implied an unrealistic *mise en scène* and colours to match. Yet the film is not entirely devoid of realism, particularly in the early sequences and in its self-reflexive nature which foregrounds cinema as uniquely capable of commenting on the troubled and passionate world of ballet. Cinematic artistry is accentuated, including camera tricks, superimpositions, matte shots and many other visual spectacles, in order to celebrate ballet and yet expose the human cost of the total dedication demanded by Boris Lermontov (Anton Walbrook). The ballet-within-the-film serves as a mini-treatment to which the feature film narrative is inextricably connected. Just as the technicians used Heckroth's filmed designs and drawings as a template for shooting the ballet sequence proper, its foregone conclusion of death acts as a portentous omen for the rest of the film.

The fairytale context of the narrative continued a generic form dating back to silent cinema and pre-cinematic media. The latent horror which is often at the heart of fairytales is exposed in *The Red Shoes* as what is initially presented as a compelling and exuberant passion for dance, represented in different ways by Vicky Page (Moira Shearer) and Lermontov, is pitted against the ambitions of composer Julian Craster (Marius Goring) who falls in love with Vicky. On several occasions the dialogue asserts that 'the music is all that matters', and the remark made by Julian that ballet is a lower art form results in him being dismissed from the company by Lermontov. As a film marked by its experiment with the 'composed film' and by Brian Easdale's score, music and cinema combine to both celebrate and disturb the ballet world.

A pair of red ballet shoes is featured from the film's title sequence and thereafter red is the colour which is presented most often in different hues and contexts. In one scene the camera tracks over rows and rows of red shoes before a stick, presumably held by Lermontov, firmly taps the floor to indicate that these are the ones to be worn by Vicky for the ballet. While a casual glance makes little or no distinction between the pairs of shoes, it is clear that the chosen pair is most clearly identifiable to an expert; we are reminded that all reds are not the same. The symbolism associated with red shoes is an integral part of transformative myths, as referenced in *The Wizard of Oz* (1939) with Dorothy's ruby slippers. As Brian Price points out, red has many different connotations including 'love *and* anger, revolution *and* madness'.[55] To this one could add the blood of life and menstruation, prestige and wealth.[56] In keeping with the musical analogy, the colour red in *The Red Shoes* is related to both the major *and* the minor. The red shoes make Vicky a ballet star and bring her together with Julian; at the same time they symbolise sexuality and initiate the course of events that results in impossible choices, emotional conflict and tragedy. They are also aligned with cinema since, as Mulvey points out: 'When the red shoes force the heroine to dance, the cinema takes over from the stage, shifting gradually into a hallucinatory world in which the movement of the cinema merges with the movement of the dance that can only stop with death.'[57] They are accorded an unusual number of close-ups which exaggerate their strangeness and their association with a loss of control. Indeed, their

The Red Shoes (Technicolor, 1948): close-up of Vicky (Moira Shearer) at the Mercury Theatre

The Red Shoes: similar shot of Vicky as she dances 'The Red Shoes' ballet

symbolic role in the film requires them to assume an unusual degree of visual importance. Contrary to Tompkins's fear that filmed ballet seldom showed the dancers' feet, *The Red Shoes* makes them fetish objects.

In keeping with this contradictory symbolism, the colour red features differently in other contexts. It marks Vicky's facial expression, her red lips in stark contrast to her pale skin, and her abundant, slightly waved auburn hair as a colour favoured by Technicolor. In a classic case of complementary colours emphasising each other, for the ballet Vicky's auburn hair is accentuated by the blue bow on her head. Her hair is invested with authenticity in one or two shots such as when she is confessing her nerves to Lermontov just before she is about to perform 'The Red Shoes', faint freckles on her neck and arms (common for auburn-haired people) are visible. While the auburn colour of her hair is thus marked as 'natural', the deep red of her lips forms a stark contrast as being aligned with artificiality, theatricality and the world of performance. As with the symbolic accentuation of red for Sister Ruth's lips in *Black Narcissus*, the bright red of Vicky's lips departs from Technicolor's recommendation to reproduce natural colouring in facial make-up.[58] In this respect their shade of red is like the red shoes, also something worn for the performance that will end in death. Red thus connects her feet and her head in a symbolic manner as the lure of the dance is associated with passion and desire, as well as with compulsive, consuming emotions. This is particularly evident in the

close-up of her face at the Mercury Theatre after the 'dizzying, zip-panned point-of-view shots as she pirouettes her way through *Swan Lake*'.[59] The close-up shows her face in a state of almost demonic possession, with her bright red lips and exaggerated eye make-up; this shot is later recalled when Vicky dances 'The Red Shoes' ballet. Red is not only on her lips but also near both tear ducts of her eyes which gives added emphasis to the impression of inspired artistry combined with horrific madness (this make-up effect also features in 'The Red Shoes' ballet). We later learn that this performance was decisive in convincing Lermontov of her potential, of her commitment to dancing to the point of self-sacrifice; she must literally lose herself in order to excel in her art. Vicky also wears red lipstick when she is not performing, indicating the formality of her role in general throughout the film. When not dancing she is dressed for formal events: when she is practising with the ballet company and as a fairytale princess, complete with crown, as she magisterially ascends the steps when summoned to Lermontov's Riviera residence. This is unlike Deborah Kerr in *Black Narcissus*, whose pale face is surrounded by her wimple except for the flashback scenes in Ireland when her red hair impresses for the comparative shock of its vivid appearance. We have no access to Vicky's past or sight of her in informal poses, with the exception of a night scene after she and Julian have left the company when Julian gets up to compose and Vicky opens a drawer containing her ballet shoes, caressing them fondly, indicating that she is missing her life with the company. Yet even this scene is theatrical, appearing almost as a stage set rather than a domestic dwelling. As advertised in the film's press book, the gowns worn by Moira Shearer and by Ludmilla Tcherina were designed by Fath and Carven of Paris and Mattli of London. Thus, the costumes also contributed to the film's consistent out-of-the-everyday feel in the presentation of its lead female characters.

Other reds appear, such as the closed burgundy curtains seen just before 'The Red Shoes' ballet begins, as well as the rare sight of Lermontov in a blue shirt with a red necktie in the scene when Vicky is told the news that she has been chosen as the lead dancer in 'The Red Shoes' ballet. Lermontov is normally dressed in formal attire, black suits and white shirts appearing, along with his pale skin and eyes shaded from the Mediterranean sunlight by dark glasses, somewhat like a vampire.[60] He does appear in red again – wearing a dark burgundy velvet jacket – in the scene when he learns of Julian and Vicky's marriage and thrusts his fist into the mirror. What is interesting here is that when his usual dark attire is departed from, red features as a connecting colour symbol with the film's demonic driver of the red shoes. In this sense not only is Vicky possessed by their attraction, but Lermontov also is under their influence. As the one who chose to put on the ballet and to select Vicky as the lead ballerina despite his colleagues' scepticism, he is complicit with the spell of the red shoes but also a victim of its logic when they appear to 'cause' Vicky's death. Lermontov's speech at the end of the film announcing that the ballet will be performed without Vicky reveals the emotional wrench he has suffered as his voice, wracked with shock, cracks and breaks in a higher pitch than usual.

The film's exterior shots, particularly of the Riviera, are sumptuous, with blue sea and bright sunlight. Throughout the film 'colour control' is exercised in the sense that shots have clearly been planned to exhibit a range of colours and 'wrong' colour or 'clashes' (in Natalie Kalmus's terms) have been avoided. One such shot is when the ballet company arrive in Monte Carlo. The sea is in the background and in the centre-left of the frame members of the company walk forward wearing white, brown and dark shades with some donning panama hats, while to the right are tourists dressed in an assortment of colours –

The Red Shoes: colour composition: the Lermontov ballet company arriving in Monte Carlo

consecutively – yellow, blue, white, red, pale blue and green dresses and blouses. This composition displays an array of colour, but it is contained in one element of the frame, and selectively so. As such the women do not distract from the scenic shot which is presented in the mode of a travelogue; it has a narrative purpose but is essentially an attraction designed to show off not only the Riviera but also Technicolor. It constitutes a brief moment of 'the cinema of colour attractions' before the narrative proper continues. Other examples of colour display involve posters. At the beginning of the film when the students rush to the gallery at Covent Garden, a red and yellow poster on the stairs announces the Lermontov ballet's world premiere of 'Heart of Fire'. In the students' anxiety to get the best seats the poster is torn as they stampede up the stairs, perhaps prefiguring the story to follow of passion, destruction and death. Later in the film Vicky, wearing the red shoes, runs down stairs, her fast steps mechanistic in their movement and implying that the shoes are in control of her suicidal destiny. In a more conventional context, bright-coloured posters feature in a montage of the locations where the Lermontov company performs. The connection between these scenes is the association of colour with metronomic syncopation as dancing, rushing and travelling on whirlwind tours are part of the consuming passion associated with ballet.

In 'The Red Shoes' ballet, colour is, of course, an essential part of its address. Hein Heckroth's designs and drawings are a fairly accurate guide to how the sequence

Hein Heckroth's preparatory drawing for 'The Red Shoes' ballet; *The Red Shoes*: the film replicates the drawing

The Red Shoes: paper dancer effect; Jack Cardiff's experimentation with shooting ballet movement

was planned, filmed as a short consisting of 141 shots, featuring Easdale's score.[61] The Heckroth film (to avoid confusion I will refer to the filmed designs and drawings as this) is very similar to the sequence in *The Red Shoes*; images such as the exterior town backdrop, which gradually becomes crowded with visitors to the fair, appear in both films. The drawings also anticipate details which became part of the main film ballet's cinematic artifice, such as the close-ups of the terrified dancer's face and the alternating male figures which become the Shoemaker, Lermontov and Julian. The menacing silhouetted hands reaching out for the dancer's feet are also drawn, as well as the skeletal newspaper figure which dances with the ballerina wearing the red shoes.[62] Including specific lighting effects in the sketches pushed the technical team to come up with non-standard

solutions to the technical challenges they invited. The hard shadows created by the hands required two 25 amp 'brutes' which had their condenser lenses replaced by sheets of plain glass. The newspaper figure was created with trick effects with its movements manipulated with wires like a puppet and then cutting on frame when the artificial figure changes into a real dancer. The scene's conclusion with the dancer leaping in the air was shot by using varying speeds from forty-eight frames per second to twenty-four.[63] The two versions are interesting to compare. The impact of 'The Red Shoes' ballet in the film has details which naturally connect it more explicitly with the rest of the narrative and emphasise cinematic technique. Near the beginning, for example, the Heckroth film has the red shoes in the shoemaker's shop frontage, with a mannequin on a podium wearing them

Hein Heckroth's shop window
scenario for 'The Red Shoes'
ballet; *The Red Shoes*: a
similar scene with Vicky
gazing at herself

Hein Heckroth's fallen,
coloured poster drawing;
cellophane is used to create
this effect in the film

which is admired by the woman onlooker. The actual
film acquires an additional perspective since the figure
modelling the shoes is a superimposition of Moira
Shearer: a mirror-image scenario is presented as the
dancer apparently is gazing at herself. While this would
lend obvious credence to a Lacanian reading of the film
in which the wearing of the red shoes represents Vicky's
entry into the Symbolic Order (the Law of the Father
represented by Lermontov and Julian) that will
ultimately destroy her, there are also other possible
interpretations of this mirror imagery. Vicky's collusion
in her obsession is credible, since she is driven to dance
and the first half of the film shows her thrilled at being
chosen by Lermontov for his company and also to dance
'The Red Shoes' ballet. In this reading the coding of red
as almost written on her body – her feet, lips and hair –

accentuates this connection and colludes with the
inevitable logic of the fairytale. It also can be linked to
the Freudian death drive associated with desire and 'a
compulsion to repeat' identified by Mulvey as applicable
to the film since the ballet 'tells the story of the red
dancing shoes that the heroine wants above all else and
that then force her to dance until she dies'.[64] Positioned
less than halfway through the film, the ballet sequence
refers to the joyous acquisition of the shoes which
connect with Vicky's rise to stardom in the Lermontov
company, as well as to the tragic events to come.

The ballet sequence in the film is generally
clearer in identifying Vicky than the Heckroth film, as
are the red shoes in the main feature. To this extent red
is more obtrusive in the film as a motif. As Vicky dances
on and on, the coloured cellophane posters and

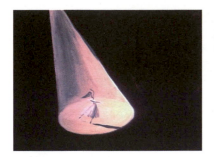

Hein Heckroth's preparatory drawings of Vicky dancing in a cone of light

The Red Shoes: translation of the drawing into a circle of light on the stage

The Red Shoes: top lighting to illuminate Vicky as she reaches towards Julian

rectangular shapes, including that of a dancer, float to the floor in the wake of her motion. The Heckroth film features the posters but they seem less ethereal because the cellophane material chosen for the film constitutes a crucial difference in creating the effect of spectral imagery which prefigures the paper dancer.[65] Another effective cinematic technique features later when Vicky is still dancing when the sun rises. In the Heckroth film a blurry light effect is indicated, but in the film specific use is made of coloured lights from within the diegesis. The special high-key spotlight used by Jack Cardiff is also anticipated in the Heckroth film but appears slightly differently in 'The Red Shoes' ballet sequence of the film. In the Heckroth film it appears as a cone, a shaft of light from above with a circular base (this is indeed replicated in the film but for a different shot), whereas in one shot in the film it is generally a pure circle on the ground with no obvious light source. While this might not appear to make much difference, the isolated light suggests that rather than being an external, technological device to highlight Vicky's performance the spotlight is in fact more closely identified with her. Indeed, the device is repeated at the end of the film when Lermontov decides to go ahead with the performance without Vicky, the spotlight substituting for her body. Other effects are facilitated by cinematic technique, such as in the film the gesture of cutting off the red shoes with a knife is seemingly frustrated by magic as the knife leaps in the air and thuds into the ground. This detail is not in the Heckroth film, constituting another example of ingenuity in the film even though the template was clearly the origin of most of the sequence's major details and overall 'look'. The experiments of *The Red Shoes* were augmented in *The*

Tales of Hoffmann, Heckroth's next major collaboration with Powell and Pressburger involving dance, colour and music as integral elements of its aesthetic address.

'MAKING COLOUR TALK': *THE TALES OF HOFFMANN*

During the filming of *The Tales of Hoffmann*, Michael Powell and Hein Heckroth explained to *Kinematograph Weekly*'s studio correspondent that colour was 'an essential part of the story' and not used 'merely as an embellishment'. Heckroth further elaborated by claiming that: 'To make a symbol that represents nature, you cannot copy nature's colouring, such pigments don't exist. You must set out to use colour dramatically like you use an actor, and it is essential that the person using the colour should be a painter.'[66] At the same time, the article revealed that despite a clear affinity for the creative deployment of colour, Powell was not convinced that in 'naturalistic films' colour was even necessary. Both were, however, appreciative of the principle of colour design. Working with colour sets, Heckroth was able to produce impressive effects relatively quickly, and collaboration with cinematographer Chris Challis and the Technicolor laboratories was productive in working with the concept of colour design.[67] Heckroth's deployment of colour symbolism (for example, yellow for frivolity; red and black for richness and nobility; silver greys, light blues and olive greens as suggestive of maturity) was grounded in the idea that, as analogous to music, colour substituted for words. Indeed, according to various sources the film has a particular coding for its various episodes. The first tale about Hoffmann's love for Olympia (Moira Shearer) features yellow floating gauze, browns and glittering cellophane to convey a light-hearted mood of 'designed frivolity'. Purple, black and gold dominate the second act set in Giulietta's palace and the last act dealing with Hoffmann's love for consumptive singer Antonia (Ann Ayars) has 'cooler' designs in grey, greens, blues and white. Each act begins with the pages of a programme being turned, giving the title and details of the main performers and each programme was in the dominant colour of each act. In the final shots of the film we are shown a book of Hoffmann's tales which is in purple with gold lettering. This is imitative of Hoffmann's purple costuming throughout the film. The demarcation of particular colours to illustrate particular spaces was an idea that was further experimented with in *Oh … Rosalinda!!* (1955).[68]

While the idea of coding has some validity, it does not do justice to the full deployment of colour in *The Tales of Hoffmann*. Natalie Kalmus does not appear in the credits; the Technicolor consultant is named as Joan Bridge. While Heckroth was responsible for general ideas on colour, Joan Bridge's expertise would have informed the specific application of Technicolor, combined with Chris Challis's input as cinematographer. In the prologue sequence of the 'Ballet of the Enchanted Dragonfly', when Stella (Moira Shearer) entrusts her servant to deliver a note confessing her love to Hoffmann (Robert Rounseville), the first entrance of Hoffmann's opponent Councillor Lindorf (Robert Helpmann) is striking for its colour impact. Ornate green and gold double doors open and he is revealed against a totally red background, including the floor. This signals his role throughout the film as menacing, for in each of the three tales Helpmann plays a character who is vengeful (Coppelius); sinister and scheming (Dapurtutto); and a harbinger of death (Dr Miracle). For Stella's performance of the ballet her dragonfly body costume has green-painted features, and green is also used for her headpiece and the small wings on her back. She is soon joined on the blue-green lily-pond effect painted flooring by the dancer performing the role of the red male dragonfly who is killed by the female after mating. Watching the ballet, Hoffmann is dressed in a purple dress coat, as he is in all three tales, creating colour consistency concerning his role. The only other character who wears the same colour in the three tales is

The Tales of Hoffmann (Technicolor, 1951): colour palette for tale no. 1; tale no. 2; tale no. 3

The Tales of Hoffmann: the
tale of Olympia (Moira
Shearer) with gauzes,
cellophane and painted
backdrops

The Tales of Hoffmann:
Venice with red, black and
green

Nicklaus (Pamela Brown), Hoffman's friend and
companion who wears a red coat.

The first tale of Olympia indeed features a wealth
of yellow gauzes, cellophane effects and painted
backdrops. The mechanical doll, played by Moira
Shearer, wears a yellow ballet dress. She reclines on an
ornate yellow couch supported by model swans, and the
yellow bed in her room appears to be suspended from
the ceiling. When Hoffmann puts on the magic glasses
made by Coppelius he sees many wondrous things
including dancing puppets dressed in soft yellows, blues
and pinks. A light-hearted tone is communicated
through colour, although the tale has a darker side
which emerges as Coppelius accepts payment to make
eyes for the doll that Hoffmann falls in love with,
believing it to be human. When Coppelius goes to the
bank to cash his cheque he learns that Spalanzani
(Leonide Massine) has tricked him. At the point of
revelation the screen momentarily goes completely green
in an unusual colour effect which in this context
indicates horror and his determination to seek revenge.
The screen splashed with green has all the more impact
since it is followed by a shot which is almost drained of
colour. The form that this takes is indeed extreme, since
he dismembers the doll after she has danced away from
Hoffmann in a manner reminiscent to Vicky's
compulsive dancing in *The Red Shoes*. Hoffmann is
shocked to learn he has been cheated and at the end of

the act the colours become darker reds and blacks.
Olympia's body is pulled apart by the protagonists, at
one point only her dancing leg is visible, and at the end
of the act the ghoulish spectacle is completed with her
head visible on the floor with a spring coming out of it.
This devastating finale is in keeping with the latent
horror at the heart of fairytales as we witness the
destruction of the 'ideal' woman created by the puppet-
maker whose construction was completed by the
addition of eyes made by Coppelius. The fact that
Hoffmann falls in love with this impossible creation
bears obvious comparison with *The Red Shoes* and
Lermontov's training of Vicky as the perfect dancer,
automaton-like herself as she dances to her death
wearing the red shoes. Pamela Brown plays Nicklaus,
Hoffmann's male companion in all three tales, who
provides the voice of reason to which Hoffman generally
does not listen. In this tale Nicklaus sees through the
doll's masquerade, seeing what Hoffmann cannot in an
ironic commentary on the nature of male fantasy.
Although the magic glasses he wears appear to give him
access to fantastical sights they obscure the truth of
Olympia's mechanical construction.

The second tale of Giulietta (Ludmilla Tcherina)
is generally regarded as having the richest colour palette.
It takes place in Venice and contains shades of red, gold,
black and green. A multitude of effects with gauzes,
lighting, textures and painted sets created the act's

spectacle of colour and sensuality. Early on in the sequence there is a scene of an orgy, the debauchery characterised by writhing bodies, bowls of fruit and wine shot from above to convey a sense of a large number of people conducting their incessant revels. Giuletta, the courtesan, with her dark tan, hair and red lips, looks very different from Moira Shearer, with her pale face and red hair. As the sinister Dapurtutto, Helpman's make-up is also striking, with green eye make-up which links with Giuletta's green head-scarf and cape worn in the earlier parts of the sequence and creates a colour connection which prefigures their collusion in tricking Hoffmann. Dapurtutto transforms wax dripping from red-, green- and mauve-coloured candles into jewels which form into a necklace worn by Giuletta which ensures that Hoffmann falls in love with her. Stop-frame replacements were used for the shots creating the effect of the wax instantly turning into jewels. The textures of both Giuletta and Dapurtutto's costumes shimmer in this scene as Giuletta's black body-suit has small glittering green jewels on the upper half and the material of Dapurtutto's dark dress coat appears to contain strands of shiny, silvery synthetic fabric. Schmeil (Leonid Massine), the character who has lost his soul, is appropriately dressed in black with almost white face make-up to make him appear ghostly. Colour and texture are also obtrusive in one shot when Hoffmann appears to pass through a green gauze curtain, the screen briefly filled with its green sheen as he rushes forward in search of Giuletta.

Antonia's tale is the final act of the film and features far more sombre colours of blue and grey in keeping with its story of the consumptive singer who, under the spell of Dr Miracle (Helpmann), pushes herself to sing in spite of her illness and against the wishes of her father and suitor, Hoffmann. While it is certainly the case that the colours are generally 'colder' shades than in the two previous acts, towards the end of Antonia's tale as she sings to her death, red flames, at one point becoming hands, appear to consume her. This scene is particularly striking since the terrifying flames contrast so markedly with the muted colours of the previous scenes. After the last tale the epilogue reverts to Luther's Beer Cellar where an exhausted and depressed Hoffmann sees Stella walk away with Councillor Lindorf. They ascend the stairs to the same multicoloured stained-glass door we saw Lindorf and

Hoffman use in the prologue. Such a detail is typical of a film which revels in displaying colour in a range of different contexts, in this case setting up the opposition between Hoffmann and Lindorf and concluding the film by underlining Hoffmann's despair as he sees Stella elude him, as has her counterpart in each tale. Beyond the obvious colour symbolism which characterises each act there are instances of interesting colour correspondences, such as when green is used for the female dragonfly who kills her mate; the flash of green when Coppelius learns he has been fleeced by Spalanzani and the green which marks Dapurtutto and Giuletta in their pact to steal souls. In these contexts green is a deathly shock, an inspiration for revenge and associated with exploitative magic. Colours are variable, assisted by texture and lighting in evoking play with symbolism as with red which has different inflections throughout the film. While indicative of Lindorf's power it also is used for Nicklaus, the voice of reason and friendship. On another occasion the material form of colour is manipulated when the soft, melting candle-wax becomes the hard, glittering jewels of the treacherous necklace. Heckroth's interest in experimenting with materials to convey a sense of three-dimensionality on screen worked well with colour in relation to the soft gauzes which indicate deep, background space and with sets such as the illusory staircase, which is in fact a flat, painted surface. The impact of lighting and different camera angles works on colour to create a challenging and shifting *mise en scène*.

Working with exceptionally gifted technicians like Jack Cardiff, Powell and Pressburger's films are notable for the pleasure they take in creating colour effects and playing with symbolism. In the 'composed film' examples the musical analogy of major and minor inflections concerning particular colours is apposite. Cornwell-Clyne's ideas about colour scores are relevant to such displays of colour mutability which emphasise multiple possibilities for inflection, nuance, shade and shifts in contextual meaning within a particular colour range. Catling's advocacy of the ballet film as a form that provided opportunities for exploring multiple planes and the nature of screen perspective are also evident. As we have observed, exploring screen colour's aesthetic possibilities was not confined to Powell and Pressburger's films and can be seen to operate in films which are not related to the fantasy or ballet film. Other genres show a far from 'restrained' deployment of colour, that is to say if 'restraint' is taken to mean colour more or less used as monochrome. Although one might refer to films such as *The Life and Death of Colonel Blimp* (1943), *This Happy Breed* (1944) or *Henry V* as being associated with 'pastel shades' or a 'restrained mode', it is clear that their colour designs were quite distinctive for their comparative variation, contextual nuance and 'colour consciousness'. The films analysed in this chapter have demonstrated the extent to which colour in postwar British cinema was characterised by traditions of aesthetic experimentation rooted in the silent era and which have influenced many subsequent film-makers. Francis Ford Coppola's *Tetro* (2010) references *The Red Shoes* and *The Tales of Hoffmann* in dream sequences that evoke a cinematic memory of screen colour. Much like Vicky Page's never-ending dance, this has undoubtedly resonated across the decades.

12 COLLABORATION AND INNOVATION IN THE 1950s
JACK CARDIFF AND OSWALD MORRIS

Cinematographers, colour consultants, directors, art directors and numerous other film technicians collaborated to produce colour in three exceptional colour films of the 1950s: *Pandora and the Flying Dutchman* (1950), *Moulin Rouge* (1953) and *Moby Dick* (1956). They were Anglo-American productions on which distinguished British cinematographers worked with others to devise innovative approaches to screen colour during a decade when technologies were in transition. While the key contributions of technicians have been referenced many times in this book, this chapter presents an opportunity to further examine the multiple contexts of creativity presented by colour. These could be complex, involving a range of professionals. For example, while Oswald 'Ossie' Morris was director of photography on *Moulin Rouge*, a biopic about Toulouse-Lautrec, he collaborated for this experimental use of colour with Joan Bridge (Technicolor colour consultant), *Life* photographer Eliot Elisofon ('Special' colour consultant), Technicolor technician Ian Craig, camera operator Freddie Francis, production designer and costumer Marcel Vertès, art director Paul Sheriff and costume supervisor Julia Squire. While the overt aesthetic experimentation of Powell and Pressburger's films tends to overshadow other colour films of the 1940s and 50s, *Moulin Rouge* and *Moby Dick* in particular explored entirely new directions.

Jack Cardiff is often accorded auteur status in terms of Technicolor innovation, even though he worked with film-makers who are often thought of themselves as auteurs. His reputation as a technician who flouted Technicolor's strictures is legendary. An advertisement for an event on restoring the Jack Cardiff catalogue at the National Film Theatre in 2010, for example, refers to him as 'Mr Technicolor', perhaps in defiance of the credit most usually associated with Herbert Kalmus and the title of his autobiography.[1] Cardiff's recruitment as the first British Technicolor cameraman was based on his knowledge of light and painting, as he always pointed out when interviewed.[2] His approach throughout his career was to draw inspiration from art and in his leisure time he adapted the styles of artists he admired on canvas such as Degas and Van Gogh.[3] He was keen to experiment with colour, particularly when working with Powell and Pressburger whose requests for particular effects inspired Cardiff's creativity. Working on films as complex and challenging as *Black Narcissus* (1947) and *The Red Shoes* (1948) necessitated a high degree of collaboration, notoriously resulting in volatile exchanges with production designer Alfred Junge on *Black Narcissus*. Such instances of creative conflict subsequently overcome to produce 'great art' were highlighted in celebratory and promotional production histories. Their tales of tempestuous behaviour combined with extraordinary creative and technical feats aligned popular cinema with artistic temperaments normally associated with high art. In these discourses individualism was prized, so cinematographers were accorded primary agency for the design of specific sequences and for solving intricate technical problems. It is not surprising that any attempts to impose conformity from an external source were resisted as interfering, and in this respect Technicolor USA and Natalie Kalmus were easy targets.

This is not to detract from the stunning achievements of Jack Cardiff and other British cinematographers, it is simply to draw attention to the broader discursive contexts within which they operated and have subsequently been appraised. It is still the case that particular films are cited more often than others at the expense of interesting examples of colour experimentation which go relatively unnoticed because they were not associated with great directors or were box-office and/or critical failures. One such film in relation to Jack Cardiff is *Pandora and the Flying Dutchman* which has been overshadowed by his work with Powell and Pressburger. Harper and Porter, for example, argue that in the 1950s 'Cardiff found it difficult to replicate his earlier visual triumphs. The challenges of *The African Queen* (1952) were logistical rather than artistic, and in *Pandora and the Flying Dutchman*, he had been more preoccupied with Ava Gardner than technical matters.'[4] Perhaps in recognition of the rather warped view of Cardiff's legacy, the British Film Institute showed the film in an extended run as part of a season of films shown in 2010, the year of Cardiff's death. In terms of production context, *Pandora* is similar to *Moulin Rouge* and *Moby Dick* as an Anglo-American production. Like *Moulin Rouge*, John and James Woolf of Independent Film Distributors and the National Film Finance Corporation co-financed the film produced by Romulus, with MGM distributing in the USA. *Pandora and the Flying Dutchman* was directed by Albert Lewin, an American who had directed *The Picture of Dorian Gray* (1945) with its similarly ghostly narrative and Technicolor insert for the infamous portrait.

Pandora and the Flying Dutchman is based on the legend of the Flying Dutchman doomed to roam the seas for eternity until a woman declares that out of love she will die for him. The Dutchman in this case is Hendrick van der Zee (James Mason), who is eventually released from his suffering by Pandora Reynolds (Ava Gardner), an attractive American woman living in Esperanza on the coast of Spain, who is the centre of attention for Stephen (Nigel Patrick), a racing driver, and Juan Montalvo (Mario Cabré), a bullfighter. Pandora's character changes when she meets the mysterious and compelling Hendrick, whose yacht is moored off the Spanish coast for one of his seven-yearly opportunities to break the curse. Pandora's experience of

Pandora and the Flying Dutchman (Technicolor, 1950): Pandora (Ava Gardner) in yellow, halter-neck dress

genuine love makes her more considerate, particularly towards the men with whose affections she has previously toyed. The film's fantastical tale involves interesting colour choices for costumes as well as locations which range from low-key, moonlit sequences to a spectacular bullfight. Lewin was reportedly fascinated with Ava Gardner and she is indeed shot very much as the film's star attraction in numerous close-ups and wearing costumes which emphasise her voluptuous, statuesque figure. Pandora's association with Hendrick invests her with an 'other-worldly' spirit; she is compelled to swim to Hendrick's yacht as if summoned by a spell and when she arrives it is as if he has been expecting her. He is painting a picture of a woman who looks exactly like her, a strange occurrence which further shifts the tone of the film into the realms of the uncanny. Her horror at this image results in her striking out the woman's face in the portrait, an act Hendrick completes in a spirit of creativity as the painting ends up resembling a surrealist portrait by Chirico, with the face covered by a semi-spherical, opaque mask.

The colour most associated with Pandora is yellow, as seen in the silk lining of a cape, or the pale shade of yellow for the robe she wears on Hendrick's yacht which is the same as that worn by the woman in his painting. A particularly distinctive yellow dress has a halter neck and material gathered into ruches to emphasise her breasts. Such costuming displays her figure while encouraging a visual resemblance to classical forms typified by her posture, slow movement and stasis or by gestures such as draping a yellow silk scarf on a statue at a key point in the narrative just before she declares her love for Hendrick. The colour yellow can be linked with conflicting cultural meanings ranging from optimism and happiness to being associated with mourning in Egypt and worn by actors in the Middle Ages to signify the dead. In *Pandora and the Flying Dutchman* yellow works to emphasise Pandora's positioning between life and death. Her encounter with Hendrick signals a renewed spirit as her character changes to being kinder, more humane; at the same time it seals her destiny to die with him as the ultimate sacrifice for love. When predicting the future Montalvo's mother is terrified when she draws the card of death which has a yellow skull.

On other occasions Pandora wears white halter-necked, long dresses which similarly emphasise her breasts and her likeness to a classical statue. This colour also links her with Hendrick since his story, read to Geoffrey, the film's narrator who asks Hendrick for help in translating the manuscript he has found which turns out to be the story of the Flying Dutchman, refers to the Dutchman's dead wife as having a face 'as white as marble'. While Ava Gardner's skin is not ashen white, since this would not show well against the more predominant costume colour of yellow, her dark hair and red lips create contrasts which further liken her to Hendrick's painting. When Pandora finally joins him on his yacht when she has decided to die for him her face is once again on the canvas having replaced the surrealist image.

Some reviewers dismissed the musings on legend as pretentious, and the 'pedantry' of the film's pace.[5] Yet the colour was commented on as remarkable, such as Caroline Lejeune's appreciation of it as investing the film with 'an almost magical, moon-spun quality'.[6] Advertisements for the film described it as being 'In Flaming Color by Technicolor!' Cardiff's skill at filming the bullfight with one camera on a high rostrum and another on the roof of a four-storey building, as well as shooting in very low light for the party scene on the beach, feature in the film's press book, but there is little detailed discussion apart from how the effect of light apparently coming from fishermen's lamps was achieved by 'sprinkling earth in graduated form over the sand and arranging studio lamps along the cliff over the bay'. He also used two large mirrors and special filters loaned from studios in Barcelona.[7] This minimal technical detail is in stark contrast to the amount available for other films worked on by Cardiff, since these are more typically considered as representative of innovative screen colour achieved with, for example, filters and experimental lighting. Dilys Powell noted John Bryan's set designs as contributing to the film's 'remarkable' visual qualities, yet the specifics of how colour interacted with set design are seldom elaborated on in contemporary commentary.[8] This is reflective of prevailing attitudes which downgraded the creation of visual artifice as relatively worthless unless accompanied by, or integrated within, a compelling narrative. Without the auteur status of Powell and Pressburger to reinforce his credentials, Cardiff's cinematography alone was not capable of elevating the film to the canon of British colour classics.

The collaborations between Ossie Morris and legendary American director John Huston, however, produced two films that were the most technically daring colour experiments of the decade. *Moulin Rouge* was a film in which the colour look was totally integral to theme, character and visual style. Working closely with director John Huston, decisions were made regarding an overall approach to colour design which encouraged Morris to negotiate technical problems creatively. An example of this is the coloured fill lights used for three different characters and fog filters on the camera for the diffused effect which likened the 'look' of the film to Toulouse-Lautrec's paintings.[9] The filming of the paintings, which feature on several occasions in the film, was executed by Cyril Knowles, a cameraman formerly associated with Technicolor. In considering this innovative production, George Ashton's review foregrounds the difficulties of apportioning a single vision. He comments, for example, that:

The use of diffusion attachments on the lens and coloured lighting are, of course, by no means novel in themselves; there are few professional motion pictures which do not include scenes with diffusion, and in fact some cameramen never make a shot without. The use of coloured light effect lighting, too, has been on the increase these last ten years: a good example which springs to mind is the last two reels of *An American in Paris*, photographed by Al Gilks. But *Moulin Rouge* is remarkable for the boldness with which these two devices have been used.[10]

The film was produced by Romulus Films, an independent production company established by John and James Woolf which aimed to collaborate with American film-makers, particularly those experiencing difficulties with the Un-American Activities Committee.[11] It received support from the National Film Finance Corporation. This production context arguably influenced the extent to which colour could push the boundaries of established conventions, an observation that is supported by Powell and Pressburger's similar degree of freedom as producers who were given considerable leeway in creative decision-making by their sponsors. Production contexts which permitted independence, the employment of specific experts as appropriate to a particular production and degrees of risk-taking, proved to be conducive to colour experimentation. George Ashton recognised this, recommending that Romulus Films 'must be congratulated in giving the responsible technicians and artists such a free hand'.[12] Unless a major studio was prepared to accord a similar degree of autonomy to its production personnel it was less likely that norms would be challenged. In addition, contextual factors such as whether a colour process was experiencing competition from newer systems influenced approaches to innovation. In the early 1950s, for example, while Technicolor's domination of the market was well established, the appearance of different processes as well as widescreen and 3-D highlighted experimentation, as a similarly competitive environment had done in the mid-1930s when three-strip Technicolor was introduced.

Moulin Rouge is an excellent example of technical innovation, and a wealth of documentation and personal recollection exists to facilitate a detailed examination. The film is an exemplary case of the style being developed for a specific purpose: to make the colour cinematography a significant part of the biopic. In view of its subject, making colour a feature of the film was hardly surprising; it was the tone and emphasis achieved by the lights and filters that was different, combined with a bold range of extreme camera angles and close-ups. Reviewers appreciated these dimensions, recognising the film as remarkable in its deployment of colour, not least in trade papers geared to box-office values: 'Out of this world Technicolor screen biography … Rare and satisfying subject, great acting, attractive cosmopolitan cast, sensitive and show-manlike direction,

strong human angle, marvellous atmosphere, amazing décor, best-ever Technicolor photography'.[13] This unequivocal view was not, however, shared by the *Monthly Film Bulletin* reviewer who described the film as 'two hours of innate boredom, relieved from time to time by some striking effects of colour'.[14]

American notices also recognised the film's innovative colour, but Eliot Elisofon was more regularly credited as being responsible than Ossie Morris, as in the *New Yorker*: 'Mr Huston has had the inspiring technical assistance of Eliot Elisofon, a photographer who can congratulate himself on having got down on celluloid the most original ideas about color that have turned up since Sir Laurence Olivier made *Henry V*.'[15] According to Morris, Elisofon's reputation for being largely responsible for the colour design was the result of an inaccurate, publicity-seeking five-page picture spread in *Life* magazine.[16] Huston more readily acknowledged several collaborators, including Vertès, Morris and Elisofon, 'all working on some way to get into color the feeling of Toulouse-Lautrec, to get color that looked real, not just splashy and bright'.[17] Morris wanted to distance himself from what he considered to be 'typical', harsh Technicolor norms, and colour tests incorporated the ideas of Sheriff and Vertès, using fog filters and smoke.[18] The initial response from Technicolor was that the process had been 'desecrated'. The early 1950s context is particularly significant since three-strip's tendency towards lack of definition was exaggerated by the increased magnification of widescreen formats so the company was concerned that deliberate diffusion would draw further attention to this perceived shortcoming. Morris recalls Technicolor's senior executive George Gunn, on viewing tests for the film in Paris, complain: 'You are ruining everything we stand for and we cannot support what you are doing.' Huston reacted explosively to this criticism and producer John Woolf received a letter from Technicolor saying the company would not accept responsibility for the final results. Once the film was made, and effusive notices began to appear about the colour cinematography, an apologetic Technicolor sent Huston and Morris letters of congratulation.[19] Thus, we have a classic account of a director and technicians blatantly ignoring Technicolor's attempts to impose consistency of application and stylistic reverence. What is not commented on is that the production nevertheless took place; Huston's independence was not punished by the removal of Technicolor cameras and, when the results were more than satisfactory, the company was prepared to acknowledge the film's achievements. George Gunn later wrote to Morris that he should have been nominated for an Oscar for colour cinematography and French director Robert Bresson also very much admired the film.[20]

Moulin Rouge is a fairly straightforward account of Henri de Toulouse-Lautrec's life, beginning with a scene in the Moulin Rouge in 1890 and then a flashback which shows how a childhood accident exacerbated a genetic weakness that resulted in the stunted growth of his legs. After being rejected by a woman he loves he resolves to leave home and become a painter in Paris. The film then resumes its present-day account of Henri's doomed love affairs; his loneliness and near-suicide attempt; success as a painter; and final descent into alcoholism. The film's distinctive stylistic choices dominate since they are intimately connected to the painter's biography. A previous Technicolor film, *The Great Mr Handel* (1942), glorified the composer's highest point of creativity by marking his inspiration to compose 'The Messiah' with bright colours, in contrast to much of the rest of the film (see Chapter 6). *Moulin Rouge*, however, imbricates colour and diffusion effects throughout most of the film (the flashback does not use this strategy to such an extent), so that the film attempts to replicate the artist's style. The iconicity of Toulouse-Lautrec's work permitted a total approach to stylistic infusion with colour being a central element that would

Moulin Rouge: dancers shot with diffused look from above; close shots of dancers with frenetic colour and movement

Moulin Rouge (Technicolor, 1953): tracking shot of the bar

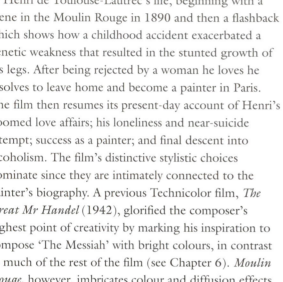

not have made sense in another context. The opening sequence in the Moulin Rouge is a remarkable case in point. The diffused look is immediately apparent as the camera surveys the nightclub in a long take exploring the set. Morris explained how the camera executed particularly fluid movements on a crane for this non-dialogue sequence since there was no need for a blimp.[21] A long tracking shot shows an effect of the patrons at the bar reflected in a high mirror above the counter, so only arms, glasses and bottles can be seen, as well as the dancers in the distance reflected from mirrors behind the bar; it is disorientating to observe two spatially disconnected areas of movement in one frame.

The ambient sensation of frenetic exaggeration is presented by the first dancers seen wearing orange, reds, white and one of them in an olive green skirt and a red blouse with white spots. They are accompanied by men in black suits and top hats, one of whom has the infamous long nose and chin memorialised in Toulouse-Lautrec's 'Moulin Rouge – La Goulue' poster design (1891). The colours are emphasised in comparison with the black-and-white sketches which we intermittently see being drawn in close-up (these were executed by Vertès) before it is revealed that the artist is Henri (Jose Ferrar), who agrees to use them as the basis for a promotional poster in exchange for a month's free drinks. It is as if the film is completing the well-known sketches by adding their colours in a holistic approach to design. As Jane Avril (Zsa Zsa Gabor) sings at the top of the red-carpeted staircase she wears an orange/red skirt with a yellow swirl on the edge of the hem, a white blouse, a hat with orange/red pom-poms, long black gloves, neck ruff and a black feather on the hat. Like with the first dancers, this palette is indicative of the colours of Toulouse-Lautrec's poster which features in close-up as background to the opening credits. The can-can dancers who feature towards the end of the sequence each wear different-coloured skirts in red, blue, green, black and yellow but their white underskirts and garments predominate, shot from close, low angles and striking for their almost luminescent quality. The end of the sequence forms an impressive contrast as the people leave and colour appears drained from the scene. Henri walks out as the cleaners wash the floor; we see his disfigured legs as the light fades. This type of effect is repeated on several occasions in the film, including instances of optical light sources within the frame being manipulated.

On other occasions colour features to assist dramatic effect, as in the sequence after Marie (Colette Marchand) has rejected Henri and he attempts suicide by turning on the gas in his apartment. The screen is bathed in blue light to emphasise his depression and in contrast with the following images when his desire to paint returns so strongly that he changes his mind, puts off the gas and opens the window to reveal the brighter hues of the rooftops of Paris. The blue lighting effect is repeated later to indicate his descent into alcoholism and again towards the end of the film when greener, deathly tones are used when he collapses and has to be forcibly removed from the bar. Ashton noted how, even though these lighting effects are most clearly visible in particular scenes, 'a certain amount of blue-green fill lighting is

Moulin Rouge: Henri attempts suicide with the screen bathed in blue; after the suicide attempt Henri looks out over the Parisian rooftops

often used and contributes to the general effect without being readily perceptible'.[22] These colour associations retain conventions of 'warm' hues of red and orange for the gaiety of the Moulin Rouge and 'cooler' colours for the low-points in Henri's life. Henri's doomed relationships with Marie Charlet and Myriamme Hayem (Suzanne Flon) were highlighted with the deployment of coloured fill lights for the actresses – violet for Marie and pink for Myriamme. The rationale was to 'help character' through colour, as when the violet for Marie emphasises her strange, quixotic mood in a scene when she has been drinking.[23] Comments on the diffused look of the colour and the lighting dominated reviews to the extent that Morris was, as it were, given permission to further experiment on *Moby Dick*, directed by John Huston but also registered as a British film because of the Associated British Picture Corporation's involvement with Moulin Productions and distributor Warner Bros. It was shot at Elstree and on location in the Irish Sea and in Fishguard. Exterior scenes set in New Bedford were shot in Youghal, southern Ireland, and other locations included Madeira and Las Palmas in the Canary Islands.

The look of *Moby Dick* could not be more different from *Moulin Rouge*. Eastmancolor stock was used but the film was printed differently with Technicolor 'by using wide-cut filter bands and then adding the black and white to restore contrast, in effect putting a grey image through their matrix system'.[24] The idea for this evolved when Morris remembered seeing the Technicolor laboratory processing Olivier's film *Richard III* (1955) for television transmission, designed to appear pastel as better suited for a system which could not easily accommodate the normal film contrast.[25] *Moby Dick* was an early opportunity to test Technicolor Ltd's Eastman developing operations by processing Eastmancolor from the stage of developed negatives for the first time.[26] For three-strip Technicolor processing the green record received direct light and so tended to have sharper contrast than the red and blue, which received reflected light. To create a balance with the latter records the green record was first printed as a half-tone black-and-white image on a blank piece of film before being used in the final process. As Haines explains, if the green record was used unmediated the contrast of the final dye-transfer print would be too dark. With the advent of Eastmancolor negative the grey

exposure was eliminated, but *Moby Dick* was unusual in that it 'used a halftone gray exposure to desaturate the colours'.[27] Technicolor Ltd was very accommodating in trying to achieve the desired style and tests took place in the autumn of 1954 and into 1955. Morris was so pleased with the results that in May 1955 he recommended to Huston that the opening sequence should be printed with the grey exposure:

> If you remember, we both thought the opening sequence would be better if printed normally. Having seen these various test rolls, I am not now so sure. I have a feeling that there may be a bad jump into the style if we do that. They have desaturated the colour so much in this sequence that the lush green foliage has gone almost neutral, but with a strong almost piercing white sky behind, which to me is quite revolutionary in appearance.[28]

By July Morris was even more convinced that the approach they were taking was perfect for the film, writing to Huston after seeing further tests produced by Technicolor:

> I must say that I was most impressed and excited by what I saw, and I genuinely believe that by taking part of each of these rolls we have the real answer to all that we may have been searching for these past months. I can't begin to tell you how relieved I felt, and the excitement and thrill I experienced in that 30-minute session in the theatre was worth all the headaches and heartaches that we have been through since you first decided to make *Moby Dick*.[29]

The resulting washed-out colour looked perfect for the desired fine grain, 'line' effect for *Moby Dick*. As with *Moulin Rouge*, the approach of fitting the colour to the theme of the film again pertained since Huston and Morris decided Melville's rugged, masculine whaling narrative required a desaturated style similar to nineteenth-century whaling prints. Yet colour was hardly absent and was controlled very precisely in the laboratory and in consultation with costume designer Elizabeth Haffenden, Joan Bridge and art director Ralph Brinton.[30] Blacks and whites were distinctive because of the 'line effect' so that desaturation did not mean a lack of tonal definition. Morris recalled that 'we could get

Moby Dick (Eastmancolor, 1956): the desaturated look of the film declared in opening scene with a waterfall introducing a white accent; grass with desaturated look

simultaneous play with the stasis of the locked door and the portentous movement of the ship; it is a visual tension in anticipation of the consequences of Ahab's quest to kill the great white whale. Like the closed door, the rigidity of his obsession never falters, while the vulnerability of the ship and its crew to the elements as represented by the swaying ship's rigging is a major theme of the film.[32]

Whiteness is associated with the whale Ahab searches for in revenge for its mutilation of him as indicated by his false leg carved from a whale's white jaw-bone and the white scar on his face. Such visual emphases of lines etched on the body extend to the harpooner Queequeg (Friedrich von Ledebur) who has dark lines tattooed on his face and body. The film differs from the novel in that Queequeg is granted with foresight in his request for his coffin to be built when he is consumed with a sense of tragic foreboding of his own death after divining with stones. In this way the etching, 'litho-line' technique chosen for the film's cinematography extends to the crew who are marked by the voyage and Ahab's doomed quest. With the lure of the golden coin Ahab has nailed to the mast as a prize for the crew member who first catches sight of the white whale, the men similarly become caught in his obsession; the visual strategy thus acquires a profound metaphorical dimension. Both movement and stasis are dangerous. At one point the ship is becalmed and there are evocative shots of the men struggling in the blistering

Moby Dick: low-angle shots of the ship at sea create stark contrasts

really dramatic effects using strong blacks and whites under quite dull conditions'.[31] In the opening sequence mentioned above, the grass is indeed very desaturated but other details of natural scenery such as the waterfall and stream sparkle with glinting whiteness. Shots of the ship at sea similarly took advantage of this effect by showing up masts and rigging from low-angle shots which emphasised their lines against the background of the sea and sky. The progressive definition enhanced a three-dimensional impression, used for creative effect, such as when the door behind which Captain Ahab (Gregory Peck) resides for much of the beginning of the voyage is shot with the dark shapes of ropes and rigging swaying in front of it. The shot's depth enhances the

heat. Morris intensified the lighting to exaggerate this impression as the men sprawl languidly on the deck, interspersed with close-ups of the golden coin nailed to the mast.[33] The tension between stasis and movement is again emphasised as the ship's physical immobility is pitted against the 'magnetising lure' of the coin which represents their desire to rapidly hunt down the whale. The gold sparkles in contrast to the 'colder' tones of black, grey and blue which typify much of the film, this being an example of colour contrast as visual spectacle and metaphor.

An impressive example of cinematographic prescience occurs in the shot when Ishmael (Richard Basehart) is arrested by the mysterious Elijah (Royal Dano), who prophesies disaster just before the ship leaves on its voyage. Elijah walks towards Ishmael (and the camera) into extreme close-up in a way that anticipates the stasis–movement dynamic which is a major theme of the film. Even though this gives us privileged knowledge of the narrative's conclusion there is still suspense as the doomed quest takes the men through waters which are becalmed and then stormy. The climactic storm sequence is animated by expressive editing between close-ups, low- and high-angle shots and a generally dynamic visual design which heightens the sensation of danger. When thunder strikes the frame is bathed in blue light which adds to the turbulent, engulfing experience whereby sea, sky, ship and crew are overwhelmed by the environment. Yet within this barrage of intense action there are shots which 'halt' the narrative by arresting attention through colour. The 'St Elmo's fire' shots feature the mast struck by lightning with the effect of the mast and then the whaling spear held by Ahab turning luminous green.[34] The colour is not green in the novel of *Moby Dick* in which Ishmael observes: 'All the yardarms were tipped with a pallid fire, and touched at each tri-pointed lightning rod-end with three tapering white flames, each of the three tall masts was silently burning in that sulphurous air, like three gigantic wax tapers before an altar.'[35] In the film the effect was created in post-production and Morris very much wanted it resemble ghostly phenomena, in this instance not opting for a clear-line approach. When viewing early tests for the effect he reported to Huston: 'They are still getting it too sharp and clear and making it look like a material thing instead of the eerie almost supernatural effect that is intended.'[36] The final shots

Moby Dick: St Elmo's fire with green effect created in post-production

did indeed create an impression of luminosity, the green serving as an appropriate colour for the effect's symbolic register of impending death while at the same time retaining a sense of the colour's ambiguous relationship with life. Ahab's defiant clutching of the green-tinged spear is taken by the crew as a sign that he beat St Elmo's fire and caused the storm to abate.

Yet the biggest threat is what follows. When crewmember Starbuck (Leo Genn) is unable to shoot Ahab, stasis again defeats action in collusion with Elijah's prophesy. Finally, after Ahab's incessant goading the whale sinks both the ship and the longboats, with only Ishmael surviving. The whale's terrifying appearance brings to a conclusion the film's meditation on whiteness. This can be perplexing because, as Melville conjectures in the novel: 'Whiteness is not so much a colour as the visible absence of colour, and at the same time the concrete of all colours; it is for these reasons that there is such a dumb blankness, full of meaning, in a wide landscape of snows – a colourless, all colour atheism from which we shrink?'[37] From this perspective the choice of colour design for the film is entirely appropriate. In a film that desaturates colour yet emphasises whites and blacks, the essence of both assume an unusually deep, symbolic quality as appropriate to the narrative. The invitation to 'read' black and white *as colours* thus distances *Moby Dick* very much from a conventional black-and-white film. Ahab's pointless, inexorable drive to hunt the white whale literally drags the ship and crew down into the depths of the sea, into the terrifying nothingness so aptly expressed in the colour design. Morris used white to good effect but in a completely different context for *Moulin Rouge*. His ingenuity with camera placement, angles and close-ups is evident in both films, as is his willingness not to be defeated by technical difficulties. Yet we must conclude that the results are the work of many collaborators and he is the first to acknowledge that his job is to work closely with others, particularly the director. Writing in the *International Projectionist*, reviewer Norman Wasserman described the desaturated effect as 'producing something quite unique in screen hues'.[38]

These extraordinary films are evidence of occasional, pluralistic approaches to screen colour in the 1950s. While these could, as with *Moulin Rouge*, be criticised by Technicolor, the company could not afford to constrain new ideas against a background of technical and economic competition. The 1950s was a period of opportunity as the imbibition printing technique continued to be used after the introduction of Eastmancolor and the film industry sought to differentiate itself from television.[39] The British technicians who contributed so centrally to the creative development of colour worked productively with independent production companies that gave them a free hand to experiment. Their adaptability, most often working freelance, meant the challenge to produce 'something unique in screen hues' was prolonged until a time when colour dominated the world's cinema screens.

CONCLUSION
CREATING COLOUR IN BRITISH CINEMA

The many films referenced in this book have indeed shown that British technicians experimented with colour in exciting ways, and were at the forefront of exploring the potential of colour aesthetics and designs for the screen. What will also have emerged clearly is that there was a national investment in making a case for a specifically British deployment of colour. There was a collective will for a quality style of colour that advocated a particular appreciation of British cinema. This was frequently associated with restraint, which reflected dominant critical conceptions of colour as underscoring rather than distracting from narrative development. The fact that many of the films displayed far more aesthetically ambitious colour palettes reveals the limits of this rhetorical position and the extent to which British films extended and enriched the concept of colour restraint. Britain was not the only country to experiment with colour, and any claims for national specificity need to take into account comparative developments while acknowledging local variation. Reductive judgments on colour as applied in Hollywood and elsewhere fail to reflect the complexities and contexts of different colour styles and aesthetics within any national experience. The task of the film historian is to understand the role colour played in British cinema's attempts to gain more of the market share while at the same time be cognisant of the wider aspirations held by many who associated colour with particular aesthetic taste cultures and wider aspirations for progress, utopianism and postwar planning. Arising from these multifaceted contexts, the number of outstanding British colour films in a variety of genres and styles constitutes a fascinating and

distinguished record. The legacy of British colour films is their imaginative exploration of colour restraint; expressive play with colour design within genre cinema, and the production of some of the most significant short and avant-garde colour films in the first half of the twentieth century.

Avant-garde film-making, short and feature productions exhibited some extraordinary colour experimentation as successive processes were tried and tested, often first in shorter film formats. The arrival of three-strip Technicolor came at a specific historical juncture when the British film industry's economic infrastructure was developing and producers aimed for international distribution. Even though World War II placed severe strains on the industry, some seminal short and feature films were produced, enabling further strides with colour to be achieved in the following decade. As we have seen, British experimentation with colour involved not only exploring chromatic variation within notions of restraint but also unconventional practices around lighting and genre to produce what Dilys Powell referred to as a 'poetic' use of colour. As many of the films analysed in this book demonstrate, working within notions of restraint could be exciting. While one might assume restraint implied 'anti-colour' and a fundamental affinity with monochromatic palettes, what British technicians achieved was as daring in its way as the more overt experimentalism of films such as *Saraband for Dead Lovers* (1948) or *The Tales of Hoffmann* (1951). In short and documentary films opportunities were taken to push the boundaries: the cinematographer's wonder at the sheer beauty of screen colour can be seen in the swimming pool shots of *XIV Olympiad: The Glory of Sport* (1948), and *This is Colour* (1942) was a creative meditation on colour at every turn. That a film was instructional and informational in content was no barrier to technical virtuosity and glorification of the sensual, visual pleasures of colour.

Technicians were inspired by the challenges of working with colour, and the fractured economic make-up of British cinema in which companies such as The Archers or Cineguild operated may well have provided them with the independent space necessary to try new things. Even though conflicts could arise, affiliation with a large distribution company such as the Rank Organisation provided a degree of security as well as access to cinemas abroad. Against this economic background British cinema's reputation for producing prestige pictures that played well in metropolitan cinemas in the USA assisted product differentiation through creative distinction with screen colour, as noted by American and French critics who admired British Technicolor films. Indeed, one of the key contexts to be negotiated was economic: the additional financial outlay required for colour processes such as Technicolor could militate against overt experimentation that might confuse audiences. If, as Adrian Cornwell-Clyne advocated, the ideal expressions of colour were those that went relatively unnoticed, then it was hardly worth the extra effort and expenditure. A delicate balance was therefore struck in most instances of colour enhancing a film's aesthetic qualities and status as a quality product while being distanced from accusations often levelled at Hollywood of garishness equated with vulgarity and low art. As well as ensuring consistency of application, one of the rationales for establishing the Color Advisory Service at Technicolor was to reassure producers that the increased production costs were justified. In view of the response of many critics to colour, judging its success or failure on arbitrary standards of realism, or whether it supported a film's narrative trajectory, it is no wonder that overt experimentation was discouraged. On the other hand, and as we have seen from many examples of British films, it was not a clear-cut case of colour occupying a consistently minor role in genre productions; in fact, the opposite could be said of many British titles which were admired in the USA for their innovative approaches.

Colour provided cinematographers with the opportunity to work closely with the latest developments in technology, carving out an area of expertise and aligning themselves with competence, flair and imagination. Jack Cardiff's talents were celebrated at the time, becoming a model for other colour cinematographers who similarly publicised their efforts at working both within and against Technicolor's norms. Since many of them aspired to work in Hollywood and in collaboration with American technicians, a strict stylistic independence was undesirable. Chris Challis, for example, said he 'tried not to have a style that was the same in every picture'. He described the training he received as 'of a very high calibre', not least that provided by American technicians who advised on early Technicolor films in Britain.[1] Presenting Natalie Kalmus as an obstructive, even ridiculous figure served as a convenient means of claiming technical expertise at a time when nationalistically inflected discourses around colour coincided with British cinema's attempts to expand its domestic production base. It is therefore useful to consider British colour films in the light of such contextual imperatives while not seeking to downgrade their distinctive and innovatory qualities that nevertheless shone through.

The legacy of British colour films has entered a new phase as many films in the recognised canon, particularly Powell and Pressburger's Technicolor classics, have been restored and re-presented to audiences on DVD and Blu-Ray formats. While a detailed discussion of film restoration is beyond the scope of this book, I will conclude by offering some brief reflections on the issues involved in projects to restore films either to an approximation of their former glory, or, as is sometimes the case, something which is markedly different. While the different personnel involved in creating colour at the time of a film's production, post-production and release have been highlighted, some films are returned to many years later as candidates for restoration. How these films are selected is often influenced by prevailing notions of which films are seminal and most worthy of the time and expense. The attention devoted to Powell and Pressburger's films is a prime example of this tendency. Yet, as this book has shown, many less well-known examples exist from the history of colour films that deserve another look. It is surprising, for example, that even though Jack Cardiff's contribution has been celebrated many times in relation to feature films, his short films, especially the seminal *World Windows* series (1937–40) and *This is Colour*, remain difficult to access. Important British colour melodramas including *Jassy* (1947), *Blanche Fury* (1948) and *Footsteps in the Fog* (1955) are also not nearly as accessible as the other titles associated with British Technicolor. To see a good print of *Wings of the Morning* (1937), the first British three-strip Technicolor feature film, one has to go to the BFI National Archive; the film is not available in DVD format in the UK and copies produced in the USA are of very poor quality. In the silent period things are even more seriously imbalanced. If the Prizmacolor classic *The Glorious Adventure* (1922) had not been restored there would have been a major gap in the history of colour films and, again, this film is only accessible at the BFI National Archive.

The availability of digital technologies to assist such projects has turned attention towards presenting restored colour classics for theatrical, DVD and Blu-Ray release. The value judgments that are involved in such projects make us more and more aware of the futility of ever being able to return a film to what it might have looked like on first release. As noted many times in this book, a range of factors militate against consistency of film colour. These include processing, projection, the differing quality of prints, chemical deterioration, the scarcity of primary sources to accurately inform a restoration project and historic differences in colour perception. The DVD of *The Open Road* (2007) is a classic case in point in which a version of the film series palatable to contemporary viewers is now in circulation rather than something which equates with how people would have encountered the films on first release. This is an extreme example and a DVD that included all the fringing problems and resulting eye-strain noted when people saw the films in the 1920s would not have been commercially viable. Yet seminal colour feature films

such as *Gone with the Wind* (1939) exist in many formats acceptable to different generations of audiences and scholars, including nitrate and viewing prints, videos, laser discs and DVDs so that there can be a great deal of colour variation even in films taken to be iconic exemplars of colour technologies as famous as Technicolor.[2] In spite of this, Technicolor films produced before the widespread introduction of monopack film in the 1950s generally preserved better because of the dyes used in the process. On the other hand, the dye-transfer process resulted in levels of saturation which cannot be duplicated by the light-sensitive dyes used in modern colour film stocks. This renders any notion of replicating the conditions of first release problematic, and we may never find ourselves experiencing colour films as E. S. Tompkins, the extraordinarily astute colour film enthusiast, did in the 1940s.

Rather than frustrate analysis, the intertwined pragmatic and ethical issues surrounding restoration projects add to colour's ability to inspire interpretation, re-viewing and comparing films in their different versions as they become available. The history of colour is a living thing as we balance evidence of contemporary reactions on first release against our own perceptions. It is this dynamic that contributes to the difficult but rewarding enterprise of investigating colour, charting a course between knowledge about the many experts involved in its creation and the end-point of individual response to chromatic sensation. For artists, technicians and viewers alike, being colour conscious was, and remains, an exacting but enthralling pursuit. That British film-makers made such distinguished contributions to the development of colour in first half of the twentieth century is a testament to their tenacity and imagination as they negotiated innovation with so many varied, remarkable and enduring films.

APPENDIX 1
KINEMATOGRAPH YEAR BOOKS, 1938–55

Colour Films in Britain

DATE TRADE SHOWN; RELEASE DATE	TITLE	DISTRIBUTOR/COUNTRY	*KINEMATOGRAPH WEEKLY* REVIEW
16/6/38 2/6/38	*The Adventures of Robin Hood*	First National/USA	23/6/38
17/5/38 9/1/39	*The Adventures of Tom Sawyer*	United Artists/USA	12/5/38
17/6/38 14/11/38	*Devil on Horseback*	ABFD (Grand National)/USA	23/6/38
13/1/38 26/9/38	*The Divorce of Lady X*	United Artists/UK	13/1/38
5/4/38 31/10/38	*Gold Is Where You Find It*	Warner/USA	14/4/38
8/3/38 7/11/38	*Goldwyn Follies*	United Artists/USA	10/3/38
8/4/38 10/10/38	*Her Jungle Love*	Paramount/USA	7/4/38
17/10/38 26/12/38	*Sixty Glorious Years*	RKO Radio/UK	20/10/38
23/3/38 19/9/38	*Snow White and the Seven Dwarfs*	RKO Radio/UK	24/2/38
18/10/38 3/4/38	*Valley of the Giants*	Warner/USA	27/10/38
1/2/38 8/8/38	*We're in the Legion Now*	ABFD (Grand National)/USA	17/2/38
4/7/39 27/11/39	*Dodge City*	Warner/USA	13/7/39
20/4/39 4/9/39	*The Four Feathers*	United Artists/UK	20/4/39

DATE TRADE SHOWN; RELEASE DATE	TITLE	DISTRIBUTOR/COUNTRY	KINEMATOGRAPH WEEKLY REVIEW
12/1/39 5/6/39	*Heart of the North*	Warner/USA	19/1/39
2/2/39 17/4/39	*Kentucky*	20th Century-Fox/USA	9/2/39
16/3/39 7/8/39	*The Little Princess*	20th Century-Fox/USA	23/3/39
11/1/39 23/10/39	*The Mikado*	GFD/UK	19/1/39
13/10/39 19/2/40	*Over the Moon*	United Artists/UK	19/10/39
2/11/39 Rel. not fixed	*Sons of the Sea*	Grand National/UK	9/11/39
15/12/38 1/5/39	*Sweethearts*	MGM/USA	22/12/38
23/4/40 26/8/40	*The Blue Bird*	20th Century-Fox/USA	25/4/40
27/6/40 4/11/40	*Dr Cyclops*	Paramount/USA	20/6/40
31/1/40 8/2/40	*Drums Along the Mohawk*	20th Century-Fox/USA	8/2/40
18/4/40 Rel. not fixed	*Gone with the Wind*	MGM/USA	25/4/40
12/1/40 22/4/40	*Gulliver's Travels*	Paramount/USA	4/1/40
15/12/39 Rel. floating	*Happy Event*	British Lion/UK	21/12/39
11/12/39 18/3/40	*Hollywood Cavalcade*	20th Century-Fox/USA	14/12/39
22/4/40 Rel. not fixed	*Isle of Destiny*	RKO Radio/USA	25/4/40
6/9/40 25/11/40	*Maryland*	20th Century-Fox/USA	12/11/40
11/12/40 Rel. not fixed	*North-West Mounted Police*	Paramount/USA	21/11/40
28/3/40 2/9/40	*Northwest Passage*	MGM/USA	4/4/40
27/3/40 28/9/40	*Pinocchio*	RKO Radio/USA	21/3/40

DATE TRADE SHOWN; RELEASE DATE	TITLE	DISTRIBUTOR/COUNTRY	*KINEMATOGRAPH WEEKLY* REVIEW
18/10/40 20/1/41	*The Return of Frank James*	20th Century-Fox/USA	24/10/40
6/3/40 5/8/40	*Swanee River*	20th Century-Fox/USA	14/3/40
8/5/40 29/7/40	*Typhoon*	Paramount/USA	2/5/40
15/5/40 22/7/40	*Untamed*	Paramount/USA	23/5/40
19/12/39 25/3/40	*The Wizard of Oz*	MGM/USA	21/12/39
Reissue rel. 29/7/40	*Wings of the Morning*	20th Century-Fox/UK	28/1/37 14/3/40
7/11/41 22/12/41	*Aloma of the South Seas*	Paramount/USA	13/11/41
25/11/41 16/3/42	*Belle Star*	20th Century-Fox/USA	27/11/41
20/8/41 20/10/41	*Billy the Kid*	MGM/USA	28/8/41
22/4/41 14/7/41	*Bitter Sweet*	MGM/USA	24/4/41
27/11/41 30/3/42	*Blood and Sand*	20th Century-Fox/USA	4/12/41
24/9/41 17/11/41	*Blossoms in the Dust*	MGM/USA	2/10/41
3/4/41 16/6/41	*Chad Hanna*	20th Century-Fox/USA	10/4/41
17/12/41 Rel. not fixed	*Dive Bomber*	Warner/USA	25/12/41
7/2/41 14/4/41	*Down Argentine Way*	20th Century-Fox/USA	20/2/41
11/12/41 Rel. not fixed	*Dumbo*	RKO Radio/USA	18/12/41
16/7/41 Rel. not fixed	*Fantasia*	RKO Radio/USA	24/7/41
9/9/41 29/12/41	*Moon Over Miami*	20th Century-Fox/USA	11/9/41
3/9/41 6/10/41	*The Reluctant Dragon*	RKO Radio/USA	11/9/41

DATE TRADE SHOWN; RELEASE DATE	TITLE	DISTRIBUTOR/COUNTRY	KINEMATOGRAPH WEEKLY REVIEW
13/11/41 6/4/41	Smilin' Through	MGM/USA	20/11/41
24/12/40 10/3/41	The Thief of Bagdad	United Artists/UK	26/12/40
25/3/41 23/6/41	Virginia	Paramount/USA	27/3/41
22/5/41 21/7/41	Western Union	20th Century-Fox/USA	29/5/41
6/2/42 18/5/42	Bahama Passage	Paramount/USA	12/2/42
13/8/42 21/12/42	Bambi	RKO Radio/USA	13/8/42
12/6/42 3/8/42	Beyond the Blue Horizon	Paramount/USA	18/6/42
27/2/42 13/7/42	Captains of the Clouds	Warner/USA	12/2/42
9/10/42 30/11/42	The Forest Rangers	Paramount/USA	15/10/42
23/9/42 9/11/42	The Great Mr Handel	GFD/UK	1/10/42
23/1/42 27/4/42	Hoppity Goes to Town	Paramount/USA	22/1/42
5/6/42 3/8/42	Jungle Book	United Artists/USA	11/6/42
19/2/42 6/4/42	Louisiana Purchase	Paramount/USA	26/2/42
23/7/42 2/11/42	My Gal Sal	20th Century-Fox/USA	30/7/42
16/11/42 14/12/42	Queen Victoria	Renown/UK	19/11/42
10/4/42 15/6/42	Reap the Wild Wind	Paramount/USA	9/4/42
18/6/42 7/9/42	Song of the Islands	20th Century-Fox/USA	25/6/42
17/6/42 14/9/42	To the Shores of Tripoli	20th Century-Fox/USA	25/6/42
1/1/42 25/5/42	Weekend in Havana	20th Century-Fox/USA	8/1/42

DATE TRADE SHOWN; RELEASE DATE	TITLE	DISTRIBUTOR/COUNTRY	*KINEMATOGRAPH WEEKLY* REVIEW
Reissue (floating)	*Cavalcade of the Navy*	Equity-British/UK	12/3/42
20/1/43 29/3/43	*Arabian Nights*	GFD/Universal/USA	28/1/43
16/3/43 14/6/43	*The Black Swan*	20th Century-Fox/USA	18/3/43
7/7/43 4/10/43	*Coney Island*	20th Century-Fox/USA	15/7/43
16/6/43 30/8/43	*Crash Dive*	20th Century-Fox/USA	24/6/43
24/11/43 21/5/43	*The Desert Song*	Warner/USA	2/12/43
2/6/43 5/7/43	*The Desperadoes*	Columbia/USA	27/5/43
13/8/43 25/10/43	*Dixie*	Paramount/USA	19/8/43
14/7/43 20/9/43	*Du Barry was a Lady*	MGM/USA	22/7/43
26/3/43 27/9/43	*Fiesta*	United Artists/USA	1/4/43
9/11/43 Rel. not fixed	*For Whom the Bell Tolls*	Paramount/USA	13/5/43
23/3/43 3/5/43	*Get Cracking*	Columbia/USA	25/3/43
2/2/43 22/2/43	*Happy Go Lucky*	Paramount/USA	4/2/43
4/8/43 1/11/43	*Heaven Can Wait*	20th Century-Fox/USA	12/8/43
3/6/43 2/8/43	*Hello, 'Frisco, Hello*	20th Century-Fox/USA	10/6/43
14/7/43 8/11/43	*My Friend Flicka*	20th Century-Fox/USA	22/7/43
30/11/43 27/3/43	*Phantom of the Opera*	Universal/USA	2/12/43
4/11/43 6/12/43	*Saludos Amigos*	RKO-Radio/USA	11/11/43
5/8/43 18/10/43	*Salute to the Marines*	MGM/USA	12/8/43

DATE TRADE SHOWN; RELEASE DATE	TITLE	DISTRIBUTOR/COUNTRY	*KINEMATOGRAPH WEEKLY* REVIEW
14/1/43 26/4/43	*Springtime in the Rockies*	20th Century-Fox/USA	21/1/43
4/11/43 24/1/44	*Sweet Rosie O'Grady*	20th Century-Fox/USA	11/11/43
1/12/43 28/2/44	*This is the Army*	Warner/USA	9/12/43
18/2/43 28/6/43	*Thunder Birds*	20th Century-Fox/USA	25/2/43
8/9/43 25/10/43	*Victory Through Air Power*	United Artists/USA	16/9/43
19/8/43 25/10/43	*White Captive*	GFD/Universal/USA	26/8/43
Reissue December 1943	*The Adventures of Robin Hood*	Warner/USA	26/8/43
Reissue 1/11/43	*The Four Feathers*	Ealing/UK	26/8/43
10/3/44 1/5/44	*Ali Baba and the Forty Thieves*	GFD/Universal/USA	9/3/44
6/9/44 8/1/45	*An American Romance*	MGM/USA	14/9/44
23/8/44 25/12/44	*Bathing Beauty*	MGM/USA	31/8/44
22/3/44 24/7/44	*Broadway Rhythm*	MGM/USA	30/3/44
14/9/44 8/1/45	*The Climax*	GFD/Universal/USA	21/9/44
25/5/44 2/10/44	*Cobra Woman*	GFD/Universal/USA	1/6/44
13/6/44 4/9/44	*Cover Girl*	Columbia/USA	15/6/44
22/12/44 12/2/45	*Frenchman's Creek*	Paramount/USA	28/12/44
13/1/44 6/3/44	*The Girls He Left Behind*	20th Century-Fox/USA	13/1/44
5/10/44 1/12/45	*Gypsy Wildcat*	GFD/Universal/USA	12/10/44
5/1/44 Rel. not fixed	*Henry V*	Eagle-Lion/UK	30/11/44

DATE TRADE SHOWN; RELEASE DATE	TITLE	DISTRIBUTOR/COUNTRY	*KINEMATOGRAPH WEEKLY* REVIEW
15/6/44 9/10/44	*Home In Indiana*	20th Century-Fox/USA	31/8/44
14/11/44 25/12/44	*Irish Eyes are Smiling*	20th Century-Fox/USA	16/11/44
13/12/44 22/1/45	*Kismet*	MGM/USA	21/12/44
1/6/44 21/8/44	*Lady in the Dark*	Paramount/USA	8/6/44
27/1/44 29/5/44	*Melody Inn*	Paramount/USA	3/2/44
9/6/44 16/10/44	*The Memphis Belle*	MGM/USA	15/6/44
25/5/44 28/8/44	*Pin-Up Girl*	20th Century-Fox/USA	1/6/44
19/12/44 2/4/45	*A Song to Remember*	Columbia/USA	23/11/44
16/6/44 25/9/44	*The Story of Dr Wassell*	Paramount/USA	22/6/44
27/4/44 7/8/44	*This Happy Breed*	Eagle-Lion/UK	4/5/44
2/2/44 20/3/44	*Thousands Cheer*	MGM/USA	10/2/44
18/4/44 14/8/44	*Up In Arms*	RKO-Radio/USA	20/4/44
9/11/44 15/1/45	*Western Approaches*	British Lion/UK	18/5/44
15/11/44 19/3/44	*Wilson*	20th Century-Fox/USA	23/11/44
Reissue floating	*The Adventures of Tom Sawyer*	New Realm/USA	24/2/44
Reissue 27/3/44	*The Divorce of Lady X*	Ealing Dist/UK	2/3/44
Reissue 20/3/44	*The Drum*	Ealing Dist/UK	6/1/44
Reissue 3/7/44	*Her Jungle Love*	Paramount/USA	22/6/44
Reissue floating	*Nothing Sacred*	Grand National/USA	11/5/44

DATE TRADE SHOWN; RELEASE DATE	TITLE	DISTRIBUTOR/COUNTRY	*KINEMATOGRAPH WEEKLY* REVIEW
Reissue 3/4/44	*Snow White and the Seven Dwarfs*	RKO-Radio/USA	24/2/44
Reissue 18/12/44	*The Thief of Bagdad*	Ealing Dist/UK	24/8/44
Reissue 12/6/44	*The Trail of the Lonesome Pine*	Paramount/USA	6/1/44
10/4/45 Rel. floating	*Blithe Spirit*	GFD/UK	12/4/45
27/4/45 9/7/45	*Bring on the Girls*	Paramount/USA	3/5/45
23/1/46 Rel. not fixed	*Caesar and Cleopatra*	Eagle-Lion/UK	13/12/45
8/2/45 2/4/45	*Can't Help Singing*	GFD/Universal/USA	15/2/45
19/6/45 20/8/45	*Diamond Horseshoe*	20th Century-Fox/USA	21/6/45
12/12/45 11/3/46	*The Dolly Sisters*	20th Century-Fox/USA	20/12/45
27/2/45 4/6/45	*The Fighting Lady*	20th Century-Fox/USA	1/3/45
17/1/45 19/3/45	*Meet Me In St Louis*	MGM/USA	25/1/45
7/3/45 6/8/45	*National Velvet*	MGM/USA	15/3/45
21/6/45 1/10/45	*Nob Hill*	20th Century-Fox/USA	28/6/45
13/2/45 13/8/45	*The Princess and the Pirate*	RKO-Radio/USA	15/2/45
21/6/45 6/8/45	*Salome, Where She Danced*	GFD-Universal/USA	28/6/45
23/1/45 30/4/45	*Something for the Boys*	20th Century-Fox/USA	25/1/45
8/8/45 29/10/45	*Son of Lassie*	MGM/USA	16/8/45
10/10/45 24/12/45	*State Fair*	20th Century-Fox/USA	18/10/45
22/6/45 3/9/45	*Steel*	20th Century-Fox/UK	5/7/45

DATE TRADE SHOWN; RELEASE DATE	TITLE	DISTRIBUTOR/COUNTRY	KINEMATOGRAPH WEEKLY REVIEW
2/5/45 18/6/45	Sudan	GFD-Universal/USA	10/5/45
5/9/45 31/12/45	A Thousand and One Nights	Columbia/USA	30/8/45
10/5/45 24/9/45	The Three Caballeros	RKO-Radio/USA	17/5/45
24/10/45 4/2/46	Thrill of a Romance	MGM/USA	1/11/45
19/4/45 16/7/45	Thunderhead, Son of Flicka	20th Century-Fox/USA	26/4/45
21/8/45 26/11/45	Where Do We Go From Here?	20th Century-Fox/USA	23/8/45
8/11/45 4/2/46	Wonder Man	RKO-Radio/USA	15/11/45
Reissue 19/11/45	Blood and Sand	20th Century-Fox/USA	4/10/45
Reissue 17/12/45	The Wizard of Oz	MGM/USA	4/10/45
Reissue 17/12/45	Wings of the Morning	20th Century-Fox/UK	16/8/45
7/1/46 22/4/46	The Bandit of Sherwood Forest	Columbia/USA	10/1/46
25/9/46 23/12/46	Blue Skies	Paramount/USA	3/10/46
15/3/46 29/4/46	The Bride Wasn't Willing	GFD/USA	21/3/46
19/11/46 Immediate	California	Paramount/USA	21/11/46
25/7/46 18/11/46	Canyon Passage	GFD/USA	1/8/46
22/11/46 24/3/47	The Caravan Trail	Pathé/USA	28/11/46
26/6/46 7/10/46	Centennial Summer	20th Century-Fox/USA	4/7/46
23/7/46 30/12/46	Colorado Serenade	Pathé/USA	25/7/46
28/6/46 23/9/46	Concerto	British Lion/USA	4/7/46

DATE TRADE SHOWN; RELEASE DATE	TITLE	DISTRIBUTOR/COUNTRY	KINEMATOGRAPH WEEKLY REVIEW
3/7/46 19/8/46	*Courage of Lassie*	MGM/USA	11/7/46
2/5/46 19/8/46	*Do You Love Me?*	20th Century-Fox/USA	9/5/46
28/3/46 5/8/46	*Easy To Wed*	MGM/USA	4/4/46
25/7/46 16/12/46	*Enchanted Forest*	Pathé/USA	1/8/46
23/10/46 20/1/47	*Gallant Bess*	MGM/USA	31/10/46
20/2/46 13/5/46	*The Harvey Girls*	MGM/USA	28/2/46
21/8/46 11/11/46	*Holiday in Mexico*	MGM/USA	29/8/46
6/11/46 6/1/47	*The Jolson Story*	Columbia/USA	7/11/46
29/10/46 3/2/46	*The Kid From Brooklyn*	RKO-Radio/USA	31/10/46
15/10/46 3/2/46	*Laughing Lady*	Anglo-American/UK	24/10/46
27/8/46 23/9/46	*London Town*	Eagle-Lion/UK	5/9/46
28/5/46 26/8/46	*Make Mine Music*	RKO-Radio/USA	30/5/46
29/8/46 Rel. immediate	*Man From Rainbow Valley*	British Lion/USA	5/9/46
12/11/46 30/12/46	*A Matter of Life and Death*	GFD/UK	7/11/46
17/5/46 2/9/46	*Meet the Navy*	Anglo-American/UK	23/5/46
18/7/46 9/9/46	*Men of Two Worlds*	GFD/UK	18/7/46
13/8/46 30/12/46	*Night and Day*	Warner/USA	22/8/46
13/6/46 26/8/46	*Night in Paradise*	GFD/USA	20/6/46
9/7/46 21/10/46	*Northwest Trail*	Exclusive/USA	11/7/46

DATE TRADE SHOWN; RELEASE DATE	TITLE	DISTRIBUTOR/COUNTRY	*KINEMATOGRAPH WEEKLY* REVIEW
25/4/46 17/6/46	*Renegades*	Columbia/USA	28/3/46
7/3/46 1/7/46	*San Antonio*	Warner/USA	14/3/46
10/7/46 14/10/46	*Smoky*	20th Century-Fox/USA	18/7/46
24/1/46 15/4/46	*The Spanish Main*	RKO-Radio/USA	31/1/46
23/4/46 25/3/46	*Sports Parade in Moscow*	GFD/USSR	21/3/46
2/10/46 2/12/46	*Three Little Girls in Blue*	20th Century-Fox/USA	10/10/46
12/2/46 17/6/46	*The Virginian*	Paramount/USA	14/2/46
14/11/46 Rel. immediate	*Wildfire* Cinecolor	Exclusive/USA	24/10/46
27/2/46 22/7/46	*Yolanda and the Thief*	MGM/USA	7/3/46
13/2/46 29/4/46	*Ziegfeld Follies*	MGM/USA	21/2/46
Reissue 2/5/46 Immediate	*Becky Sharp*	Grand National/USA	9/5/46
Reissue 12/9/46 4/11/46	*Blossoms in the Dust*	MGM/USA	19/9/46
Reissue 30/10/46 Immediate	*Over the Moon*	British Lion/UK	7/11/46
Reissue 26/2/46 8/4/46	*Pinocchio*	RKO-Radio/USA	28/2/46
Rel. not fixed	*An Ideal Husband*	British Lion/UK	20/11/47
24/11/47	*The Assassin*	Columbia/USA	14/8/47
26/5/47	*Black Narcissus*	GFD/UK	24/4/47
25/8/47	*Bob, Son of Battle*	20th Century-Fox/USA	3/7/47
21/7/47	*Carnival in Costa Rica*	20th Century-Fox/USA	24/4/47
17/11/47	*Desert Fury*	Paramount/USA	11/9/47

RELEASE DATE	TITLE	DISTRIBUTOR/COUNTRY	*KINEMATOGRAPH WEEKLY* REVIEW
1/9/47	*Down to Earth*	Columbia/USA	24/7/47
20/10/47	*Duel in the Sun*	Selznick Inc/USA	22/5/47
29/9/47	*Fiesta*	MGM/USA	7/8/47
June 1947	*God's Country*	Exclusive US	27/3/47
15/12/47	*I Wonder Who's Kissing Her Now*	20th Century-Fox/USA	17/7/47
8/9/47	*Jassy*	GFD/UK	14/8/47
19/5/47	*The Man Within*	GFD/UK	10/4/47
24/3/47	*Margie*	20th Century-Fox/USA	9/1/47
11/8/47	*The Perils of Pauline*	Paramount/USA	29/5/47
Rel. not fixed	*The Red Stallion* Cinecolor	GFD/USA	31/7/47
20/10/47	*Romance in the West*	MGM/USA	24/7/47
9/6/47	*The Shocking Miss Pilgrim*	20th Century-Fox/USA	27/3/47
18/8/47	*Sinbad the Sailor*	RKO-Radio/USA	19/6/47
22/12/47	*Slave Girl*	GFD/USA	21/8/47
21/7/47	*Song of Scheherazade*	GFD/USA	1/5/47
Rel. not fixed	*The Stone Flower*	Film Traders/USSR	1/5/47
Rel. not fixed	*Tale of Navajos*	MGM/USA	31/7/47
7/4/47	*Till the Clouds Roll By*	MGM/USA	6/3/47
19/5/47	*The Time, the Place, and the Girl*	Warner/USA	9/1/47
22/9/47	*The Vigilante's Return* Cinecolor	GFD/USA	24/7/47
3/11/47	*Wake up and Dream*	20th Century-Fox/USA	2/10/47
Reissue Rel. not fixed	*For Whom the Bell Tolls*	Paramount/USA	21/8/47
Reissue Immediate	*Jungle Book*	British Lion/USA	30/10/47
Reissue Immediate	*Queen Victoria*	Renown/UK	16/1/47
15/11/48	*The Birds and the Bees*	MGM/USA	22/7/48
5/7/48	*Black Gold* Cinecolor	Pathé/USA	10/6/48

RELEASE DATE	TITLE	DISTRIBUTOR/COUNTRY	*KINEMATOGRAPH WEEKLY* REVIEW
22/3/48	*Blanche Fury*	GFD/UK	26/2/48
Rel. not fixed	*Bonnie Prince Charlie*	British Lion/UK	4/11/48
Rel. not fixed	*A Date with Judy*	MGM/USA	18/11/48
Rel. not fixed	*Easter Parade*	MGM/USA	11/11/48
Rel. not fixed	*The Emperor Waltz*	Paramount/USA	6/5/48
27/9/48	*Forever Amber*	20th Century-Fox/USA	27/9/48
16/2/48	*Fun and Fancy Free*	RKO-Radio/USA	8/1/48
Rel. not fixed	*Give My Regards to Broadway*	20th Century-Fox/USA	25/11/48
Rel. not fixed	*Good News*	MGM/USA	23/9/48
Rel. not fixed	*Green Grass of Wyoming*	20th Century-Fox/USA	18/11/48
Rel. not fixed	*Highland Story* Radiantcolor	Excusive/UK	15/4/48
11/10/48	*Life with Father*	Warner/USA	24/6/48
Rel. not fixed	*Luxury Liner*	MGM/USA	25/11/48
24/1/48	*The Man From Colorado*	Columbia/USA	15/7/48
Rel. not fixed	*Master of Lassie*	MGM/USA	11/11/48
Rel. not fixed	*Mother Wore Tights*	20th Century-Fox/USA	23/9/48
27/12/48	*My Wild Irish Rose*	Warner/USA	3/6/48
Rel. not fixed	*On an Island with You*	MGM/USA	18/11/48
Rel. not fixed	*Paleface*	Paramount/USA	26/8/48
27/12/48	*The Prince of Thieves*	Columbia/USA	22/7/48
6/9/48	*The Red Shoes*	GFD/UK	22/7/48
11/10/48	*Relentless*	Columbia/USA	13/5/48
13/12/48	*River Lady*	GFD/USA	28/10/48
4/10/48	*The Pirate*	MGM/USA	8/7/48
4/10/48	*Saraband for Dead Lovers*	GFD/UK	9/9/48
Rel. not fixed	*Say it with Flowers* (short)	Dan Fish/UK	23/9/48
Rel. not fixed	*Secret Life of Walter Mitty*	RKO-Radio/USA	7/10/48
Rel. not fixed	*Silver City*	Paramount/USA	30/9/8

RELEASE DATE	TITLE	DISTRIBUTOR/COUNTRY	*KINEMATOGRAPH WEEKLY* REVIEW
10/1/48	*Summer Holiday*	MGM/USA	5/8/48
Rel. not fixed	*Summer Lightning*	20th Century-Fox/USA	2/9/48
8/3/48	*The Swordsman*	Columbia/USA	11/12/48
3/1/48	*This Time for Keeps*	MGM/USA	5/8/48
30/8/48	*Unconquered*	Paramount/USA	4/3/48
9/8/48	*The Unfinished Dance*	MGM/USA	3/6/48
24/5/48	*Wild West* Cinecolor	Pathé/USA	8/4/48
20/9/48	*XIV Olympiad*	GFD/UK	2/9/48
Reissue 12/4/48	*Bambi*	RKO-Radio/USA	12/2/48
Reissue Rel. not fixed	*The Bandit of Sherwood Forest*	Columbia/USA	18/12/47
Reissue Rel. not fixed	*Blithe Spirit*	ABFD/UK	18/12/47
Reissue Rel. floating	*Buffalo Bill*	20th Century-Fox/USA	25/12/47
Reissue Rel. not fixed	*Cover Girl*	Columbia/USA	25/12/47
Reissue Rel. floating	*Dancing Pirate*	New Realm/USA	11/3/48
Reissue Rel. not fixed	*The Four Feathers*	British Lion/UK	29/1/48
Reissue 12/4/48	*Northwest Passage*	MGM/USA	1/4/48
Reissue Rel. floating	*A Star is Born*	New Realm/USA	11/3/48
Reissue 22/3/48	*Sweethearts*	MGM/USA	11/3/48
Reissue Rel. not fixed	*The Thief of Bagdad*	British Lion/UK	10/6/48
11/4/49	*Apartment for Peggy*	20th Century-Fox/USA	20/1/49
24/10/49	*The Barkleys of Broadway*	MGM/USA	28/7/49
26/12/49	*The Big Cat*	GFD/USA	24/11/49
18/4/49	*The Blue Lagoon*	GFD/UK	3/3/49

RELEASE DATE	TITLE	DISTRIBUTOR/COUNTRY	*KINEMATOGRAPH WEEKLY* REVIEW
2/1/50	*Calamity Jane and Sam Bass*	GFD/USA	27/10/49
26/9/49	*Captain from Castile*	Paramount/USA	14/4/49
Rel. not fixed	*Coroner Creek*	Columbia/USA	9/12/48
5/9/49	*Christopher Columbus*	GFD/UK	16/6/49
Rel. floating	*Date with Destiny*	Columbia/USA	28/7/49
Rel. not fixed	*Elizabeth of Ladymead*	British Lion/UK	23/12/48
3/10/49	*Everybody's Cheering*	MGM/USA	21/7/49
Rel. not fixed	*The Forsyth Saga*	MGM/USA	24/11/49
25/4/49	*The Gallant Blade*	Columbia/USA	16/12/48
23/1/50	*The Gal Who Took the West*	GFD/USA	3/11/49
12/12/49	*In the Good Old Summertime*	MGM/USA	22/9/49
25/7/49	*It's Magic*	Warner/USA	17/3/49
10/10/49	*Joan of Arc*	RKO-Radio/USA	7/4/49
13/6/49	*The Kissing Bandit*	MGM/USA	17/4/49
25/7/49	*Last of the Redskins*	Columbia/USA	14/4/49
26/12/49	*Little Women*	MGM/USA	4/8/49
30/6/50	*Look for the Silver Lining*	Warner/USA	10/11/49
Rel. not fixed	*The Loves of Carmen*	Columbia/USA	17/2/49
14/9/49	*Maytime in Mayfair*	British Lion/UK	26/5/49
11/7/49	*Melody Time*	RKO-Radio/USA	9/12/48
7/11/49	*Mother Knows Best*	20th Century-Fox/USA	1/9/49
10/10/49	*My Dream is Yours*	Warner/USA	11/8/49
7/11/49	*The New Adventures of Don Juan*	Warner/USA	28/7/49
14/3/49	*Pirates of Monterey*	GFD/USA	13/1/49
Rel. not fixed	*Red Canyon*	Eros/USA	7/7/49
Rel. not fixed	*The Red Pony*	British Lion/USA	18/8/49
12/12/49	*Ride, Ryder, Ride* Cinecolor	AB-Pathé/USA	3/11/49
7/3/49	*Scott of the Antarctic*	GFD/UK	2/12/48

RELEASE DATE	TITLE	DISTRIBUTOR/COUNTRY	*KINEMATOGRAPH WEEKLY* REVIEW
18/4/49	*The Secret Land*	MGM/USA	20/1/49
Rel. not fixed	*So Dear to my Heart*	RKO-Radio/USA	25/8/49
17/10/49	*Sofia* Cinecolor	ABFD/USA	8/9/49
17/10/49	*A Song is Born*	RKO-Radio/USA	7/7/49
5/9/49	*The Sun Comes Up*	MGM/USA	12/5/49
27/2/50	*Task Force*	Warner/USA	10/11/49
8/8/49	*That Lady in Ermine*	20th Century-Fox/USA	14/4/49
Rel. not fixed	*That Midnight Kiss*	MGM/USA	27/10/49
2/5/49	*Three Godfathers*	MGM/USA	27/1/49
Rel. not fixed	*The Tinderbox* Gevacolor	Adelphi/Danish	31/3/49
12/9/49	*Trottie True*	GFD/UK	11/8/49
Rel. not fixed	*Tap Roots*	GFD/USA	2/12/49
1/8/49	*Tulsa*	GFD/USA	7/4/49
Rel. not fixed	*Two Texas Knights*	Warner/USA	14/7/49
Rel. not fixed	*Tycoon*	RKO-Radio/USA	9/12/48
2/1/50	*Under Capricorn*	Warner/UK	6/10/49
Rel. not fixed	*Untamed Breed*	Columbia/USA	16/12/48
12/12/49	*When My Baby Smiles at Me*	20th Century-Fox/USA	1/9/49
4/4/49	*Whispering Smith*	Paramount/USA	20/1/49
15/8/49	*Words and Music*	MGM/USA	28/4/49
18/4/49	*A Yankee at King Arthur's Court*	Paramount/USA	10/2/49
Rel. not fixed	*The Younger Brothers*	Warner/USA	14/7/49
20/3/50	*Adventures of Gallant Bess*	AB-Pathé/USA	23/2/50
26/6/50	*The Adventures of Ichabod and Mr Toad*	RKO-Radio/USA	18/5/50
9/10/50	*Annie Get Your Gun*	MGM/USA	29/6/50
2/4/50	*Bagdad*	GFD/USA	2/3/50
24/7/50	*Barricade*	Warner/USA	4/5/50

RELEASE DATE	TITLE	DISTRIBUTOR/COUNTRY	KINEMATOGRAPH WEEKLY REVIEW
24/4/50	*Beautiful Blonde from Bashful Bend*	20th Century-Fox/USA	15/12/49
25/9/50	*The Black Rose*	20th Century-Fox/UK	13/7/50
19/6/50	*The Boy with the Green Hair*	RKO-Radio/USA	8/6/50
2/10/50	*Broken Arrow*	20th Century-Fox/USA	20/7/50
13/3/50	*Buccaneer's Girl*	GFD/USA	26/1/50
5/6/50	*Canadian Pacific*	20th Century-Fox/USA	13/4/50
Rel. floating	*The Cariboo Trail*	20th Century-Fox/USA	21/9/50
6/3/50	*Challenge to Lassie*	MGM/USA	26/1/50
26/6/50	*Cheaper by the Dozen*	20th Century-Fox/USA	20/4/50
11/12/50	*Colt. 45*	Warner/USA	10/8/50
17/7/50	*Comanche Territory*	GFD/USA	15/6/50
3/4/50	*Copper Canyon*	Paramount/USA	2/2/50
Rel. floating	*Dakota Lil*	20th Century-Fox/USA	21/9/50
22/5/50	*Dancing in the Dark*	20th Century-Fox/USA	16/5/50
4/9/50	*The Dancing Years*	AB-Pathé/UK	13/4/50
Rel. floating	*Death Valley*	Exclusive/USA	2/3/50
22/1/51	*The Desert Hawk*	GFD/USA	5/10/50
26/9/50	*Destination Moon*	GFD/USA	17/8/50
2/12/49	*Die Fledermaus* Agfacolor	Archway/Gmy	8/12/49
19/6/50	*Double Crossbones*	GFD/USA	18/5/50
Rel. floating	*Drums for a Holiday* (short)	British Lion/UK	26/1/50
11/9/50	*Duchess of Idaho*	MGM/USA	17/8/50
31/7/50	*The Eagle and the Hawk*	Paramount/USA	18/5/50
1/1/51	*The Elusive Pimpernel*	British Lion/UK	9/11/50
4/9/50	*Fancy Pants*	Paramount/USA	27/7/50
12/2/51	*Fighting Man of the Plains*	20th Century-Fox/USA	14/9/50
12/2/51	*The Flame and the Arrow*	Warner/USA	9/11/50
4/12/50	*Frenchie*	GFD/USA	16/11/50

RELEASE DATE	TITLE	DISTRIBUTOR/COUNTRY	*KINEMATOGRAPH WEEKLY* REVIEW
6/11/50	*Gone to Earth*	British Lion/UK	28/9/50
25/9/50	*High Lonesome*	GFD/USA	17/8/50
25/9/50	*Hills of the Brave*	Columbia/USA	1/6/50
8/1/51	*If You Feel Like Singing*	MGM/USA	2/11/50
27/3/50	*It's a Great Feeling*	Warner/USA	9/2/50
13/2/50	*Jolson Sings Again*	Columbia/USA	13/12/49
18/12/50	*Let's Dance*	Paramount/USA	17/8/50
2/10/50	*Man from Nevada*	Columbia/USA	1/6/50
11/12/50	*The Man on the Eiffel Tower*	British Lion-Independent/USA	23/11/50
17/4/50	*Mickey*	AB-Pathé/USA	30/3/50
2/7/50	*Montana*	Warner/USA	27/4/50
Rel. immediate	*Monmartre* (short)	ABFD/UK	20/7/50
6/11/50	*My Blue Heaven*	20th Century-Fox/USA	21/9/50
11/9/50	*Nancy Goes to Rio*	MGM/USA	24/8/50
13/3/50	*Neptune's Daughter*	MGM/USA	22/12/49
20/2/50	*Northwest Stampede*	AB-Pathé/USA	2/2/50
15/5/50	*Oh, You Beautiful Doll*	20th Century-Fox/USA	30/3/50
14/8/50	*On the Town*	MGM/USA	22/2/50
3/7/50	*One Sunday Afternoon*	Warner/USA	4/5/50
30/10/50	*The Outriders*	MGM/USA	21/9/50
28/8/50	*Peggy*	GFD/USA	13/7/50
Rel. floating	*Perilous Crossing* Technicolor	New Realm/Swed	22/12/49
8/5/50	*Pride of Kentucky*	Warner/USA	16/3/50
11/6/51	*Return of the Frontiersman*	Warner/USA	2/11/50
11/11/50	*Rogues of Sherwood Forest*	Columbia/USA	17/8/50
7/8/50	*Roll, Thunder Roll!*	AB-Pathé/USA	4/5/50
2/10/50	*Saddle Tramp*	GFD/USA	14/9/50
20/2/50	*Sand*	20th Century-Fox/USA	8/12/50

RELEASE DATE	TITLE	DISTRIBUTOR/COUNTRY	*KINEMATOGRAPH WEEKLY* REVIEW
8/5/50	*She Wore a Yellow Ribbon*	RKO-Radio/USA	12/1/50
Rel. not fixed	*The Singing Smuggler* Agfacolor	Five Ocean Films/Fr	12/1/50
8/5/50	*South of St Louis*	Warner/USA	16/2/50
Rel. floating	*Take the Stage*	Eros/USA	19/1/50
Rel. floating	*Texas Kid, Outlaw*	Eros/USA	14/9/50
18/12/50	*Three Little Words*	MGM/USA	14/9/50
July 1950	*A Ticket to Tomahawk*	20th Century-Fox/USA	1/6/50
31/7/50	*Treasure Island*	RKO-Radio/UK	8/6/50
8/1/50	*Tripoli*	Paramount/USA	9/11/50
29/1/51	*Two Weeks with Love*	MGM/USA	9/11/50
Rel. floating	*Unknown Island*	International/USA	25/5/50
Rel. floating	*The Vatican* (short)	Columbia/UK	17/8/50
12/7/50	*Wabash Avenue*	20th Century-Fox/USA	20/4/50
11/9/50	*The White Tower*	RKO-Radio/USA	17/8/50
20/11/50	*Wyoming Mail*	GFD/USA	9/11/50
Rel. not fixed	*Yes, Sir, That's My Baby*	GFD/USA	2/2/50
6/3/50	*You're My Everything*	20th Century-Fox/USA	15/12/49
Rel. floating Reissue	*Blanche Fury*	ABFD/UK	13/7/50
Rel. floating Reissue	*Dr Cyclops*	Paramount/USA	17/8/50
23/10/50 Reissue	*The Forest Rangers*	Paramount/USA	17/8/50
Rel. floating Reissue	*Hello, Frisco, Hello*	20th Century-Fox/USA	26/1/50
10/7/50 Reissue	*North-West Mounted Police*	Paramount/USA	29/6/50
22/10/51	*Across the Wide Missouri*	MGM/USA	4/10/51
14/5/51	*Al Jennings of Oklahoma*	Columbia/USA	5/4/51
6/8/51	*Alice in Wonderland*	RKO-Radio/USA	12/4/51
22/10/51	*An American in Paris*	MGM/USA	16/8/51

RELEASE DATE	TITLE	DISTRIBUTOR/COUNTRY	KINEMATOGRAPH WEEKLY REVIEW
18/2/51	Anne of the Indies	20th Century-Fox/USA	18/10/51
9/7/51	Apache Drums	GFD/USA	7/6/51
5/3/51	Battle of Powder River	GFD/USA	25/1/51
6/8/51	Bird of Paradise	20th Century-Fox/USA	7/6/51
29/10/51	Blue Grass of Kentucky	AB-Pathé/USA	21/7/51
26/2/51	Branded	Paramount/USA	7/12/51
2/7/51	Call Me Mister	20th Century-Fox/USA	26/4/51
1/10/51	Captain Horatio Hornblower R N	Warner/UK	12/4/51
30/7/51	Cattle Drive	GFD/USA	28/6/51
19/11/51	Cave of Outlaws	GFD/USA	8/11/51
8/10/51	Chicago Masquerade	GFD/USA	2/8/51
14/5/51	Cinderella	RKO-Radio/USA	21/12/51
17/12/51	County Fair	AB-Pathé/USA	27/9/51
15/10/51	Crosswinds	Paramount/USA	23/8/51
17/12/51	Curley	Eros/?	8/2/51
3/12/51	Dallas	Warner/USA	23/8/51
Rel. floating	Daughter of the West	International/USA	12/7/51
24/12/51	David and Bathsheba	20th Century-Fox/USA	6/9/51
Rel. floating	Dollars to Spend	Butcher's/UK	27/9/51
16/7/51	Excuse my Dust	MGM/USA	21/6/51
28/5/51	The Fighting Redhead	AB-Pathé/USA	8/3/51
12/11/51	Flaming Feather	Paramount/USA	18/10/51
22/10/51	Flying Leathernecks	RKO-Radio/USA	27/9/51
24/9/51	The Golden Horde	GFD/USA	16/8/51
15/11/51	Golden Stallion	Republic/USA	18/10/51
2/4/51	The Great Missouri Raid	Paramount/USA	1/2/51
24/9/51	Half Angel	20th Century-Fox/USA	5/7/51
7/5/51	Halls of Montezuma	20th Century-Fox/USA	8/3/51
Rel. floating	Happy Go Lovely	AB-Pathé/UK	8/3/51

RELEASE DATE	TITLE	DISTRIBUTOR/COUNTRY	KINEMATOGRAPH WEEKLY REVIEW
21/5/51	*High Venture*	Paramount/USA	17/5/51
10/12/51	*High Vermilion*	Paramount/USA	22/11/51
Rel. floating	*Honeychile*	Republic/USA	27/9/51
11/1/52	*House in the Square*	20th Century-Fox/UK	11/10/51
29/1/51	*I Shall Return*	20th Century-Fox/USA	14/12/51
23/7/51	*I'd Climb the Highest Mountain*	20th Century-Fox/USA	24/5/51
19/2/51	*I'll Get By*	20th Century-Fox/USA	14/12/51
Rel. immediate	*In the Forest*	Carlyle/Canadian	12/4/51
26/2/51	*Kansas Raiders*	GFD/USA	1/2/51
5/3/51	*Kim*	MGM/USA	18/1/51
26/3/51	*King Solomon's Mines*	MGM/USA	7/12/50
3/12/51	*The Lady from Texas*	GFD/USA	8/11/51
5/2/51	*Last of the Buchaneers*	Columbia/USA	7/12/50
13/8/51	*Lorna Doone*	Columbia/USA	26/7/51
6/8/51	*Lost Stage Valley*	Columbia/USA	5/7/51
31/12/51	*Lullaby of Broadway*	Warner/USA	27/9/51
19/9/51	*The Magic Box*	British Lion/UK	20/9/51
5/11/51	*Mark of the Renegade*	GFD/USA	11/10/51
26/11/51	*Mask of the Avenger*	Columbia/USA	20/9/51
10/12/51	*Meet me after the Show*	20th Century-Fox/USA	30/8/51
30/7/51	*On the Riviera*	20th Century-Fox/USA	31/5/51
30/4/51	*Pagan Love Song*	MGM/USA	5/4/51
25/6/51	*The Painted Hills*	MGM/USA	31/5/51
5/3/51	*Pandora and the Flying Dutchman*	British Lion-Independent/UK	1/2/51
Rel. floating	*Prehistoric Women* Cinecolor	Eros/USA	21/6/51
27/8/51	*The Prince Who Was A Thief*	GFD/USA	12/7/51
Rel. floating	*Quebec*	Paramount/USA	29/3/51
3/9/51	*Red Mountain*	Paramount/USA	19/7/51

RELEASE DATE	TITLE	DISTRIBUTOR/COUNTRY	KINEMATOGRAPH WEEKLY REVIEW
5/3/51	*Red Stallion in the Rockies*	AB-Pathé/USA	22/2/51
26/3/51	*Samson and Delilah*	Paramount/USA	21/12/50
1/10/51	*Sante Fe*	Columbia/USA	16/8/51
24/9/51	*Showboat*	MGM/USA	7/6/51
Rel. floating	*Sinister House*	Eros/USA	15/11/51
7/5/51	*Smuggler's Island*	GFD/USA	12/4/51
Rel. immediate	*Sugarfoot*	Warner/USA	2/8/51
10/12/51	*The Sword of Monte Cristo*	20th Century-Fox/USA	6/9/51
Rel. immediate	*Tale of Siberia*	Concorde/USSR	23/8/51
26/11/51	*The Tales of Hoffmann*	British Lion/UK	26/4/51
14/5/51	*Tea for Two*	Warner/USA	7/12/50
3/12/51	*Texas Carnival*	MGM/USA	4/10/51
9/7/51	*There is Another Sun*	Butchers/USA	5/4/51
3/4/51	*Thunder in the Dust*	Eros/USA	15/3/51
18/6/51	*Toast of New Orleans*	MGM/USA	28/12/51
22/12/50	*Transcontinent Express*	Republic/USA	21/12/50
8/10/51	*Valentino*	Columbia/USA	30/8/51
9/4/51	*Vengeance Valley*	MGM/USA	8/3/51
7/5/51	*Wedding Bells*	MGM/USA	8/3/51
12/11/51	*When the Redskins Rode*	Columbia/USA	27/9/51
15/10/51	*When Worlds Collide*	Paramount/USA	23/8/51
7/1/52	*Where No Vultures Fly*	GFD/UK	8/11/51
25/6/51	*You Belong to My Heart*	MGM/USA	14/6/51
2/7/51 Reissue	*Aloma of the South Seas*	Paramount/USA	26/4/51
Rel. floating Reissue	*Arabian Nights*	Eros/USA	15/2/51
4/6/51 Reissue	*Dixie*	Paramount/USA	2/8/51
Rel. floating Reissue	*The Jolson Story*	Columbia/USA	18/1/51

RELEASE DATE	TITLE	DISTRIBUTOR/COUNTRY	*KINEMATOGRAPH WEEKLY* REVIEW
7/5/51 Reissue	*Reap the Wild Wind*	Paramount/USA	3/5/51
30/7/51 Reissue	*The Story of Dr Wassel*	Paramount/USA	31/5/51
3/11/52	*About Face*	Warner/USA	9/10/52
10/3/52	*The African Queen*	British Lion/Independent FD/UK	10/1/52
16/2/52	*Against all Flags*	GFD/USA	23/10/52
29/12/52	*Aladdin and His Lamp*	AB-Pathé/USA	12/6/52
26/5/52	*The Barefoot Mailman*	Columbia/USA	14/2/52
2/6/52	*The Battle at Apache Pass*	GFD/USA	8/5/52
29/12/52	*Because You're Mine*	MGM/USA	30/10/52
21/4/52	*The Belle of New York*	MGM/USA	28/2/52
26/5/52	*Belles on their Toes*	20th Century-Fox/USA	10/4/52
7/1/52	*Best of the Badmen*	RKO-Radio/USA	6/12/52
26/10/52	*The Big Top* (short) Sovcolor	Continental Concorde/USSR	14/8/52
31/3/52	*The Big Trees*	Warner/USA	6/3/52
29/12/52	*Bloodhounds of Broadway*	20th Century-Fox/USA	27/11/52
21/1/52	*The Blue Blood*	AB-Pathé/USA	20/12/51
25/8/52	*Brave People* Agfacolor	Continental Concorde/USSR	12/6/52
13/10/52	*Brave Warrior*	Columbia/USA	10/7/52
20/10/52	*The Brigand*	Columbia/USA	17/7/52
19/5/52	*Bronco Buster*	GFD/USA	8/5/52
2/6/52	*Bugles in the Afternoon*	Warner/USA	10/4/52
8/9/52	*Californian Conquest*	Columbia/USA	12/6/52
Rel. floating	*Call of the Land* (short)	Exclusive/UK	22/5/52
22/9/52	*Captain Blood, Fugitive*	Columbia/USA	17/7/52
Rel. floating	*Captain Scarlett*	United Artists/USA	21/8/52
3/11/52	*Carson City*	Warner/USA	4/9/52

RELEASE DATE	TITLE	DISTRIBUTOR/COUNTRY	KINEMATOGRAPH WEEKLY REVIEW
28/1/52	Cavalry Scout	AB-Pathé/USA	13/12/51
23/2/53	The Crimson Pirate	Warner/UK	6/11/52
2/6/52	Denver and Rio Grande	Paramount/USA	24/4/52
21/4/52	Distant Drums	Warner/USA	13/3/52
16/6/52	Down Among the Sheltering Palms	20th Century-Fox/USA	10/4/52
13/10/52	Drums in the Deep South	RKO-Radio/USA	25/9/52
8/9/52	The Duel at Silver Creek	GFD/USA	21/8/52
20/7/52	The Fall of Berlin Agfacolor	Continentale Concorde/USSR	8/5/52
24/11/52	Father's Doing Fine	AB-Pathé/UK	21/8/52
11/2/52	Flame of Araby	GFD/USA	17/1/52
2/6/52	Flight to Mars	AB-Pathé/USA	27/3/52
15/5/52	Fort Defiance	United Artists/USA	15/5/52
25/8/52	Fort Osage	AB-Pathé/USA	19/6/52
7/4/52	Fort Worth	Warner/USA	6/3/52
17/3/52	Golden Girl	20th Century-Fox/USA	6/12/51
17/11/52	The Golden Hawk	Columbia/USA	24/7/52
7/4/52	The Greatest Show on Earth	Paramount/USA	17/1/52
7/7/52	The Half Breed	RKO-Radio/USA	12/6/52
23/6/52	Has Anybody Seen My Girl	GFD/USA	12/6/52
16/6/52	The Highwayman	AB-Pathé/USA	20/3/52
11/2/52	Hong Kong	Paramount/USA	24/1/52
17/11/52	Horizons West	GFD/USA	16/10/52
24/3/52	Hurricane Island	Columbia/USA	14/2/52
1/9/52	The Importance of Being Earnest	GFD/UK	12/6/52
1/9/52	Indian Uprising	Columbia/USA	24/7/52
16/3/52	The Iron Mistress	Warner/USA	6/11/52
24/11/52	It Started in Paradise	GFD/UK	16/10/52
8/9/52	Ivanhoe	MGM/UK	12/6/52

RELEASE DATE	TITLE	DISTRIBUTOR/COUNTRY	*KINEMATOGRAPH WEEKLY* REVIEW
5/1/53	*Jack and the Beanstalk*	Warner/USA	30/10/52
Rel. not fixed	*Johnny Lion-Heart*	Regent/?	1/5/52
29/9/52	*Just For You*	Paramount/USA	14/8/52
4/8/52	*Kangaroo*	20th Century-Fox/USA	12/6/52
26/1/53	*The Lion and the Horse*	Warner/USA	6/11/52
20/10/52	*Lovely to Look at*	MGM/USA	3/7/52
13/10/52	*Lure of the Wilderness*	20th Century-Fox/USA	21/8/52
21//52	*Lydia Bailey*	20th Century-Fox/USA	10/4/52
22/12/52	*Made in Heaven*	GFD/UK	13/11/52
14/4/52	*The Magic Carpet*	Columbia/USA	6/3/52
12/5/52	*Marshmallow Moon*	Paramount/USA	15/5/52
6/10/52	*Meet Me Tonight*	GFD/UK	11/9/52
17/11/52	*The Merry Widow*	MGM/USA	28/8/52
27/4/52	*Michurin* Agfacolor	Continental Concorde/USSR	22/5/52
22/9/52	*Montana Territory*	Columbia/USA	24/7/52
Rel. floating	*Mutiny*	United Artists/USA	28/8/52
Rel. floating	*New Mexico*	United Artists/USA	26/6/52
7/4/52	*On Moonlight Bay*	Warner/USA	24/1/2
18/8/52	*The Outcast*	Columbia/USA	26/6/52
25/2/52	*Painting the Clouds with Sunshine*	Warner/USA	20/12/51
18/8/52	*Penny Princess*	GFD/UK	10/7/52
21/7/52	*The Quiet Man*	Republic/USA	1/5/52
Rel. not fixed	*Quo Vadis*	MGM/USA	31/1/52
10/11/52	*The Raiders*	GFD/USA	30/10/52
15/9/52	*Rainbow 'Round My Shoulder*	Columbia/USA	28/8/52
12/5/52	*Rancho Notorious*	RKO-Radio/USA	3/4/52
7/4/52	*Red Skies of Montana*	20th Century-Fox/USA	7/2/52
24/4/52	*The River*	United Artists/UK	1/5/52

RELEASE DATE	TITLE	DISTRIBUTOR/COUNTRY	*KINEMATOGRAPH WEEKLY* REVIEW
14/4/52	*Robin Hood and his Merrie Men*	RKO-Radio/UK	13/3/52
Rel. immediate	*The Rose of Baghdad* Technicolor	Grand Natonal/UK/Italy	25/9/52
1/12/52	*Rose of Cimarron*	20th Century-Fox/USA	23/10/52
18/2/52	*Royal Journey*	GFD/UK (Canada)	10/1/52
21/4/52	*Saturday Island*	RKO-Radio/UK	6/3/52
1/12/52	*The Savage*	Paramount/USA	11/9/52
10/3/52	*Savage Splendour*	RKO-Radio/USA	21/2/52
22/9/52	*Scaramouche*	MGM/USA	10/7/52
21/7/52	*Scarlet Angel*	GFD/USA	19/6/52
26/1/53	*She's Working Her Way Through College*	Warner/USA	16/10/52
5/5/52	*Singin' in the Rain*	MGM/USA	3/4/52
28/7/52	*Skirts Ahoy!*	MGM/USA	15/5/52
1/9/52	*Slaughter Trail*	RKO-Radio/USA	31/7/52
9/2/52	*The Snows of Kilimanjaro*	20th Century-Fox/USA	16/10/52
2/1/52	*Somebody Loves Me*	Paramount/USA	20/11/52
27/10/52	*Son of Ali Baba*	GFD/USA	4/9/52
8/9/52	*Son of Paleface*	Paramount/USA	24/7/52
10/3/52	*Sons of the Musketeers*	RKO-Radio/USA	21/2/52
11/8/52	*Sound Off*	Columbia/USA	17/7/52
30/3/52	*South of Algiers*	AB-Pathé/UK	30/3/52
24/3/52	*Steel Town*	GFD/USA	21/2/52
29/9/52	*The Story of Will Rogers*	Warner/USA	28/8/52
17/3/52	*Sunny Side of the Street*	Columbia/USA	14/2/52
25/2/52	*Take Care of My Little Girl*	20th Century-Fox/USA	13/12/51
7/4/52	*Ten Tall Men*	Columbia/USA	10/1/52
4/8/52	*Thief of Damascus*	Columbia/USA	29/5/52
January 1953	*Three for Bedroom C*	International/USA	23/10/52
11/2/52	*The Treasure of Lost Canyon*	GFD/USA	24/1/52

RELEASE DATE	TITLE	DISTRIBUTOR/COUNTRY	*KINEMATOGRAPH WEEKLY* REVIEW
27/10/52	*24 Hours in a Woman's Life*	AB-Pathé/UK	21/8/52
4/2/52	*Two Tickets to Broadway*	RKO-Radio/USA	10/1/52
18/8/52	*Untamed Frontier*	GFD/USA	3/7/52
5/1/53	*Wagons West*	AB-Pathé/USA	6/11/52
14/7/52	*Wait 'Til the Sun Shines Nellie*	20th Century-Fox/USA	5/6/52
10/3/52	*Warpath*	Paramount/USA	21/2/52
14/4/52	*Where the River Bends*	GFD/USA	6/3/52
29/9/52	*Where's Charley?*	Warner/USA	26/6/52
31/3/52	*The Wild North*	MGM/USA	24/1/52
6/10/52	*Wild Stallion*	AB-Pathé/USA	21/8/52
19/5/52	*With a Song in My Heart*	20th Century-Fox/USA	28/2/52
17/11/52	*Woman of the North Country*	Republic/USA	6/11/52
15/9/52	*The World in His Arms*	GFD/USA	10/7/52
15/12/52	*Yankee Buccaneer*	GFD/USA	20/11/52
Rel. floating Reissue	*Dumbo*	RKO-Radio/USA	8/5/52
Rel. floating Reissue	*Phantom of the Opera*	Eros/USA	6/3/52
Rel. floating Reissue	*To the Shores of Tripoli*	20th Century-Fox/USA	12/6/52
Rel. floating Reissue	*Trail of the Lonesome Pine*	Eros/USA	14/8/52
Rel. floating Reissue	*Wonder Man*	RKO-Radio/USA	1/5/52
17/8/53	*Abbott and Costello meet Captain Kidd*	Warner/USA	30/4/53
23/3/53	*All Ashore*	Columbia/USA	5/3/53
14/9/53	*Ambush at Tomahawk Gap*	Columbia/USA	27/8/53
6/4/53	*April in Paris*	Warner/USA	12/2/53
Rel. floating	*Babes in Bagdad*	United Artists/USA	1/1/53
30/11/53	*Back to God's Country*	GFD/USA	22/10/53
1/3/54	*The Band Wagon*	MGM/USA	12/11/53

RELEASE DATE	TITLE	DISTRIBUTOR/COUNTRY	KINEMATOGRAPH WEEKLY REVIEW
5/10/53	*The Beggar's Opera*	British Lion/UK	11/6/53
9/3/53	*Blackbeard the Pirate*	RKO-Radio/USA	12/2/53
12/1/53	*The Blazing Forest*	Paramount/USA	11/12/53
26/1/53	*Botany Bay*	Paramount/USA	1/1/53
14/9/53	*By the Light of the Silvery Moon*	Warner/USA	9/7/53
21/9/53	*Call Me Madam*	20th Century-Fox/USA	21/5/53
23/2/53	*Caribbean Gold*	Paramount/USA	18/12/53
13/7/53	*The Cimarron Kid*	GFD/USA	7/5/53
25/5/53	*City Beneath the Sea*	GFD/USA	2/4/53
2/11/53	*City of Bad Men*	20th Century-Fox/USA	17/9/53
21/12/53	*Column South*	GFD/USA	15/10/53
Rel. immediate	*The Composer Glinka/ Glinka (Man of Music)* Sovcolor	Gala/USSR	15/10/53
5/1/54	*Conquest of Cochise*	Columbia/USA	26/11/53
30/11/53	*The Conquest of Everest*	British Lion/UK	29/10/53
26/1/53	*Cripple Creek*	Columbia/USA	18/12/52
3/8/53	*Cruisin' Down the River*	Columbia/USA	9/7/53
14/12/53	*Dangerous When Wet*	MGM/USA	3/9/53
16/2/53	*Decameron Nights*	Eros/UK	26/3/53
20/4/53	*Desert Legion*	GFD/USA	26/3/53
27/4/53	*Destination Gobi*	20th Century-Fox/USA	9/4/53
31/8/53	*Eagles of the Fleet*	AB-Pathé/USA	16/7/53
5/10/53	*East of Sumatra*	GFD/USA	17/9/53
8/6/53	*Elizabeth is Queen* Warnercolor	AB-Pathé/UK	11/6/53
January 1953	*The Emperor's Nightingale* Technicolor from Agfacolor original	Bond/Czech	5/2/53
25/5/53	*Everything I Have is Yours*	MGM/USA	4/12/52
22/6/53	*Fair Wind to Java*	Republic/USA	21/5/53
29/6/53	*The Farmer Takes a Wife*	20th Century-Fox/USA	14/5/53

RELEASE DATE	TITLE	DISTRIBUTOR/COUNTRY	KINEMATOGRAPH WEEKLY REVIEW
5/10/53	*Flame of Calcutta*	Columbia/USA	6/8/53
14/12/53	*Flight to Tangier*	Paramount/USA	26/11/53
28/12/53	*Fort Vengeance*	AB-Pathé/USA	18/6/53
Rel. immediate	*Gala Festival* Sovcolor	Gala/USSR	18/12/53
24/8/53	*Genevieve*	GFD/USA	28/5/53
7/12/53	*The Girl Next Door*	20th Century-Fox/USA	22/10/53
Rel. not fixed	*The Girls of Pleasure Island*	Paramount/USA	4/6/53
2/11/53	*The Great Sioux Uprising*	GFD/USA	15/10/53
Rel. floating	*Gun Belt*	United Artists/USA	29/10/53
13/7/53	*Gunsmoke*	GFD/USA	21/5/53
17/8/53	*Hans Christian Anderson*	RKO-Radio/USA	25/12/52
16/3/53	*Hangman's Knot*	Columbia/USA	5/3/53
21/12/53	*Here Come the Girls*	Paramount/USA	20/8/53
3/8/53	*Hiawatha*	AB-Pathé/USA	14/5/53
Rel. not fixed	*Himalayan Epic*	Films de France	26/11/53
11/1/54	*Houdini*	Paramount/USA	5/11/53
23/3/53	*Hurricane Smith*	Paramount/USA	12/3/53
4/5/53	*The 'I Don't Care' Girl*	20th Century-Fox/USA	12/2/53
29/6/53	*I Love Melvin*	MGM/USA	5/3/53
16/11/53	*Isn't Life Wonderful?*	AB-Pathé/USA	4/6/53
20/4/53	*Jack McCall Desperado*	Columbia/USA	12/3/53
20/7/53	*Jamaica Inn*	Paramount/USA	11/6/53
Rel. floating	*Jungle Headhunters*	RKO-Radio/USA	30/7/53
4/1/54	*Kansas Pacific*	AB-Pathé/USA	24/9/53
Rel. immediate	*A Kingdom on the Waters*	G & S/Hungarian	23/4/53
16/8/53	*The Lady Wants Mink*	Republic/USA	27/8/53
7/12/53	*Latin Lovers*	MGM/USA	15/10/53
19/10/53	*Laughing Anne*	Republic/UK	10/9/53

RELEASE DATE	TITLE	DISTRIBUTOR/COUNTRY	*KINEMATOGRAPH WEEKLY* REVIEW
14/9/53	*Law and Order*	GFD/USA	6/8/53
5/1/53	*The Lawless Breed*	GFD/USA	18/12/52
14/9/53	*Let's Do It Again*	Columbia/USA	6/8/53
31/8/53	*Lili*	MGM/USA	12/3/53
9/11/53	*The Lone Hand*	GFD/USA	7/5/53
10/8/53	*Macdonald of the Canadian Mounties*	20th Century-Fox/USA	14/5/53
6/7/53	*The Man Behind the Gun*	Warner/USA	26/2/53
16/11/53	*The Man from the Alamo*	GFD/USA	24/9/53
26/1/53	*The Man Who Watched Trains Go By*	Eros/UK	11/12/52
23/2/53	*Marching Along*	20th Century-Fox/USA	25/12/52
19/10/53	*The Master of Ballantrae*	Warner/UK	9/7/53
22/6/53	*Meet Me at the Fair*	GFD/USA	28/5/53
12/10/53	*Melba*	United Artists/UK	3/9/53
27/4/53	*The Miracle of Fatima*	Warner/USA	26/2/53
30/3/53	*Mississippi Gambler*	GFD/USA	29/1/53
4/1/54	*Mogambo*	MGM/USA	29/10/53
Rel. immediate	*Monsoon* Technicolor	Grand National/India	26/3/53
19/1/53	*Montana Belle*	RKO-Radio/USA	25/12/52
5/10/53	*Moulin Rouge*	Independent/USA	12/3/53
Rel. immediate	*Moussorgsky* Sovcolor	Gala/USSR	12/3/53
11/5/53	*The Naked Spur*	MGM/USA	12/2/53
11/5/53	*Niagara*	20th Century-Fox/USA	26/2/53
19/1/53	*The One-Piece Bathing Suit*	MGM/USA	11/12/52
Rel.floating	*Outlaw Women* Cinecolor	Exclusive/USA	16/4/53
30/3/53	*The Pathfinder*	Columbia/USA	5/3/53
20/7/53	*Peter Pan*	RKO-Radio/USA	26/3/53
9/3/53	*Plymouth Adventure*	MGM/USA	18/12/52

RELEASE DATE	TITLE	DISTRIBUTOR/COUNTRY	*KINEMATOGRAPH WEEKLY* REVIEW
Rel. floating	*Pony Express*	Paramount/USA	3/9/53
7/9/53	*Powder River*	20th Century-Fox/USA	25/6/53
20/7/53	*Prince of Pirates*	Columbia/USA	28/5/53
9/2/53	*The Prisoner of Zenda*	MGM/USA	11/12/52
8/6/53	*A Queen is Crowned*	GFD/UK	11/6/53
29/6/53	*Raiders of the Seven Seas*	United Artists/USA	4/6/53
28/9/53	*The Red Beret*	Columbia/USA	20/8/53
9/2/53	*The Redhead from Wyoming*	GFD/USA	29/1/53
Rel. immediate	*The Return of Rin Tin Tin*	Grand National/USA	11/12/52
19/10/53	*Return to Paradise*	United Artists/USA	10/9/53
11/5/53	*Ride the Man Down*	Republic/USA	16/4/53
23/11/53	*Ride, Vaquero!*	MGM/USA	27/8/53
29/12/52	*Road to Bali*	Paramount/USA	4/12/52
11/1/54	*Rob Roy*	RKO-Radio-Disney/UK	29/10/53
Rel. not fixed	*The Robe*	20th Century-Fox/USA	26/11/53
27/4/53	*Rodeo*	AB-Pathé/USA	26/3/53
16/3/53	*Rose Bowl Story*	AB-Pathé/USA	5/2/53
14/12/53	*The Sabre and the Arrow*	Columbia/USA	9/7/53
7/9/53	*Salome*	Columbia/USA	18/6/53
26/10/53	*Scandal at Scourie*	MGM/USA	4/6/53
25/5/53	*Sea Devils*	RKO-Radio/UK	2/4/53
30/11/53	*Second Chance*	RKO-Radio/USA	29/10/53
18/5/53	*Seminole*	GFD/USA	9/4/53
14/12/53	*Serpent on the Nile*	Columbia/USA	12/11/53
26/10/53	*Shane*	Paramount/USA	23/7/53
17/8/53	*She's Back on Broadway*	Warner/USA	16/7/53
16/11/53	*Siren of Bagdad*	Columbia/USA	6/8/53
21/12/53	*Slaves of Babylon*	Columbia/USA	12/11/53
22/6/53	*Small Town Girl*	MGM/USA	19/3/53

RELEASE DATE	TITLE	DISTRIBUTOR/COUNTRY	*KINEMATOGRAPH WEEKLY* REVIEW
12/10/53	*Sombrero*	MGM/USA	4/6/53
28/12/53	*Spring on Ice* Agfacolor	Gala/Austria	5/11/53
16/3/53	*Speingfield Rifle*	Warner/USA	22/1/53
1/6/53	*The Stars are Singing*	Paramount/USA	19/2/53
29/6/53	*Stop, You're Killing Me*	Warner/USA	26/3/53
7/9/53	*The Story of Gilbert and Sullivan*	British Lion/UK	14/5/53
18/5/53	*The Story of Three Loves*	MGM/USA	5/3/53
26/10/53	*The Sword and the Rose*	RKO-Radio/UK	20/8/53
5/10/53	*Take Me to Town*	GFD/USA	11/6/53
14/12/53	*Those Redheads from Seattle*	Paramount/USA	26/11/53
3/8/53	*Thunder Bay*	GFD/USA	18/6/53
6/4/53	*The Titfield Thunderbolt*	GFD/UK	12/3/53
27/4/53	*Tonight We Sing*	20th Century-Fox/USA	26/2/53
2/3/53	*Toughest Man in Arizona*	Republic/USA	22/1/53
13/4/53	*Treasure of the Golden Condor*	20th Century-Fox/USA	5/2/53
15/6/53	*Tropic Zone*	Paramount/USA	21/5/53
17/8/53	*The Vanquished*	Paramount/USA	18/6/53
30/11/53	*The Veils of Bagdad*	GFD/USA	22/10/53
2/11/53	*Walking My Baby Back Home*	GFD/USA	15/10/53
4/5/53	*The War of the Worlds*	Paramount/USA	26/3/53
24/8/53	*Way of a Gaucho*	20th Century-Fox/USA	14/5/53
5/1/53	*What Price Glory*	20th Century-Fox/USA	4/12/53
12/10/53	*White Witch Doctor*	20th Century-Fox/USA	23/7/53
24/8/53	*Will Any Gentleman?*	AB-Pathé/UK	21/5/53
4/1/54	*Wings of the Hawk*	GFD/USA	19/11/53
10/8/53	*Young Bess*	MGM/USA	21/5/53
Rel. floating Reissue	*Duel in the Sun*	Eros/USA	26/11/53
Rel. floating Reissue	*Her Jungle Love*	Eros/USA	13/8/53

RELEASE DATE	TITLE	DISTRIBUTOR/COUNTRY	*KINEMATOGRAPH WEEKLY* REVIEW
Rel. floating Reissue	*The Private Lives of Elizabeth and Essex*	Warner/USA	23/7/53
Rel. floating Reissue	*Savage Princess (Aan)* Technicolor	British Lion/India	27/8/53
12/4/53 Reissue	*Snow White and the Seven Dwarfs*	RKO-Radio/USA	22/10/53
Rel. floating Reissue	*Untamed*	Eros/USA	12/2/53
20/12/54	*Africa Adventure*	RKO-Radio-US	18/11/54
1/2/54	*All the Brothers were Valiant*	MGM/USA	10/12/53
Rel. floating	*Anna Cross* Agfacolor	Gala/USSR	21/10/54
20/9/53	*Appointment in Honduras*	RKO-Radio/USA	20/12/53
17/5/54	*Arena*	MGM/USA	28/1/54
17/1/55	*Armand and Michaela Denis Under the Southern Cross*	GFD/UK	23/12/54
22/11/54	*Arrow in the Dust*	AB-Pathé/USA	14/10/54
11/1/54	*Arrowhead*	Paramount/USA	3/12/54
20/12/54	*Athena*	MGM/USA	16/12/54
3/1/54	*The Barefoot Contessa*	United Artists/USA	11/11/54
19/7/54	*Battle of the Rogue River*	Columbia/USA	1/7/54
13/9/54	*The Beachcomber*	GFD/UK	5/8/54
31/5/54	*Beachhead*	United Artists/USA	6/5/54
20/12/54	*Beau Brummell*	MGM/UK	18/11/54
23/8/54	*Below the Sahara*	RKO-Radio/USA	17/6/54
12/4/54	*Beneath the 12-Mile Reef*	20th Century-Fox/USA	4/3/54
20/9/54	*Betrayed*	MGM/USA	12/8/54
6/9/54	*Black Horse Canyon*	GFD/USA	19/8/54
20/9/54	*The Black Knight*	Columbia/UK	26/8/54
8/11/54	*The Black Shield of Falworth*	GFD/USA	2/9/54
Rel. floating	*The Blakes Slept Here* (short?)	New Realm/UK	27/5/54
Rel. floating	*Bongolo and the Black Princess* Gevacolor	Astarte/Belgium	23/9/54

RELEASE DATE	TITLE	DISTRIBUTOR/COUNTRY	*KINEMATOGRAPH WEEKLY* REVIEW
22/2/54	*Border River*	GFD/USA	11/2/54
13/12/54	*The Bounty Hunter*	Warner/USA	21/10/54
7/2/55	*The Bridges at Toko-Ri*	Paramount/USA	23/12/54
10/1/55	*Broken Lance*	20th Century-Fox/USA	23/9/54
1/11/54	*A Bullet is Waiting*	Columbia/USA	14/10/54
4/7/54	*Burning Arrows*	United Artists/USA	10/6/54
4/10/54	*The Caine Mutiny*	Columbia/USA	29/7/54
15/3/54	*Calamity Jane*	Warner/USA	14/1/54
12/7/54	*Camels West*	United Artists/USA	24/6/54
20/9/54	*Captain Kidd and the Slave Girl*	United Artists/USA	19/8/54
14/6/54	*Carnival Story*	RKO-Radio/USA	13/5/54
3/5/54	*Casanova's Big Night*	Paramount/USA	4/3/54
26/4/54	*Charge of the Lancers*	Columbia/USA	8/4/54
16/8/54	*The Command*	Warner/USA	8/4/54
Rel. floating	*Concert of Stars* (short) Sovcolor	Gala/USSR	31/12/53
28/6/54	*Crossed Swords*	United Artists/USA	17/6/54
23/8/54	*Dance Little Lady*	Renown/UK	1/7/54
28/6/54	*Dangerous Mission*	RKO-Radio/USA	3/6/54
25/10/54	*Dawn at Socorro*	GFD/USA	30/9/54
Oct 1954	*Demetrius and the Gladiators*	20th Century-Fox/USA	16/9/54
Rel. not fixed	*Devil's Canyon*	RKO-Radio/USA	17/12/54
23/8/54	*Dial M for Murder*	Warner/USA	22/7/54
31/5/54	*The Diamond Queen*	Warner/USA	13/5/54
26/4/54	*Doctor in the House*	GFD/UK	18/3/54
14/2/55	*Dragnet*	Warner/USA	4/11/54
6/3/54	*Drum Beat*	Warner/USA	30/12/54
27/9/54	*Drums Across the River*	GFD/USA	9/9/54
14/6/54	*Drums of Tahiti*	Columbia/USA	3/6/54

RELEASE DATE	TITLE	DISTRIBUTOR/COUNTRY	*KINEMATOGRAPH WEEKLY* REVIEW
6/9/54	*Duel in the Jungle*	AB-Pathé/UK	17/6/54
10/5/54	*Easy to Love*	MGM/USA	4/3/54
15/2/54	*The Eddie Cantor Story*	Warner/USA	28/1/54
28/2/54	*The Egyptian*	20th Century-Fox/USA	14/10/54
23/8/54	*Elephant Walk*	Paramount/USA	3/6/54
Rel. floating	*Emperor's Baker (The Return of the Golem)* Agfacolor	Gala/Czech	25/3/54
7/6/54	*Escape from Fort Bravo*	MGM/USA	4/3/54
30/8/54	*The Far Country*	GFD/USA	29/7/54
6/9/54	*Fighter Attack*	AB-Pathé/USA	29/7/54
3/5/54	*The 5,000 Fingers of Dr T*	Columbia/USA	15/4/54
8/11/54	*Flame and the Flesh*	MGM/USA	19/8/54
22/7/54	*Flame of Africa* Eastmancolor	United Artists/South Africa	22/7/54
7/6/54	*Flight of the White Heron*	20th Century-Fox/USA	10/6/54
10/1/55	*For Better, for Worse*	AB-Pathé/UK	30/9/54
6/6/54	*The Fortune Hunter*	Republic/USA	13/5/54
13/12/54	*Four Guns to the Border*	GFD/USA	2/12/54
24/5/54	*The French Line*	RKO-Radio/USA	29/4/54
15/11/54	*Garden of Evil*	20th Century-Fox/USA	16/9/54
Rel. floating	*Gate of Hell* Eastmancolor	London Films/Japan	10/6/54
28/6/54	*Give a Girl a Break*	MGM/USA	24/12/53
3/3/54	*The Glenn Miller Story*	GFD/USA	14/1/54
18/10/54	*Gog*	United Artists/USA	23/9/54
18/1/54	*The Golden Blade*	GFD/USA	3/12/54
Rel. floating	*The Golden Coach*	Films de France/Fr/It	17/12/53
6/12/54	*Golden Ivory*	AB-Pathé/UK	7/10/54
16/8/54	*Gorilla at Large*	20th Century-Fox/USA	27/5/54
18/1/54	*The Grace Moore Story*	Warner/USA	3/12/54

RELEASE DATE	TITLE	DISTRIBUTOR/COUNTRY	*KINEMATOGRAPH WEEKLY* REVIEW
29/4/54	*The Great Jesse James Raid*	Exclusive/USA	1/4/54
11/10/54	*Green Fire*	MGM/USA	30/12/54
15/3/54	*Gun Fury*	Columbia/USA	25/2/54
10/5/54	*Gypsy Colt*	MGM/USA	18/3/54
24/1/55	*Hansel and Gretel*	RKO-Radio/USA	23/12/54
2/8/54	*Happy Ever After*	AB-Pathé/UK	17/6/54
7/6/54	*Hell and High Water*	20th Century-Fox/USA	6/5/54
15/2/54	*Hell Below Zero*	Columbia/USA	14/1/54
11/10/54	*Her Twelve Men*	MGM/USA	16/9/54
1/11/54	*The High and Mighty*	Warner/USA	2/9/54
26/7/54	*His Majesty O'Keefe*	Warner/UK	6/5/54
5/4/54	*Hondo*	Warner/USA	18/2/54
1/2/54	*How to Marry a Millionaire*	20th Century-Fox/USA	14/1/54
8/11/54	*Hunters of the Deep* (short) Super Cinecolor	Monarch/USA	7/10/54
Rel. floating	*The Inspecting General* Sovcolor	Gala/USSR	7/10/54
14/3/54	*Invaders from Mars*	British Lion/USA	14/10/54
27/9/54	*The Iron Glove*	Columbia/USA	12/8/54
13/12/54	*The Jazz Singer*	Warner/USA	17/12/54
27/9/54	*Jesse James vs the Daltons*	Columbia/USA	12/8/54
2/8/54	*Johnny Dark*	GFD/USA	22/7/54
5/7/54	*Johnny Guitar*	Republic/USA	3/6/54
22/3/54	*Jubilee Trail*	Republic/USA	18/2/54
26/7/54	*Jungle Spell*	20th Century-Fox/USA	27/5/54
10/5/54	*King of the Khyber Rifles*	20th Century-Fox/USA	8/4/54
27/12/54	*King Richard and the Crusaders*	Warner/USA	14/10/54
12/4/54	*Kiss Me Kate*	MGM/USA	21/1/54
4/10/54	*Knights of the Round Table*	MGM/UK	20/5/54
7/6/54	*Knock on Wood*	Paramount/USA	8/4/54

RELEASE DATE	TITLE	DISTRIBUTOR/COUNTRY	*KINEMATOGRAPH WEEKLY* REVIEW
15/3/54	*Lady in the Iron Mask*	20th Century-Fox/USA	11/3/54
21/3/54	*The Last Time I Saw Paris*	MGM/USA	23/12/54
8/11/54	*Lease of Life*	GFD/UK	7/10/54
24/1/55	*Lilacs in the Spring*	Republic/UK	9/12/54
Rel. floating	*A Lion is in the Streets*	Warner/USA	28/1/54
13/12/54	*The Living Desert* (short?)	Walt Disney FD/USA	13/5/54
13/9/54	*Living It Up*	Paramount/USA	29/7/54
28/6/54	*The Lone Gun*	United Artists/USA	17/6/54
27/12/54	*Long John Silver*	20th Century-Fox/USA	16/12/54
7/6/54	*The Long, Long Trailer*	MGM/USA	15/4/54
8/3/54	*Lost Treasure of the Amazon*	Paramount/USA	11/2/54
1/3/54	*The Love Lottery*	GFD/UK	28/1/54
13/9/54	*Lucky Me*	Warner/USA	3/6/54
20/12/54	*Mad About Men*	GFD/UK	28/12/54
20/12/54	*Magnificent Obsession*	GFD/USA	4/11/54
2/5/54	*Make me an Offer*	British Lion/UK	9/12/54
9/8/54	*Malaga*	British Lion/UK	1/7/54
6/12/54	*Men of Sherwood Forest*	Exclusive/UK	4/11/54
11/10/54	*Men of the Fighting Lady*	MGM/USA	23/9/54
8/2/54	*The Million Pound Note*	GFD/UK	14/1/54
21/6/54	*Miss Sadie Thompson*	Columbia/USA	27/5/54
8/2/54	*Money From Home*	Paramount/USA	10/12/53
14/6/54	*The Naked Jungle*	Paramount/USA	15/4/54
10/5/54	*The Nebraskan*	Columbia/USA	8/4/54
Rel. floating	*New Faces*	British Lion/USA	21/10/54
26/7/54	*Night People*	20th Century-Fox/USA	17/6/54
Rel. floating	*Oilmen of the Caspian Sea* (short), Sovcolor	Gala/USSR	9/12/54
29/3/54	*O'Rourke of the Royal Mounted*	GFD/USA	11/3/54

RELEASE DATE	TITLE	DISTRIBUTOR/COUNTRY	KINEMATOGRAPH WEEKLY REVIEW
1/2/54	*Our Girl Friday*	Renown/UK	17/12/54
Rel. floating	*Overland Pacific*	United Artists/USA	22/7/54
Rel. floating	*Pamposh* Gevacolor	Gala/India	30/9/54
29/11/54	*Passion*	RKO-Radio/USA	11/11/54
12/7/54	*Phantom of the Rue Morgue*	Warner/USA	3/6/54
16/8/54	*Prince of the Blue Grass*	AB-Pathé/USA	5/8/54
4/10/54	*Princess of the Nile*	20th Century-Fox/USA	9/9/54
18/10/54	*The Purple Plain*	GFD/UK	23/9/54
14/6/54	*The Queen in Australia* (short)	GFD/UK	20/5/54
21/6/54	*Racing Blood*	20th Century-Fox/USA	1/4/54
November 1954	*The Raid*	20th Century-Fox/USA	16/9/54
10/5/54	*Rails into Laramie*	GFD/USA	22/4/54
7/6/54	*Rainbow Jacket*	GFD/UK	3/6/54
15/11/54	*Rear Window*	Paramount/USA	12/8/54
3/5/54	*Red Garters*	Paramount/USA	25/2/54
Rel. floating	*Return to Treasure Island*	United Artists/USA	28/10/54
Rel. not fixed	*Rhapsody*	MGM/USA	4/3/54
22/3/54	*Ride Clear of Diablo*	GFD/USA	4/3/54
31/5/54	*Riders to the Stars*	United Artists/USA	6/5/54
13/12/54	*Riding Shotgun*	Warner/USA	30/9/54
17/1/54	*Ring of Fear*	Warner/USA	4/11/54
13/9/54	*River of No Return*	20th Century-Fox/USA	24/6/54
25/10/54	*Romeo and Juliet*	GFD/UK	9/9/54
11/10/54	*Rose Marie*	MGM/USA	12/8/54
1/3/54	*Royal New Zealand Journey* (short)	GFD/UK	18/2/54
8/2/54	*Royal Symphony* (short)	GFD/UK	21/1/54
28/6/54	*Saadia*	MGM/USA	10/6/54
1/8/54	*Sabre Jet*	United Artists/USA	3/12/54
19/7/54	*The Saracen Blade*	Columbia/USA	8/7/54

RELEASE DATE	TITLE	DISTRIBUTOR/COUNTRY	*KINEMATOGRAPH WEEKLY* REVIEW
28/3/54	*The Scarlet Spear*	United Artists/UK	11/2/54
28/6/54	*The Sea Around Us*	RKO-Radio/USA	8/4/54
9/8/54	*Secret of the Incas*	Paramount/USA	15/7/54
6/9/54	*The Seekers*	GFD/UK	24/6/54
31/1/54	*Seven Brides for Seven Brothers*	MGM/USA	21/10/54
17/5/54	*Shark River*	United Artists/USA	8/4/54
26/7/54	*The Siege of Red River*	20th Century-Fox/USA	29/4/54
10/1/55	*Sign of the Pagan*	GFD/USA	2/12/54
17/5/54	*Sins of Jezebel*	Exclusive/USA	13/5/54
Rel. floating	*The Snow Maiden* Sovcolor	Gala/USSR	17/12/53
1/2/54	*Son of Belle Star*	AB-Pathé/USA	24/12/53
22/2/54	*Stand at Apache River*	GFD/USA	21/1/54
29/3/54	*Star of India*	Eros/UK	11/2/54
7/6/54	*Storm Over Africa*	AB-Pathé/USA	25/2/54
13/12/54	*Stormy, the Thoroughbred*	Walt Disney FD/USA	3/6/54
25/1/54	*The Stranger Wore a Gun*	Columbia/USA	21/1/54
Rel. floating	*The Stratford Adventure* (short?)	Archway/UK	21/10/54
27/12/54	*The Student Prince*	MGM/USA	14/10/54
23/8/54	*Susan Slept Here*	RKO-Radio/USA	5/8/54
17/1/55	*Svengali*	Renown/UK	9/12/54
28/6/54	*Take the High Ground*	MGM/USA	20/5/54
2/8/54	*Tanganyika*	GFD/USA	29/7/54
17/5/54	*Taza, Son of Cochise*	GFD/USA	13/5/54
24/5/54	*Tembo*	RKO-Radio/USA	29/4/54
31/1/55	*Tennessee Champ*	MGM/USA	11/11/54
8/3/54	*They Who Dare*	British Lion/UK	4/2/54
23/8/54	*Three Coins in the Fountain*	20th Century-Fox/USA	24/6/54
3/1/55	*Three Hours to Kill*	Columbia/USA	16/12/54

RELEASE DATE	TITLE	DISTRIBUTOR/COUNTRY	*KINEMATOGRAPH WEEKLY* REVIEW
24/1/54	*Three Ring Circus*	Paramount/USA	2/12/54
5/4/54	*Three Sailors and a Girl*	Warner/USA	4/3/54
19/7/54	*Three Young Texans*	20th Century-Fox/USA	8/7/54
15/2/54	*Thunder Over the Plains*	Warner/USA	24/12/54
1/3/54	*Torch Song*	MGM/USA	3/12/53
Rel. floating	*Trio-Ballet* Sovcolor	Gala/USSR	1/7/54
26/7/54	*Trouble in the Glen*	Republic/UK	17/6/54
4/1/54	*Tumbleweed*	GFD/USA	17/12/53
Rel. not fixed	*Under the Caribbean*	British Lion/USA	9/12/54
30/8/54	*Valley of the Kings*	MGM/USA	29/7/54
15/3/54	*War Arrow*	GFD/USA	18/2/54
22/2/54	*War Paint*	United Artists/USA	18/2/54
24/5/54	*Welcome the Queen!* (short)	AB-Pathé/UK	27/5/54
19/4/54	*West of Zanzibar*	GFD/UK	1/4/54
27/12/54	*White Christmas*	Paramount/USA	23/9/54
7/2/54	*Woman's World*	20th Century-Fox/USA	25/11/54
3/5/54	*Yankee Pasha*	GFD/USA	15/4/54
22/11/54	*The Yellow Tomahawk*	United Artists/USA	4/11/54
8/11/54	*Yellow Mountain*	GFD/USA	21/10/54
8/3/54	*You Know What Sailors Are*	GFD/UK	11/2/54
Rel. floating Reissue	*Fiesta* (short)	New Realm/USA	27/5/54
Rel. floating Reissue	*Lassie Come Home*	Eros/USA	17/6/54
21/4/55	*The Adventures of Hajji Baba*	20th Century-Fox/USA	20/1/55
15/8/55	*African Fury*	AB-Pathé/USA	18/8/55
13/6/55	*Ain't Misbehavin'*	JARFID/USA	19/5/55
27/2/55	*Aleko* Agfacolor	Gala/USSR	27/1/55
26/9/55	*All That Heaven Allows*	JARFID/USA	25/8/55

RELEASE DATE	TITLE	DISTRIBUTOR/COUNTRY	*KINEMATOGRAPH WEEKLY* REVIEW
19/12/55	*An Alligator Named Daisy*	JARFID/UK	1/12/55
31/1/55	*The Americano*	RKO-Radio/USA	20/1/55
Rel. floating	*Animal Farm*	AB-Pathé/UK	13/1/55
31/10/55	*Armand and Michaela Denis Among the Headhunters* (short, Eastmancolor print)	JARFID/UK	22/9/55
11/4/55	*Armand and Michaela Denis on the Barrier Reef* (short, Eastmancolor print)	JARFID/UK	31/3/55
11/4/55	*As Long as They're Happy*	JARFID/UK	10/3/55
16/5/55	*Bad Day at Black Rock*	MGM/USA	24/2/55
18/9/55	*Battle Cry*	Warner/USA	5/5/55
Rel. floating	*The Beach/La Spiaggia* Ferraniacolor	Gala/It/Fr	19/5/55
25/7/55	*Bedevilled*	MGM/USA	16/6/55
23/5/55	*The Black Dakotas*	Columbia/USA	28/4/55
6/6/55	*Black Widow*	20th Century-Fox/USA	27/1/55
15/8/55	*The Blue and the Gold*	AB-Pathé/USA	18/8/55
5/12/55	*The Blue Peter*	British Lion/UK	24/11/55
Rel. floating	*Bluebeard*	Films de France/Fr	7/7/55
28/2/55	*Break in the Circle*	Exclusive/UK	17/2/55
1/8/55	*Brigadoon*	MGM/USA	14/4/55
1/8/55	*Bring Your Smile Along*	Columbia/USA	21/7/55
9/5/55	*Captain Lightfoot*	JARFID/USA	24/3/55
28/3/55	*Carmen Jones*	20th Century-Fox/USA	6/1/55
4/7/55	*Cattle Queen of Montana*	RKO-Radio/USA	16/6/55
23/1/56	*Cockleshell Heroes*	Columbia/UK	17/11/55
2/5/55	*Conquest of Space*	Paramount/USA	2/5/55
16/5/55	*The Constant Husband*	British Lion/UK	7/4/55
13/6/55	*Contraband-Spain*	AB-Pathé/UK	17/3/55
2/12/55	*Count Three and Pray*	Columbia/USA	24/11/55

RELEASE DATE	TITLE	DISTRIBUTOR/COUNTRY	*KINEMATOGRAPH WEEKLY* REVIEW
11/4/55	*The Cowboy* (short)	Exclusive/USA	11/4/55
31/7/55	*Daddy Long Legs*	20th Century-Fox/USA	9/6/55
25/4/55	*The Dark Avenger*	20th Century-Fox/UK	21/4/55
16/12/55	*Davy Crockett*	Walt Disney/USA	15/12/55
17/10/55	*The Deep Blue Sea*	20th Century-Fox/UK	25/8/55
2/5/55	*Deep in My Heart*	MGM/USA	24/2/55
21/11/55	*Desert Sands*	United Artists/USA	17/11/55
7/3/55	*Desiree*	20th Century-Fox/USA	20/1/55
24/1/55	*Destry*	JARFID/USA	6/1/55
29/8/55	*Doctor at Sea*	JARFID/UK	14/7/55
21/11/55	*Duel in the Mississippi*	Columbia/USA	10/11/55
9/10/55	*East of Eden*	Warner/USA	26/5/55
20/6/55	*Escape to Burma*	RKO-Radio/USA	28/4/55
Rel. floating	*The Face that Launched a Thousand Ships*	Republic/USA	30/6/55
4/7/55	*The Far Horizons*	Paramount/USA	12/5/55
19/1/55	*Five Boys from Barska Street* Agfacolor	Synchro-Cine/Poland	24/11/55
14/11/55	*Five Guns West*	Anglo-Amalgamated/USA	15/9/55
12/12/55	*Flame of the Islands*	Republic/USA	1/12/55
12/9/55	*Footsteps in the Fog*	Columbia/UK	7/7/55
18/4/55	*Foxfire*	JARFID/USA	24/3/55
8/1/56	*French Can Can*	Miracle/FR	1/9/55
19/9/55	*Fury in Paradise*	British Lion-Monarch/USA	25/8/55
20/6/55	*The Gambler from Natchez*	20th Century-Fox/USA	9/6/55
23/1/56	*Gateway to the Antarctic* (short)	Republic/UK	9/12/55
17/10/55	*Gentlemen Marry Brunettes*	United Artists/USA	22/9/55
3/10/55	*Geordie*	British Lion/UK	11/8/55
30/1/55	*The Girl in the Red Velvet Swing*	20th Century-Fox/USA	10/11/55
5/12/55	*The Girl Rush*	Paramount/USA	27/10/55

RELEASE DATE	TITLE	DISTRIBUTOR/COUNTRY	KINEMATOGRAPH WEEKLY REVIEW
5/12/55	*The Glass Slipper*	MGM/USA	11/8/55
Rel. immediate	*The Golden Age/Un Siècle d'Or Gevacolor*	Film Traders/Belgium	7/7/55
31/1/55	*The Golden Mistress*	United Artists/USA	6/1/55
12/9/55	*The Gun that Won the West*	Columbia/USA	4/8/55
2/5/55	*Hell's Island*	Paramount/USA	7/4/55
1/8/55	*Hit the Deck*	MGM/USA	12/5/55
21/11/55	*House of Bamboo*	20th Century-Fox/USA	1/9/55
28/11/55	*How to be Very, Very Popular*	20th Century-Fox/USA	8/9/55
19/3/55	*I Died a Thousand Times*	Warner/UK	1/12/55
12/12/55	*I had Seven Daughters*	Columbia/USA	24/11/55
29/8/55	*Interrupted Melody*	MGM/USA	14/7/55
26/12/55	*It's Always Fair Weather*	MGM/USA	6/10/55
8/8/55	*John and Julie*	British Lion/UK	16/6/55
16/1/56	*Josephine and Men*	British Lion/UK	10/1/55
18/7/55	*Jupiter's Darling*	MGM/USA	14/4/55
10/10/55	*The Kentuckian*	United Artists/USA	15/9/55
31/1/55	*Khyber Patrol*	United Artists/USA	6/1/55
15/8/55	*A Kid for Two Farthings*	British Lion-Independent/UK	28/4/55
23/1/56	*King's Rhapsody*	British Lion/UK	27/10/55
17/10/55	*The King's Thief*	MGM/USA	11/8/55
4/7/55	*Kiss of Fire*	JARFID/USA	19/5/55
1/1/56	*Lady and the Tramp*	Walt Disney/USA	1/9/55
30/5/55	*Lady Godiva of Coventry*	JARFID/USA	5/5/55
2/1/56	*The Ladykillers*	JARFID/UK	8/12/55
5/2/56	*Land of the Pharaohs*	Warner/USA	5/2/56
15/8/55	*The Last Command*	Republic/USA	28/7/55
2/1/56	*Laughing in the Sunshine*	United Artists/USA	22/12/55
28/3/55	*The Law Versus Bill the Kid*	Columbia/USA	3/2/55

RELEASE DATE	TITLE *WEEKLY* REVIEW	DISTRIBUTOR/COUNTRY	*KINEMATOGRAPH*
16/1/56	*Left Hand of God*	20th Century-Fox/USA	6/10/55
4/4/55	*The Long Grey Line*	Columbia/USA	3/3/55
9/2/55	*Love is a Many-Splendored Thing*	20th Century-Fox/USA	13/10/55
26/9/55	*Love Me or Leave Me*	MGM/USA	7/7/55
Rel. not fixed	*Lucretia Borgia*	United Artists/USA	31/3/55
24/10/55	*Lucy Gallant*	Paramount/USA	21/7/55
Rel. floating	*Madame Butterfly*	Films de France/It/Japan	4/8/55
5/9/55	*A Man Alone*	Republic/USA	25/8/55
13/6/55	*A Man Called Peter*	20th Century-Fox/USA	31/3/55
14/3/55	*The Man from Bitter Ridge*	JARFID/USA	24/2/55
3/10/55	*The Man from Laramie*	Columbia/USA	28/7/55
Rel. not fixed	*Man of Africa*	Regent/UK	1/12/55
7/2/55	*The Man Who Loved Redheads*	British Lion/UK	20/1/55
4/4/55	*Man Without a Star*	JARFID/USA	24/3/55
6/6/55	*Many Rivers to Cross*	MGM/USA	7/4/55
11/7/55	*The Marauders*	MGM/USA	9/6/55
21/2/55	*Masterson of Kansas*	Columbia/USA	17/2/55
21/11/55	*Mister Roberts*	Warner/USA	29/9/55
18/7/55	*Moonfleet*	MGM/USA	9/6/55
17/10/55	*My Sister Eileen*	Columbia/USA	8/9/55
Rel. not fixed	*The Naked Dawn*	JARFID/USA	11/8/55
9/1/56	*Never Say Goodbye*	JARFID/USA	29/12/55
Rel. not fixed	*On Such a Night*	JARFID/UK	1/12/55
4/7/55	*One Desire*	JARFID/USA	9/6/55
14/3/55	*Our of the Clouds*	JARFID/UK	3/2/55
29/8/55	*The Outlaw's Daughter*	20th Century-Fox/USA	16/6/55
7/3/55	*The Outlaw Stallion*	Columbia/USA	3/2/55
25/7/55	*Pearl of the South Pacific*	RKO-Radio/USA	30/6/55
11/10/55	*Pete Kelly's Blues*	Warner/USA	22/9/55

RELEASE DATE	TITLE	DISTRIBUTOR/COUNTRY	*KINEMATOGRAPH WEEKLY* REVIEW
18/7/55	*Pirates of Tripoli*	Columbia/USA	2/6/55
3/10/55	*Prince of Players*	20th Century-Fox/USA	3/3/55
8/8/55	*The Private War of Major Benson*	JARFID/USA	21/7/55
21/3/55	*A Prize of Gold*	Columbia/UK	17/2/55
12/9/55	*The Prodigal*	MGM/USA	7/7/55
13/6/55	*The Purple Mask*	JARFID/USA	12/5/55
21/3/55	*Quest for the Lost City*	RKO-Radio/USA	3/3/55
14/11/55	*Rage at Dawn*	RKO-Radio/USA	26/4/55
11/4/55	*Raising a Riot*	British Lion/UK	24/2/55
24/10/55	*The Rawhide Years*	JARFID/USA	13/10/55
16/4/55	*Richard III*	British Lion-Independent/UK	15/12/55
7/11/55	*The Road to Denver*	Republic/USA	20/10/55
17/10/55	*Robbers' Roost*	United Artists/USA	6/10/55
25/7/55	*Rough Company*	Columbia/USA	14/2/55
26/9/55	*Run for Cover*	Paramount/USA	28/4/55
26/9/55	*Sante Fe Passage*	Republic/USA	15/9/55
28/8/55	*The Sea Chase*	Warner/USA	14/7/55
20/6/55	*The Secret*	Eros/UK	2/6/55
27/2/56	*Secret Interlude*	20th Century-Fox/USA	22/12/55
Rel. floating	*Secret of the Mountain Lake* Agfacolor	Gala/USSR	31/3/55
20/10/55	*Seven Cities of Gold*	20th Century-Fox/USA	20/10/55
29/8/55	*The Seven Little Foys*	Paramount/USA	12/5/55
14/11/55	*The Seven Year Itch*	20th Century-Fox/USA	28/7/55
Rel. not fixed	*Shotgun*	AB-Pathé/USA	15/9/55
20/6/55	*The Silver Chalice*	Warner/USA	28/4/55
14/2/55	*Simba*	JARFID/UK	20/1/55
26/12/55	*Simon and Laura*	JARFID/UK	24/11/55
5/2/55	*Sincerely Yours*	Warner/USA	29/12/55

RELEASE DATE	TITLE	DISTRIBUTOR/COUNTRY	*KINEMATOGRAPH WEEKLY* REVIEW
28/2/55	*Sitting Bull*	United Artists/USA	3/2/55
7/3/55	*Smoke Signal*	JARFID/USA	24/2/55
24/1/55	*So This is Paris*	JARFID/USA	6/1/55
24/10/55	*Soldier of Fortune*	20th Century-Fox/USA	30/6/55
3/10/55	*Son of Sinbad*	RKO-Radio/USA	8/9/55
3/10/55	*The Spoilers*	JARFID/USA	8/9/55
26/12/55	*Storm Over the Nile*	British Lion-Independent/UK	10/11/55
27/6/55	*Strange Lady in Town*	Warner/USA	27/6/55
27/6/55	*Stranger on Horseback*	United Artists/USA	16/6/55
8/8/55	*Strategic Air Command*	Paramount/USA	28/4/55
15/5/55	*Such Men are Dangerous*	20th Century-Fox/USA	5/5/55
7/11/55	*Summer Madness*	British Lion-Independent/USA	15/9/55
20/11/55	*Tall Man Riding*	Warner/USA	11/8/55
19/12/55	*The Tall Men*	20th Century-Fox/USA	20/10/55
Rel. immediate	*Team from Our Street* Agfacolor	Plato/USSR	19/5/55
14/3/55	*Ten Wanted Men*	Columbia/USA	17/2/55
30/1/56	*The Tender Trap*	MGM/USA	24/11/55
19/12/55	*Tennessee's Partner*	RKO-Radio/USA	17/11/55
4/4/55	*That Lady*	20th Century-Fox/UK	17/3/55
19/1/55	*Theodora, the Slave Empress/ Teodora, Imperatrice de Bisanzio* Eastmancolor	Archway/It/Fr	27/1/55
14/2/55	*There's No Business Like Show Business*	20th Century-Fox/USA	27/1/55
18/7/55	*They Rode West*	Columbia/USA	7/7/55
27/6/55	*This Island Earth*	JARFID/USA	12/5/55
6/6/55	*Three for the Show*	Columbia/USA	5/5/55
18/12/55	*Tiger in the Sky*	Warner/USA	27/10/55
7/3/55	*Timberjack*	Republic/USA	10/2/55
20/12/55	*To Catch a Thief*	Paramount/USA	3/11/55

RELEASE DATE	TITLE	DISTRIBUTOR/COUNTRY	*KINEMATOGRAPH WEEKLY* REVIEW
6/2/55	*To Hell and Back*	JARFID/USA	3/11/55
7/2/55	*To Paris With Love*	JARFID/UK	6/1/55
31/10/55	*Touch and Go*	JARFID/UK	29/9/55
25/4/55	*Track of the Cat*	Warner/USA	14/4/55
30/1/56	*The Treasure of Pancho Villa*	RKO-Radio/USA	22/12/55
1/8/55	*20,000 Leagues Under the Sea*	Walt Disney/USA	19/5/55
25/5/55	*Ulysses*	Archway/It	2/6/55
21/3/55	*Underwater*	RKO-Radio/USA	24/2/55
22/5/55	*Untamed*	20th Century-Fox/USA	12/5/55
30/5/55	*Valley of Fury*	JARFID/USA	28/4/55
19/9/55	*Value for Money*	JARFID/UK	11/8/55
18/7/55	*The Vanishing Prairie*	Walt Disney/USA	7/4/55
28/3/55	*Vera Cruz*	United Artists/USA	10/2/55
17/7/55	*Violent Saturday*	20th Century-Fox/USA	26/5/55
12/12/55	*The Virgin Queen*	20th Century-Fox/USA	22/9/55
12/9/55	*We're No Angels*	Paramount/USA	9/6/55
25/7/55	*White Feather*	20th Century-Fox/USA	24/3/55
25/4/55	*The White Orchid*	United Artists/USA	31/3/55
12/12/55	*Wichita*	AB-Pathé/USA	27/10/55
Rel. floating	*Winged Guardians* Agfacolor	Gala/USSR	31/3/55
26/9/55	*The Woman for Joe*	JARFID/UK	1/9/55
1/8/55	*Wyoming Renegades*	Columbia/USA	21/7/55
12/12/55	*A Yank in Ermine*	British Lion-Monarch/USA	1/12/55
Rel. floating	*Yellowneck*	Republic/USA	23/6/55
14/11/55	*You're Never Too Young*	Paramount/USA	18/8/55
10/4/55	*Young at Heart*	Warner/USA	3/2/55
Rel. floating Reissue	*For Whom the Bell Tolls*	Eros/USA	27/1/55

RELEASE DATE	TITLE	DISTRIBUTOR/COUNTRY	*KINEMATOGRAPH WEEKLY* REVIEW
2/1/56 Reissue	*Meet Me in St Louis*	MGM/USA	1/9/55
Rel floating Reissue	*Pamposh/Lotus of Kashmir* Gevacolor	New Realm/India	29/12/55
3/10/55 Reissue	*Thousands Cheer!*	MGM/USA	1/9/55

TOTALS: COLOUR FILMS, BRITISH AND US

YEAR	TOTAL FILMS RELEASED (INC. REISSUES)	TOTAL COLOUR FILMS RELEASED	BRITISH COLOUR FILMS	US COLOUR FILMS
1939	603	9	4	5
1940	540	18	2	16
1941	573	17	1	16
1942	605	16	3	13
1943	537	29	3	26
1944	552	33	6	27
1945	544	27	4	23
1946	532	42	6	35 (+ 1 USSR)
1947	571	26	6	19 (+ 1 USSR)
1948	705	45	10	35
1949	693	54	7	46 (+ 1 Danish)
1950	689	83		
1951	670	90		
1952	674	127		
1953	645	150		
1954	639	216		
1955	530	202		
TOTAL	10302	1184		

APPENDIX 2
TECHNICAL APPENDIX

Simon Brown

This appendix offers supporting information on the colour processes discussed in this book. As such this is not designed to be an overview of all the colour processes developed between 1900 and 1955. Indeed hundreds of such processes were developed, some going into full, often limited, commercial production, others little more than a name on a patent. Instead, the reason for including a particular system in this section is based primarily upon its relevance to the examples cited in this book. The majority of processes included, therefore, have a British connection. Either they were developed in Britain by a British company, or developed in Britain by an overseas company, or had some form of significant exploitation within, or impact upon, the British film industry. The concept of 'significant' is applied relatively here. In some cases the process was barely screened, and in one case it never went beyond the development stage, but it is included if the process is relevant to the development and exploitation of colour in British cinema. Each entry covers the technical information as to how the process worked, the historical background, a representative filmography, and details of further reading. As such, this section is envisaged as both a companion piece to the main body of text, and a reference guide in its own right.

The approach taken in the technical descriptions is to be accurate yet accessible. To do so inevitably involves the inclusion of a certain amount of technical detail and to this end a glossary of key terms is included at the start. The descriptions should not, therefore, be taken as comprehensive by those wishing to explore more fully the complex optical or laboratory processes

used in these processes. Fuller descriptions can often be found in patent applications or in the key technical work on colour, the three editions of Adrian Klein (later Adrian Cornwell-Clyne)'s *Colour Cinematography*. This is not the case for all the processes included. Sometimes the only descriptions available are brief comments in reviews of public demonstrations, while patent applications are often vague and can bear little resemblance to the process in practice.

Each entry begins with the name or names of the process, a description of what kind of process it was, and key dates. Identifying exact dates is sometimes difficult. In some cases a great deal of information is available from a variety of sources; in others the available information is limited. This is particularly true in relation to the demise of a particular process. While in the case of Kinemacolor, for example, it is possible to identify when the process ceased to be exploited, for others, such as Spectracolor or Zoechrome, this is much more difficult to determine, since they simply cease to be mentioned in the trade press. Files in the National Archives, notably Board of Trade files, can, in certain cases, provide information as to when the company was wound up, but the detail of the events which led to this can often only be speculated upon. Equally, it is not always straightforward to identify a specific year in which a process started, nor indeed what that means. Does, for example, a process begin with the patent, with the formation of a company to develop it, or with commercial exploitation? Thomas Albert Mills, for example, first registered a patent for **Zoechrome** in 1911, forming a company in 1912. The system was not publicly demonstrated until 1929 and was offered for sale in 1932. Those dates are straightforward. **Cinechrome**, on the other hand, had a more complex period of development. The company was formed in 1912 from a company first registered in 1908, and the system was based on patents from both 1905 and 1911. In this case 1912 marks the point where the system and the name come together, so that is the start date that has been chosen.

The filmographies are representative rather than comprehensive for several reasons. In some cases there is evidence that films were shown during trade or public presentations of a process, but reports of the screenings describe the content of the films rather than the titles, if indeed they had titles at all, which they may not have if they were test films. In some instances, therefore, only one or two titles can be identified. At the other extreme, commercially successful processes were used in vast numbers of films – far more than can be included here. Pathécolor was commonly used for titles from the prolific Pathé Frères between 1905 and the early 1930s, and likewise tinting and toning was commonplace in the majority of silent films for approximately twenty years, and so it would be impossible and highly reductive to try and identify a handful of key titles. As the focus of both this book and this appendix is British cinema, I have concentrated upon British films.

Finally, each entry ends with several key references for additional readings. Again, these are not comprehensive but represent the key sources for information on specific processes, either from books, journals or trade papers.

GLOSSARY

Additive processes

The first attempts to put the colours of nature on screen fall generally into the category of additive processes. Additive colour was superseded by subtractive colour in the 1930s, due in part to the commercial and aesthetic success of three-strip Technicolor. The principle behind additive colour was that a broad spectrum of colours could be achieved through the combination of red, blue and green light. All three of these colours together produce white light, and by combining them in different ways other colours can be achieved. In practice all additive colour systems consisted of splitting the spectrum of light into two or three of those primary colours, recording those colours, and then recombining them on the screen in projection. This idea was first presented by James Clerk Maxwell to the Royal Institution in London in 1861. He exposed the image of a piece of tartan onto three separate glass slides through red, green and blue filters, and then projected the slides simultaneously, superimposed one upon the other, through similar filters. The results offered a relatively faithful rendition of the original. The principle remains the same for additive cinematographic processes. The majority of additive systems were two-colour processes, combining only red and green, although three-colour systems were developed. In a standard two-colour additive system, the image was taken through red and green filters, creating two black-and-white negative images of varying densities representing the red and green components of the spectrum. The method for capturing the two, or three, negative images varied as new systems developed, including capturing the images successively one after the other on a single film strip and using a **beam splitter** to record two images simultaneously on the same or separate film strips.

From these negatives, black-and-white positives were made and then projected in such a way as to recombine the colours and the images to form a colour representation of the original. Methods for achieving this also varied. They included projecting each image through a corresponding colour filter, or staining each successive frame or print the correct colour, so the red record was stained red, the green record green.

Additive processes suffered from a number of significant problems. Those such as **Kinemacolor**, which recorded the red and green images successively and projected them together, found that the fraction of a second of time lapse between the moment the first and second image was taken meant that the two images were not identical, so when projected together they exhibited what is known as 'fringing' or time/parallax error, where moving objects would be followed by 'vapour-trails' of colour. In addition, additive colour was based on the principle of adding colour to white light through, for example, staining or filters, meaning the final image could be quite dark, since a portion of the light was absorbed by the added colour. Perhaps most damaging to additive colour was that many of the processes required that often costly new pieces of equipment be attached to a projector in order to work, making them unattractive to many exhibitors. Ultimately, the impetus for colour on screen was taken over by **subtractive processes**, which required no such additional equipment in projection.

Beam splitting

When a frame of film is exposed, the light from the scene passes through the camera lens and hits the frame, recording onto it a negative image. This is then printed to make a positive image for projection. Usually each frame/image is recorded one at a time. So, for example, in a successive-frame colour system like **Kinemacolor**, where each colour frame is recorded one after the other, to capture the red portions of the scene before the camera the light would pass through a red filter in front of the lens, then the lens itself, and register a single negative image on the film. The film would wind on and the next frame would be exposed through a green filter. As mentioned above (see **Additive processes**), this resulted in the two images being different, since they were taken a fraction of a second apart, meaning that when they were recombined on the screen, they were not quite identical, resulting in fringing. Beam splitting is a way of manipulating the light so that instead of multiple images being recorded successively (one after the other), the light that hits the camera passes through a lens and hits a prism which splits it into two or three beams. These pass through different-coloured filters and are recorded on the negative simultaneously. Sometimes the two or three images are registered successively, one after the other, on the negative. Other systems reduce the size of the image and record two or three in the space of a normal film frame.

Bipack film

The principle of bipack was first proposed by French pioneer in colour photography Louis Ducos du Hauron in 1895. Bipack film is two films placed together, and run through the camera emulsion to emulsion. Each film is sensitised to a different part of the spectrum and one is exposed through the other. In the camera the front element of the bipack is an **orthochromatic film** coated with a red dye. The dye prevents all but the orange-red parts of the spectrum from passing through the orthochromatic negative onto the **panchromatic** negative. The orthochromatic negative therefore records the blue-green elements of the scene while the rear element, which is exposed in contact with the red dye, is a panchromatic emulsion, onto which the red-orange record of the scene passes.

Double-coated/duplitised film stock and dye positive conversion/dye-toning

Duplitised stock is positive film which has a sensitive emulsion on both sides of the base, rather than the usual one side and was used predominantly in **subtractive processes**. Two colour negatives are produced, using in some cases a beam splitter and in others bipack film, and then printed onto either side of the double-coated positive in precise register. The two colour records are then dyed with a complementary subtractive colour. Thus, in a two-colour process the red record is dyed blue-green, and the green record red-orange (see **Subtractive processes** for an explanation of complementary colour).

Dye transfer/dye imbibition

The dye-transfer process, also known as dye imbibition, was developed in 1928 by Technicolor. The negative was taken through colour filters, recording each colour record of the scene on separate negatives – so, for example, one negative would be a record of the red portions of the scene. From that negative a positive dyed relief image was made, known as the matrix, which had been developed by Technicolor in 1922. This was a special film stock which combined the silver halides in black-and-white stock, which are the light-sensitive silver compound used to capture the image, with a special gelatine. The image on the negative was exposed onto the base of the matrix stock. The developing solution contained the normal chemicals which developed the silver halides into a latent image, plus a chemical agent that hardened the gelatine in the same areas where the latent image lay. The remaining gelatine was washed away, therefore rendering a latent image in relief. The next stage of dye transfer was to coat this relief image with the correct complementary subtractive colour (see **Subtractive processes**). The matrix was then pressed against a blank film coated with gelatine that absorbed the dye from the relief image, which was then locked by a **mordant**. The next colour matrix was added the same way. At the end of the process a full-colour record of the original scene was visible.

Mordant/mordanting

A mordant is a chemical compound to which a dye can attach itself. In colour cinematography it was used primarily in subtractive processes to lock into dyes which have been transferred to a print, thus preventing the dyes and, therefore, the colour from smearing or being rubbed off. It was also used in the silent era as a method of **toning**.

Natural colour/applied colour

The majority of the processes discussed in this appendix are examples of natural colour, meaning attempts to re-create on film and in projection the actual colours of the original scene before the camera. Applied colour, on the other hand, refers to processes whereby colour was added to the film in a more interpretive manner, trying less to capture the actual colours before the camera than either to approximate them or offer an entirely abstract flavour of colour. Thus, what are described here as 'Applied colour' are Pathécolor, and also tinting and toning.

Orthochromatic and panchromatic film

Orthochromatic film is sensitive to blue, green and, to a lesser extent, yellow light. The development of orthochromatic film was an important step towards the reproduction of colour. Originally developed for still photography by H. W. Vogel in 1873, orthochromatic film replaced earlier film stock, which was not uniformly sensitive to the entire spectrum of light, only to blue and ultra-violet light. Vogel discovered that by treating the film with dyes, he could expand the sensitivity of the emulsion to include green light, thus extending the accuracy of the image.

The development of panchromatic black-and-white film was an important step forward in the representation of the whole colour spectrum, because it was sensitive to all colours equally. As colour needed to be added to black-and-white film, it was important that the black-and-white film was sensitive to the entire colour spectrum. Panchromatic stock was the result of further experiments regarding the sensitivity of film to the spectrum of light. In 1903 Adolf Meithe and Arthur Traube found a way of sensitising photographic plates to red light. This was put into commercial production in 1906 by a British firm, Wratten and Wainwright, who produced the first commercially available panchromatic film for still photography, sensitised to all colours equally, thus allowing for an accurate black-and-white, and colour, representation of the subject. The majority of early colour experimenters with cinematography were, however, limited to using orthochromatic stock which had to go through a panchromatising process before it was used, which involved submerging the orthochromatic stock into a panchromatising agent prior to use. Owing to the short life span of the panchromatising agent, film stock treated in this way had to be used within three or four days, making it impractical for commercial use. The first panchromatic cine film was introduced in 1913 by Eastman Kodak, originally for the Gaumont Chronochrome process, before being made commercially available generally.

Subtractive processes

By the 1930s developments of subtractive colour processes superseded those of additive colour processes, a transition cemented by the commercial success of **Technicolor**. The principal advantage that subtractive processes had was that they did not absorb light in the way that additive processes did, and therefore produced a much brighter picture, and also they generally required no additional mechanisms in projection.

The basis of subtractive colour stems from a description by Louis Ducos du Hauron in 1868, and although far simpler to use than additive colour in terms of projection, the principles of subtractive colour are much more difficult to describe. Subtractive colour begins with white light – a combination of all the colours of the spectrum – and subtracts from it unnecessary colours, leaving only the mixture of the primary colours of the scene in place. So, again, the image is made up of a combination of red, blue and green, but these primary colours as they appear on the screen are what remain of the white of the projection beam. Whereas to make the colour red appear on the screen in an additive process red is added to white light (by passing white light through a red filter, for example), in a subtractive process, all other colours *except* red are subtracted from the white light, by dying the film with complementary colours which control how much red is allowed to pass through.

For example, red, blue and green added together make white. If one were to subtract red, then only blue and green would remain and together they make the colour cyan, which is the complementary colour for red. Magenta is the complementary colour for green, being a mixture of blue and red, while yellow is the complementary colour for blue, being a mixture of red and green. Thus, if you were to project white light through a magenta filter, the two colours red and blue would pass through the filter, and green would be stopped, or subtracted from the white light.

By extension, therefore, if you were to make a filter consisting of a layer of magenta and a layer of yellow, the magenta would only allow red and blue light to pass through, stopping green light, and the yellow filter would allow only red and green light to pass through and stop blue light. As green light has already been stopped by the magenta filter, only red light will pass through both layers. This assumes that the filters are of an even density – that is, they block all green and blue light equally. But by varying the density of the magenta and yellow filters, it is possible to control the amount of green or blue light that gets through, with the result that the final image becomes a mixture of red, green and blue. This is the essence of subtractive colour in film. The original negative record is of a scene which is a mixture of primary colours, which will be of varying density depending upon the amount of red, blue or green in any given part of the scene. The release print that is made is made up of varying densities of magenta, cyan and yellow, which control the amount of red, green and blue light which pass through, thus projects an accurate rendition of the original scene.

COLOUR PROCESSES

Biocolour (1911–13)
Two-colour additive process
Developed by William Friese-Greene, Biocolour was not a technical or commercial success. Its principal historical significance lies in its rivalry with the first commercially successful **natural colour** process, **Kinemacolor**. The two processes shared an identical system in the camera. The film was exposed at 32 frames per second (fps), twice the normal speed, through alternate red and green filters. This resulted in a negative consisting of successive frames, which were alternately records of the red and green components of the original spectrum, from which a positive was made. It is at this point that Biocolour diverged from **Kinemacolor**, since while the latter projected the image at the same speed through similar

red and green filters, with Biocolour the individual frames were alternately stained red and green. When projected at twice the normal speed, the theory was that persistence of vision would allow the red and green colours to blur, creating the illusion of a full colour record. However, as with **Kinemacolor** (see also **Additive processes** and **Beam splitting**), the two frames were taken successively, one after the other, and so were not identical. This resulted in a fringing effect, where moving objects would leave red and green colour trails behind them as they moved.

Biocolour developed out of William Friese-Greene's experiments while working in Brighton for William Norman Lascelles Davidson between 1905 and 1906. At this time Friese-Greene was trying to perfect two different methods of bringing natural colour to the screen. One system involved the use of a prism. In 1903 Davidson and his then partner, Benjamin Jumeaux, had filed a patent for a three-colour system of colour cinematography using mirrors or prisms, with a provision for a two-colour version, which Friese-Greene adapted in 1905 to register his own patent, no. 9465. This patent suggested the use of a prism behind the camera lens to split the light from the object into two, half of which passed through a red-blue filter, the other half through a yellow-orange filter, and then the two images were registered side by side on the negative. Friese-Greene was also working on a successive-frame process, whereby successive images were taken through red and green filters, and then the film stained red and green. In 1906 Friese-Greene demonstrated both versions to various witnesses, using a special projector built by Robert Royou Beard which allowed for the mechanism for each system to be switched. In 1908 Friese-Greene moved into a workshop above the Queen's Electric Theatre in Brighton, a cinema owned by Walter Harold Speer, where he continued his experiments. Speer, who was in the process of moving from the exhibition sector into production by forming the Brighton and County Film Company, later Brightonia, in 1911, backed the successive-frame process and Biocolour Ltd was formed in August 1911 for its exploitation. The following month it was announced in the trade press that Biocolour was poised to enter the market, having signed an exclusive deal with the exhibitor Montagu Pyke, and having constructed a lab and studio in Brighton, although the claims about the lab and studio were almost certainly exaggerated. Part of the reason for the formation of Biocolour was to acquire the rights to the 1905 patent for the prism system, which perhaps suggests that Speer had doubts about the long-term effectiveness of the successive-frame system. As it was, Charles Urban immediately sued Biocolour for infringement of the 1906 patent filed by George Albert Smith which was the basis for **Kinemacolor**, resulting in Biocolour having to cease trading and enter a lengthy court battle. At the same time, despite being owned by Biocolour, the prism system was developed elsewhere to become **Cinechrome**.

To fund the court case with **Kinemacolor**, Speer turned to the man who was backing Brighton and County, a wealthy motorist and cyclist, Selwyn Francis Edge. Edge bought most of the Biocolour shares and set up a new company, Bioschemes Ltd, which petitioned for the revoking of Smith's 1906 patent. This was denied in December 1913 but the decision was overturned in March 1914, when Smith's patent was declared invalid. Urban appealed again, but lost in 1915. This was a pyrrhic victory for Biocolour. Only one fiction film was made using the process, *The Earl of Camelot*, released in November 1914. This was produced by Aurora Films, which had been set up by Claude Friese-Greene, William's son, to make films in the Biocolour process. However, the film was poorly received, and if there were any future projects planned they were interrupted when Claude joined up to fight in World War I. The Biocolour process quietly died out, although it was adapted by Claude in the 1920s as the basis for his **Friese-Greene Natural Colour** process.

Filmography
The Earl of Camelot (1914)

Further reading

Brown, Simon, 'The Brighton School and the Quest for Natural Colour – Redux', in Simon Brown, Sarah Street and Liz Watkins (eds), *Colour and the Moving Image* (New York: Routledge, 2012), pp. 13–22.

Coe, Brian, *The History of Movie Photography* (London: Ash & Grant, 1981), pp. 118–19.

McKernan, Luke, 'The Brighton School and the Quest for Natural Colour', in Vanessa Toulmin and Simon Popple (eds), *Visual Delights Two: Exhibition and Reception* (Sydney: John Libbey and Co., 2004), pp. 205–18.

Brewstercolor (c. 1912–35)
Two/three-colour subtractive process

Brewstercolor was not a great commercial success, but is nevertheless significant because it was involved in two important firsts in the history of colour on film. Percy Douglas Brewster developed his process in the USA in the early 1910s, registering a number of British and French patents as his system evolved. The process used a camera with a **beam splitter** that split the light through red and green filters and through a double gate and recorded the two images on two negatives running parallel. The negatives were then printed onto **double-coated** stock, the red image on one side and the green on the other. The red image was then dyed green, and the green image was dyed red.

By 1915 Brewster had set up the Brewster Film Corporation at 147 Broadway in New York but there is very little information to suggest that the process achieved wide commercial success. It evidently did manage some measure of commercial exploitation because in 1920 American animator John Randolph Bray, whose company Bray Pictures Corporation had recently struck a distribution deal with Sam Goldwyn, used Brewstercolor to produced the first full-colour cartoon, *The Debut of Thomas Katt* (1920, also known as *Thomas Cat*). Despite good results the process was deemed too expensive and Bray never used it again.

In the 1930s Brewstercolor was modified into a three-colour system. It used the same principles as before, red and green, with yellow being added chemically. For the three-colour version the camera had rotating mirrors which split the light and directed it onto three separate negatives. The negatives were printed onto **double-coated** stock with the red and green exposures **dye-toned** to cyan and magenta. The yellow record was added using **dye imbibition**. A relief image was made which was dyed, and the dye was transferred by being brought into contact with the final print. The three-colour version was demonstrated to the Colour Society of the Royal Photographic Society on 12 April 1935. One of the films shown was *Let's Look at London* while the second was scenes taken at Shepherd's Bush. *Let's Look at London* had apparently been previously screened to the society since the *Kinematograph Weekly* described the print as a considerable improvement on the previous copy. It contained footage of the Limehouse Pool, the changing of the guard, a cabaret show at Grosvenor House and a mannequin parade, and was the first three-colour film shot in Britain. The scenes were shot in the summer of 1934 and processed in America. Both films were made by the commercial film production company Revelation Films under their managing director Stanley Neal, Revelation Films having been founded in 1934.

At this point Revelation Films and Brewstercolor seemed poised for success. Immediately after the trade show Revelation were commissioned to make twelve films using the Brewstercolor process, while Warner Bros. picked up the US distribution rights to *Let's Look at London*. In addition, Charles A. Cochran, chairman of Revelation Films, went to America to purchase three more Brewstercolor cameras. At the same time Neal hired legendary American animator Ub Iwerks to supervise the animated shorts

Yet the cost of three-colour Brewstercolor was high, effectively doubling the average budget of a Revelation film from £1,850 to £3,500. Brewstercolor and Revelation's ambitious projects came to nothing, and after 1935 no more was heard of Brewstercolor.

Filmography

Barnum was Wrong (1930), *Mendelssohn's Spring Song* (1931), *Let's Look at London* (1935), *See How they Won* (1935)

Further reading

Coe, Brian, *The History of Movie Photography* (London: Ash & Grant, 1981), pp. 131–2.

The Commercial Film, February 1935, p. 12.

The Commercial Film, April 1935, p. 1.

Cornwell-Clyne, Adrian, *Colour Cinematography* (London: Chapman & Hall, 3rd edn, 1951), pp. 23–5, 410–12.

Crafton, Donald, *Before Mickey: The Animated Film 1898–1928* (Massachusetts: MIT Press, 1984), pp. 160–1.

Ryan, Roderick T., *A History of Motion Picture Colour Technology* (New York: Focal Press, 1977), pp. 72–5.

British Tricolour (1943–47)

Three–colour subtractive process

British Tricolour was devised by a British inventor named Jack Coote. In 1943 he began working on a system in which the camera ran at 72fps and captured three-colour images successively on a film strip. This method, however, suffered from fringing problems endemic to all successive-frame processes. In 1944 a private company, British Tricolour Processes Ltd, was set up and in 1945 work began on developing a new system. That same year Tricolour was used to film scenes of the VE day celebrations which were released as *Victory Comes to London*. By 1947 his company had designed and built, in association with Wray Optical Works Ltd, a camera similar to a three-strip Technicolor camera which used a **beam splitter** to reflect some of the light through filters and onto a bipack film, which composed the red and blue records, while the remaining light registered on a single film strip through a green filter, giving a three-colour negative record.

After 1945 the process achieved modest exposure in the field of advertising shorts, and in 1947 it was announced that the process was ready to go into full commercial production. The roll-out was, however, held up pending planning permission for the construction of a commercial lab. Coote had found a suitable site at Maidenhead, but the regional Town and Country planning officials at Reading refused permission, and the matter was to be sent to the government for arbitration. This delayed the start of construction, which was scheduled to take a year to complete. In the intervening period Dufay-Chromex approached British Tricolour about acquiring the patents. Coote agreed, and went with the patents to Dufay-Chromex's plant in Thames Ditton in south-west London. British Tricolour was then developed under the name of **Dufaychrome**, and technically the two processes were identical (see **Dufaychrome** for details of the printing process).

Filmography

Victory Comes to London (1945)

Further reading

Cornwell-Clyne, Adrian, *Colour Cinematography* (London: Chapman & Hall, 3rd edn, 1951), p. 414.

Journal of the Society of Motion Picture Engineers, June 1948, pp. 543–53.

Kinematograph Weekly, 3 April 1947, pp. xix–xx.

Kinematograph Weekly, 22 May 1947, p. xix.

Chemicolor (1936–39)

Two-colour subtractive process

Chemicolor was the name under which the German Ufacolor Process was marketed in Britain. Ufacolor was also marketed under the name **Spectracolor**. The process used Agfa **bipack** negatives loaded with the emulsion sides facing and separated by a colour filter. The negatives were printed onto **double-coated** film and toned with complementary colours. The process was formally demonstrated on 27 August 1936 at Elstree Studios. About 1,200 feet of film was screened, mostly outdoor subjects of European tours and indoor costume shots.

At the time of the demonstration, Austrian director Karl Grune, who had left Germany in 1931 and settled in Britain, was using Chemicolor in a film of the opera *Pagliacci* for Capitol Films, under managing director Max Schach. Grune was the managing director of British Chemicolor, which was, along with Capitol Films, part of the Schach Group. Evidently Grune and Schach had been testing the process because in April or May of 1936 Grune went to America with colour film of *Pagliacci* and persuaded William Fox to come out of retirement as an executive director of British Chemicolor to help with the development and commercial exploitation of the process.

Chemicolor was sold in part on its simplicity. The process only required 10–12 per cent more light than black-and-white film for shooting and, before the first demonstration, in July, 6,000 feet of Chemicolor film was shown in cinemas around the country to show that no additional light was required in projection. It was announced that colour prints could be ready for the screen in two days and that producing large numbers of release prints was unproblematic. Further reports stated that make-up tests showed that women needed less make-up than for black-and-white film, and men no make up at all. Any camera could be used 'adapted only by a special device', while any cameraman could achieve perfect results after a little experimenting with the process.

Pagliacci, starring celebrated singer Richard Tauber, was released in 1936 with Chemicolor sections. Though the film was well received little more was heard about Chemicolor and British Chemicolor was in receivership by 1939, possibly due to the increasing concern over Germany and German companies operating in the UK in the run up to World War II.

Filmography

Pagliacci (1936)

Further reading

Coe, Brian, *The History of Movie Photography* (London: Ash & Grant, 1981), p. 129

Cornwell-Clyne, Adrian, *Colour Cinematography* (London: Chapman & Hall, 3rd edn, 1951), p. 331.

Kinematograph Weekly, 30 July 1936, p. 1.

Today's Cinema, 24 August 1936, p. 4.

Today's Cinema, 28 August 1936, p. 2.

Today's Cinema, 7 October 1936, p. xiv.

Today's Cinema, 20 May 1937, p. 1.

Limbacher, James L., *Four Aspects of the Film: A History of the Development of Color, Sound, 3-D and Widescreen Films and their Contribution to the Art of the Motion Picture* (New York: Brussel and Brussel, 1968), p. 40.

Low, Rachael, *Film Making in 1930s Britain* (London: Allen and Unwin, 1985), p. 107.

Cinechrome/Cinecolor (1912–37)
Two-colour additive process

Cinechrome was adapted from a 1905 patent by William Friese-Greene (see **Biocolour** above), which described a system in the camera whereby a prism split the light from the object and passed it through two colour filters, one red-blue and one yellow-orange, and then through the lens, registering two images side by side on the negative. After a brief period running a photographic shop, in 1907 Friese-Greene returned to inventing and continued to develop this process alongside a successive-frame process which would become **Biocolour**.

At this point the history becomes complicated. An engineer named Allan Ramsay acquired the rights to all of Friese-Greene's patents (excluding the 1905 patent which was not available) and set up a company to develop them, named Friese-Greene Patents Ltd. Friese-Greene was hired as technical director for a period of four years but was lured away by his friend, the exhibitor Walter Harold Speer, who set up **Biocolour** in 1911 and acquired the services of Friese-Greene plus the rights to the 1905 patent, the only one not owned by Ramsay and Friese-Greene Patents Ltd. Curiously, therefore, despite Friese-Greene Patents Ltd not owning the 1905 patent, the prism system which it outlined formed the basis of the process which the company would ultimately develop, while **Biocolour** would attempt to exploit the successive-frame system, despite owning the rights to the prism system in the 1905 patent.

In 1911 the film journalist Colin Noel Bennett patented a colour system which used two small lenses, one above the other, placed behind a rotating shutter with cut-away sections which worked in synch to expose two frames simultaneously. Before the lenses were two filters, one red and one green. Both the red and green images were therefore recorded simultaneously but successively. A further patent in 1912 was for a complementary projection system wherein light from the source passed through red and green filters and through two lenses, the upper of which was adjustable in order to accomplish precise register with the lower and ensure the picture on screen was in focus. The film gate was double the width, so the light passed through two frames at once, and the projector moved the film on two frames at a time. Further patents in 1912 refined the system, abandoning the use of two small lenses in the camera and replacing it with a prism that split the light so that it passed through two filters and recorded the images successively. It was later refined again so that the two images were recorded in a smaller size side by side on a single film frame. Bennett was adamant in his original 1911 patent that his system did not use a prism and so was not derivative of Davidson and Jumeaux's 1903 patent and, by extension, Friese-Greene's 1905 patent, but these revisions clearly derived from those earlier patents and suggest that Bennett was fostering links with Friese-Greene. Indeed, Bennett granted the rights to his 1911 patent to Friese-Greene, facilitating a link between himself and Friese-Greene Patents Ltd. The company was reformed in 1912 as Colin Bennett Ltd, with financing provided by Sir William Pickles Hartley of Hartley's Jams, whose son-in-law, John Sharp Higham, was on the board of directors. For reasons unknown, at this point Bennett turned his back on inventing and returned to journalism. Further patents refining his process were filed in 1915 under Higham's name and also the names of Frank Twynam and Harold Workman, both of whom worked for a company called Adam Hilger Ltd. That same year Colin Bennett Ltd was re-formed as Cinechrome Ltd, without Bennett but still with Hartley and Higham.

Over the next few years the system underwent further development until it reached the high-point of its success. In 1921 Cinechrome was used to film the state visit of the Prince of Wales – later Edward VIII – to India, which was premiered at the Royal Society of Arts in 1922 and later had a public run at the Stoll Picture Theatre. By this point the process used a prism which split the beam of light from the object and recorded two colour records side by side on an extra-wide film with perforations down both sides and in the middle. The special film and the special projector required to show it proved a stumbling block to commercial exploitation, and the system was revised again, this time by Cox and Demetre Daponte, who had also worked for Adam Hilger Ltd and who took over the running of Cinechrome with Cox in 1922 after Hartley's death. The wide film was dispensed with and the two images were registered sideways on a single 35mm frame. In 1929 Cox and Daponte renamed the company, and the process, Cinecolor Ltd and the process was adapted again, dispensing with the two sideways images in favour of two images registered the right way up in a single frame and a projection system which used an adjustable prism to enable the two images to be registered precisely – a system ironically not far removed from that originally proposed by Bennett in 1911. Commercial success, however, remained elusive. In 1937 the Cinecolor patents were acquired by a holding company, Chromex Ltd, and passed to Dufay-Chromex, which was at that time exploiting the additive **Dufaycolor** process but looking for ideas to develop a subtractive process.

Filmography

Cinechrome Colour Test with Soap Boxes and Packets (1920), *Through India and Burma with HRH The Prince of Wales* (aka *With The Prince of Wales Through India and Burma*) (1922), *Edward Prince of Wales' Tour of India: Madras. Bangalore, Mysore and Hyderabad* (1922), *Edward Prince of Wales' Tour of India: Peshawar, The Khyber Pass and Rawl Pindi* (1922), *Edward Prince of Wales' Tour of India: Calcutta and Delhi* (1921), *Edward Prince of Wales' Tour of India: Bombay, Poona, Barodajodhpur and Bikaner* (1920s), *Edward Prince of Wales' Tour of India: Bikaner, Lucknow, Benares, Nepal and Great Tiger Shoot* (1920s), *Edward Prince of Wales' Tour of India: Indore, Bhopal, Gwalior and Delhi* (1920s), *Edward Prince of Wales' Tour of India: Malakand, Kapurthala and Dehra Dun* (1920s)

Further reading

Brown, Simon, 'The Brighton School and the Quest for Natural Colour – Redux' in Simon Brown, Sarah Street and Liz Watkins, (eds), *Colour and the Moving Image* (New York: Routledge, 2012), pp. 13–22.

Coe, Brian, *The History of Movie Photography* (London: Ash & Grant, 1981), p. 120.

McKernan, Luke, 'The Brighton School and the Quest for Natural Colour', in Vanessa Toulmin and Simon Popple (eds), *Visual Delights Two: Exhibition and Reception* (Sydney: John Libbey and Co., 2004), pp. 205–18.

BT 31/18498/98940, Friese-Greene Patents Ltd, 1908, National Archives.

BT 31/21043/125384, Colin Bennett Ltd, 1912, National Archives.

BT 31/22949/141281 Cinechrome Ltd, 1915, National Archives.

Dufaychrome (1948–c. 53)

Three-colour subtractive process

Dufaychrome was a subtractive colour system developed by Dufay-Chromex to replace its additive **Dufaycolor** system. Dufaychrome used a prism in the camera which allowed part of the light to pass through to a film gate along the axis, and diverted the remaining light from the source by 90 degrees to a second gate. The diverted image, consisting of the blue and red records, was recorded on **bipack** film, the non-diverted image – the green record – on a single film. An alternative successive-frame version was also proposed, specifically for animated films, which recorded blue, red and green images successively on a single film strip. Each record was printed onto the same piece of film, one at a time, the film having been treated with the complementary subtractive colour. So the blue record was printed first onto an emulsion layer which had been treated so it contained a yellow coupler, a colourless substance in the emulsion which is transformed into a colour dye by the developing process. This was not processed, and the film was then resensitised using a magenta coupler (magenta being the complementary colour to green) onto which the green record was printed. Finally, the film was resensitised containing a cyan coupler onto which the red record was printed, creating a three-layered colour record which was then processed, bringing out the colour dyes in the couplers.

Dufaychrome was launched by Dufay-Chromex after World War II. With the success of **Technicolor** in the mid-1930s, it became clear that subtractive colour was to become the industry standard. At that time **Dufaycolor** was achieving some success in the field of commercial shorts but only limited use in feature films

owing to various technical problems and issues of cost. Seeking to develop a subtractive process, in 1937 Dufay acquired the rights to **Cinecolor**, but any development was stalled after the company gave over many of its factories to essential war work in 1940. In 1943 Dufay-Chromex proposed a deal with Kodak in the UK to pool resources to develop a colour process but the discussions came to nothing.

By the end of World War II Dufay-Chromex was in financial trouble, with losses of almost £15,000 in the financial year 1946–47. The board responded with an aggressive expansion plan, prompted in part by a perceived gap in the market left by the demise of the German Agfacolor company after the war. Supported by the Board of Trade, Dufay was given the opportunity to develop a colour process to rival Technicolor. In 1948 it acquired the rights to the **British Tricolour** process, which would form the basis of Dufaychrome.

In July 1948 Adrian Klein announced that development of Dufaychrome was underway but that organising the provision of lab facilities was slowing down the process of commercial exploitation. Klein reported that the labs would be fully functional within eighteen months, but that a limited service would be available in eight months. Part of the plan for the labs was for Dufay-Chromex to bring the coating of the Dufaychrome film stock in-house, this having been contracted out to this point. At the same time he announced that Rank was to make a feature using Dufaychrome.

The proposed film with Rank does not seem to have emerged, and neither did the ambitious expansion plans. Instead, Dufay-Chromex's fortunes did not improve. The following year the company's losses increased to £101,223 and in 1949 Dufay-Chromex began a process of overall retrenchment. Many factories were closed and the work transferred to the main factory at Elstree, while the focus of the company shifted to the making of colour and black-and-white roll film, mostly for the amateur market, and also the making and selling of its line of inexpensive box cameras for still photography.

At the end of 1949 Eric Lightfoot, the chairman of Dufay-Chromex, announced that it was the intention of the company to continue to maintain and develop both Dufaycolor and Dufaychrome, but not to go into large-scale production until such time as market conditions improved. Although clearly Dufaychrome did achieve limited commercial exploitation there is very little to suggest it was used regularly or with any great success. A series of commercial advertising films, dating from 1950, are held in the BFI National Archive. These are very short, lasting only a few seconds and mostly consisting of a single shot of a product over which a title is placed. Whether this was a compilation of commissioned films or films which were specifically taken to sell the process is unknown. In 1952 a screen test of Audrey Hepburn was recorded, so attempts to promote the commercial use of the process were still ongoing by then, but as commercially exploitable products both Dufaycolor and Dufaychrome were effectively finished by 1955.

Filmography

Dufaychrome Advertising Compilation (1950)
The Audrey Hepburn Screen Test (1952)

Further reading

Cornwell-Clyne, Adrian, *Colour Cinematography* (London: Chapman & Hall, 3rd edn, 1951), pp. 414–18, 522–8.
HM Treasury Capital Issues Committee File No T266 161, Dufay-Chromex Ltd, National Archives.
Today's Cinema, 2 July 1948, p. 3.

Dufaycolor (UK, 1931–c. 52)

Three-colour additive process

Dufaycolor was based upon a four-colour screen still photography process invented by the Frenchman Louis Dufay in 1908 called the Diopticolore process (which went on the market in 1909 as Dioptichrome). The colour photographic image consisted of pairs of lines of complementary colours, such as magenta and green, placed at right angles to a series of non-complementary colours, such as cyan and yellow. This produced a mosaic pattern of green lines interspersed with rows of red and green squares. By 1912 the mosaic had been changed to consist of blue lines alternating with rows of red and green elements shaped like capsules, and by 1917 the name of the process had been changed to Dufay Versicolor. A company, also called Versicolor, was formed to exploit it and to develop it for cine film but in 1920 it ran into financial difficulties and T. Thorne Baker, a colour expert from Britain working for Versicolor, was asked by the British paper manufacturing

firm Spicers to report back to them on the possibilities of the process. In 1926 Spicers bought the process, and set up Spicer-Dufay the same year.

Spicers successfully adapted the process for cine film between 1926 and 1931 under Thorne Baker's direction at the Spicer plant in Sawston, Cambridgeshire. They altered Dufay's original process with a new mosaic pattern, called the *réseau*, made up of red and green lines overlaid at right angles. The *réseau* was printed onto the back of the film stock. In the camera the film was loaded with the base facing the lens and the light passed through the *réseau*, through the base and onto the emulsion. In projection the light had to shine first through the emulsion, then the base, then the *réseau*, meaning that in projection the print had to be laced with the emulsion facing away from the screen, the opposite of normal projection. The research was presented as Dufaycolor in 1931, first at the Royal Society in March, and then at the British Kinematograph Society (BKS) in September.

Despite being well received, Dufaycolor had significant problems. First, although the angles of the lines of the *réseau* had been chosen to minimise its visibility on projection, by Spicer-Dufay's own admission, the lines were visible as a series of diamond shapes on the image from the first six rows of any cinema. Second, the process as displayed to the BKS was a 16mm reversal process, which was more in keeping with home movies than commercial production, which relied upon a negative to positive printing process. Third, as the film had to be laced a different way from normal in both the camera and the projector, when using Dufaycolor both projectors and cameras required recalibrating. In addition, because the image on the emulsion was projected through the base, the image was darker than normal film and, on films with a combined soundtrack, the sound was quieter, meaning more light was required in projection.

Having raised their profile with the presentations in 1931, Spicer-Dufay continued research and a 35mm reversal film was launched at the end of 1932. The same year the British photographic firm Ilford invested in the company and the process and Spicer-Dufay (British) Ltd was registered in February 1933 with a capital of £600,000. Ilford's main objective was the development of a 16mm colour cine film for the amateur market, and this was the direction taken by the company throughout that year and most of the next. The new 16mm colour film, along with an improved 35mm stock, was presented at the Savoy Hotel in April 1934, and the 16mm film was released onto the market in September to great success.

Having broken into the amateur market and fulfilled the aims of Ilford, Spicer-Dufay turned its attention to the problems which prevented a breakthrough in professional production, notably the cost of using the process, problems with shooting in artificial light and the fact that Dufaycolor was a reversal process and unsuitable for negative to positive printing. Dufaycolor prints cost around 3.5 pence per foot to make, about three and a half times that of black-and-white prints. For a film with a length of 1,000ft, this expense was considerable but not disastrous, but for feature-length films of 6,000ft or more, the extra few pence a foot added a substantial amount to the budget. In addition, although Dufaycolor was simple to use out of doors, requiring only a gelatine filter and some minor adjustments in the camera, its use in artificial light was problematic. It required at least one and a half times the usual amount of light for interior lighting, and also required that light sources were not mixed – for example, arc lamps and tungsten lamps – in order to maintain neutral balance in the colours.

The added complications of interior shooting, plus the extra cost involved, served to limit the attractiveness of Dufaycolor for the feature market, but did not prohibit its use in shorter subjects. In 1935 Spicer-Dufay (British) Ltd struck a deal with British Movietone News to film the Silver Jubilee of King George V. That same year Len Lye completed his abstract film *The Colour Box*, in Dufaycolor, and it was acquired by John Grierson for the GPO Film Unit as an advert for the sixpenny parcel post. Although in December the British feature film *Radio Parade of 1935* was released, featuring two sequences in Dufaycolor, and raised the profile of the process, it did not mark the start of a profitable relationship between Dufaycolor and the feature film sector.

In January 1936 Spicer-Dufay became Dufay-Chromex, having merged with Chromex, a holding company formed to take over British **Cinecolor**, and in October 1936 the company finally solved the problem of reversal printing and announced the perfection of a negative to positive printing process, which went into full-scale production in April 1937. The arrival, also in 1937, of Adrian Klein, who had previously worked for **Gasparcolor**, signalled the start of Dufaycolor's most productive phase. Keen to promote the process for commercial use, Klein instigated a series of short films to be produced in-house. Humphrey Jennings was hired as director since he had previously worked in Gasparcolor on the Shell advertising film *The Birth of the Robot* (1936). At the same time, Dufay-Chromex perfected a reduction process whereby 16mm Dufaycolor prints could be made from 35mm negatives, an ideal situation for the shorts market, which was predominantly distributed on 16mm. Following on from Klein's successful experiments with Jennings, independent commercial companies including Rayant Wanderfilms, Inspiration Films, Publicity Films and Merton Park adopted the Dufaycolor process, with 1938 and 1939 seeing the release of over fifty short films in Dufaycolor. Finally, in 1939, a complete feature was made in the process, *Sons of the Sea*, directed by Maurice Elvey. A second film was announced, but stalled with the start of World War II. Dufay handed its labs over to war work, expanding on their work with filters to become one of the world's largest suppliers of plastic glass substitutes, and by the time the war ended, Technicolor and subtractive colour was dominant. In response, Dufay-Chromex began to develop its own subtractive process, **Dufaychrome**.

Filmography
London Zoological Society (1931), *Glimpses of 1935* (1935), *Kaleidoscope* (1935), *A Colour Box* (1936), *Coronation of King George VI* (Pathé Gazette) (1937), *Design for Spring/Making Fashion* (1938), *St Moritz* (1938), *Sam Goes Shopping* (1938), *Behind the Dykes* (1939), *English Harvest* (1939), *The Farm* (1939), *Farewell Topsails* (1939), *Garden of the Sea* (1939), *The HPO* (1939), *Old Soldiers* (1939), *Sons of the Sea* (1939), *Calling Mr Smith* (1943), *Our Inheritance* (1945)

Further reading

Brown, Simon, 'Dufaycolor: The Spectacle of Reality and British National Cinema', www.bftv.ac.uk/projects/dufaycolor.htm [Note: This entry has been adapted from material previously published in this article.]

Coe, Brian, *The History of Movie Photography* (London: Ash & Grant, 1981), pp. 125–6.

Hercock, Robert J. and Jones, George A., *Silver by the Ton: The History of Ilford Ltd 1879–1979* (New York: McGraw-Hill, 1979).

Cornwell-Clyne, Adrian, *Colour Cinematography* (London: Chapman & Hall, 3rd edn, 1951), pp. 285–316.

Dunningcolor (c. 1932–39)

Two/three-colour subtractive process

Dunningcolor was developed in the 1930s by American Caroll H. Dunning, who also invented the Dunning process for travelling matte photography, used most famously in the original *King Kong* (1933). Dunning also collaborated with William Van Doren Kelley on the short-lived Kesdacolor process (see **Prizamcolor**). Originally, Dunningcolor was a two-colour process using a specially built camera in which two separate **panchromatic** negatives ran side by side. The light from the source was split through two filters, with the red record registered on one film and the green on the other. An average of 65 per cent more light was needed and the camera had a built-in control system allowing for the cameraman to make adjustments depending upon the light source. Colour prints were made on **duplitised** stock. Rushes from the red record could be printed in black and white and were suitable for release.

Rarely used for live action, Dunningcolor achieved modest success in the field of animated shorts, and in particular was adopted by the English animator Anson Dyer who, having set up his own animation studio in 1935, used Dunningcolor for many of his most popular films between 1935 and 1937.

Dunningcolor was altered to a three-colour process in 1937. In the three-colour version, a **beam splitter** was used in the camera to split the image though two gates, positioned side by side. Through one was a **panchromatic** negative, through the other a **bipack** negative. Prints were made on **duplitised** positive film from three separation negatives. The red record negative was printed on one side and dyed cyan, while the green record was printed on the other and dyed magenta. Yellow was added by **imbibition** from a matrix printed from the blue record negative.

In July 1939 Dunning announced that the three-colour process was ready for commercial use. It was estimated the cost for Dunningcolor films would be about twice that of normal monochrome prints. In Britain it was expected that George Humphries would

process Dunningcolor films, as Humphries labs were already capable of handling 10 million feet of two-colour Dunningcolor per year and just needed new equipment to handle the addition of a third colour. Almost immediately afterwards, Dunningcolor faded away. Why the process never achieved commercial exploitation is unknown, but the most likely scenario is that the outbreak of World War II prevented any further development. Film stock became scarcer and the market more problematic as imports and exports were affected by the war at sea, the government tightened control over factory production and technicians and staff went off to fight. The exact manner in which this affected Dunningcolor is yet to be determined, but it was never commercially exploited in Britain after 1939.

Filmography

All the Fun of the 'Air (1935), *Sam and his Musket* (1935), *Carmen* (1936), *Sam's Medal* (1936), *Alt! 'Oo Goes There* (1936), *Beat the Retreat* (1936), *Drummed Out* (1937), *The Lion and Albert* (1937), *Three Ha'Pence a Foot* (1937), *Gunner Sam* (1937), *The King with the Terrible Temper* (1938)

Further reading

Cornwell-Clyne, Adrian, *Colour Cinematography* (London: Chapman & Hall, 3rd edn, 1951), p. 418.

The Commercial Film, May–June 1936, p. 6.

Kinematograph Weekly, 3 December 1936, p. 308.

Ryan, Roderick T., *A History of Motion Picture Colour Technology* (New York: Focal Press, 1977), p. 106.

Today's Cinema, 8 July 1939, p. 1.

Friese-Greene Natural Colour process (c. 1924–26)

Two-colour additive process

Friese-Greene Natural Colour, which is also sometimes referred to as the Spectrum Colour process after the company formed to promote it, was an adaptation by Claude Friese-Greene of his father William's work with **Biocolour**. In the earlier process, a rotating disc was placed before the camera lens which exposed the film through alternate red and green filters, the resulting print consisting of alternating red and green records which were then dyed red and green, respectively. Claude Friese-Greene retained the rotating disc and the red filter but replaced the green filter with an open aperture partly filled by a yellow filter. This unusual combination was the result of a number of years of experimentation with alternatives to red and green, which were the standard for two-colour additive processes, and which Claude Friese-Greene felt was partly the cause of headache-inducing flickering which had dogged previous processes (see also **Kinemacolor** and **Additive processes**). The completed film was then processed to make a black-and-white negative record which was then put through a machine which tinted red the frames taken through the red filter, and cyan (blue/green) the frames taken through the yellow filter/open aperture. Upon projection, using the principle of persistence of vision, the alternating tinted frames blurred together to produce a full two-colour image, but there is some debate as to whether the print was shown at 24fps or 32fps. It is logical to assume that the speed, as with **Kinemacolor**, was 30–2fps, which was twice the normal silent speed, but the existing material in the BFI National Archive runs satisfactorily at 24fps.

Like his father, Claude Friese-Greene was a man with big ideas. After a number of test films he embarked on a motor tour of Britain from Land's End to John O'Groats, taking colour film along the way. His vision was to release twenty-six short films, each detailing one particular leg of the journey, under the umbrella title of *The Open Road* (1925). Initially Friese-Greene's experiments caused considerable excitement in the film industry in London, so much so that the *British Journal of Photography* declared 1925 a landmark year for colour cinematography because of the success of both Friese-Greene's process and **Technicolor** in presenting images in natural colour. Yet despite this seemingly favourable response, neither the process nor *The Open Road* developed further, and it is unlikely that all twenty-six episodes were ever exhibited. Friese-Greene Natural Colour still suffered from flickering and the fact that the two frames were taken successively and were therefore not identical caused the fringing endemic to all successive-frame systems. Claude Friese-Greene became an efficient cinematographer, including working on the single **Dufaycolor** feature film, *Sons of the Sea* (1939), directed by Maurice Elvey, and the material he shot for *The Open Road* was deposited in the then National Film Archive in the 1950s.

Interest in both his process and his film was revived in the twenty-first century thanks to a BBC/BFI co-production, *The Lost World of Claude Friese-Greene* (2006), in which presenter Dan Cruickshank re-created the original route taken in 1924. The programme used prints which had been copied photochemically from Friese-Greene's original unedited material in the 1980s by the BFI National Archive. Around the same time the BBC was making the programme, the BFI experimented with a new digital restoration of the process which substantially reduced the fringing and flickering. A sixty-five-minute section of this new restoration was then edited and released on DVD as *The Open Road* (2007). While both of these restorations are controversial in that they use modern techniques to overcome the problems of Friese-Greene's original process, and are thus not faithful renditions of what audiences originally saw, they demonstrate that Friese-Greene was an excellent cameraman with a keen eye and a gentle sense of humour, and provide a fascinating colour snapshot of Britain in the 1920s.

Filmography
Moonbeam Magic (1924), *Dance of the Moods* (1924), *Quest for Colour* (1924), *The Open Road* (1925)

Further reading
British Journal of Photography, 9 April 1925, p. 215.
British Journal of Photography Colour Supplement, 4 January 1924, pp. 1–2.
Coe, Brian, *The History of Movie Photography*, (London: Ash & Grant, 1981), p. 119.
Dixon, Bryony and Genaitay, Sonia, 'Early Colour Film Restoration at the BFI National Archive', *Journal of British Cinema and Television* vol. 7 no. 1, April 2010, pp. 131–46.

Gasparcolor (c. 1933–c. 41)
Three-colour subtractive process
Gasparcolor was a forerunner of modern colour film as an early example of a film with three layers, each of which could be sensitised to one of the three primary colours and processed to give three complementary dyed images. Gasparcolor used a special film, manufactured in Belgium by Gevaert, which was coated with three emulsions all containing dyes. On one side the emulsion was sensitised to red light and contained a cyan dye, on the other two emulsions were sensitised to green and blue light and contained respectively magenta and yellow dyes.

Gasparcolor prints could be made either from three separation negatives taken through appropriate filters, or from a single negative comprising three successive frames. From the negatives three black-and-white positive prints were made. The positives were then printed onto the special Gasparcolor film. During processing the dyes in the three layers were destroyed in proportion to the developed silver image, so that when the silver image was bleached away, three positive dye images were left. The soundtrack was printed with white light on the same side of the film as the double emulsion layers and developed separately.

Gasparcolor was the work of the Hungarian chemist Dr Belá Gaspar. Initially Gaspar was working to develop his process in Germany in collaboration with the avant-garde film-maker Oskar Fischinger, who made the film *Circles* (1933) in Gasparcolor; but Gaspar fled to the UK in 1934. There he formed Gasparcolor Ltd, and Gasparcolor films were shown to the Film Society towards the end of that same year. The process showed considerable promise. The demonstration at the Film Society was well received and even before it had taken place Gasparcolor had been commissioned to make three films for national advertisers. Gasparcolor was presented at the Royal Photographic Society on 25 January 1935 by Major Adrian Klein and in July it was presented at the International Congress of Photography in Paris.

Gasparcolor was exploited not just in Britain but also in Europe and Scandinavia. The process was, for example, used extensively in Norway for advertising shorts. The complex technical nature of production meant it was used more for animated short films than for live action, and indeed only one live-action film was taken in Britain using the process, *Colour on the Thames* (1935), directed by Adrian Klein and featuring film of the riverbank at Richmond, the pool of London, Tower Bridge and Docklands. The film was made to test the live-action capabilities of the process and, although the results were good, the process remained strictly within the purview of the animation industry, being used in Britain by George Pál on his *Puppetoons* series (1932–47), by Len Lye on his film *Rainbow Dance* (1936) and by Lye again, this time working with Humphrey Jennings, on the advertising film for Shell *The Birth of the Robot* (1936). With the outbreak of World War II Gevaert, the Belgian company which manufactured the stock, closed down its operation and

Gasparcolor Ltd folded in Britain. Dr Gaspar moved to America to continue his research, forming an American branch of Gasparcolor which was unsuccessful, partly due to the lack of availability of the film stock from German-occupied Belgium. Based on the principles of Gasparcolor, he went on to focus on colour still photography, developing a process called Cibachrome, which would go on to be known as Ilfrachrome.

Filmography

The Ship of the Ether (1934), *Red Box Fantasy* (1935), *Colour on the Thames* (1935), *The Birth of the Robot* (1936), *Rainbow Dance* (1936), *On Parade* (1936), *Phosferine* (1937), *How the Motor Works* (1938), *Colour Flight* (1939)

Further reading

British Journal of Photography Colour Supplement, 4 August 1933, pp. 29–31.

British Journal of Photography Colour Supplement, 6 October 1933, pp. 37–8.

Coe, Brian, *The History of Movie Photography* (London: Ash & Grant, 1981), pp. 133, 136.

The Commercial Film, March 1936, p. 10.

Cornwell-Clyne, Adrian, *Colour Cinematography* (London: Chapman & Hall, 3rd edn, 1951), pp. 419–27.

Today's Cinema, 17 January 1935, p. 1.

Today's Cinema, 6 February 1935, p. xviii.

Harmonicolor (1935–36)

Two-colour subtractive process

Harmonicolor was developed by French chemist Maurice Combes. It was first formally demonstrated in London by Harmonicolor Films Ltd, of 4 Great Winchester Street, on the 23 March 1936 at the Curzon Soho with the film *Talking Hands*, produced at Nettlefold studios at Walton on Thames. The process used **bipack** negative in the camera to record two negatives taken through colour filters. These were printed onto **double-coated** positive film which was stained magenta and yellow-orange on one side, and green and blue-violet on the other. The dyes were then fixed to the silver image using a **mordant** and the silver image washed away. The idea behind using a range of dyes was to leave an image which had a greater variety of colours than was traditionally achieved through a two-colour process. Thus, on one side of the film lighter areas would be more yellow and, on the other side, green, while darker areas would be orange-red on one side and blue-violet on the other. The chief selling point of the process was that it was relatively cheap, prints costing only 30–40 per cent more than standard black and white.

Apart from the demonstration in 1936 there is no evidence that the process was used for any other films or commercially exploited.

Filmography
Talking Hands (1936)

Further reading
Coe, Brian, *The History of Movie Photography* (London: Ash & Grant, 1981), p. 129.
Cornwell-Clyne, Adrian, *Colour Cinematography* (London: Chapman & Hall, 3rd edn, 1951), pp. 333–4.
Today's Cinema, 10 January 1935, p. 1.

Hillman Colour (1930–35)
Two-colour additive process

While it was never commercially exploited, Hillman Colour is nevertheless an interesting footnote in the history of colour cinematography in Britain. At the fifth annual general meeting of Gerrard Wire Tying Machines Co. Ltd, part of Gerrard Industries, held in July 1930, Chairman Kay Harrison announced to the shareholders that Gerrard had acquired world rights – excluding the USA and Canada – for a new process for printing colour images on paper at great speed. The system was known as Colourgravure and to exploit it a subsidiary of Gerrard, known as Colourgravure Ltd, was set up. In announcing this development, Harrison noted that the process was to be used for the printing of packing labels but that 'the process will involve revolutionary changes in other directions from which the company should derive considerable benefit'. One of those 'other directions' was the acquisition and development of patents in an additive process which was being developed by Albert George Hillman, known as the Hillman process. Hillman had previously worked on **Cinecolor** with Demetre Daponte and Sydney Cox.

In the Hillman process, two frames were taken simultaneously through two lenses, one above the other. This was done through the use of two mirrors before the two lenses. The light hit the upper mirror which was perforated, allowing some of the light through to the upper lens, and reflecting the rest of the light down to the lower mirror, which was angled to direct the light onto the lower lens. The frames were taken through an oscillating filter containing three filter elements: red, green and red. Two frames were exposed, one through the red filter and one through the green, and then the film moved on one frame, as did the filter, so that the same frame was exposed through its filter twice, once in the upper gate, once in the lower. By this method a red frame would be exposed through the red filter in the upper gate, then moved on one frame with the filter to be exposed again through the red filter in the lower gate. At the same time, a new unexposed frame would be exposed through the green filter in the upper gate, before being moved on to the lower gate to be exposed again. As reported by Cornwell-Clyne, the shutter on the camera moved in the opposite direction, so the second exposure of each frame effectively began before the first exposure of the following frame. The aim of this was to reduce the time between the exposure of each frame and thus reduce fringing.

In 1934 meetings began between Gerrard Industries and Alexander Korda of London Film Productions, at that time Britain's most celebrated production company thanks to the success of *The Private Life of Henry VIII* (1933), to discuss the possibility of London Films using the Hillman process. These negotiations were probably prompted by the Prudential, who had a stake in both Gerrard and London Films. In December 1934 it was agreed that London Films would assist with the development of the Hillman process.

Testing of the process took place in the early part of 1935, but it was evident that it was not yet ready for commercial exploitation, while simultaneously in America the first three-strip **Technicolor** feature, *Becky Sharp* (1935), was in production. According to Charles Drazin, after successful previews of *Becky Sharp*, Technicolor founder Herbert Kalmus came to Britain to sell the process and began negotiations with a financier, Sir Adrian Baillie, out of which came a British production company, Tower Films, which was to make only Technicolor films. The fact that Korda's American distributor and partner, United Artists, agreed to distribute Tower Films' output prompted Korda to join the negotiations around this already-proven process. Gerrard Industries were also involved, with Kay Harrison set to become managing director of Technicolor Ltd, so with both major developers now aligned with Technicolor, the Hillman process faded away at the end of 1935.

Further reading

British Journal of Photography, 8 August 1930, p. 482.

Drazin, Charles, 'Korda, Technicolor and the Zeitgeist', *Journal of British Cinema and Television* vol. 7 no. 1, April 2010, pp. 5–20.

Cornwell-Clyne, Adrian, *Colour Cinematography* (London: Chapman & Hall, 3rd edn, 1951), pp. 275–6, 556–9.

Today's Cinema, 23 September 1935, p. 1.

Kinemacolor (1906–15)
Two-colour additive process

Kinemacolor was the first commercially successful natural colour motion picture process. It was developed between 1902 and 1906 by British film pioneer George Albert Smith under the patronage of American film producer Charles Urban. In 1902, while managing director of the Warwick Trading Company, Urban purchased the rights to the patents for an additive colour process filed by **Lee and Turner** from Turner's widow, believing that a working system could be developed from Lee and Turner's experiments. He handed the task over to Smith, who was at that time doing processing work for Urban. From 1903 onwards Smith, who had been successfully making and selling his own films, gave up film-making and focused his attention on the development of this colour system. His major breakthrough was to abandon the idea of three additive primary colours in favour of two, red and green. This discovery addressed two significant problems with the Lee and Turner process, the first of which was the complex projection system. The second problem was one of fringing (see **Additive processes**), which Smith solved only partially.

Smith's simplified version was patented in November 1906. The process recorded successive frames on a single strip of film through an alternating red and green filter. The frames were taken successively at 30–2fps, up to twice the normal speed of 16fps. In projection the positive copy was projected, again at 30–2fps, through corresponding red and green filters. After several test films in 1907, the system was launched in May 1908 at Urbanora House in Wardour Street.

The first public screenings took place at the Palace Theatre in February 1909. In March Urban formed the Natural Color Kinematograph Co. Ltd to exploit the system commercially. Urban took the decision to retain the rights to the process and make money purely from exhibition and overseas patent rights sales. Thus, the Natural Color Kinematograph Co. Ltd controlled the exhibition and patent rights to the process.

Kinemacolor was a great success in the UK, running continuously for eighteen months at the Palace Theatre and swiftly moving out from London to the rest of Britain. While at first all Kinemacolor films were non-fiction, in 1910 Urban hired Theo Bowmeester, who had previously worked for Cecil Hepworth, to direct fiction films in Kinemacolor. In 1911 Urban hired the Scala Cinema in central London as a flagship venue for Kinemacolor films.

Urban then focused his attention on overseas development, selling international licences to the process. However, Kinemacolor achieved only limited international success, due in part to the problems with fringing but also because the system required a special projector in order to show it, which limited its attractiveness to exhibitors. This proved less of an issue in the UK where many highly successful royal-themed films offered an additional attraction, culminating in 1911–12 with the epic coverage of the Delhi Durbar. Ultimately it was not these problems which caused the demise of the system, but William Friese-Greene and **Biocolour**. When Biocolour was launched in August 1911 Urban sued for infringement of Smith's 1906 patent and ordered that Biocolour cease all trading. The dispute continued until December 1912 when Bioschemes – a company set up to fight Kinemacolor in the courts – petitioned for the revoking of Smith's 1906 patent on the grounds that it was insufficiently detailed. This was rejected, but Bioschemes appealed and in March 1914 Smith's patent was revoked on the grounds that its implicit claims to offer the colour blue were not proven. Urban lost his monopoly on natural colour, and immediately liquidated the Natural Color Kinematograph Co., although he carried on the business under the name of Colorfilms until 1915, the same year his appeal against the 1914 ruling was rejected. Internationally, Kinemacolor survived a little longer, with Kinemacolor films being exhibited in Japan until 1917.

Filmography

A Visit to the Seaside (1908), *A Kinemacolor Puzzle* (1909), *SS Olympic* (1910), *From Bud to Blossom* (1910), *From Factory Girl to Prima Donna* (1910), *By Order of Napoleon* (1910), *King Edward's Funeral* (1910), *Refreshments* (1910), *A Lucky Escape: The Story Of The French Revolution* (1911), *The Coronation of King George V and Queen Mary* (1911), *Unveiling of the Queen Victoria Memorial* (1911), *The Flower Girl of Florence* (1911), *Fall of Babylon* (1911), *Telemachus: A Mythological Play* (1911), *A Love Story of Charles II* (1911), *The King of Indigo* (1911), *Scenes in the Indian Camp at Hampton Court, 18 June 1911* (1911), *With our King and Queen Through India* (1912), *Gerald's Butterfly* (1912), *Studies in Natural Colour* (1913), *With the Fighting Forces of Europe* (1914), *The World, the Flesh and the Devil* (1914), *Britain Prepared* (1915) (monochrome film with Kinemacolor sequences)

Further reading

British Journal of Photography, 14 April 1911, p. 286.

McKernan, Luke, '"Something More than a Mere Picture Show": Charles Urban and the Early Non-Fiction Film in Great Britain and America, 1897–1925', unpublished PhD thesis, University of London, 2003. Chapter 3 on Kinemacolor, 'The Eighth Wonder of the World', is available at www.lukemckernan.com/kinemacolor.pdf

Thomas, David B., *The First Colour Motion Pictures* (London: HMSO, 2nd edn, 1983).

Lee and Turner colour process (1899–1903)

Three-colour additive process

Lee and Turner's original design was a camera with a shutter consisting of three opaque sections interspersed with red, green and blue colour filters. Three images were taken in succession, comprising the red, green and blue records, on a single strip of 38mm film. The projection system involved a triple gate, which meant that three frames were projected simultaneously, and each frame was projected three times. The film was projected through a filter wheel with three concentric colour bands. One band ran blue, red, green from the inner part of the wheel to the rim, the second green, blue, red and the third red, green, blue. Thus, the red record would be projected three times, each time through the red filter in one of the concentric bands, which were designed to balance the amount of light reaching the screen, since the bands at the outer rim were larger.

The Lee and Turner process proved to be unworkable but it did have important implications for the early development of additive colour cinematography. Edward Raymond Turner had been working in London for an American inventor, Frederic Ives, who had been developing a process for still colour photography. Ives's process produced a stereoscopic colour image viewed in a machine called a Kromskop. In 1898 Turner went into partnership with a financier, Frederick Marshall Lee, and together they sought to adapt some of the ideas behind the Kromskop into a workable colour process for cinematography. The system described above was patented in March 1899. That same year, Lee and Turner obtained funding from the Warwick Trading Company, which brought them into contact with two men who would develop **Kinemacolor**, managing director Charles Urban and George Albert Smith, pioneer film-maker and inventor, who at this time was responsible for Warwick's processing work. With Urban's support a camera was constructed by Alfred Darling of Brighton in 1901, with a projector following in 1902. Despite this apparent progress the system did not work, and Lee withdrew his backing in 1902. When Turner died in 1903 Urban acquired the patents and turned to Smith to continue the work. The patents acquired by Urban formed the basis of Smith's experiments which led to his simplification of Lee and Turner's process into the two-colour **Kinemacolor** system. There are surviving fragments of film from Lee and Turner's original process. A much-replicated still image of a boy and girl by a swing is held in Bradford's National Media Museum, while the BFI National Archive holds two of Lee and Turner's experiments, *Parrot on Perch* and *Fish in Bowl*.

Filmography

Parrot on Perch (1901), *Fish in Bowl* (1901)

Further reading

Coe, Brian, *The History of Movie Photography* (London: Ash & Grant, 2000), p. 117.

McKernan, Luke, 'The Brighton School and the Quest for Natural Colour', in Vanessa Toulmin and Simon Popple (eds), *Visual Delights Two: Exhibition and Reception* (Sydney: John Libbey and Co., 2004), pp. 205–18.

Morganacolor (1931–37)

Two-colour additive process

Morganacolor was analogous to a 16mm home movie version of **Kinemacolor**. In the camera successive frames of the film were exposed through red and blue-green filters. The film was then reversal processed. The projection system was elaborate with each frame being projected three times, twice while running forward and once backwards through a rotating wheel divided into red and blue sectors, which were in turn divided into smaller sectors with transparent spacings. The projection speed was 72fps, but the forwards/backwards motion meant that it corresponded to 24fps and this complex process served to reduce fringing and flicker.

It was based on patents filed by Sydney George Short of London and Lady Juliet Evangeline Williams of Pontyclud. Lady Williams and her husband Sir Rhys Williams set up a small syndicate company in February 1931 with a nominal capital of £100 to take on the rights to the patents and to look into the possibilities of exploiting the system. Both had been involved the previous year with **Talkicolor**, as had fellow members of the syndicate Elinor Glyn (Lady Williams's mother) and Lady Margot Davson (Lady Williams's sister). In May it was agreed that Rhys and Juliet Williams should enter into negotiations with appropriate companies and by the autumn Rhys Williams was in America having talks with Joseph McNabb, President of Bell and Howell in Chicago. An agreement for Bell and Howell to commercially exploit the system was reached in December 1931, at which time the capital of the company was raised from £100 to £5,100. It was agreed that Bell and Howell would pay a royalty fee to the Morgana Syndicate. By April 1932 McNabb had successfully shown the system to the Chicago Cinema Club and was poised for production, but the commercial exploitation was at the mercy of the Great Depression. McNabb requested in May 1932 that the royalty payment be reduced by 50 per cent and by 1933 the whole venture was losing money.

The registrar was informed to dissolve the company in February 1937 and it was noted at this point that the Morgana patents had been allowed to lapse and that the agreement will Bell and Howell was therefore valueless.

Further reading

BT 31/33242/254470, Morgana Syndicate Ltd, 1931, National Archives.

Cornwell-Clyne, Adrian, *Colour Cinematography* (London: Chapman & Hall, 3rd edn, 1951), p. 270.

Elinor Glyn Collection, University of Reading Special Collection UoR MS-4059.

Pathécolor (1905–c. 30)

Applied colour process

Pathé introduced a process of colouring films using stencils in 1905 and in developing this between 1905 and 1908 they industrialised the painstaking traditional method of hand-colouring film by painting directly onto the frame. Initially Pathé's stencil process was equally laborious and not unique, similar processes being used by both Gaumont and Georges Méliès. A print was made for each colour which was to be added, and the area to be coloured was cut out with a scalpel to make a stencil. Each stencil was then overlaid one at a time on a release print and an operator would brush paint onto the stencil and thus through the cut out and onto the film. By 1906, hundreds of women were employed in the stencil laboratory in Pathé's studio complex at Vincennes. However, as the length of films and the number of prints required increased, due mainly to Pathé's aggressive expansion at the time, this system, like hand-colouring, became impractical. In 1908 the system was mechanised. Stencils were cut by projecting each frame onto a ground glass screen, where an operator would outline elements to be coloured a certain colour using a pointer. This was linked to a cutter which moved over a blank film strip, cutting out the same area and making a series of stencils for different colours. The prints were run through dyeing machines in which the print and the stencil were overlaid in precise register on a wheel and held in place by sprockets. The dye was applied via a velvet ribbon. The process would be repeated with the same print, but a different stencil and different-coloured dye until all the colours had been added. This process was named Pathécolor.

Pathécolor offered the prestige of high-class colour presentation at a fraction of the cost of hand-colouring, and helped Pathé in its bid to make its product stand out in the marketplace. Although Pathé's interpretive stencil process was initially threatened by the commercial success of **Kinemacolor**, it nevertheless remained successful until the 1920s. However, in December 1924 a lecture on the current methods used for Pathécolor was given at the Royal Photographic Society, and the system had barely changed since 1908. It was noted at that time that it took one hour to cut three feet of stencil strip for a single tinting. In the age of the feature film, what was once Pathé's mechanical innovation was very old fashioned and labour intensive. Pathé closed its stencil-colouring labs in 1928 and renamed the process Pathéchrome in 1929. The use of stencil colouring continued into the early 1930s.

Further reading

Abel, Richard, *The Ciné Goes to Town: French Cinema 1896–1915* (Berkeley: University of California Press, 1994), pp. 20–5.

Coe, Brian, *The History of Movie Photography* (London: Ash & Grant, 2000), pp. 113–15.

Lameris, Bregtje, 'Pathécolor: Perfect in their Rendition of the Colours of Nature', *Living Pictures* vol. 2 no. 2, 2003, pp. 46–58.

Read, Paul, 'Unnatural Colour: An Introduction to Colouring Techniques in Silent Era Movies', *Film History* vol. 21 no. 1, 2009, pp. 9–47.

Cherchi Usai, Paolo, *Silent Cinema: An Introduction* (London : BFI, 2000), pp. 21–43.

Polychromide/Verachrome (1922–37)

Two/four-colour subtractive process

Polychromide was developed initially as a process for still photography between 1911 and 1914 by the American Aaron Hamburger, who owned a photographic studio in Dover Street in London. Hamburger went on to become the editor for the Gaumont cinemagazine *Around the Town* when it began in 1919, by which time he was adapting his still colour process for moving images, first patenting and demonstrating his process for cinematography in 1922. Ostensibly this was a two-colour process, although four coloured dyes were used in the processing stage, giving a broader palette than standard two colour could offer. A **beam splitter** in the camera split the light from the object and recorded the red-yellow portion of the scene on one film and the blue-green on another. This was eventually replaced by the use of **bipack film**. The two negatives were then printed onto **duplitised** stock, one on each side in precise register simultaneously using a specially developed printer. The blue-green image was then dyed with a mixture of red and yellow, while the red-yellow image was dyed with a mixture of blue and green. One important innovation made by Hamburger was that the process was the first to fix dyes using a chemical **mordant**. This would become standard for the majority of **subtractive processes**, including **Technicolor**.

British Polychromide Ltd was formed to exploit the process, and Polychromide was adopted by British Pathé News in the 1920s for occasional use in its *Pathé Pictorial* and *Eve's Film Review* cinemagazines alongside Pathécolor. It was briefly marketed by Pathé under the name Verachrome between 1923 and 1925. An interesting scientific coup came in 1927 when British Polychromide Ltd took a colour film of the total eclipse of the sun which took place on 29 June. The film was taken in Giggleswick in North Yorkshire and was shown on 11 November to the Royal Astronomical Society. In 1928 the delegates of the Seventh International Congress of Photography visited the Polychromide works where both still and moving images were printed.

Hamburger died in 1932, and his patents were taken over by a new company, British Colour Films Ltd, registered in 1933 to market the process. This was, however, unsuccessful and the processing plant was disbanded in 1937.

Filmography

The BFI National Archive holds a compilation from 1926 entitled 'Selections Illustrating the British Polychromide Colour Process' which includes the 1927 film of the eclipse.

The film *How I Play Tennis by Mlle Suzanne Lenglen* (1925) is available to view via the British Pathé News website at http://www.britishpathe.com/record.php?id=75159. The colour is not replicated online but the intertitles state that sections are in Veracolor.

Further reading

'Polychromide Colour Process: Photographic Congress Delegates Visit Hamburger's Studio', *Kinematograph Weekly*, 19 July 1928, p. 59.

Coe, Brian, *The History of Movie Photography* (London: Ash & Grant, 1981), p. 128.

Cornwell-Clyne, Adrian, *Colour Cinematography* (London: Chapman & Hall, 3rd edn, 1951), pp.18, 339–41.

Ryan, Roderick T., *A History of Motion Picture Colour Technology* (New York: Focal Press, 1977), pp. 75–7.

Prizmacolor (c. 1917–28)

Four/three/two-colour additive process/two-colour subtractive process

Prizmacolor was developed by the American William Van Doren Kelley and went through a number of different names and processes. Kelley's initial invention in 1913 was called Panchromotion. This was a four-colour additive process using a revolving filter wheel in front of the lens divided into four colour segments – red, green, yellow and blue – each separated by a clear section which was included to give the picture clarity. Each frame was exposed through one colour filter and the clear section. When Panchromotion failed, Kelley continued to develop his four-colour process, which he renamed Prizmacolor, forming a new company, Prizma Inc., sometime before 1917. Like Panchromotion, this version of Prizmacolor used a rotating disc with four filters, the fifth clear filter having been dispensed with. To compensate for the drop in brightness caused by eliminating the clear filter, the saturation level of the colours on the Prizma filter wheel were reduced from the centre outwards, so the saturation of the colours of the filter was less at the outside of the wheel. In projection only two filters were used, red-orange and blue-green, so that the film was shown at twice the normal speed, rather than four times. In February 1917 a demonstration of Prizmacolor took place at the American Museum of Natural History in New York, and the New York Academy of Sciences, and the first commercially released Prizmacolor film, *Our Navy*, was shown in New York the same year.

After this test, Prizmacolor was reworked first as a three- and then a two-colour additive system shooting, like **Kinemacolor** and **Biocolour**, successive frames through a rotating disc comprising red and green filters. For the three-colour version the same filter was used in projection, but for the two-colour version Kelley tried staining alternate frames red and green, as Friese-Greene had done with **Biocolour**.

Around the same time in 1918 Kelley also developed a process known as Kesdacolor with Caroll H. Dunning, who would go on to invent **Dunningcolor**. The process was used for only one film, *Our American Flag*, shown in September 1918. It used a camera with two lenses and a screen banded with vertical red and green lines. The scene was recorded through one lens and through the banded screen. In front of the other lens was a prism arranged so that it did not record the scene at all, but only sunlight. In the camera the film moved forward two frames at a time, the result being that two frames were exposed simultaneously, one recording the latent red and green spectrum of the scene, the other recording only the red and green records from the colour screen. In printing, the two frames were superimposed on **duplitised** film stock, and the record of the screen, which was on one side, was dyed red and blue-green, resulting in a double-sided positive with the banded red and green picture on one side, and the banded red and green filter on the other. The filter was therefore part of the release print.

Kelley subsequently returned to Prizmacolor and Prizma Inc., bringing Dunning with him as vice-president, and revamped Prizma as a subtractive process, using some of the principles of Kesdacolor. The film was taken through a colour filter disc before the camera lens in traditional fashion, the camera recording successive red and blue-green records of the original scene. These records were printed onto a **double-sided** positive. The side with the blue-green record was dyed red-orange and the other, the red record, was dyed blue-green. A one-reel travelogue, *Everywhere with Prizma*, was shown in New York in 1919 at the Rivoli theatre. The first Prizma feature film was *Bali the Unknown*, produced by Myron Selznick and premiered at the Capitol Theatre in New York in February 1921.

Prizmacolor was premiered in the UK in 1921 at the Alhambra Theatre, in a special two-hour private programme of shorts for British exhibitors. In the same year James Stuart Blackton, who was born in Sheffield but had been working for Vitagraph in the USA, decided to use Prizmacolor to make *The Glorious Adventure* (1922) for the Stoll Picture Company. The film was shot by William T. Crespinel who, like Blackton, was born in England and who had worked for Blackton at Vitagraph in 1915, having moved to America with **Kinemacolor** in 1912, after working for them in London. Crespinel joined Prizma from Vitagraph to work with Kelley in 1917. The film was processed at the Prizma labs in America, and premiered in January 1922 at the Royal Opera House in Covent Garden. In 1923 Blackton made *The Virgin Queen* in England, which featured sections in Prizmacolor. This was followed the same year in America by Goldwyn's *Vanity Fair*. Problems with fringing made the system problematic for feature use but it flourished in the shorts and animated market. In 1922, Prizma released twenty-six short films which by the end of that year had developed into three separate series, Prizma Master Pictures, Music Films and Prizma Color Cartoons by Pinto Colvig. Yet, despite being seemingly poised for success, by the end of 1922, with a flourishing number of shorts and several features, Prizmacolor died quickly, and the company was in severe trouble by the end of 1923. William T. Crespinel put this down to the location of the labs in Jersey City and the failure to move out to California. Kelley started work on a new process called Kelleycolor and, in 1928, the Prizma patents were acquired by Consolidated Film Industries, part of Republic Pictures; the process name was changed to Magnacolor.

Filmography

The Glorious Adventure (1922), *The Virgin Queen* (1923), *Vanity Fair* (1923), *Flames of Passion* (1923, sequences), *Pagliacci* (1923, sequences)

Further reading

British Journal of Photography Colour Supplement, 6 April 1917, p. 14.

British Journal of Photography Colour Supplement, 6 May 1921, pp. 18–19.

Cherchi Usai, Paolo, *Silent Cinema: An Introduction* (London: BFI, 2000), p. 35.

Crespinel, William A., 'Pioneer Days in Color Motion Pictures with William T. Crespinel', *Film History* vol. 12 no. 1, 2000, pp. 57–71.

Limbacher, James L., *Four Aspects of the Film: A History of the Development of Color, Sound, 3-D and Widescreen Films and their Contribution to the Art of the Motion Picture* (New York: Brussel and Brussel, 1968), pp. 18–20.

Nowotny, Robert A., *The Way of All Flesh Tones: A History of Color Motion Picture Processes, 1895–1929* (New York and London: Garland, 1983), pp. 154–85.

Raycol (1928–35)

Two-colour additive process

Raycol used a **beam splitter** to produce two quarter-sized pictures in the normal frame area. At first the two images were diagonal in the frame, but later this was adjusted so that they were placed one directly above the other. The images were projected through two half-lenses one above the other, which could be adjusted to

ensure that correct superimposition of the two images was achieved on the screen. Initially, upon projection the images were superimposed, one through a red filter and one through no filter, which made the picture brighter than normal and offered a surprising range of colours considering only one filter was used. This system was eventually replaced by using coloured lenses, one red-orange glass and one green glass.

Raycol was the invention of the Austrian chemist Anton Bernardi. Bernardi moved to Britain in 1926, changing his name to Anthony Bernardi, to raise capital for the development of his new colour process. His initial attempts failed, resulting in him being adjudged bankrupt in 1928. The judgment was, however, reversed because Bernardi patented his process in February 1928 and while in the bankruptcy courts he sold the rights to Charles Bolton, director of the mining company Wheal Reeth Tin Ltd, who formed a company, Raycol Ltd, to acquire them. Raycol Ltd was quickly wound up and Bernardi and Bolton formed a holding company, Temple Holdings Ltd, to prepare for the formation in 1929 of Raycol British Corporation Ltd. Bernardi was hired as technical advisor, while on the board sat Bolton, along with Charles Henry, the Duke of Richmond and Gordon, Major John Sewell Courtauld MP and the film-maker Maurice Elvey, who was also managing director of the company. With such heavyweight personalities on the board, Raycol was clearly aiming at a big success. In 1929 author Elinor Glyn announced she was producing a sound version of one of her novels, *Knowing Men*, and Elvey offered on behalf of Raycol to bankroll the production if she made it using the process. The deal quickly fell through and Glyn instead used the **Talkicolor** process, but the offer to fund the production indicates the ambition of Raycol British. Elvey demonstrated the process to the trade in July 1930 and in September announced that six shorts and seven features would go into production early in 1931. However, the only film made was the short *The School for Scandal*, directed by Elvey in 1930, which has the distinction of being the first British colour sound film. Bernardi moved on in 1930 to work on the development of **Talkicolor**.

Over the next three years Raycol was used for shorts and animated films before production of the first Raycol feature film, *The Skipper of the Osprey* (1933). Like most additive processes the drawback with Raycol was that it needed special projection equipment and very precise adjustment on the part of the projectionist, resulting in frequent problems at screenings of the film. In December 1933 a new company, Raycol British Productions Ltd, was formed and granted sole and exclusive rights to the Raycol process, but nothing came of the venture. Elvey and Bolton ceased to be involved, and in 1935 Raycol's development continued under Basil Dean's Associated Talking Pictures (ATP). This deal was negotiated by Jack and Stephen Courtald who were directors of both Raycol and ATP. ATP announced plans to transform Raycol from a two- to a three-colour process in July 1935, the same week that *Becky Sharp* was premiered. Dean announced plans in September to use Raycol to film colour versions of *Twelfth Night* and *The Tempest*. However, nothing came of these plans. Raycol British and Raycol British Productions were both wound up. In 1934 Bernardi took on the directorship and development of Omnicolor.

Filmography

The School for Scandal (1930), *The Cane Bottomed Chair* (1932), *Hastings* (1932), *The Skipper of the Osprey* (1933), *On the Farm* (1933), *The Scilly Isles* (1933), *Zoo Oddities* (1933), *Colonel Capers* (1933), *Barnacle Bill No 1: Treasure Island* (1934)

Further reading

BT 31/33013/234772, Raycol Ltd, 1928, National Archives.

BT 31/33090/239872, Raycol British Corporation Ltd, 1929, National Archives.

BT 31/35591/282398 Raycol Productions Ltd, 1933, National Archives.

Coe, Brian, *The History of Movie Photography* (London: Ash & Grant, 1981), p. 120.

Cornwell-Clyne, Adrian, *Colour Cinematography* (London: Chapman & Hall, 3rd edn, 1951), pp. 265–8.

Rhys Williams Collection, London School of Economics British Library of Political and Economic Science (Rhys_Williams_J_16/2/1, 16/2/2, 16/2/3).

Realita/Francita/Opticolor (1931–39)

Three-colour additive process

For a few years in the 1930s the French Francita process was marketed in the UK, first by Opticolor Ltd and then by the British Realita Syndicate Ltd, so that reports in the British trade press refer to the process both as Opticolor and Realita. They are, in fact, the same. The process was developed in France by Maurice Velle, initially starting out by registering three small images within a normal film frame, one above the other two in a pyramid shape. This version was first demonstrated in 1931 but by 1933, when it was demonstrated as Opticolor in the USA, it had undergone revisions based on patents submitted by Jean Marie Guttman and Pierre Angenieux. The system now registered small-sized images representing the red and green records diagonally across the film frame, after which the film was wound on half a frame and the blue record was registered in the remaining empty space, resulting in a frame with two records on the left-hand side of the frame one above the other, and one on the right. This system meant that the process required only two lenses for a three-colour image. The pictures were taken at 48fps. A black-and-white print was then made from the negative and projected through a corresponding series of filters mounted in an adjustable mechanism which allowed for the three images to be moved into registration on the screen. Precise registration was impossible because the blue record was registered a fraction later than the red and green records.

While the process enjoyed some modest success in France, being used for the only two colour feature films released in France before World War II, *Jeunes Filles à Marier* (1935) and *La Terre qui Meurt* (1936), in Britain the exploitation of the process was prevented by a complex and fractious period of development. The French Francita company was formed in 1932 with a capital of 4 million francs and in 1934 acquired the patent rights excluding certain territories, among them Britain. Francita formed the Société Realita in 1933 to acquire the rights to the remaining territories. In 1936 the British rights were granted to Opticolor Ltd, formed by Mary Murillo. Murillo had become interested in the process in early 1935 and in January 1936 signed an agreement with Société Realita to acquire the UK licence by forming a company with capital of £1 million by November. However, the investors which she had lined up pulled out after a disastrous demonstration of the process, leaving Murillo in need of short-term capital to make interim payments of £1,000 per month to Realita, which she persuaded businessman Sir Thomas Bazley to cover. Murillo claimed that Realita had delivered faulty lenses for the demonstration, and in July

1936 she refused to continue the payments. Bazley inspected both the books and the process and decided that the process was viable but that Opticolor as a business was not, and so resigned from the board and set up British Realita Syndicate to take on the rights.

While technical development proceeded, including working with Vintens to produce new lenses, the company was unable to go into full-scale commercial development because Murillo and Opticolor refused to accept that they were in breach of their contract. The grounds were that Opticolor had defaulted on its payments, but Murillo argued that this was because Société Realita had defaulted on their agreement to supply the correct lenses. With British Realita unable to confirm sole ownership of the rights to the process, they were unable to attract investors.

Limited production nevertheless took place in 1937. The first film was of the Coronation procession of King George VI. In a major coup, British Realita managed to get the film processed in time to screen it that same afternoon in the Cameo News Cinema in London. While this was a great achievement, the film was not widely distributed because most British cinemas did not have the mechanism required for projection. The film was shown in Manchester, Bristol and Birmingham, but received much wider distribution outside the UK in Holland, Belgium and Canada, where the Francita system was more established and more cinemas had the necessary equipment. The publicity surrounding the speedy projection of the Coronation film was, however, sufficient to encourage cinema owners to invest and within days orders for the projection mechanism were coming in from the UK, while the Italian rights to the process were also sold. Realita immediately announced it was filming the Naval Review, the Trooping of the Colour and the Aldershot Tattoo. These projects were successful enough to encourage the company in June 1937 to make their first studio film about a collection of rare masks from 200BC to the present day, photographed by John Odle, the company's chief technician and managing director.

Despite considerable pressure from British Realita, Société Realita did not pursue a resolution regarding the Opticolor situation. Having already paid out around £40,000, British Realita refused to pay more until the situation was resolved to the satisfaction of potential investors, meaning that by May 1938 British

Realita still had not received a licence from France. Furthermore, Thomas Bazley was approached by two separate individuals offering the chance to buy a controlling interest in Société Realita, and discovered that neither individual was aware of the other, strongly suggesting serious problems in France. With almost no capital, no licence and little prospect of getting one, 1938 saw British Realita selling off its assets and closing its offices. John Odle and British Realita's other technician, the American Lars Moen, abandoned Realita and went to Belgium to develop a process which they called Truecolor. Hopes were raised in 1939 when William Fox agreed to meet Moen and Bazley in Paris to discuss the possibility of using Truecolor/Realita, having previously been involved with **Chemicolor**. The prospect of war, however, caused him to cancel his trip, while the invasion of Belgium by Germany at the outbreak of the war caused Moen to close down his lab in Belgium, effectively signalling the end of British Realita. Francita in France continued in business after the war, attempting to develop a subtractive process under the Francita/Realita banner.

Filmography
The Coronation of Their Majesties King George VI and Queen Elizabeth (1937), *Coronation Naval Review* (1937), *RAF Review at Hendon* (1937)

Further reading
Cornwell-Clyne, Adrian, *Colour Cinematography* (London: Chapman & Hall, 3rd edn, 1951), pp. 279–80.
Crisp, Colin G., *The Classic French Cinema 1930–1960* (Bloomington: Indiana University Press, 1993), p. 136.
Dixon, Bryony and Genaitay, Sonia, 'Early Colour Film Restoration at the BFI National Archive', *Journal of British Cinema and Television* vol. 7 no. 1, April 2010, pp. 131–46.
Thomas Bazley Collection Gloucestershire Archives, D540/48 to D540/59.
Today's Cinema, 2 June 1937, p. xi.
Today's Cinema, 16 June 1937, p. 31.

Spectracolor (1935–c. 37)
Two-colour subtractive process
Spectracolor was a derivation of the German Ufacolor system which was briefly marketed in the UK in the mid-1930s and found moderate success in commercial

advertising films. The process was similar to **Chemicolor** which was also based on the UFA system and marketed in Britain around the same time. In the camera a red and blue image was recorded on a **bipack** negative. The negative was printed onto each side of **double-coated** film stock which was then **dye-toned** blue-green on one side and red-orange on the other and fixed using a **mordant**. The relationship between Chemicolor and Spectracolor is unclear. Limbacher, for example, states that Chemicolor later became Spectracolor, when in fact the two processes were unveiled almost simultaneously. Interestingly, Ufacolor itself was not widely used in Germany during the 1930s.

The process was launched in April 1935 by Publicity Picture Productions with a special presentation at the Curzon Cinema in Mayfair. Two films made by Herbert Hopkins and Reginald Wire were shown at the launch, an animated short which was part of a series called *Cheery Tunes* (obviously derived from Disney's *Silly Symphony* series), plus *Faust*, a live-action feature which had been shot at Publicity's Bushey Studios.

Publicity Pictures developed, wrote and produced films to order for commercial clients who would approach them with an idea for an advertising film. From 1935 they offered to make their films in Spectracolor if the client desired, and also offered an in-house Spectracolor printing service to other companies. At a time when considerable debate was taking place in the trade paper *The Commercial Film* about the value of colour to the advertising sector, a number of clients took up the option of using Spectracolor. One of the earliest films to use the process was an advertising film for the Marconiphone, released to tie into the Jubilee celebrations for George V in 1935. The film was moderately successful, with twelve copies released. In August 1935 Publicity Pictures Ltd used the process for the first advertising film ever commissioned by Mackintosh's Toffee, while in February 1936 the Dorland Advertising Agency produced a film called *Fashion Sketches* for Clark's Anchor Tricoton in Spectracolor.

There is very little information to indicate what happened to Spectracolor. Most likely, given its close links to the German system, the gathering clouds of war in the late 1930s hampered its development as relations between Britain and Germany strained and finally collapsed.

Filmography

Faust (1935), *Morris May Day* (1935), *The Jolly Farmer* (1935), *The Marconiphone* (1935), *The Midshipman* (1935), *The Baronial Beanfeast* (1935), *Carnival Capers* (1935), *The Gay Cavalier* (1936), *Railroad Rhythm* (1936), *Fashion Sketches* (1936)

Further reading

The Commercial Film, April 1935, pp. 2, 14.

The Commercial Film, January–February 1936, p. 11.

The Commercial Film, May–June 1936, p. 6.

Cornwell-Clyne, Adrian, *Colour Cinematography* (London: Chapman & Hall, 3rd edn, 1951), p. 342.

Limbacher, James L., *Four Aspects of the Film: A History of the Development of Color, Sound, 3-D and Widescreen Films and their Contribution to the Art of the Motion Picture* (New York: Brussel and Brussel, 1968), p. 40.

Talkicolor (1929–37)
Two-colour additive process

Talkicolor was developed by Percy James Pearce along with Dr Anthony Bernardi who was also involved in the development of **Raycol**. The process was funded mainly by the author Elinor Glyn through her company Elinor Glyn Ltd, run by her daughter Juliet Evangeline Williams and her husband Sir Rhys Williams, assisted by her other daughter, Lady Margot Davson, all of whom were also involved in the development of **Morganacolor**. In 1929 Glyn decided to adapt one of her novels, *Knowing Men*, into a sound film. She had previously adapted it for silent film and so hired writer Edward Knoblock to rework the silent scenario for sound. The film, to be produced by a small syndicate company called Talking and Sound Films Ltd, was due to start shooting on 1 October 1929 and, by August, Glyn was considering making the film in colour, entering into discussions with Maurice Elvey and Raycol. Raycol agreed not only to allow Glyn to use the process free of charge but also to fund the production in order to publicise their process. By September this arrangement had broken down. Elvey insisted upon producing, a role that Glyn was doing herself, while Glyn insisted that the film be available in both colour and black and white, a decision with which Elvey did not agree. Lady Williams hired lawyers who found the Raycol patents to be unreliable. Looking around for an alternative, Rhys Williams signed a deal in September with Bernardi for the rights to use Talkicolor for two films, *Knowing Men* and *The Price of Things* (both 1931). Bernardi was bought out of his contract with Raycol and hired to develop the process, and a company, Talkicolor Ltd, was formally set up in September 1929, backed by Elinor Glyn Ltd.

The process used a **bipack** film in the camera. The front layer was sensitised to blue light and dyed orange to prevent blue and green rays from passing through to the second emulsion which recorded the red portion of the spectrum. The two negatives were separated and then printed successively onto positive stock, so that each frame of the red record alternated with each frame of the blue record. The film was then projected at double speed through an alternating red and clear filter, the red record being projected through the red filter, the blue-green record being projected through a clear filter. An alternate projection method was also suggested to dye the red record red, and to leave the blue-green record black and white. Which version was actually used is not known.

As production of *Knowing Men* and *The Price of Things* continued, in January 1930 Sir Rhys Williams signed an agreement with United Artists (UA) to distribute the film internationally in both silent and sound versions, for which UA paid an advance of £15,000. Both films were family affairs. Glyn both wrote and produced *Knowing Men* (ending up in a bitter dispute with Edward Knoblock), while *The Price of Things* was directed by Juliet Williams and designed by Lady Davson. Costumes for both were provided by designer Lucy Duff-Gordon, Glyn's sister. By August 1930 it was clear that the process was technically flawed. At a board meeting it was reported that the results were disappointing and that it was highly unlikely that the colour version of *The Price of Things* could ever be shown. Both films lost considerable sums of money, *Knowing Men* never making back the £15,000 which United Artists had advanced, and Talkicolor started retrenching by selling off assets and laying off staff. In September the company cancelled its agreements with Bernardi. By 1933 there was talk of winding up the company once the bookings on *Knowing Men* were officially closed. In 1937 Lady Williams wrote to the registrar of companies in Britain to formally request that Talkicolor be dissolved.

Filmography
Knowing Men (1931), *The Price of Things* (1931)

Further reading
BT 31/33126/242400 Talkicolor Company Ltd, 1929, National Archives.
Elinor Glyn Collection, University of Reading Special Collections (UoR MS 4059).
Rhys Williams Collection, London School of Economics British Library of Political and Economic Science (Rhys_Williams_J_16/2/1, 16/2/2, 16/2/3).

Technicolor (1917–55)

Two-colour additive process/two-colour subtractive process/three-colour subtractive process
Founded in the USA as the Technicolor Motion Picture Corporation in 1915 by Herbert Kalmus, Daniel Comstock and W. Burton Westcott, in the 1930s Technicolor swept aside all the competition to become the most commercially successful colour film company and process. Most often the name is associated with three-strip Technicolor – used for such key 1930s colour films as *Becky Sharp* (1935), *Gone with the Wind* (1939) and *The Wizard of Oz* (1939) – which is officially known as Technicolor Process No. 4. The name gives testament to the fact that the rapid success of Technicolor was in fact the result of years of painstaking trial and error in the area of research, coupled with an aggressive campaign of commercial exploitation.

The first Technicolor process, unveiled in 1917, was an additive system which used a **beam splitter** in the camera to record two frames simultaneously through red and green filters. The two images were registered successively on the negative and processed into a positive. In projection the successive images were projected through the corresponding filters and through a prism which could be adjusted to bring the successive frames into precise register.

Technicolor's two-colour subtractive process was actually two processes, the second one being a refinement of the first, which was developed in 1922. Technicolor's first subtractive process – known as Technicolor Process No. 2 – used a **beam splitter** to create two separate colour record negatives, as the additive system had done, but with significant variations. The camera exposed the red and green images simultaneously through filters, but a new prism was included that exposed the green record upside down.

From the two negatives two dyed positive relief images were made using special stock known as the matrix (see **Dye transfer/Dye imbibition**). The two relief images were cemented back to back and then dyed red-orange on the green side and green on the red side, making a subtractive print that was the normal thickness and could be used on any conventional projector. The system was successful but had problems, notably that in time one of the two cemented images would frequently break away from the other, causing the print to go out of focus.

In 1928 the processing was improved by virtue of a **dye-transfer** process, which became known as Technicolor Process No. 3. The two relief images were produced as they had been in Process No. 2 and two matrices were created but instead of being cemented together they remained separate. Still in relief, and dyed with the correct colours, the matrices were then pressed using pressured rollers against a blank film coated with gelatine to which the dyed images were transferred by embossing the relief images onto the blank film with the dye, the dyes being locked by the use of a **mordant**. By this method multiple layers could be registered on a single film strip.

Even as Process No. 3 was being rolled out commercially, Kalmus continued his research to figure out a way to use three colours, thus making possible the rendering of the full colour spectrum. The dye-transfer process had effectively solved one of the problems of three-colour cinematography, which was that even by using **double-sided** film there was still the challenge of how to register the third colour on the print. Imbibition allowed two or more colour images to be transferred via the matrices onto the print, provided that the images were in precise register. Kalmus therefore focused on producing a working three-colour camera. Initial experiments with a successive-frame system were abandoned in favour of a camera which used a **beam splitter** to split the light from the source through filters, the green record passing straight through a green filter onto a film strip, while the red and blue records were captured on a **bipack** film through a magenta filter. The camera therefore produced three negatives, one red, one blue, one green. As with the two-colour process, gelatine relief matrices were made which were then dyed complementary subtractive colours and pressed one after the other against a blank film which absorbed the dye.

The success of Technicolor has as much to do with the way in which Kalmus ran the business as the quality of the process itself. As stated, Technicolor Process No. 2 suffered from a number of problems – not only the cement joining the two thin emulsions coming apart, but also cupping, where the heat from repeated projections would cause one emulsion to shrink slightly and throw the images out of register. While not sharing the same problems in projection, three-strip Technicolor was expensive and involved the use of a large, cumbersome camera, making location shooting difficult. Similar issues had led to the demise of other processes, but despite the fact that for years the company lost money, Kalmus managed to keep finding investors to back his work and film directors willing to experiment. From the first feature using the original two-colour additive system – *The Gulf Between* (1917) – Technicolor in all its incarnations appeared in some of the biggest Hollywood films of the day, albeit often only in short sequences. Thus, after being used for the first time to make *The Toll of the Sea* (1922), the cemented positive process was used for significant scenes in films including *The Ten Commandments* (1923), *The Phantom of the Opera* (1925) and *Ben Hur* (1926). Also in 1926 the commercial exploitation of Technicolor received a boost when Douglas Fairbanks decided to make *The Black Pirate* entirely in Technicolor, but the success of the film only proved how unworkable the cemented positive system was as Technicolor struggled to cope with the large number of prints required and the increased number of problems which consequentially arose. Technicolor was making losses and enjoying only very moderate success, yet Kalmus continued to develop his ideas even after the conversion to sound was followed by the Great Depression, which saw a shift in aesthetics in Hollywood towards black and white and away from colour.

Three-strip Technicolor led to the company becoming the industry leader. In 1932 Kalmus approached Walt Disney, who used three-strip Technicolor for a number of his *Silly Symphony* shorts. Shortly afterwards, in 1934, the first live-action Technicolor short was released, *La Cucaracha*, followed by the first feature film, *Becky Sharp* (1935). It was the global success of this film which propelled three-strip Technicolor forward, and it was the impact of *Becky Sharp* in the UK, as well as the quality of the image, which first attracted Alexander Korda to the process and encouraged him to abandon his plans to use **Hillman**

colour, thus bringing the Technicolor brand to the UK. The first British film made using the process was *Wings of the Morning* (1937), and Technicolor would ultimately be used for some of the most respected British films of the 1940s, including *Black Narcissus* (1947) and *The Red Shoes* (1948).

Filmography
See Appendix 1 for list of British three-strip Technicolor films

Further reading
Basten, Fred E., *Glorious Technicolor: The Movies' Magic Rainbow* (New Jersey: A. S. Barnes and Co., 1980).
Coe, Brian, *The History of Movie Photography* (London: Ash & Grant, 1981), pp. 132–5.
Cornwell-Clyne, Adrian, *Colour Cinematography* (London: Chapman & Hall, 3rd edn, 1951), pp. 451–507.
Haines, Richard W., *Technicolor Movies: The History of Dye Transfer Printing* (London: McFarland and Co., 1993).
Higgins, Scott, *Harnessing the Technicolor Rainbow: Colour Design in the 1930s* (Austin: University of Texas Press, 2007).
Huntley, John, *British Technicolor Films* (London: Skelton Robinson, 1949).

Tinting and toning (c. 1900–c. 30)
Applied colour process
Tinting and toning became the standard method of adding colour to black-and-white films in the silent era, to the extent that Paolo Cherchi Usai has suggested that as much as 85 per cent of the total production of silent films was either tinted, or toned, or both, based upon surviving nitrate copies.

Although they are routinely discussed together, tinting and toning were two different technical processes which could be applied in tandem or separately. The simpler of the two was tinting. Initially, tinting was done by applying coloured varnish to the print with a brush, but this was prone to streaking and so the process adapted into a system of immersing black-and-white positive film into a dye, which was absorbed by the gelatine in the emulsion and so gave a uniform colour. The colouring of tinting became standardised and was chosen to suit the scene in terms of the setting, action or general mood. Night-time scenes were commonly tinted blue, and yellow was used for day-time scenes or interiors. Fire scenes were tinted red. In 1912 the

Belgian Gevaert company released a range of pre-tinted stock which was gradually adopted by the industry to become commonplace by the 1920s. Kodak responded to the coming of sound on film in the late 1920s and early 30s with Sonochrome, pre-coloured film stock designed for sound use.

Toning was much more complicated. While tinting effectively coloured the lighter areas of the frame, since the colour was more visible in the lighter areas, toning was a chemical process which coloured the darker areas. Toning involved the alteration or replacement of the silver salts which made up the image in a frame of nitrate film into or with another, coloured, metallic compound. Toning, therefore, did not provide a 'wash' of colour like tinting. It only affected the parts of the image where the silver was at its densest. White images would, therefore, remain pure white during the toning process. The main method of toning was to use one solution to convert the silver that forms the image into colourless silver salts, a process known as bleaching, and then a second solution that replaced those silver salts with another coloured metal compound, such as iron, which would produce a blue-green colour. In the latter half of the 1910s another method was developed using **mordanting**. After bleaching, the silver salts acted as a mordant to which a dye could attach itself. Mordanting allowed for organic colours to be used, broadening the range of available colours previously limited by the available metallic compounds such as iron, copper and uranium.

Tinting and toning was widely adopted around 1907, having been used from approximately 1900, and remained the standard until the mid-1920s. The reasons for their decline have not been fully established. A common belief is that tinting and toning affected the density of the soundtrack when sound films arrived. This, however, is challenged by the development of Sonochrome film, which was adopted by the industry but not to the same extent as pre-tinted stock. One of the problems with Sonochrome was that sound films were edited in a different way. Silent film release prints were assembled from tinted and toned sections, and were therefore full of joins. Sound films, on the other hand, were assembled in the negative stage and printed in such a way that a 1,000ft reel had no joins, so with Sonochrome it was largely necessary to have each 1,000ft reel the same colour, rather than made up of different-coloured sections, a limitation which defeated the point of tinting and toning. Other theories suggest that the introduction of sound added an element of realism to film with which the expressionist tinting and toning clashed, focusing attention away from non-natural colour and spurring the development of natural colour. Whatever the reasons, by the early 1930s tinting and toning had largely disappeared.

Further reading
Coe, Brian, *The History of Movie Photography* (London: Ash & Grant, 1981), pp. 114, 116.

Read, Paul, 'Unnatural Colour: An Introduction to Colouring Techniques in Silent Era Movies', *Film History* vol. 21 no. 1, 2009, pp. 9–47.

Cherchi Usai, Paolo, *Silent Cinema: An Introduction* (London: BFI, 2000), pp. 21–43.

Zoechrome (1911–32)
Two/three-colour subtractive process
Zoechrome was developed Thomas Albert Mills over an extended period. He first patented a successive-frame system for two- or three-colour cinematography in December 1911. This was a complicated system in which, for two-colour, successive images were captured through blue and orange filters. After printing the successive frames were toned blue and orange and then the film was coated with emulsion on the back and the same images printed one frame out of register and toned identically, so behind each blue-toned frame on the print was an orange-toned frame. Zoechrome Ltd was registered in February 1912 with a nominal capital of £15,000 in £1 shares to acquire the rights Mill's patents. From 1921 the process was significantly revised and by the time it was first demonstrated in 1929 it used one large and three smaller lenses. Successive frames were registered, one through the large, normal-sized lens creating a full-frame picture, and the next through the three smaller lenses resulting in three small images registered on a normal-sized frame. This created a negative which alternated between one full-sized frame and one frame with three smaller images. Each single frame image was printed to produce a black-and-white print of the full-frame image. This was then fixed with varnish and then recoated with emulsion. One of the three smaller images was then enlarged and printed over the full-frame image in register. The print was then **dye-toned** with the correct subtractive colour, and the process repeated with the other two colours. The function of the single, black-and-white full-frame image was effectively to override any parallax issues from the three smaller images, the larger one being much clearer and more dominant.

The first public demonstration of the process took place on 12 March 1929 at the New Gallery in London, featuring footage of the sea, country lanes and flowers. Despite a favourable review the following day in *The Times*, the company appears to have never traded and an official receiver was appointed in April 1931. When the process was offered for sale in 1932 there were no buyers and it ceased development.

Further reading
BT 31/32118/120350, Zoechrome Ltd, 1912, National Archives.

Coe, Brian, *The History of Movie Photography* (London: Ash & Grant, 1981), pp. 130–1.

Cornwell-Clyne, Adrian, *Colour Cinematography* (London: Chapman & Hall, 3rd edn, 1951), p. 536.

Neale, Steve, *Cinema and Technology: Image, Sound, Colour* (London: BFI, 1985), p. 123.

Cherchi Usai, Paolo, *Silent Cinema: An Introduction* (London: BFI, 2000), p. 36.

NOTES

INTRODUCTION

1. Alexander Korda, 'They Talk Colour', *Cine-Technician* vol. 3 no. 14, March–April 1937–8, p. 192.

2. As Chapter 1 details, estimates for the percentage of coloured films in the silent era are high, as much as 80–85 per cent.

3. See Scott Higgins, *Harnessing the Technicolor Rainbow: Color Design in the 1930s* (Austin: University of Texas Press, 2007) and Dudley Andrew, 'The Post-War Struggle for Colour', in Angela Dalle Vacche and Brian Price (eds), *Color: The Film Reader* (New York: Routledge, 2006).

4. Huntley (1921–2003) was a writer and educationalist. In the 1950s he was a member of the British Film Institute's executive and head of regional development. He was also a film collector, establishing the Huntley Archives in the mid-1980s. See *Guardian* obituary, 11 August 2003.

5. John Huntley, *British Technicolor Films* (London: Skelton Robinson, 1949), p. 19.

6. Dilys Powell, quoted in Huntley, ibid., pp. 20, 144.

7. Roland Dailly writing in *L'Ecran Francaise* in 1948, quoted in Andrew, 'The Post-War Struggle for Colour', p. 45.

8. Andrew, 'The Post-War Struggle for Colour', p. 46.

9. A 'roadshow', identified with American exhibition practices, involved a film being released selectively in a few key cities before general release. Several British films in the 1940s were released in this way to build up audiences for them when released in the USA.

10. Charles O'Brien, *Cinema's Conversion to Sound: Technology and Film Style in France and the US* (Bloomington and Indianapolis: Indiana University Press, 2005).

11. Ibid., p. 7.

12. Immanuel Kant, *Critique of Asethetic Judgement* and Roland Barthes, *Camera Lucida: Reflections on Photography* (London: Vintage, 1982), p. 81, quoted in David Batchelor, *Chromophobia* (London: Reaktion, 2000), p. 53, emphasis added.

13. Béla Balázs, *Early Film Theory: Visible Man and the Spirit of Film*, ed. Erica Carter (New York and Oxford: Berghahn, 2010), pp. 76–9.

14. Scott Higgins, 'Deft Trajectories for the Eye: Bringing Arnheim to Vincente Minnelli's Color Design', in Scott Higgins (ed.), *Arnheim for Film and Media Studies* (New York: Routledge, 2011), pp. 107–8.

15. Andrew, 'The Post-War Struggle for Colour', p. 40, emphasis in original.

16. Jack Cardiff, 'Foreword' to Huntley, *British Technicolor Films*, p. 9.

17. Some of these periods are covered in Simon Brown and Sarah Street (eds), 'Colour in British Cinema and Television', special issue of *Journal of British Cinema and Television* vol. 7 no. 1, 2010.

18. Michael Powell, *Million Dollar Movie* (London: Heinemann, 1992), p. 35.

1 COLOUR IN SILENT BRITAIN

1. *Collier's: The National Weekly*, 3 May 1924, p. 28. This is somewhat different from Griffith's views in 1916, when he argued that the reproduction of natural colours would be 'carrying realism too far' since black and white was often 'more artistic', *New York Times*, 10 December 1916, X8.

2. The Griffith article annotated with Urban's comment can be located in URB, 9/3-8 (56), Urban papers, National Media Museum, Bradford. Kinecrom was a patent process developed by Urban and Henry Joy during World War I, described by Urban as 'destined to solve the problem of producing actual natural colours by light rays only from machines which will run any existing standard gauge film as well as Kinekrom, produced at one-third the cost of Kinemacolor', in 'Terse History of Natural

Kinematography', unpublished typescript, 1921; URB 9/1, Urban archive, National Media Museum, Bradford. Kinecrom was never fully perfected and was still being prepared for commercial production when Urban's business collapsed in 1924.

3. For a listing of patents registered for colour processes in Britain, 1893–1930 see Benjamin Pask, 'Capturing Colour: The British Pursuit of Natural Colour Cinema during the Silent Period', unpublished MA thesis, University of East Anglia, 2004, pp. 78–87.

4. Tom Gunning, 'Colorful Metaphors: The Attraction of Color in early Silent Cinema', *Fotogenia 1: Il Colore nel Cinema/Color in the Cinema*, 1994, reproduced in *Living Pictures: The Journal of the Popular and Projected Image before 1914* vol. 2 no. 2, 2003, pp. 4–13.

5. Simon Brown, 'Colouring the Nation: Spectacle, Reality and British Natural Colour in the Silent and Early Sound Era', *Film History* vol. 21 no. 2, 2009, pp. 139–49. The term 'spectacle of reality' was developed by Vanessa R. Schwartz in *Spectacular Realities: Early Mass Culture in Fin-de-Siècle Paris* (Berkeley: University of California Press, 1998).

6. Paolo Cherchi Usai, *Silent Cinema: An Introduction* (London: BFI, 2000), p. 23, and Giovanna Fossati, in Daan Hertogs and Nico de Klerk (eds), *'Disorderly Order': Colours in Silent Film* (Amsterdam: Stichting Nederlands Filmmuseum, 1996), p. 12.

7. Paul Read, 'Tinting and Toning Techniques and their Adaptation for the Restoration of Archive Film', in *All the Colours of the World: Colours in Early Mass Media, 1900–30* (Reggio Emilia: Edizioni Diabasis, 1998), p. 160.

8. Cherchi Usai, *Silent Cinema*, p. 39, and Gunning, in Hertogs and de Klerk, *'Disorderly Order'*, p. 18.

9. Particularly notable studies include Brian Coe, *The History of Movie Photography* (London: Ash & Grant, 1981), pp. 112–39; Richard Abel, *The Red Rooster Scare: Making Cinema American, 1900–1910* (Berkeley: University of California Press, 1999) has a section on Pathé and colour; Joshua Yumibe, 'Moving Color: An Aesthetic History of Applied Color Technologies in Silent Cinema', unpublished PhD thesis, University of Chicago, 2007; special issues of *Film History* vol. 21, nos 1 and 2, 2009; Eirik Frisvold Hanssen, *Early Discourses on Colour and Cinema: Origins, Functions, Meanings* (Stockholm: Stockholm University, 2006); special issue of *Living Pictures*, Luke McKernan (ed.), vol. 2 no. 2, 2003.

10. For a discussion of current practices and examples, see Sonia Genaitay and Bryony Dixon, 'Early Colour Film Restoration at the BFI National Archive', *Journal of British Cinema and Television* vol. 7 no. 1, 2010, pp. 131–46.

11. Coe, *The History of Movie Photography*, p. 112.

12. Yumibe, 'Moving Color', pp. 173–4, 178.

13. Coe, *The History of Movie Photography*, pp. 113–15.

14. This is based on a survey of *Kinematograph Weekly* of second-hand film advertisements in January 1909, Pask, 'Capturing Colour', p. 13.

15. *Kinematograph and Lantern Weekly*, 6 June 1907, p. 66, and 21 November 1907, p. 26.

16. I am grateful to Vicky Jackson for conducting this survey.

17. *Kinematograph and Lantern Weekly*, 30 May 1907, p. 45.

18 *Kinematograph and Lantern Weekly*, 9 July 1908, p. 207.

19. *Kinematograph and Lantern Weekly*, 18 February 1909, p. 1121.

20. *Kinematograph and Lantern Weekly*, 19 September 1907, p. 317.

21. Yumibe, 'Moving Color', p. 123.

22. Ibid., pp. 191–201.

23. Pask, 'Capturing Colour', pp. 78–87. The list was created from British Patent Office records.

24. For the rivalry between Friese-Greene and Urban, see Luke McKernan, 'The Brighton School and the Quest for Natural Colour', *Visual Delights Two*, 2004, and Simon Brown, 'The Brighton School and the Quest for Natural Colour – Redux', unpublished paper given at Colour and the Moving Image conference, Bristol 2009.

25. Christine Macleod, *Heroes of Invention: Technology, Liberalism and British Identity, 1750–1914* (Cambridge: Cambridge University Press, 2007), pp. 9–10.

26. Pask, 'Capturing Colour', p. 28.

27. Ibid., pp. 34–5.

28. Luke McKernan, ' "Something More than a Mere Picture Show": Charles Urban and the early non-fiction film in Great Britain and America, 1897–25', unpublished PhD thesis, University of London, 2003, pp. 189–93.

29. Edward Branagan, 'Color and Cinema: Problems in the Writing of History', in Paul Kerr (ed.), *The Hollywood Film Industry* (London and New York: Routledge & Kegan Paul, 1986), pp. 120–47.

30. Ibid., p. 137.

31. Quotation from W. W. Harmon, *Moving Picture World*, 25 December 1910, reprinted in *Kinemacolor Handbook*, September 1910 (Natural Color Kinematograph Co. Ltd), p. 10.

32. *Kinemacolor Supplement to the Kinematograph and Lantern Weekly*, 12 September 1912.

33. McKernan, ' "Something More than a Mere Picture Show" ', chapter 3 and Hanssen, *Early Discourses on Colour and Cinema*.

34. A short history of the process is presented in the Technical Appendix of this book.

35. G. A. Smith, 'Animated Photographs in Natural Colours', paper delivered 9 December 1908 to Fourth Ordinary Meeting of the Royal Society, *Journal of the Royal Society of Arts* vol. LVII no. 2925, 11 December 1908, pp. 70–6.

36. Ibid., pp. 75–6.

37. The Autochrome process was additive and dominated still colour photography in the early years of the twentieth century. The plates consisted of fine red/orange, green and violet grains of potato starch, forming a three-colour filter; they were coated with a panchromatic emulsion. For further details of Autochromes see Michel Frizot, 'A Natural Strangeness: The Hypothesis of Color', in Michel Frizot (ed.), *A New History of Photography* (Köln: Könemann, 1998 English language edition), p. 414.

38. Victoria Jackson, 'Reviving the Lost Experience of Kinemacolor: David Cleveland and Brian Pritchard' (interview), *Journal of British Cinema and Television* vol. 7 no. 1, 2010, p. 149.

39. Gorham Kindem, 'The Demise of Kinemacolor: Technological, Legal, Economic, and Aesthetic Problems in Early Color Cinema History', *Cinema Journal* vol. 20 no. 2, Spring 1981, pp. 7–9.

40. Luke McKernan, '"The Modern Elixir of Life": Kinemacolor, Royalty and the Delhi Durbar', *Film* History vol. 21 no. 2, 2009, pp. 122–36.

41. Ibid., p. 131.

42. Charles Raleigh, 'Remiscences of Commercial Colour Cinematography – its Possibilities', *British Journal of Photography*, colour supplement, vol. XVI no. 189, 4 August 1922, pp. 30–2; vol. XVI no. 190, 1 September 1922, pp. 35–6; vol. XVI no. 191, 6 October 1922, pp. 37–8.

43. William A. Crespinell, 'Pioneer Days in Colour Motion Pictures with William T. Crespinel', *Film History* vol. 12 no. 1, 2000, p. 59.

44. John Scotland, *The Talkies* (London: C. Lockwood & Son, 1930), p. 166.

45. *The Bioscope*, 4 March 1909, p. 23.

46. McKernan, '"Something More than a Mere Picture Show"', pp. 172–82.

47. Theodore Brown, 'My Impressions of Kinemacolor', *Kinematograph and Lantern Weekly* vol. 6 no. 151, 31 March 1910.

48. *The Bioscope*, 8 February 1912.

49. Cherchi Usai, *Silent Cinema*, p. 29.

50. G. A. Smith, unpublished evidence in URB 7/2/6, pp. 292. This reference is also cited by McKernan, '"Something More than a Mere Picture Show"', p. 179.

51. *Catalogue of Kinemacolor Film Subjects, 1912–13*, (Natural Color Kinematograph Co.).

52. *British Journal of Photography*, colour supplement, vol. XVI no. 189, 4 August 1922, p. 31.

53. This point was made by Nick Hiley, in Hertogs and de Klerk, *'Disorderly Order'*, pp. 31–2.

54. Victoria Jackson, 'The Distribution and Exhibition of Kinemacolor in the UK Provinces, 1909–15', unpublished PhD thesis, University of Bristol.

55. *Kinematograph Monthly Film Record*, April 1913, pp. 24–5.

56. Ibid., p. 25.

57. One is reminded of the ending of *Stella Dallas* (1937), when Barbara Stanwyck gazes through the window at her daughter in an opulent house.

58. *Catalogue of Kinemacolor Film Subjects*, p. 125.

59. McKernan, '"Something More than a Mere Picture Show"', p. 180.

60. *Catalogue of Kinemacolor Film Subjects*, p. 16.

61. Ibid., p. 309.

62. For the relevant documents on the case see URB 7/2/6 and summary in *The Bioscope*, 9 April 1914, pp. 141–2. McKernan also discusses the case, '"Something More than a Mere Picture Show"', pp. 182–9.

63. URB 3/2, p. 60. See also Jackson, 'The Distribution and Exhibition of Kinemacolor'.

64. *Kinemacolor Supplement to the Kinematograph and Lantern Weekly*, 15 August 1912.

65. Ibid., 29 August 1912.

66. Jackson, 'The Distribution and Exhibition of Kinemacolor'.

67. McKernan, '"Something More than a Mere Picture Show"', pp. 163–72.

68. Urban, 'Terse History', URB9/1, p. 14.

69. Hanssen, *Early Discourses on Colour and Cinema*, pp. 31–87.

70. Tom Gunning, 'The Cinema of Attractions: Early Film, Its Spectator and the Avant-Garde', in Thomas Elsaesser and Adam Barker (eds), *Early Film* (London: BFI, 1989). The idea is that early cinema was primarily a demonstrative mode in which visual display and attraction was the major source of appeal rather than continuous narrative development. The spectacle of colour can be usefully linked to this idea as developed in Gunning's 'Colorful Metaphors' article.

71. *Kinematograph Monthly Film Record*, March 1913, p. 6.

72. All subsequent descriptions of Kinemacolor films are taken from the *Catalogue of Kinemacolor Film Subjects, 1912–13*.

73. *Kinematograph Monthly Film Record*, May 1913, p. 102, emphasis in original (referring to *Studies in Natural Colour*).

74. *Kinemacolor Supplement to the Kinematograph and Lantern Weekly*, 10 October 1912.

75. The relationship between Kinemacolor and applied methods is discussed in Bregt Lameris, 'Pathécolor: "Perfect in their Rendition of the Colours of Nature"', *Living Pictures: The Journal of the Popular and Projected Images Before 1914* vol. 2 no. 2, 2003, pp. 46–58.

76. See Hanssen, *Early Discourses on Colour and Cinema*, p. 40.

77. Joshua Yumibe, '"Harmonious Sensations of Sound by Means of Colors": Vernacular Colour Abstractions in Silent Cinema', *Film History* vol. 21 no. 2, 2009, pp. 164–76.

78. *Kinematograph and Lantern Weekly*, 18 February 1909, p. 1121.

79. *Catalogue of Kinemacolor Film Subjects, 1912–13*, pp. 216–7.

80. *The Bioscope*, 26 October 1911, p. 283.

81. Jackson, 'The Distribution and Exhibition of Kinemacolor'.

82. Rachael Low, *The History of the British Film, 1918–29* (London: Allen & Unwin, 1971), p. 280.

83. Read, 'Tinting and Toning Techniques and their Adaption for the Restoration of Archive Film', p. 161.

84. Low, *The History of the British Film*, p. 283, quoting H. G. Wells from *The King Who Was a King*.

85. *Kinemacolor Supplement to the Kinematograph and Lantern Weekly*, 5 September 1912.

86. For further details on the concept of Orientalism see Edward Said, *Orientalism* (London: Routledge, 1978).

87. *British Journal of Photography*, colour supplement, vol. XVI no. 189, 8 August 1922, p. 30.

88. Ulrich Ruedel, 'The Technicolor Notebooks at the George Eastman House', *Film History* vol. 21 no. 1, 2009, p. 49.

89. 'Kinemacolor versus "Colour" Cinematography', introduced by Luke McKernan and reproduced in *Living Pictures: The Journal of the Popular and Projected Image before 1914* vol. 2 no. 1, 2003, p. 89.

90. There is a section discussing colour patents in the introduction to the *Catalogue of Kinemacolor Film Subjects, 1912–13*, in which Urban dismisses all other 'ghostly rivals', pp. 10–12.

2 COLOUR ADVENTURES WITH PRIZMA AND CLAUDE FRIESE-GREENE IN THE 1920s

1. David Robertson, 'Natural-Colour Films', *Motion Picture Studio* vol. 1 no. 39, 4 March 1922, p. 12.

2. J. S. Blackton, reply to Robertson in *Motion Picture Studio* vol. 1 no. 39, 4 March 1922, pp. 12–13.

3. According to Brian Coe, Kesdacolor involved double-coated film 'printed on each side from negatives exposed through a fine screen of red and green lines', *The History of Motion Picture Photography* (London: Ash & Grant, 1981), p. 127.

4. William A. Crespinel, 'Pioneer Days in Colour Motion Pictures with William T. Crespinel', *Film History* vol. 12 no. 1, 2000, pp. 57–71.

5. Adrian Cornwell-Clyne, *Colour Cinematography* (London: Chapman & Hall, 3rd edn, 1951), p. 335.

6. *Exhibitors Herald*, 15 April 1922, p. 4.

7. An example of advertising the film as a 'high-class', quality product can be found in *Illustrated London News*, 21 January 1922, pp. 88–9, which comments on 'enormous interest' being aroused by the film at the premiere at the Royal Opera House, Covent Garden, on 18 January 1922. Lady Diana's aristocratic connections were emphasised, as well as Hon. Lois Sturt, the younger daughter of Lord and Lady Alington, who plays Nell Gwynn.

8. J. S. Blackton, 'A Milestone Passed', *Motion Picture Studio* vol. 1 no. 25, 26 November 1921, p. 14.

9. *British Journal of Photography*, colour supplement, 6 May 1921, pp. 18–19.

10. *The Times*, 9 April 1921, p. 6, issue 42690.

11. *British Journal of Photography*, colour supplement, 5 August 1921, p. 32. The reference to three images is somewhat puzzling since Prizma was clearly a two-colour process.

12. Henry Albert Phillips, 'Pictures in Natural Colours', *Motion Picture Magazine*, November 1923, p. 95.

13. *Kine Technicalities* supplement to *Kinematograph Weekly* vol. 59 no. 770, 26 January 1922, p. vi.

14. Charles Raleigh, 'Reminisces of Commercial Colour Cinematography – Its Possibilities', *British Journal of Photography*, colour supplement, 5 October 1922, p. 37.

15. J. S. Blackton, as reported in *British Journal of Photography*, colour supplement, 1 July 1921, p. 28.

16. J. S. Blackton, 'A Future for British Films', *Motion Picture Studio* vol. 1 no. 2, 19 August 1922, p. 21.

17. Jon Burrows, *Legitimate Cinema: Theatre Stars in Silent British Films, 1908–18* (Exeter: University of Exeter Press, 2003), p. 229.

18. Rachael Low, *The History of the British Film, 1918–29* (London: Allen & Unwin, 1971), p. 126.

19. Mirian Blackton Trimble, *J. Stuart Blackton: A Personal Biography by his Daughter* (Metuchen, NJ, and London: Scarecrow Press, 1985), p. 108.

20. *Kinematograph Weekly* vol. 59 no. 767, 5 January 1922, p. 17.

21. *Film Renter and Moving Picture News*, 'The Progress of Colour Kinematography', 28 January 1922, p. 10.

22. Ibid.

23. *Kinematograph Weekly* vol. 59 no. 769, 19 January 1922, p. 63.

24. Henry Albert Phillips, 'Pictures in Natural Colours', *Motion Picture Magazine*, November 1923, p. 95.

25. Restored by Paul de Burgh for the BFI National Archive in the 1991. The source material for the restoration was a 1922 Prizmacolor print duped onto internegative stock, from which a new copy was made. This may have been printed optically and as a consequence there would be a slight increase in the contrast. At the time of the restoration this was probably as good a result as you could get with the available technology: Eastmancolor negative stock only gives a close but not exact rendition of the original colours. The film was based on a scenario written by Felix Orman and published in *Picturegoer Monthly* vol. 3 no. 13, January 1922, pp. 35–8, 58–9, 61, and in vol. 3 no. 14, February 1922, pp. 54, 56, 58.

26. I am grateful to Joshua Yumibe for discussing this point with me.

27. Phillips, 'Pictures in Natural Colours', p. 95.

28. Paul Nash, 'The Colour Film', in Charles Davy (ed.), *Footnotes to the Film* (London: Lovat Dickson, Readers' Union, 1938), p. 124.

29. *Picturegoer Monthly* vol. 2 no. 7, July 1921, p. 11.

30. *Picturegoer Monthly*, January 1922, p. 36.

31. Tom Gunning, quoted in Daan Hertogs and Nico de Klerk, '*Disorderly Order': Colours in Silent Cinema* (Amsterdam: Stichting Nederlands Museum, 1996), p. 39.

32. Sergei Eisenstein, *The Film Sense* (1942), trans. Jay Leyda (London: Faber and Faber, 1968), pp. 120–1, emphasis in original.

33. Urban papers, National Media Museum (NMM), Bradford: URB 9/10/1, report by Charles Urban on Prizma, 11 October 1916.

34. *Daily News* (n.d.), article by E. A. Saunders, in clippings file of Claude Friese-Green collection, C 35/S2, box 5, NMM.

35. *British Journal of Photography* vol. XVI no. 183, colour supplement, 3 February 1922, p. 8.

36. *Motion Picture Studio* vol. 1 no. 30, 31 December 1921, p. 15.

37. Blackton, 'A Milestone Passed', p. 14.

38. *Motion Picture Studio* vol. 2 no. 63, 19 August 1922, p. 11.

39. J. S. Blackton, quoting from *Conquest* in *Motion Picture Studio* vol. 1 no. 25, 26 November 1921, p. 14.

40. Blackton, 'A Milestone Passed', p. 14.

41. Blackton Trimble, *J. Stuart Blackton*, p. 108.

42. Christine Gledhill, *Reframing British Cinema, 1918–29: Between Restraint and Passion* (London: BFI, 2003), pp. 62–89.

43. *Picturegoer Monthly* vol. 2 no. 7, July 1921, p. 10.

44. Blackton, 'A Milestone Passed', p. 14.

45. *Kinematograph Monthly Film Record*, November 1912, p. 25.

46. Joshua Yumibe, 'Moving Color: An Aesthetic History of Applied Color Technologies in Silent Cinema', unpublished PhD thesis, University of Chicago, 2007, p. 168.

47. *British Journal of Photography*, colour supplement, 2 February 1923, p. 8.

48. W. T. Crespinel, *American Cinematographer*, March 1929, p. 5.

49. William Friese-Greene to Claude, 5 May 1918, C35/S2: Box 9, Claude Friese-Greene papers, National Media Museum, Bradford.

50. For example, Claude Friese-Greene, 'Colour Cinematography by Photographic Impression', *The Bioscope*, Equipment and Technical section, 29 April 1926, p. iii.

51. It is not clear whether 24 or 32fps was the speed, although Claude Friese-Greene wrote in *Film Weekly*, 28 September 1934, p. 13, that the speed of silent film (16fps) was too slow for his colour films and that 24 would have been better.

52. *Film Renter and Moving Picture News*, 29 March 1924, p. 8.

53. Typed copy of Claude Friese-Greene's report for *Journal of the Royal Photographic Society*, FG C33/S4, Bradford.

54. *The Bioscope*, 2 October 1924, p. 33.

55. *Kinematograph Weekly*, 16 October 1924.

56. See report in *Exhibitors Trade Review*, an American publication (n.d.) in FG: C33/S4, scrapbook, NMM.

57. *Manchester Guardian*, 27 March 1924.

58. *New York Telegraph*, 17 July 1924.

59. *The Bioscope*, 25 September 1924, p. 71.

60. *Cinema*, 29 October 1924.

61. Will Day to Claude Friese-Greene, 14 May 1926, FG papers, C35/S2, Box 4, NMM.

62. FG to Day, 22 July 1926, FG papers, C35/S2, Box 4, NMM.

63. Low, *The History of the British Film*, p. 281.

64. For an account of the restoration see Sonia Genaitay and Bryony Dixon, 'Early Colour Film Restoration at the BFI National Archive', *Journal of British Cinema and Television* vol. 7 no. 1, 2010, pp. 138–41.

65. *Times of India*, 8 December 1925.

66. *Film Weekly*, supplement, 28 September 1935, p. 13.

67. Quotation from *Daily Film Renter*, 31 October 1925, reproduced in marketing leaflet for *The Open Road*.

68. Margaret Dickinson and Sarah Street, *Cinema and State: The Film Industry and the British Government, 1927–84* (London: BFI, 1985), pp. 5–33.

69. *Pictures and Picturegoer*, March 1924, p. 38.

3 DEBATING COLOUR IN THE 1930s

1. *Today's Cinema*, Construction and Equipment supplement, 5 June 1935, p. iv.

2. *Today's Cinema*, 1 May 1935, Construction and Equipment supplement, p. iii; and Shirley R. Simpson, 'A Plea for Natural Colour', *Kinematograph Weekly*, 26 August 1937, p. 4.

3. Adrian Cornwell-Clyne, *Colour Cinematography* (London: Chapman & Hall, 3rd edn, 1951). All references are from 1951 edition.

4. Ibid., p. 660.

5. Ibid, pp. 661–2, emphasis in original.

6. Ibid., p. 663.

7. Rachael Low, *The History of the British Film, 1918–29* (London: Allen & Unwin, 1971), pp. 282–3.

8. All quotations from *Kinematograph Weekly* vol. 74 no. 385, p. 65.

9. *The Bioscope* vol. 66 no. 101, 11 March 1926, p. 57.

10. *The Bioscope*, 1 April 1926, Equipment and Technical section, p. iii. The triple-lens Chronochrome was

considered to be a high-quality process but was ultimately stymied by mechanical complications and because it required a special projector. See Paolo Cherchi Usai, *Silent Cinema: An Introduction* (London: BFI, 2000), pp. 30–1.

11. Elliott Hammett, 'Competing Colour Systems', *The Commercial Film* vol. 1 no. 2, 1935, pp. 8. 19.

12. Scott Higgins, *Harnessing the Technicolor Rainbow: Color Design in the 1930s* (Austin: University of Texas Press, 2007), p. 4.

13. *Cinematograph* vol. 4 no. 82, 28 June 1930, p. 40.

14. See Simon Brown, 'Colouring the Nation: Spectacle, Reality and British Natural Colour in the Silent and Early Sound Period', *Film History* vol. 21 no. 2, 2009, pp. 140–1.

15. Rudolf Arnheim, *Film as Art* (Berkeley: University of California Press, 1957), pp. 1, 154.

16. Brian Coe, *The History of Movie Photography* (London: Ash & Grant, 1981), pp. 119–20 and Cornwell-Clyne, *Colour Cinematography*, p. 10.

17. Ibid., pp. 130–1.

18. Ibid., pp. 210–21.

19. Hammett, 'Competing Colour Systems', p. 8.

20. Cornwell-Clyne, *Colour Cinematography*, p. 331.

21. Coe, *The History of Movie Photography*, p. 129.

22. *Kinematograph Weekly*, 19 March 1936, p. 53.

23. D. A. Spencer, 'What is the Present Position of Color Cinematography?', *The International Projectionist* vol. 12, March 1937, p. 11.

24. Paul Nash, 'The Colour Film', in Charles Davy (ed.), *Footnotes to the Film* (London: Lovat Dickson, Readers' Union, 1938), pp. 125–6.

25. The information on Dufaycolor presented in this paragraph is based on Simon Brown's article, 'Dufaycolor – The spectacle of reality and British national cinema', http://www.bftv.ac.uk/projects/dufaycolor.htm. See also *Commercial Film* vol. 1 no. 9, October 1935, pp. 13, 16.

26. Hammett, 'Competing Colour Systems', p. 19.

27. Report on colour systems in *The Era*, 11 September 1935.

28. *Kinematograph Weekly* vol. 259 no. 1640, 22 September 1938, p. 39. The debate on screen illumination was supported by demonstrations of the impact of varying intensities on both Technicolor and Dufaycolor, such as at the Odeon, Leicester Square, in November 1938. See report in *Kinematograph Weekly* vol. 261 no. 1649, 24 November 1938, p. 37. A report on the situation in Germany noted that screen brightness in first-run cinemas was ten times that of the subsequent-run halls. This meant that prints for the latter had to be of greater density than for the first-run venues. See *Kinematograph Weekly* vol. 262 no. 1654, 29 December 1938, p. 19.

29. See Victor Gray (ed.), *The Colours of Another Age: The Rothschild Autochromes 1908–12* (London: The Rothschild Archive, 2007).

30. Brown, 'Dufaycolor', p. 10.

31. Ibid., p. 13.

32. The print I viewed of *Making Fashion* was a BFI restoration, so presumably no attempt was made to 'correct' the colours.

33. Humphrey Jennings, 'They Talk Colour', *Cine-Technician* vol. 3 no. 14, March–April 1937–38, p. 194.

34. *Kinematograph Weekly* vol. 251 no. 1604, 13 January 1938, p. 165.

35. See Eirik Frisvold Hanssen, *Early Discourses on Colour and Cinema: Origins, Functions, Meanings* (Stockholm: Stockholm University, 2006), pp. 41–5.

36. Leo Enticknap, 'Technology and the GPO Film Unit', in Scott Anthony and James Mansell (eds), *The Projection of Britain: A History of the GPO Film Unit* (London: BFI/Palgrave Macmillan, 2011), p. 192.

37. *The Commercial Film* vol.1 no. 2, March 1935, p. 6.

38. Kenneth Gordon, *Journal of the Association of Cine-Technicians* vol. 1 no. 1, May 1935, p. 9.

39. *The Commercial Film* vol. 1 no. 7, August 1935, p. 8, letter from H. P. Weiner from Twickenham.

40. *The Commercial Film* vol. 1 no. 3, April 1935, p. 5.

41. Ibid.

42. Brown, 'Colouring the Nation', p. 146.

43. Alvin Wyckoff, '*Puppetoons* – George Pal's Three-Dimensional Animations', *American Cinematographer* vol. 22 no. 12, pp. 563, 588.

44. Cornwell-Clyne, *Colour Cinematography*, p. 419.

45. Spencer, 'What is the Present Position of Color Cinematography?', p. 32.

46. Ibid.

47. George Pearson, 'They Talk Colour', *Cine-Technician* vol. 3 no. 14, March–April 1937–38, p. 196, emphasis in original.

48. *Kinematograph Weekly*, 27 May 1937, p. 50. I have been unable to discover information on Kinechrome.

49. *The Times*, 18 May 1937.

50. F. Watts, 'They Talk Colour', *Cine-Technician* vol. 3 no. 14, March–April 1937–38, p. 194.

51. *Kinematograph Weekly*, 20 May 1937, p. 33.

52. Alexander Korda, 'They Talk Colour', *Cine-Technician* vol. 3 no. 14, March–April 1937–38, p. 192.

53. Higgins, *Harnessing the Technicolor Rainbow*, p. 133.

54. *Kinematograph Weekly*, 9 April 1936, p. 6.

55. C. P. Metcalfe, 'They Talk Colour', *Cine-Technician* vol. 3 no. 14, March–April 1937–38 p. 193.

56. Arthur Dent, 'They Talk Colour', *Cine-Technician* vol. 3 no. 14, March–April 1937–38, p. 193.

57. Ibid.

58. Nash, 'The Colour Film', p. 120.

59. Bernard Knowles, 'Colour – The New Technique', *Cine-Technician* vol. 4 no. 18, November–December 1938, p. 110.

60. Review in *Monthly Film Bulletin* vol. 6 no. 61, January 1939, p. 1.

61. *Kinematograph Weekly* vol. 263 no. 1655, 5 January 1939, pp. 25–32.

62. *Kinematograph Weekly* vol. 263 no. 1655, 5 January 1939, studio survey by H. Chevalier, p. 125, and review, *Kinematograph Weekly* vol. 263 no. 1656, 19 January 1939, p. 32.

4 GLORIOUS TECHNICOLOR COMES TO BRITAIN

1. *Today's Cinema*, 1 May 1935, Construction and Equipment supplement, p. iii.

2. Shirley R. Simpson, 'A Plea for Natural Colour', *Kinematograph Weekly*, 26 August 1937, p. 4

3. Contemporary studies include Adrian Bernard Klein/Cornwell-Clyne, *Colour Cinematography* (London: Chapman & Hall, 1936, 1939 and 1951 edns) and John Huntley, *British Technicolor Films* (London: Skelton Robinson, 1949). Technicolor has received detailed attention from classic books, including Steve Neale's, *Cinema and Technology: Image, Sound, Colour* (London: Macmillan, 1985) and, more recently, Scott Higgins's, *Harnessing the Technicolor Rainbow: Color Design in the 1930s* (Texas: Texas University Press, 2007). For reprints of key articles on Technicolor see Angela Dalle Vacche and Brian Price (eds), *Color: The Film Reader* (London: Routledge, 2006).

4. For full technical details of Technicolor, see Leo Enticknap, *Moving Image Technology from Zoetrope to Digital* (London: Wallflower, 2005), pp. 87–8.

5. See Higgins, *Harnessing the Technicolor Rainbow*, pp. 39–47.

6. *Technicolor News and Views* vol. 1 no. 2, May 1939, p. 3. For details of the Color Advisory Service, see Natalie Kalmus collection, 2 f. 29. Technicolor Control Department, 1938–44, Margaret Herrick Library, Los Angeles.

7. Ivor Montagu, 'They Talk Colour', *Cine-Technician* vol. 3 no. 14, March–April 1937–38, p. 205.

8. Sarah Street, *Transatlantic Crossings: British Feature Films in the USA* (New York: Continuum, 2002).

9. Joshua Yumibe, 'Moving Color: An Aesthetic History of Applied Color Technologies in Silent Cinema', PhD thesis, University of Chicago, 2007.

10. Natalie Kalmus, 'Color Consciousness', *Journal of the Society of Motion Picture Engineers*, August 1935, reprinted in Dalle Vacche and Price, *Color*, p. 24.

11. Ibid., p. 25.

12. Albert Munsell, *A Color Notation* (Baltimore: Hoffman Brothers, 7th edn, 1926), pp. 18–31, quoted in Higgins, *Harnessing the Technicolor Rainbow*, p. 15.

13. Kalmus, 'Color Consciousness', p. 28.

14. Ibid., p. 29.

15. Duncan Petrie, *The British Cinematographer* (London: BFI, 1996), pp. 42–5.

16. David Batchelor, *Chromophobia* (London: Reaktion, 2000), pp. 93–4.

17. Hanssen, *Early Discourses on Colour and Cinema*, p. 179.

18. Sergei Eisenstein, *The Film Sense*, trans. Jay Leyda (first published 1942; London: Faber and Faber, 1968), pp. 120–1, italics in original. For an analysis of Eisenstein's writings on colour, see Eirik Hanssen, 'Eisenstein in Colour', *Konsthistorisk Tidskrift* vol. 73 no. 4, 2004, pp. 212–27.

19. Street, *Transatlantic Crossings*.

20. *Variety*, 13 November 1929, p. 5.

21. Technicolor Archives, George Eastman House, Box 2, doc 0986.

22. Herbert Kalmus to Seelye (London), 27 December 1930, Technicolor Archives, George Eastman House, Box 2, doc 0047.

23. *Today's Cinema*, 23 September 1935, p. 1, and Margaret Dickinson and Sarah Street, *Cinema and State: The Film Industry and the British Government, 1927–84* (London: BFI, 1985), p. 82. The Hillman process was abandoned in favour of creating links with Technicolor.

24. *Today's Cinema*, 1 May 1935, Construction and Equipment supplement, p. iii.

25. *Today's Cinema*, 10 July 1935, p. 13.

26. Ibid., p. 1.

27. Bernstein questionnaires, 1937 and 1946–47, British Film Institute Library.

28. *Picturegoer* vol. 3 no. 146, 10 March 1934, p. 42.

29. Higgins, *Harnessing the Technicolor Rainbow*, p. 19.

30. Scott Higgins, 'Demonstrating Three-color Technicolor: Early Three-colour Aesthetics and Design', *Film History* vol. 12 no. 4 (2000), pp. 358–83. See also Higgins, *Harnessing the Technicolor Rainbow*.

31. *Today's Cinema*, 4 September 1935, Construction and Equipment supplement, p. iv.

32. *Picturegoer* vol. 4 no. 175, 29 September 1934, p. 5.

33. See report of an address by Dr Spencer to the Royal Photographic Society in *Kinematograph Weekly*, 4 March 1937, p. 46.

34. *Kinematograph Weekly*, 'When Colour Comes', 7 October 1937, p. 4.

35. J. P. Mayer, *British Cinemas and their Audiences* (London: Dennis Dobson, 1948), p. 42.

36. See Charles Drazin, 'Korda, Technicolor and the Zeitgeist', *Journal of British Cinema and Television* vol. 7 no. 1, 2010, pp. 5–20.

37. *Today's Cinema*, 28 May 1935, p. 1.

38. *Financial Times*, 19 March 1956.

39. *Today's Cinema*, 25 July 1935, p. 3.

40. Huntley, *British Technicolor Films*, p. 18.

41. *Today's Cinema*, 24 September 1935, p. 1.

42. *Kinematograph Weekly*, 7 May 1936, p. 14.

43. See, for example, an article by Kalmus, which quotes her 'color consciousness' ideas in *Cinema*, Construction and Equipment section, 2 January 1936, p. xxix.

44. *Cinema*, report in 'Onlooker' section, 30 April 1936, p. 1.

45. See *Photoplay* article with Kalmus declared as 'Technicolor's first star!', described as 'one of the most romantic figures of the day', vol. 37 no. 5, April 1930, p. 67.

46. Natalie Kalmus papers, 1-f.7, Ray Dannenbaum. The file has details of an article written by Dannenbaum that was published under Kalmus's name in *Popular Photography*, 25 September 1942.

47. Sarah Street, 'Negotiating the Archives: The Natalie Kalmus Papers and the "Branding" of Technicolor in Britain and the United States', *The Moving Image* vol. 11 no. 1, Spring 2011, p. 11.

48. Although they were divorced this was not publicly known until 1948, when Natalie Kalmus filed a law suit against Herbert for a monetary settlement. See Herbert T. Kalmus with Eleanore King Kalmus, *Mr Technicolor* (New Jersey: MagicImage Film, 1993) for a far from impartial history.

49. Freddie Young BECTU interview, no. 4, 1 April 1987.

50. Natalie Kalmus papers (NK papers), Herrick library, LA; Maude Churchill to Natalie Kalmus, 28 April 1938, *Queen of Destiny* folder, 1-f-2.

51. NK papers, Kay Harrison, no. II, NK to KH, 24 September 1935.

52. Art director L. P. Williams's BECTU interview, no. 381, 12 August 1993, claims that Natalie Kalmus spent much of her time in England at the races.

53. NK papers, Kay Harrison, no. II, KH to NK, 10 October 1939.

54. Jack Cardiff, in Justin Bowyer, *Conversations with Jack Cardiff* (London: Batsford, 2003), p. 42.

55. The scope for colour in avant-garde films is more open to experimentation than in those operating within classical narrative norms. This was commented on by artist Paul Nash, who wrote about the films of Len Lye in 'The Colour Film', in Charles Davy (ed.), *Footnotes to the Film* (London: Lovat Dickson, 1938), pp. 116–34.

56. For a discussion of the production context see Anthony Slide, '*Wings of the Morning*, an Important Film', *American Cinematographer*, February 1986, pp. 36–40.

57. Natalie Kalmus, quoted in Huntley, *British Technicolor Films*, p. 22.

58. Interview with Jack Houshold, 18 June 1991, BECTU interview collection, tape 199, BFI Library.

59. 'Color Films Mark Return to Nature', article (n.d.) in *Wings of the Morning* press file microfiche, British Film Institute library.

60. Neale, *Cinema and Technology*, p. 147.

61. Nash, 'The Colour Film', p. 125.

62. *Variety*, 19 January 1938.

63. *Kinematograph Weekly*, 28 January 1937, p. 35, and in 'Technicolor Supplement' of the same issue, p. 52.

64. *Kinematograph Weekly*, 28 January 1937, p. 52.

65. Huntley, *British Technicolor Films*, p. 21.

66. The derby was a common feature of newsreels, including shots of gypsy encampments at Epsom, which would have added to the novelty of the colour derby sequence in *Wings of the Morning*.

67. Charlotte Brunsdon, *London in Cinema: The Cinematic City since 1945* (London: BFI, 2007), p. 21.

68. Howard Barnes, *New York Times* (n.d.), British Film Institute microfiche.

69. Nash, 'The Colour Film', p. 118.

70. Higgins, *Harnessing the Technicolor Rainbow*, p. 6.

71. Nash, 'The Colour Film', p. 120.

72. Mayer, *British Cinemas and their Audiences*, p. 231.

73. Michael Powell, *A Life in Movies: An Autobiography* (London: Heinemann, 1986), p. 406.

74. Michael Powell, *Million Dollar Movie* (London: Heinemann, 1992), p. 35.

75. See *Filmfax* no. 60, April/May 1997, pp. 60–3.

76. Mohja Kahf, 'The Image of the Muslim Woman in American Cinema: Two Colonialist Fantasy Films', *Cinefocus* vol. 3, 1995, pp. 19–25.

77. Ibid., p. 21.

78. Eisenstein, *The Film Sense*, p. 121, emphasis added.

79. Virginia Wright in *LA News* (n.d.), quoted in *Technicolor News and Views* vol. 2 no. 9, October 1940.

80. Elsa Schiaperelli, quoted in *Technicolor News and Views* vol. 2 no. 10, November 1940.

81. *New York Times*, 6 December 1946

82. For example, *New York Sun*, 6 December 1940.

5 COLOUR ENTHUSIASTS

1. For an account of a wartime screening of the *World Windows* films, see Jack Cardiff, 'Travelogue Photography in Technicolor', *Photographic Journal* vol. LXXXII, December 1942, pp. 404–5.

2. The *Kinematograph Year Books* for 1939 and 1940 list eleven titles trade shown in 1938 and nine in 1939.

3. *Kinematograph Weekly* vol. 270 no. 1689, 31 August 1939, p. 27.

4. See reports by Howard Cricks in *Kinematograph Weekly* vol. 258 no. 1635, 18 August 1938, p. 27, and vol. 259 no. 1640, 22 September 1938, p. 39. For a general discussion of the technical difficulties of using early three-strip Technicolor, see Duncan Petrie, *The British Cinematographer* (London: BFI, 1996), pp. 42–5.

5. Points noted in review of Adrian Klein's first edition of *Colour Cinematography* in *The Commercial Film* vol. 2 no. 4, July–August 1936, p. 7.

6. D. A. Spencer, 'What is the Present Position of Color Cinematography?', *The International Projectionist* vol. 12, March 1937, p. 11.

7. *Kinematograph Weekly* vol. 265 no. 1664, 9 March 1939, p. 55.

8. *Kinematograph Weekly* vol. 251 no. 1604, 13 January 1938, p. 17.

9. *Kinematograph Weekly* vol. 261 no. 1647, 10 November 1938, p. 48.

10. Alexander Korda, in 'They Talk Colour', *Cine-Technician* vol. 3 no. 14, March–April 1937–38, p. 192.

11. Annette Kuhn, *An Everyday Magic: Cinema and Cultural Memory* (London: I.B. Tauris, 2002), p. 133.

12. The British Colour Council's aims were to 'place colour determination for the British Empire in British hands; to obtain advance information about fashion colour tendencies; and to provide standard names for colours, with a view to eliminating the confusion which at present exists', *The British Colour Council Dictionary of Colour Standards* (London: British Colour Council, 1934), p. 5.

13. *British Journal of Photography* vol. XC no. 4330, 30 April 1943, pp. 158–9.

14. *British Journal of Photography* vol. XCII no. 4459, 19 October 1945, p. 338.

15. Fred Bond, Kodachrome expert, writing in *American Photography*, December 1942, p. 12, and reported in *British Journal of Photography* vol. XC no. 4330, 30 April 1943, p. 159.

16. Anthony Aldgate and Jeffrey Richards, *Britain Can Take It: The British Cinema in the Second World War* (Oxford: Blackwell, 1986), pp. 2–3.

17. Bernard Happé collection, LBH/1/1, report by Happé, 6 November 1939, British Film Institute National Archive, London. See also George Elvin, 'British Film Technicians and the War', *American Cinematographer* vol. 23 no. 7, July 1942, pp. 294–5, 334.

18. Kay Harrison to Natalie Kalmus, 23 November 1939. Natalie Kalmus papers, correspondence with Kay Harrison, Margaret Herrick Library, Los Angeles.

19. *Technicolor News and Views* vol. 5 no. 2, June 1943.

20. Bernard Happé papers, LBH/1/1: report by Happé, 6 November 1939; British Film Institute Special Collections.

21. *The Times*, 2 March 1953, p. 14, issue 52559, and 19 March 1956, p. 17, issue 53483.

22. *Kinematograph Year Book*, 1841, p. 272.

23. *Technicolor News and Views*, London Letter, vol. 1 no. 7, October 1939, p. 3.

24. *Technicolor News and Views* vol. 4 no. 2, April 1942, (report from Walter Davenport in *Collier's Magazine*, 21 March 1942, quoting Elkan Allan of Fleet Street, London).

25. *British Journal of Photography* vol. LXXXIX no. 4293, 14 August 1942, p. 307.

26. *The Times*, 18 August 1939, p. 8, issue 48387.

27. *Kinematograph Year Book*, 1946, p. 260.

28. *British Journal of Photography*, vol. LXXXIX no. 4270, 6 March 1942, p. 87.

29. Harry Walden, 'New 16mm Colour Film Invention', *The Commercial Film* vol. 1 no. 6, July 1935, pp. 4, 9.

30. *Kinematograph Weekly* vol. 266 no. 1668, 6 April 1939, p. 25.

31. *British Journal of Photography* vol. XCI no. 4374, 3 March 1944, p. 74. For Tompkins's earlier review of *The Life and Death of Colonel Blimp*, see *British Journal of Photography* vol. XC no. 4345, 13 August 1943, pp. 292–3.

32. Sergei Eisenstein, *The Film Sense*, trans. Jay Leyda (first published 1942; London: Faber and Faber, 1968), pp. 120–1.

33. *British Journal of Photography* vol. XC no. 4324, 19 March 1943, pp. 102–3.

34. *Photographic Journal* vol. LXXXII, February 1942, p. 48.

35. *British Journal of Photography* vol. LXXXIX no. 4278, 1 May 1942, p. 162.

36. *British Journal of Photography* vol. XC no. 4327, 9 April 1943, p. 131.

37. *British Journal of Photography* vol. XC no. 4317, 29 January 1943, p. 38.

38. *British Journal of Photography* vol. LXXXIX no. 4285, 19 June 1942, p. 226.

39. J. P. Mayer, *British Cinemas and their Audiences* (London: Dennis Dobson, 1948), p. 42.

40. *British Journal of Photography* vol. LXXXIX no. 4301, 9 October 1942, p. 378.

41. Ibid.

42. *British Journal of Photography* vol. LXXXIX no. 4270, 6 March 1942, p. 87.

43. Pat Kirkham, 'Fashioning the Feminine: Dress, Appearance and Femininity in Wartime Britain', in Christine Gledhill and Gillian Swanson (eds), *Nationalising Femininity: Culture, Sexuality and British Cinema in the Second World War* (Manchester: Manchester University Press, 1996), p. 157.

44. Jonathan Walford, *Forties Fashion: From Siren Suits to the New Look* (London: Thames & Hudson, 2008), p. 43.

45. Kirkham, 'Fashioning the Feminine', p. 157.

46. Ibid., p. 158.

47. *British Journal of Photography* vol. XC no. 4322, 5 March 1943, p. 85.

48. Ibid.

49. *British Journal of Photography* vol. XCII no. 4465, 30 November 1945, pp. 391–2.

50. Interview with Michael Powell, Finland, 1987, printed in David Lazar (ed.), *Michael Powell Interviews* (Oxford, MS: University Press of Mississippi, 2003), p. 145.

51. E. S. Tompkins discusses *Discovery of a New Pigment* in

Journal of British Photography vol. XCL no. 4392, 7 July 1944, p. 240, and Adrian Cornwell-Clyne refers to Monastral blue in *Colour Cinematography* (London: Chapman & Hall, 3rd edn, 1951), p. 102.

52. Philip Ball, *Bright Earth: The Invention of Colour* (London: Penguin, 2001), p. 279.

53. See account of production by Catling in *British Journal of Photography* vol. XCI no. 4397, 11 August 1944, pp. 282–4.

54. Aldgate and Richards, *Britain Can Take It*, pp. 246–76.

55. *British Journal of Photography* vol. LXXXIX no. 4308, 27 November 1942, p. 443.

56. *British Journal of Photography* vol. XCI no. 4387, 2 June 1944, pp. 192–3.

57. Robert Murphy notes that throughout the war at least three-quarters of the films shown in Britain were American in *British Cinema and the Second World War* (New York: Continuum, 2000), p. 10.

6 BRITISH COLOUR FEATURE FILMS IN WARTIME

1. *Kinematograph Year Book*, 1944, p. 285.

2. Data from *Kinematograph Year Books*, 1938–46.

3. *Kinematograph Weekly* vol. 272 no. 1696, 19 October 1939, p. 5.

4. *Kinematograph Weekly* vol. 273 no. 1699, 9 November 1939, p. 15, and *Monthly Film Bulletin* vol. 6, 1939, p. 202.

5. John Huntley, *British Technicolor Films* (London: Skelton Robinson, 1949), p. 50.

6. *Hollywood Review*, 16 June 1944, and note in Natalie Kalmus papers, 2-f.24 screenings file, May 1943, Margaret Herrick Library, Los Angeles.

7. *British Journal of Photography* vol. LXXXIX no. 4305, 6 November 1942, p. 416.

8. *Kinematograph Year Book*, 1943, p. 284.

9. For a discussion of the controversy see James Chapman, '*The Life and Death of Colonel Blimp* (1943) Reconsidered', *Historical Journal of Film, Radio and Television* vol. 15 no. 1, March 1995, pp. 19–54. See also documents relating to the controversy reproduced in Ian Christie (ed.), *The Life and Death of Colonel Blimp (Script)* (London: Faber and Faber, 1994).

10. For a discussion of the marketing of *Colonel Blimp* in the USA see Sarah Street, *Transatlantic Crossings: British Feature Films in the USA* (New York: Continuum, 2002), p. 97.

11. Interview with Thelma Shoonmaker on DVD of *The Red Shoes* restored version, 2009 (ITV DVD 37115 31983).

12. Andrew Moor, *Powell & Pressburger: A Cinema of Magic Spaces* (London: I.B.Tauris, 2005), pp. 56–7.

13. Ibid., p. 70.

14. Michael Powell, *A Life in Movies* (London: Heinemann, 1986), p. 536.

15. Jack Cardiff, *Magic Hour* (London: Faber and Faber, 1996), p. 83. Interestingly, on the Criterion DVD commentary Michael Powell considers this scene to be too long, drawn out and ponderous, remarking that Max Ophuls would have done it better.

16. *Motion Picture Herald*, 24 March 1945.

17. Jeffrey Richards and Dorothy Sheridan (eds), *Mass Observation at the Movies* (London: Routledge and Kegan Paul, 1987), pp. 263, 271, 282.

18. There is some discussion of the qualities of London water in Frank Littlejohn's BECTU interview, no. 91, 13 June 1989.

19. British cinematographer Ossie Morris cited the difference in light as crucial since it affected shooting and processing for three-strip Technicolor, interview with Sarah Street and Liz Watkins, 8 August 2008. Frank Littlejohn said that in the Technicolor Ltd labs 'we found that the composition of the water had a damned important effect on the characteristics of transfer'. BECTU interview no. 91, 13 June 1989.

20. *British Journal of Photography* vol. LXXXIX no. 4299, 25 September 1942, p. 360.

21. For a discussion of such terms, see Scott Higgins, *Harnessing the Technicolor Rainbow: Color Design in the 1930s* (Austin: University of Texas Press, 2007), p. 15. For a contemporary discussion of standard terms of reference for colour and its variants, see 'Colour Nomenclature', *British Journal of Photography* vol. XC no. 4329, 23 April 1943, p. 148.

22. *British Journal of Photography* vol. XCI no. 4374, 3 March 1944, p. 74.

23. *British Journal of Photography* vol. XC no. 4345, 13 August 1943, p. 293.

24. All quotations in this paragraph are from Alfred Junge, 'The Art Director and His Work', *The Artist*, parts 2 and 3, April and May 1944.

25. Daily Notes, 8 and 15 June 1942, Natalie Kalmus papers, Margaret Herrick Library, Los Angeles.

26. Michael Powell comments on the Criterion DVD (2002, no. 173) on *Colonel Blimp* that he thought she was 'overdressed' in this scene but that he was enthusiastic about her hats in the film.

27. Michael Powell recalled that this detail was researched by Emeric Pressburger for the film, Criterion DVD commentary.

28. Moor, *Powell & Pressburger*, pp. 76–7.

29. Paul Nash, 'The Colour Film', in Charles Davy (ed.), *Footnotes to the Film* (London: Lovat Dickson, Readers' Union, 1938), pp. 125–6.

30. Michael Powell, Criterion Collection DVD commentary.

31. Ibid.

32. *British Journal of Photography* vol. XC no. 4345, 13 August 1943, p. 293.

33. See scene as described in Christie, *The Life and Death of Colonel Blimp*, sequence 97, pp. 258–60.

34. Michael Powell, Criterion Collection DVD commentary.

35. Moor, *Powell & Pressburger*, p. 60.

36. *Technicolor News and Views* vol. X no. 33, December 1948, p. 2.

37. Ronald Neame with B. Roisman Cooper, *Straight from the Horses's Mouth* (Lanham, MA, and Oxford: Scarecrow Press, 2003), p. 77.

38. *British Journal of Photography* vol. XCI no. 4390, 23 June 1944, p. 220.

39. As in the British Film Institute's restoration of 2008, sponsored by the David Lean Foundation.

40. Quotations from *Newsweek*, 28 April 1947; *Philadelphia Enquirer*, 1947; *Hollywood Reporter*, 21 April 1947, all from clippings file, Margaret Herrick Library, Los Angeles.

41. For example, *Box Office*, 19 April 1947.

42. *Blithe Spirit* press book, BFI Special Collections.

43. Kevin Brownlow, *David Lean* (London: Faber and Faber, 1996), p. 196.

44. Ibid., n. 21: 759.

45. My reading of *Blithe Spirit* is based on Carlton International's 'Rank Collection' DVD released in 2003 and also on the BFI, Granada International and Studio Canal's restoration released theatrically in 2008.

46. John Lahr, *Coward, The Playwright* (London: Methuen, 1982), p. 131.

47. Ibid., pp. 116–7.

48. Robert Murphy, *Realism and Tinsel: Cinema and Society in Britain, 1939–49*, (London: Routledge, 1992), p. 93.

49. *Kinematograph Weekly,* 20 December 1945, p. 51.

50. Brownlow, *David Lean*, p. 191.

51. J. P. Mayer, *British Cinemas and their Audiences* (London: Dennis Dobson, 1948), p. 195.

52. Ibid., pp. 178, 167.

53. *New York Times*, 27: 2, 4 October 1945.

54. G. K. Nelson, *Spiritualism and Society* (London: Routledge and Kegan Paul, 1969), p. 166.

55. Lahr, *Coward*, p. 117.

56. *Motion Picture Herald* 28 April 1945.

57. Ronald Neame, 'A Talk on Technicolor', *Cine-Technician* vol. 10, 1944, p. 37.

58. Ibid.

59. Mayer, *British Cinemas and their Audiences*, pp. 194–5.

60. Neame, 'A Talk on Technicolor', p. 40.

61. Brownlow, *David Lean*, p. 173.

62. Natalie Kalmus, 'Color Consciousness' (1935), reprinted in A. Dalle Vache and Brian Price (eds), *Color: The Film Reader* (London: Routledge, 2006), pp. 24–9.

63. Richard Allen, 'Hitchcock's Colour Designs', in Dalle Vache and Price, *Color*, p. 137.

64. Sergei Eisenstein, *The Film Sense*, trans. Jay Leyda (first published 1942; London: Faber and Faber, 1968), pp. 100–1.

65. Kalmus, 'Color Consciousness', p. 29.

66. Sarah Street, 'Colour Consciousness', *Screen* vol. 50 no. 2, 2009, pp. 191–215.

67. *British Journal of Photography* vol. XCII no. 4435, 4 May 1945, p. 148.

68. Sarah Berry, *Screen Style: Fashion and Femininity in 1930s Hollywood* (Minneapolis: University of Minnesota Press, 2000), pp. 117–26.

69. See Jack Cardiff, 'Shooting *Western Approaches*', *Cine-Technician* vol. 10 no. 51, November–December 1944, pp. 112–6; BECTU interview with Pat Jackson, no. 185, 22 March 1991.

70. Anthony Aldgate and Jeffrey Richards, *Britain Can Take It: The British Cinema in the Second World War* (Oxford: Blackwell, 1986), pp. 247–76.

71. Dalrymple to Beddington, 26 January 1942 in Ministry of Information, INF 1/213, National Archives, quoted in Aldgate and Richards, *Britain Can Take It*, p. 250.

72. Cardiff, 'Shooting *Western Approaches*', p. 112.

73. The initial treatment was by Owen Rutter, and the focus was on the Royal Navy.

74. Cardiff, 'Shooting *Western Approaches*', p. 113.

75. Ibid.

76. Ibid., p. 114.

77. Jackson, BECTU interview no. 185.

78. Kay Harrison to Jack Beddington, 30 Mar 1944, INF 1/213, quoted in Aldgate and Richards, *Britain Can Take It*, p. 265.

79. Jackson, BECTU interview no. 185.

80. *British Journal of Photography* vol. VCI no. 4397, 11 August 1944, p. 282.

81. Cardiff, *Magic Hour*, p. 80.

82. Adrian Cornwell-Clyne, *Colour Cinematography* (London: Chapman & Hall, 3rd edn 1951), p. 132.

83. Aldgate and Richards, *Britain Can Take It*, p. 267.

84. The following viewing notes are from the Imperial War Museum's DVD of *Western Approaches* (digitally remastered, DD 06167).

85. *British Journal of Photography* vol. XCI no. 4417, 29 December 1944, p. 457.

86. *New York Times*, 13: 2, 28 September 1946.

87. *New Statesman*, 9 December 1944.

88. *British Journal of Photography* vol. XCI no. 4417, 29 December 1944, p. 457.

89. *News Chronicle*, 11 December 1944.

90. Cardiff, 'Shooting *Western Approaches*', p. 116.

91. Cardiff, *Magic Hour*, pp. 74–82, and Justin Bowyer, *Conversations with Jack Cardiff* (London: Batsford, 2003), pp. 51–4.

92. See particularly James Chapman, *The British at War: Cinema, State and Propaganda, 1939–45* (London:

I.B.Tauris, 1998), pp. 244–8. For *Henry V*'s marketing, distribution and exhibition in the USA see Street, *Transatlantic Crossings*, pp. 96–104.

93. *British Journal of Photography* vol. XCI no. 4417, 29 December 1944, p. 456.

94. *New Yorker*, 22 June 1946.

95. Charles Barr, 'Amnesia and Schizophrenia', in Barr (ed.), *All Our Yesterdays: 90 Years of British Cinema* (London: BFI, 1986), p. 12. Some of the arguments developed by Barr in relation to 'heritage' and 'quality' were taken up and extended by Andrew Higson in 'Re-Presenting the National Past: Nostalgia and Pastiche in the Heritage Film', in Lester Friedman (ed.), *British Cinema and Thatcherism* (London: University College of London Press, 1993).

96. Barr, 'Amnesia and Schizophrenia', p. 12.

97. *New York Times*, 18 June 1946. The 1937 Coronation had been shot as a Technicolor newsreel.

98. *British Journal of Photography* vol. XCII no. 4445, 13 July 1945, pp. 225–6.

7 INTO A POSTWAR WORLD OF COLOUR

1. *Observer*, 2 July 1944.

2. Dudley Andrew, 'The Post-War Struggle for Colour', in Angela Dalle Vacche and Brian Price (eds), *Color: The Film Reader* (New York: Routledge, 2006), pp. 40–9.

3. Jack H. Coote, 'Survey of Current Processes of Color Kinematography in England', *American Cinematographer*, vol. 27 no. 5, May 1946, pp. 164, 184–5.

4. Jack H. Coote, 'British Tricolour', *Film Industry* vol. 3 no. 13, July 1947, pp. 12–13, 26, and see also Adrian Cornwell-Clyne, *Colour Cinematography* (London: Chapman & Hall, 3rd edn, 1951), p. 32.

5. John Belton, 'Cinecolor', *Film History* vol. 12 no. 4, 2000, pp. 344–57.

6. *Kinematograph Weekly* vol. 366 no. 2101, 7 August 1947, p. 12.

7. *Kinematograph Weekly* vol. 388 no. 2197, 9 June 1949, p. 19.

8. *Kinematograph Weekly* vol. 367 no. 2105, 4 September 1947, p. 34, and see Sarah Street, *British National Cinema* (London: Routledge, 1997, 2nd edn, 2009), pp. 16–17.

9. R. Howard Cricks, 'Two Colours are Better than None', *Kinematograph Weekly*, British Studio Supplement, 10 July 1947, p. xxix.

10. Jack Coote estimated in 1946 that 90 per cent of colour in commercial cinemas was the result of a beam-splitter camera. Quoted in *British Journal of Photography* vol. XCIII no. 4478, 1 March 1946, p. 77.

11. *Kinematograph Weekly* vol. 414 no. 2309, 27 September 1951, *Studio Review*, p. 9.

12. Comment on *The Magic Box* in *Kinematograph Weekly* vol. 415 no. 2310, 4 October 1951, p. 5, and on *Where No Vultures Fly* in *Kinematograph Weekly* vol. 416 no. 2315, 8 November 1951, p. 18. By this time E. S. Tompkins was no longer writing the 'Colour Enthusiast' page in the *British Journal of Photography*.

13. R. Howard Cricks, 'Colour Films Demand the Highest Projection Standards', *Kinematograph Weekly*, 'The Ideal Kinema supplement', vol. XVII no. 186, 8 February 1951, pp. 15–16.

14. *British Journal of Photography*, vol. XCIII no. 4482, 29 March 1946, quotation p. 113, article pp. 113–4.

15. Ibid.

16. *British Journal of Photography* vol. XCIII no. 4483, 5 April 1946, p. 120.

17. *British Journal of Photography* vol. XCV no. 4584, 26 March 1948, p. 119.

18. *British Journal of Photography* vol. XCIV no. 4546, 4 July 1947, p. 231, emphasis in original.

19. Ibid.

20. Kay Harrison, quoted in *Technicolor News and Views* vol. 8 no. 3, September 1946.

21. *British Journal of Photography* vol. XCL no. 4373, 23 February 1944, p. 65.

22. Watterson R. Rothacker, 'The Laboratory and its Functions', *Motion Picture Studio* vol. II no. 108, 30 June 1923, p. 14.

23. Challis, BECTU interview no. 59, 11 October 1988.

24. For extracts and commentary on these interviews see Sarah Street, Liz Watkins and Simon Brown (eds), *British Colour Cinema: Practices and Theories* (London: BFI/Palgrave Macmillan, 2012).

25. A matrix was a single strip of film that transferred a coloured dye to a positive print in imbibition printing. Three were used, each transferring a complementary colour for one of the primary colours and, through a subtractive process, the properly coloured image was projected onto the screen.

26. Happé, BECTU interview no. 92, 13 June 1989.

27. Ibid.

28. Bernard Happé papers, LBH/1/1: report by Happé, 6 November 1939; British Film Institute Special Collections.

29. *Kinematograph Weekly* vol. 444 no. 2439, Studio Review, 25 March 1954, pp. ix, xvi.

30. Syd Wilson, BECTU interview no. 69, 18 June 1991.

31. Jack Cardiff in Justin Bowyer, *Conversations with Jack Cardiff* (London: Batsford, 2003), p. 53.

32. Ibid., p. 61.

33. John Huntley, *British Technicolor Films* (London: Shelton Robinson, 1949), p. 106.

34. Herb A. Lightman, 'Two Worlds in Technicolor', *American Cinematographer* vol. 28 no. 7, July 1947, pp. 236–7, 263, and E. S. Tompkins, *British Journal of Photography* vol. XCIV no. 4524, 17 January 1947,

pp. 31–2. For a discussion of the context of release and reception see James Chapman, ' "The True Business of the British Movie"? *A Matter of Life and Death* and British Film Culture', *Screen* vol. 46 no. 1, Spring 2005, pp. 33–49.

35. Michael Powell, *A Life in Movies* (London: Heinemann, 1986), p. 536.

36. Ian Christie, *A Matter of Life and Death* (London: BFI, 2000), pp. 43–9.

37. Lightman, 'Two Worlds in Technicolor', p. 237.

38. Powell, *A Life in Movies*, p. 498.

39. Lightman, 'Two Worlds in Technicolor', pp. 236–7.

40. E. S. Tompkins, *British Journal of Photography* vol. XCII no. 4430, 30 March 1945, p. 107.

41. Lightman, 'Two Worlds in Technicolor', p. 237, emphasis in original.

42. Daan Hertogs and Nico de Klerk (eds), '*Disorderly Order': Colours in Silent Cinema* (Amsterdam: Stichting Nederlands Filmmuseum, 1996), p. 39.

43. Powell, *A Life in Movies*, p. 541.

44. Jack Cardiff, *Magic Hour* (London: Faber and Faber, 1996), pp. 85–6.

45. *British Journal of Photography* vol. LXXXIX no. 4284, 12 June 1942, p. 217.

46. Damian Sutton, 'Rediagnosing *A Matter of Life and Death*', *Screen* vol. 46 no. 1, Spring 2005, p. 52.

47. Laura Mulvey, *Death 24x a Second: Stillness and the Moving Image* (London: Reaktion, 2006), p. 37.

48. Siegfried Kracauer, *Theory of Film: The Redemption of Physical Reality* (Princeton, NJ: Princeton University Press, 1997 edition, first published 1960), p. 48.

49. Gilles Deleuze, *The Movement-Image*, trans. Hugh Tomlinson and Barbara Habberjam (Minneapolis: University of Minnesota Press, 1986), p. 87.

50. In this I suggest that the screen bathed in colour is different from its impact melodramas such as *Black Narcissus*, *Blanche Fury* and *Marnie*, which all use a constant colour to fill the frame and as linked to traumas experienced by the female protagonists.

51. As theorised by Giuliana Bruno, *Atlas of Emotion: Journeys in Art, Architecture, and Film* (New York: Verso, 2002), p. 56.

52. Frank Littlejohn, transcript of BECTU interview no. 91, interviewed 13 June 1989.

53. *The Times*, 5 August 1952, p. 9, issue 52382. Technicolor Ltd was charged Excess Profits Tax, however, which affected its financial performance.

8 COLOUR GENRES IN POSTWAR CINEMA 1

1. For 'repetition and difference and 'regimes of verisimilitude', see Steve Neale, 'Questions of Genre', *Screen* vol. 31 no. 1, 1990, pp. 45–66.

2. *British Journal of Photography* vol. LXXXIX no. 4278,

p. 162.

3. *Kinemacolor Supplement to the Kinematograph and Lantern Weekly*, 3 October 1912.

4. Advertising material for Kinemacolor quoted in Luke McKernan, ' "The Modern Elixir of Life": Kinemacolor, Royalty and the Delhi Durbar', *Film History* vol. 21 no. 2, 2009, p. 127.

5. *The Times*, 28 May 1910, p. 12, quoted in ibid., p. 123.

6. *Catalogue of Kinemacolor Film Subjects, 1912–13* (London: Natural Colour Kinematograph Company), p. 14.

7. Ibid., pp. 78–9.

8. Ibid., pp. 112, 147.

9. Ibid., p. 166.

10. Ibid., p. 309.

11. McKernan, ' "The Modern Elixir of Life" ', p. 123.

12. Brian Winston, *Technologies of Seeing: Photography, Cinematography and Television* (London: BFI, 1996), pp. 39–57.

13. *Catalogue of Kinemacolor Film Subjects, 1912–13*, pp. 304, 307.

14. W. T. Crespinel, 'How Color was Made at the Last Coronation', *American Cinematographer*, May 1937, p. 187. I am grateful for a reader's report on this book which pointed out that a note of caution should be signalled regarding this incident since it may be an apocryphal appropriation of a more famous story from 1901 in which Edward VII heard the noise of a film camera during Queen Victoria's funeral procession and directly acknowledged it (and this one is seemingly corroborated by filmic evidence).

15. The cinematographers who filmed the 1953 Coronation using 3-D cameras reunited to make a television programme using 3-D to film Queen Elizabeth II in 2009. They commented that the Queen – then and now – would never appear to address the camera or look at it directly.

16. Quoted in *Catalogue of Kinemacolor Film Subjects, 1912–13*, p. 311.

17. *Kinematograph Monthly Film Record*, 'The Story of the Films, February, 1913', p. 26.

18. *Catalogue of Kinemacolor Film Subjects, 1912–13*, p. 305.

19. Eirik Frisvold Hanssen, *Early Discourses on Colour and Cinema: Origins, Functions, Meanings* (Stockholm University, 2006), pp. 65–9.

20. *Kinemacolor Supplement to the Kinematograph and Lantern Weekly*, 19 September 1912.

21. *Catalogue of Kinemacolor Film Subjects, 1912–13*, p. 306.

22. URB 3/1/1, programme from Guildhall, Cambridge, 23–8 October, 1913.

23. URB 7/2/6, published appendix to Lords Appeal case of Natural Colour Kinematograph Co. Ltd vs Bioschemes. Examination of G. A. Smith, pp. 290–1.

24. Paolo Cherchi Usai, *Silent Cinema: An Introduction* (London: BFI, 2000), p. 29.

25. Crespinel, 'How Color was Made at Last Coronation', pp. 186–7.

26. *Kinematograph Weekly*, 20 May 1937, p. 33, and 27 May 1937, p. 50.

27. *Kinematograph Weekly* vol. 418 no. 2325, 17 January 1952, pp. 6–7.

28. *Kinematograph Weekly* vol. 374 no. 2137, 15 April 1948, p. 9.

29. *Kinematograph Weekly* vol. 422 no. 2344, 29 May 1953, p. 15. For details of Warnercolor, see *American Cinematographer* vol. 33 no. 9, September 1952, pp. 384–5, 402. In this article it is described as a negative–positive process using Eastmancolor film.

30. *Kinematograph Weekly* vol. 427 no. 2362, 2 October 1952, Studio Review, p. 5.

31. *British Journal of Photography* vol. XCIX no. 4823, 24 October 1952, p. 521.

32. 'Processing the Coronation Colour Films', *Kinematograph Weekly* vol. 435 no. 2398, 11 June 1953, p. 34.

33. *Kinematograph Weekly* vol. 434 no. 2396, 28 May 1953, p. 19.

34. *Kinematograph Weekly* vol. 435 no. 2398, 11 June 1953, p. 5.

35. *Monthly Film Bulletin* vol. 20 no. 234, 1953, pp. 112–13.

36. *British Journal of Photography* vol. C no. 4856, 12 June 1953, p. 304.

37. *British Journal of Photography* vol. C no. 4837, 30 January 1953, p. 61, and vol. C no. 4856, 12 June 1953, p. 304.

38. *The Queen in 3-D*, Channel 4, broadcast 16 November 2009. The producer of *Royal Review* was Bob Angell and cinematographer Arthur Wooster.

39. As recorded in 'The People's Coronation', *Timewatch*, BBC2, 2 June 2010.

40. Quoted in *British Journal of Photography* vol. C no. 4856, 12 June 1953, p. 304.

41. Interestingly, in the 16mm print of *Elizabeth is Queen* I viewed, the shot of the Queen of Tonga in shows her costume more as red than pink.

42. *Kinematograph Weekly* vol. 432 no. 2384, 5 March 1953, pp. 17–20.

43. *Kinematograph Weekly* vol. 438 no. 2412, 17 September 1953, p. 2.

44. *Kinematograph Weekly* vol. 435 no. 2398, 11 June 1953, p. 21.

45. James Chapman, 'Cinema, Monarchy and the Making of Heritage: *A Queen is Crowned*', in Claire Monk and Amy Sargeant (eds), *British Historical Cinema* (London: Routledge, 2002), pp. 82–91.

46. *Kinematograph Weekly* vol. 434 no. 2396, 28 May 1952, p. 16.

47. Marcia Landy, *British Genres: Cinema and Society, 1930–60* (Princeton, NJ: Princeton University Press, 1991), p. 95.

48. John Huntley, 'The XIV Olympiad', in *Film Industry* vol. 5 no. 28, 12 August 1948, p. 8.

49. Castleton Knight, 'Filming the *XIVth Olympiad*: Production Problems', *Cine-Technician* vol. 15 no. 76, January–February 1949, p. 10. Many of the following details are taken from this account, pp. 10–13, 19–20, 22.

50. Review in *Film Industry* vol. 5 no. 30, 9 September 1948, p. 5.

51. Huntley, 'The XIV Olympiad', p. 9.

52. Ibid., p. 19.

53. *Monthly Film Bulletin* vol. 19 no. 218, March 1951, p. 10.

54. For a more detailed analysis of the Festival of Britain films see Sarah Street, 'Cinema, Colour and the Festival of Britain, 1951', in *Visual Culture in Britain* vol. 13, 2012.

55. *Kinematograph Weekly*, 27 May 1937, p. 50.

56. *Kinematograph Weekly*, 28 September 1937, p. 24.

57. *The Spectator*, 24 September 1937, p. 499.

58. James Agate, 'Victoria the Little', 29 September 1937, from *The Tatler*, quoted in James Agate, *Around Cinemas* (London: Home & Van Thal, 1946), p. 185.

59. John Huntley, *British Technicolor Films* (London: Skelton Robinson, 1949), p. 30.

60. For a case study of Anna Neagle see Sarah Street, *British National Cinema* (London: Routledge, 2nd edn, 2009), pp. 163–73.

61. Huntley, *British Technicolor Films*, p. 30.

62. *Film Industry* vol. 5 no. 36, 2 December 1948, p. 10.

63. Jack Cardiff, *Magic Hour* (London: Faber and Faber, 1996), p. 102.

64. 'Ealing's Royal Command Film: How *Scott of the Antarctic* was Filmed', *Film Industry* vol. 5 no. 36, 2 December 1948, pp. 10–11, 18.

65. Ibid., pp. 102–3.

66. Roger Manvell in *Chichester Quarterly*, Spring 1949.

67. *Daily Mail*, 30 November 1948.

68. Jack Cardiff in Justin Bowyer, *Conversations with Jack Cardiff* (London: Batsford, 2003), p. 63.

69. David Raglan in *Woman's Own*, 17 January 1952.

70. Sue Harper and Vincent Porter, *British Cinema of the 1950s: The Decline of Deference* (Oxford: Oxford University Press, 2003), p. 16.

71. *Picturegoer*, 19 January 1952.

72. *Catalogue of Kinemacolor Film Subjects, 1912–13*, p. 287.

73. Ibid., pp. 284–5.

74. Hanssen, *Early Discourses on Colour and Cinema*, p. 69.

75. See Hans Neiter, '*World Window* Series', in Huntley, *British Technicolor Films*, pp. 125–7.

76. Chris Challis interview with Sarah Street and Liz Watkins, 17 October 2008.

77. Bowyer, *Conversations with Jack Cardiff*, p. 46.

78. Jack Cardiff, 'Travelogue Photography in Technicolor', *Photographic Journal* vol. LXXXII, December 1942, p. 404, emphasis in original.

79. Neiter, '*World Window* Series'.

80. As seen in *The Thirties in Colour*, BBC4, 2008.

81. Ibid., p. 127.

82. Chris Challis interview with Sarah Street and Liz Watkins, 17 October 2008.

83. Cardiff, *Magic Hour*, pp. 59–60.

84. Cardiff, 'Travelogue Photography in Technicolor', p. 404.

85. Cardiff, *Magic Hour*, p. 63.

86. Ibid., p. 64.

87. Ibid., p. 54.

88. Cardiff, 'Travelogue Photography in Technicolor', p. 404.

89. Cardiff, *Magic Hour*, p. 64.

90. Dallas Bower, 'British Films in the Orient', *Great Britain and the East*, 24 June 1937, p. 909, quoted in Priya Jaikumar, *Cinema and the End of Empire: A Politics of the Transition in Britain and India* (Durham and London: Duke University Press, 2006), p. 141.

91. Street, *British National Cinema*, pp. 52–5, and Jaikumar, *Cinema and the End of Empire*, pp. 138–64.

92. *British Journal of Photography* vol. LXXXIX no. 4301, 9 October 1942, pp. 378–9.

93. Steve Neale, *Cinema and Technology: Image, Sound, Colour* (London: Macmillan, 1985), p. 152.

94. Richard Dyer, *White* (London: Routledge, 1997), pp. 184–206.

95. Jaikumar, *Cinema and the End of Empire*, p. 159.

96. Prem Chowdhry, *Colonial India and the Making of Empire Cinema: Image, Ideology and Identity* (Manchester: Manchester University Press, 2000), p. 89.

97. Winston, *Technologies of Seeing*, p. 39.

98. Jaikumar, *Cinema and the End of Empire*, p. 159.

99. See, for example, James Chapman and Nicholas J. Cull, *Projecting Empire: Imperialism and Popular Culture* (London: I.B.Tauris, 2009), pp. 21–6; Jaikumar, *Cinema and the End of Empire*, pp. 136–7, 160–2; Landy, *British Genres*, pp. 105–6.

100. *British Journal of Photography*, vol. LXXXIX no. 301, 9 October 1942, p. 378.

101. Ibid.

102. Dickinson, quoted in Huntley, *British Technicolor Films*, pp. 89–103.

103. Ibid., p. 97.

104. Gilles Deleuze, *Cinema 1: The Movement Image* (Minneapolis: University of Minnesota Press, 1997), p. 118.

105. Huntley, *British Technicolor Films*, p. 101.

106. Roland Barthes, *Camera Lucida* (New York: Hill and Wang, 1981).

9 COLOUR GENRES IN POSTWAR CINEMA 2

1. Thomas Elsaesser, 'Tales of Sound and Fury: Observations on the Family Melodrama', *Monogram* no. 4, 1972, p. 2.

2. Mary Beth Haralovich, '*All That Heaven Allows*: Color, Narrative Space, and Melodrama', in Angela Dalle Vacche and Brian Price (eds), *Color: The Film Reader* (London: Routledge, 2006), p. 147.

3. Ibid., p. 150.

4. As argued by Frederic Jameson in *Signatures of the Visible* (London: Routledge, 2007), p. 194.

5. Elsaesser, 'Tales of Sound and Fury', reprinted in Marcia Landy (ed.), *Imitations of Life: A Reader on Film and Television Melodrama* (Detroit: Wayne State University Press, 1991), p. 75.

6. See Sue Harper, *Picturing the Past: The Rise and Fall of the British Costume Film* (London: BFI, 1994) and Pam Cook, *Fashioning the Nation: Costume and Identity in British Cinema* (London: BFI, 1996).

7. Sarah Street, *British National Cinema* (London: Routledge, 2nd edn, 2009), pp. 67–70.

8. Bernard Knowles, 'Colour – The New Technique', *Cine-Technician* vol. 4 no. 18, November–December 1938, pp. 110–11.

9. John Huntley, *British Technicolor Films* (London: Skelton Robinson, 1949), p. 109.

10. Robert Murphy, *Realism and Tinsel: Cinema and Society in Britain, 1939–49* (London: Routledge, 1989), p. 126.

11. *British Journal of Photography* vol. XCVIII no. 4736, 23 February 1951, pp. 96–7.

12. Basil Wright, *The Spectator*, 18 April 1947, quoted by Sue Harper in Sue Aspinall and Robert Murphy (eds), *Gainsborough Melodrama*, BFI Dossier no. 18 (London: BFI, 1983), p. 79.

13. Maurice Carter, quotation from interview with Sue Harper in Aspinall and Murphy, *Gainsborough Melodrama*, p. 83.

14. *Jassy* press book, BFI Library.

15. C. A. Lejeune, *Observer*, 7 August 1947.

16. Duncan Petrie, 'Innovation and Economy: The Contribution of the Gainsborough Cinematographer', in Pam Cook (ed.), *Gainsborough Pictures* (London: Cassell, 1997), pp. 132–3.

17. Darrel Catling, 'Colour Question', *British Journal of Photography* vol. XCIV no. 4546, 4 July 1947, p. 232.

18. *Jassy* press book, BFI Library.

19. Scott Higgins, *Harnessing the Technicolor Rainbow: Color Design in the 1930s* (Austin: University of Texas Press, 2007), p. 180.

20. Sergei Eisenstein, 'On colour', reprinted in Dalle Vacche and Price, *Color*, p. 107.

21. For an analysis of Lockwood's star persona and image see Sarah Street, *British Cinema in Documents* (London: Routledge, 2000), pp. 80–107.

22. Murphy, *Realism and Tinsel*, p. 141.

23. Petrie, 'Innovation and Economy', p. 132.

24. *Blanche Fury* press book, comments reproduced in Huntley, *British Technicolor Films*, pp. 117–8.

25. Ibid., p. 118.

26. Ibid. Rudolf Arnheim later termed this 'partial illusion' for black-and-white conventions that were full of expressive potential. See Arnheim, *Film as Art* (Berkeley: University of California Press, 1957), pp. 26–8.

27. Stanley Cavell, *The World Viewed* (Cambridge, MA: Harvard University Press, 1971; enlarged edition, 1979), pp. 90–1.

28. *Blanche Fury* press book, comments reproduced in Huntley, *British Technicolor Films*, p. 118.

29. Ibid.

30. Elsaesser, 'Tales of Sound and Fury', in Landy, *Imitations of Life*, p. 74, and Liz Watkins, 'Colour Consciousness and Design in *Blanche Fury* as Technicolor Melodrama', in Simon Brown and Sarah Street (eds), colour issue of *Journal of British Cinema and Television* vol. 7 no. 1, 2010, p. 58.

31. Ibid., p. 57.

32. Richard W. Haines, *Technicolor Movies: The History of Dye Transfer Printing* (Jefferson, NC, and London: McFarland and Co., 1993), p. 20.

33. *Blanche Fury* press book.

34. *Kinematograph Weekly* vol. 377 no. 2151, 22 July 1947, p. 29.

35. Watkins, 'Colour Consciousness', p. 57.

36. *Kinematograph Weekly* vol. 372 no. 2130, 26 February 1948, p. 15.

37. *Blanche Fury* press book.

38. Patrick Keating, *Hollywood Lighting from the Silent Era to Film Noir* (New York: Columbia University Press, 2010), pp. 207, 217.

39. The possible connections between the two films have also been noted by Watkins, 'Colour Consciousness', n. 13, p. 67.

40. *Motion Picture Herald* vol. 172 no. 9, 28 August 1948, product digest review, p. 4290.

41. *Kinematograph Weekly* vol. 459 no. 2504, 23 June 1955, p. 12.

42. Higgins, *Harnessing the Technicolor Rainbow*, p. 98.

43. Dilys Powell, *Sunday Times*, 21 August 1955, p. 11.

44. *British Journal of Photography* vol. XCIV no. 4546, 4 July 1947, p. 231.

45. Production notes, BFI micfofiche on *Footsteps in the Fog*.

46. *Kinematograph Weekly* vol. 460 no. 2506, 7 July 1955, p. 16.

47. The standard ratio was 1.33:1, so 1.66:1 was an early widescreen format that was wider than usual but not as wide as other formats introduced in the 1950s.

48. For a discussion of Michael Balcon's aspirations for the film and its production context, see Keith Johnston, 'Ealing's Colour Aesthetic: *Saraband for Dead Lovers*', in Simon Brown and Sarah Street (eds), colour issue of the *Journal of British Cinema and Television* vol. 7 no. 1, 2010, pp. 21–4.

49. Harper, *Picturing the Past*, p. 117.

50. Douglas Slocombe, BECTU interview no. 68, 1996, quoted in Johnston, 'Ealing's Colour Aesthetic', p. 23. See also Slocombe, 'Colour Through the Camera', in *Saraband for Dead Lovers: The Film and its Production* (London: Convoy, 1948), pp. 85–7.

51. Douglas Slocombe, 'Learning to See Again', *Film Industry* vol. 4 no. 21, March 1948, p. 4.

52. Michael Relph, 'Designing a Colour Film', in *Saraband for Dead Lovers: The Film and its Production*, pp. 77–8.

53. Johnston, 'Ealing's Colour Aesthetic', p. 28.

54. Relph, 'Designing a Colour Film', pp. 83–4.

55. Sophie-Dorothea's face in close-up, wearing a red mask and with red lips resembles the disorientated Vicky Page in 'The Red Shoes' ballet sequence when she similarly encounters a succession of disturbing scenes.

56. Harper, *Picturing the Past*, p. 116.

57. Ibid., p. 117.

58. Relph, 'Designing a Colour Film', p. 80.

59. Higgins, *Harnessing the Technicolor Rainbow*, p. 195. Selznick rescued the production when Korda was in financial difficulties. Selznick, however, disapproved of the final cut and took Powell and Pressburger to court, claiming that they had not shot the agreed script. He lost the case, but was so incensed that he hired Rouben Mamoulian to direct, and his version of Webb's novel was released as *The Wild Heart*. In the latter there are fewer shots of the Shropshire countryside. See Michael Powell, *Million Dollar Movie* (London: Heinemann, 1992), pp. 81–3, and Ian Christie, *Gone to Earth* DVD feature.

60. Higgins notes how coloured lighting and manipulations of colour temperature enhanced similar firelight effects in *Gone with the Wind*. See *Harnessing the Technicolor Rainbow*, p. 184.

61. The significance of the white dress is also discussed by Natacha Thiéry in 'That Obscure Subject of Desire: Powell's Women, 1945–50', in Ian Christie and Andrew Moor (eds), *The Cinema of Michael Powell: International Perspectives on an English Film-Maker* (London: BFI, 2005), pp. 228–9.

62. The screen becoming black is reminiscent to this device as in *Black Narcissus* in one of Sister Clodagh's flashbacks when she opens a door to meet her fiancé Con. In this instance the blackness is a portent of the end of their relationship. See Sarah Street, *Black Narcissus* (London: I.B.Tauris, 2005), p. 45.

63. For a discussion of gypsy/foreign characters in Gainsborough melodramas see Cook, *Fashioning the Nation*, pp. 91–115

64. *Kinematograph Weekly* vol. 377 no. 2148, 1 July 1948, p. 39; vol. 377 no. 2150, 15 July 1948, p. 43; vol. 377 no. 2152, 29 July 1948, p. 41.

65. Harper, *Picturing the Past*, p. 117, and Johnston, 'Ealing's Colour Aesthetic', p. 23.

66. Harper's view is that it was 'out of kilter with popular taste', despite being formally innovatory. *Picturing the Past*, p. 173.

67. Higgins's *Harnessing the Technicolor Rainbow* presents case studies from the 1930s to illustrate three modes: demonstration, restrained and assertive.

68. This would support Geoffrey Nowell-Smith's conception of excess and *mise en scène* in melodrama in 'Minnelli and Melodrama', *Screen* vol. 18 no. 2, 1977, p. 117.

69. Andrew Higson, 'The Heritage Film and British Cinema', in Higson (ed.), *Dissolving Views: Key Writings in British Cinema* (London: Cassell, 1996), pp. 236–8.

10 COLOUR GENRES IN POSTWAR CINEMA 3

1. Sarah Street, *British National Cinema* (London: Routledge, 2nd edn, 2009), pp. 37, 41–2, 45–6, 55–9, 65–7, 70–1, 76–82, 109–12, 138–9, 142, 150, 242.

2. *British Journal of Photography* vol. XCI no. 4376, 17 March 1946, p. 92.

3. *British Journal of Photography* vol. XCIII no. 4516, 22 November 1946, p. 422.

4. Joanne Lacey, 'Seeing through Happiness: Hollywood Musicals and the Construction of the American Dream in Liverpool in the 1950s', in Annette Kuhn and Sarah Street (eds), *Audiences and Reception in Britain*, special issue of the *Journal of British Cinema and Television*, 2, 1999, p. 54.

5. Sue Harper and Vincent Porter, *British Cinema of the 1950s: The Decline of Deference* (Oxford: Oxford University Press, 2003), p. 259.

6. Steve Neale, 'The Musical', in Pam Cook (ed.), *The Cinema Book* (London: BFI, 3rd edn, 2007), pp. 333–43.

7. Mike Cormack, *Ideology and Cinematography in Hollywood, 1930–39* (Basingstoke and London: Macmillan, 1994), p. 84.

8. *British Journal of Photography* vol. XCI no. 4376, 17 March 1944, p. 92.

9. Stanley Cavell, *The World Viewed* (Cambridge, MA: Harvard University Press, 1971; enlarged edition, 1979), pp. 90–1.

10. *British Journal of Photography* vol. LXXXIX no. 4305, 6 November 1942, p. 416.

11. *British Journal of Photography* vol. XCI no. 4405, 6 October 1944, p. 356.

12. *British Journal of Photography* vol. XCII no. 4439, 1 June 1945, p. 180.

13. *British Journal of Photography* vol. XCIII no. 4516, 22 November 1946, p. 422.

14. J. P. Mayer, *British Cinemas and their Audiences* (London: Dennis Dobson: 1948), p. 116.

15. J. P. Mayer, *Sociology of Film* (London: Faber and Faber, 1946), p. 256.

16. Duncan Petrie, *The British Cinematographer* (London: BFI, 1996), p. 109.

17. John Huntley, *British Technicolor Films* (London: Skelton Robinson, 1949), p. 103.

18. *British Journal of Photography* vol. XCIII no. 4513, 1 November 1946, p. 391.

19. *Monthly Film Bulletin* vol. 13 no. 154, October 1946, p. 134.

20. The colour lilac was also used in dialogue as a comic subtext for homosexuality in *Pillow Talk* (1959). Along with other floral referents, lilac was a slang term for homosexuality, see Ed Madden, 'Flowers and Birds', in George E. Haggerty (ed.), *Gay Histories and Cultures* (New York: Garland, 2000), p. 332.

21. Harper and Porter, *British Cinema of the 1950s*, p. 260.

22. On 'genre mixing', see Rick Altman, *Film/Genre* (London: BFI, 1999), pp. 123–43.

23. For discussions of 'indigenous' and 'exportable' categories of film see Andrew Higson, 'The Instability of the National', and Sarah Street, 'Stepping Westward: The Distribution of British Feature Films in America, and the Case of *The Private Life of Henry VIII*', in Justine Ashby and Andrew Higson (eds), *British Cinema, Past and Present* (London: Routledge, 2000), pp. 35–47, 51–62.

24. *Time and Tide*, July 1952.

25. Harper and Porter, *British Cinema of the 1950s*, p. 205.

26. Virginia Graham in *The Spectator*, 27 June 1952.

27. Harper and Porter, *British Cinema of the 1950*, pp. 49, 249.

28. Christine Geraghty, *British Cinema in the Fifties: Gender, Genre and the 'New Look'* (London: BFI, 2000), p. 163.

29. Ibid., p. 164.

30. For a discussion of comic suspense and surprise see Steve Neale and Frank Krutnik, *Popular Film and Television Comedy* (London: Routledge, 1990), pp. 33–42.

31. Charles Barr, *Ealing Studios* (London and Newton Abbot: Cameron & Tayleur and David & Charles, 1977), p. 162.

32. Ibid., p. 159.

33. Duncan Petrie terms it thus in *The British Cinematographer*, p. 103.

34. Barr, *Ealing Studios*, p. 171.

11 COLOUR AESTHETICS IN POSTWAR CINEMA

1. Tom Gunning, in Daan Hertogs and Nico de Klerk (eds), *'Disorderly Order': Colours in Silent Cinema* (Amsterdam: Stichting Nederlands Filmmuseum, 1996), p. 39.

2. I use this term as an adaptation of Tom Gunning's seminal formulation, 'The Cinema of Attractions: Early Film, Its Spectator and the Avant-Garde', in Thomas Elsaesser and Adam Barker (eds), *Early Film* (London: BFI, 1989).

Colour was very much a part of cinema's appeal to early film audiences but as examples from selected films from the sound period show, colour continued to constitute an attraction beyond the silent era.

3. Adrian Cornwell-Clyne, *Colour Cinematography* (London: Chapman & Hall, 3rd edn, 1951), pp. 661–2.

4. *Catalogue of Kinemacolor Subjects, 1912–13* (Natural Color Kinematograph Co.), p. 5.

5. Eirik Frisvold Hanssen, *Early Discourses on Colour and Cinema: Origins, Functions, Meanings* (Stockholm University, 2006), pp. 37–8.

6. *Catalogue of Kinemacolor Film Subjects, 1912–13*, p. 65.

7. Similar claims about Kinemacolor exceeding normal perception had been made about early cinema, so in some ways this rhetoric about colour is repeating earlier discourses.

8. Theodore Brown, *Kinematograph Weekly* vol. 6 no. 151, 31 March 1910, p. 1134.

9. Antonia Lant with Ingrid Periz (eds), *The Red Velvet Seat: Women's Writing on the First Fifty Years of Cinema* (London: Verso, 2006), pp. 25–7.

10. Ibid., p. 24.

11. Natalie Kalmus, 'Color Consciousness', reprinted in Angela Dalle Vacche and Brian Price (eds), *Color: The Film Reader* (New York: Routledge, 2006), p. 29, and Sergei Eisenstein, trans. Jay Leyda, *The Film Sense* (first published 1942; London: Faber and Faber, 1968), pp. 120–1.

12. Tom Gunning in Hertogs and de Klerk, '*Disorderly Order*', p. 67.

13. E. S. Tompkins, 'Colour Enthusiast at the Cinema', *British Journal of Photography* vol. XCII no. 4426, 2 March 1945, p. 73.

14. Paul Nash, ' The Colour Film', in Charles Davy (ed.), *Footnotes to the Film* (London: Lovat Dickson, 1938), p. 125.

15. Michael Powell, *A Life in Movies* (London: Heinemann, 1986), pp. 562–3.

16. *Kinematograph Weekly* vol. 371 no. 2126, 29 January 1948, p. 27.

17. David Batchelor, *Chromophobia* (London: Reaktion, 2000), pp. 23–48. Andrew Moor discusses the colour red in *Black Narcissus* in *Powell & Pressburger: A Cinema of Magic Spaces* (London: I.B.Tauris, 2005), pp. 184–5.

18. Scott Higgins, *Harnessing the Technicolor Rainbow: Colour Design in the 1930s* (Austin: University of Texas Press, 2007), p. 35.

19. Jack Cardiff, in Justin Bowyer, *Conversations with Jack Cardiff* (London: Batsford, 2003), p. 74.

20. Sarah Street, *Black Narcissus* (London: I.B.Tauris, 2005), pp. 21–2.

21. Sergei Eisenstein, 'One Path to Color: An Autobiographical Fragment', trans. Jay Leyda, in Lewis Jacobs (ed.), *The Movies as Medium* (New York: Farra, Straus & Gironox, 1970), pp. 206–7.

22. Interview with Jack Cardiff on Craig McCall's 'Painting with Light', documentary (Modus Operandi Films and Smoke & Mirrors Film Productions, 2000).

23. Jack Cardiff, 'Technicolor Cameraman', *Cine-Technician* vol. 16 no. 82, January–February 1950, pp. 30, 32.

24. Sergei Eisenstein, 'On Colour', reprinted in Dalle Vacche and Price, *Color*, p. 107, emphasis in original.

25. BFI library microfiche on *Wings of the Morning*, Rennahan, 'Color Films Mark Return to Nature' article, n.d.

26. Ossie Morris's experiments with colour in *Moulin Rouge* and *Moby Dick* (1956) are detailed in his autobiography *Huston, We Have a Problem* (Lanham, MA, and Oxford: Scarecrow Press, 2006), pp. 66–75, 83–91.

27. Scott Higgins, 'Technology and Aesthetics: Technicolor Cinematography and Design in the Late 1930's, *Film History* vol. 11 (1999), p. 64.

28. Higgins, *Harnessing the Technicolor Rainbow*, p. 213.

29. These examples are quoted in Joshua Yumibe, 'Moving Color: An Aesthetic History of Applied Color Techniques in Silent Cinema', unpublished PhD thesis, University of Chicago, 2007, p. 110.

30. Higgins, *Harnessing the Technicolor Rainbow*, p. 34.

31. Robert Ernest Jones, 'The Crisis of Color', *New York Times*, 19 May 1935, quoted by Higgins, *Harnessing the Technicolor Rainbow*, p. 28.

32. William Stull, 'Will Color Help of Hinder?', *American Cinematographer*, March 1935, pp. 106–7.

33. Robert Surtees, 'Color is Different', *American Cinematographer*, January 1948, p. 11.

34. Darrel Catling, 'Colour and the Ballet Film', *British Journal of Photography* vol. XC no. 4313, 1 January 1943, pp. 2–3.

35. Ibid., p. 2.

36. Ibid.

37. Ibid., p. 3.

38. E. S. Tompkins, 'Ballet Film Problems', *British Journal of Photography* vol. XC no. 4336, 11 June 1943, pp. 212–3.

39. Rick Altman, *The American Film Musical* (Bloomington: Indiana University Press, 1987), p. 188.

40. *British Journal of Photography*, vol. XCIII no. 4516, 22 November 1946, pp. 422–3.

41. Ibid.

42. Adrian Klein, *Colour-Music: The Art of Light* (London: Crosby Lockwood & Son, 2nd edn, 1930).

43. Ibid., p. 150.

44. Other writers have also highlighted the importance of Cornwell-Clyne's writings on colour-music and on narrative cinema. See Hanssen, *Early Discourses on Colour and Cinema*, pp. 140–7; Liz Watkins, 'Colour Consciousness and Design in *Blanche Fury* (1947) as

Technicolor Melodrama', *Journal of British Cinema and Television*, 2010, pp. 56–7.

45. Cornwell-Clyne, *Colour Cinematography*, pp. 659–60.

46. Ibid., p. 659.

47. The colour scores do not appear to have survived in any of the archives with Technicolor holdings. Natalie Kalmus, 'Color Consciousness', reprinted in Dalle Vacche and Price (eds), *Color*, p. 28.

48. Mark Connolly, *The Red Shoes* (London: I.B.Tauris, 2005), p. 30.

49. Herb Lightman, 'The Red Shoes', *American Cinematographer*, March 1949, p. 82.

50. Edward Carrick, 'The Influence of the Graphic Artist on Films', address to the Royal Society of Arts, 18 January 1950, published in *Journal of the Royal Society of Arts* vol. 98 no. 4817, pp. 368–84.

51. Edward Carrick, *Designing for Films* (London: Studio, 2nd edn, 1949), p. 66.

52. Cardiff, quoted in Lightman, 'The Red Shoes', p. 83.

53. Jack Cardiff, *Magic Hour* (London: Faber & Faber, 1996), p. 95.

54. Jack Cardiff, quoted in John Huntley, *British Technicolor Films* (London: Skelton Robinson, 1949), pp. 123–4. These technical details are also recorded in Lightman, 'The Red Shoes', pp. 83, 99–100.

55. Brian Price, 'Introduction' in Dalle Vacche and Price, *Color*, p. 5, emphasis in original.

56. For a discussion of the varied symbolic meanings of red in different cultures, see John Gage, *Colour and Meaning: Art, Science and Symbolism* (London: Thames and Hudson, 1999), pp. 110–12.

57. Laura Mulvey, *Death 24x a Second* (London: Reaktion, 2006), p. 74.

58. See interview with Max Factor, 'Make-up for the New Technicolor Process', *American Cinematographer*, August 1936, pp. 331, 334.

59. Moor, *Powell & Pressburger*, p. 209.

60. This point is made by Moor, ibid., pp. 218–9.

61. The film made from Heckroth's drawings is available as an extra on the ITV DVD of *The Red Shoes* (no. 3711531983). For a discussion of Heckroth's work with Powell and Pressburger, see Nanette Aldred, 'Hein Heckroth and the Archers', in Ian Christie and Andrew Moor (eds), *The Cinema of Michael Powell: International Perspectives on an English Filmmaker* (London: BFI, 2005), pp. 187–206.

62. The newspaper effect was criticised by Marian Eames in *Films in Review* vol. 1 no. 19, December 1950, pp. 21–2.

63. Lightman, 'The Red Shoes', p. 100.

64. Mulvey, *Death 24x a Second*, pp. 75–6.

65. Lightman comments on the cellophane shapes (he refers to them as 'leaves') being shot at varying speeds, 'The Red Shoes', p. 100.

66. Michael Powell and Hein Heckroth, 'Making Colour Talk', in *Kinematograph Weekly*, British Studio Supplement, 9 November 1950, p. 5.

67. Ibid.

68. Aldred, 'Hein Heckroth and the Archers', p. 199. Michael Powell's account of the colour coding is that Heckroth planned this at an early stage, yellow for the first act and the second act dominated by red. The idea that blue dominated the third act came from Emeric Pressburger. See Powell, *Million-Dollar Movie* (London: Heinemann, 1992), p. 90. A more specific explanation of this coding is is provided in Chris Challis, 'Hoffman Sets New Pattern in Film Making Technique', *American Cinematographer* vol. 32 no. 5, May 1951, p. 195.

12 COLLABORATION AND INNOVATION IN THE 1950s

1. *BFI Southbank*, May 2010, p. 20, and Herbert T. Kalmus with Eleanore King Kalmus, *Mr Technicolor* (Absecon, NJ: MagicImage Film, 1993).

2. Justin Bowyer, *Conversations with Jack Cardiff* (London: Batsford, 2003), pp. 40–1.

3. As seen in Craig Mccall's documentary *Cameraman: The Life and Work of Jack Cardiff* (Modus Operandi Films, UK Film Council in association with Smoke & Mirrors, 2010).

4. Sue Harper and Vincent Porter, *British Cinema of the 1950s: The Decline of Deference* (Oxford: Oxford University Press, 2003), p. 207.

5. For example, David Robinson in *The Times*, when the film was reissued, 2 August 1985, p. 15.

6. *Britain Today*, April 1951.

7. Press book for *Pandora and the Flying Dutchman*, BFI Library.

8. *Sunday Times*, 4 February 1951.

9. Sarah Street and Liz Watkins, interview with Ossie Morris, 8 August 2008.

10. *British Journal of Photography* vol. C no. 4847, 10 April 1953, p. 187.

11. Harper and Porter, *British Cinema of the 1950s*, p. 179.

12. *British Journal of Photography* vol. C no. 4847, 10 April 1953, p. 188.

13. *Kinematography Weekly* vol. 432 no. 2385, 12 March 1953, p. 19.

14. *Monthly Film Bulletin* vol. 20 no. 231, April 1953, p. 48.

15. *New Yorker*, 21 February 1953.

16. Oswald Morris with Geoffrey Bull, *Huston, We Have a Problem* (Lanham, MD, and Oxford: Scarecrow Press, 2006), p. 74.

17. *Holiday*, April 1953.

18. Morris, *Huston, We Have a Problem*, p. 69.

19. Duncan Petrie, *The British Cinematographer* (London: BFI, 1996), pp. 124–5.

20. Morris, *Huston, We Have a Problem*, p. 73.

21. Morris interview, 8 August 2008.

22. *British Journal of Photography* vol. C no. 4847, 10 April 1953, p. 187.

23. Morris interview, 8 August 2008.

24. Morris, *Huston, We Have a Problem*, p. 85. Other accounts of the system used are in *American Cinematographer* vol. 84 no. 11, November 2003, p. 120, and Petrie, *The British Cinematographer*, p. 126.

25. Morris interview, 8 August 2008.

26. ABPC inter-office memorandum, Lee Katz to Morris and Huston, 16 July 1954; John Huston Papers, I 392, Margaret Herrick Library, Los Angeles.

27. R. W. Haines, *Technicolor Movies: The History of Dye Transfer Printing* (Jefferson, NC, and London: McFarland and Co., 2003), p. 24.

28. Morris to Huston, 1 May 1955; John Huston Papers, I 392, Margaret Herrick Library, Los Angeles.

29. Morris to Huston, 21 July 1955, ibid.

30. D. Hill, '*Moby Dick* sets New Style in Color Cinematography', *American Cinematographer*, September 1956, p. 535.

31. Ibid., p. 556.

32. I am grateful to Ossie Morris and Liz Watkins for their discussion on this scene when we viewed *Moby Dick* together.

33. Gordon Gow, 'The Right Look', *Films and Filming* vol. 23 no. 7, April 1977, p. 13, has details of Morris's lighting effects in this scene.

34. St Elmo's fire is an electrical weather phenomenon in which a luminous plasma is created by a coronal discharge originating from a grounded object in an atmospheric electric field as generated by a thunderstorm.

35. Herman Melville, *Moby-Dick or, the Whale*, first published 1851 (Oxford: Oxford World Classics edn, 1998), ch. CXIX, 'The Candles', p. 447.

36. Morris to Huston, 1 May 1955; John Huston Papers, I 392.

37. Melville, *Moby-Dick*, p. 212.

38. Norman Wasserman, 'Muted Colors in *Moby Dick*', *International Projectionist*, August 1956, p. 15.

39. Haines, *Technicolor Movies*, p. 65.

CONCLUSION

1. Challis, Broadcasting, Entertainment, Cinematograph and Theatre Union (BECTU) History Project interview no. 59, 11 October 1988.

2. For a discussion of the many versions of *Gone with the Wind*, see Scott Higgins, *Harnessing the Technicolor Rainbow: Color Design in the 1930s* (Austin: University of Texas Press, 2007), pp. 9–13.

SELECT BIBLIOGRAPHY

ARCHIVES AND ARCHIVAL SOURCES

BECTU Film History Project interviews, BFI National Library

Billy Rose Theatre Collection, New York Public Library

British Film Institute National Archive

Claude Friese-Greene papers, National Media Museum, Bradford

Bernard Happé papers, BFI National Library

Natalie Kalmus papers, Margaret Herrick Library, Los Angeles

Technicolor papers, George Eastman House, Rochester

United Artists papers, State Historical Society, Madison

Charles Urban papers, National Media Museum, Bradford

PERIODICALS AND JOURNALS

American Cinematographer

The Bioscope

British Journal of Photography

Cinematograph Times

Cinema

Cine-Technician

Close-Up

The Commercial Film

Daily Film Renter

Exhibitors' Herald

Films and Filming

Film History

Film Industry

Films in Review

Framework

Historical Journal of Film, Radio and Television

The International Projectionist

Journal of British Cinema and Television

Journal of the Royal Society of Arts

Kinematograph Weekly

Kinematograph Monthly Film Record

Kinematograph Year Books

Living Pictures: The Journal of the Popular and Projected Image before 1914

Monthly Film Bulletin

Motion Picture Herald

Motion Picture Magazine

Motion Picture Studio

Photographic Journal

Picturegoer

Screen

Sight & Sound

Technicolor News and Views

The Times

Today's Cinema

Variety

BOOKS AND KEY ARTICLES/CHAPTERS

Andrew, Dudley, 'The Post-War Struggle for Colour', in Angela Dalle Vacche and Brian Price (eds), *Color: The Film Reader* (New York: Routledge, 2006), pp. 40–9.

Ball, Philip, *Bright Earth: The Invention of Colour* (London: Penguin, 2001).

Basten, Fred E., *Glorious Technicolor: The Movies' Magic Rainbow* (Camarillo: Technicolor, 2005).

Batchelor, David, *Chromophobia* (London: Reaktion, 2000).

Belton, John, 'Cinecolor', *Film History* vol. 12 no. 4, 2000, pp. 344–57.

Bowyer, Justin, *Conversations with Jack Cardiff* (London: Batsford, 2003).

Branagan, Edward, 'Color and Cinema: Problems in the

Writing of History', in Paul Kerr (ed.), *The Hollywood Film Industry* (London and New York: Routledge & Kegan Paul, 1986), pp. 120–47.

Brown, Simon, 'Dufaycolor: The Spectacle of Reality and British National Cinema' (2002), available at www.bftv.ac.uk/projects/dufaycolor.htm

Brown, Simon, 'Colouring the Nation: Spectacle, Reality and British Natural Colour in the Silent and Early Sound Era', *Film History* vol. 21 no. 2, 2009, pp. 139–49.

Cardiff, Jack, *Magic Hour* (London: Faber and Faber, 1996).

Carrick, Edward, *Designing for Films* (London: Studio, 2nd edn, 1949).

Cherchi Usai, Paolo, *Silent Cinema: An Introduction* (London: BFI, 2000).

Coe, Brian, *The History of Movie Photography* (London: Ash & Grant, 1981).

Cornwell-Clyne, Adrian, *Colour Cinematography* (London: Chapman & Hall, 3rd edn, 1951).

Crespinell, William A., 'Pioneer Days in Colour Motion Pictures with William T. Crespinel', *Film History* vol. 12 no. 1, 2000, pp. 57–71.

Dalle Vacche, Angela and Price, Brian (eds), *Color: The Film Reader* (London: Routledge, 2006).

Drazin, Charles, 'Korda, Technicolor and the Zeitgeist', *Journal of British Cinema and Television* vol. 7 no. 1, 2010, pp. 5–20.

Dyer, Richard, *White* (London: Routledge, 1997).

Eisenstein, Sergei, *The Film Sense*, trans. Jay Leyda (first published 1942; London: Faber and Faber, 1968).

Enticknap, Leo, *Moving Image Technology from Zoetrope to Digital* (London: Wallflower, 2005).

Genaitay, Sonia and Dixon, Bryony, 'Early Colour Film Restoration at the BFI National Archive', *Journal of British Cinema and Television* vol. 7 no. 1, 2010, pp. 131–46.

Gunning, Tom, 'Colorful Metaphors: The Attraction of Color in Early Silent Cinema', *Fotogenia 1: Il Colore nel Cinema/Color in the Cinema*, 1994, reproduced in *Living Pictures: The Journal of the Popular and Projected Image before 1914* vol. 2 no. 2, 2003, pp. 4–13.

Haines, Richard W., *Technicolor Movies: The History of Dye Transfer Printing* (Jefferson, NC, and London: McFarland and Co., 1993).

Hanssen, Eirik Frisvold, *Early Discourses on Colour and Cinema: Origins, Functions, Meanings* (Stockholm: Stockholm University, 2006).

Harris, Neil, *Cultural Excursions: Marketing Appetites and Cultural Tastes in Modern America* (Chicago and London:

Chicago University Press, 1990).

Hertogs, Daan and de Klerk, Nico (eds), *'Disorderly Order': Colours in Silent Film* (Amsterdam: Stichting Nederlands Filmmuseum, 1996).

Higgins, Scott, *Harnessing the Technicolor Rainbow: Color Design in the 1930s* (Austin: University of Texas Press, 2007).

Huntley, John, *British Technicolor Films* (London: Skelton Robinson, 1949).

Johnston, Keith, 'Ealing's Colour Aesthetic: *Saraband for Dead Lovers*', in Simon Brown and Sarah Street (eds), colour issue of the *Journal of British Cinema and Television* vol. 7 no. 1, 2010, pp. 21–33.

Kalmus, Natalie, 'Color Consciousness', reprinted in Angela Dalle Vacche and Brian Price (eds), *Color: The Film Reader* (New York: Routledge, 2006), pp. 24–9.

Kindem, Gorham, 'The Demise of Kinemacolor: Technological, Legal, Economic, and Aesthetic Problems in Early Color Cinema History', *Cinema Journal* vol. 20 no. 2, Spring 1981, pp. 3–14.

Kindem, Gorham, 'Hollywood's Conversion to Color: The Technological, Economic and Aesthetic Factors', in Gorham Kindem (ed.), *The American Movie Industry: The Business of Motion Pictures* (Carbondale/Edwardsville: Southern Illinois University Press, 1982), pp. 146–58.

Klein, Adrian, *Colour-Music: The Art of Light* (London: Crosby Lockwood & Son, 2nd edn, 1930).

Klein, Adrian Bernard, *Colour Cinematography* (London: Chapman & Hall, 1936, 1939).

Lightman, Herb A., 'Two Worlds in Technicolor', *American Cinematographer* vol. 28 no. 7, July 1947, pp. 236–7, 263.

Mayer, J. P., *British Cinemas and their Audiences* (London: Dennis Dobson, 1948).

McKernan, Luke, ' "Something More than a Mere Picture Show": Charles Urban and the Early Non-fiction Film in Great Britain and America, 1897–25', unpublished PhD thesis, University of London, 2003.

McKernan, Luke, 'The Brighton School and the Quest for Natural Colour', in Vanessa Toulmin and Simon Popple (eds), *Visual Delights Two: Exhibition and Reception* (Sydney: John Libbey and Co., 2004).

McKernan, Luke, ' "The Modern Elixir of Life": Kinemacolor, Royalty and the Delhi Durbar', *Film History* vol. 21 no. 2, 2009, pp. 122–36.

Moor, Andrew, *Powell & Pressburger: A Cinema of Magic Spaces* (London: I.B.Tauris, 2005).

Morris, Oswald, *Huston, We Have a Problem* (Lanham, MA, and Oxford: Scarecrow Press, 2006).

Nash, Paul, 'The Colour Film', in Charles Davy (ed.), *Footnotes to the Film* (London: Lovat Dickson, Readers' Union, 1938), pp. 116–34.

Neale, Steve, *Cinema and Technology: Image, Sound, Colour* (London: Macmillan, 1985).

Nowotny, Robert A., *The Way of All Flesh Tones: A History of Color Motion Picture Processes, 1895–1929* (New York and London: Garland, 1983).

Petrie, Duncan, *The British Cinematographer* (London: BFI, 1996).

Powell, Michael, *A Life in Movies: An Autobiography* (London: Heinemann, 1986).

Powell, Michael, *Million Dollar Movie* (London: Heinemann, 1992).

Slide, Anthony, '*Wings of the Morning*, an Important Film', *American Cinematographer*, February 1986, pp. 36–40.

Smith, G. A., 'Animated Photographs in Natural Colours', paper delivered 9 December 1908 to Fourth Ordinary Meeting of the Royal Society, *Journal of the Royal Society of Arts* vol. LVII no. 2925 11 December 1908, pp. 70–6.

Street, Sarah, *Black Narcissus* (London: I.B.Tauris, 2005).

Street, Sarah, *British National Cinema* (London: Routledge, 2nd edn, 2009).

Street, Sarah, '"In Blushing Technicolor": Colour in *Blithe Spirit*', *Journal of British Cinema and Television*, 2010, pp. 34–52.

Street, Sarah, 'Negotiating the Archives: The Natalie Kalmus Papers and the "Branding" of Technicolor in Britain and the United States', *The Moving Image* vol. 11 no. 1, Spring 2011, pp. 1–24.

Urban, Charles, 'Terse History of Natural Colour Kinematography' (1921), in *Living Pictures* vol. 2 no. 2, 2003, pp. 59–68.

Watkins, Liz, 'Colour Consciousness and Design in *Blanche Fury* (1947) as Technicolor Melodrama', *Journal of British Cinema and Television*, 2010, pp. 53–68.

Winston, Brian, *Technologies of Seeing: Photography, Cinematography and Television* (London: BFI, 1996).

Yumibe, Joshua, 'Moving Color: An Aesthetic History of Applied Color Technologies in Silent Cinema', unpublished PhD thesis, University of Chicago, 2007.

Yumibe, Joshua, '"Harmonious Sensations of Sound by Means of Colors": Vernacular Colour Abstractions in Silent Cinema', *Film History* vol. 21 no. 2, 2009, pp. 164–76.

INDEX

LIST OF ILLUSTRATIONS

While considerable effort has been made to correctly identify the copyright holders, this has not been possible in all cases. We apologise for any apparent negligence and any omissions or corrections brought to our attention will be remedied in any future editions.

At the Villa Rose, Stoll Film Company; *The Glorious Adventure*, J. Stuart Blackton Photoplays; *The Open Road*, © BFI; *A Colour Box*, GPO Film Unit; *The HPO – Heavenly Post Office*, GPO Film Unit; *Making Fashion*, Dufay-Chromex Ltd; *Rainbow Dance*, GPO Film Unit; *On Parade*, J. Walter Thompson; *The Mikado*, G and S Films; *Wings of the Morning*, 20th Century-Fox Film Corporation/New World Pictures; *The Thief of Bagdad*, © Alexander Korda Film Productions; *Queen Cotton*, Merton Park; *This is Colour*, Strand Film Company; *Sons of the Sea*, British Consolidated Pictures; *The Life and Death of Colonel Blimp*, Archers Film Productions/Independent Pictures; *This Happy Breed*, Cineguild; *Blithe Spirit*, Two Cities Films/Cineguild; *Western Approaches*, Crown Film Unit; *Henry V*, Two Cities Films; *A Matter of Life and Death*, Independent Producers/Archers Film Productions; *A Queen is Crowned*, © General Film Distributors; *XIV Olympiad: The Glory of Sport*, Olympic Games (1948) Film Company; *Festival in London*, Crown Film Unit; *Scott of the Antarctic*, © Ealing Studios Ltd; *Arabian Bazaar*, World Windows; *Blanche Fury*, Cineguild/Independent Pictures; *Footsteps in the Fog*, Film Locations Ltd; *Saraband for Dead Lovers*, Ealing Studios; *Gone to Earth*, London Film Productions/British Lion Film Corporation/Vanguard Films; *London Town*, Wesley Ruggles Productions; *The Importance of Being Earnest*, British Film Makers Ltd/Javelin Films; *Genevieve*, © Sirius Productions; *The Ladykillers*, Ealing Studios/© Canal+; *Black Narcissus*, © Independent Producers; *The Red Shoes*, © Independent Pictures; *The Tales of Hoffmann*, London Film Productions/Michael Powell & Emeric Pressburger Productions/British Lion Film Corporation; *Pandora and the Flying Dutchman*, © Dorkay Productions Inc.; *Moulin Rouge*, © Romulus Films; *Moby Dick*, © Moulin Productions.